3 9082 02836 7350

WATERFORD TWP. PUBLIC LIBRARY
5168 Civic Center Drive
Waterford, MI 48329

#64

Michigan:
Heart of the Great Lakes

Richard A. Santer Ph.D
Associate Professor of Geography
Ferris State College

KENDALL/HUNT PUBLISHING COMPANY
2460 Kerper Boulevard, Dubuque, Iowa 52001

Cover Photo

Frontispiece Photo

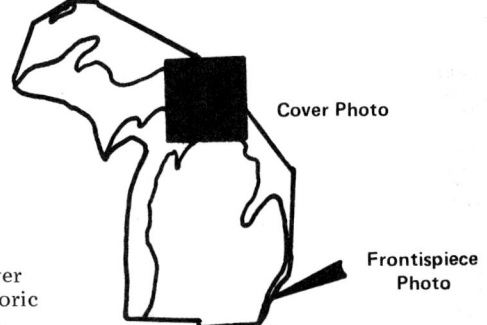

Cover Photo: NASA-ERTS photo of the tip of the Lower Peninsula and eastern area of the Upper Peninsula. Historic Straits of Mackinac and the Soo Locks can be observed.

Frontispiece Photo: The photo illustrates the critical transportation interfaces in the City of Detroit with the Detroit River and Ambassador Bridge in the background, the ConRail yard to the left and the intersection of the I-75 (Fisher) and I-96 (Jeffries) Freeways in the foreground. (Photo: Michigan Travel Commission)

Copyright © 1977 by Kendall/Hunt Publishing Company

Library of Congress Catalog Card Number: 76-53268

ISBN 0—8403—1698—4

All rights reserved. No part of this publication may be reproduced, stored in a retrieval system, or transmitted, in any form or by any means, electronic, mechanical, photocopying, recording, or otherwise, without the prior written permission of the copyright owner.

Printed in the United States of America

401698 01

Contents

List of Figures, ix

List of Tables, xiii

Preface, xvii

Acknowledgments, xix

Prologue: Geography in Relation to Other Geo-Disciplines, xxi

Chapter One   An Introduction to the Geography of Michigan, **1**

Chapter Two   Historical Geographic Origins of Michigan, **13**
      Naming of Michigan, **13**
      American Indian Land Occupance Areas, **15**
      Post-French Contact Indian Occupance Patterns, **18**
      The Colonial Occupance Era of the French, British, and Spanish, **25**
      The Spanish in Michigan, **34**
      Michigan Under the British Monarchy, **35**

Chapter Three   The Political Geographic Evolution of Michigan, **41**
      Establishing the Michigan-Canadian Boundary, **41**
      Americans Gain Control of the Peninsulas, **43**
      Political Geographic Land Preparations for American Settlement, **44**
      Michigan Territory Created, **46**
      American Indian Land Treaties, **47**
      Michigan Statehood and Boundaries, **50**
      The Federal Land Surveys and County Evolution, **55**
      Survey and Civil Township Establishment, **59**
      Nineteenth Century County Evolution, **62**
      Spatial Aspects of Regional and Economic Development Acts, **66**

Chapter Four	Michigan's Geology and Mining Resources, **75**
	Earliest Geologic History and Contemporary Resource Activity, **75**
	The Paleozoic Seas: Deposits and Contemporary Resources, **84**
	Fossils from the Paleozoic Seas, **88**
	Michigan Energy Demands and Petroleum Production, **89**
Chapter Five	The Glacial Lakes and Ice Sculptured Land, **93**
	Evidence for Glaciation, **93**
	The Economic Value of the Pleistocene Sands and Gravels, **98**
	The Water Wonderland of Michigan, **99**
	The Formation of the Great Lakes, **106**
	Fluctuation of Lake Levels and Contemporary Shoreline Erosion Problems, **115**
Chapter Six	Climate, Soil, Vegetation, and Lumber Resources, **119**
	The Weather and Climate Resources of Michigan, **119**
	Michigan Meteorites, **135**
	Michigan's Soil, **135**
	Michigan's Forests, Logging, and Wood Products Industry, **139**
	Exploitation of the Northern Pine and Hardwood Forest, **140**
Chapter Seven	Population and Settlement, **155**
	Growth and Composition of Michigan's Contemporary Population, **155**
	Historic Migration Influences on Michigan's Population, **166**
	Territorial Inland Settlement 1817-1829, **167**
	Race and Ethnic Groups of Michigan, **169**
Chapter Eight	Population and Settlement Patterns of Michigan's Fourteen Planning and Development Regions, **175**
	Detroit, Region One: Michigan's Core Area, **175**
	Jackson, Region Two: The Auto Parts, General Livestock and Corn Production Area, **184**
	Kalamazoo-Battle Creek, Region Three: A Pharmaceutical and Cereal Products Manufacturing Area, **191**
	Benton Harbor-St. Joseph, Region Four: A Fruit Raising and Processing Area, **193**
	Flint, Region Five: An Automobile Manufacturing Area, **194**
	Lansing, Region Six: The Capital Area, **196**
	Saginaw-Bay City, Region Seven: The Eastern Transition Area from the Agricultural-Industrial South to Forested North, **199**
	Grand Rapids, Region Eight: The Heartland of the Western Lower Peninsula, **201**
	Alpena-Gaylord, Region Nine: The Northeast Forest, Recreation, and Limestone Area, **205**
	Traverse City, Region Ten: The Cherry Capital Area, **209**
	The Upper Peninsula, Regions Eleven, Twelve, Thirteen: The North Country of Forest, Mining, and Recreation, **213**
	Muskegon, Region Fourteen: The West Shore Area of Lower Michigan, **215**

Chapter Nine   Michigan's Economic Geography, 223
- Michigan's Labor Force and Diversity of Production Activities, 223
- Diversification of the Economy Dominated by Motor Vehicles, Agriculture and Recreation, 224
- Agriculture: Primary Within the Michigan Economy, 226
- A World View and the Future Needs of Michigan Agriculture, 244
- The Economic Geography of the Automobile Industry, 250
- Michigan's Leisure Time Industry, 254
- Economic Development and International Trade, 262
- Planning for Modern Industrial Expansion, 266
- Education and Economics, 267.

Chapter Ten   Michigan's Transportation and Communication Systems, 277
- Highways in Michigan, 278
- Rediversifying the Michigan Transportation System, 287
- Railroads in Michigan, 288
- Great Lakes Transportation, 294
- Closing Michigan's Utility Frontier, 296
- Michigan Aviation, 302
- Communication by Newspaper, Radio, Television, and Mail, 305

Chapter Eleven   The Quest for a Quality Environment, 315
- National Forest Management, 316
- The Innovative Muskegon Waste Water System, 317
- Misplaced Chemicals in the Environment, 321
- Michigan State Police and a Quality Environment, 322
- Mental Health Service Areas, 324
- Flood Plain Management, 326
- Land Use Management, Open Space and Historic Site Preservation, 336

List of Sources, 339

Index, 353

List of Figures

Figure
1.1 Michigan including its Great Lakes boundaries, **2**
1.2 Kirtland's warbler nesting area warning sign, **3**
1.3 Great Seal of Michigan, **4**
1.4 Industrial core area of the United States and Canada, **6**
1.5 Typical logos depicting Michigan without the Upper Peninsula, **9**
1.6a Original Michigan Bicentennial Commission logo, **10**
1.6b Apology logo used by the Michigan Bicentennial Commission, **10**
1.7 Proposed boundaries for the United States, **11**

2.1 States and names proposed by Jefferson for the area northwest of the Ohio River, **14**
2.2 Isabella County Indian Reservations, **21**
2.3 Indian children in the Lansing Public Schools 1969-1970, **24**
2.4 Reconstructed Fort Michilimackinac, **29**
2.5 Map of Monroe County illustrating the French long-lot and Federal Survey Systems, **31**

3.1 Boundary proposals of British fur merchants 1791, **43**
3.2 American Indian treaty cessions affecting Michigan, **48**
3.3 Portion of Mitchell's 1755 Map of North America, **51**
3.4 Portion of Michigan-Ohio boundary at mouth of Maumee River, **53**
3.5 Michigan-Wisconsin boundary on the Montreal River to Lac Vieux Desert, **54**
3.6 Michigan-Wisconsin boundary in Green Bay, **56**
3.7 Michigan Survey Townships, **58**
3.8 Map illustrating Federal Survey description of land, **60**
3.9 Michigan county organization 1818, **62**
3.10 Michigan county organization 1828, **63**
3.11 Michigan county organization 1836, **63**
3.12 Michigan county organization 1840, **64**
3.13 Michigan county organization 1867, **64**

Figure

3.14   Michigan county organization 1876, **65**
3.15   Michigan Planning Regions 1976, **69**

4.1   Michigan bedrock formations, **76**
4.2   Michigan bedrock patterns, **78**
4.3   Michigan iron mines, **81**
4.4   Copper region of Michigan, **83**
4.5   Sandstone outcrop north of original State Prison site in City of Jackson, **87**
4.6   Sandstone wall of original State Prison in Jackson, **87**

5.1   Glacial landforms developed during glaciation, **95**
5.2   Typical post-glacial landforms, **95**
5.3   Land types of Michigan, **97**
5.4   Canadian Lakes, Morton Township, Mecosta County, **101**
5.5   River pattern in Michigan, **104**
5.6   Grand Rapids fish ladder, **105**
5.7   Principal moraines in the Great Lakes region, **108**
5.8   Ice front approximately 16,000 years ago, **109**
5.9   Ice front approximately 14,000 years ago, **109**
5.10   Ice front approximately 12,500 years ago, **109**
5.11   Ice front approximately 11,000 years ago, **110**
5.12   The Great Lakes 9,500 years ago, **111**
5.13   The Great Lakes 3,500-4,500 years ago, **112**
5.14   Sand dune areas in Michigan, **114**
5.15   Example of bluff recession, **117**

6.1   Mean annual temperature, **122**
6.2   Mean annual January temperature, **123**
6.3   Mean annual July temperature, **124**
6.4   Average number of days in growing season, **128**
6.5   Mean annual precipitation, **129**
6.6   Mean annual snowfall, **131**
6.7   General soil regions of Michigan and limits of white pine, beech vegetation, **137**
6.8   Modern soil survey map, **138**
6.9   Major forest types in Michigan, **144**

7.1   Michigan Standard Metropolitan Statistical Areas 1970, **157**
7.2   Graph of Michigan population by age 1960 and 1970, **162**
7.3   Population by age and sex Keweenaw County 1970, **163**
7.4   Population by age and sex Mecosta County 1970, **164**
7.5   Population by age and sex Lake County 1970, **165**
7.6   Murder distribution in the United States 1968, **172**
7.7   Total index of crime distribution for the United States, **173**

8.1   Murder and assault pattern in Detroit, **179**
8.2   Industrial corridors of Metropolitan Detroit, **181**

Figure

8.3	Political units of Metropolitan Detroit, **182**	
8.4	Selfridge Air National Guard Base on Anchor Bay, **183**	
8.5	Region Two—Jackson Planning Area, **186**	
8.6	Negro and foreign-born housing pattern, Jackson 1870, **187**	
8.7	Negro and Polish housing pattern, Jackson 1910, **188**	
8.8	Negro distribution by wards, Jackson 1930, **189**	
8.9	Negro and foreign-born distribution by census tract, Jackson 1960, **190**	
8.10	Region Three—Kalamazoo-Battle Creek, minor civil divisions, **192**	
8.11	1877 Flint carriage, buggy, and wagon advertisement, **195**	
8.12	The Lansing Capital Complex and central business district, **198**	
8.13	Region Eight—Grand Rapids, **203**	
8.14	Otsego County-City Building, Gaylord, **207**	
8.15	Region Nine—Alpena, percent of employed who cross a county line in their journey to work, **208**	
8.16	Traverse City on the west arm of Grand Traverse Bay, **210**	
8.17	Average number of visitors per day by month to Antrim, Benzie, Grand Traverse, Kalkaska, and Leelanau counties, **211**	
8.18	Muskegon Service Area, **216**	
9.1	Corn, **230**	
9.2	Wheat, **231**	
9.3	Oats, **232**	
9.4	Dry beans, **233**	
9.5	Soybeans, **234**	
9.6	Sugar beets, **235**	
9.7	Cattle, **236**	
9.8	Milk cows, **237**	
9.9	Hogs and pigs, **238**	
9.10	Egg producing chickens, **239**	
9.11	Sheep, **240**	
9.12	Trend of land in farms 1945-1972 with projection to 2000 A.D., **248**	
9.13	The automobile realm, **253**	
9.14	Sign of the times, **258**	
9.15	Sign at private campground 1976, **260**	
10.1	Change in status of major highways in southern Michigan 1919-1965, **281**	
10.2	Relative advantage of highway improvements, **283**	
10.3	Michigan's basic highway network, **285**	
10.4	Michigan's railroad network and hub in Jackson in the 1870s, **290**	
10.5	Michigan and ConRail reorganization of the Penn Central and Ann Arbor rail network, **292**	
10.6	Flow of coal to Great Lakes ports, **293**	
10.7	Ports of the Great Lakes, **295**	
10.8	Base Rate Area and Local Telephone Tariff Zone for Big Rapids, **300**	
10.9	Rural route postal address, **308**	

Figure
- 11.1 Muskegon Waste Water facility, **319**
- 11.2 Center pivot sprayer in operation at the Muskegon Waste Water facility, **319**
- 11.3 Method of waste water use at the Muskegon Waste Water facility, **320**
- 11.4 Percent change in Index Crime by county 1970-1975, **323**
- 11.5 Community Mental Health Board Service Areas, **325**
- 11.6 Federal Mental Health Catchment Areas, **327**
- 11.7 State centers for mentally retarded, **328**
- 11.8 State hospitals for mentally ill, **329**
- 11.9 Typical flood plain folders, **335**
- 11.10 Application process for open space and farmland preservation, **337**

Photo Essay
- A Fur Trade at the Straits of Mackinac, **72**
- B The Natural Environment of Michigan, **148**
- C Michigan Settlement Features 1830-1976, **218**
- D Leisure Time and Agriculture, **269**
- E Twentieth Century Water and Highway Transportation, **309**
- F Houses and Water, **330**

List of Tables

Table
1 Geography and Related Disciplines with Greek Meanings and Modern Focus, **xxii**
1.1 Areas of the States Contiguous to Michigan, **7**
4.1 Generalized Geologic Time Scale, **79**
4.2 Number Active Iron Mines, Employment and Shipments 1950-1972, **82**
5.1 Major Inland Lakes of Michigan, **100**
6.1 Season Reversal of Temperature Due to Lake Michigan, **121**
6.2 Selected Michigan Average Annual Degree Days, Snow Accumulation, and Temperatures by Station, **126**
6.3 Tornadoes and Loss of Life 1953-1969, **133**
6.4 Great Lakes States Commercial Timber Land 1970, **143**
6.5 Ownership of Michigan Commercial Forestland, **143**
6.6 Major Pulpwood Producing Counties by Peninsula 1969, **146**
7.1 Michigan Population Growth and Daily Increase by Decade 1810-1975, **156**
7.2 Michigan Nonregional Center Cities with 50,000 People 1970, **156**
7.3 Selected Densities of Population in Comparison to Michigan 1974, **158**
7.4 Crematories Under Regulation of Michigan Cemetery Commission 1976, **159**
7.5 Number of Residents in Michigan in 1970 Residing in Another State in 1965, **160**
7.6 Michigan Past and Future Population with Approximate Rates and Dates to Add One Million 1810-1990, **161**
7.7 Michigan Sex Ratio 1900-1990 and Estimated Population by Sex 1975-1990, **161**
7.8 Certified Land Sales in Acres at Detroit 1820-1836, **166**
7.9 1810-1840 Population of Michigan, Illinois, Indiana, and Ohio, **167**
7.10 Land Sales Receipts 1823-1837 USA, Ohio, Illinois, Indiana, Michigan ($1,000), **167**
7.11 Racial Composition of Michigan 1860-1970, **169**

Table

7.12	Nationality Composition of Michigan 1880 and 1970,	**170**
7.13	Ethnic-Race-Religious Groups Location and Cultural Landscape Features,	**171**
8.1	Population and Land-Water Areas of Michigan's Planning and Development Regions 1970,	**176**
8.2	Vertical Space Enclosure in Major USA Cities 1954 and 1974,	**177**
8.3	Region One: Place of Work by County,	**180**
8.4	Region One: State Parks and Selected Historic Attractions,	**184**
8.5	Regions Two, Three, Four: State Parks and Selected Historic Attractions,	**191**
8.6	Regions Five, Six, and Seven: State Parks and Selected Historic Attractions,	**197**
8.7	Regions Eight and Fourteen: State Parks and Selected Historic Attractions,	**205**
8.8	Regions Nine and Ten: State Parks and Selected Historic Attractions,	**209**
8.9	Upper Peninsula Regions: State Parks and Selected Historic Attractions,	**215**
9.1	Civilian Labor Force and Unemployment 1970-1975,	**224**
9.2	Unemployment Percent for Selected Michigan Areas,	**224**
9.3	Distribution of Employment in Michigan Manufacturing Industries 1975,	**225**
9.4	Michigan Rank in Agricultural Products 1975,	**227**
9.5	Farms, Farm Size, and Farmland 1920-1975,	**228**
9.6	Great Lakes State Farm Comparisons 1969,	**228**
9.7	Usual County Rank for Selected Agricultural Products,	**229**
9.8	Crop and Livestock Comparisons 1880-1975,	**229**
9.9	Number of Dairy Processing Plants 1940-1970,	**243**
9.10	Selected Facts on Vegetable Production and Location 1975,	**244**
9.11	Selected Facts on Fruit Production and Location 1975,	**245**
9.12	Selected Food Products, Location and US Rank 1975,	**246**
9.13	Average Number Employees in Automobile Production by State 1972,	**250**
9.14	Passenger Cars Assembled by City 1973,	**250**
9.15	United States Automobile Production for Selected Years 1900-1975,	**251**
9.16	Method of Shipment of Motor Vehicles by Percent 1950-1974,	**252**
9.17	Leisure Time Terms and Space Relationships,	**255**
9.18	Most Used State Parks by Category 1973,	**257**
9.19	Foreign Investments in Michigan by Nation and Community 1975,	**263**
9.20	New Incorporations and Industrial Commercial Failures 1955-1975,	**264**
9.21	Michigan-USA Mobile Home Production 1963-1975,	**266**
9.22	Criteria and Point Scale Used for Certifying Industrial Parks,	**267**
9.23	Public School District Consolidation with Number of Teachers and Pupils 1952-1970,	**268**
10.1	Michigan Road Lengths and Type 1905,	**279**
10.2	Total Length of Michigan Highway Network by Category,	**282**
10.3	Michigan Central Railroad Report 1870,	**289**
10.4	Major Michigan Rail Systems and Connected Communities 1976,	**291**
10.5	Relative Energy Efficiency of Freight Transportation by Mode,	**294**
10.6	Major Great Lakes Port Clusters Ranked by Weight of General Cargo 1975,	**295**
10.7	Characteristics of Major Great Lakes Vessel Types,	**297**

Table
- 10.8 Location of Telephone Company and Number of Main Stations, Michigan Telephone Network 1976, **298**
- 10.9 Michigan Franchised Gas Utilities and Pipeline Companies 1976, **303**
- 10.10 Aircraft Operation at FAA Traffic Control Tower Airports 1973, **304**
- 10.11 AM Radio Stations in Operation Since 1920s, **306**
- 10.12 Michigan Sectional Center Facilities and Number of Post Offices 1976, **307**
- 11.1 Michigan National Forests, **316**
- 11.2 DDT, PCBs, and Mercury in Fish 1969-1974, **322**
- 11.3 Number of State Police Posts by Region and Police Reporting Agencies, **324**

Preface

Michigan: its peninsular lands surrounded by the greatest bodies of fresh water on the earth and occupied by nine million native and immigrant people from scores of nations, is a region of fascinating uniqueness. The physical landscape features of Michigan have been molded by over a billion years of incessant change including the rumble of volcanoes and earthquakes, the inundations of saltwater oceans, and the fickleness of tropical rainforest, desert, and arctic climates. Even today, Michigan is being etched by the flow of hundreds of miles of postglacial age streams and is pocked by thousands of inland lakes that had their origin a scant 10,000 years ago.

The combination of these diverse earth-shaping processes has resulted in a place of uncalculable wealth with numerous vistas and pleasant environments—a place which millions continue to enjoy for everyday living, recreation, and employment.

Michigan's cultural landscape has been created by the inhabitants through the use of a thousand years of material technology (agriculture, mining, urbanization, transportation, industry) and social institutions (education, political, economic, and religious systems). Today these cultural processes shaping the state are more dynamic than the slower paced physical processes in having a devastating impact on the region's land and water resources.

In this text the geographic method of inquiry is utilized. The generalist-holistic approach, used by geographers ideally suits the task of describing the region's vast array of spatially related phenomena. The author heartily embraces the geographic tradition of practicing "the art of scientific trespass" by borrowing data freely from several scientific disciplines, as well as the technical and applied arts, to develop this short but comprehensive study of Michigan.

Within the several chapters, photos, tables, and graphs have been utilized to complement the narrative. The several maps integrated into the text have been drawn from numerous sources allowing the reader an opportunity to evaluate differing mapping techniques. In anticipation of the United States' conversion to the metric system, most distance and areal units have been converted using the National Bureau of Standards, Special Publication 365, November 1972. Contemporary Michigan is emphasized, however, the historical foundation of the state's political, economic, and demographic evolution has been laid throughout the topical chapters to enhance the analysis of the region during the last quarter of the twentieth century.

The narrative is written with the expectation that it will be read primarily by college-age and noncollege mature students of Michigan. Anticipating the needs of a diverse audience who possess different background and motives for studying the state, the amount of technical geographic jargon is limited and infrequently used terms are italicized. Thus, both the lay person and geography student alike should find the book useful in heightening their awareness of Michigan. In the end, it is hoped that this text will stimulate its readers to further research, inquiry, and participation in the shaping of a better state in which to live and work.

Acknowledgments

This modest *Geography of Michigan* could only be completed with the encouragement and continual prompt assistance of numerous individuals. I am most appreciative of all those in state, local, and private agencies who helped in gathering the basic data, as well as those who willingly took time to share with me their specialized knowledge on various aspects of Michigan. I further appreciate the grant of a sabbatical leave from Ferris State College during the Spring Quarter, 1976, to pursue research which has been incorporated into this text.

Although there are many unnamed individuals and agencies whose contributions were no less significant than those listed below, I want to especially record assistance from several persons. Mary Braun, Ann Breitenwischer, Raymond Dickinson, Margene Fennell, Sara Krumins, and Elaine Nienhouse on the Ferris State College Library staff, were most helpful in securing materials locally and through interlibrary loan. Professor emeritus Proctor Maynard and Steven Voorhees provided valuable assistance concerning the Upper Peninsula and photography, respectively. Several public servants in the Department of Natural Resources provided timely aid and counsel including: Allen Billings, Larry Folks, Wendell Hoover, Martin Jannereth, Irvin Kuehner, Kenneth MacKellar, Norman Smith, Ronald Webster, and Steven Wilson.

In other state agencies, generous assistance was received from: Gil Clark and John Maters, Michigan Travel Commission; Philip Hogan, III, Department of State Police; Charles Hines, Crop Reporting Service; Robert Otstot and Frank VanCamp, Public Service Commission; Donald Riel, Department of State Highways and Transportation; and John Sarver, Department of Mental Health. Critical comments and encouragement by my students and colleagues of Michigan geography during the last several years have also been appreciated.

Finally, without the unfailing support, labor, and sacrifices of my family, this effort would have remained an unfulfilled task.

> "Geography is not merely useful. It is exciting for its own sake."
> Jan O. M. Broek

Prologue
Geography in Relation to Other Geo-Disciplines

Geography, geology, geometry, geomorphology, geodesy. What's geography? Geography is recognized as one of the ancient, time-honored, generalist disciplines, predating the age of exploration. Modern geographers continue to build on the tradition of describing people and the places they inhabit. Unfortunately geography as a subject is frequently confused with the many related specialized "geo-" disciplines.

The prefix *geo-* is the Greek word for *earth,* thus words or courses with the *geo-* prefix will deal in some respect with the earth. The *geo-* word endings or suffixes indicate a special focus of interest in regards to the earth. In the case of geography, *-graphy* means *description.* Thus, geography deals with the description of various aspects of the earth including both natural and human phenomena. The following chart outlines the basic translation and focus of several fields of study associated with geography. Fuller definitions of the word meanings and their focus can be found in general introductory textbooks of the specific disciplines and in unabridged dictionaries (table 1).[1]

Ecology, Economics, Demography in Relation to Geography

From the translation of the prefix and suffix parts, the relationship of ecology, economics, and demography to geography can also be easily seen illustrating a close association between these disciplines and geography. The earth is the "home of man," whether it is studied by ecologists or described by geographers. Further, how it is managed is of vital interest to the economists and geographers alike. Additionally, the dividing line between demography and

---

1. *Webster's New World Dictionary of the English Language,* 2nd College Ed. (New York: World Publishing Co., 1970).
The Random House Dictionary of the English Language, Unabridged Ed. (New York: Random House Inc., 1966).
The Oxford English Dictionary (Oxford: Clarendon Press, 1933).
Funk and Wagnalls New "Standard" Dictionary of the English Language (New York: Funk and Wagnalls, 1956).

geography is exceedingly narrow due to their mutual concern for human population relationships. Therefore, the geographer associates closely with and openly borrows from these disciplines and others in a quest to describe and explain earth activity.

TABLE 1
Geography and Related Disciplines with
Greek Meanings and Modern Focus

Prefix	Suffix	Simple Greek Meaning	Modern-Day Focus of Discipline
geo-		Earth	Earth
eco- (oikes)		House	House or home
demo-		People	People
historia-		Learned factual information	History: a record of times and facts of human events usually with philosophic explanation of their causes.
	-graphy	Description	Geography: description of the earth's physical-natural and cultural-human features and their spatial relationships. Demography: description of vital social statistics and relation to human activity.
	-ology	Study of	Geology: study of the earth's history from the location of rock and minerals generally beneath its surface. Ecology: study of the mutual relations between organisms and their living environment.
	-metry	Measure	Geometry: branch of mathematics which measures the properties and relationships of surfaces, lines, and angles.
	-*morph*ology	Form	Geomorphology: study of the origin and change of the earth's **landforms** and distribution of its land and water surfaces.
	-odesy	Divide	Geodesy: surveying, applied branch of mathematics which determines exact points, lines, and locations of the earth.
	-nomic (-nomos)	Manage	Economics: investigation of management affecting production, distribution, and consumption of resources in the world.

If there is one apparent distinction between geography and the previously identified fields of knowledge, it is the geographers' constant use of maps and mappable phenomena to illustrate *spatial* or space relationships between places of the earth and its people, as well as its generalist interdisciplinary focus.

Geography and History

History, like geography, is not confined to a narrow, well-defined, specialized scope of happenings, but rather both embrace the broadest spectrum of human activities on the earth. The point of divergence between the two disciplines would be the geographers' close link to the physical sciences and determining spatial relationships, while the historians' focus is usually on *human and time* references.

The Role of Modern Geography

Considering only the discussion of geography and its primary related disciplines up to this point, it could be assumed that from the time of the ancient Greek scholars to the present, the role of geography has been limited to "mere description." However, such is not the case. Modern geographers, possessing social consciousness and not being content with descriptive activities alone, have expanded their work to include: (1) the analysis of the earth's environment, (2) the identification of problems related to the earth from both a social and natural viewpoint, but within a spatial framework, (3) the search, with other disciplines, for solutions to common problems which affect the earth, and (4) the advancement of planning and environmental management for the future of the earth.

> ". . . and the means of education shall forever be encouraged."
> Northwest Ordinance 1787

Chapter One

An Introduction to the Geography of Michigan

The time-honored way to help a person conceptualize the shape of Michigan is to have the individual visualize the shape of two hands or mittens. The right hand with palm up and thumb separated easily represents the Lower Peninsula including its Thumb Area. The left hand held horizontal and above the right hand with the thumb extended at a slight angle is analogous to the Upper and Keweenaw Peninsulas. Although the mitten conceptualization of Michigan's *basic land shape* is useful, it remains an incomplete, elementary, and misleading model of the state's total area and shape, for the analogy omits the water area which makes Michigan the Great Lakes State.

A mature perception of Michigan should include its Great Lakes water boundaries. Then, a holistic mental map image of the shape and area of the state can emerge (fig. 1.1). By visualizing Michigan as more than a mitten, the individual is encouraged to expand his perception to not only the Great Lakes, but also their major islands including: (1) Isle Royale National Park, Lake Superior's largest island, 215,712 hectares [ha] (539,280 ac), eighty kilometers [km] (50 mi) northeast of the Keweenaw Peninsula, (2) Drummond, Mackinac, and Bois Blanc Islands near the Straits of Mackinac at the head of Lake Huron, (3) the Green Bay Island chain lying between the Door Peninsula of Wisconsin and the Garden Peninsula, and finally (4) Beaver, Fox, and the Manitou Islands off the northwest shore of the Lower Peninsula. These peripheral islands and waters are significant for the roles which they have played in history, recreation, transportation, and the potential they hold for future use. Further, had there been greater awareness, understanding, and concern in the past by Michigan citizens of its total area, they might have prevented the loss of nearly 780 sq km (300 sq mi) of Lake Erie to the state of Ohio in 1972.

Figure 1.1. Michigan including its Great Lakes boundaries. (Map: Department of Natural Resources.)

Michigan's Symbols of Statehood—Iconography

Like most political entities Michigan has a profusion of state symbols or modern-day icons, which, when collected or displayed, create a sense of pride and identification with the state. Michigan's official symbols include: seal, flag, bird, fish, tree, flower, stone, and gem. During the American Revolution Bicentennial, the Kirtland's warbler was also recognized (fig. 1.2).

Figure 1.2. Kirtland's warbler nesting area warning sign near Lovells, Crawford County, 1975.

In analyzing the iconography of the state, a sense of mixed emotion can be experienced, for these symbols so representative of the state's natural heritage are constantly being threatened due to the losses and changes in the natural habitats. To be sure, the twentieth century environmental movement has resulted in some progress in their protection. Nevertheless, the moose and elk which are displayed on the original state seal and flag only exist on Isle Royale and a small portion of the Pigeon River Country State Forest respectively. Even the elk that survive in Michigan are not native, as they were reintroduced from the West in the early part of this century by the Michigan Department of Conservation. The robin and Kirtland's warbler continue to have their survival challenged with sprays and chemicals intended for other purposes. The Kirtland's warbler's advocates have also had to seek cooperation from the National Guard in protecting their nesting area as it is not only threatened by its natural parasite, the destroying cowbird, but it also lies primarily within the Camp Grayling Military Reservation tank-artillery maneuver area.

Trout, the state fish, has been affected by DDT, PCB's, and mercury to the point that the State Department of Public Health warns citizens against their unrestricted consumption. Further, thousands of dollars have been spent in trying to determine how to get lake trout to reproduce naturally again in Lake Michigan. White Pine, the state tree, has been timbered and burned relentlessly, and remains in its original grandeur on only 20 ha (49 ac) of the Hartwick Pines State Park in Lower Michigan. Even this small area of native pines is a remnant of 34 ha (86 ac) which existed as recently as 1941. Although the state flower (apple blossom), stone (petoskey), and gem (greenstone) appear to have withstood the ravages of time, many of the state's 24,000 ha (60,000 ac) of apple orchards are seriously threatened with alternate forms of land development.

In spite of the deteriorated conditions for some of the state's natural symbols, Michigan's Latin motto still endures: *Si quaeris peninsulam amoenam circumspice* (If you seek a pleasant peninsula, look about you). Similarly, *Tuebor* (I will defend) which holds the central place in the state's great seal today, still challenges Michigan citizens to defend those things which it treasures (fig. 1.3).

Figure 1.3. Great Seal of Michigan.

Problems Confronting Contemporary Michigan

In this introductory chapter it is valuable to focus attention on several problems confronting contemporary Michigan on which there is a need for further reflection and which will be discussed in the body of the text. Certainly problems are nothing new to be pondered. Each age has had to overcome what may have appeared to be insurmountable challenges to survival: traumatic climatic changes, rampant disease, sparce populations, unreliable food supplies from hunting, fishing, or gathering, and swarms of insects. Nevertheless, "man the chooser" has always made the choices which have allowed for survival.[1] Thus, it is hypothesized that the citizens of Michigan will make the necessary decisions to allow for survival through the protection of its environment. Yet, it can be predicted that, in the near future, without the deliberate altering of existing land practices, Michigan's qualities for life will be significantly diminished.

Michigan is, in many respects, a microcosm of the nation and the industrial world. Therefore, it follows that many of Michigan's problems are the same as those of the world of which it is a part. It is hoped that the reader will ponder and conclude for himself: (1) which of the following problems are the most important, (2) which problems are inseparably interrelated, and (3) which problems he or she would personally devote efforts to solving.

Agricultural land loss
Urban decay with suburban sprawl
Population growth
Economic instability
Resource depletion
Transportation-communication congestion
Leisure time increases
Decay of social-physical environments
    Crime
    Pollution
    Education
    Health service

To seek solutions to today's problems, is neither to imply that their solution alone will lead mystically to future utopia, nor that to ignore them, will cause them mystically to go away.

Relative Location and Comparative Area

Michigan is located in the northern tier of the United States and extends north 740 km (445 mi) from the Ohio border. It shares a 1,200 km (720 mi) international water boundary with the Canadian Province of Ontario. Within the world scheme of locations, Michigan's Mid-Polar-Equator Trail helps to create an awareness of the state's position in the midsection of the Northern Hemisphere. The trail, established in the 1970s for motorists, cyclists, and hikers, follows the 45th parallel and also nearly coincides with a line drawn halfway between the Lake Superior, Ohio-Indiana borders. The communities of Menominee, Bellaire, Gaylord, and Alpena are each situated within ten kilometers of the 45° north latitude line.

---

1. Daniel Jacobson, "Man the Chooser and Mankind's Most Important Choices," *Journal of Geography*, LXIX (September 1970) pp. 326-34.

Longitudinally, Michigan is located within the midsection of the Western Hemisphere. Ironwood (90°10′W) situated at the western end of the Upper Peninsula is at the midpoint of the Western Hemisphere while Port Huron (82°30′W) is located 625 km (385 mi) east on the St. Clair River.

As a result of the territorial expansion of the United States, Michigan has had a succession of locational references which continue to reoccur as anachronisms of the past. *The Victors,* song of the University of Michigan, proclaims Michigan to be the "Champions of the West." During its territorial years Michigan was a "Northwest" Territory. More recently it has been known as a "Mid-Western" state much to the amazement of Iowans and Missourians who travel into the state's vast northern forested expanses. Some of its college teams play in the "Mid-American" conference, while the Association of American Geographers places it in its East-Lakes Region. On the other hand, the U.S. Census Bureau places Michigan in the category of the "East-North Central" states.

From a social, economic, and demographic point of view, Michigan's southern Lower Peninsula is a part of the industrial *core area* of the United States and Canada which encompasses an oblong-shaped area from eastern Iowa to the Atlantic Coast and south of the Bay-Muskegon Line to the Ohio River Valley (fig. 1.4). The core area which comprises about 15 percent of the nation's area has within it a major portion of the nation's population, industrial employment and income, major libraries and educational institutions.

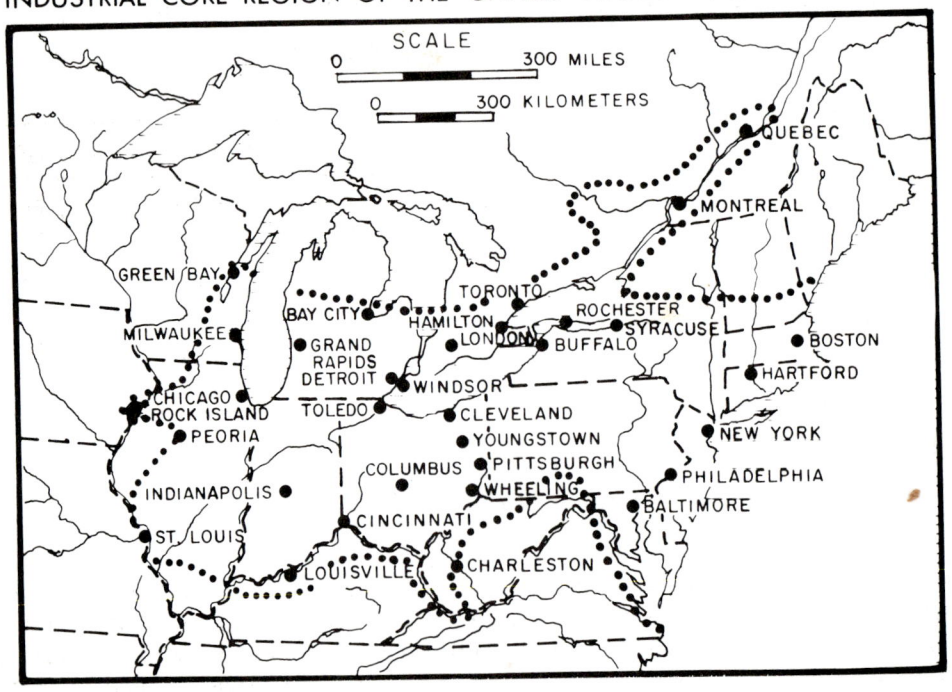

Figure 1.4. Industrial core area of the United States and Canada. (Map: University of Wisconsin Sea Grant College Program, Technical Report No. 230.)

In recent years the nation's core area has expanded well into the region north of the Bay-Muskegon Line. Indication of the core expansion into the northern Lower Peninsula is its improved accessibility, educational opportunities, stabilizing migration of population, and industrial employment opportunities. The Upper Peninsula dominated by mining, forestry, and tourism lies outside the core area of the nation. However, its expanded educational facilities maintain a strong link to the core area of the state.

The term *Heartland,* popularized by the work of the British geographer MacKinder, includes the industrial core area plus the section of country which is of basic agricultural importance to the strength of the nation. Michigan's southern Lower Peninsula again is considered to be a part of the Heartland, while the northern Lower Peninsula and Upper Peninsula are peripheral to it. Isle Royale lies on the wilderness fringe of the United States surrounded by Lake Superior.

Sizing up Michigan: Its Comparative Land-Water Areas

The land area of Michigan including inland lakes is 150,779 sq km (58,216 sq mi), ranking it 23rd among the fifty states. However, it should be observed that, in reality, the area continually varies with the process of shoreline erosion, soil deposition, and Great Lakes water level fluctuation. While these changes are not enormous, it remains that official land figures are close approximations. Its contiguous states, Illinois and Wisconsin, are similar in land area ranking 24th and 26th respectively, while Minnesota with 217,736 sq km (84,068 sq mi) ranks 12th. Ohio and Indiana are about one-third smaller, ranking 35th and 38th (table 1.1).

TABLE 1.1
Areas of the States Contiguous to Michigan

State	Land Area with Inland Waters[a]		Noninland Water Area[b]	
	Sq Km	Sq Mi	Sq Km	Sq Mi
Illinois	146,076	56,400	3,952	1,526
Indiana	93,994	36,291	591	228
Michigan	150,779	58,216	99,908	38,575
Minnesota	217,736	84,068	5,729	2,212
Ohio	106,765	41,222	8,954	3,457
Wisconsin	145,439	56,154	26,060	10,062

[a] Inland waters are permanent lakes, reservoirs of 40 acres or more.
[b] Great Lakes water surfaces within a state's boundaries.
SOURCE: *Statistical Abstract of the United States 1975.* pp. 176-177.

In the computation of areal statistics, the U.S. Census Bureau generally segregates the noninland waters from the general area figure. In most instances such a practice has a negligible effect on the overall figures. However, in the case of Michigan and other Great Lakes and coastal ocean states, the total area which its citizens are responsible for administering is distorted. For instance, Michigan manages a Great Lakes water area of 99,908 sq km (38,575 sq mi), an area larger than the state of Maine. Further, Michigan's shoreline provides its citizens a land-water ecotone of 5,176 km (3,235 mi) which is unsurpassed by any of the conterminous forty-eight states. There can be little doubt that the resources and aesthetic beauty of the state's water area justify its claim as the "Great Lakes State." Notwithstanding, the cost to manage and protect such a vast water resource is considerable even though there are no permanent inhabitants of the Great Lakes themselves. By combining both land and water areas, the area of Michigan totals 250,687 sq km (96,791 sq mi).

In comparison to the size of nations of the world, Michigan in land area alone, is larger than Greece, Nepal, Malawi, Liberia, the Koreas, and Hungary, twice the size of Ireland, and three and one half times the size of Denmark. Using the combined land-water area, Michigan is larger than the United Kingdom, West Germany, Laos, Ghana, or Romania. Alone, the Upper Peninsula is larger than Belgium, Switzerland, and nearly twice the size of El Salvador.

From a political geographic viewpoint, Michigan's shape lacks compactness due to the boundary protruding to the Northwest. This lack of compactness has created problems of both distance and social interaction which has challenged the state since the earliest days of statehood. The extension westward can perhaps best be visualized when one realizes that Ironwood is located as far west as St. Louis, Missouri, the "Gateway to the West." One of the oddities of the shape of the southeastern water boundary is the protrusion of the Ontario Lake Lowland Peninsula eastward beneath the Thumb of the Lower Peninsula. As a result, it is possible to travel due south from the Thumb Area into Canada. Both the Ambassador and Blue Water Bridges at Detroit and Port Huron extend east-west, thus in Michigan the expression "going *over to* Canada" is as common as "going *up into* Canada."

The Upper Peninsula Dilemma of Distance and Isolation

To further understand the distance from Michigan's major population center to its extreme frontier, one can observe that the straight distance between Detroit and Ironwood is as great as that between Detroit and New York or Detroit and St. Louis, 720 km (450 mi). In comparison, Minneapolis and Milwaukee are only 280 and 440 km (168 and 264 mi) respectively from Ironwood. Similarly, Marquette, the Upper Peninsula's largest city, is 160 km (100 mi) or about two hours driving time nearer to both metropolitan Milwaukee and Minneapolis than Detroit.

Logos from various Lower Peninsula organizations provide indications that the Upper Peninsula is frequently perceived as a peripheral entity of Michigan (fig. 1.5). Inadvertent depictions of the state without the Upper Peninsula through the years have become especially irksome to the state's most northern and western residents. Michigan's American Revolution Bicentennial Commission even fell victim to the graphic error of omission. The uprising in the Upper Peninsula was so great that it promptly adopted a new logo plus a special one created especially for the Upper Peninsula to smooth the ruffled feathers of that region's taxpayers (fig. 1.6).

Futuristic Boundary Proposals

Periodically, proposals are advanced by Upper Michigan citizens for the creation of a state of Superior. In the 1890s and 1970s, separate statehood proposals gained more than the usual latent support. In 1975, sixteen northern Wisconsin counties also indicated a willingness to join with the Upper Peninsula as a state. Generally, most northern residents who express support for statehood realize the unlikelihood of either the Michigan Legislature or the United States Con-

Figure 1.5. Typical logos depicting Michigan without the Upper Peninsula.

Figure 1.6a. Original Michigan Bicentennial Commission logo with the western Upper Peninsula omitted.

Suggested alteration of "76" design.
No letters, please ... we're only kidding!

OOPS – SORRY!

Figure 1.6b. Logo used by the Michigan Bicentennial Commission to apologize to western Upper Peninsula citizens for omitting part of the Upper Peninsula and Isle Royale in the original logo.

gress approving separation. Nevertheless, the periodic ritual of news releases, rallies, and advisory votes undoubtedly plays a constructive role, for it refocuses attention on the unique needs of the Upper Peninsula.

Political geographers and political scientists have cited for years instances of states which are confronted with boundary problems. In most situations the boundary malfunctions have developed out of a necessity for a political compromise or the semipermanent nature of borders established at a time when the United States had a small sedentary rural population engaged in agriculture. Ernest Tugwell, the political scientist of the 1930s, Etzel Pearcy, and Stanley Brunn, geographers in the 1970s, gained national mass media attention with their "discussion proposals" suggesting that the United States reduce its number of states through relocating the state boundaries. Professor Brunn's map illustrates that Michigan could become parts of three states functioning around the urban hubs of Detroit, Chicago, and Minneapolis (fig. 1.7). It is felt that the boundaries proposed delineate more accurately interactions based on present-day social, political, and economic realities.

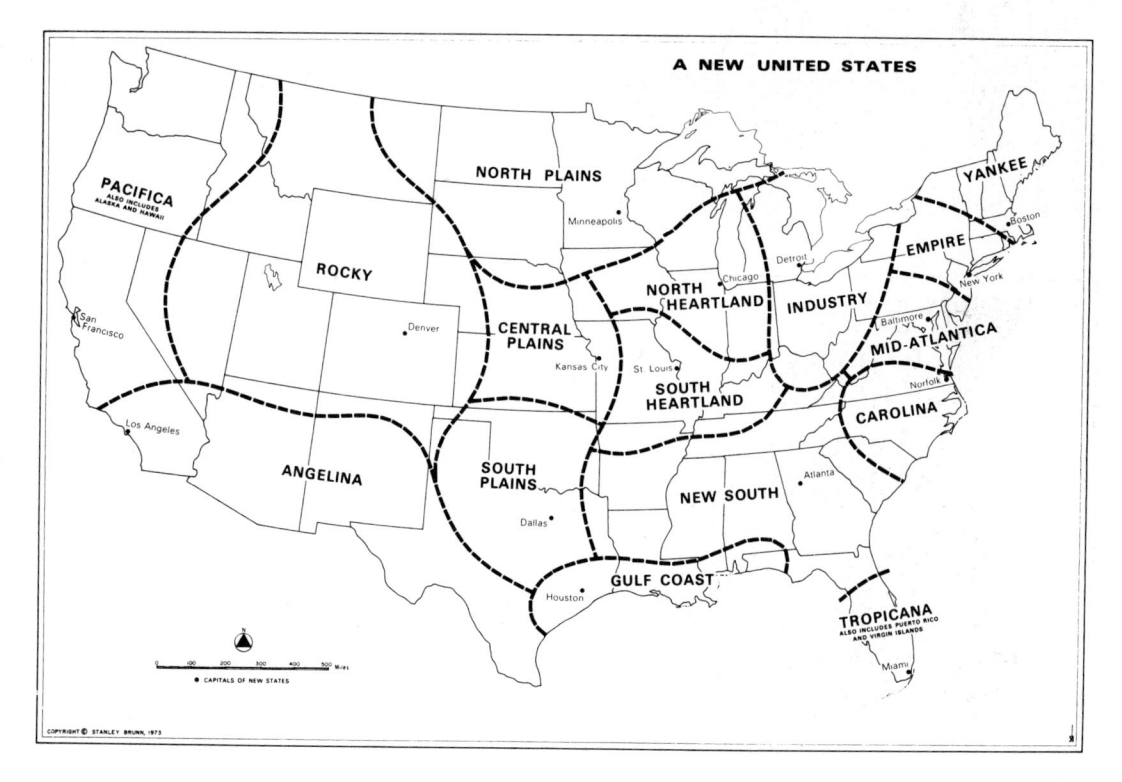

Figure 1.7. Proposed boundaries for the United States. (Source: Stanley Brunn, used with permission.)

Although national boundary reorganization is not imminent, political geographic changes have occurred at all levels of government since World War II. In many respects, boundary changes have become common including those changed for school consolidation, city annexation, county home rule, and public service districting at the local level; while nationally and internationally, territorial waters areas have shifted from 3 to 6 to 12 to 200 miles or the continental shelf.

Observing the local, national, and world political geographic boundary currents which have stirred in the last quarter century, it can be anticipated that Michigan with its high level of citizen education and communication networks will also witness a continual transition in its boundary composition.

"Michi Gama—Great Lake"
In the language of the Algonquians

Chapter Two

Historical Geographic Origins of Michigan

Few words other than *Michi Gama* (Great Lake) can describe the awesome sight as one gazes at Lake Michigan from the promontory of Sleeping Bear Dune into the westward wind and setting sun. To what lake *Michi Gama* was first applied when spoken by the ancient Indian can never be known. Nonetheless, the earliest known use of the term Lake Michigan appears on a French map in 1681, long after Jean Nicolet's credited discovery of the lake in 1634. Until the beginning of the eighteenth century, Lac Ilinois was the map name most consistently used as a title for the lake west of the Lower Peninsula.

Naming of Michigan

One of the earliest recorded applications of the word *Michigan* to a land area was by Thomas Jefferson in 1784 in his proposal for states and names to be developed in the territory northwest of the Ohio River. Surprising to many is that Jefferson's "Michigania" was originally located in what is presently northern Wisconsin and extended from eastern Lake Michigan to the Mississippi River (fig. 2.1). Had Jefferson's proposal been adopted, the Upper Peninsula would have been the state of Sylvania, the Lower Peninsula the state of Cherronesus, and the extreme southern part of Michigan the state of Metropoliana. In analyzing regions of the state in the contemporary era there is an uncanny closeness between Jefferson's names and present-day conditions: Sylvania—forest area, Cherronesus—peninsula, and Metropoliana—chief city area. It is a small point to ponder—however, it is ironic that when Michigan is depicted by outline of only its land area, such representation ignores the Indian root meaning of Michigan—"Great Lake." Therefore, perhaps Jefferson's Cherronesus, or peninsula, best fits what many citizens have perceived to be the state.

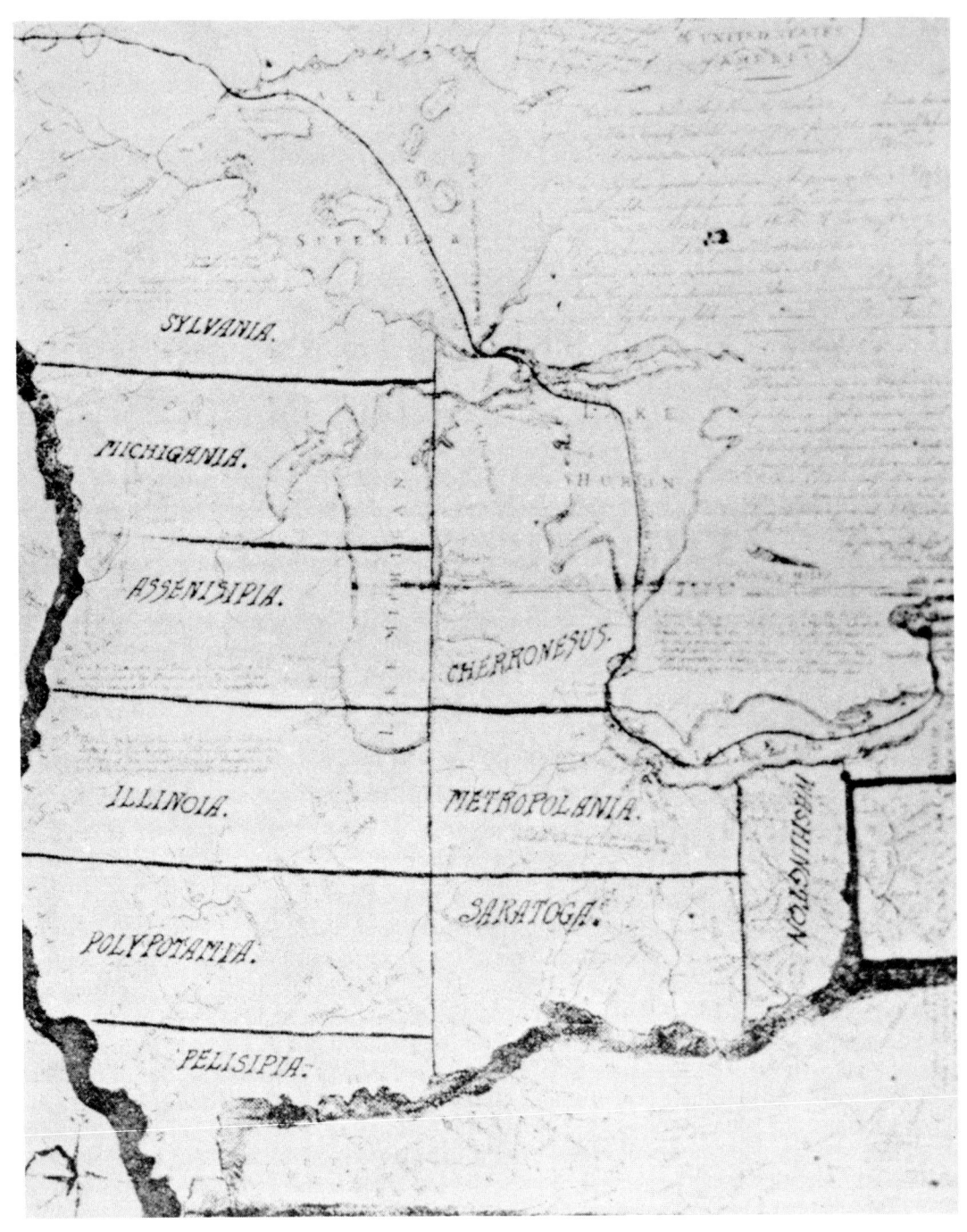

Figure 2.1. States and names proposed by Jefferson for the area northwest of the Ohio River. (John Fitch, 1785, in Karpinski's *Map Bibliography of Michigan*.)

American Indian Land Occupance Areas

To fix precise boundaries on the areas occupied by Michigan's prehistoric and the American Indian people, prior to the arrival of the first French, is a task subject to error. The aborigines of North America were composed of a large number of wandering nomads, not unlike contemporary Michigan residents. Nevertheless, territoriality among native Americans did exist in the form of a shifting core area with an undemarcated, sometimes uncontested, jointly shared frontier zone. Perhaps the noted Shawnee chief and eloquent orator, Tecumseh, best stated the aborigines' concept of territoriality:

> . . . land, as it was at first and should be yet; for it was never divided, but belongs to all for the use of each. That no part (sic party) has the right to sell, even to each other, . . .[1]

Although significant migrations occurred and land was considered to be communal, the archaeological and historical records which continue to be expanded upon by scholars provide a general pattern of native American occupancy and way of life in Michigan. Considerable landscape evidence of the early inhabitants has been found in copper mines of the Lake Superior area, garden beds in the southwestern counties, beach ridge sites in southeastern counties, and numerous mounds in southern Lower Michigan. Gratifying it is, to many Michigan citizens, tourists, and scholars, that a few relics and mound sites of the state's first residents have survived the plunder of artifacts by thoughtless treasure seekers and the unfortunate destruction by the plow and bulldozer during the state's modern development process.

Study of these sites and other archaeological evidence shows that between 11,000 B.P. (before present) and 1600 A.D., three prehistoric periods of cultural activity can be differentiated in Michigan: (1) 11,000-4500 B.P., the Paleo-Indian Hunter Period, (2) 4000-2500 B.P., the Archaic Period, and (3) 2500 B.P. to the French contact, the Woodland Period.

The Paleo-Indian Hunter

The earliest inhabitants of Michigan were what the archaeologists and anthropologists call the Paleo-Indian hunters. These people probably did not continuously occupy the peninsulas, but wandered in and out in relationship to opportunities for hunting, fishing, and gathering which were closely linked to the changing postglacial natural environment. Theories concerning the state's first residents are formulated from evidence at Michigan's oldest archaeological site on an ancient glacial lake beach ridge just north of Detroit, as well as at other professionally excavated sites. The north Detroit site, dated about 11,000 B.P., contained broken stone-crafted tools, caribou bones, and a fire hearth. The projectile points were both fluted and unfluted lanceolates. It is surmised from archaeological and historical evidence that the Paleo-Indian hunters were offspring of those that migrated out of Asia across the Bering land bridge only a few generations earlier. Undoubtedly, the Paleo-hunters followed the retreat of the Wisconsin ice sheet northward along shorelines and water courses, thus colonizing the state at the same time as postglacial flora and fauna became established. Survival in Michigan one hundred centuries ago undoubtedly depended upon the skill and cooperative efforts of small groups of male hunters in subduing the great barren ground caribou and other large animals plus the foraging expertise and success of the clan's women members.

1. T. C. McLuhan, *Touch the Earth* (New York: Promontory Press, 1971), p. 85.

It is further surmised by archaeologists that the varying glacial Great Lakes levels influenced not only the location of the early inhabitants' living site, but also their dearth in contemporary Michigan. If it is accepted that early Indians occupied lakeshore sites like present-day Monroe, Detroit, Saginaw, Bay City, and Muskegon, then the sites established up to about 9000 B.P. when the Great Lakes were about 125 meters [m] (400 ft) lower, would now be hidden, undetectable under several meters of water. Fortunately for the archaeologist, the peninsula of northern Michigan has been rebounding from its weight of glacial ice more rapidly than the rise of the Great Lakes, thus opening opportunities for site discovery even though they are scattered and hard to find.

Between 9000 B.P. and 4500 B.P. the lakes rose to drown shoreline forests, create swamps along the shore and other unfavorable habitats for animals which the hunting people depended upon for survival. Archaeologists hypothesize that in this period the human population declined. In support of this conjecture, the recorded number of sites for the period are few, and material retrieved, meager.

Indians of the Archaic Period

Approximately 4000 B.P., the natural environment again favored hunting, fishing and gathering activities. As a result, people in increasing numbers moved into the state from the south. The Archaic people, as they have been named, brought with them as "cultural baggage" a rich ceremonial life centered around a burial cult. Their burial ground artifacts frequently consisted of magnificent copper tools from the vicinity of Lake Superior, gray flint "turkey tail" points from Indiana, carved stone objects and shell gorgets from the Gulf Coast of Florida. The unused appearance of some recovered small triangular projectile points gives the impression that they were specifically made for burials. From their relics it is surmised that the Archaic Period was a time of village life in addition to hunting, fishing and gathering attuned to changing seasons. Further, it can be surmised from the diversity of artifacts that extensive trade contacts on the continent existed.

Indians of the Woodland Period

The Woodland Period of Indian activity extended from 2500 B.P. to the time of European contact. The Woodland Period is distinctive from the Archaic in that pottery was produced. Similarly, they were distinct from the Indians of historic record in that they constructed mounds and garden beds which were not a part of the traditions of the Indians with whom the French first encountered. The making of pottery and the inevitable discard of broken pieces or shards allow a specialist to determine style variations between times, as well as between groups living at the same time. From pottery relics and other site debris, a basic understanding of the Woodland Indians' land use, economic and social organization can be gained. From the present knowledge, the Woodland cultural period is divided into stages: early, middle, and late.

The Early Woodland stage of cultural evolution in Michigan was evidenced on the land by the introduction of burial mounds. The earliest known burial mound in Michigan was located along the lower Muskegon River. Perhaps also initiated at that time was the planting, cultivation and harvesting of plants. The pottery relics of the Early Woodland stage are of a thick variety, with cord impressions on both the interior and outside surfaces. It is hypothesized that women were the original crafters of pottery, while men continued in the time-consuming hunting and fishing tasks. From excavation of the Early Woodland Period sites, a decline in the quantity and quality of materials committed with the dead is observed, further suggesting a change in social order in comparison to the Archaic Indians.

The Middle Woodland stage, also known in Illinois and Ohio as the Hopewell or "Mound Builder" period, commenced about 100 B.C. By the time of World War II, 1,068 mounds, mostly Hopewell in age, had been identified. In most instances these mounds dotted the landscape along the St. Joseph, Grand, and Muskegon water courses and the Saginaw Valley. The most impressive of the mound sites is the Norton Mound Group located near Grand Rapids which was excavated under the direction of the staff of the Grand Rapids Public Museum and the University of Michigan in 1963-1964. The relics found mutely testify to what many consider to be the highest degree of artistry attained by the prehistoric residents. From that period were found skillfully decorated pottery, worked copper and mica ornaments, arrowheads, hammers, knives, drills, hoes, spades, pipes, and large and small effigies. Although many artifacts have been professionally uncovered, it is felt that the greatest bulk of Mound Builder artifacts are scattered throughout the state in unclassified amateur collections. In some cases the original relics have been subject to modern imitations which have been unsuspectingly sold as native artifacts.

In northern Michigan the village sites of the Middle Woodland stage are classified as belonging to the "lake forest" people. Their village sites are as large as those found in southern Michigan, however they do not have the elements of an elaborate ceremonial complex in comparison to the Hopewell culture. Although lake forest villages were common in their day, debris from their sites suggests that the people lacked a social organization associated with sedentary agriculture; thus hunting, fishing, and gathering undoubtedly persisted.

The Late Woodland stage started about 700 A.D. in Michigan with more widespread participation in the neolithic agricultural revolution. Seasonal ways of life were adopted so that the role of agricultural planting, cultivating, and harvesting could be expanded. The first evidence of corn in the state was found at a site in Monroe County dated about 1000 A.D. During this stage economic linkages were also strengthened with the Indian communities to the south in Mississippi, Cahokia (Illinois), Angle Site (Indiana), and the Fort Ancient Group (Ohio). Even though Michigan's early people interacted with these southern groups, they did not construct temple mounds and plazas which might suggest contact with the great cultural centers of Meso-America. Nonetheless, a Michigan custom, rarely encountered north of Mexico, was the trephining of skulls. Most specimens uncovered indicate that the process was performed near or after death. However, the University Museum at Ann Arbor has a skull showing evidence of well-advanced healing that could only have occurred during life. This early form of neurosurgery may have been performed to relieve severe headaches or brain tumors. Mississippian cultural diffusion influences can be identified in the trade pottery and in style modifications on ceramic materials. James Fitting, the former State Archaeologist, speculates that the Late Woodland people in Michigan fulfilled a role similar to that of the early historic people who carried on agriculture, plus specializing in part, in the trapping of furs. Instead of marketing furs in Europe, the Woodland people could have traded them in the Indian centers of the Midwest and South. The increased dependence upon agriculture during the Late Woodland stage is reflected in an increase of population based on the number of village sites and burial grounds which have been found to be associated with that period.

By about 1000 A.D. the regional economic patterns similar to those found by the Europeans had been established. Native Indian regional activities varied primarily with the state's natural environment. Although the knowledge of agriculture was undoubtedly spread throughout the state, it could not be practiced as readily in the north. Thus, the early northern Michiganians adopted a system with a greater focus on fishing. Family units would gather into large assemblies near the rewarding fishing sites of the Upper Straits during spring and summer. With the onset of fall and winter individual families and clans would disperse to survive on the success of hunting and trapping.[2]

In the quest to expand knowledge about Michigan's first inhabitants, two basic problems face the professional researcher. One problem dates from the formative days of Euro-American settlement which brought a widespread disregard for sacred sites and relic features of the aborigines. The unwitting disturbance of prehistoric sites not only has angered native Indians for years, but also reduces knowledgeable analysis based on cooperative efforts between finders, landowners, native Americans, and archaeologists. A second and perhaps more serious problem facing researchers concerning early life in Michigan is the unabating destruction or damage to both known and unknown archaeological-historical sites as residential, recreational, industrial, and transportation systems expand with population and life-style changes.

The statutory responsibility for the recovery and preservation of the state's archaeological materials rests with the two-person Archaeology Section, Michigan History Division of the Department of State. Undoubtedly, with such a small staff but great responsibility, Michigan runs the risk of the further loss of its prehistorical geographic landscape and relic features. Lacking expanded efforts by its citizens, Frank Angelo's 1975 opening remark in *Yesterday's Michigan*, ". . ., but little is known yet of the very first Indians who came to make it home," will remain true.[3]

Post-French Contact Indian Occupance Patterns

In contrast to the knowledge about Paleo-Indians, Indian history originating at their contact with the French is voluminous, widely known, and studied continuously. A summary of the regional activities of the immediate ancestors of Michigan's native American population is desirable to illustrate similarities and contrasts with the present-day Indian citizens.

The Tribes of Michigan

The history of Indians of Michigan is generally associated with three different tribal groups which occupied varying sections of the state during their seminomadic era of inhabitation. At the time of contact with the French, it has been estimated that 15,000 Indians resided in the state, with the majority (12,000) situated in the southern Lower Peninsula. The three primary tribes of the Algonquian-speaking group, Chippewa, Ottawa, and Potawatomi, occupied both peninsulas. The Chippewas or Ojibiwas, as they are also known, spoke a dialect nearly identical to the Ottawa. It is from these tribal languages that Michigan has derived many of its present-day Indian place names such as: Okemos, Osceola, Negaunee, Mecosta, Kalamazoo, Tah-

---

2. James E. Fitting, "Archaeology in Michigan: Present Knowledge and Prospects," *Great Lake Informant,* Series One, Number One (Lansing: Department of State, 1973), pp. 1-4.
3. Frank Angelo, *Yesterday's Michigan* (Miami, Florida: E. A. Seemann Publishing, Inc., 1975), p. 11.

quamenon, Kitchitikipi, and Ontonagon. Although the acculturation process of transferring the English language to the contemporary Indians is nearly complete, the native languages of the seventeenth century can still be heard in the vicinity of the present-day reservations, Dowagiac, and on Sugar Island at Sault Ste. Marie.

The Chippewa-Ojibiwa. The core area occupied by the Chippewa-Ojibawa was the Upper Peninsula, the Canadian shore of the Upper Great Lakes, and the northern Lower Peninsula. They were "northerners;" however, with the founding of Detroit in 1701 by Cadillac, many moved southward from the Straits of Mackinac to the Lower Straits area while other Chippewas congregated near Saginaw. The basic life-supporting activity of the Chippewa was, like their ancestors of the Late Woodland stage, fishing, especially the harvesting of the tasty white fish. Their continued engagement in fishing in the contemporary era has brought the northern Indians into conflict with the state between the management and interpretations of fishing rights granted in the treaties of land cession.

The Ottawa. The French first encountered the Ottawa, which translates as "traders," on Manitoulin Island (Ontario) near the headwaters of Lake Huron. As early as 1615 the Ottawas began their western movement from Canada's Ottawa River Basin. Since the early seventeenth century they resided at several locales along the eastern shore of Lake Michigan extending at one time as far south as the Benton Harbor area. They also periodically occupied widespread sites throughout the northern Lower Peninsula. About 1742, approximately 180 Ottawas moved with their families to L'Arbre Croche near Harbor Springs on the Little Traverse Bay whose influence in that section continues to be felt.

The Ottawa, while at times living in areas in which agriculture could be continuously undertaken, appear to have kept it in secondary importance within their economy. Preferred was their role as traders, exchanging furs for agricultural products. The Ottawa occupied large village sites which were rarely fortified and were relocated frequently. In the winter season it was common for small groups of men to travel long distances into the interior reaches of the state to hunt. Hinsdale, in his monumental *Archaeological Atlas of Michigan* in 1931, quotes Black Bird, ". . . that his people abandoned their village in the fall for their favorite winter quarters among the hardwood trees somewhere above Big Rapids on the Muskegon . . ." After maple sugaring in early spring, they would return to the L'Arbre Croche area to cultivate corn and other plants.

The Potawatomis. The Potawatomis were originally found in Wisconsin in the mid-1600s, but moved into the basin of the St. Joseph River during the late seventeenth century. Hundreds of the descendants of this tribe avoided the removal and reservation attempts during the 1830s and 1840s. Thus, today there remain scores of Potawatomis, living and working in the vicinity of Dowagiac Township in Cass County.

Several small tribes and subtribes occupied portions of the state for short lengths of time, frequently being driven in or out by their tribal adversaries. Tribes having such a history included the Miami, Wyandot (Huron), Menominee, and Salk. Subtribal groups in southwestern Michigan included the Piankashaw, Eel River, and Wea. The Sauk, Miami, and Menominee were Algonquian-speaking tribes who lived at times respectively in the Saginaw Valley, southwestern Lower Peninsula, and southwestern Upper Peninsula.

The Menominees were basically a Wisconsin tribe whose area of habitation expanded into Michigan in association with wild rice gathering activities. The Miami, a mild-mannered tribe according to French explorers, were closely related to the Illinois Indians. After the War of

1812, the Miami resettled in Oklahoma. Both the Miami and Potawatomi were agricultural people although they also hunted buffalo. Unlike the Ottawa, the southwestern Indians built large stockaded villages near their farms. During the winter months all but the very old would join extended hunting trips away from their permanent villages.

The Huron-Wyandot. Huron is a French word meaning "unkempt person" which was unceremoniously applied to the Wyandot tribe. The Wyandots were an Iroquian-speaking group; however, even with their off-shoot relationship to the Iroquois, they were not a member of the Five Nations or Iroquois Longhouse. The Hurons, like several other Michigan tribes, had associations with both the Upper and Lower Straits areas, but after 1650 they lived mainly in the vicinity of the present-day city of Wyandotte. Iroquois Point on Lake Superior, northwest of the Bay Mills Reservation, indicates the place in 1653 where an Iroquois war party met a disastrous defeat in its attempt to extend its control into the Upper Great Lakes region after receiving weapons from the Dutch.

Cultural Features. House shelters constructed by Michigan Indians were usually dome-shaped bark or mat-covered wigwam enclosures with a rectangular floor pattern. An example of a typical bark lodge has been preserved on Mackinac Island. The teepee is popularly associated with Indians in general; however, in Michigan the Chippewa summer residence, with a low conical shape covered with skins and bark, was the native Americans' closest link to the classical teepee. The interior of lodges was furnished with reed and cedar bark mats, splint woven baskets, and bags for storage. Wood, bark, and pottery were formed into vessels while stone, bone, antlers, and copper provided resources for other utensils. Common within the nearly 750 village sites which have been found in Michigan were small corn storage cribs. Pits similar to present-day ground silos were also used for caches of grain. In comparison to village sites, about one-third as many native burial grounds have been identified in the state.

In concluding a historical sketch of Indian life, the noted Michigan Indian authority, Emerson F. Greenman, provides the following sensitive observation:

> The white settlers of Michigan were inclined to look upon the Indians as savages. Such has always been the relationship between people with a superior technology and those they have conquered. Neither side, until quite recently, have informed themselves in matters of history, folklore, and anthropology. The Indians of Michigan, and all Indians for that matter, were civilized in their own way. With strict rules of conduct and manners, and ideas that come under the head of religion. . . . The clans were at once political, social and religious in character.[4]

Contemporary Indian Reservations and Urbanization

Government actions in the early twentieth century have had significant impact on the lives of Michigan's small Amerind population. In 1924 the native Indians were granted citizenship—for many, a difficult concept to grasp having lived in Michigan all their lives. Ten years later the Indian Reorganization Act reversed previous federal policy which encouraged the breakup of tribes and the allotment of land to individuals. Subsequent to 1934 efforts have been made to assist the tribes in regaining land holdings to reestablish a self-sustaining economy and social organization. Contemporary Michigan has four Indian reservations with three in the

---

4. Emerson Greenman, "The Indians of Michigan," Information Series No. 1 (Lansing: Michigan Historical Commission, 1957), p. 2.

Upper Peninsula: L'Anse, Hannahville, and Bay Mills. In the central Lower Peninsula the Isabella Reservation near Mt. Pleasant was reorganized under the 1934 Act. Although the term reservation is used, the modern-day Indians are not required to reside on them to be considered tribal members. Further, while it is common to refer to a specific reservation as Indian, the actual ownership of the combined land holdings of 9120 ha (22,800 ac) continues to be held by the United States Government.

The Mt. Pleasant Reserve. The reservation at Mt. Pleasant, first established in 1855, illustrates the land-holding changes as the government has experimented with various Indian policies during the last century and a quarter. In 1855 a treaty was concluded to create a land reserve in the sparsely settled frontier county of Isabella for "Chippewas of Saginaw, Swan Creek, and Black River." The Chippewa by this period were in fact a mixture of Chippewa, Potawatomi, Wyandot, Ottawa, and other tribes. The reserve comprised all unsold lands in a total of six survey townships (fig. 2.2). From the reservation lands each family head was

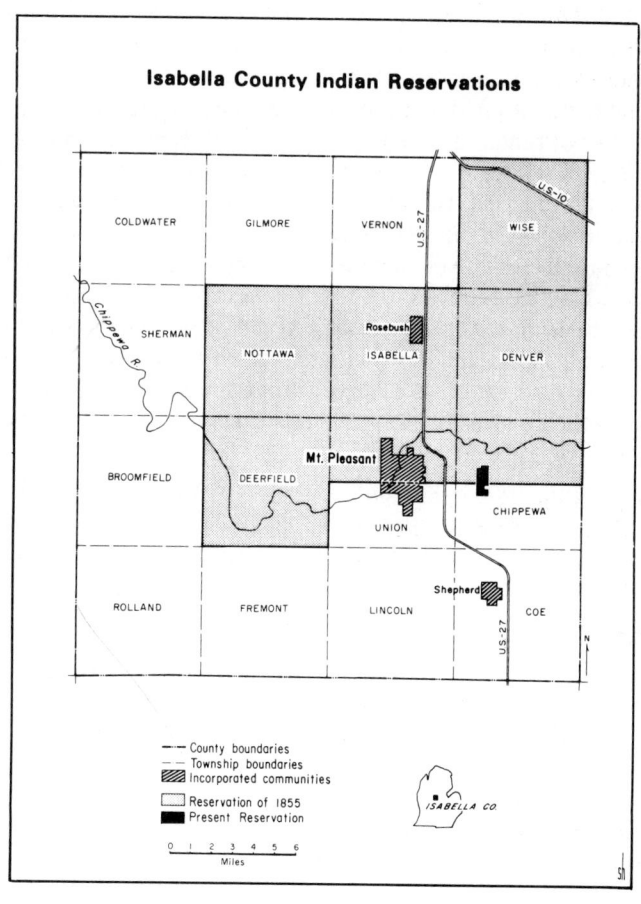

Figure 2.2. Isabella County Indian Reservations. (Source: D. Kyser, *The Peninsular,* 1974.)

allowed to select eighty acres to be held in "severality" (individual ownership). Additionally, each person over twenty-one years of age and each orphan was allotted forty acres. The land not selected in the initial five years remained government property, again reserved, but only for the exclusive purchase by Indians at the set land sale rates. The provisions of the treaty reserve barred white settlement only temporarily from an area of nearly 55,200 ha (138,000 ac), as those lands granted to Indians classified as "competent" could be sold to white settlers. The pressure on the Isabella Indians to sell mounted after 1871 when unrestricted titles began to be conveyed to them. Those classified by Indian agents as "not so competent" were granted land titles with provisos limiting transfer with the consent of the Secretary of the Interior. Notwithstanding the government's desire to create a stable community of Indian farmers, the rapid transfer of Indian farmland to white owners illustrates the experiment's failure. In 1860 Isabella County's Indian population numbered 848; however, by 1880 it had declined to 479. In contrast, white population rose from 595 in 1860 to 11,679 twenty years later. The ambitious reserve program, which attempted to acculturate rapidly a society of primarily hunters, fishers, and gatherers with minimum agricultural traditions into a sedentary agricultural society, did not fail to recognize the need for a community saw and grist mill and blacksmith shop. These primary activities were set up as early as 1857, along with provisions for the purchase of tools, livestock, and other materials needed in establishing an agricultural tradition.

In the area of the original reserve there are a few plots of land still held by native Americans. A vexing contemporary problem has been created by the "not so competent" proviso land grants. The unauthorized transfer of these grants has resulted in "clouded land titles" on the lands recently purchased in the reserve area.

The Isabella Indian Reservation in contemporary existence is much smaller than the original 1855 reserve whose boundaries are still frequently depicted on highway maps and in school atlases. Under the Indian Reorganization Act of 1934 a new Chippewa tribe was officially formed. A block of 180 ha (450 ac) was secured which partially laid outside the original reserve. The modern-day reservation is controlled in common by all members in the tribe. In addition to a few farm houses already along the new reservation's county roads, the Bureau of Indian Affairs added about another two dozen homes, stringing them along the roads. In 1966 an apartment complex with twenty-one units for Indians was constructed on the reservation. The farmland is rented to local farmers with the income divided among the members listed on the tribal roll. Isabella County's 1970 Indian population of 439 includes: (1) tribal members who live on the reservation, (2) tribal members living off the reservation, and (3) Indians who are not associated with the Isabella Reservation tribal roll.

The Nonreservation Potawatomis. The Potawatomi Indians in southwestern Michigan, unlike the four other Indian communities (L'Anse, Hannahville, Bay Mills, and Isabella) in the 1930s, exercised their traditional independence by voting not to accept a reservation consisting of two sections of muck land in Silver Creek Township and options for additional highland suitable for fruit cultivation. Everett Claspy, the historian of the southwest Michigan Potawatomis, observed that, "The tribal officers now realize that a tactical mistake was made in not coming under the Act."[5]

Although the Michigan contingent of Potawatomis have avoided two reservation experiments a century apart in the 1830s and 1930s, the Silver Creek Indians have adapted themselves fairly well to the 100 years of economic change. At first, in the nineteenth century,

---

5. Everett Claspy, *The Potawatomi Indians of Southwestern Michigan* (Dowagiac: 1966). p. 30.

the Potawatomis pursued their tradition of farming, securing work on white-owned farms in Cass County, and became pickers in the Fruit Belt. With the need for ever-increasing amounts of farmland and displacement by Chicano migrants, the rural Potawatomis, like other citizens, sought employment in urban centers.

At the L'Anse Reservation an attempt is currently being made to stimulate the local Indian economy and employment opportunities. Dr. Duane Cummings, a physician who has established a growing bison herd near Stanwood, 70 km (45 mi) northeast of Muskegon, has undertaken the difficult task of introducing and nurturing a buffalo herd operation at L'Anse. If successful, the grass-eating buffalo should provide both a source of meat and a tourist interest. Additionally, the buffalo may help to maintain in part the traditional out-of-doors lifestyle historically associated with the Indian.

Indian Education. Up to the mid-twentieth century the education of Michigan Indians was controlled by the federal government. At first schools were established in areas with high concentrations of Indians such as the historic school on Mackinac Island. Later in the nineteenth century, boarding schools came into existence including one at Mt. Pleasant. In 1934 the State of Michigan assumed increased responsibility for the education of the children included in the state's total of 7,000 Indians. The state education policy then, and now, is to integrate the youngsters into the public schools. While Michigan is responsible for the educational needs of its Amerind minority, the federal government periodically distributes money to the school districts with the greatest proportion of Indian pupil enrollment. For instance, in 1971-1972, $50,000 was allocated to six school districts to aid Indian children. Such aid is generally in the form of home-school coordinators, tutors, and teacher aides.

The Urbanization of the Michigan Indian. The Michigan Indian, in spite of efforts, policies, or desires which may conflict, is continually being assimilated into urban life. The acculturation process is apparent by their place of residence, intermarriages, and occupations increasingly in factories and service activities, as well as college enrollment trends. Of the seven counties with an Indian population over 300, only Chippewa has a rural condition. Wayne and Kent Counties with 4,419 and 1,121 Indian citizens respectively, account for one-third of the state's total Indian population. Oakland, Ingham, Genesee, Macomb, Muskegon, Emmet, and Isabella Counties also have significant Indian populations. With the exception of Emmet and Isabella Counties, each attracted Indian migrants with its factory employment opportunities. Emmet County has retained its Indian population due to the lasting impact of the historic Ottawa village, L'Arbre Croche. The present-day Amerind population of 17,000 is only slightly larger than the estimates of the number of Indians by the early French.

The case study map of the Indian students in the Lansing School District illustrates the locational pattern of the urbanizing Indian families near industrial sites and lower cost housing (fig. 2.3). While contemporary Indian family units are found to be in close proximity to industry, there is a lack of heavy concentration in ghettos or multifamily housing projects. Mullally's conclusions concerning the urbanized Indians are significant as evidence that by the time the American Indian reaches the city, acculturation is nearly complete:

> The Indians of Lansing . . . lack a formalized organization or sense of unity. Many Indians are satisfied with being assimilated into the population and do not seek to be associated with other Indians; others seek an Indian identity.[6]

---

6. Lee J. Mullally, "An Historical Analysis of the American Indians of Lansing, Michigan," *The Peninsular*, Vol. I (1974), p. 26.

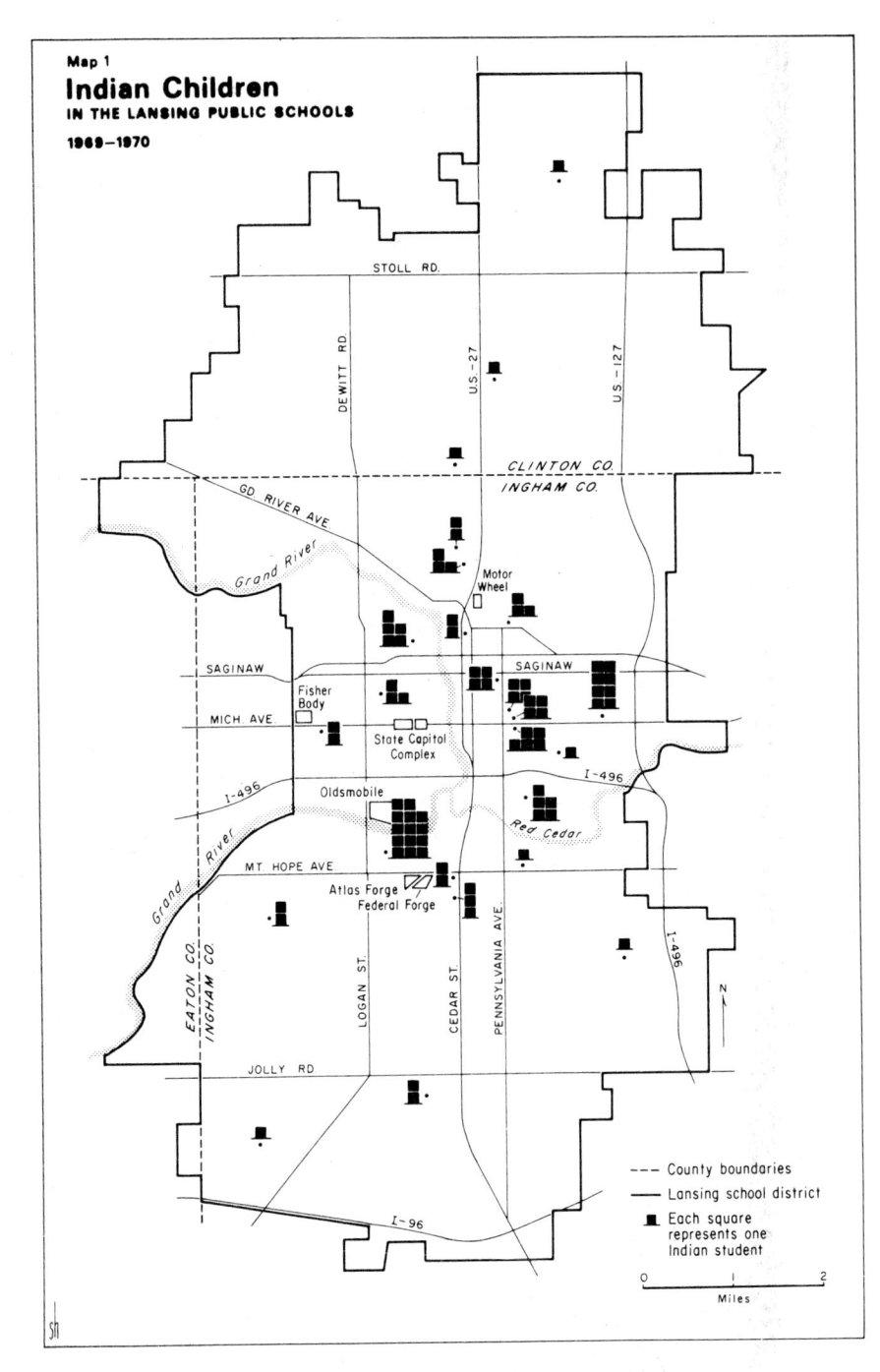

Figure 2.3. Indian children in the Lansing Public Schools, 1969-1970. (Source: L. Mullally, *The Peninsular,* 1974.)

The Colonial Occupance Era of the French, British and Spanish

Half of Michigan's four centuries of inhabitation by people of European cultural heritage has been within the French and British colonial empires claimed by discovery. Only the Hudson River Dutch and Pacific Coast Russians of the well-known North American colonizers failed to penetrate the peninsulas. While not qualifying as Michigan colonialists, some Spanish did spend a day or two near Niles at Fort St. Joseph and vicinity. Whether the Phoenicians or Vikings reached Michigan can be debated. Nonetheless, significant evidence to support an argument that settlement occurred is sparce.[7]

The written record describing Michigan's people and physical environment began to accumulate with the westward movement of French explorers and Roman Catholic priests. The first Frenchmen, who came into the state via its waterways after the Grand Banks fisheries were established off the mouth of the St. Lawrence River, were questing for something other than unknown wealth which the interior might possess. The magnet that drew the explorers to the Great Lakes was a desire to find a water route to the known riches of Asia.

French Claims and Explorer Impact

Even in 1534, when Jacques Cartier gained credit for the discovery of the St. Lawrence River, fishing ships were already off its mouth.[8] Nonetheless, his voyages up the St. Lawrence to Montreal and claims for the French Royal Crown of the St. Lawrence Valley set the stage for the knowledge to be gained by the explorers sent out by Champlain three-quarters of a century later. The fur that Cartier and his agents found, plus the land claimed, became more important to the settlement of Michigan than their not finding legendary Cathay which had been sought.

Discovery of Michigan. Considering the combined events of the 10,000 years of settlement by the American Indians and the unheralded logistic support necessary for exploration, it is perhaps dubious to focus on the individuals who were the first Europeans to reach the shores of Michigan. Nonetheless, the events of discovery are important to geography as they help to identify shifts in the chronology of ethnic impacts on the landscape. Two Frenchmen have gained credit from historians as the first to reach present-day Michigan. According to Gabriel Sagard's *Histoire du Canada* published in 1636, Etienne Brule, an interpreter and agent of Champlain is alleged to have wintered near Sault Ste. Marie in 1618-1619. Perhaps two years later he was accompanied by Grenoble up the St. Mary's River into Lake Superior. Their return with copper nuggets and a description of the Upper Peninsula lends credibility to the assumption that they were also the first Europeans to sense the potential wealth of the area.

Environmental Perception. Beginning in the early 1600s Champlain began to submit reports on the natural conditions of New France which were realistically frank in comparison to those of Cartier. He repeatedly warned against inferring that the climate was similar to that of the homeland simply from the resemblances of vegetation and similar latitudes. Up to his time, it had been popular to consider the North American area as literally a "New" France.[9] With a

---

7. Harland Hatcher and Erich Walter, *A Pictorial History of the Great Lakes* (New York: Bonanza Books, 1963), pp. 38-39; Willis Dunbar, *Michigan: A History of the Wolverine State* (Grand Rapids: Wm. B. Eerdmans Publishing Co., 1966), p. 47.
8. Ralph H. Brown, *Historical Geography of the United States* (New York: Harcourt, Brace & World, Inc., 1948), p. 24.
9. *Ibid.*, p. 10.

more accurate knowledge of the land, including low fertility of soil, short growing season, and long snowy winters, the unfounded expectation by the French of being able to transfer easily the life-style of their homeland to the St. Lawrence watershed was doomed. On the other hand, the reports that interior areas held a potential with their abundant fur-bearing animals found interest with the government. This was especially so when it was noted that the native Indians, when treated with a semblance of respect, would cooperate in trade of pelts. Champlain's, missionaries', and other people's analyses resulted in the setting into motion of the flow of valuable furs from the Great Lakes region to the profitable markets of France and Europe.

French Occupance Activities

If one could have flown over Michigan at the beginning of the French era of occupancy and duplicated the flight 150 years later after the British had gained control of the Great Lakes as a result of the arduous French and Indian War, only a small percentage of change in the natural landscape would have been discernible. At no time in the colonial period did the French population exceed four thousand. Their population was characteristically of low density made up mostly of men scattered along fur trade routes. The small number of French women and families that did settle were huddled in protection at the villages of Mackinac, Sault Ste. Marie, Detroit, and later, Frenchtown. While the French were meager in numbers and did not alter the physical environment greatly, their contribution to Michigan historical and cultural geography has been enduring. Especially significant was the French fur trade which gave birth to the state's largest city.

French Fur Trade. Following the water routes of the explorers, scores of fur traders made contact with the Indians and began blending the ways of Europe with native American cultures. Transportation was by canoe and along the ancient foot paths. The trader was welcomed into the bark wigwams. In time, daughters were offered in marriage, and children were born to these French-Indian parents. These wives and children cemented relationships with the Europeans and thereby served the expansion of the fur trade. Food was secured by the isolated trader in the manner of the Indian. In exchange for the Indians' efforts of skillfully trapping and collecting beaver, mink, otter, and other skins, the fur trader provided cloth, guns, knives, blankets, beads, and numerous other items.

French Fur Trade Settlements

Trading of goods and protection of the developing economic system necessitated a few well-situated exchange sites. At these places the French influence became most apparent, and the finer elements of sedentary French culture emerged. Michilimackinac, later shortened to Mackinac, Sault Ste. Marie, and Detroit emerged as the paramount places of both the French and British fur eras. Each of these sites commanded narrow straits with defensive attributes. They also were relatively easily linked to Montreal, more than 800 km (500 mi) away, which at the time was the head of ocean navigation. These communities were also sites of native Indian tribal congregation. The sites were near places of abundant fish which could be easily secured, an important consideration for the "fish-day" French Catholic.

Portages and Waterways. The headwaters and tributaries of the Mississippi River and St. Lawrence River watershed are divided by low moraines and lake ridges. In ancient times the best portage points were located between the two watersheds. Some of them occurred within former river channels which occasionally flooded, making even short portages unnecessary. The historic significance of the drainage pattern created by glacial actions has been its contribution to easier transportation. Portages most important to the fur trade centered on Michigan included: the Fox-Wisconsin, Chicago-DesPlaines, the Fort Wayne linking the Maumee and Wabash, the Georgian Bay and Grand Portage at the west end of Lake Superior. The long and difficult portage around Niagara Falls was usually avoided by the French in the initial period of settlement. Hostilities of the Iroquois, allied to the British, were a major factor contributing to the shunting of the southern trade route in the formative days of French fur trade.

Missionary Efforts. Concurrently associated with the opening of the Great Lakes to fur trade was the Christian missionary work among the Indians by various Catholic Orders, especially the Jesuits. Mission churches were a notable feature of the trading communities. Without the unselfish and tireless efforts of these Christians in their detailed mapping and journal recordings of observations while engaged in mission work, the bulk of historical geography of the initial European entrance into the Great Lakes region would have been lost. The volume and accuracy of the priests' work under hardship and privation remains awesome to the present-day researcher.

Sault Ste. Marie and St. Ignace. The Upper Straits French communities, Sault Ste. Marie at the falls of the St. Mary's River in 1668 and St. Ignace in 1671, became the first permanently settled European communities in Michigan with the establishment of their Catholic missions. To further strengthen French control of the Straits of Mackinac and protect the fur trade, the French government later stationed troops at St. Ignace in 1683 and at Fort Michilimackinac (Mackinac City) on the tip of the Lower Peninsula.

Michilimackinac. For thirty years the Straits of Mackinac was held by means of a fortified trading post and missionary center. During the first decade of the eighteenth century, while Cadillac was establishing Detroit, the number of French in the Upper Straits area declined. Nevertheless, with renewed emphasis on the importance of the Upper Straits, modest population growth and construction of a fort in 1715 led to Michilimackinac's international fame as the foremost Great Lakes fur center. In addition to a garrison of 425 military personnel, the fur traders, master carpenters, skilled artisans, blacksmiths, and farmers with their wives and children provided a distinctive French-American character to the outpost. Although "fort" was a part of the Fort Michilimackinac place name, the community's *raison-d-etre* at the site was not so much fortification but rather the *fortunes* to be made in the exchange of pelts.

To secure wealth from the trade of fur, two groups of men were of critical importance. The *coureurs de bois,* or wood rangers, lived with the Indians and bargained for the furs. Those who came without valid trading licenses spent the majority of their lives in the woods and became similar to Indians in life-style. The *voyageurs* were the French boatmen who paddled and portaged the valued trade between Quebec, Montreal and the strategic lakeside settlements. The Montreal-type canoe, eleven meters long and two meters wide, could carry a five ton burden with ten men.

After the British gained control of the Upper Straits in 1761, the cultural landscape remained substantially the same as a result of liberal terms of peace. Unlike the Acadian French, those at Mackinac were allowed to remain in their homes, keep their possessions, real estate, and religion. Furthermore, the region's economic stability was maintained by the British encouraging the French traders, craftsmen, and farmers to remain at Mackinac. As the American Revolutionary War raged, the British in control of the Upper Straits decided that the most defensible location for the fort, in order to command the straits and carry on active trading, would be one of the islands between Lake Huron and Lake Michigan. Thus, in 1781 the fort and trading community were relocated for the third time, to a bluff on Mackinac Island. The new stone-walled fortification and buildings were simply named Fort Mackinac. British, French, and Indians all joined the abandonment of the old fort site at the tip of the Lower Peninsula and made the island their permanent home.[10]

The government of the United States finally gained control of Fort Mackinac and the area it controlled in 1796. The War Department utilized it until 1895, except for the three years the British occupied it during the War of 1812. In 1875 Mackinac Island was made the nation's second national park still under the jurisdiction of the War Department. When Michigan's interest in establishing a State Park System materialized, Mackinac National Park was turned over to the state, and it became Michigan's first state park. Nine years later, in 1904, the site of Fort Michilimackinac was acquired also for use as a state park.

Contemporary French-American Activities at the Straits

The construction of the Mackinac Bridge in the late 1950s rekindled interest in the Upper Straits. Since that time archaeological work done by Michigan State University personnel in cooperation with the Park Commission of the Department of Natural Resources (DNR) has revealed an increasing amount of knowledge about the cultural geography of the region. In 1974 a significant breakthrough occurred with the identification of a 1749 French map of Fort Michilimackinac which included by location the names of individual family homes such as Langlade, Amiot, Ains, Blondeau, and Chevalier. The sites of the church, Jesuit priest's house, blacksmith shops, powder magazine, stables, ice house, bake oven, and other places are clearly indicated. Undoubtedly, this map will help the thousands of tourists who visit the straits area to identify more closely with the French individuals who opened Michigan's fur trading frontier. The 1749 French map will also assist in the more accurate reconstruction and interpretation of the fort, as previous work and analysis were based on three English maps of the 1760s.[11]

The painstaking authentic restoration work so far accomplished at the two state parks at Mackinac provides excellent examples of the house types of Michigan's earliest European settlers. The realistic structural materials used in the reconstructions, as well as fabrication and design, help to explode the myth which has tended to emphasize that nearly all European immigrant pioneers lived in log cabins (fig. 2.4).

The heritage of the French is indelibly etched on the landscape of the Upper Straits. Place names abound with Gaulic antecedents including: Pointe Aux Pins, Bois Blanc, Les Cheneaux, Pointe La Barbe, Gros Cap, Epoufette, Pointe Aux Chenes, and De Tour. These lesser known places, as well as the popularly known St. Ignace and Sault Ste. Marie, continually proclaim the impact and onetime dominance of the French.

---

10. Eugene Peterson, *France at Mackinac: A Pictorial Record of French Life and Culture 1715-1760* (Mackinac Island: Mackinac Island State Park Commission, 1968), pp. 3-38; "Mackinac Island State Park 1895-1976," *Michigan Natural Resources,* vol. 45, no. 3 (May-June 1976), pp. 42-43.

11. "French Map from 1749 called 'Greatest Find of the Year,'" *Michigan Natural Resources,* vol. 43, no. 5 (September-October 1974), p. 30.

Figure 2.4. Reconstructed Fort Michilimackinac. (Photo: Michigan Travel Commission.)

Contemporarily, numerous descendants from the French fur trading era are active businessmen and service workers participating in the recreation economy which supports the region. Their children are still baptized, married, and registered at St. Anne's Church on Mackinac Island. When death inevitably overcomes life, the soil of the Catholic cemetery becomes a final resting place.

French at the Lower Straits—Detroit

In the late seventeenth century, Cadillac, commandant at Michilimackinac, reasoned that the fur trade could best be protected from a British-Iroquois encroachment by congregating the Indians friendly to the French in the vicinity of the Lower Straits. Strengthening the argument to establish a strong settlement at Detroit was the conclusion that the physical environment to the south would be less rigorous and more conducive to agricultural labors. Place names such as: Grosse Pointe, Grosse Isle, River Rouge, Ecorse, Frenchtown, and Gabriel Richard, which appear on contemporary maps, provide testimony to Antoine de la Mothe Cadillac's bold determination to maintain his and France's economic hold on the Great Lakes region of New France. Through the years the place-name "Detroit River" has caused confusion. "Detroit" is the French word for strait (a narrow waterway between two larger water bodies); however, the British appended the English word "river" to the strait which created the continuing geographic and linguistic absurdity.

Fort Pontchartrain at Detroit. The decision to create a settlement at Detroit did not initially receive sympathetic support from the religious leaders at St. Ignace nor the merchant elite of the Mackinac region. Nonetheless, the fur trade, military force, substantial missionary activity, and Indians shifted to the Lower Straits once 1,500 livres of financial aid from Count Pontchartrain in Quebec were assured.

Although the site of Detroit has been continuously occupied since the summer of 1701 when Cadillac constructed Fort Pontchartrain, there is some evidence that indicates a temporary French trading post had operated there as much as fifteen years earlier.[12] Farmer, in his monumental *History of Detroit,* observes that the critical element in the plan to gain prominence for the Lower Straits was to agglomerate the friendly Indians there so that the *coureurs de bois* could secure neither pelts nor favors elsewhere. Acculturation and equality between the Indians and French were stimulated by the open encouragement of intermarriage at Detroit and the learning of the French language by native Americans so that they could communicate on an independent basis with the French government. Undoubtedly the interpreters and Jesuits were not altogether delighted with the "social-political" advancements of teaching and communication which began to diffuse from the new town.

Early Detroit. The initial Fort Pontchartrain complex which emerged in 1701 consisted of a small stockade with a sunken timber palisade, chapel, powder magazine, and a few dwellings. By fall the soil was tilled and sown to wheat. Requiring less change to the local landscape was the Wyandot Indian village which was laid out nearby in the early winter to accommodate that tribe which came from the north.

The population at Detroit in its first decade did not witness a boom, even though 150 settlers arrived in 1706 with cattle, horses, and other farming and craftsmen materials. By the end of the next two years the efforts of these people and others had resulted in only 140 ha (350 ac) of cleared land including twenty-nine farm and habitat lots outside the fort along the waterfront. After Cadillac's appointment as governor of Louisiana and the rekindled interest in Michilimackinac, the settlement at Detroit languished. What growth did occur was through natural increases of the local inhabitants; one mother is credited with bearing thirty offspring at the settlement.[13]

French Ribbon Farms. Emerging with the slow growth in the Lower Straits area was the distinctive colonial French settlement pattern of "ribbon farms." Close observation today reveals that the property lines of these original farms still coincide with the streets, and seedlings from the original French-planted trees shade motorists as they travel through the French sector of old Detroit and Monroe County (fig. 2.5). The "ribbon farm" is unquestionably the most

---

12. Silas Farmer, *History of Detroit and Wayne County and Early Michigan,* 3rd ed. (New York: Munsell and Co., 1890), p. 331.
13. *Ibid.,* p. 332-33.

Figure 2.5. This map of Monroe County illustrates the French long lot and Federal Survey Systems. (Map: Michigan Department of State Highways and Transportation.)

impressed French landscape feature in Michigan. The popular name is derived, of course, from their shape which is a narrow band of land extending perpendicular back from a waterfront. Generally the farmholding lines were spaced every 120 to 270 m (133-300 yds) consecutively along the flowing water courses and extended back into the woods about 3,168 m (3,520 yds). As a result of the division of the land into narrow strips, plus the essential need for water to provide both sustenance and transportation, dwelling houses were strung along the waterfront as beads on a necklace. Other features of the farm pattern included: (1) a front yard garden plot which included both herbs and plants adopted from the Indians and some introduced from Europe; (2) immediately behind the dwellings, orchards of pears, several dozen apple, cherry, and sometimes quince trees were planted which typically displayed the beauty of tender care; and (3) intervening before the wilderness of trees were small fields of wheat, corn, and other hardy cereal grains, pasture, and a woodlot.

The apple trees nurtured in the eighteenth century frequently had a hybrid origin. The wild thorn or crab apple, native to Michigan, was called mish-i-min in the Algonquian language. Cuttings from European apple stock were commonly grafted to the roots of the native trees by the French to establish the early orchards to increase hardiness and survivability. In 1897 the Michigan Legislature designated the blossom of the European-origin apple rather than the native blossom as the State Flower.[14]

Dotting the shoreline every few miles at Detroit were large stone-based windmills, some of which were still producing energy as recently as the 1890s.[15] Some settlers maintained the French farm village tradition of living inside the stockade which provided an opportunity for greater social interaction and safety. Inside the fort the largest lots would not exceed 225 sq m (2,500 sq ft).

Homes of the higher class French were well-built as described by Hubbard:

> The better class of dwellings of the French habitants were of quite a substantial character, . . . They were built of logs, squared and covered with clapboards, and the roofs shingled with cedar. They were one or two stories, according to the need or ability of the owner, the upper or half story, being chiefly within the roof, which was high, and lighted by small dormer windows, projecting on the front and rear sides. The entrance was in the centre, and a hall ran from front to rear. A low and perfectly plain veranda was another usual feature.[16]

Why the Long Lots. Why did the French introduce the long lot farm pattern into Michigan? The ribbon farm was not the dominant rural division of the land in seventeenth century France; thus, the easy answer that the Gauls brought their distinctive farm shape with them as so much "cultural baggage" is not acceptable. Yet, wherever the French settled in America, the long lots appear on the landscape: St. Lawrence Valley, Kaskaskia (Illinois), Wisconsin, Mississippi Valley, and Michigan. Perhaps the explanation can be linked with the Dutch, France's homeland neighbor. First, the Dutch utilized what are known as "dike villages," homes placed on the meander of the dikes with the farms extending in narrow strips behind them. Secondly, the windmills, described by Hubbard, which were common along Detroit's waterfront, might suggest also a Dutch origin. The adoption of the pattern may also be

---

14. Bela Hubbard, *Memorials of a Half Century* (New York: G. P. Putnam's Sons, 1887), p. 128; R. H. Brown, *op. cit.*, p. 35; Albert F. Butler, "Thoreau's Week in Michigan," *Michigan Natural Resources*, vol. 45, no. 3 (May-June 1976), pp. 16-19.
15. Hubbard, *op. cit.*, p. 135.
16. *Ibid.*, p. 131.

associated with the demands for "fish days" by the Catholic Church. By sharing the waterfront, each family had an equal opportunity to secure the bounty of fish that were readily available near the doorstep.

One of the most obvious disadvantages of the ribbon farms was the difficulty of maintaining social interaction between farm families as they had only two adjoining neighbors. Further, the exclusive use of the shoreline by the first inhabitants choked off water access when increased population forced farms to be formed to the rear. However, with an intent to keep the population density low, perhaps exclusive riverfront occupance was not thought of as a disadvantage. One condition which early British and American observers objected to in the French farm settlement pattern was the wretched, unhealthy water quality in front of stretches of French homes, especially where the water velocity was slow.[17]

Whatever the true reason for the French adoption of the ribbon farm pattern with its river access, they shared with the Indian the bounty of the Great Lakes fishery long before its commercial exploitation. They relished the white fish and gained much pleasure and excitement in its harvest. Lake trout and sturgeon were also caught in large numbers. These fish were a major addition to the habitants' larder considering the sturgeon weighed up to 31 kilograms [kg] (70 lb) and trout 4 to 9 kg (10-20 lb).

French-American Land Claims. Between the years 1807 and 1818 the United States Government authenticated and registered the land claims of the French which by that time occupied the territory from Grosse Pointe to the mouth of the River Rouge and upstream from it. Establishing clear land titles was difficult in the early American period as the United States was the fourth holder of the land. Fires, diverse record systems, mutilated documents, and questionable surveys added to the challenge of discovering who rightfully owned what land. In the final analysis, two things are apparent: (1) a great deal of care was exercised in the recording of French-held property, and (2) the American Land Commissions were generous in the settlement of claims. One example illustrates the pains taken to insure equitable treatment of the native French. Recognizing that woodlots on the established "ribbon farms" had been depleted and the farm families by practice had extended cutting directly into the woods off their farms, an additional concession of several hectares, depending on the situation, was approved in nearly one hundred cases. Out of the total of over seven hundred French-American land claims registered, nearly three hundred were in Wayne County.[18] As a result of these actions such old Detroit French families as La Badie, Cicot, Chene, Dequindre, Moran, Campau, Beaubien, Desrocher, and Audrey had their rights to free ownership and sale of property in Michigan assured by the American Government. With compassion towards the French rather than ethnic shunting, Detroit's section of Redford Township attracted such French farm families as: Chavey, Besancon, Du Toise, Du Bois, and others in the mid to latter nineteenth century. Later, Du Boisville thrived as a small farm hamlet on the River Rouge.[19] Five years after the opening of the Public Land Office at Detroit the French population was cohesive enough to elect Father Richard to Congress. By the time of statehood, one-sixth of Detroit was still French and the language was commonly heard; however, amalgamation with the pioneer immigrant population was rapidly occurring.

17. George N. Fuller, *Economic and Social Beginnings of Michigan* (Lansing: Wynkoop-Hallenbeck Crawford Co., 1916), pp. 98-108.
18. Farmer, *op. cit.*, pp. 21-22.
19. Map of "Redford Township: 1876" (Redford Historical Commission, Reprint 1976).

After four centuries in Michigan, the French have been through the acculturation process which typifies the American "melting pot" theory. From the foot-loose *coureurs de bois* of the seventeenth-eighteenth centuries to the sedentary farmer of the nineteenth century, one finds today indistinguishable suburban living, English-speaking, French descendants. Yet the map, with its place names, holds the memories of when Michigan was New France. In communities throughout Michigan, especially along water courses, citizens in search of knowledge of the founding of their town frequently discover that an unheralded French fur trader or trapper had preceded the land-seeking American pioneer who claimed the site for a new community. Such is the hidden legacy of the French in Michigan.

The Spanish in Michigan

As the American Revolutionary War progressed towards its ultimate political division of the English Colonies from the ancestral homeland, the Spanish, not allied with the United States, had also declared war on the British. During the winter of 1780-1781, the Spanish at St. Louis seized an opportunity to foray into southwestern Michigan. What exactly prompted the Spaniards to venture into the Lower Peninsula is debated by historians.[20] Nevertheless, the Spanish, with Frenchmen from Cahokia, Illinois, and friendly Indians, marched to the present-day community of Niles. Using the Kankakee-St. Joseph portage, the party arrived at Fort St. Joseph February 12, 1781, and flew the flag of Spain for a day before returning to St. Louis. A word of caution is inserted here to note that Fort St. Joseph at Niles should not be confused with the French fort of the same name sited at Port Huron between 1686 and 1688.

Suggestions advanced for the brief interlude of the Spanish in Michigan include the following: (1) they wanted to establish a claim for Spain east of the Mississippi River on the Great Lakes; (2) they wanted to gain loot by the sacking of a fort in British territory; and (3) they wanted to assist the French in gaining revenge for their losses at the hands of a British detachment from Fort Michilimackinac.

The occupation of Fort St. Joseph may not have been the first effort to put Michigan into the hands of the Spanish. In 1765 Major Rogers at Michilimackinac was charged with treason, stemming from a scheme to induce the Indians to support Spanish interests which may have led to the New Orleans authorities gaining control of the fort.[21]

A careful examination of the Michigan Highway Map reveals several place names of Spanish origin. While the Spanish only ventured into Michigan for a few hours, the origin of the contemporary Spanish place names cannot be linked to the colonial era as is the case with the French. In contrast, it was Americans who introduced the Spanish names to Michigan. Corunna is named for the town in Spain from which one of its founders brought sheep into the Old Northwest. California is undoubtedly associated with the gold rush of the 1850s, while Palo, Alamo, and Buena Vista memorialize battle sites with the Mexicans. Santiago commemorates a victory at that place in Cuba during the Spanish-American War.[22]

20. Dunbar, *op. cit.,* p. 145.
21. Dunbar, *op. cit.,* pp. 144-45; Thomas M. Cooley, *Michigan: A History of Government* (Boston: Houghton Mifflin Co., 1913), p. 78; F. Clever Bald, *Michigan in Four Centuries* (New York: Harper and Brothers, Pub., 1954), pp. 83-84.
22. Map: "Spain's Role in U.S. History" (The Spain-U.S. Chamber of Commerce, undated @ 1976), 21 × 27.5 cm; Walter Romig, *Michigan Place Names* (Grosse Pointe, undated @ 1972).

All of Michigan's place names of Spanish origin are located in the Lower Peninsula. Due to their more recent arrival in Michigan, there are no place names which can be directly associated with the thousands of Spanish-surnamed migrants who have labored in the state's Fruit Belt and vegetable fields. However, under the Voting Rights Act, Spanish-English elections are held in two cities, Saginaw and Adrian, and in the townships of Orangeville, Imlay, Madison, Grant, and Buena Vista.

Michigan Under the British Monarchy

At the beginning of the four decades of rule by the British, starting in 1760, the region's activities and settlement patterns were similar to the French, but the techniques of operation varied. London replaced Paris, while Ottawa, Quebec, and Montreal continued their royal administrative functions in North America. The settlements established by the French, especially at Detroit and Mackinac, continued to operate with little visible change. Fur trade economically reigned supreme, however, missionary and exploration efforts were curtailed. The restrictive migration policy designed to protect the fur producing environment eventually was rendered null and void by the American Revolution and the counterpolicy of unrestricted exploitation of the fur-bearing animals. Thus, both the zenith and the decline of fur trading was witnessed during the short British colonial control over the Lakes Region.

Michigan as a British Political Geographic Entity

While the basic way of life during the English period witnessed a gradual change, the political geographic units of government in which the peninsulas were included also went through a succession of changes as the King and Privy Council attempted to control the Crown's interests in the Great Lakes area. Between 1760 and 1814 Michigan was part of the following British political areas:

1. 1760-1763—British-occupied New France
2. 1763-1774—Indian Country under the direct rule of King George III
3. 1774-1791—Quebec Province Canada, Department of Hesse
4. 1791-1796—Upper Canada, Counties of Kent and Essex
5. 1812-1814—British occupied Territory of Michigan

British-American Colonial Boundary Claims. The negotiations of the Treaty of Paris 1782-1783 led to the establishment of the international boundary between the United States and Canada which follows the center of Lakes Erie, Huron, Superior, and the connecting waterways. Direct control of the Great Lakes region by the United States and Michigan was delayed for several more years. In 1796 the forts in Michigan were finally turned over to the United States by the British military. Nonetheless, Drummond Island remained under English control as part of Upper Canada until 1828. Sugar Island, formerly known as St. George's, an island in the St. Mary's River with a large number of Indian residents, came under the administration of the State of Michigan in 1842 after action of a joint American-British commission.[23]

---

23. Dunbar, *op. cit.*, p. 150; Clarence M. Burton, "The Boundary Lines of the United States under the Treaty of 1782," *Michigan Pioneer and Historical Collection,* Vol. XXXVIII, pp. 130-39.

Throughout the United State's first decade of existence, several of the Atlantic seaboard states possessed overlapping claims with the British, United States, and themselves. A part of the first tier of counties in the Lower Peninsula was claimed by Connecticut until 1786. Massachusetts maintained a claim until 1785 of the entire area south of a line drawn east from the vicinity of Ludington. New York claimed the entire Lower Peninsula until 1782, while Virginia maintained its claim to the Lower Peninsula and central and western Upper Peninsula until 1784.

British Michigan Fur Trade

Whether the British or French were in control of the Great Lakes, fur trading was the immediate reward of holding the area. It is the contrasting method of operation of trade in the formative years of British control which can be associated with the succession of political geographic territorial changes in the region. As soon as the British military had gained control of the French outposts, tough dealing, unlicensed, British and Dutch traders and a few farm families came to supply the rudimentary needs of the troops. The new fur traders soon gained a reputation among the Indians, who had been used to the adaptive ways of the *coureurs de bois*, as being greedy and unscrupulous cheaters.[24] These characterizations were perhaps deserved, as the initial British policy was to discontinue or be less liberal in the exchange of goods on which the Indians had become dependent during the French era. Psychologically, the English policy seemed to be to rely on punishment rather than reward to gain cooperative behavior.

During the initial transfer phase of control from the French to the British Crown, confusion over who really owned the land plagued the minds of native Indian leaders. Vexing to them was the question: How could the French who had only received permission to use the land for fur trade, be able to give the land to the British King? "Discovery rights," after having lived in the area for a thousand years, was nonsensical to the Indians. A more direct concern was that the British colonialists were moving westward and were actually settling on their land.

Pontiac's Plan to Keep Michigan Indian Country. Based on fears for the future, Pontiac, an Ottawa chief whose village was across the strait from Detroit, organized the Ottawa allies for the overthrow of the British in the Lakes and Ohio River region. The British outposts were defeated at Sandusky, St. Joseph, Miami, Ouiatanon, Presque Isle, Venango, and Michilimackinac. Only Detroit, even after the longest Indian seige, 157 days, survived the attempt of the Ottawa allies to regain control of the region. Critical to Detroit's survival was the ability to resupply it by *batteaux* vessels traveling through Lake Erie and up the Detroit River. Although trade was temporarily ruined, the frontier depopulated, routes closed, and cargoes plundered, the most strategic place in Michigan, Detroit, was maintained.

Proclamation of 1763. The Ottawa victories resulted in King George III issuing the Proclamation of 1763. A significant feature of this proclamation was the omission of the Great Lakes and Ohio River regions from inclusion within the Province of Quebec. By omitting the area, it was anticipated that the Indians would be more easily mollified to the fact that the King was sympathetic to their fears of settlements. Further, by restricting colonial settlement to the watersheds of the Atlantic rivers and the Lower St. Lawrence River "for the present" as the Proclamation states, credibility among the Indians could be rekindled. The political efforts were successful; settlement of the Great Lakes region was slowed, the natives were quieted and

---

24. Almon E. Parkins, *The Historical Geography of Detroit* (Lansing: Michigan Historical Commission, 1918), p. 87.

more willing to resume the fur trading partnership. Another political motive for the creation of Indian Country directly under the control of King George III was a possible hedge against a time when the British might be forced to return its acquired lands in North America to France. The point was that if the British designated the Great Lakes and the Ohio River area as "Indian Country," a simple territorial extension of their historic five-nation Iroquois allies, then only the "less valuable" Canadian lands of Quebec and the Maritime Provinces would be returned to France.[25]

There was an awareness that lawlessness could be a problem in vast "Indian Country" which was not under the direct supervision of a colonial governor. Therefore, the King's military and civil officers operating in the territory were required to police the area of fugitives:

> . . . All officers whatever, . . . within the territories reserved . . . for the said Indians, to seize and apprehend all persons whatever, who standing charged with treason murder and other felonies or misdemeanors, shall fly from justice and take refuge in the said territory and send them under proper guard to the colony where the crime was committed. . .[26]

Michigan Within the Province of Quebec. As the storm clouds of revolution gathered across the Atlantic, the King and Privy Council recognized the need for closer administrative control over the royally proclaimed Indian Country with its smattering of French habitants and English subjects. The Quebec Act of 1774 heralded Michigan's next political geographic step. Quebec Province was expanded to include all of the area northwest of the Ohio River as far west as the Mississippi River. Lieutenant Governors were appointed at Detroit, Michilimackinac, Illinois country, and Vincennes. To curry Roman Catholic favor, the church's right to exist was formally assured, the French also were allowed to rule their civil affairs as they had before British occupation, but English Law prevailed in criminal cases. Courts were established at Detroit and Michilimackinac and linked with Superior Courts at Quebec and Montreal.

Michigan Remains in British Hands After Revolution. The fur trade operated as a free enterprise system under the British, open to all who could provide security for a license. Under the system the trade expanded to embrace the far-flung reaches of the continent. The Northwest Fur Company was able to consolidate many smaller operations with Ottawa offices. The value of the exchange of animal pelts became so great that the British became unyielding in transferring control of the Great Lakes to the Americans. At the end of the 1780s, it was estimated that Detroit and Mackinac and the Lakes region still created at least 180,000 British pounds' worth of trade for Great Britain, even though Detroit's fur activity had begun to diminish as early as the 1780s.

In spite of the profits, the fur trade costs to the British were not insignificant. Although inexpensive water transportation was used for shipping, in total it still represented a significant expense. The quantity and variety of goods listed below, transported from Europe to the break-in-bulk point at Montreal for subsequent reshipment to Detroit or Mackinac, indicates a small fraction of the cost and trade interaction in 1782.

---

25. Burton, *op. cit.*, p. 133.
26. "Proclamation of 1763," *Michigan Pioneer and Historical Collection,* Vol. XXXVI, p. 19.

9,400 blankets	10,000 large silver broaches
10,000 lbs tobacco	47 nests of kettles
450 felt hats	120 guns
94 saddles	10,000 lbs gun powder
250 bridles	35,000 lbs shot and ball[27]

Food was another cost of the fur trade. Even with a sparse population, the established French farms, and military gardens, production was inadequate to meet the local demand. To overcome the yearly shortages, food was imported from eastern settlements at a much higher rate than if locally produced. The need to import food into the frontier should not lead to the conclusion that the settlers' farming efforts were insignificant. Under the British at Detroit nearly 5,508 ha (13,770 ac) of land were under cultivation according to the de Peyster Census of 1782. The majority was sown to wheat, while oats, 740 ha (1,849 ac) and corn, 210 ha (521 ac), potatoes and peas were the other major crops. Detroit residents under British control cared for 1,112 horses with 452 yearlings, 413 oxen, 807 cows, 447 sheep, and 1,307 hogs. Flax, hemp, hops, and cider also contributed to the agricultural economy.

The Detroit and Mackinac Settlements Under the British

Throughout the Revolutionary War, Detroit was regarded as having strategic importance due to its command of the entrance to the Upper Lakes. Further, the several Indian villages which were located nearby and posed little threat after the Pontiac Siege, facilitated communication with other Indian bands which frequently visited the Michigan tribes. Throughout the Revolutionary War, the King's 8th Regiment operated from Michigan. However its predecessor, the 10th Regiment, while enroute to England from Michigan, was rerouted at Quebec because of the "war threat" and became involved in the clash at Concord Bridge.[28] From the stronghold at Detroit, the British launched harrassing missions against the American frontiersmen which drew the attention of Washington in an analysis sent to Jefferson:

> . . . the reduction of the post of Detroit would be the only certain means of giving peace and security to the whole western frontier, . . . but such has been the reduced state of our Continental forces, and such the low ebb of our funds, . . . that I have never had it in my power to make the attempt.[29]

The Detroit Cultural Landscape During the American Revolution.

The landscape changes which the British made at Detroit were many—however, few of their original changes remain. Nevertheless, to the keen observer, clues to the past impact of the British at Detroit can be visualized. To many, the intersection in Detroit of Fort Street and Washington Boulevard may appear to be just another modern-day city banking corner. However, others may visualize at that intersection the fort which Washington prized as critical to the nation's future.

The construction of Fort Lernoult, started in 1779, began the dramatic changes at Detroit. By the end of the Revolution, the settlement complex consisted of several new elements. Most

---

27. Parkins, *op. cit.*, p. 116.
28. David A. Armour, "The Revolution Begins," *Michigan Department of Natural Resources Feature* (Information Education Division, May 1976), pp. 1-5.
29. Parkins, *op. cit.*, p. 98; Charles J. Snell, "This Was Fort Lernoult 1782," *Michigan Natural Resources,* vol. 45, no. 1 (January-February 1976), pp. 38-41.

dominant was the fort, later named Shelby, which had an irregular four-sided shape of approximately 300 meters, each surrounded by a high, thick earthen rampart and ditch. It was sited on a low interlobate hill-moraine, several meters inland from the river and old Fort Pontchartrain which would enable it to better withstand cannon fire of its day. Hundreds of trees were destroyed to provide pickets, fortified building materials, four bastions, and stockading which surrounded the village to the south of the fort. The fort's location away from the water's edge made it necessary to dig a well to secure fresh water inside the fort. Also within the fort were a dozen buildings including officers' quarters, barracks, and a storehouse. A naval yard with storage buildings and two wharves dotted the river bank to accommodate the one brig and twelve schooners which normally served the trade and military needs of the settlement. Some of the schooners even at that date were larger than those plying the Atlantic-West Indies Trade Route. A rectangular-shaped citadel with one- and two-story wooden structures was located near the waterway. A government house, council house, guard house, and two Catholic Churches, combined with over sixty one-story houses completed the basic community ensemble. Absent from the town landscape was an English Church. Nevertheless, religion was a strong influence on the street names. The first five streets north of the waterfront carried French and religious names: Chemin du Ronde, St. Louis, St. Ann, St. James, and St. Joseph. However, McDougall Alley, perpendicular to the river and just east of the public wharf, evidenced the commercial influence of Great Britain.

Population at Detroit at the End of the British Era. By the end of the British occupation at Detroit, the population had become more heterogeneous than when they had first entered Michigan. A diversity of Indians, French, English, German, Irish, Scotch, Yankees, and Blacks combined their skills to make the community function. The men and women operated about twenty retail stores and tended farms that extended 6.4 km (4 mi) below and 19.2 km (12 mi) above the fort on both sides of the strait. Indian villages were situated at three places: (1) the Potawatomis, 3.2 km (2 mi) below the fort near the present-day Ambassador Bridge, (2) the Hurons in Windsor, and (3) the Ottawas across from Belle Isle. There were, in total, about 4,000 non-Indian residents throughout the Lower Straits area.

British Attempts at Mining

Under the British, two feeble attempts were launched to tap the riches of the Upper Peninsula mining country. As early as 1765, Alexander Henry participated in a proposal to explore and open the ancient Indian copper mines. The difficulties precipitated by Pontiac's Uprising curtailed the effort in its initial stage of development. A more ambitious effort was made by a few Englishmen and the son of the Russian Consul in London. In the early 1770s a skilled mining team arrived from London, examined the mineral data and specimens at Michilimackinac and were convinced of the profitability of tapping the copper and hoped for silver and gold. A company was formed, funds secured, and a fort and shipyard were erected at Sault Ste. Marie. In spite of the plans, the project was abandoned by 1773 with the assaying furnace never having burned its expected nuggets.

Land Surveys Under the British

When the peninsulas were made a part of Quebec Province, the necessity for a British surveyor became more critical. At that time interest in landownership grew, conflicts over property lines became more frequent and fair land rent required accurate field measurement to keep peace between neighbors. On April 21, 1774, the Commandant at Detroit appointed James Sterling, an experienced surveyor to unravel the more serious disputes. Philip Frey, Thomas Smith, and P. McNiff followed him as surveyors through 1799 in establishing property lines.

A significant point in the state's history was reached when the Americans gained possession of the "Heart of the Great Lakes" region in the waning days of the eighteenth century. In the following two centuries American control brought an increasing rate of development of the state's natural resources. Acculturation of the Amerind, French, and British inhabitants into American society obliterated much of what they had previously established. In spite of the Americanization which has occurred since 1800, the legacy of Michigan's early residents can be readily observed. State maps record a host of distinctive place names, survey patterns, and transportation routes. State parks and museums hold treasures of artifacts, ancient burial mounds, and reconstructed forts of the Indian fur trade missionary era. From the records of the past, contemporary citizens can reflect on the contributions of those who lived in the wilderness prior to its settlement by the pioneer Americans.

> *Tandem fit surlulus arbor—from the sapling comes the tree.*
> *Great Seal of the Territory of Michigan*

Chapter Three

The Political Geographic Evolution of Michigan

This chapter outlines the political geographic evolution of Michigan, beginning with the critical period of American and British treaty negotiations to determine the international boundary, through the territorial stages of Michigan, and concluding with an analysis of present-day regional organization.

Well-placed functional boundaries are critical to the wise management of land, as well as to peace among neighbors. In western society accurately placed boundaries are also fundamental to the operation of its political and economic systems. Throughout the nineteenth and twentieth centuries, Michigan has been affected by continuing problems of cartographic, map, and survey errors which have necessitated Supreme Court action. These problems, including the Michigan-Ohio boundary determination, will also be examined.

Establishing the Michigan-Canadian Boundary

Had it not been for the determined efforts of the Americans involved in the peace settlement of the Revolutionary War, Michigan north of the 45th parallel would be within Canada. Further, the boundary decisions made for the Treaty of Paris 1783 have had profound effects on the shape, economy, and patterns of growth of Michigan. Alone, the placement of the geologic wealth of the Upper Peninsula in Canada would have had incalculable ramifications on the state. In the initial stage of negotiations the United States rejected a simple geometric straight line border with British Canada along the 45th north latitude. Franklin, for the Americans, advocated the rights of the historic claims of the former colonies of Virginia, New York, Connecticut, and Massachusetts. Specifically, the United States wanted all of Canada that was added to Quebec Province in the Act of 1774. Had the British accepted Franklin's proposal, the international boundary would have run totally north of Lake Superior. In early November 1782, renewed efforts were made by the two nations to settle the boundary question. Another alternative that the Americans presented included the possibility of a physical geographic boundary line placed in the center of the Great Lakes and connecting waterways. This alternative was accepted at 11 p.m., November 29, 1782; thus paving the way for the inclusion of the Upper Peninsula and the northern tip of the Lower Peninsula as a part of Michigan.

Division of the islands along the center line with a boundary, it was agreed, would unnecessarily fragment the islands and perhaps lead to future problems between the two nations. As a result, Bois Blanc Island at the mouth of the Detroit River which had historically been used by the people of Detroit as a source of fine red cedar, became Canadian along with Fighting Island. Later, posttreaty negotiations finally assigned Sugar, Neebish, and Drummond Islands to the United States, while Britain maintained St. Joseph, Cockburn, and Manitoulin Islands. The use of Mitchell's 1755 map of North America with its imaginary and grossly misplaced islands in Lake Superior undoubtedly led to Isle Royale being placed in the United States. The later mislocation of Isle Royale led to its placement in Michigan even though it is closer to Minnesota. Isle Royale is only 13 km (8 mi) from Minnesota's shoreline but lies 77 km (48 mi) from the Keweenaw Peninsula, Michigan's nearest mainland point. The attachment of the state's largest island to a county has also plagued the Legislature for several years. Successively Isle Royale was attached to Ontonagon, Houghton, and Keweenaw counties before becoming a separate county in 1875. In 1891 it was reattached to Keweenaw County and has remained tied to it even though the island was later designated a National Park. The costs to Keweenaw residents to extend services such as health and police to the island from the Michigan mainland rather than from Minnesota could prove to be an interesting calculation.

Boundary Demarcation Delays

The actual surveys of the boundary between the United States and British America agreed to in 1782 were delayed for several years by the British continuation of occupation of the Lakes region. The Treaty of Ghent in 1814 addressed the delay and provided for a joint survey. In between these two dates it is of interest that the elite merchants controlling the fur trade suggested to the English government six boundaries, one of which they felt should be established to insure continued access to the best fur-bearing region. Of the six fur trader boundary proposals which followed interior trade routes, the first three in priority would have placed Michigan entirely within Canada. Successive compromise lines were prepared using for the eastern boundary of Canada tributaries of the (1) Ohio, (2) French, or (3) Wabash Rivers. The south and west lines were proposed to be the Ohio and Mississippi Rivers. A fourth proposal would have placed a water boundary through Lakes Erie and Huron to the Straits of Mackinac and through Lake Michigan to the Chicago Portage. The fifth and sixth proposals would have used the Fox River in Wisconsin or circled the Upper Peninsula to a place near Ashland then followed the Chippewa River to the Mississippi River (fig. 3.1). In each of these proposals of 1791 the key point which the fur merchants wanted to control was the Grand Portage at the west end of Lake Superior. Although none of the fur interests' boundaries were adopted, the British did reorganize the Province of Quebec into Upper and Lower Canada. The Lakes Lowland Peninsula was strengthened by the settlement of many Loyalists. The settlement of Detroit was made a part of the Department of Hesse, Upper Canada, with court held on the Canadian side in Sandwich.

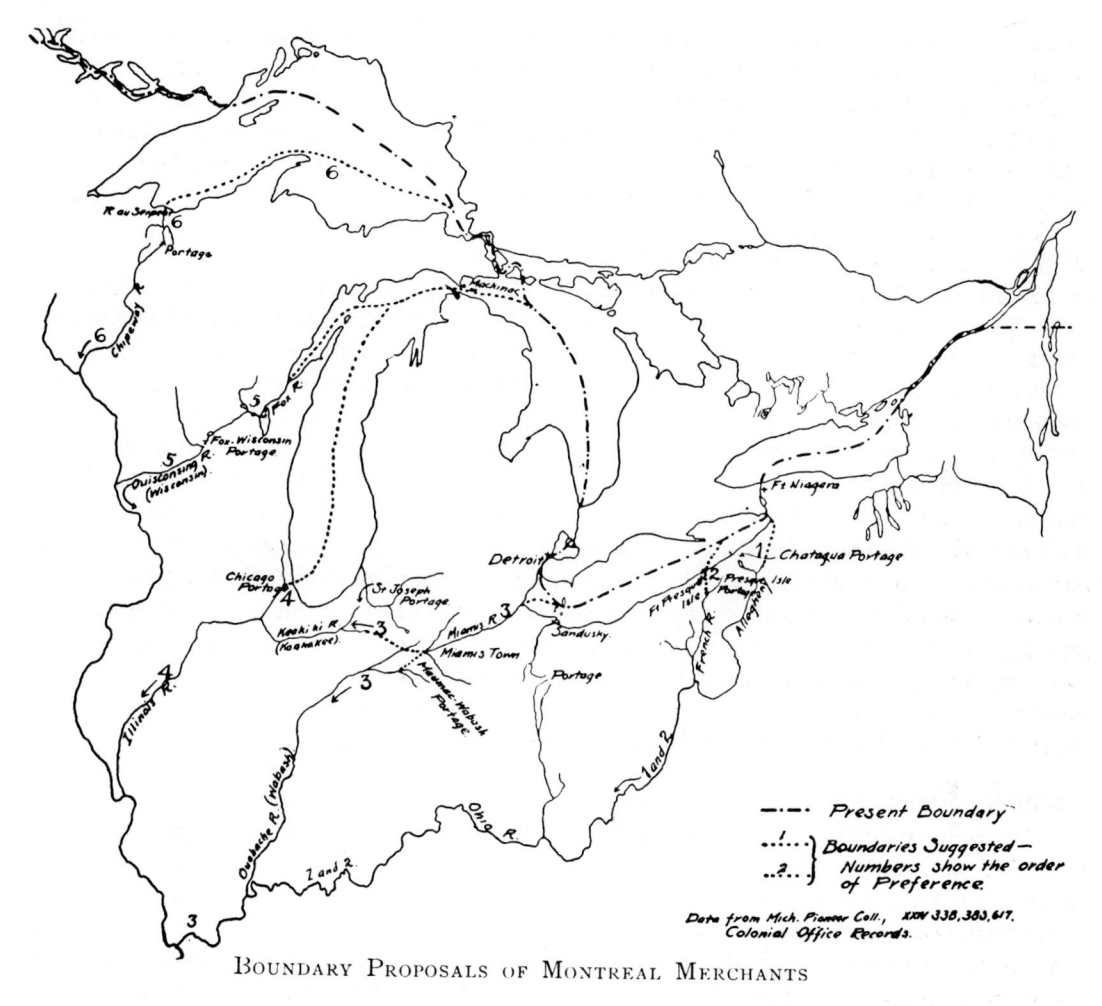

Figure 3.1. Boundary proposals of British fur merchants 1791. (Map: A.E. Parkins, *The Historical Geography of Detroit,* Michigan Historical Commission.)

Americans Gain Control of the Peninsulas

In 1783 President Washington sent Baron Steuben to take possession of the Lake ports; however the British refused, giving several reasons: (1) lack of evacuation orders, (2) treaty violations such as debt collections by the Loyalists, (3) compensation for losses to the Loyalists, perhaps the most important, and (4) time for the fur traders to gather and transport their materials out of American territory. The delays continued until Anthony Wayne, for whom Wayne County is named, scored a decisive victory over the British Indian allies at Fallen Timbers. That victory near Toledo in 1794, characterized by Teddy Roosevelt as the greatest battle in forty years of competition with the tribesmen, finally convinced the British that the

Americans had gained enough strength to take and hold Detroit.[1] While most Indian leaders of the Ohio and Great Lakes region were at Fort Greenville in Ohio making peace with the Americans, a few British subjects tried to insure their continued hold on Michigan. In July of 1795, British traders at a council with Michigan Indians bought an area equal to a dozen counties for 25,000 pounds. Later this purchase was not recognized by the United States government.

Transfer of Michigan to Americans

After thirteen years of supposed ownership, on July 11, 1796 and September 1, 1796, the stars and stripes were raised for the first times over Fort Lernoult and Fort Mackinac respectively. In August, 1796 General Wayne and Winthrop Sargent, Acting Governor of the Northwest Territory, arrived and established Wayne County, thus initiating organized American civil government in Michigan.

British interest in the resources of Michigan did not end with the lowering of military colors. The British envisioned that lasting support of the Indians could be gained by turning the region north of the Ohio River once again into an Indian Reserve. This idea and other factors manifested themselves in the War of 1812 in which both the forts and settlements of Detroit and Mackinac were lost to the British. The British occupation the second time was brief and without significant political geographic change. Perry's victory on Lake Erie and the American troops' victory under William Henry Harrison at the Thames River across from Detroit, in which the great Indian leader Tecumseh was killed, led eventually to the enduring peace.

Peaceful International Boundaries Since 1815

The second British occupation of Michigan did not change the cultural landscape significantly, although subsequent agreements with the British have had an important impact on the landscape. The international cooperation between the United States, Britain, and Canada is perhaps best interpreted from what is absent from the land. With exceptions of the American-built Fort Brady 1822-1892 at Sault Ste. Marie and Fort Wayne at Detroit which was completed in 1851, the border has been notably free from antagonistic fortifications. The waterways also have been a model for the war-torn world as a result of the successful operation of the Rush-Bagot Agreement of 1817 which limited naval armaments on the Great Lakes and connecting waters. The International Joint Commission has continually met to resolve mutual peaceful problems affecting the border, including such present-day ones as shipping, air pollution, border crossings, fishing, and water quality.

Political Geographic Land Preparations for American Settlement

Virginia Cessions and the Northwest Ordinance

The early American settlement pattern of Michigan reflects the federal government's policies for fair treatment of previous land occupants, controlled settlement of the land, and land management planning, not only to reduce anticipated problems, but also to guide the

---

1. E. H. Roseboom and F. P. Weisenburger, *A History of Ohio* (Columbus: The Ohio Historical Society, 1973), p. 62.

future land-use pattern and political geographic organization of the state. The primary documents which have influenced the political geography of Michigan are the Articles of Virginia Cession, an Ordinance for the Government of the Territory of the United States Northwest of the River Ohio, and several Indian treaties. While it may be tempting to relegate these documents to unimportance simply because of age, they in fact are still used in resolving present-day legal questions from boundaries to water rights.

Prior to the enactment of the Northwest Ordinance, the Commonwealth of Virginia conditioned the cession of its backcountry. The original Virginia Cession if left unamended would have forced Congress to create relatively small areas for states:

> . . . that the territory so ceded shall be laid out and formed into states, containing a suitable extent of territory, not less than one hundred, nor more than one hundred and fifty, miles square, or as near thereto as circumstances will admit.[2]

The Continental Congress later obtained more knowledge about the natural conditions of the tract northwest of the Ohio River, and became alarmed about the boundary conditions of the Virginia statutes. Specifically feared was the small areal requirement for states which the congressional members reasoned would produce many inconveniences, including states: (1) being isolated from navigable water, (2) being improperly intersected by lakes, rivers, and mountains, (3) having too great a proportion of unproductive land, and (4) being unable to gain sufficient population to form a respectable government entitling it to a voice in the national government. Congress further recorded that, by basing state boundaries on a "variety of circumstances" which come with time and experience, rather than just area, the future prosperity of the interior and its people could be best protected.

Reacting to Congress's fears and to additional knowledge of the Ohio and Great Lakes region, the Virginia Assembly amended its original cession position and confirmed the boundary provisions of the Northwest Ordinance. The Virginia Statute and the Northwest Ordinance of 1787 have been the basis of Michigan-Ohio-Indiana-Illinois boundary questions which have periodically sapped the energies of the Attorney General's Office staff up to the present day. Article Five of the Northwest Ordinance provides for not only a state line running due east and west from the southerly extreme of Lake Michigan, but also the creation of "not less than three nor more than five states" in the Northwest Territory.

Life-Shaping Principles of the Northwest Ordinance. The Northwest Ordinance is significant to the student of geography for more than its boundary provisions. Its approximate 2,800 words have provided a guide for the lives and activities of the people, as well as land development. In comparison to earlier nations, the initial provision of the Northwest Ordinance established that in the United States land and estates to be inherited would be divided equally among children "either brother or sister" and in no case a distinction be made between children of second marriages. By forbidding primogeniture which favored the first born son, Michigan farms have tended to be fragmented or sold to convert the land into more easily divisible collateral. Additionally, farms sold in estates frequently have been consolidated into larger commercial operations or are transferred from farmland into idle speculation property.

---

2. Supreme Court of the United States, October Term, 1970, No. 30, original, State of Michigan v. State of Ohio, p. 5, quotes Hening's Statutes of Virginia, vol. 11 (1782-1784), p. 572.

In spite of the fact that contemporary school millages fail and churches witness changes in attendance, one does not have to travel far to view the impact of the Northwest Ordinance Third Article:

> Religion, morality and knowledge, being necessary to good government and happiness of mankind, schools and the means of education shall forever be encouraged.

In comparison, there is less evidence on the land, perhaps, for the adherence to the requirements in the Articles for morality, equal taxation, and protection of Indian rights.

> The utmost good faith shall always be observed towards the Indians; their lands and property shall never be taken from them without their consent . . . in no case shall nonresident properties be taxed higher than resident's. . . .

Michigan Areal Changes Under the Northwest Ordinance. Between 1787 and 1796 Michigan was simultaneously a part of the Northwest Territory of the United States with its seat of government in Cincinnati, as well as Upper Canada. Due to the British occupation, Michigan as a total geographic entity, unlike the southern part of the Northwest Territory, was only governed for four years by the original Territorial Council. In 1800 Congress created Indiana Territory west of a boundary drawn due north from the Ohio River at Fort Recovery near the present Ohio-Indiana state line. Until 1803 the east half of the Lower Peninsula and east tip of the Upper Peninsula remained in the original Northwest Territory while the west half became oriented to Indiana. When Ohio was admitted to statehood, the peninsulas, in their entirety became a part of Indiana Territory.

Michigan Territory Created

On January 11, 1805, by Section 1 of "An Act to Divide Indiana Territory into Two Separate Governments," Congress established Michigan Territory out of the northeastern part of Indiana Territory. At that time the Michigan-Indiana Boundary was placed at:

> the southern bend or extreme of Lake Michigan, until it shall intersect Lake Erie, . . .

That Act also defined the Lakes Michigan-Superior boundary as:

> through the middle of said Lake Michigan to its northern extremity, and thence due north to the northern boundary of the United States.

Michigan Territory Expanded to the Mississippi River

After the admission of Indiana and Illinois to statehood, in 1816 and 1818 respectively, the residual area of Illinois Territory was attached to Michigan. The Michigan Territorial Government at Detroit had to expand its concerns to the unceded Indian lands lying between the Illinois and Canadian borders and west to the Mississippi River. In 1823 the people interested in the creation of Wisconsin Territory lobbied the officials at Detroit to create a separate judicial district in the area west of Mackinac. The desire for Wisconsin Territorial status, however, was less than universal. Michigan's hand of government, it was evident, reached weakly from

Detroit into the West, but many American fur trappers and frontier residents found it strong enough. Michigan had initially organized the district into two large counties, Brown and Crawford, which included as county officers, land assessors and tax collectors. The isolated frontier people in Wisconsin undoubtedly felt that territorial and state government plus pioneer farmers would come soon enough without premature urgings which would necessitate packing themselves and the Indians further west.[3] Chippewa County along Lake Superior including parts of both Michigan and Wisconsin was organized in 1826 and Iowa County in southern Wisconsin was set apart from Crawford County in 1829.

Michigan Territory Expanded to the Missouri River 1834-1836

For several years people of Michigan waited impatiently for the territorial, state, and national politicians to work out the timing for elevation to statehood which included, at the time, pairing with a slave state. During the wait, Michigan Territory was enlarged into the Louisiana Purchase area. For two years Michigan officials strived to control the territory with its largest geographical extent. Between 1834-1836 Michigan Territory reached as far west as the Missouri River including all land north of the state of Missouri. In that huge area Dubuque County and Des Moines County in the south were established. In the year 1834, the southern part of Brown County was placed in Milwaukee County.

American Indian Land Treaties

Concurrent with territorial and state organizational process was the policy of Indian Treaty cessions which preceded for the most part American pioneer settlement. When the United States government acquired treaty or statutory rights to the area northwest of the Ohio River from Great Britain and its colonies, the Indians still roamed the forest and occupied seasonal villages. Moral questions faced the fledgling nation created out of the forces of equality, justice, and human rights. Two fundamental questions had to be immediately answered: (1) Did the native Americans have rights of civilization?, and (2) Should the Indians be removed from their ancestral territory by a new government without compensation?

Some men in Congress felt that by the traditions of European discovery, occupance, conquest, and treaty, the United States had complete ownership of the interior lands without obligation to the aborigines or their tribal nations. General Knox, Secretary of War, President Washington, and others held different opinions. Needed, they argued, were treaties of amicable cession by the tribal nations of their prior and continued occupied lands. Congress adopted the Washington philosophy and created the system of Indian treaties which provided for: (1) cessions by common consent of tribal leaders in places of public council, and (2) purchase of territory by payment of money, gifts, and services. Since the treaty land system was instituted, incalculable sums have been paid, and continue to be paid, out of the public treasury for the priceless gift of living space.

Indian Treaties in Michigan

The purchase of the territory within Michigan borders is encompassed in about a dozen major treaties between the Indians and federal government extending between 1784 and 1842

---

3. Robert C. Nesbit, *Wisconsin: A History* (Madison: University of Wisconsin Press, 1973), p. 122.

(fig. 3.2). In addition to the major treaties, there were numerous other small parcel transfers of titles and reserves. In three Indian treaties: (1) Fort Stanwix 1784, (2) Fort McIntosh 1785, and (3) Fort Harmar 1789, the land at the vicinity of Detroit and Mackinac was ceded by the Iroquois Federation, Wyandot, Ottawa, Chippewa, Potawatomi, and Sac nations. As the English were still firmly in control of the peninsulas, the treaties only set a precedent for eventual American ownership.

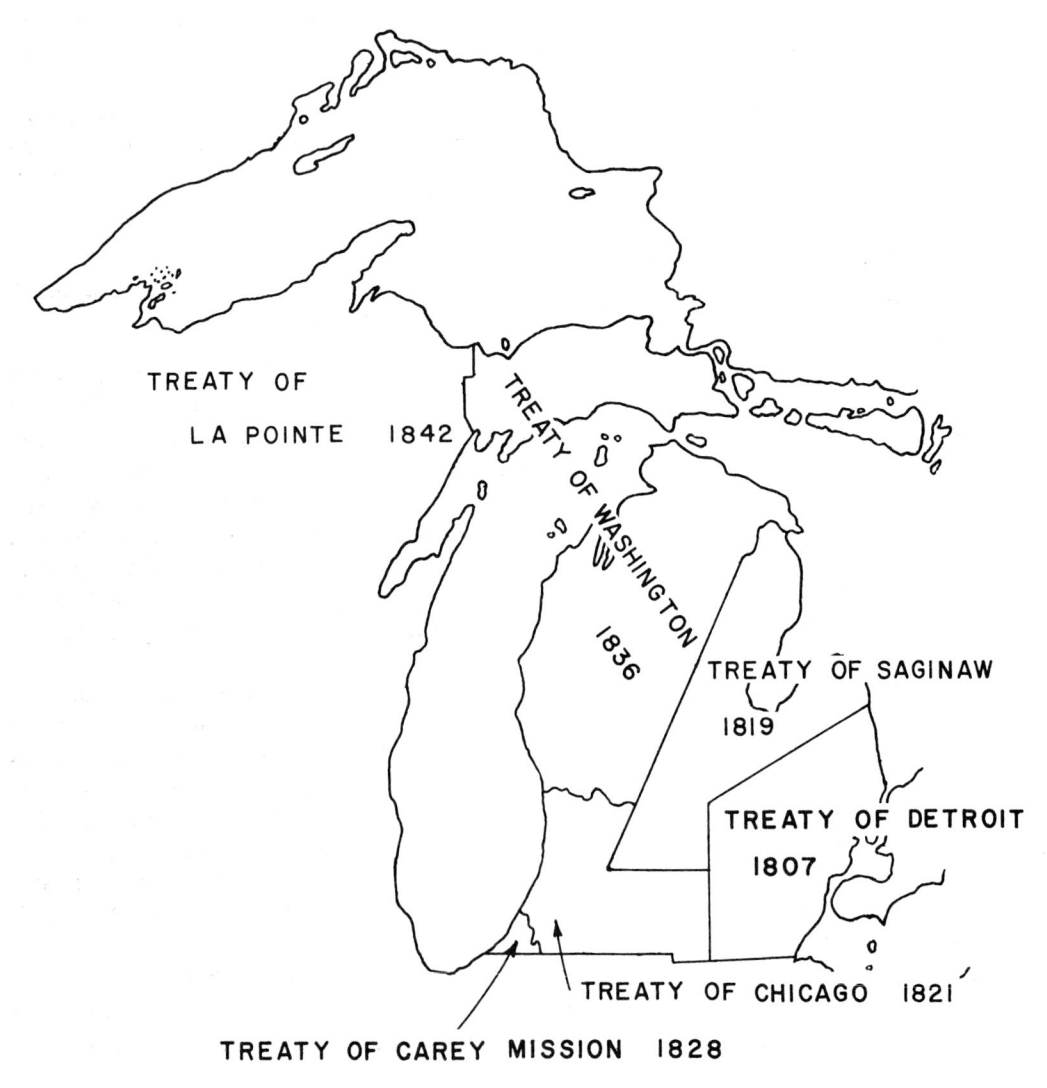

Figure 3.2. American Indian treaty cessions affecting Michigan. (Map: R. Welch, *County Evolution in Michigan 1790-1897,* Michigan Department of Education.)

The Fort Greenville Treaty, March 1795, was one of the most important territorial treaties of North American geography. Leading representatives from twelve tribes of the Indian country and the United States met in an out-of-doors setting for days of speeches, negotiation, and deliberation relative to the future of the environment and the solemn transfer of the land. Of specific interest to Michigan from the extensive amount of land transfers was the conveyance of an area extending 9.6 km (6 mi) inland from the waterfront between the River Raisin and the head of Lake St. Clair which included Detroit. Additionally, Mackinac Island and a 9.6 km (6 mi) frontage at St. Ignace extending inland 4.8 km (3 mi) was acquired on the Straits of Mackinac. Bois Blanc Island was granted as an extra gift of the Chippewa nation. The previous random French and English land grants were also transferred to the federal government by the Indians.

An indication of the ability of the Indians to communicate and the size of the native Indian communication network can be determined from a speech made by Chief Masass of the Chippewa at Greenville. In presenting a treaty belt with nine squares made from white beads, he said:

> This great Calumet comes not from the little lake near us but from the great Lake Superior to the north, . . . You therefore see that your words have gone a great ways . . . The white beads in this belt denote the number of large villages from the north who have heard your word.[4]

The Treaty of Detroit 1807 did more than create a large settlement area for potential pioneers. The treaty also created a meridian from which all federally surveyed lands in Michigan are legally described. The western boundary described in the Treaty of Detroit emerged as the Michigan Meridian, the legal dividing line between east and west Michigan, as well as one of the refernce lines for registering deeds to land. The Meridian Mall in Lansing and US-127 south of Hudson are today on the Detroit Treaty boundary. To determine the specific location of the boundary, a line was projected north from the mouth of the Au Glaze River at the present site of Defiance, Ohio. In the Detroit Treaty the Wyandots were granted a 2,000 ha (4996 ac) reserve near Flat Rock on the Huron River in Huron Township which they maintained until 1842.

The Treaty of Saginaw 1819 secured the riches of the Saginaw Valley, River, and Bay. Significantly, it also brought into use the Michigan Baseline, the second primary line used for surveying land in Michigan. The Saginaw Treaty's southern boundary line was drawn six miles or "one town width" below the Baseline and extended inland nearly to Kalamazoo. The Thunder Bay River and its head provided the northern boundary for the area which was ceded one year after the opening of the Detroit Land Office. Included in the Saginaw Treaty area were 40,000 ha (100,000 ac) in sixteen separate tracts which were reserved for the Indians at various locations. The first of two treaties affecting the Sault Ste. Marie site occurred in 1820 in which about 31 sq km (12 sq mi) fronting on the St. Mary's River were ceded.

Four southwestern Michigan treaties involving mostly Potawatomis, Chippewas, and Ottawas transferred the land south of the Grand and St. Joseph Rivers. In 1827 the Potawatomis exchanged their five reserve tracts and two village sites for ninety-nine sections in a block in

---

4. Alpheus Felch, "The Indians of Michigan and the Cession of Their Lands to the United States by Treaties," *Michigan Pioneer and Historical Collections,* XXVI (1895), p. 282.

Kalamazoo and St. Joseph Counties. In spite of the educational efforts among the Indians at Carry Mission, by 1833 most of the lands in the ninety-nine sections were also given up by the Indians.

The 1836 Treaty of Washington negotiated by Henry Schoolcraft involved Michigan's largest amount of land which included portions of thirty-five present-day counties. The Treaty of Washington completed the purchase of the Lower Peninsula except for reserves, and added Chippewa lands east of the Chocolate and Escanaba Rivers in the Upper Peninsula. The small Menominee area in the south central Upper Peninsula was also ceded in 1836.

Robert Stuart, Michigan's state treasurer, concluded the last major treaty, LaPointe, in 1842. The cession line was placed on the then undelineated Michigan-Wisconsin boundary. Over 56,000 ha (142,000 ac) in five separate parcels were reserved for the Chippewas and Ottawas. Those tracts plus numerous small islands and plots were to be held in common by the two tribes. Until the tribal dissolutions in 1855, the Upper Peninsula treaty lands had not been surveyed.

The importance of the water area of the Great Lakes was recognized in the Indian treaties since they included descriptions of boundary lines extending from the land to the Canadian border. In an attempt to insure validity, justice, and liberality of the government, it was common to pay compensation more than once for the same territory in successive treaties.

Michigan Statehood and Boundaries

Books of law, history, political geography and surveying are filled with references to and descriptions about the problems of demarcating satisfactory boundaries. Since its territorial era, Michigan, along with its neighboring states, has contributed more than its share of costly examples. Except for the repetitiously told story of the "Toledo War," Michigan's boundary disputes have been fought in courtrooms and by surveyors fighting miring mud, blistering sun, numbing cold, and mosquitoes.

It has not always been easy to answer the simple question, "What are the geographic boundaries of Michigan?" Fortunately, on the basis of two twentieth century Supreme Court decisions, the answer can be more specific now than at any other time in the state's history.

Michigan-Ohio Boundary

The simple phrase "east and west line drawn through the southerly bend or extreme of Lake Michigan," plus the words "northeast" and "north by east," as well as the persistent use of the 1755 John Mitchell map of North America which represented the head of Lake Michigan several miles north of its true location, have been the crux of Michigan's boundary disputes (fig. 3.3). Karpinski in his *Map Bibliography of Michigan* has identified at least two maps, Hutchin's 1778 and Scott's 1805, which if accepted as authoritative at crucial periods when early boundary decisions were being made, may have avoided prolonged discussion and locational problems associated with the state line.

A strict Michigan interpretation of the 1805 Michigan territorial boundary description would place Toledo, its harbor, and 1,820 sq km (700 sq mi) of land and water in the state of Michigan because of their location north of the head of Lake Michigan. Nevertheless in 1802, Ohio in its Enabling Act maintained a flexible position in regards to boundaries: (1) it was willing to include the eastern half of the Lower Peninsula and eastern tip of the Upper Penin-

Figure 3.3. Portion of Mitchell's 1755 Map of North America illustrating Lake Michigan's headwaters north of Maumee Bay. (Source: Michigan Law Library, Lansing.)

sula in its state, and (2) being uncertain of the extent of Lake Michigan it inserted a proviso, that the north boundary drawn from the head of Lake Michigan,

> . . . should intersect the said Lake Erie east of the mouth of the Miami [Maumee] River of the lake, then, and in that case, with the assent of Congress . . ., the northern boundary of this State shall be . . ., a direct line, running from the southernly extremity of Lake Michigan to the most northerly cape of the Miami Bay, . . . thence northeast to the territorial line, . . .

Congress accepted the Ohio Constitution with the proviso. Unfortunately, the exception from the Northwest Ordinance state boundary description has stimulated a string of surveys to determine the relative positions of the two sides of the peninsula; and finally Supreme Court action.

The following outline summarizes the activities relating to the Michigan-Ohio Boundary between 1787 and 1973.

Michigan-Ohio Boundary Chronology

1. 1787 — Northwest Ordinance provides for states north of line drawn due east and west from head of Lake Michigan.
2. 1802 — Ohio inserts proviso in Enabling Act to place boundary line through north cape of Maumee River drawn from head of Lake Michigan.
3. 1805 — Michigan territorial boundary based on line drawn due east from head of Lake Michigan.
4. 1812 — President authorized to have boundary ascertained.
5. 1815 — Hough placed north cape of Maumee River at 41°51′50″N.
6. 1817 — Harris placed south extreme of Lake Michigan at 41°37′19″N or 41°38′58″N and computed north cape of Maumee to be 7 miles 49 chains north of the head of Lake Michigan. Harris surveyed from Indiana-Ohio line to north cape of Maumee.
7. 1818 — Fulton surveyed line due east from Lake Michigan, reached Lake Erie about 12 miles east of mouth of Maumee.
8. 1834-35 — Talcott placed north cape of Maumee River at 83°18′55″W-41°44′07″N and the head of Lake Michigan 41°37′07″N.
9. 1836 — Congress accepted Ohio Proviso and set Ohio-Michigan state boundary on tangent from the head of Lake Michigan to north cape of Maumee River and from the cape northeast to the Canadian border. Action followed precedent of Indiana and Illinois boundaries which were previously set north of south end of Lake Michigan. Award of Upper Peninsula to Michigan for "Toledo Strip" enrages some Wisconsin interests.
10. 1844 — Army Corps of Engineers placed state line in Lake Erie at 45° angle from north cape of Maumee River—no question raised by Michigan.
11. 1915 — Joint Michigan-Ohio survey party resurvey Harris line, but varied line as agreed by landowners adjacent to state line and set seventy-one stone boundary markers at one-mile intervals.
12. 1933 and 1945 — Joint resolutions of Michigan and Ohio legislatures seeking clarification of boundary.
13. 1952 — United States Geological Survey Erie Quadrangle published with collaboration of Michigan Highway Commissioner indicating Lake Erie boundary at 45° angle from north cape of Maumee River.
14. 1967-73 — U.S. Supreme Court awarded disputed Lake Erie area to Ohio, "northeast" in regards to Lake Erie boundary accepted to mean half-way between due north and east.[5]

The Lost Peninsula. The years of activity to define the Michigan-Ohio boundary by survey, state, congressional, and Supreme Court action have failed to eliminate a boundary quirk on the Lost Peninsula. Michigan possesses the tip of the Lost Peninsula which extends as a spur of land north of Toledo. The boundary illustrates again the disadvantages of straight line geometric boundaries. In order for Michigan residents or local public servants to reach the Michigan portion of the Lost Peninsula by land, they must first pass through Ohio (fig. 3.4).

---

5. Supreme Court of the United States, October Term, 1970, No. 30 original, State of Michigan v. State of Ohio, pp. 5-24.

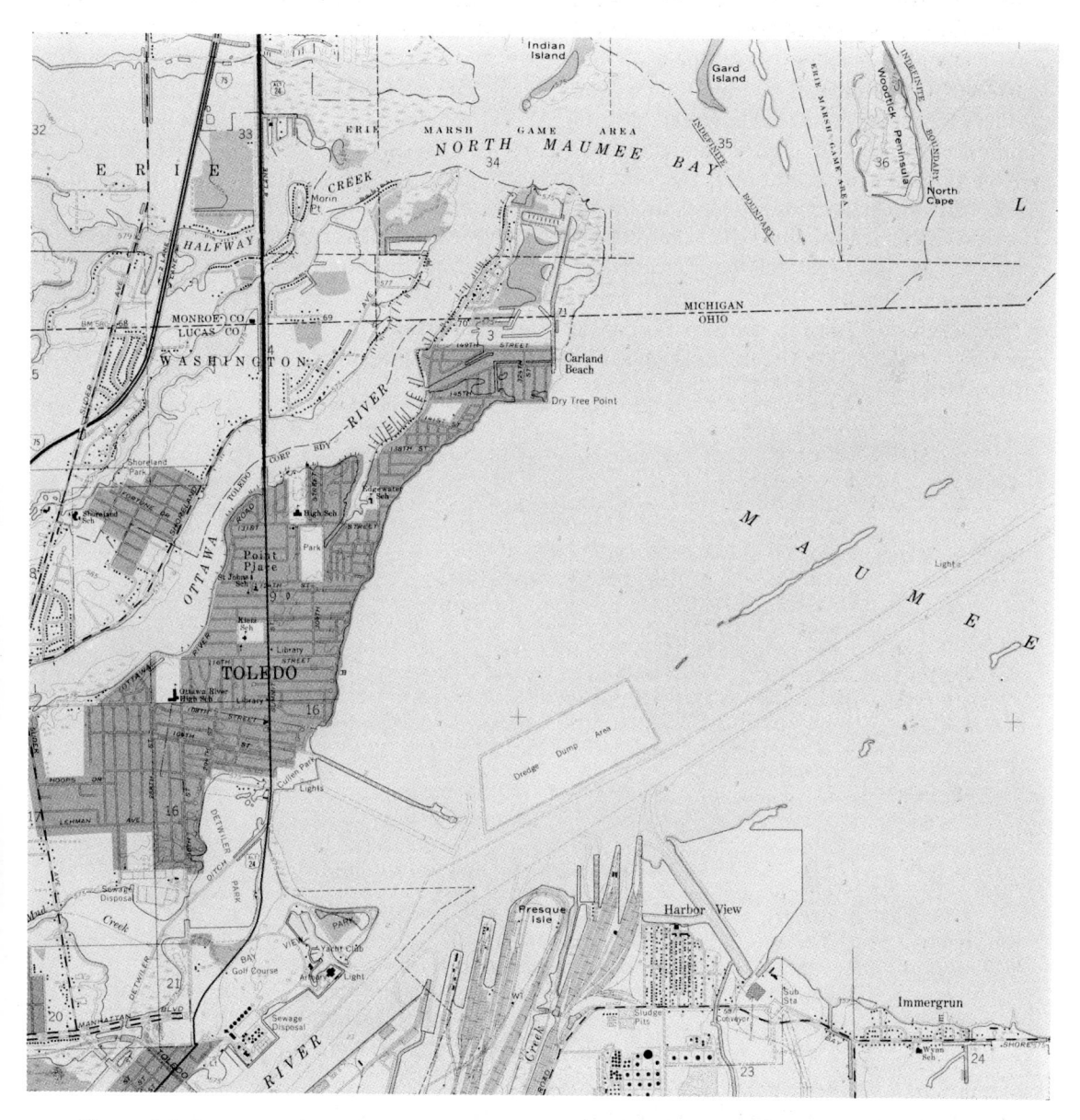

Figure 3.4. Portion of Michigan-Ohio boundary at mouth of Maumee River. The Lost Peninsula is shown extending into North Maumee Bay. (Map: Oregon Quadrangle Ohio-Michigan, U.S. Geological Survey.)

Michigan-Wisconsin Boundary

Michigan's Supreme Court action with the State of Wisconsin in the 1920s to determine and find an amicable solution to its joint boundary dilemma has been less known in comparison to the one with Ohio. The Michigan Statehood Act and Wisconsin Territorial Act both described the common boundary in essentially the same language. In 1841 William Burt, Michigan's state geologist, however, determined that the boundary defined was a geographic impossibility and "absolutely impracticable." Later, Wisconsin, in cooperation with Michigan, wrote a different description for the joint boundary in preparation for its request for statehood. The 1850 Michigan Constitution adopted similar wording as the Wisconsin Enabling Act; however, Michigan claimed the headwaters of the River Montreal as a turning point. The determination of the Montreal River headwaters came before the Supreme Court in 1923 with Michigan contending the true "head" was on the Montreal branch which flowed from Island Lake. The Court ruled in favor of Wisconsin's claim and placed the boundary turning point at Lehmen's (Layman's) Creek confluence about 13 km (8 mi) upstream from Ironwood rather than at Island Lake (fig. 3.5).

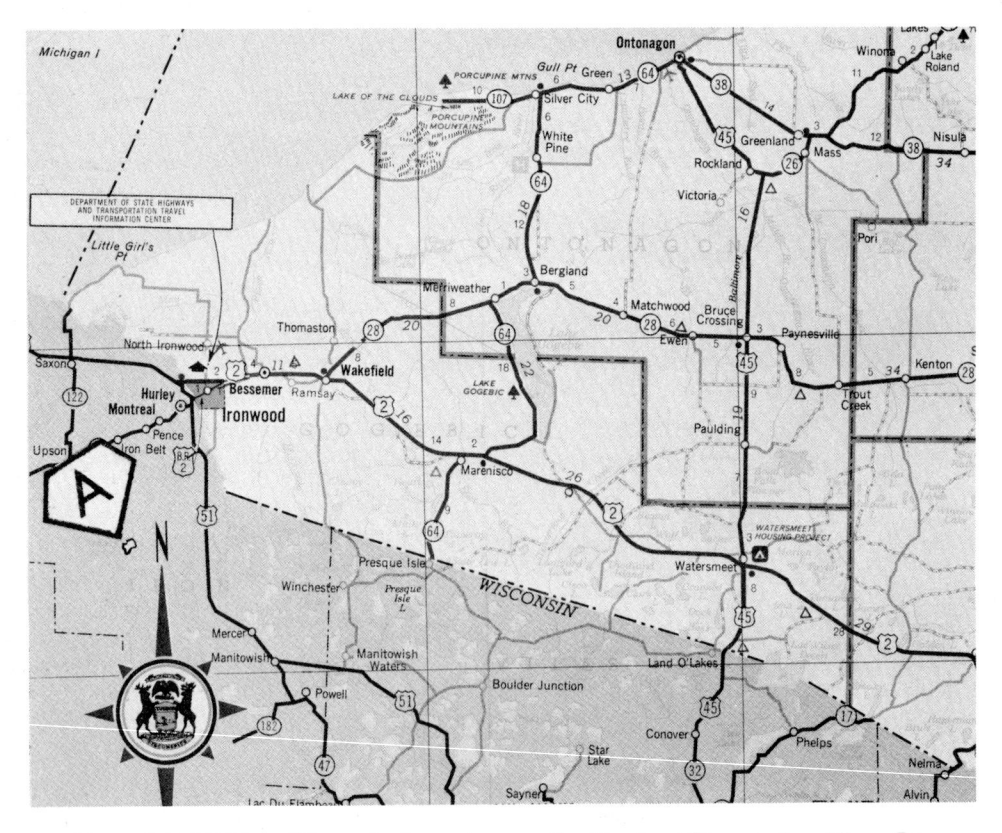

Figure 3.5. Michigan-Wisconsin boundary on the Montreal River to Lac Vieux Desert. Michigan claimed Island Lake (A) as the boundary turning point during the Supreme Court actions 1923-1926. (Map: Michigan Department of State Highways and Transportation.)

The Supreme Court reconfirmed at the same time the division of river islands earlier agreed upon by the states. The islands of the Brule and Menominee rivers upstream from Quinnesec Falls were placed in Michigan and the downstream islands located in Wisconsin. By assigning islands using various stretches of river, the problem of determining the center or main stream were avoided. To determine "main channel" is extremely difficult for surveyors: (1) Is it the deepest part of the river? (2) Is it the widest part? (3) Is it the fastest flowing? (4) Is it the one which passes the highest volume of water? (5) Where is the main channel when a river passes an island and all factors appear equal?

The Green Bay Boundary. Between the 1830s and 1920s two distinct ship channels were commonly used to connect Menominee-Marinette with Lake Michigan. Unfortunately, the Michigan-Wisconsin Boundary Acts designated the "most usual" channel to be the state water boundary. Michigan claimed in the 1920s before the U.S. Supreme Court that a ship channel which ran easterly across Green Bay nearly to the shore of the Door Peninsula, then northerly through Death's Door Channel south of Plum Island, to be the "most usual" channel. Wisconsin claimed its boundary to be the channel northeast from Marinette-Menominee to a point opposite Rock Island passage then southeast to the center of Lake Michigan. The Supreme Court awarded the Wisconsin claim in 1926 based on its long-established possession of the islands south of the Rock Island passage (fig. 3.6).[6]

Lawrence Martin in his *The Physical Geography of Wisconsin,* 1932, observes that the Supreme Court erred in the technical description of its 1926 recorded decree by using the words "north by east" instead of the word *northeast.* In strictly following the High Court description of angles and distances, Martin suggests that it would have: ". . . technically transferred 707 sq mi of water and 4,253 acres of land from Michigan to Wisconsin."

If the question were returned before the Supreme Court for correction and the Supreme Court continued the precedent of awarding claims based on the principle of historic possession, exercise of dominion, and tax collections, the Michigan-Wisconsin boundary would in no way be altered (fig. 3.7).

The Federal Land Surveys and County Evolution

The Continental Congress in 1784 was faced with a multitude of problems, some of which included how to overcome war debts, gain financial credibility for the new republic, and acquire and protect its lands in the Northwest. In confronting these problems, Congressional discussions centered on the best means to use the land. In the end, Congress agreed to one pledge: that the lands be disposed of for the common benefit of the United States. Eventually the Land Ordinance of 1785 was formulated and passed after borrowing from European antecedents, New England colonial, and Southern plantation experiences. (When one observes aerial photographs of Michigan today, the most apparent cultural landscape feature is the section line-square mile road pattern which developed as a result of the land ordinance.)

At the start Jefferson and the Land Ordinance Committee were sensitive to the conditions in the nation. They set about developing a federal land ownership to private land control system which would meet the "common benefit" principle including provisions for: (1) a national

---

6. Supreme Court of the United States, October Term 1925, No. 9, original, State of Michigan v. State of Wisconsin (272 U.S. 298; 270 U.S. 295), decided November 22, 1926.

source of revenue, and (2) assistance in the dispersion and settlement of a pioneer population. These two points, however, were in conflict. If the sale of 572,000 sq km (220,000 sq mi) of land in the Northwest were to raise money, it should be at the highest price which would limit the number of purchasers. Yet, if the defensive advantages of a well-dispersed population occupying the land was encouraged, the land sales price should be relatively inexpensive.

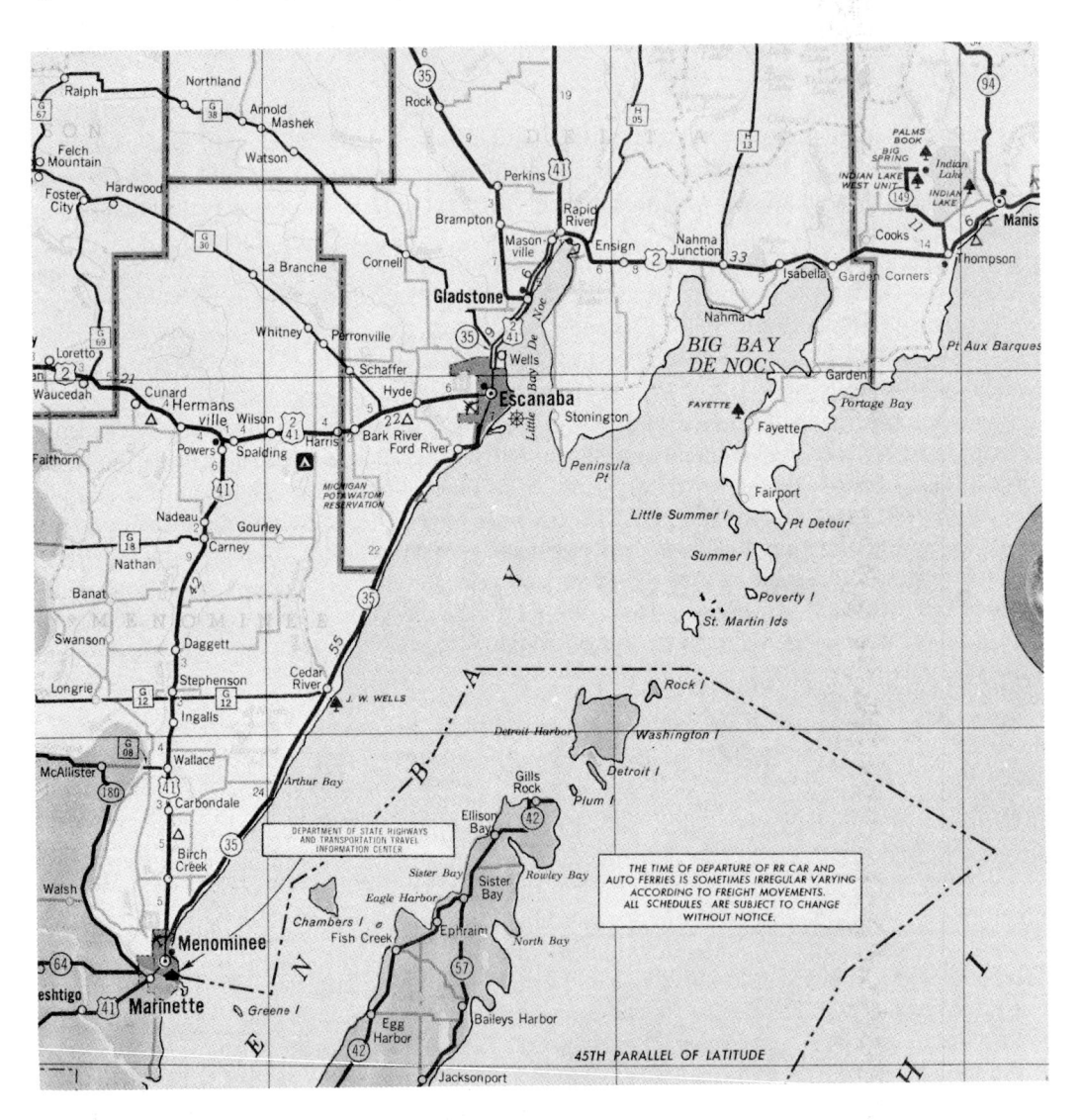

Figure 3.6. Michigan-Wisconsin boundary in Green Bay. Michigan claimed during the Supreme Court actions 1923-1926 that the boundary should be placed east of Chambers Island and south of Plum Island. (Map: Michigan Department of State Highways and Transportation.)

Rectangular Survey Replaces Metes and Bound Surveys

By the process of political compromise came the policy of the Jefferson, Congressional, Federal, or Rectangular Survey System as it has been variously named. The system embodied features both to raise revenue and to control land sales to avoid willy-nilly settlement. Other features included: (1) accurate federal surveys prior to land sale or settlement, (2) school section reserves, (3) survey of ranges of townships six miles by six miles on a side consisting of thirty-six one-mile square sections of 640 acres, (4) location of the survey townships in accordance with designated Baselines and Principle Meridians, (5) careful registering of deeds of land title, and (6) transfer control of federal land on the basis of "value received" or services rendered to prevent lavish grants to political favorites.[7]

By adopting the square mile survey system using a predetermined Baseline (42°26′30″) extending east-west across the state and a Michigan Principle Meridian (84°22′24″W) extending north-south through the length of the state, surveying could be done more speedily in comparison to the *metes and bounds* system.

Surveying Michigan

The Federal Land Survey of Michigan originated in areas already settled in the southeast and progressed into nearby areas following the establishment of the Baseline and Michigan Meridian. The formal survey of the state began with a contract to Benjamin Hough to mark the first segment of the Michigan Meridian. His party started at Fort Defiance, Ohio, in 1815 and set mile markers to the vicinity of Leslie 40 km (25 mi) south of Lansing. A quarter century later the William Burt survey team completed the last segment of the Michigan Meridian in the Upper Peninsula near Sault Ste. Marie (fig. 3.7). The survey of the Baseline began in 1824 with the line being done in several small sections. Some survey parties worked west from Detroit and others moved west to east from the meridian. West of the Michigan Meridian, the Baseline was established in a separate operation from the Baseline to its east. As a result of the segmented survey and applying a straight line system to the circular earth, correction lines had to be established. Periodic jogs in section line roads and the less than 640 acres in the "take-up" sections along the Meridian and township boundaries are constant reminders that "round and square" shapes can only be fit together with adjustment. Therefore, if a specific amount of land is critical to a decision or for meeting a legal requirement, a prospective land purchaser should investigate the actual acreage in a given plot and not rely on the theoretical amount. The Meridian-Baseline State Historic Park on the Jackson-Ingham County line commemorates both the significance of these lines as well as the 937.4 ft mismatch in the Baseline.

Surveyors in the Field

The surveyors could be called the state's first American pioneers. They were rugged individuals who frequently had to wade through muck and water up to their knees for hours on end, yet keep patient while recording notes and making detailed maps. Bending the law was illegal and subject to penalties, but it still was not enough to prevent some discouraged surveyor

---

7. P. J. Treat, "Origin of National Land System under the Confederation," Reprinted in *The Public Lands* (Madison: University of Wisconsin, 1968), pp. 7-14.

Figure 3.7. Michigan Survey Townships. (Map: Michigan Department of Natural Resources.)

from producing some imaginary maps. Frequently, to overcome the nuisances of mosquitoes, swamps, and poor sight lines, the surveys were done in the fall and winter when the ground was frozen.

The survey parties blazed trails, rated the quality and character of the land, and keyed their maps with Indian trails, haymarshes, bogs, lakes, and streams where they crossed the section lines. At each half mile a monument was established by posts, trees, pins, stones, or mounds. In addition, nearby trees were identified as *witness trees* with notes taken to include their diameter at chest height and species. Generally, there were four witness trees for a section corner while two were used for quarter post identification. At the monuments, blazes with inscribed marks to indicate township, range, and section number were made as follows:

        T7S
        R6E
        S4

Survey parties in the field consisted of several men; a surveyor-leader, ax men to clear sight lines, chain and rod men. The federal government through the Secretary of Treasury, General Land Officer, and Territorial Surveyor contracted, if possible, experienced surveyors. The surveyor had to organize and hire a party including equipping and paying the members. Under threat of fines, the survey, maps, and notes had to be completed in a designated period of time. Harvey Parke's contract for surveying six townships stipulated three months, with a $1,000 fine if turned in late. The highest sum paid for a federal land survey contract went to William Burt at $18.00 per mile to mark the tortuous Michigan and Wisconsin boundary in 1847.

The field equipment to support a pioneer survey team included: (1) a tripod mounted magnetic compass or solar compass after 1840, (2) a 66-foot chain with 100 links of 7.92 inches, (3) a dozen marking pins with a ring for looping sighting flags, (4) sighting rods, (5) axes, (6) timber scribe, and (7) pencils, pens, and paper. Essential for the protection of the notes and maps produced was a good quality waterproof box or pouch. To sustain five to eight team members the surveyor would provision a base camp with: tenting, blankets, ground cloths, tin plates, cups, pails, knives, and forks. Food items included salt pork, beans, rice, flour, baking soda, coffee, salt, pepper, and dried apples.

Survey and Civil Township Establishment

Under the Land Survey Ordinance, townships intended for settlement were to be surveyed well in advance of the land seekers' arrival. Michigan fit the model. One year after the opening of the Erie Canal, Farmer's 1826 Map of Michigan shows townships surveyed and section lines drawn throughout the southeastern one-third of the Lower Peninsula. Ready for purchase were lands from Saginaw County on the north to Hillsdale County on the west. Survey townships were created by utilizing the Baseline and placing *town lines* parallel to it at each six miles and numbering the intervals consecutively north 1 to 59 and Isle Royale 63 to 67. South of the Baseline, town line intervals number 1 to 9. Similarly, *range lines* were placed at six-mile intervals parallel to the Michigan Meridian and numbered consecutively east 1 to 17 and west 1 to 49. The 36 square mile area resulting from these town (T) and range (R) lines are known as *survey townships*. At one-mile intervals north-south and east-west, *section lines* were marked within the survey townships. After 1796 these one square mile *sections* were identified by consecutive numbers 1-36, starting in the survey township's northeast section even if the area was submerged by water. By using terms north half (N 1/2) or east half (E 1/2) a 320-acre parcel could be identified within a section. Similarly, northeast-quarter (NE 1/4) or southwest-quarter (SW 1/4), etc., could identify a 160-acre "quarter section." To identify a 40-acre farm or "quarter of a quarter" the following would be combined and used, NE 1/4 of SW 1/4, signifying the land was in the northeast quarter of the southwest quarter of a section. By further careful descriptions, farm parcels as small as 5 or even 2.5 acres could be specifically identified. By placing in a series the town number and direction (T2S), range number and direction (R1W), section number (Sect. 34), and half or quarter acreage identification (SE 1/4 160 ac) a farm holding or community can be uniquely described without the possibility of a conflicting description throughout the entire state. Thus, T2S, R1W, Sect. 34, SE 1/4 160 ac is the site of the city of Jackson in Jackson County (figs. 2.5 and 3.8).

BLACKMAN'S LOCATION

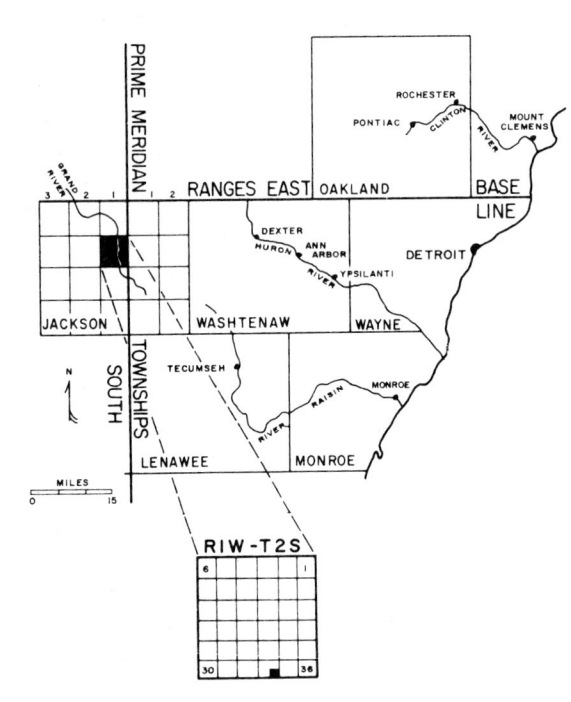

Figure 3.8. This map illustrates the Federal Survey description of land. In this example the land described as R1W-T2S, Section 34, SE¼ 160 acres was sold to Horace Blackman, the pioneer purchaser of the site of the City of Jackson.

In certain instances near lakes, rivers, or in extremely difficult terrain the intitial surveyors would designate an irregularly-shaped parcel of land by a *government lot number*. Along the state borders where two state surveys met, fractions of sections resulting from an imperfect fit would receive a section number corresponding to its respective state survey system. The overall simplicity of the rectangular land survey system allowed a vast population of semi-illiterate pioneers to enter the frontier, roam the land, seek, locate, and make claim to land with a minimum of conflict. More importantly, land could be purchased at the Land Office sometimes scores of miles away with assuredness that what was specifically seen staked as a claim was the land bought. The section line markers allowed for orientation and reorientation to a known place nearly every mile. Thus, the bane of being lost was reduced to the point that the pioneer would eagerly invest his family's future on the strength and simple organization of the land survey system.

In the contemporary period, the ability to be able to understand town-range descriptions is important due to their continued legal use in public notices, real estate transactions, as well as rural place descriptions.

Initially in Michigan Territory there was no government organization below county level. As surveys and settlement increased, smaller counties were organized out of the large frontier era counties. In 1825 Congress authorized the Michigan Territorial Governor and Council to further divide the counties into *civil townships* and concurrently organize a more local government.

Following the shape of the survey townships from which they were quickly formed, most civil townships and counties have retained straight line boundaries. The area and shape of many civil townships and counties of the central and northern peninsula are also uniformly square with sixteen survey townships to a county. In contrast, several counties vary from uniformity of size; Oakland County comprises a square with twenty-five survey townships while Jackson and Washtenaw Counties are made up of twenty survey townships. The state's smallest county, Benzie, is comprised of less than ten survey townships while the state's largest county, Marquette, has an area of over fifty-two survey townships. In 1972 Michigan's eighty-three counties had organized within them 1,248 civil townships which is slightly less than the 1,265 in 1942.

In the process of developing representative government at the local level, the civil townships were established with a distinguishing name, i.e., Bunker Hill, Prairie Ronde, Texas, Grant, Green, Fruit Land, Pine River, Deerfield, and Redford. In numerous counties throughout the state, to provide greater accessibility and a more viable township government, the civil township's boundaries would be altered from the survey township lines. Depending on conditions, the following types of civil townships have been created from the survey township base: (1) a survey-civil township occupying the same territory, (2) one survey township split into two civil townships, i.e., Lenawee County's Clinton and Tecumseh Townships, (3) two or more survey townships combined to form one civil township due to sparce population, i.e., Roscommon Township, and (4) civil townships with river boundaries, i.e., Allendale Township, Ottawa County. Unfortunately, as a result of the dual meaning of the word "township" and nonconformity between civil and survey township borders, care has to be continually exercised in its legal and political use.

Nineteenth Century County Evolution

The constant mutation of the political geographic composition of Michigan during its pioneer century can best be illustrated by the several adjoining maps (figs. 3.9 to 3.14). Between 1818, when the Land Sales Office was opened at Detroit, and 1897, when the contemporary county boundaries were fixed, the state government attempted to adjust continually to the settlement realities of its people. The state's altering of the size, number, and shape of the counties as the population swelled from 8,896 in 1820 to 2,420,982 in 1900, enhanced the opportunity for local governments to solve their problems.

Since 1897, eighty-three organized counties have governed immediately below the state level. This does not represent the highest number of counties organized. During the 1880s the list was longer and included island counties such as Manitou and Isle Royale. Some former county names also no longer appear on the map: Washington, Knox, Brown, Wyandot, nor the tongue twisting Michilimackinac. County names concocted by Schoolcraft and some counties with Indian names have also been replaced: i.e., Wabassee, Okkuddo, Megisee, Kaykakee, and Anomickee.

Figure 3.9. Michigan county organization 1818. (Map: R. Welch, *County Evolution in Michigan 1790-1897*, Michigan Department of of Education.)

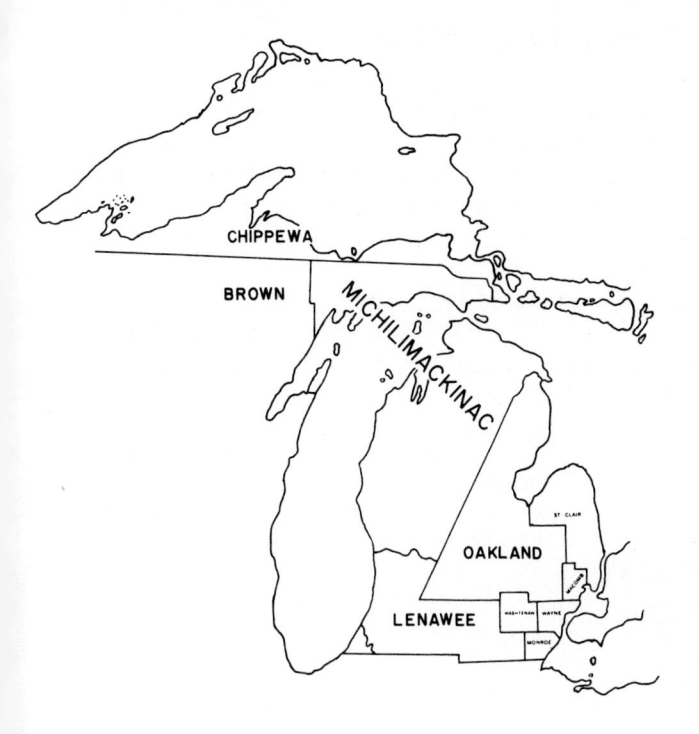

Figure 3.10. Michigan county organization 1828. (Map: R. Welch, *County Evolution in Michigan 1790-1897,* Michigan Department of Education.)

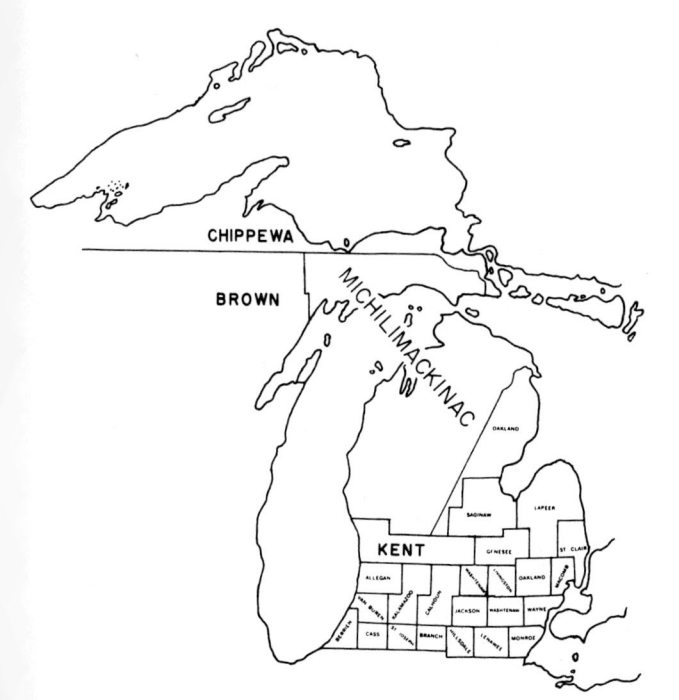

Figure 3.11. Michigan county organization 1836. (Map: R. Welch, *County Evolution in Michigan 1790-1897,* Michigan Department of Education.)

Figure 3.12. Michigan county organization 1840. (Map: R. Welch, *County Evolution in Michigan 1790-1897,* Michigan Department of Education.)

Figure 3.13. Michigan county organization 1867. (Map: R. Welch, *County Evolution in Michigan 1790-1897,* Michigan Department of Education.)

Figure 3.14. Michigan county organization 1876. (Map: R. Welch, *County Evolution in Michigan 1790-1897*, Michigan Department of Education.)

Counties and County Seats

In the process of evolving legal counties, three steps were taken. Their identifying terms are easily confused due to similarity in popular usage. The first step was to *setoff* or establish a county by designating a certain area and providing it with a name. The second step was to *attach* the named county to an organized county for civil, judicial, tax, and census purposes. Sometimes the "attached" county would be shifted from one organized county to another before reaching the third step. Thus, it is not unusual to locate the initial land records of a county in one or more counties. Similarly, a pioneer family while not moving its residence may be listed on the census schedules as having lived in more than one county. After the number of permanent residents increased sufficiently, a request was made to the state legislature to be formally *organized* and thereby be legally entitled to elect its own county officials and maintain its own records.

County Seats. Contrary to widespread belief, most Michigan county seats are nongeographically centered within county areas. Although centrality has had some influence on the siting of a few county seats, i.e., Jackson, Cassopolis, Ithaca, and Marshall, most were located in relationship to transportation accessibility, density of population, and natural features. Political astuteness was also rewarded in gaining the economic advantage of a seat of greater political activity. People in counties adjacent to the Great Lakes invariably selected their largest city on the shoreline as the county seat, i.e., Monroe, Detroit, Alpena, Muskegon, St. Joseph, Escanaba, and Marquette. Noncentrally located interior county seats are represented by Grand Rapids, Big Rapids, Reed City, Grayling, Iron Mountain, Crystal Falls, Ironwood,

Baldwin, and Hastings. Tecumseh is a rare example of a town which lost to the argument of centrality when Adrian was made the Lenawee county seat. Waldron, the historian of Tecumseh, has stated that if Tecumseh citizens had been more politically alert when the decision was made, their community would still be the place of county government.[8]

Spatial Aspects of Regional and Economic Development Acts

From the earliest days of the republic the people of Michigan have participated in the planned economic and land-use development of the nation. The national policies of Indian treaties, purchase of Indian ceded land, surveys prior to land sales, land sales to meet national financial needs, restricted areas of frontier settlement to provide for an orderly extension of government services, plus the state's constant adjustment of county boundaries, were deliberate plans by the United States and Michigan founders to avert disruptive development conditions and costly alternatives.

Based on historic political geographic traditions of the nation and state, the twentieth century government of Michigan has continued to participate with the federal government and other states in the evolving policy of economic and regional land-use management. By the 1930s the political geographic complexities and problems of a rapidly growing, large, mobile, and urbanized population spreading across fixed county lines, had become easily observable. Appearing in the eyes of millions of Michiganians were skyscrapered office space, interurbans, automobile-clogged streets, smoke-filled air, and rich farmland being lost in the race of speculative development. By 1940 the state population alone was more than a million and a quarter larger than the nation's total when it was first counted in 1790. Zoning had begun to sweep the state's cities in the 1920s, but the laws tended to fix in place already existing urban land-use patterns. Subsequently, it became recognized that zoning alone was not an effective tool in coping with the state's multicounty and wastershed problems.

Regional Concept

The most recent attempt to avert land-use and economic adversities has been the creation of regional and economic planning bodies. In Michigan, Regional Planning Commissions became legal in 1945 with Public Act 281. Philosophically, regional organization allows for a voluntary, cooperative combination of local government areas. When combined, local governments are thought to have a better opportunity to meet the citizen's desires and needs without having to seek state or federal aid. Theoretically, regional management represents a trend toward more local government rather than greater state and federal centralization. For instance, the metropolitan center to which a citizen travels to purchase major items, to seek advanced medical or hospital care, or to enjoy professional and cultural entertainment, is personally more important to that individual than the more distant Lansing or Washington. Further, if the citizens of the greater metropolitan regional community cooperate in meeting their more specialized and common needs with a regional government embracing the area in which the citizens normally interact, it is anticipated there will be less need to interact directly with the bureaucracies centered in the state and national capitals. In effect, regional organization allows

---

8. Clara Waldron, *One Hundred Years a Country Town* (Tecumseh: T. A. Riordan, 1968), pp. 82-83.

for the placing of the locus of governmental initiative closer to citizen's homes. Regional organization also allows for the formalization of a political body around a level of community activity which is already functioning economically, but not governmentally.

Since World War II numerous regional commissions have been created. However, they lack two primary attributes of traditional American government units such as school boards, townships, counties, or the state: (1) direct election of the commission members, and (2) direct financial responsibility and financing by regional citizens. In contrast to traditions of the nation, the appointment of representatives and the indirect state and federal financing may have created negative impacts on the functioning activities within the state's regional communities.

The Diffusion of Regional Organizations

In spite of a general lack of mass education relative to regional government, misunderstanding of roles and duties of commission members, and jealousy between metropolitan and nonmetropolitan counties over priority of needs and representation, regional organization has proliferated in all parts of the state. By 1970 there were ninety-eight multicounty regions; ten of these were general purpose in scope of operation, and covered sixty-one counties. Two additional state acts have stimulated the adoption of regional organization: the Economic Development Commission Act 1966 and Urban Cooperation Act 1967. United States presidents have also recognized that the nation's federal government alone is incapable of meeting the ever-increasing duplicate requests of state and local communities to assist in making their communities a worthwhile place to live. President Johnson in a 1966 memorandum, "Coordination for Development Planning," encouraged cooperation and uniform regional boundaries:

> State and local development planning agencies should be encouraged to work together in using common or consistent planning bases (i.e., statistical and economic estimates), and in sharing facilities and resources.
> Boundaries for planning and development districts assisted by the Federal Government should be the same and should be consistent with established state planning districts and regions.[9]

In analyzing the roles of the several state regions which have emerged, two broad categories can be identified. The general purpose regional and economic development areas are the fewest in number. This type is best represented by the fourteen State Planning and Development Regions created between 1968 and 1973. Single purpose regions were the earliest and most numerous type of regional functioning unit. Examples of this category are hospital districts, water and sewage districts, and mental health regions. Other early regions were established for law enforcement, legal services, watershed management, transportation, employment security, libraries, tourism, mail distribution, conservation, park, fire, and forestry. Of all these regions and districts, rarely do the boundaries coincide. Since the establishment of the fourteen State Planning Regions, many of the single purpose regions have adjusted their boundaries to conform with the uniform Planning and Development Regions. In some cases to reduce administrative costs and still serve citizen needs, the area of two uniform regions has been combined into one single purpose region. Law enforcement and other bodies have established subregional centers to be more responsive to local conditions.

9. Office of the Governor, *Planning and Development Regions for Michigan,* Tech. Rep. 14 (February 1968), p. 13.

Defining and Determining Michigan's Contemporary Regions

The word "region" has been defined in a variety of ways; however, in geography the term is used to describe an area which can be bound into a land-water unit having the presence of at least one or more common characteristics. Some *homogeneous regions* are based on natural features: climate, soil, landforms, vegetation, or river basins. Others are derived from cultural features: language, agriculture, economic activity, religion, life-style, and other human activities. A *nodal region* functions around a single place, usually a city, which has several transportation access lines into it. Human ecologists, cultural geographers, and sociologists are frequently concerned with identifying "communities of interest" measured by indices of social, economic, and political cohesiveness. Usually such communities manifest a regional consciousness which potentially can be marshaled to deal with its local problems. While each approach to the identification of a region is useful, no single feature is ideally suited to every purpose. For administrative governmental purposes, regions based on functional cultural features are generally most realistic for delimiting areas to meet and deliver human services.

Value of Regions. As citizens demand more services from their government, regional governments have the following advantages:

1. Improvement of communication between governments and levels of government.
2. Economy in providing service.
3. Greater ability to design programs to meet regional needs.
4. Creation of common information and statistical units to assist in analysis and solving problems.

Former Lieutenant Governor Brickley in his analysis of regional benefits includes: elimination of first-come-first-served government reaction to requests, reduction in duplication of services, local government's greater opportunity to develop and finance their own programs, opportunity for local leaders to develop leadership skills in a larger population setting, and a system more fitting a mobile society.[10]

Fourteen Nodal Regional Communities

When one looks at a map of the fourteen uniform State Planning Regions and observes straight lines for regional boundaries, suspicion should be aroused as to the accuracy of their location (fig. 3.15). Neither natural features nor human functional communities have so abrupt and precise geometric patterns. On the other hand, political units, due to their ease of drawing, popularly have straight lines for limits. While the straight line regional boundaries alert users to the fact that nonnatural forces were involved, the irregularity in size and shape indicates attempts to fit the boundaries to human conditions.

The fourteen nodal regions of Michigan are a product of both the political process and modern-day social behavioral scientific knowledge. In the creation of the fourteen planning regions, the number and boundaries were constrained by the political decision to: (1) limit number of regions to fourteen, (2) make the minimum region area at least three counties, and (3) adjust the region boundaries to existing county lines. Had township lines been acceptable

---

10. James H. Brickley, "Solve Problems, Provide Services Via Regionalism," *Detroit Free Press* (October 23, 1973), p. 7A.

for boundary use, a higher degree of fit between the region areas and the regional centers could have emerged. In spite of the political interplay and given constraints, Michigan's fourteen "communities of interest" have been initially acceptable. It is to the credit of the individuals preparing the regional plan for the Governor's office that, during the five years following the process of state and local review, only one major adjustment occurred. Muskegon County, having earlier established itself with Ottawa and Oceana Counties in 1966 for "west shore planning purposes," negotiated the relocation of Region Fourteen from the Upper Peninsula. As a result, Region Eight became three counties smaller and the Upper Peninsula was redelineated into three rather than four regions.

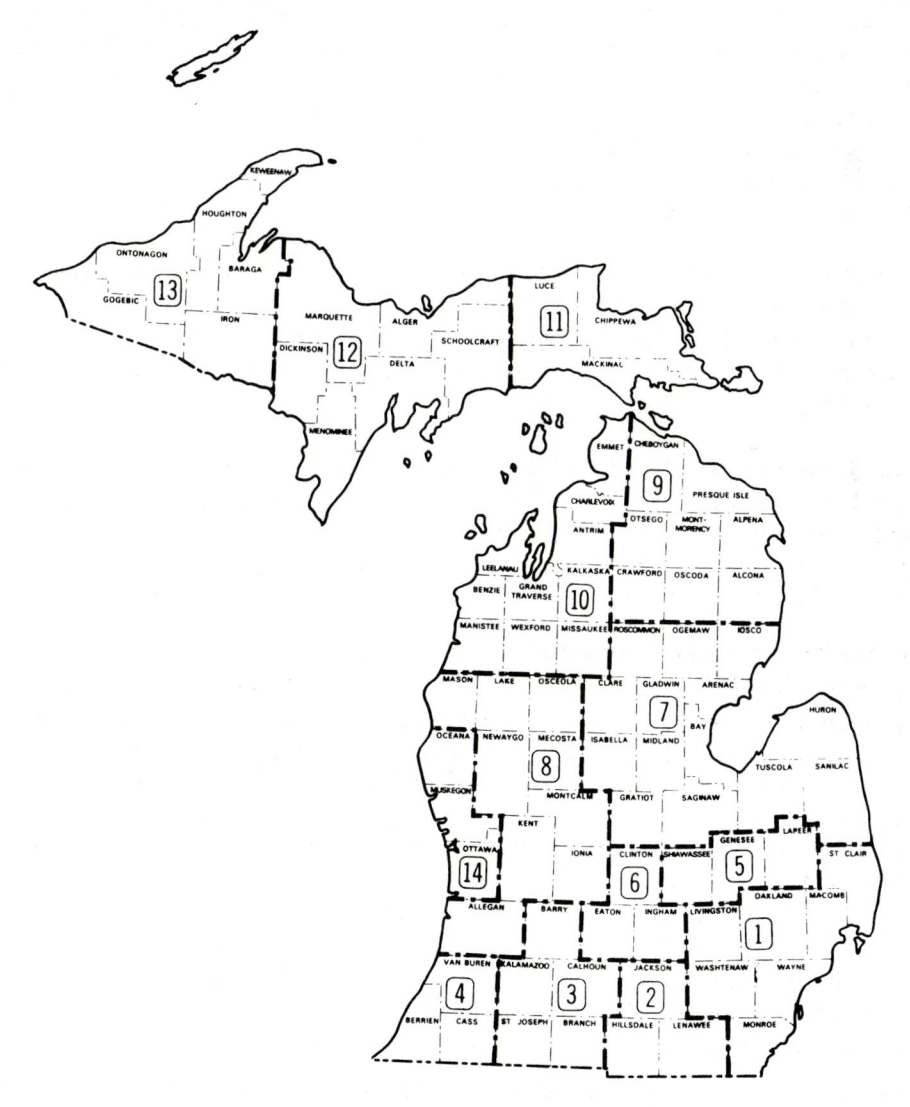

Figure 3.15. Michigan Planning Regions 1976.

Regions Based on Urban Centers. The state's uniform nodal regions have been based on major cities for they are not only centers of people, but also of production, employment, trade, communication, transportation, finance, and education. Unlike the creation of counties which were "set off" with arbitrary dimensions and sometimes even before rural settlement, the modern-day regions were bounded after a small number of significant, dispersed urban places were carefully selected as representative regional centers. If regional communities of interest are to function effectively, their center or node must be both significant in terms of its relationship to the region, as well as reasonably accessible from outlying parts of the community region.

The following criteria were used in selecting Michigan's fourteen regional centers:

1. General population distribution and economic activity patterns.
2. County rankings based on per capita retail sales, wholesale sales, selected service receipts, plus total bank deposits, manufacturing payroll, and nonagricultural labor force.
3. Population density 100 per square mile in southern Lower Michigan and 33 per square mile in the northern part of the state with each density related to a city or township area.
4. Time and distance transportation data.
5. Intercounty commuting to a place of employment.

Objectively using the data, the fourteen regional centers were selected: (1) Detroit, (2) Jackson, (3) Kalamazoo, (4) Benton Harbor, (5) Flint, (6) Lansing, (7) Saginaw, (8) Grand Rapids, (9) Alpena, (10) Traverse City, (11) Sault Ste. Marie, (12) Marquette, (13) Ironwood, and (14) Muskegon. Ann Arbor and Port Huron act as designated subregional centers in the Detroit area, while Big Rapids serves a similar function for Grand Rapids. By virtue of selection as one of the fourteen major communities of Michigan, the people in these centers have perhaps the greatest responsibility below state level in the determination of the future of Michigan.

Delineation of Regional Boundaries. The functional area of a regional center is inseparably tied to its transportation network which allows "centripetal forces" to pull people into its center. A simple test to determine where a boundary lies between two cities is to identify where people come from to view a first-run motion picture which is being shown in the two cities simultaneously. By interview or automobile license plate observation, the relative dividing line between the two places can be established. Because each city is unique in its own way, the dividing line will rarely be equidistant. Repetition of this and scores of other observations have been used successfully to determine nodal region boundaries. In Michigan, the fourteen Planning Region boundaries were established by five criteria:

1. Circulation of the regional center's afternoon daily newspaper, a general indicator of social and economic interest.
2. "Journey to work" commuting data.
3. Minimum traffic flow maps from highway count data.

4. A "gravity model," mathematical measure of attraction shoppers based on population, commercial retail floor space, travel time, and distance.
5. State economic areas derived in the 1950s from agricultural data.

To make the actual boundary determination, the raw data was mapped and the boundaries adjusted to the nearest county line. By overlaying the resulting maps, composite and well-defined boundaries were identified. In areas where a breaking point was only weakly revealed, subjective disinterested judgments determined the actual regional boundary placement.

Regional Comparisons

In most regions the driving time from outlying areas to the regional center is less than one and a half hours; however, in some cases isolation from a main road may cause a person to be two hours away from the regional center. By comparison, in animal power days the county seats were probably no further away in time from the out-county areas than the regional centers of contemporary time. Chapter Eight in this book describes the people and their activities in the state's fourteen Planning Regions.

Michigan has witnessed an abundance of changes in its political geographic boundaries from the days of Indian occupation by three major tribes to the eighty-three counties in the twentieth century. Since 1945, regions have appeared on the map indicating again the people's desire to find a political geographic organization which will satisfy their demands. What political geographic organization the twenty-first century will bring, time and the readers of this chapter will in part determine.

Photo Essay A

FUR TRADE AT THE STRAITS OF MACKINAC

A-1 Reconstructed Fort Michilimackinac originally established by the French in 1715.
A-2 Fort Mackinac, Mackinac Island, established in 1780 by the British.
A-3 Rural Quebec housetype 1780, Mackinac Island.
A-4 American Fur Company trade offices built in 1817.
A-5 Indian dormitory 1838.

All photos in this essay courtesy Michigan Travel Commission.

A-1

A-2

A-3

A-4

A-5

> "Now we face the question whether a still higher 'standard of living' is worth the cost of things natural..."
>
> *Aldo Leopold, 1948*

Chapter Four

Michigan's Geology and Mining Resources

The physical geography of Michigan is directly tied to the geology of the state's bedrock and its associated mining activities. Equally important in the analysis of physical geography are climate, soil, vegetation, astronomical impacts, glaciation, geomorphology, and hydrology which will be discussed in the following two chapters. Woven throughout these three chapters will be the present-day condition and economic uses of the physical resources created by nature.

Earliest Geologic History and Contemporary Resource Activity

The awe-inspiring beauty and wealth of resources held in trust by Michigan citizens have emerged from a complex of all the physical earth-shaping processes. In addition to the uplift of ancient mountains from surrounding oceans, the tectonic processes of folding, faulting, volcanic eruptions, lava flows, and earthquakes have also left their mark on the state. Exposed land has been attacked by the gradational forces of wind, water, freezing, and thawing, plus at least four advances and retreats of the continental glaciers. In some places the ice sheets exposed layers of igneous, metamorphic, and sedimentary bedrock, while covering other places deep with sand, gravels, and clay, which have weathered into the soil we work today. How all of these processes worked and what resulted from them will be presented as "fact." Yet, by necessity, the descriptions carry with them an element of conjecture. The basics of the formation of Michigan's land and lakes are widely agreed upon, nevertheless individual interpretations of well logs and field observations are continually debated and revised by physiographers in seeking knowledge of the state's earth history.

The Michigan Basin

The Precambrian granitic rock of the *Michigan Basin* is the foundation of the earth's crust upon which Michigan is built (fig. 4.1). In the dim past of two billion years ago the Huron

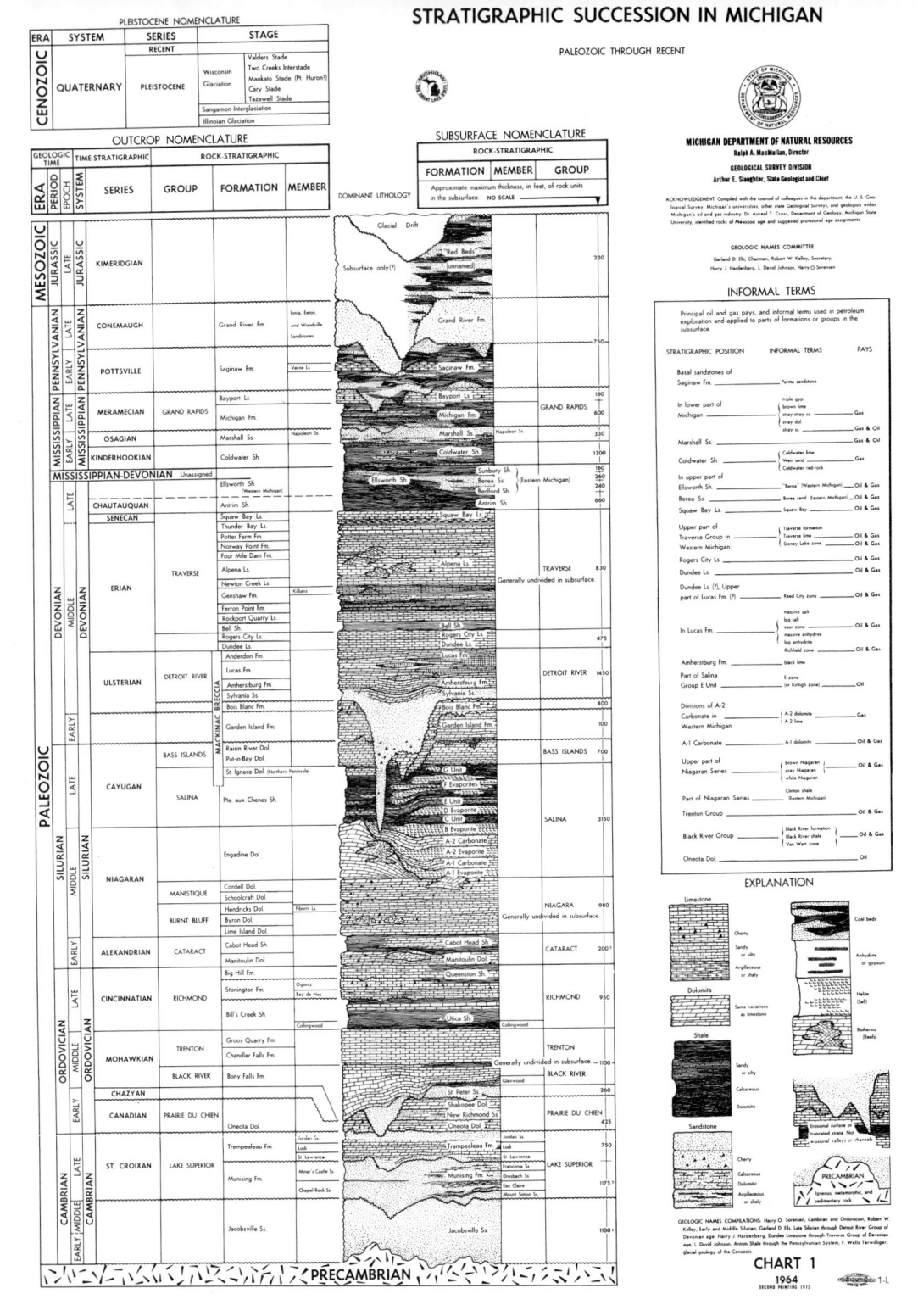

Figure 4.1. Michigan bedrock formations. (Chart: Michigan Department of Natural Resources.)

Mountains in the western Upper Peninsula were the only land area in Michigan exposed to the sun. These highlands were a part of the 5.2 million sq km (2 million sq mi) "U"-shaped Canadian Shield centered around Hudson Bay. The Appalachians, Ozark Highlands, and Canadian Shield formed a rim for a vast shallow saltwater sea which occupied a deep basin or syncline. It has been determined by drillings that the deepest part of this ancient ocean which covered Michigan was in the Lower Peninsula. Holes drilled over 1,600 meters deep in Newaygo County and 3,890 meters deep in Ogemaw County in 1960 failed to strike the tell-tale granites of the ancient Precambrian ocean floor. In 1975 the state's deepest well 5,240 m (17,466 ft) near Ithaca reached a controversially interpreted red shale at 3,648 m (12,193 ft), and finally "basement" rock at its maximum depth.[1]

In spite of the lack of complete geologic knowledge and the need to simplify the perpetual occurrences of uplifts, contractions, and alternate periods of weathering which came with changing climates, a general concept of Michigan's bedrock formation can be developed. Nested on top of the Precambriam rock basin have been formed six successively smaller layers of rocks similar to saucers with irregular edges and thicknesses. In between these primary layers, like padding, are wedges of bedrock sediments which do not reach entirely across the six saucer layers (fig. 4.2).

The Precambrian Iron and Copper Ranges Development

Two billion years ago when the earth was relatively young, igneous magma and volcanic lava flows cooled and hardened into the oldest granitic rocks of the Canadian Shield including the Huron Mountains in Marquette County. Eventually these rocks by gradational weathering and transportation, furnished the iron and silica which became the great ore deposits of Michigan, Wisconsin, and Minnesota. During the Huronian stage of the Precambrian Era, a depression formed over these states and into it flowed waters saturated with suspended silica-sand and iron rust which had eroded from iron bearing volcanic rocks. These minerals separated out in the quiet recess of a lake. In time taconite ore 100-250 meters thick of twenty-five percent iron content was deposited. Erosion continued to remove material from the Canadian Shield and bury the ore beneath massive beds of sand, silts, and clay. With heat from the earth, pressure from above, and time, sandstone and shales formed. The continued *metamorphic process* altered the sandstones into quartzites, and the shale into slate. Afterwards changes began to appear in the taconite as a result of its elevation above the groundwater table. In numerous places gravitationally flowing water seeped through the deposits of ore dissolving and removing the sand, leaving enriched iron beds. Some of the iron ore deposits became concentrated with over sixty-five percent iron content.

Soon after the discovery and verification of the iron ore deposits by Michigan surveyors and geologists in the 1840s, it was found that these ores had a major commercial development advantage. Natural iron with a high concentration could be shipped directly from the mines to iron and steel foundries without an on-site up-grading or beneficiation process. High-grade, direct ship hematite dominated the Michigan iron market through the World War II-Korean War era. Since 1960 lower-grade taconite, magnetite, and jaspolite mined primarily by the Cleveland-Cliffs Iron Company near Ishpeming have become most important.

---

1. "Deepest Well Dug at Ithaca," *Michigan Natural Resources,* vol. 45, no. 2 (March-April 1976), p. 42.

Selected Minerals By Geological Formation

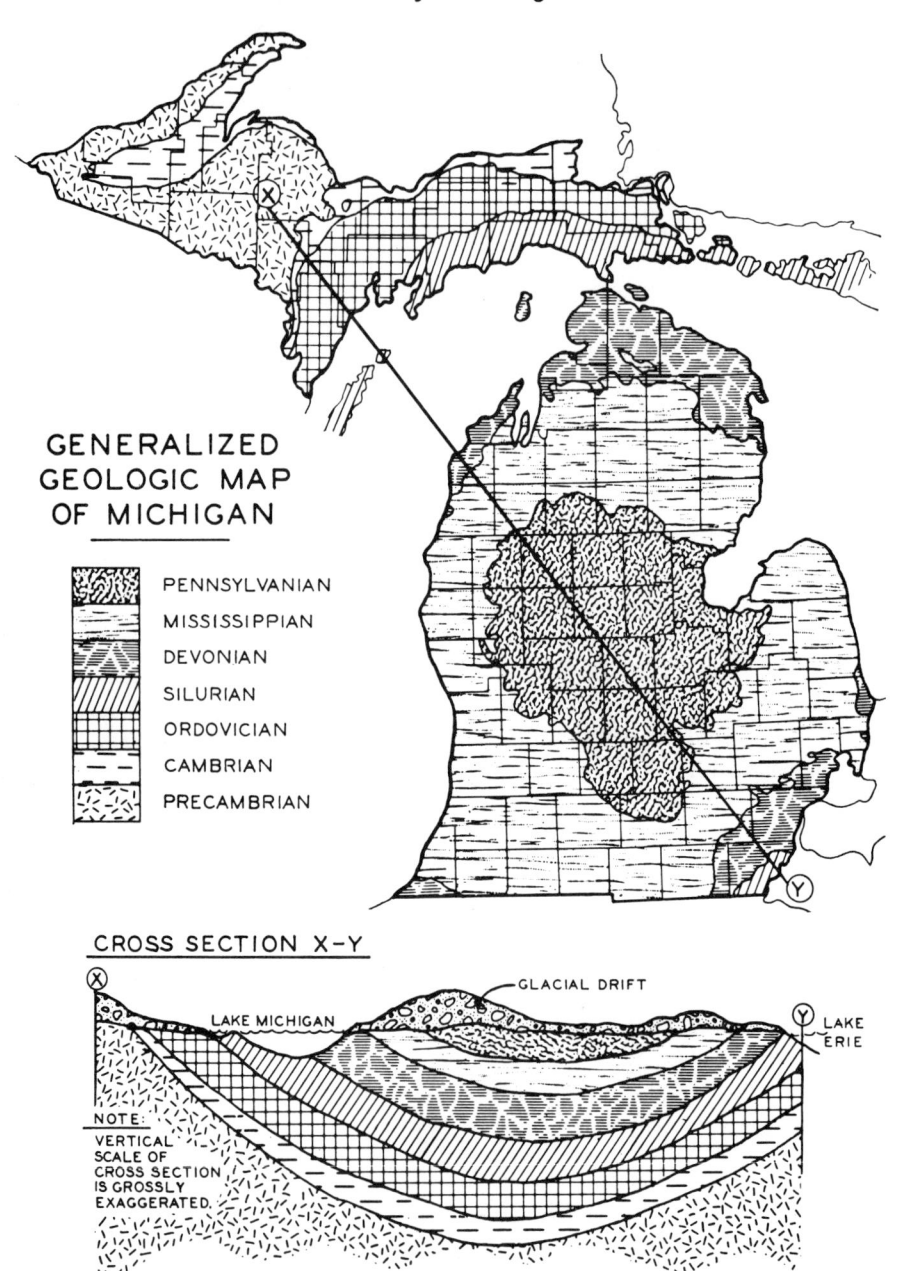

Figure 4.2. Michigan bedrock patterns. (Map: J.D. Lewis, *Michigan Mineral Producers 1975,* Michigan Geological Survey Division.)

TABLE 4.1
Generalized Geologic Time Scale

Era	Period	Epoch	Time (million years ago)
Cenozoic	Quaternary	Recent	0.004
		Pleistocene	0.5-2.0
	Tertiary		58
Mesozoic			63
Paleozoic	Permian		220
	Pennsylvanian		280
	Mississippian		310
	Devonian		345
	Silurian		405
	Ordovician		425
	Cambrian		500
Precambrian	Proterozoic		600
	Archeozoic (oldest rock date)		3,500
	Origin of earth		4,500-5,000

Adapted from Dorr and Eschman, *Geology of Michigan*, 1971.

Iron Ore Beneficiation. It is not economically profitable to ship low-grade iron ores as they come from the mine to distant markets. Thus, a process of *beneficiation* is undertaken at or near the shipping point to alter the iron ore into an economically transportable material. *Wash grade ores* are comparatively inexpensive to upgrade by crushing and rinsing the sand away leaving the cobbles in an enriched state. In winter, due to freezing, washed ore is generally unsuitable for shipment. Lower-grade ores have to be upgraded by a longer, more costly and energy-consuming process. Ores with 20-36 percent iron content are mined, crushed, and ground into a fine dust at a beneficiation plant. Iron particles are separated by one of several methods depending on the type of ore to be upgraded. The state's first pelletizing plant at the Republic Mine in 1952 used a *liquid flotation* process which allows the iron to be skimmed off the top of a ferrosilicon mixture. At the Empire Mine a *magnetic separator* process was developed in 1966 to upgrade magnetite. The Tilden Plant, established in 1972, Ishpeming, separates ground hematic particles off the bottom of a vat of caustic soda, cooked cornstarch, and water. The finely ground iron dust is manufactured into marble-sized pellets of about sixty-five percent iron content using bentonite as a bonding agent, and hardened in kilns heated to 1,338 °C (2,440 °F). The dry iron pellets can be easily loaded and shipped anytime of the year which has enabled the extension of the lake shipping season.

The beneficiation process has extended the economic life of the Upper Peninsula mines, as well as created mine-related indoor factory employment. Interregional interdependency has also increased with the expansion of the flow of resources such as bentonite, cornstarch, coal, natural gas, and other resources from outside the state to support pelletizing operations.

Beneficiation Wastes and the Environment. The disposal of inorganic crushed rock waste created in the pelletizing process has vexed managers of iron mines and ecologists for several years. For over a decade in Minnesota, a beneficiating plant deposited 60,000 tons of waste per day into Lake Superior. The discovery of asbestos fibers in the municipal water supply of Duluth and other Lake Superior communities prompted a demand for land deposition which was ordered by a Federal Court in 1976. In Michigan, for two decades, waste from pelletizing plants has been spread on the land. Land disposal problems occurring in Michigan have included: filling of wetland swamps, runoff into streams, blowing dust, and stack emissions. These constant problems near the beneficiation plants, coupled with greater environmental awareness, have led corporations to initiate extensive projects to reclaim the land by revegetating inert tailing basins with grasses, shrubs, and trees. Over ninety percent of the water used in the processing plants is recycled, and scrubbers and electrostatic precipitators have been designed to control ninety-nine percent of stack particulate matter. Further, the Cleveland-Cliff's 560 ha (1,400 ac) Greenwood Reservoir which is used for iron processing has been open to the public for multiple recreational uses.

The Iron Ranges

At the western end of Lake Superior are two iron ranges, the *Gogebic Range* of Michigan and the giant-sized *Mesabi Range* of Minnesota. The two ranges have iron beds 200-325 meters thick which were probably formed at the same time, but were later separated by a huge downfold in the earth's crust. The Gogebic Range is a narrow, 125 km (80 mi) long area, dotted by the communities of Ironwood, Bessemer, and Wakefield. In 1967 the range's last operating mine, the Peterson, closed; however, as recently as 1956 the Gogebic Range produced nearly one-quarter of the state's total iron ore. The six iron ranges in the Upper Peninsula's eastern district: Marquette, Guinn, Amasa, Iron River-Crystal Falls, Felch, and Iron Mountain, were made commercially accessible by downwarping and removal of overburden by glacial action. Of these ranges, the Marquette dominates the iron mining area with over three-quarters of the state's total production coming from its four mines. Most iron production is from open pit mines such as the Empire, Republic, and Tilden Mines which yield magnetite and hemetic ores. The Tilden operation also produces martite. The Mather and Sherwood Mines in the Iron River-Crystal Falls range are the only two underground iron mines in operation. The less extensive Iron Mountain range, now inactive, was created when a fault exposed its steeply dipped beds. The combined closings of the Amasa and Gwinn Mines, as well as improvements in mining equipment, have resulted in employment decreasing to one-third of its 1950s level (fig. 4.3).

In the years of transition from direct ship ore to pelletized iron and reduced employment, Michigan has been able to maintain its historical rank as the second leading producer of iron. During the 1970s production has averaged between twelve and fourteen million tons of iron ore which is about one-third below the peak productions of World Wars One and Two (table 4.2). Although production is lower than during earlier peaks, the value of the mined ore continues to increase due to demand and inflation. The annual value of iron ore in the midseventies exceeds 250 million dollars.

Historical Discovery and Production of Iron Ore. The earliest discovery of commercial iron ore by Americans was in 1844 at Negaunee by the survey party of William Burt when they encountered difficulty with their compass. The erratic deflections in the compass were soon found to be caused by the magnetic attraction of the iron beds. A year later twenty citizens from Jackson opened the Jackson Pit in the Upper Peninsula near Teal Lake, and shipped 90 kg (200 lb) of iron ore. In 1846 a blacksmith cast the ore into iron which marked the first productive use of the Lake Superior iron ore deposits. On May 12, 1975, the Mather Mine in the Marquette Range yielded its 50 millionth ton of iron ore, the largest tonnage of any active underground mine, but still short of the 53.8 million tons hoisted to the surface from the Gogebic Range's Norrie-Pabst-Aurora Mine before it closed in 1935.

MICHIGAN IRON RESOURCES AND MINES

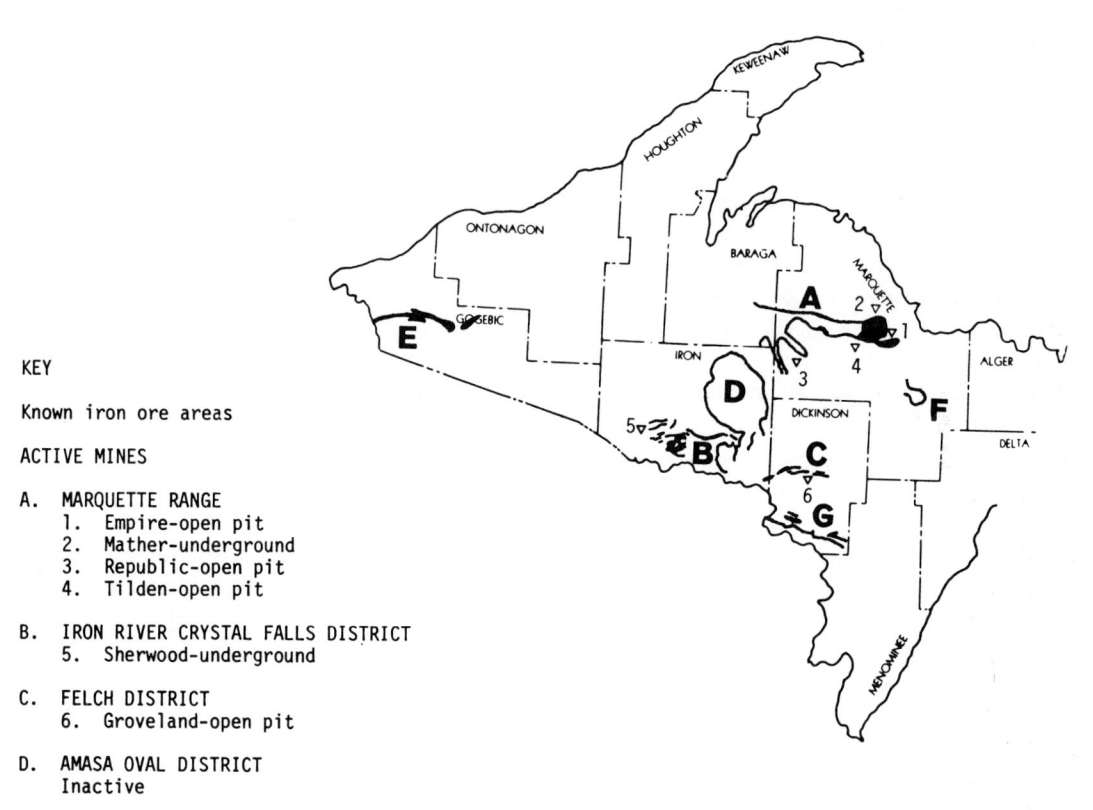

KEY

Known iron ore areas

ACTIVE MINES

A. MARQUETTE RANGE
   1. Empire-open pit
   2. Mather-underground
   3. Republic-open pit
   4. Tilden-open pit

B. IRON RIVER CRYSTAL FALLS DISTRICT
   5. Sherwood-underground

C. FELCH DISTRICT
   6. Groveland-open pit

D. AMASA OVAL DISTRICT
   Inactive

E. GOGEBIC RANGE
   Inactive

F. GWINN DISTRICT
   Inactive

G. IRON MOUNTAIN RANGE
   Inactive

Figure 4.3. Michigan iron mines. (Map: J.D. Lewis, *Michigan Mineral Producers 1975*, Michigan Geological Survey Division.)

TABLE 4.2
Number Active Iron Mines, Employment and Shipments 1950-1972

Year	Active Mines	Employment	Production* Marquette	Production* Menominee	Production* Gogebic
1950	37	6,809	4,955	4,144	3,827
1955	37	6,093	6,640	4,326	3,183
1960	27	4,735	4,945	4,121	1,890
1965	16	3,775	8,925	4,361	773
1970	7	2,798	10,336	2,925	0
1972	6	2,226	9,251	2,577	0

*Thousand long ton.
SOURCE: *Michigan Statistical Abstract*, 10th ed., 1974, p. 360.

Since the 1840s over a billion tons of ore have been shipped from the Upper Peninsula. Natural direct ship ores represent ninety percent of the total, but this is decreasing annually as beneficiated ore production increases. As a result of capital investments in beneficiation plants, a potential of 16.5 tons of pelletized ore can be shipped annually. The iron formations suitable for concentration into pellets are widely distributed in the Precambrian rock. The total resource of iron has not been measured, but it is estimated that tens of billions of tons are in reserve.

Copper Range on the Keweenaw Fault

In the late Precambrian era, the copper-rich spine of the Keweenaw Peninsula was thrust upward over 200 meters by a massive fault. The face and fault escarpment, now well-eroded, can still be traced for over 240 km (150 mi) in an area 1.6-13 km (1-8 mi) wide between Copper Harbor and northern Wisconsin. Along this giant crack in the earth's crust occurred explosive volcanoes followed by quiet lava flows of copper-bearing magma which were interrupted with deposits of sandstone and conglomerates. This copper and other valuable minerals were deposited in three ways as the materials cooled: (1) in dikes, fissures, and veins of otherwise solid basalt rock (Phoenix Central Mine, Central), (2) in amygdaloids or gas bubble voids in the basalt rock (Quincy and Pewabic Mines, Hancock), and (3) in the mixed conglomerate rock (Calumet and Hecla Mine, Calumet). As a result of these geologic processes the greatest native copper deposits found in the world were created.

Pure sheets and globs of native copper which occurred near the surface were mined from shallow pits by Michigan's early Indians on both the Keweenaw Peninsula and Isle Royale. The native copper, which is rarely found in other parts of the world, was traded in its natural condition and also crafted before exchange. In 1841 Michigan's first State Geologist, Douglass Houghton, explored, mapped, and reported on the economic potential of the 1,040 sq km (400 sq mi) of copper country. By 1844 the first of the modern-day miners arrived at Copper Harbor and Eagle River from Cornwall, England, bringing with them not only mining skills, but also the regionally distinctive lunch bucket pasty. The Cliff Mine at Eagle River became the initial copper deposit to be systematically mined and the world's first pure native copper mine. The original copper mines tapped fissures and veins in the basalt in comparison to present-day mining of stratified deposits in shales, conglomerates, and lava flows.

Copper Production. Since the opening of commercial mining, 5.5 million tons of native copper and one million tons of lower-grade copper ores have been shipped to refining plants. Through the 1800s Michigan was the nation's leading copper-producing state and reached a peak in production in 1916; however, with only two active mines still producing, Centennial north of Calumet and White Pine, the state has slipped to fifth place in copper production. Although the copper country is no longer the nation's foremost copper region, the reserves of inferred copper have been judged to be the largest in the United States. Should mining and refining methods continue to improve, the importance of Michigan copper will increase economically (fig. 4.4).

In addition to the iron and copper deposits found in the Precambrian rock, there are several other minerals with commercial potentials in the Upper Peninsula: zinc, lead, nickel, cobalt, platinum, gold, silver, and uranium. It is estimated that the Ropes Gold Mine near Ishpeming holds a million dollar potential beyond the $700,000 worth of gold it yielded between 1883 and 1897 at $28 per ounce.

LOCATION OF NATIVE COPPER DEPOSITS

96 percent of copper production

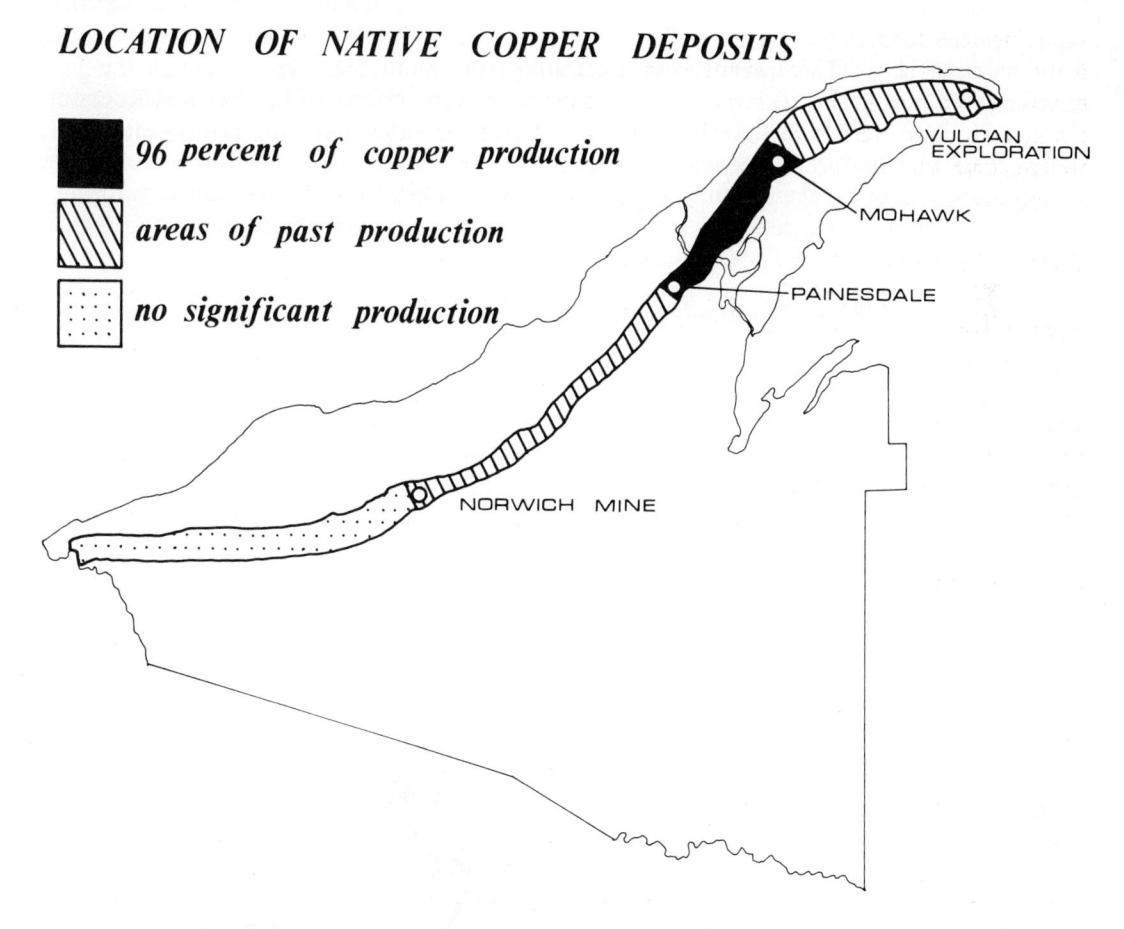

areas of past production

no significant production

Figure 4.4. Copper region of Michigan. (Map: Western Upper Peninsula Planning and Development Region.)

The Paleozoic Seas: Deposits and Contemporary Resources

During the 350 million years of the Paleozoic Era, oceans alternately expanded and withdrew which geologists have named the Seas of the Cambrian, Ordovician, Silurian, Devonian, Mississippian, and Pennsylvania periods. Each succeeding sea became smaller in area and shallower until the entire Michigan Basin was filled with sediments and the remains of teaming sea and plant life which solidified into a registry of former days. The original Cambrian Sea was 735 km (460 mi) in diameter and perhaps 5 km (3 mi) deep. In comparison, the final Pennsylvanian Sea was only 200 km (125 mi) wide and 180 meters deep. Complicating the geologic history of Michigan are the deposits of as many as fifty-five minor ebbs and flows of seas. The bedrock stratas produced by the sediments of the seas, plus the intervening periods of desert and rain forest climate, are best known for their nonmetallic minerals, fossil fuels, and water resources.

The Cambrian Sea and Pictured Rocks

The Cambrian Sea and its sedimentary bedrock covered the entire Lower Peninsula, eastern Upper Peninsula, as well as part of Wisconsin, Illinois, Indiana, and Ohio. Its northern sandy beaches formed the southern edge of Lake Superior and hardened into sandstone with a resistant outer layer. These sandstones are found from Sault Ste. Marie through the Tahquamenon Falls, and then exhibit themselves in the majestic beauty of the Pictured Rocks between Marquette and Munising. The fossil-laced Cambrian sandstones attained prominence in Indian times and have now become a famous national treasure. A further attraction of the Cambrian rock area are the streams which brilliantly tumble over an escarpment face forming picturesque waterfalls which delight tourists, local Chambers of Commerce, and earth scientists alike.

The Ordovician Sea and Relatively Soft Limestone

The Ordovician Sea existed for seventy million years. Its sediments produced a bedrock of limestone and shales which now hold some potential for oil production. These rocks appear as an arc about 24 km (15 mi) wide from Neebish Island to Big Bay De Noc. On its center axis are the towns of Newberry, McMillian, Seney, and Escanaba. Most of the ordovician limestone is relatively soft. As a result of the easy erodibility of ordovician limestone several bays indent its water-exposed edge including: Georgian Bay, North Channel, Big Bay De Noc, and Green Bay.

The Silurian Sea: Limestone, Salt, and the Great Lakes

The Silurian Sea existed for 25 million years with warm salt waters that supported coral growths. The later deposits formed on the Silurian Sea bed have also made several resource contributions to the state. In addition to its treasure of resources, the peninsular shape of Michigan may have been determined by the deposits of the Silurian Period. Among the most impressive features of the Silurian-aged rocks are the clifflike cuestas of Niagara limestone which have been exposed by the erosion of the softer Ordovician limestone. The cuesta forms the backbone of Drummond Island and appears as a band of rock 24 km (15 mi) wide across the southeastern Upper Peninsula and the Garden Peninsula. In Monroe County the limestone reappears and can be seen used in several nineteenth century homes. Fayette State Park on the Garden Peninsula preserves the structures of the iron-casting community which utilized the limestone, local hardwoods for charcoal, and iron ore from Negaunee. Active quarrying of the industrial dolomite and limestone still occurs along the southern edge of Schoolcraft and Mackinac counties.

Salt Products. The most important products from the Silurian Period are its brines and rock salt from which Michigan chemical producers have earned international fame. By locating near the edge of the former Silurian Sea where the brine and rock salt deposits are closest to the surface, Dow Chemical in Midland and several other companies in Manistee, Ludington, Mayville, Marysville, St. Louis, Wyandotte, and Muskegon have been able to minimize extraction costs. Brines are the most valuable for sodium salts such as iodine, fluorine, bromine, caustic soda, and soda ash. Natural brines have also been a commercial source of sodium chloride (table salt) since the mid-1800s. Michigan ranks first in the nation in the production of natural salines.

Michigan salts are usually mined by a solution method. In the process fresh hot water is injected into the salt horizon where the rock is dissolved into a brine and returned to the surface by another well placed about 300 meters away. The state's only underground rock salt-mining operation lies 300 meters beneath metropolitan Detroit where huge quantities of salt are annually hoisted to the surface for use in snow and ice removal. Michigan has 66 trillion tons of salt in reserves, but it ranks only fifth in rock salt production. Grand Rapids even imports salt from Louisiana for wintertime use. Since 1957 Michigan's salt beds have been considered as a possible place to store long-term radioactive wastes. The salt beds in the vicinity of Alpena and Presque Isle counties are usually advocated as the most desirable sites. One major consideration for storage of atomic wastes is their long-term relationship to the fresh water supply of the Great Lakes.

Salt Beds and the Great Lakes. The separation of the state's two major peninsulas at the Straits of Mackinac has also been attributed to the Silurian salt deposits. It is hypothesized that an underground stream formed in the salt beds between Lakes Michigan and Huron, and while carrying water between them dissolved out salt up to 100 meters thick and several meters wide. As a result, the later formed Devonian-aged limestone blocks and Pt. Aux Chenes shale became unsupported and collapsed into the void to form the initial channel. Eventually the collapsed limestone blocks were recemented by nature into a *breccia limestone* formation. On Mackinac Island and near St. Ignace, Arch Rock, Castle Rock, and several other rock stacks are from this formation. The downfolding of the limestone can be seen in rock cuts on US 2 and I-75 on the north approach to the Mackinac Bridge. Later during the Pleistocene Lake stages, the depression was widened again.

From the knowledge gained at the Straits of Mackinac and by comparing the thickness of the Silurian salt beds with the depths of the Lake Michigan-Lake Huron basins, it has been suggested that the preglacial drainage channels could have been created by the same process as that which formed the initial Straits of Mackinac. On Grosse Isle a 39 m (130 ft) deep water-filled large crater suddenly formed in 1971, presumably because of twenty years of salt removal activity 390 m (1,300 ft) below, which may illustrate a modern man-made example of the collapse process.

The Devonian Sea: Coral, Limestone, and Petroleum

The Devonian Sea deposited corals, limestone, and shales in thick layers which are found primarily at the northern tip and southern corners of the Lower Peninsula. The state stone, the fossilized coral found at Petoskey and Alpena, commonly called the "Petoskey Stone" originally was formed in a warm water coral reef near the margin of the Devonian Sea.

Devonian limestone and cement manufactured from it has become the state's most valuable nonmetallic mineral resource. Its production is valued at over 120 million dollars annually. Quarries operated solely for the manufacture of cement, both portland and masonry, are located at Alpena, Charlevoix, Petoskey, and Dundee. The world's largest limestone quarry is found at Rogers City, where the US Steel Corporation operates its calcite quarry to provide a flux for steel production. Burning lime, stone aggregate, and stone for the chemical industry is also secured from the Devonian Sea sediments.

Shales, also related to the Devonian Era, are probably most noted for construction problems which they generate as a result of gases they release when exposed to air. Especially damaging shale gases have created tunnel explosions and well blowouts such as at Port Huron and Williamsburg. Shale gas water tap fires in homes having private wells in southeastern Michigan have also periodically occurred. In contrast, the troublesome shales have been successfully used in the manufacture of cement and drain tile.

Karst Topography. A small karst or sinkhole region occurs north and west of Alpena. The pocked topography was developed by the action of atmospheric water gravitationally flowing into the limestone beds. The characteristic sinkholes and sunken lakes are observable at Lachine, Long Rapids, Fletcher Park, and at the narrow outlet channel for Long Lake. Most of the thirty prominent sinks are 15-30 m (50-100 ft) in diameter with vertical rock walls of 25-30 m (75-100 ft).

The Mississippian Sea: Sandstone and Gypsum

The Mississippian Sea came to an end when dry arid winds of a desert climate evaporated its water after it had covered only the Lower Peninsula south of Cheboygan and Alpena counties. Sandstone and gypsum have become the most used minerals of those formed during the Mississippian Period. In addition, colorful black, pastel blue, and greenish-yellow shales, limestone, salt, and alabaster were also formed. Easily mined gypsum beds appear as outcrops at Grand Rapids, National City, and Alabaster in Iosco County. These quarries yield materials for gypsum board and fertilizer. In the 1970s the state's gypsum became a five million dollar resource from a production of eight million tons of raw material. More recently an underground gypsum mine in Grand Rapids has been adapted for constant temperature storage use.

Marshall sandstone, named for a village in Calhoun County, has been extensively used for fences, stepping stones, fireplaces, plus other decorative and functional purposes. Napoleon has produced commercial sandstone since the 1830s when it challenged both Jackson and Marshall for the site of the State Prison. The city of Jackson has tapped the high quality of water found in the formation's outer margin for its metropolitan water supply system. In the more central parts of the Marshall sandstone formation, the water quality is reduced by brine contamination.

Marshall sandstone also was an important factor in determining the original location of the State Prison in 1837. At first, the legislature's prison site selection committee favored the village of Marshall because of its supply of sandstone which could be used for the prison. Nonetheless, politically active Jackson politicians argued: (1) that Jackson had a more easily quarried outcrop of sandstone, and (2) it would also save the state transportation money because Jackson was closer to the eastern part of the state, the area of the expected largest number of convicts. To clinch a favorable decision Jackson citizens also donated land with sandstone to the state. During the 1840s convicts labored to quarry and build the sandstone-walled fortress which served the state's prison needs for the following nine decades (figs. 4.5 and 4.6).

Figure 4.5. Sandstone outcrop north of original State Prison site in City of Jackson.

Figure 4.6. Sandstone wall of original State Prison in Jackson. Left portion built in 1840s, right portion of wall erected in early 1900s.

The Pennsylvanian Sea: Low-Grade Coal

The Pennsylvanian Sea was both the smallest and last of the six major seas which developed in the Michigan Basin. It occupied only the central portion of the Lower Peninsula. Near the end of the Pennsylvanian Period, a lush tropical rainforest gathered and stored the energy of the sun. Drenching rains and poor drainage created brackish swamps which accumulated organic matter and converted the vegetational material into peat. Eventually some of the organic matter was compressed by a sedimentary veneer and metamorphosed into a low-grade bituminous coal. In the Civil War years several Michigan communities developed both surface and shaft coal-mining operations including Flint, Saginaw, Jackson, Bay City, and Unionville. The peak production of coal was reached in 1907 with a yield of two million short tons. By World War I most coal-mining operations had been discontinued. During the Great Depression a minor resurgence occurred with a small amount of mining continuing until 1952. Traces of the former underground coal mine rooms can be seen above one of the century-old mines in Jackson where the rotted timber supports have let their ceilings collapse.

In comparison to other states, Michigan's coal deposits are generally of poor quality and thinly bedded; nonetheless, in 1975 due to increases in the cost of competing energy sources, the Michigan Aggregates Corporation opened a strip mine near Williamston to supply coal for an electric plant in Lansing. The state's coal reserves may be as high as 110 million tons, depending on its use, with most of the recoverable deposits in Tuscola, Bay, Saginaw, Midland, and Genesee counties.

Permian Red Bed Mystery

The Mesozoic Era in Michigan until recently had been known as the "lost interval" because no rocks of its periods (Triassic, Jurassic, and Cretaceous) had been recognized. In 1964 Dr. Aureal Cross of Michigan State University claimed, based on his palynology research, that the "red beds" of the state which up to that time had been placed in the Permain Period held fossil spores and pollen of the Mesozoic Era. His studies are not yet conclusive, but progress is being made in filling this gap in Michigan's geologic history.[2]

Fossils from the Paleozoic Seas

Fossils found in Michigan usually date from one of the six Paleozoic Era seas. The various depths, temperatures, salinity, and clarity of the water provided a diversity of niches for an abundance of ocean life. Upon dying and settling to the bottom, fossilization could begin. Undoubtedly, only a small portion of the seas' early life ever became fossils, however the fossils found today are probably representative of the most common sea life. Fossil preservation of organic life involves a chemical process whereby the original organic material is replaced by calcite or silica.

Excellent displays of Michigan's fossilized early life can be found in the museums at Michigan State University, Cranbrook Institute, University of Michigan, and Grand Rapids. In the viewing for enjoyment and collecting of fossil specimens, there is a moral obligation to take precautions to protect these unique and ancient resources of the state. Taking care to prevent damage in extraction, handling, and transportation, and identification of the exact place of col-

---

2. J. A. Dorr, Jr., D. R. Eschman, *Geology of Michigan* (Ann Arbor: University of Michigan Press, 1971), pp. 439-440.

lection of unique specimens, assists professional scientists in unraveling and understanding the mysteries of the earth. The best places to look for fossils are in areas of Paleozoic bedrock outcrops and in gravel pits which hold transported fossils. Particularly good areas for collecting fossils are Monroe, Alpena, Presque Isle, Charlevoix, Chippewa, Schoolcraft, and Delta counties. Michigan possesses a wide diversity of types of fossils which are classified as follows:

1. Fossilized plants.
2. Crinoids (pronounced "cry-noids") including starfish, sea urchins, and sand dollars.
3. Solitary corals and colony corals.
4. Cephalopods (pronounced "Sef-a-lo-pods"), creatures with tentacles about the head. The octopus and chambered nautilus are modern examples of the ancient life of Michigan.
5. Brachiopods, clams, and snails.
6. Trilobites, perhaps related to modern-day lobsters, crabs, crayfish, and scorpions.[3]

Michigan Energy Demands and Petroleum Production

Massive anticlinal domelike geologic formations have proven worldwide to be the best source of natural gas and crude oil. The concaved or synclinal Michigan Basin structure is not generally conducive to trapping natural gas and oil. Nevertheless, as a result of a few natural folds in the rock layers, some minidomes have formed and provide a minor source of petroleum. These domes usually vary in age between the Ordovician and Mississippian periods. The Devonian Period's Dundee, Monroe, and Detroit River formations have been extensively tapped and have yielded a small, but reliable supply of energy. In the final analysis, the total production from these fields is grossly insufficient to meet the constant demands of Michigan's citizens and industries.

In recent years Michigan has produced about twenty-five percent of its crude oil needs which has placed it in seventeenth place among the states. In 1973 all the state's producing fields yielded only 45,000 barrels of oil per day while the daily consumption was 165,000 barrels. In the case of natural gas, the import need situation is even greater. In 1973, forty-four billion cubic feet of Michigan natural gas were marketed while the state used one trillion cubic feet. To overcome the state's natural gas shortage, pipelines from Texas, Kansas, and Canada have been installed. To meet peak demands in the winter season, natural gas is pumped into the former Austin Gas Field geologic formation in Mecosta County, and temporarily held underground until redistribution. In spite of shortages in meeting daily demands, Michigan's bedrock still holds a huge quantity of petroleum. Based on yields per cubic mile of sedimentary rock, the oil reserves under the peninsulas are estimated to be 1.25 billion barrels. Additional unestimated potentials are undoubtedly held under the waters of the Great Lakes.

Historical Summary of Michigan Oil and Gas Production

Michigan's first oil well is claimed to have been drilled near Port Huron in 1886 in the Dundee formation at a depth of 173 m (575 ft). Later wells developed in the Port Huron Field continued to produce up to the post-World War I era. The state's first natural gas field was

---

3. Robert W. Kelly, *Guide to Michigan Fossils,* Geological Survey Pamphlet 3 (1962), pp. 1-16.

established in St. Clair County by the Diamond Crystal Salt Company in connection with a salt well in 1927 and continued to produce for six more years. One of the state's more prominent producing oil-gas fields is the *Albion-Scipio trend* opened in 1957 when the Houseknecht well was drilled in Scipio Township, Hillsdale County. Since then one-third of Michigan's crude oil, one-quarter of the state's natural gases, and over half of the liquid petroleum gas (LPG) has come from that field making it historically the greatest oil-producing region of the state.

Using knowledge gained from drilling brine wells, geologists and speculators in 1925-1926 opened the *Saginaw Oil and Gas Field* by tapping structural closures in the Berea sandstones at 540 m (1800 ft). The producing life of this field was shortened due to its location within the city limits of Saginaw where close spaced urban-lot drilling occurred. Additionally, the crude oil yield was reduced because natural gas was released as waste preventing the gas from expanding below ground to complement the recovery of the oil.[4]

In 1927 the *Muskegon Field* was discovered and attracted the attention of major oil companies and wildcatters. During the following decade oil and gas fields were tapped between Muskegon and Saginaw counties with the Mt. Pleasant or *Central Michigan Field* emerging as the state's major field after 1928.

Since the early days of petroleum operations, it is estimated that 30,000 test wells have been drilled in Michigan. From the wells drilled, oil has been found in fifty-six of the sixty-eight counties of the Lower Peninsula, but none in the Upper Peninsula. Wildcat drilling still takes place in Michigan, but the cost of an unproductive dry hole can reach between $65,000 to over $100,000. Thus, today's costs of drilling generally dictate the use of seismographic computer interpretation of the subsurface strata.

In the early 1970s Midland, Osceola, and Isabella counties became the leading crude oil producing counties while St. Clair, Clare, and Montcalm counties led in natural gas production. The deposits of the Niagara reef reservoirs have gained much attention and hold potential for future development. Otsego, Kalkaska, Grand Traverse, Manistee, and Mason counties are included in the northern area of petroleum development with Kalkaska being the center of activities. Additional drilling operations in the area north of Interstate-94 (I-94) and south of Charlotte, and in the vicinity of Mason have been established by Mobil Oil, Michigan Gas Utilities, Michigan Consolidated, and Peninsular Oil and Gas.

Crude oil is refined at Detroit, Trenton, Flat Rock, Bay City, Alma, and West Branch. The largest refinery is the Marathon Oil Company plant in Melvindale which has a storage capacity of 448 million liters (118 million gal) of refined petroleum and 2,394,000 liters (630,000 gal) of LPG. Some of the state's crude oil is also piped to and refined in Toledo.

Oil and Gas Drilling on State Land. Public Act 61 of 1939 and its amendment in 1973 gives the DNR supervision over the drilling operations at all the state's oil and gas well sites. The amount of gas taken from a well, however, is regulated by the Public Service Commission. The DNR also controls the leasing of state land for petroleum operations. In major gas field development areas, one or two wells are established per square mile. On the other hand, oil fields may have as many as one well for each three hectares (8 ac).

The Pigeon River Country State Forest has provided a model of conflict between those desiring to maintain the only significantly large wilderness tract in the Lower Peninsula and those who desire to utilize the leases granted by the DNR in the late 1960s for drilling and oil

---

4. Bert Hudgins, *Michigan: Geographic Backgrounds in the Development of the Commonwealth* (Ann Arbor: Edwards Brothers, 1961), p. 54.

production operations. The Pigeon River State Forest is a 37,800 ha (94,500 ac) area in Otsego, Cheboygan, and Montmorency counties. Its terrain and wildlife are varied and exist in almost pristine splendor. The forest sits atop a large petroleum reserve. Three-fourths of it was leased in 1968 for oil drilling. As a result of later citizen interest, the granting of the leases was emotionally and academically questioned in the mid-1970s. In situations of conflict such as in the Pigeon River Country, no perfect answer can be satisfactory to all, only a solution which appears to be less damaging, less objectionable, and philosophically more fair than others. In the case of the oil beneath Pigeon River State Forest, the following choices emerged:

1. Ban all drilling in response to citizen concern.
2. Allow drilling freely in the leased area as a legal right.
3. Ban drilling but extend leases until a greater need arises.
4. Drill only in the southern third of the forest where most of the potential oil exists and is most accessible to drillers.[5]

Undoubtedly as the demand for energy continues, the citizens, regulatory agencies of government, and commercial interests will come under increasing pressure to seek decisions which will weigh the impact of resource development in comparison to the damage to the natural environment. While Michigan has a potential to expand its energy production from natural sources, it must be concluded that traditional energy resources are very limited in the long run. As long as the people of the state can produce goods and services which will pay for imported fuels, the economic health of the state can be maintained. However, even with import supplies from domestic and foreign sources, the state's citizens will have to continue to face critical energy supply decisions. In Michigan's future, its landscape will undoubtedly be dotted with devices using complementary sources of power, such as wind, solar, hydroelectric, pump storage, and atomic generation of electricity, whose initial imprints can already be seen.

Earthquakes in Michigan

Earthquake activity in Michigan was most common thousands of years ago when folding and faulting occurred in the bedrocks of the Precambrian and Paleozoic eras. In the present-day the Michigan Basin structure is not noted for earthquakes because it is a great distance from any of the active edges of the several *Tectonic Plates* which have spawned devastating tremors in the twentieth century. Nevertheless, earthquakes still occasionally occur in the state causing minor damage, and a considerable number of calls to police, newspaper offices, librarians, and university geologists.

On February 2, 1976, an earthquake registering 3.25 on the Richter Scale affected ten southern Wayne County communities between Trenton and Rockwood. A quarter century earlier in August of 1947, a slightly stronger shock occurred in the Branch County area whose effects stretched from Detroit to Chicago and included the felling of some chimneys.

What future impact the removal of groundwater and petroleum will have on the state's bedrock is not known. Parallels with localized occurrences in Western states may be assumed. U.S. Geological Survey research has discovered significant evidence of earth surface sinking in both Texas and California. It is expected that problems of sinking will multiply with larger withdrawals of subsurface liquid and gas resources.

5. *Grand Rapids Press,* May 12, 1976, p. 14 A.

> *"The mill cannot grind with water that's past."*
> W. Brewster

Chapter Five

The Glacial Lakes and Ice Sculptured Land

The purpose of this chapter is to describe Michigan's geomorphic and hydrologic features, including the creation of its ice age landforms, Great Lakes, inland lakes, rivers, and waterfalls. Further, the present-day economic uses of the resources formed during the Pleistocene are identified. The more recent land-use management problems associated with these physical geographic features are also discussed including the Natural Rivers Act and the Shoreline Erosion Protection and Management Act.

Sun, wind, and pelting rains beat down on the land and watery depression of ancient Michigan for 220 million years following the era of the Paleozoic Seas. These weathering forces sculptured Michigan into three highland areas which formed in the western Upper Peninsula, the northern, and southern parts of the Lower Peninsula. The modern-day Great Lakes areas are, it is believed by geomorphologists, valleys of the ancient North American continent's preglacial river system. In the years following the Paleozoic, plants and roving animals established themselves, multiplied and contributed to the diversity of the state's ancient biomass. Suddenly, for reasons still debated, a huge ice sheet 1.6-3.2 km (1-2 mi) thick skidded southward from Hudson Bay and buried the northern part of the continent under ice to the margins of the Ohio and Missouri rivers and east to Long Island. At the same time the ocean levels were lowered about 100 meters as their waters were converted to ice that also covered parts of Eurasia and South America. Four times during the million or more years of the Cenozoic Era, Pleistocene Age, glaciers advanced over Michigan leaving distinctive deposits identified by state names: Nebraskan, Kansan, Illinoian, and the most recent Wisconsin.

Evidence for Glaciation

In the mid-nineteenth century, years after the early pioneers had sent their first letters back East to relatives describing Michigan's hilly interior dotted with thousands of lakes and poorly drained plains, Louis Agassiz's explanations of glaciers as the primary shaping force of the land surface became accepted. Previously it was thought that just a great flood had washed the rubble of mixed clay, sand, and gravel southward and icebergs had drifted and rafted the large boulders which dot fields in an erratic pattern. The general term for the soil which covers the bedrock is *drift* derived from the early theory of deposition, but more recently referred to as *till*. As the history of the ice age is unraveled, geomorphologists have been able to identify patterns and shapes which other people view as just another hill or lake. Benefiting the early interpretations of Michigan's landforms was the nearly complete stripping of the original forest which opened to the eye the naked vistas of these landforms. Thus, when Leverett and Taylor made their classic studies they had an advantage which contemporary students do not enjoy.[1] To advance the understanding of landforms today, satellite photography and computer mapping is used which reduces field observations in many instances.

Even with the later land-healing growth of forests, evidence of glaciation is abundant and can be seen by both the casual and keen observers. While working and traveling throughout Michigan, several landscape features can be identified which provide conclusive arguments for the occurrence of an ice age followed by channelized torrents of flooding. Several categories of evidence observed include:

1. Rock minerals such as copper carried great distances from their bedrock source.
2. Soils unrelated to their underlying bedrock.
3. River valleys much wider than the present-day rivers even in their greatest flood stage.
4. Grooved, scratched, striated, and highly polished rock surfaces in a constant direction and above river channels.
5. Hills containing a random mix of clay, sand, gravel, and boulders without characteristics of water layered deposition.
6. Unique shapes of hillocks such as drumlins, eskers, kames, kettles, and beach ridges (figs. 5.1 and 5.2).

The Wisconsin Ice Lobes

Ten thousand years ago, but only yesterday in geologic time, the last stage of the Wisconsin glacier melted away from the shores of Lake Superior after blanketing Michigan for several millenniums. The melting waters from its continual retreat and the land rebounding after the crushing pressure, however, significantly affected the levels of the Great Lakes until about two thousand years ago. Prior to its retreat, the Wisconsin ice sheet advanced across Michigan with an uneven front consisting of three or four principal lobes; the *Erie Lobe* entered from the east while the *Saginaw-Huron* and *Michigan Lobes* followed the preglacial drainage channels and entered from the northeast and north respectively. As the lobes pushed forward by pressures of accumulated snow and ice, they slid, skidded, ground and mixed soil with rock fragments, and also carved the exposed bedrock in their paths with their transported load of debris.

Moraines and Till Plains

The rock and soil debris was dumped by the ice lobes when the glacier stopped movement as a result of reduced pressure on the front edge and melting due to exposure to warmer

---

1. F. Leverett and F. B. Taylor, *Pleistocene of Indiana and Michigan and the History of the Great Lakes,* United States Geological Survey Monograph 53 (1915), p. 529.

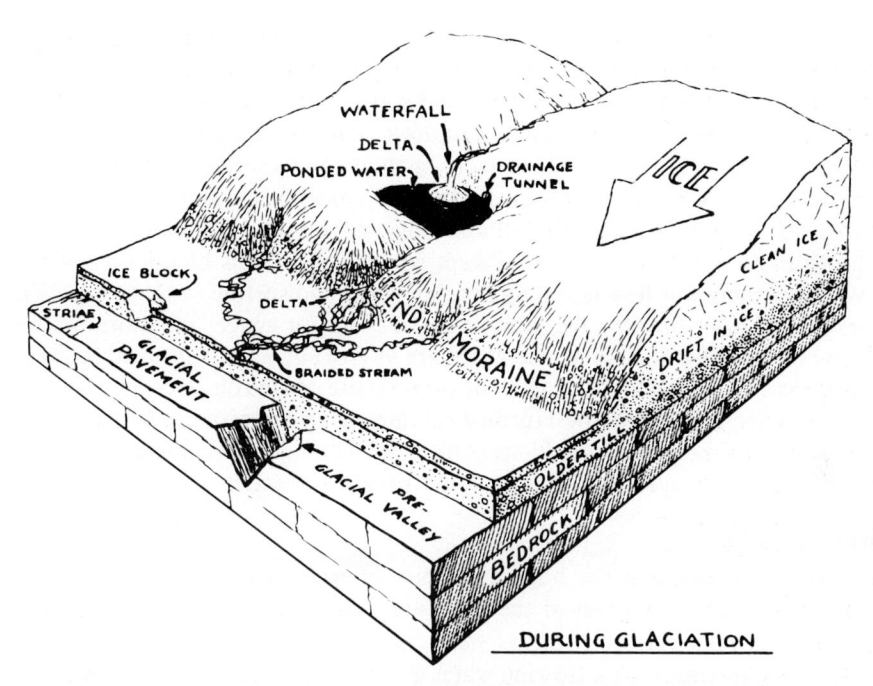

Figure 5.1. Glacial landforms developed during glaciation. (Drawing: J.M. Campbell in, *The Glacial Lakes around Michigan*, Geological Survey.)

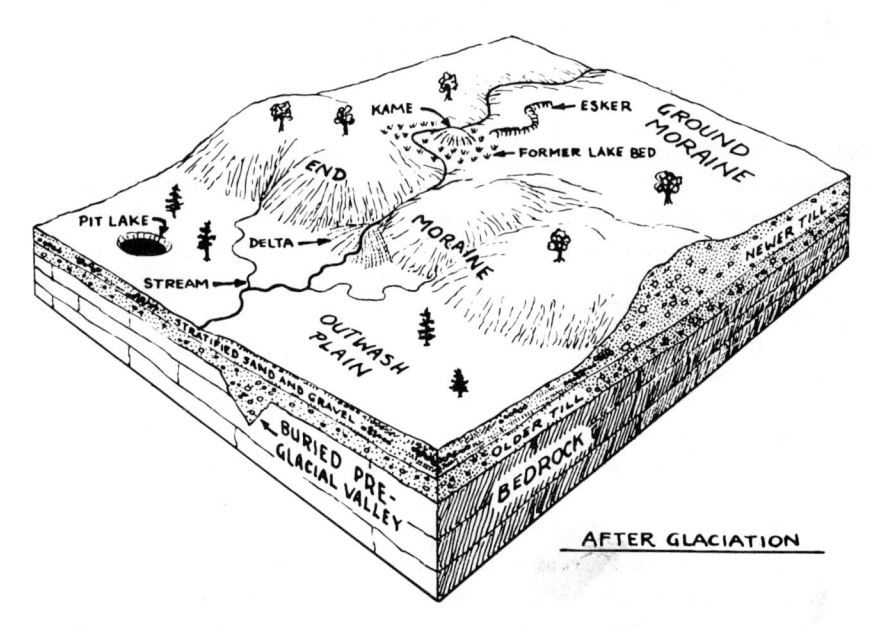

Figure 5.2. Typical post-glacial landforms. (Drawing: J.M. Campbell in, *The Glacial Lakes around Michigan*, Geological Survey.)

weather. *Hilly end moraines* were formed in a stationary situation when the ice front was replenished at nearly the same rate as it melted. Under such conditions the jumble of sand, gravel, and boulders was piled in a hummocky belt along the lobe face for hundreds of kilometers. The Port Huron, Kalamazoo, Charlotte, and West Branch Moraines are examples of this feature. Gently rolling *ground moraines* or *till plains* were created when the ice stagnated and its large surface area evaporated rapidly and somewhat evenly, dropping its load of sediments (fig. 5.3). In later years the till plains usually became cultivated farmland while the steeper sloped moraines were pastured or kept wooded. The soils of the till plains tend to be more clayey since there was less action by running water and sorting of materials. Where two or more lobes melted after pushing together and jockeying for space, the moraines were shaped into a variety of picturesque hills whose vistas are in great demand for housing sites. Although less dramatic than most interlobate areas, the original site of Detroit selected by Cadillac was on the relatively higher ground of the Huron-Erie interlobate moraine. The Irish Hills is an interlobate recreation area, as are the ski areas developed along the Michigan-Saginaw Lobe contact line in Wexford, Missaukee, Kalkaska, and Crawford counties.

Meltwater Features

It is difficult to envision the huge quantities of water which once flowed from the ice sheets; however, the carving forces of the meltwater can be frequently observed when traveling on the state's highways. *Outwash plains* were created when the glaciers melted rapidly providing a broad expanse of swiftly flowing water away from the ice front. In the rushing flow of water, sediments would be segregated with the heavier rocks dropped first while gravel and sands were sorted and spread out, further leveling the till plains. In north central Michigan, US-10, US-131, and M-37 follow beautiful outwash plains in the vicinity of Evart, Reed City, Big Rapids, and Bitley. Many outwash plains have been opened for sand and gravel mining especially in the Commerce, Drayton Plains, and Oxford area of Oakland County. Narrow, fast-flowing glacial rivers hemmed in by steep sloped moraines created boulder-lined *valley trains*. These trains of larger gravels, cobbles, and boulders when located have provided an excellent source of heavy base material for construction projects. Examples of valley trains are found just south of Northville and two miles northeast of Bloomfield Hills. *Kettles, kettle lakes,* and *pitted outwash plains* can be identified by their uniformly round or pit shapes. These "pot holes" were probably formed in till and outwash plains when blocks of ice broke away from the ice face, then rock debris buried or surrounded them. Later when they melted, water-filled lakes or pits remained. Frain Lake north of Ypsilanti on M-14 is a metropolitan area example of a kettle lake.

Kames, Eskers, and Drumlins. Kames, eskers, and drumlins are hills with smooth-sided profiles which formed in direct contact with the ice. When the lobes stagnated, small rivers would flow on top and in cracks of the ice sheets washing out debris from the glacier and layering it in the channels. *Eskers* or "hog backs" as pioneers named them, were formed as the ice evaporated. The rubble in the meltwater river bottom would be laid down on the new till plain creating a hump above the plain. Between Howell and Olivet, and Jackson and Lansing, numerous eskers can be identified and seen from I-96 and old US-16. These former ice-channeled river bottoms vary in length from a few meters to the Mason Esker whose profitable gravels, scenic parks and homesite vistas can be traced for nearly 50 km (30 mi). *Kames* have a

MICHIGAN'S LAND TYPES
Department of Conservation

Swamps

Moraines

Outwash plains

Till plains

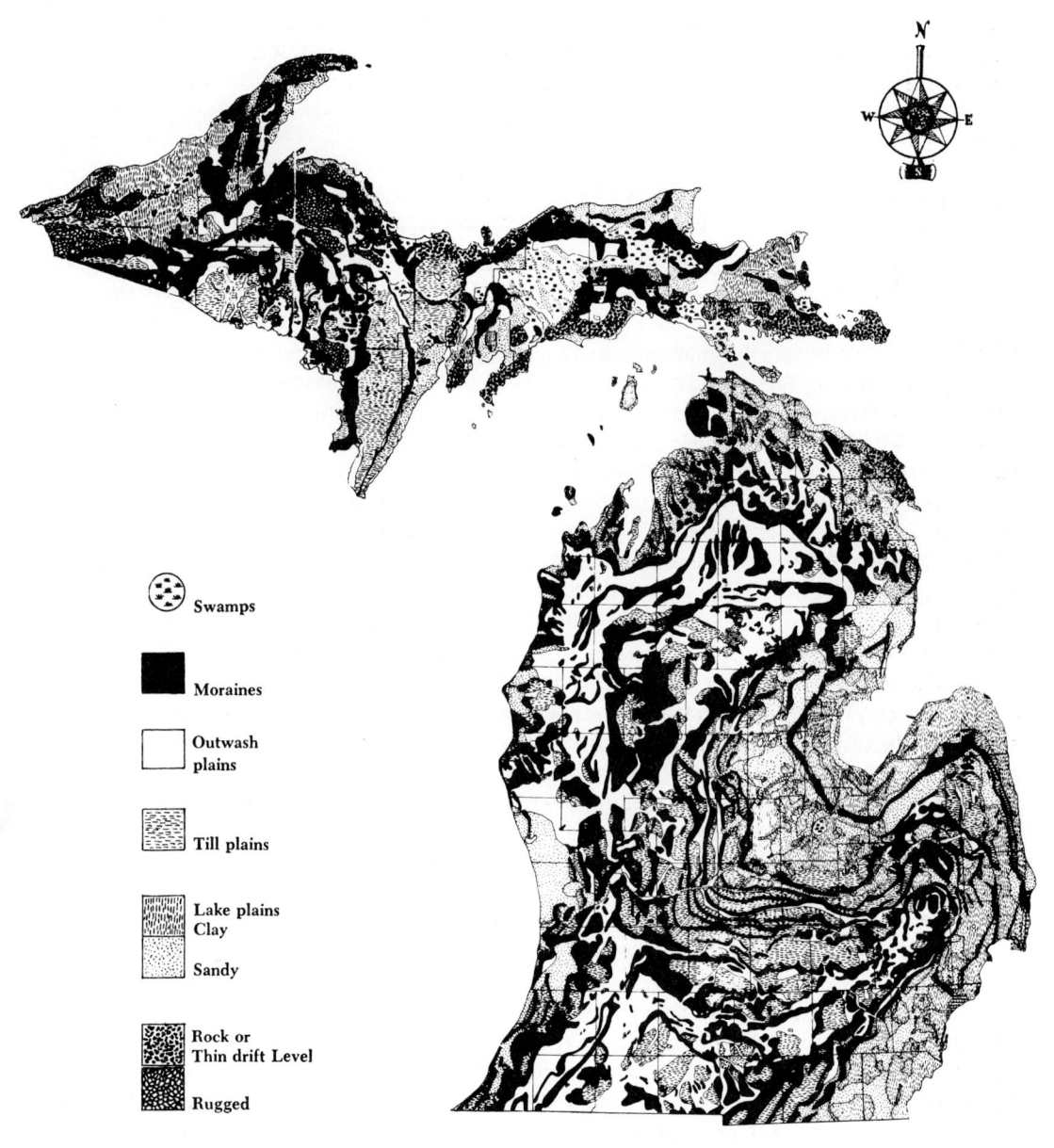

Lake plains Clay

Sandy

Rock or Thin drift Level

Rugged

Figure 5.3. Land types of Michigan. (Map: Michigan Department of Natural Resources.)

conical hill shape which formed as the ice-channeled rivers flowed over the ice face at an indentation point or into a crevice where the till could be confined while being piled up. Several kames appear in the vicinity of Boyne Falls, Boyne City, Barker Creek, and Rapid City. *Drumlins* were formed under the ice sheets and appear today as fields of inverted spoon-shaped low hills on the axis of the glaciers' retreat. Many drumlins may be 2,000 meters long and 400 meters wide at their face, then narrowing to a pointed tail. Scenic fields of these rounded hillocks can be seen north of Suttons Bay in Leelanau County and along Lake Michigan in Antrim and Charlevoix counties. A field of drumlins of lower relief is identifiable along US-2 between Kinross and Sault Ste. Marie.

The Economic Value of the Pleistocene Sands and Gravels

Separate from the aesthetic and recreational benefits of the glacial landforms, their deposits of sand and gravel have been developed into a valuable part of the state's economy. Although the gravel excavators have not stimulated romantic imaginations in comparison to copper and gold miners, the mundane daily contributions to the state by these mining operations is considerable. The sand and gravel industry, primarily organized since 1900, now ranks second in the nation with an annual production of sixty million short tons valued at $7 million. Compared with Michigan's other nonmetallic minerals, only cement returns a higher income. Most of the state's 250 sand and gravel excavation operations are confined to outwash plains, eskers, and kames with gravel material being at least 25 percent of the material. Deposits with chert and ironstone which cause pitting in concrete are generally avoided. Sand and gravel pits are generally located near expanding urban areas, highway, bridge, dam, and other large construction projects due to their low unit values.

Clay, Peat, and Marl

Clay materials deposited by the glaciers support twenty manufacturing operations including pottery, brick, tile, and light-weight aggregate. Michigan ranks first in the nation in the annual production of peat with a yield of 20,000 tons. Michigan peat, generally not satisfactory as a fuel, developed under natural conditions from decaying vegetation. Michigan's reserves of peat are estimated at one billion dry tons with 80 percent located in the Upper Peninsula. Postglacial marl deposits, as well as peat are used almost exclusively as soil conditioners.

The necessity to rent open the earth to seize the postglacial mineral resources has earned gravel pits a dangerous reputation. As citizens and their governments act to protect people and the land from the dangers of excavations and abandoned pits, operators in the excavation industry are finding it more difficult to open new sites. Given the low unit value of peat, clay, sand, and gravel, and the market site economic necessity of operation, changes in the industry's management will undoubtedly emerge in the foreseeable future. Local planning and zoning boards meeting with excavation operators to solve the basic conflicts may have to negotiate a higher standard of land reconditioning and safer operating standards in proximity to dense population centers. Without such accommodations, the production and transportation costs from low density areas will have serious construction cost implications for the state.

The Water Wonderland of Michigan

The melting torrents of water which surged from the glaciers' fronts did more than initially shape the land. Their water, now sustained by spring rains and winter snow, turned Michigan into a proudly proclaimed "water wonderland." The original icy meltwater provided moisture which helped to give birth to the protecting forests that would soon surround the thousands of sparkling inland lakes whose reflections in a twilight sun rekindle the spirits of their observers.

The Inland Lakes

Michigan's over 11,000 inland lakes which filled depressions as the glaciers retreated have provided the state with an incalculable resource for homes and recreational area. These lakes. though, are subject to natural eutrophication, a process which filled the former glacial lakes in the adjoining states to the south. In the process, the shallower inland lakes, warmed by the sun, produce abundant aquatic plant life around their edges. When the water plants die, they accumulate on the bottom. As the lake edges fill, nonaquatic plants inch forward and take root in the spongy organic matter. Then concentric rings of plant life and soil slowly fill a lake depression until a wooded area is established. Today, artificial impoundments behind dams frequently show evidence of eutrophication. The common practice of cutting water weeds and letting them drop to the bottom rather than removing them, tends to speed the water-to-land succession process. The drainage of septic wastes and lawn fertilizers into small lakes also provides additional nutrients on which water plants can survive, thus accelerating the process of organic filling. Perhaps the harvesting of aquatic plants and utilizing them as soil conditioners is the solution for slowing natural eutrophication and enhancing water contact sports. At the same time, those involved in water management also have to take into consideration the needs of fish in relation to aquatic plants. The Pinckney State Recreation Area has many lakes which exhibit the lake-land filling process, while lake levels in the Haymarsh State Game Area in Mecosta County are controlled for aquatic plant life used by ducks.

Many of the state's former small and shallow ponds and lakes have already been filled with rotting organic matter and covered with vegetation. Some of these depressions provide valuable soils for muck land truck farming of vegetables such as celery, onions, potatoes, and sod farm operation, as well as peat mining. In bogs of muck and peat, remains of ice-aged mammoths, mastodons, musk ox, caribou, and other extinct animals which once lived in the state are sometimes found. Frequently bog lands have been drained to secure additional farmland ignoring the fact that bogs play an important role in maintaining the water table which helps to increase the productivity of surrounding uplands. On the other hand, the untiring efforts of farmers and engineers in tiling and draining fields have led to not only a bounty of food, but also to the reversal of the bleak prophecy held for Michigan in the 1815 "Tiffin Report:"

> . . . Taking the country altogether, so far as has been explored, and all appearances, together with the information received concerning the balance is as bad, there could not be more than one acre out of a hundred if there would be one of a thousand, that would in any case admit to cultivation.[2]

---

2. United States, *American State Papers, Public Lands,* III, pp. 164-65.

In spite of historic advantages of draining Michigan's lowlands, how much drainage, where and when and under what conditions, are questions which are becoming increasingly important as the state's population continues to multiply without increases in water frontage except through dredging and filling activities (fig. 5.4).

Inland Lakes by the Thousands. Michigan's license plates proclaim it to be "The Great Lake State." *Lake* rather than *lakes* is used to imply that Michigan is not only bound by four of the Great Lakes, but also holds a great treasure of inland lakes. Seven Michigan counties possess more than 300 lakes: Marquette, 835; Luce, 571; Gogebic, 488; Oakland, 447; Schoolcraft, 340; and Barry, 327 (table 5.1). In contrast, four counties are without recognized lakes (Gratiot, Macomb, Sanilac, and Shiawassee), each of which is on the margin of former large glacial lakes whose sediments and water obliterated depressions. Houghton Lake is the state's largest lake covering 80 sq km (30.8 sq mi). Gogebic Lake south of the Keweenaw Fault is the Upper Peninsula's largest lake, covering 52 sq km (20 sq mi) and ranks sixth in the state. Other counties with large areas of water surface include Cheboygan, 18,688 ha (46,720 ac); Chippewa, 18,176 ha (45,440 ac); and Mackinac, 17,152 ha (42,880 ac). The challenge facing civil authorities in regards to lake management today is how to best provide public services to both surrounding land owners and public user demand. Further conflicts exist between those with summertime interests in public access, fishing, motor boating, water skiing, and swimming. The wintertime operations of snowmobiles and ice boats, as well as timely ice shanty removal are also increasing problems having to be faced.

TABLE 5.1
Major Inland Lakes of Michigan

Rank	Name	Area Sq Km	Area Sq Mi	County
1.	Houghton	80.0	30.8	Roscommon
2.	Torch	74.1	28.5	Antrim
3.	Burt	72.3	27.8	Cheboygan
4.	Charlevoix	69.4	26.7	Charlevoix
5.	Mullet	64.7	24.9	Cheboygan
6.	Gogebic	52.0	20.0	Gogetic-Ontonagon
7.	Portage	46.8	18.0	Houghton
8.	Crystal	41.6	16.0	Benzie
9.	Manistique	41.1	15.8	Mackinac-Luce
10.	Black	40.1	15.7	Cheboygan-Presque Isle
11.	Higgins	40.0	15.5	Roscommon
12.	Hubbard	35.1	13.5	Alcona

SOURCE: Hudgins, *Michigan*, p. 29.

The Problem of Duplication in Lake Names. The duplication of common lake names in close proximity to each other, i.e., Long, Little, Big, Round, Bass, Mud, Crooked, Silver, and Pickerel, has frequently confused fishermen and those doing historical research. More tragic, however, has been the delays in rendering public services to lake residents and users such as fire, medical assistance, mail delivery, and law enforcement. As a result, for several years the

Figure 5.4. Canadian Lakes, Morton Township (T14N-R8W), Mecosta County, is a group of lakes which have been regenerated by the removal of organic material. (Photo: ASCS, U.S. Department of Agriculture, 1972.)

Geographic Names Unit of the DNR has acted as a clearing house for information, procedures on selecting and revising place names, plus processing name changes through the U.S. Board of Geographic Names.

Historic Uses of Inland Lakes

During the nineteenth century, the inland lakes provided the loggers with floating collection points for timber as it was removed from surrounding forests. On some large lakes, huge rafts of logs ready to be cut into lumber would be sent to lumber mills established at a strategic point such as Otsego Lake Village at the south end of Otsego Lake. Other times, logs were boomed through lake outlets to mills further downstream. The early cottage era recreationalist found the lakes not only pleasant places to swim and fish, but also a pure source of drinking water and ice. Throughout the years of use, inland lakes have probably provided recreation for more people and yielded more fish on a per acre basis than the Great Lakes. In recent years the inland lakes have been overshadowed in the news media by the successful introduction of salmon into the Great Lakes. Yet, the inland lakes still hold outstanding potentials for increased yields of warm water fish for food, as well as sport fishing.

Rivers in Michigan

It is difficult to overstate the important role that the 58,160 km (36,350 mi) of classified rivers has played in the history and present-day economy of the state. In the DNR Inventory of Michigan Waterways, 120 rivers are identified as major waterways. However, none are judged to be a principal river of the United States because of their shortness and small volume of water discharged as a result of the peninsular shape of the state. The major rivers, as well as the numerous smaller ones, have served the needs of Michigan residents in countless ways. Rivers and streams were significant in: determining town, mill, and hydroelectric power sites; providing water for drinking, irrigation, sewage treatment, and transportation. Rubbled river bottoms have provided spawning beds for fish and habitats for other aquatic life necessary for their survival.

Frequently in a modern urbanized society, people fail to interact daily with the flowing streams of their community, especially those that may have been channeled with concrete banks and lined with buildings, or put underground by hundreds of meters of sewer conduits. Yet, the influence of rivers on the daily lives of citizens has undoubtedly increased in importance as population and technology have grown. While a skyscraper water tower may proclaim an engineering achievement of a proud community, what needs to be appreciated is that the lifegiving waters which it holds still come from an out-of-sight pipe in a flowing river or well whose purity must continually be protected. Sensitive naturalists of many backgrounds have become weary and disquieted due to the ceaseless disruption of protective vegetation along river banks, erosion, and tons of silts which fill fishing holes and clog hydroelectric power impoundments. Further questions requiring contemporary social, political, and technological answers are how to constructively mesh private rights and public responsibility along waterways and how to resolve or reduce the conflicts between fishermen, canoeists, and water frontage owners.

River and Watershed Characteristics. The melted waters which were released by the glaciers immediately began their battle with the land to reach the ocean. The early skirmishes of this classic fight of nature are etched into Michigan with evidence of abandoned river channels, giant step-sided valleys whose contemporary streams are minute in comparison to former torrents which once flowed, "check-shaped" river courses which indicate reversals in direction of the flow of water such as the St. Joseph River and Pine River of Gratiot County. The rivers which flow through the gently rolling southern Michigan agricultural till plains and flat *lacustrine plains* of the former glacial lake bottoms contrast dramatically with the thunderous, splashing, waterfall-dotted rocky rivers of the Upper Peninsula. Also in contrast are the northern Lower Peninsula rivers that flow under shady forests and over sandy cobblestone-littered bottoms.

Waterfalls. All of Michigan's larger waterfalls, and most of its smaller ones, totaling about 150, are found in picturesque settings in the Upper Peninsula. Over 100,000 visitors annually are attracted to the Upper Tahquamenon Falls which cascade over a 14 m (48 ft) sandstone ledge. The Black River in Gogebic County has eleven falls and many stretches of wild turbulent rapids. Other important waterfalls include Miners, Bond, Agate, Munising, and Laughing Whitfish. The St. Mary's Falls at Sault Ste. Marie which dropped more than 6.3 m (20 ft) was eliminated when the Soo Locks were constructed to connect shipping between Lake Superior and Lake Huron. Most of the Upper Peninsula waterfalls were created when the river channels cut down to the more resistant hardened layer of Cambrian sandstone.

The dominant waterfall area of the Lower Peninsula is found in Presque Isle County with the Ocqueoc Falls and Rainy River Falls which descend a Devonian-aged rock ledge. The rivers of southern Michigan generally lack natural waterfalls, however, some have spillways of dams, as well as aesthetic beauty with patches of rapids and riffles, and stretches of scenic countryside.

Michigan's Major Watersheds. The areas of Michigan watersheds vary with the disordered and blocked drainage patterns created by the glacial moraines (fig. 5.5). Many watersheds, especially in the Upper Peninsula, have narrow truncated basins with few tributaries. Other watersheds such as the Saginaw, Grand, Muskegon, Menominee, Kalamazoo, and St. Joseph drain more than 5,200 sq km (2,000 sq mi) and reach more than half way across the state. The state's longest river, the Grand River whose headwaters form in Jackson County, flows 360 km (225 mi) before it reaches its mouth at Grand Haven. The Saginaw Basin with its fan of tributaries reaching in all directions drains nearly 15,600 sq km (6,000 sq mi). Except for a small area in the vicinity of Lac Vieux Desert drained by the Wisconsin River into the Mississippi River system, Michigan's watersheds are connected by the Great Lakes and Niagara Falls to the St. Lawrence River.

Most of Michigan's rivers are what physiographers refer to as *extended rivers*. The characteristic mouth of extended rivers developed as the levels of the Great Lakes lowered causing the streams to lengthen their channels to reach the lakes. Another characteristic of western Michigan rivers' mouth areas is the action of the sanddunes which tends to block the river openings to Lake Michigan. Thus, most of these rivers empty first into small natural impoundments before flowing into the Great Lakes. Muskegon, White, Pentwater, Hamlin, and Manistee are examples of these natural reservoirs along the Lake Michigan shore.

Large upstream shipping activity on Michigan rivers is limited because of the shallow depth of rivers and the competitive advantages of protected shoreline harbors. There are, nevertheless, two notable exceptions to the general pattern of river use: (1) the St. Mary's, whose locks have helped to make it one of the world's busiest waterways for bulk movement of iron and wheat, and (2) the Saginaw River, which carries large vessels inland to serve the heavy industrial complex in the vicinity of Saginaw.

Figure 5.5. River pattern in Michigan. (Map: Michigan Department of Natural Resources.)

Twentieth Century Dams. The practice of building dams for water power was introduced extensively by the founders of the pioneer villages. Later, generally after the large scale timber harvest was completed, high earthen and reinforced concrete dams to produce hydroelectric power became a common sight along the state's rivers. As a legacy of the dam building era, over 220 dams exist on Michigan water courses. Many of these dams, due to the silting of their impoundments and maintenance costs, as well as obsolete equipment and operations, in less than a century have become unsightly abandoned relics. On the other hand, well-designed and maintained dams can provide many advantages for flood control, scenic views, recreation, plus locally produced electric energy. Perhaps, as energy costs become more critical economically, a few well-selected river sites will again witness a resurgence in the development of community or privately operated small hydroelectric plants whose potentially usable energy is renewed with each rainfall and melt of snow in its watershed. In meeting the needs for both a dam and spawning salmon, the city of Grand Rapids became a pacesetting urban community by constructing a successful and attractive fish ladder which combined the efforts of biologists, artists, and government administrators, with a blending of community pride and support (fig. 5.6).

Figure 5.6. The Grand Rapids fish ladder is an artistic and functional solution to the problem of a dam blocking the upstream movement of fish. (Photo: *The Grand Rapids Press,* June 1975.)

The Natural Rivers Act

By the 1960s the accumulations of research data quietly and patiently recorded by scholars concerning the rapidly changing condition of Michigan's rivers became recognized as significant when nationally distributed paperback books and the mass media rejuvenated the aging turn-of-the-century and Depression era conservation movements by popularizing a "new" ecology-environmental movement. Aroused by the knowledge of a deteriorating environment, not only nationally, but also in Michigan, citizens supported legislators in the passage of several new acts to protect and improve the public management of the state resources.

In 1970, Public Act 231—*The Natural Rivers Act* inaugurated the legal authority to establish a system of designated natural rivers meeting certain criteria and to protect the natural quality of these rivers from unwise use and development. Initially the DNR field personnel, local groups, and private organizations recommended thirty of Michigan's rivers for further study and possible designation as a "natural river." Additional streams may be recommended at any time by community action. The Natural Rivers Program has within it three categories of possible designation. These may be for the entire length of a river or for a portion of it which generally is at least a 16 km (10 mi) segment. The designations for natural rivers are:

1. *Wilderness River,* a river in an extensive wilderness or primitive setting, with qualities associated with undeveloped settings.
2. *Wild Scenic River,* a river with wild or forested borders or backlands, in close proximity to man-made development.
3. *Country Scenic River,* a river generally in an agricultural setting with narrow bands of woods or pastoral borders, often with farms and other developments viewable from the river.

Under the Natural Rivers Act, local zoning is encouraged for carrying out the proposals in a river management plan developed by a local planning body with active citizen participation and assistance from the DNR. Property along a designated segment of a natural river, if private, remains private property and any use of it *must* have the owner's permission. Under the act, provisions for setback of structures and maintenance of natural vegetation strips are included, however, persons with vested rights cannot be prohibited from making reasonable use of their private property or be required to relocate existing houses.

The Formation of the Great Lakes

The birth of the Great Lakes is recorded on the land in a series of beach ridges, shoreline cliffs, lakeside terraces, former lake bottom plains, and abandoned river deltas. These former lake edge features are not only useful to the earth scientists in studying the aging process of the lakes, but they also hold many of the sites which archaeologists and anthropologists use to unravel the mysteries of the first Indian settlers in the state. A description of the evolution of the Great Lakes begins with the drainage and ponding of the glacial meltwaters in preglacial river channels between the ice front and the moraines which constricted their outlet to the Mississippi River. Only a summary of the basic ice stages can be presented in a short geography of Michigan. However, outstanding detailed accounts can be found in Hough's 1958 *Geology of the Great Lakes* and in Leverett and Taylor's 1915 *Pleistocene of Indiana and Michigan and the History of the Great Lakes*. In the summary which follows with illustrations by James Campbell, the Kelley and Farrand Geological Survey publication of 1967, *The Glacial Lakes around Michigan* has been a primary source.

Early Lakes Chicago and Maumee

In the years of transition from ice advance to retreat, the Saginaw Lobe melted back more rapidly than the lobes on either side of it. As it released its load of ice, the area of South Central Michigan in the vicinity of Sturgis became the first land area in the state to reappear. Soon afterwards the *Kalamazoo and Tekonsha* moraines were formed (fig. 5.7). Therefore, that area of Michigan has the oldest soils on the lower Peninsula. About 16,000 years ago a warming climate melted the ice further and in the process created the *Valpariso-Charlotte and Fort Wayne* belt of moraines (fig. 5.8). The waters trapped behind the belt of moraines formed glacial lakes Chicago and Maumee, the predecessors of modern-day lakes Michigan and Erie. These early lakes extented far inland and covered the sites of both Detroit and Chicago. The extensive *Lake Border* moraine system hills allowed for further lake expansion after the ice front stabilized following a period of retreat and readvance. At this stage of development, Lake Maumee was drained by two outlets: (1) southwest through the Maumee-Wabash River system, and (2) west to Lake Chicago through the *Imlay Outlet* which bisected the lower Peninsula. Lake Chicago was drained by the *Chicago Outlet* into the Des Plaines River system (fig. 5.9).

Canals in the Former Outlets. In 1900 the former Chicago Outlet was reopened to create the Chicago Sanitary and Ship Canal. In 1922 the Calumet River was modified and its drainage diverted from emptying into Lake Michigan so that it would flow into the Sag Canal and Chicago Sanitary and Ship Canal. The waters that have been redirected today reach the Atlantic Ocean via the Gulf of Mexico as in the glacial period. The regulated diversion of Lake Michigan waters further helps to solve transportation, pollution, and sanitation problems at the head of Lake Michigan. During low water level cycles on the Great Lakes, the diversion of water into the Mississippi River usually becomes a point of conflict between Great Lakes shipping and Chicago interests. The Imlay Outlet has frequently caught the imagination of politicians, business speculators, and engineers who would like to dredge the former outlet channel following the Flint River, Maple River, or Stony Creek and Grand River to connect the east and west sides of the Lower Peninsula.

Lake Arkona-Lake Whittlesey, Port Huron Moraine

As the Huron, Erie, and Saginaw Lobes retreated to the east and northeast, Lake Erie became the first Great Lake to be freed of ice. The meltwaters of this retreat created Lake Arkona which spread over the land from the Saginaw Lowland to Syracuse, New York, but continued to be drained by the elongated Grand River and Chicago Outlet. Again, the ice readvanced and halted along the line of the spectacular Port Huron moraine belt which can be traced between Minnesota and New York. At this stage 12,500 years ago, *Lake Whittlesey* occupied the Erie Basin and extended inland nearly to Adrian, Macon, Ypsilanti, Sandusky, and Ubly (fig. 5.10). Water also quietly ponded between present-day Port Huron and Ubly in the Black River Valley. At Ubly the flow turned to the southwest into the Cass River Valley and

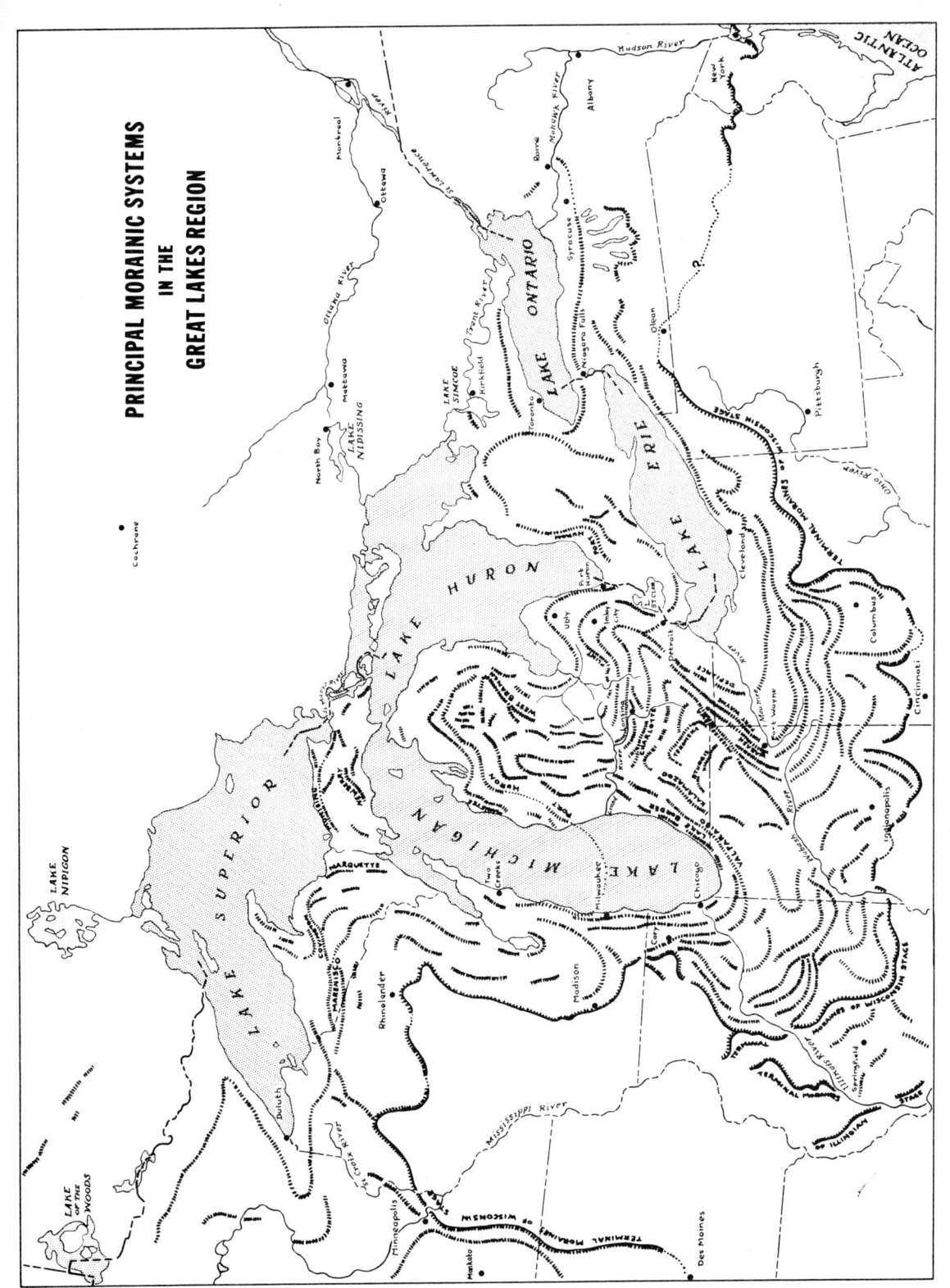

Figure 5.7. Principal moraines in the Great Lakes region. (Source: *The Glacial Lakes around Michigan*, Geological Survey.)

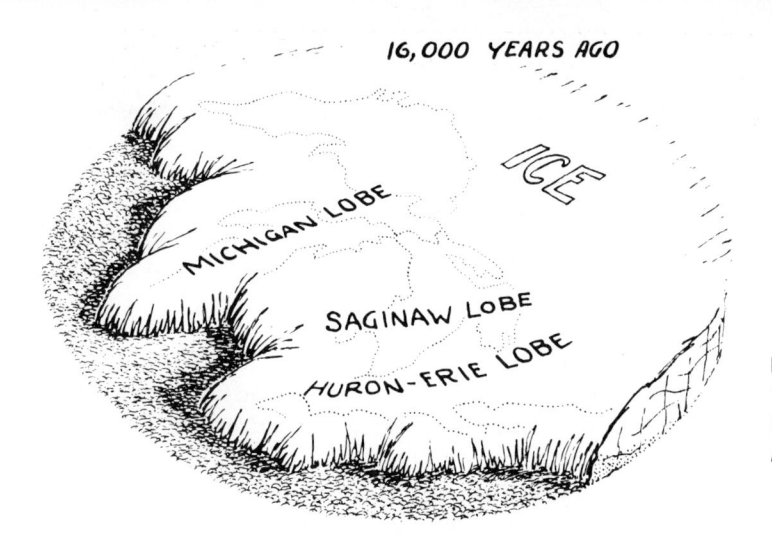

Figure 5.8. Ice front approximately 16,000 years ago. (Drawing: J.M. Campbell in, *The Glacial Lakes around Michigan,* Geological Survey.)

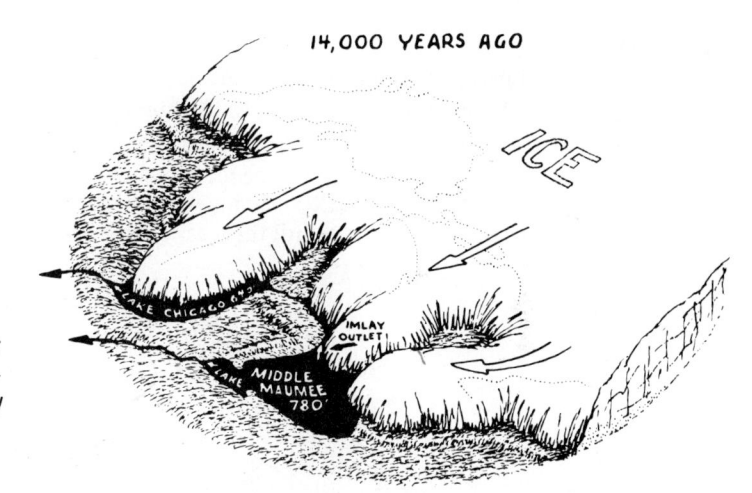

Figure 5.9. Ice front approximately 14,000 years ago. (Drawing: J.M. Campbell in, *The Glacial Lakes around Michigan,* Geological Survey.)

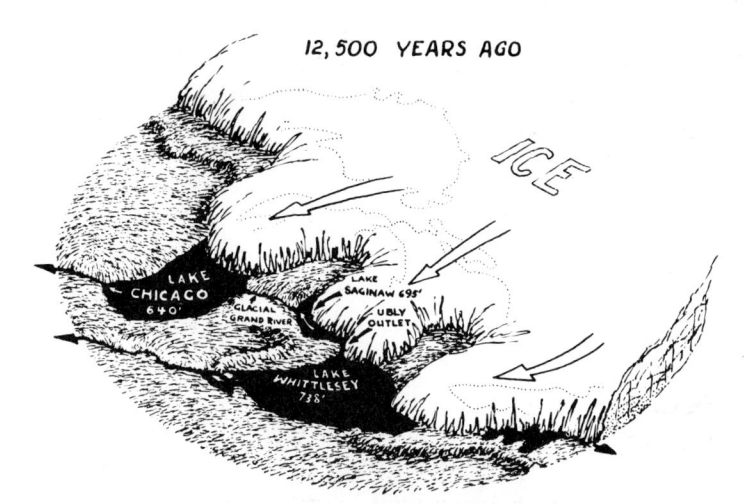

Figure 5.10. Ice front approximately 12,500 years ago. (Drawing: J.M. Campbell in, *The Glacial Lakes around Michigan,* Geological Survey.)

began a 10 km (6 mi) wide torrent for 80 km (50 mi) past Cass City, Caro, and Vassar into glacial *Lake Saginaw* between Pine Run and Frankenmuth. As the outlets to the east were still blocked by ice, the flow was into the lower Lake Chicago and its outlet to the Mississippi River. Later sporadic advances and retreats of the ice front would create the glacial lake stages of Lake Huron and Erie known as Lakes Warren, Wayne, Grassmere, and Lundy. In these later lake stages the Lower Lakes began their drainage to the east using the Mohawk Outlet and the Hudson River.

The Upper Great Lakes

For a short interval known as the *Two Creeks,* the Straits of Mackinac were temporarily exposed and connected to glacial *Lake Keweenaw* which covered the east end of the Upper Peninsula. At the same time about 12,000 years ago ice withdrew from northern New York, and opened Niagara Falls. Glacial Lake Keweenaw was drained by a channel connecting the Au Train and Whitefish rivers south into an enlarged Lake Chicago. Like other glacial outlet channels, this one is periodically advocated as a route for a modern-day canal which would bypass the aging Soo Locks. Also uncovered was the *Trent Outlet* which cut eastward across the lowland Ontario Peninsula from present-day Georgian Bay to Lake Ontario. The *Valders stage* was the last glacier readvancement into Michigan, carrying with it trees and vegetation. Reddish soils are characteristic of the Valders moraines. The Mohawk Outlet, the later day route of the Erie Canal, was again blocked by the ice advance. *Glacial Lake Algonquin* formed the ponded backwaters in the basin of Lakes Michigan and Huron to create an island out of the tip of the Lower Peninsula which lasted until the ice melted back again (fig. 5.11).

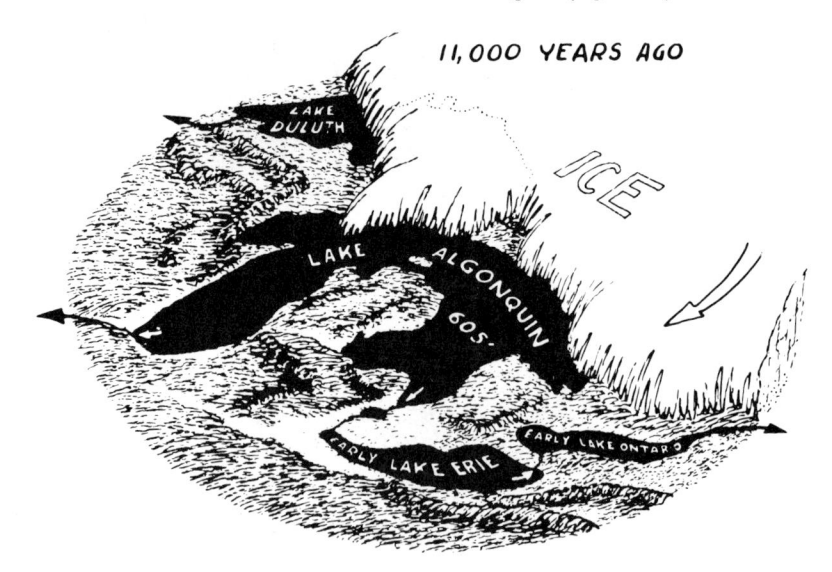

Figure 5.11. Ice front approximately 11,000 years ago. (Drawing: J.M. Campbell in, *The Glacial Lakes around Michigan,* Geological Survey.)

About 9500 B.P. a succession of lower eastern outlets were uncovered which significantly lowered the early glacial lakes (fig. 5.12). Three lakes much smaller in area than their immediate predecessors known as glacial Lakes Houghton (Superior), Chippewa (Michigan), and Stanley (Huron) were drained by the *North Bay Outlet* through the Ottawa Channel into a salt water St. Lawrence Sea which occupied the basin of that present-day river. During this drainage stage, Lake Chippewa cut a tremendous vertical-sided gorge 1,080 m (1,200 yd) wide and 105 m (115 yd) deep into the weak Mackinac Breccia limestone. The water level at the surface of the straits dropped to 69 m (230 ft) above sea level in comparison to 174 m (579 ft), the surface level today. During the lower stage of Great Lake water levels, inland sand dunes were formed by the wind blowing over the dried sands of the former lake bottoms. At that time also native Paleo-Indian villages were undoubtedly relocated towards the lower lake shore only to be drowned by the later rise in the lake levels.

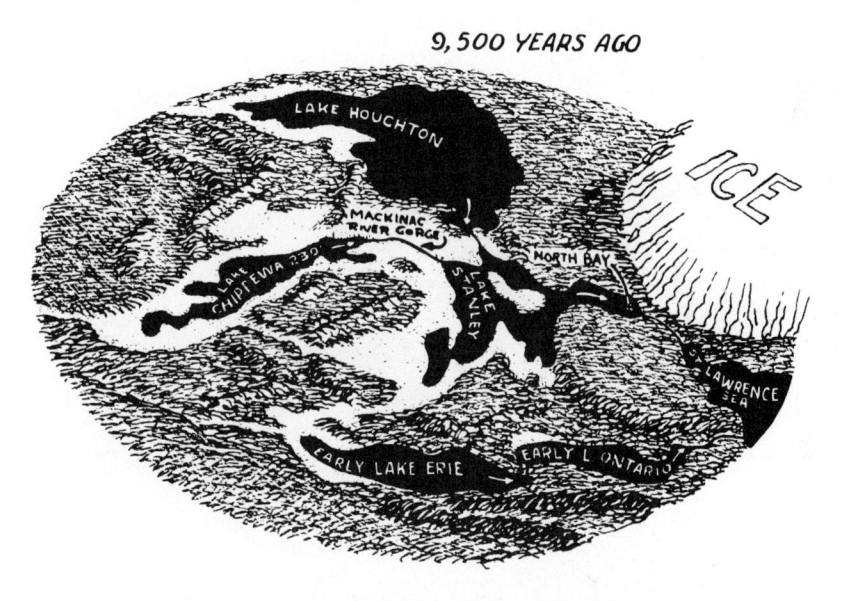

Figure 5.12. The Great Lakes 9,500 years ago. (Drawing: J.M. Campbell in, *The Glacial Lakes around Michigan,* Geological Survey.)

The Postglacial Earth Crust Rebound Stage

Throughout the 70,000 years of the Wisconsin glacial stages the mass of the ice sheet may have exerted up to 250 tons pressure per square foot. This immense weight depressed the earth's crust especially in Northern Michigan. When the load of ice was removed the crust began to rebound and this is still occurring at the rate of about 15 cm (6 in) per century. Due to the variations in the thickness of ice and distance from the source area of the glaciers, the land has rebounded at different rates north and south of what are known as *hinge lines* which are taken into consideration by physiographers in comparing elevations of glacial features of the same age in different areas of the state and nation. As a result of the earth's rebound, the North Bay Outlet, formerly near sea level, has been elevated nearly 210 m (700 ft). Until the North Bay Outlet rose above the Port Huron and Chicago Outlets, it remained as the exclusive drainage way for the Upper Great Lakes. When the North Bay Outlet rose to 181 m (605 ft), which was the elevation of the Chicago and Port Huron Outlets, they were able to reestablish themselves as the Upper Great Lakes outlets (fig. 5.13). Postglacial Lake Nipissing, the largest of all the Great Lakes, combined and filled all of the former lake basins and existed for about 1,000 years with the three outlets. In time, the Port Huron Outlet captured all the Upper Great Lakes drainage because the Chicago Outlet met a resistant limestone sill while the Port Huron Outlet continued to cut into its glacial drift channel. When the level of lake waters dropped below the Chicago Outlet, the present-day Lake Michigan and Lake Huron were established. Continued rebound of the Upper Peninsula sandstone sill, coupled with the continued cutting and lowering in the St. Clair River channel, separated Lake Superior except at the St. Mary's River. During the last two thousand years the shape and area of the Great Lakes have persisted. What the future will bring in about 5,000 years when it is estimated that the limestone of Niagara Falls will erode, is open to debate and speculation.

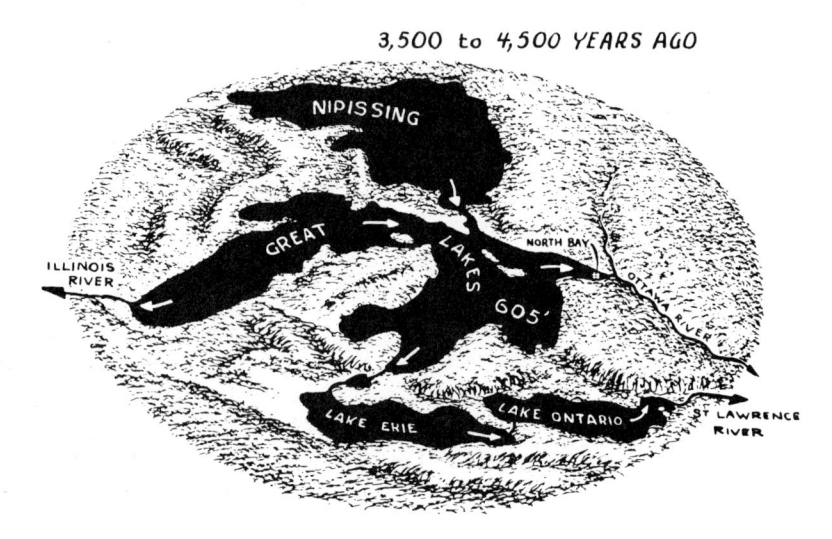

Figure 5.13. The Great Lakes 3,500-4,500 years ago. (Drawing: J.M. Campbell in, *The Glacial Lakes around Michigan,* Geological Survey.)

The Sand Dunes and Other Great Lakes Land Features

Michigan's sand dunes have become one of the state's most attractive glacial landscape features. Residents and tourists, as well as the mining industry, have each found them desirable for various purposes. The dunes are the state's youngest hill-like feature, in fact they are so new on the earth that in many places soil has not developed. Additionally, the dunes are still being built by the constant westerly winds. The sand dune building process generally follows a three-step *saltation* process: (1) the wind carries dry sand which skips, jumps, and bounces against an object, usually vegetation, which can trap and hold the sand grains, (2) the pile of trapped sand forms a foundation and obstruction which forces the wind to change its speed which continues to pile more sand on the original obstruction, and (3) dune stability with a gentle windward slope and steep lee slope is reached when vegetation establishes itself and covers the exposed sand.

The cyclical fluctuation of the Great Lakes region's precipitation and water levels further contributes to the sand building process. During high water, the sand particles are reground by wave action. In low water periods they become dried and available for transportation by the wind. Gentle winds of 11-13 KPH (7-8 MPH) can move sand, however, most dune building occurs when winds exceed 32 KPH (20 MPH). Winds of gale force 120 KPH (75 MPH) or more can roll 7.62 cm (3 in) cobbles. Both the east shore of Lake Michigan plus the Keweenaw and Grand Sable shores on Lake Superior display dramatic examples of sand dunes reaching heights of 30-120 m (100-400 ft).

The Michigan dune sand is usually found to be about 90 percent quartz grains from glacial drift mixed with magnetite, hornblende, calcite, tourmaline, and other materials.

The Sleeping Bear Dune has gained international acclaim and is the central feature of the Sleeping Bear Dune National Seashore Park area. The spectacular dune reaches 135 m (450 ft) above Lake Michigan; however, because its foundation is a moraine plateau, it is not strictly a sand dune. Grand Sable which rises 115 m (380 ft) is also perched on top of former glacial deposits. The Silver Lake sand dune area at Little Sable Point, Oceana County, also contains dunes in excess of 100 m (300 ft).

Dune Features. Within the shoreline margins where dunes are found, several distinctive dune features are observable including:

1. *Fore dunes,* low 9-15 m (30-50 ft) dunes parallel to beaches.
2. *Blowouts,* dune areas which have been reexposed to the wind due to the vegetative cover's injury or removal by natural or human occurrences such as the operation of trail bikes and dune buggies. They generally have saddle-shaped depressions.
3. *Dune Ridges,* a further extension of blowouts with pronounced "U"-shaped topography, unlike anything observable in arid lands. Along southern Lake Michigan they may rise over 75 m (250 ft) and stretch inland a thousand meters.
4. *Migratory Dunes,* in their classic desert form, rarely develop in Michigan, however, evidence of some dune migration includes the reexposure of dune-buried forests and the building of backslopes at the rate of 1.5-3 m (5-10 ft) per year.

Economic Uses of Sand Dunes

The high purity and uniformity of Michigan dune sand has stimulated a great demand for it as a heavy industry resource. In recent years Michigan has led the nation in the production of industrial sand of which 90 percent is used in the automobile and associated manufacturing processes especially for cores and foundry molds. Industrial sands are chiefly produced along the shores of Lake Michigan where nearness to low-cost water transportation is a basic advantage. Tuscola, Wexford, Saginaw, and Bay counties also participate in the industrial sand market activities. Additional commercial uses for dune sand include: mortar, plaster, asphalt dressing, locomotive rail traction dressing, furnace linings, fiberglass, and recreation. Continued extensive mining of the dunes has not only eliminated some dunes, but also threatens many others. Again, the question of priorities of use, protection, and management is a critical one facing the dune sand excavation and tourist industries, as well as citizens and governments (fig. 5.14).[3]

---

3. *Michigan's Sand Dunes: A Geological Sketch* (Michigan Department of Conservation, 1962), pp. 1-22.

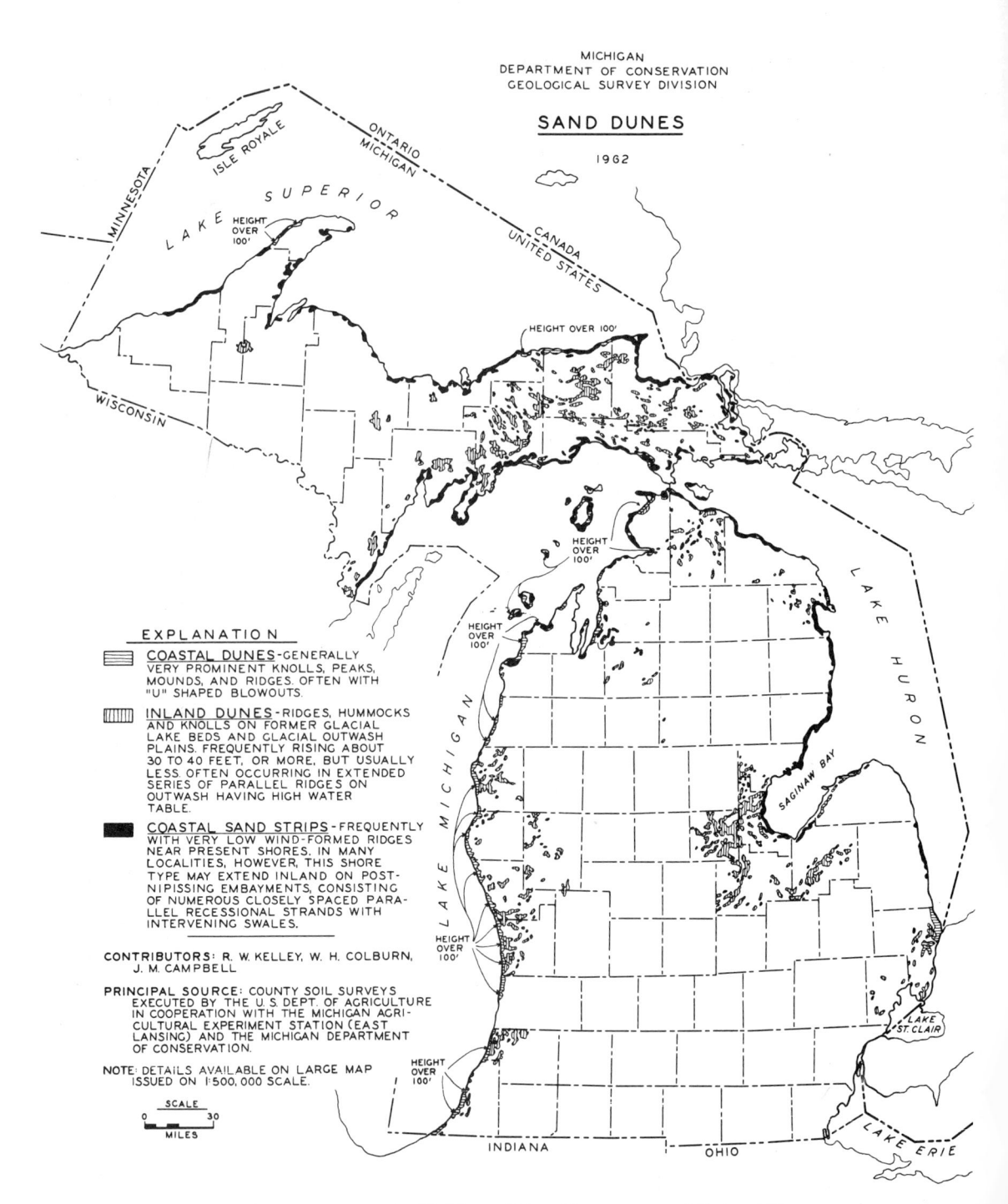

Figure 5.14. Sand dune areas in Michigan. (Map: Department of Natural Resources.)

Glacial Lake Bed Deposits and Features

The numerous water level stages in the creation of the Great Lakes between a low of 54 m (180 ft) and a high of 240 m (800 ft) above sea level produced a variety of beach ridges, lake terraces, and lake bed lacustrine plains. Ancient beach ridges were formed out of sand and gravel material along the margins of the lakes and piled into ribbons 1.5-3 m (5-10 ft) high and 30 m (100 ft) wide. In the Detroit area several of these ancient beach ridges still exist having been preserved by their use as cemeteries and parks. Others have been completely mined to serve the construction needs of the lake plain urban communities. *The Sand Hill Monthly,* the publication of the Redford Masonic organization, was named for the former existence of this type of terrain on Grand River Avenue between the Southfield Freeway and Telegraph Road. Burgess Park and Mt. Hazel Cemetery, about two blocks off the main business artery, still hold the former beach sands of glacial Lake Wayne.

Glacial and postglacial lacustrine plains are found wherever the Great Lakes invaded the land. The largest Michigan lake plain dominates the physiographic region extending from Toledo north to Port Huron, inland to the belted moraines and includes the Saginaw Lowland which is interrupted by successive beach ridges. A smaller embayment plain was created between Muskegon and South Haven. The clayey sediment soils of the lacustrine plains have become the most valuable agricultural producing land in the state.

Shoreline cut cliffs and lake terraces are features which were gouged into moraines, drumlins, and rocks by wave action. Beautiful terraces dating from the Lake Nipissing and Algonquian stages cut from limestone can be seen at Mackinac City. Another limestone terrace was cut into the Old Mission Peninsula, north of Traverse City.

Fluctuation of Lake Levels and Contemporary Shoreline Erosion Problems

As early as 1749 Lotbiniere recorded observations of earlier French inhabitants at Fort Michilimackinac who stated that the lake levels rose and fell about equal amounts in 10-12 year cycles.[4] Ninety years later the Michigan topographer, S. W. Higgins, again confirmed the periodic fluctuation in levels and attributed the cycles to surface drainage and climate. "The flood of the century" in 1839 which inundated the orchards along the Detroit and St. Clair rivers plus caused additional destruction, prompted early calculations on how to best manage the shoreline to reduce recurring community hardships due to high water.[5]

In the early 1950s high water levels on the Great Lakes again caused millions of dollars of damage to Michigan's shorelands. During the following years, spurred by population, economic, and technologic changes, in conjunction with a cycle of low water levels, many homes were built too close to the lakes to assure their survival. When high lake levels returned in the late 1960s and 1970s, the cost in damages to homes and other structures continued the increasing cost spiral. By April 1976, over 800 homes had been identified as being in immediate danger of severe damage or destruction due to shoreline erosion.

---

4. "Fort Michilimackinac in 1749," *Mackinac History,* Vol. II Leaflet No. 5 (1976), p. 10. ("Lotbiniere's Plan and Description," translated by Marie Gerin-Lajoie).
5. *Geological Reports of Douglass Houghton* (Lansing: Michigan Historical Commission, 1928), pp. 263-66.

Shorelands Protection and Management Act

Recognizing the high cost to individuals and state taxpayers, plus the damage done to shorelands due to unplanned individual uses and in some instances, ignorant development along the shorelines which affected the greater state community, the legislature passed in 1970 "The Shorelands Protection and Management Act (Public Act 245). The Act requires that the DNR determine high risk shoreline areas to be regulated to prevent property loss. The rules of the act require:

> Upon designation of a high risk erosion area, the director shall also set forth recommended shoreline use restrictions based on a thirty-year period of life of a permanent building or structure. . .

Under the Act, 840 km (525 mi) of Michigan's 3,715 km (2,322 mi) of nonisland Great Lakes shoreline were identified as being subject to high risk erosion. High risk is interpreted to mean a long-term bluff recession rate of 30.5 cm (12 in) per year. The process of natural shoreline erosion is a continuous powerful force which is difficult and costly to manage or control. Reducing the losses due to bluff recession is made more complex by the development that occurred prior to 1970. Only unplatted areas at the time of the Act's passage can be designated by the DNR. Consequently, only 10 percent of Michigan's high risk shoreline is within the regulatory power of PA 245. Therefore, the majority of the efforts to minimize the impact of natural shoreline erosion rests with the individual property owners, their voluntary cooperative associations and local government.

Shoreline Management Strategies. Initially, three options of protecting Michigan's remaining undeveloped shoreline subject to rapid bluff erosion were analyzed, including:

1. Setbacks from bluff lines to provide 30 years of protection to buildings and sanitation systems.
2. Construction of relocatable buildings and septic systems.
3. Construction of protective works such as groins, seawalls, and revetments.

Of the options, the third is the most expensive in relationship to public funds and perhaps least effective due to the unpredictable actions of adjoining property owners. The adoption of setbacks has met with the greatest amount of acceptance perhaps due to the graphic observation of losses to individuals when homes are seen falling into the lakes (fig. 5.15). While not scientifically verified, a "rule of thumb" seems to be operating which suggests that "structures 9 m (30 ft) or closer to a bluff line frequently lose property value at a disproportionately rapid rate." In one instance in Van Buren County, a recession of 33 m (110 ft) in two years has been observed. South of Grand Haven State Park between 1970 and 1976, scores of homes were lost, torn down or relocated at an estimated cost of $7,500 apiece.

Shoreline Bluff Erosion Determination. To determine the rate of bluff recession is at best a difficult task. To gain a reasonable degree of accuracy, trained natural scientists walked a portion of the Great Lakes shoreline, photographed, and noted conditions of the shore including: vegetation, sand exposure, beach width, slope and bank slumpage, water action, condition of land, protective control structures, and unusual angle of the repose of ground material. Additionally, based on early air photos, original survey field notes, and maps, bluff recession distances from the 1800s and 1930s to the 1970s could be measured. After determining

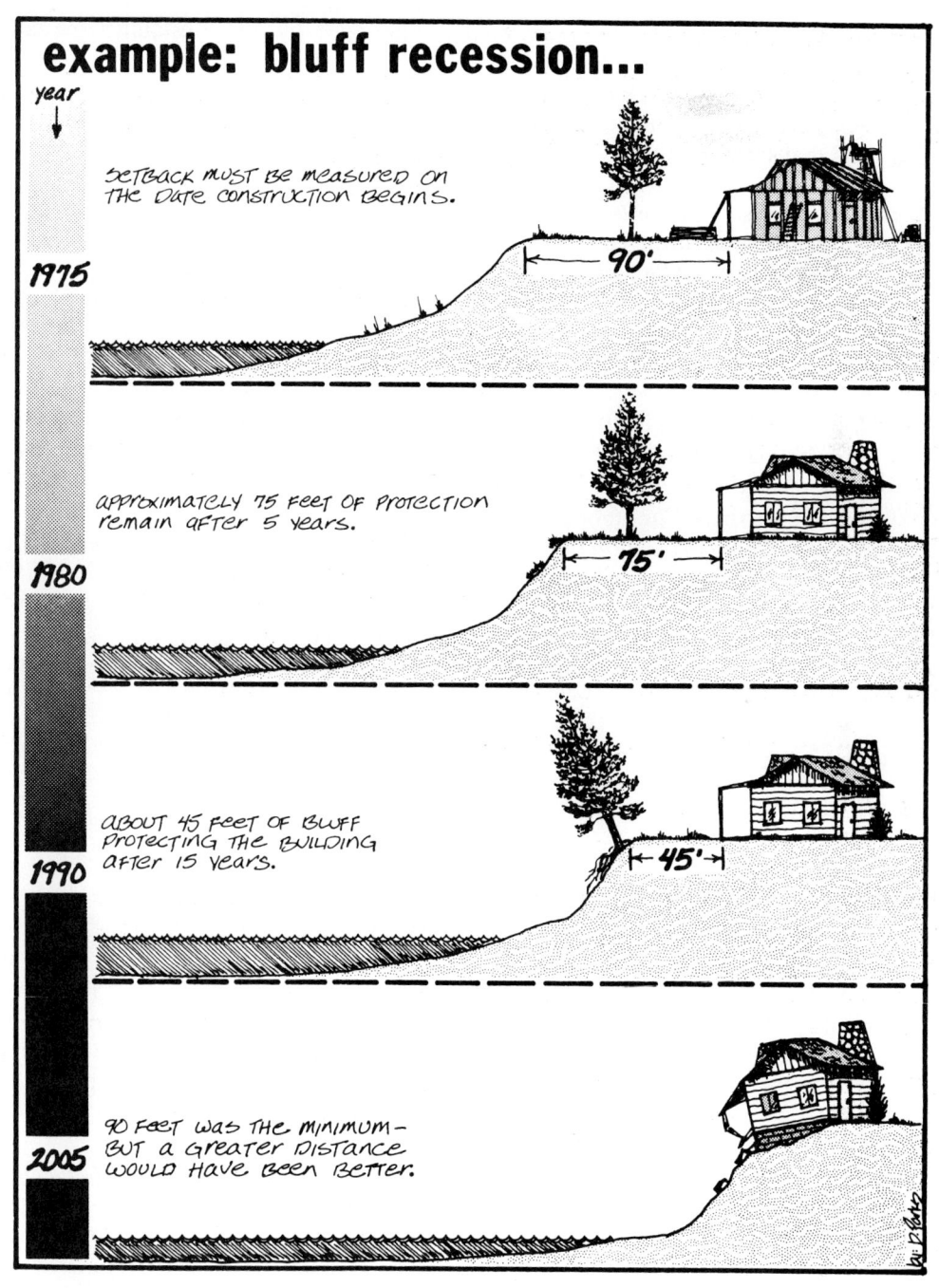

Figure 5.15. Example of bluff recession in relationship to PA 245-1970 Shorelands Protection and Management Act. (Source: *Erosion*, Michigan Department of Natural Resources.)

the average annual bluff recession distance, it is multiplied by 30 to establish the lawful shoreline setback under PA 245.

Ultimately, whether the DNR exercises its power to determine setbacks in high erosion risk areas is determined by the action of local units of government. If they initiate local zoning, planning, and management, those actions could preclude the necessity of further state regulation.

Numerous efforts by property owners and the government to protect investments in land and buildings can be seen in traveling along the Great Lakes shoreline. All too often seawalls and jetties represent efforts which have had limited individual success. The effectiveness of protective devices depends not only on design, construction, space protected, and money, but also cooperation of the several affected shoreline property owners. Two of the best publications to help individuals and associations in their quest to protect the Great Lakes shoreline are:

1. *Help Yourself,* a discussion of the critical erosion problems on the Great Lakes and alternate methods of shore protection. This roadmap-like folded publication by the Corps of Engineers, North Central Division, has over 45 simple line drawings of do's and don'ts to make the labor and cost of installation beneficial.
2. *Low Cost Shore Protection for the Great Lakes,* Lake Hydraulics Laboratory, U of M and Water Resources Commission, DNR, reprinted 1975.

It is hoped that the use of these self-help booklets plus other active local, state, and federal cooperative efforts will result in a continually attractive Great Lakes shoreline for generations yet unborn.

> "No simple formula can be devised for the solution of the many problems of land and water use history has left in our laps."
>
> Samuel T. Dana, 1955

Chapter Six

Climate, Soil, Vegetation, and Lumber Resources

The puzzles and blessings of the close relationship between climate, soil, and vegetation in support of agriculture and forest resources have been observed, discussed, and recorded since ancient time. The use of these resources for the enrichment of present-day life and that of future generations necessitates recycling of nonrenewable resources and continued wise management of all resources. While education holds a promise for improved utilization of Michigan's resources, discipline and enlightened ethical behavior by citizens is also necessary. Whether they enjoy food from its soil, water from its snow and rain, air, scenery, or sitting in suburban comfort enjoying the flickering flames of a fireplace tindered with logs from its trees, everyone in Michigan uses its resources. Therefore, everyone shares a responsibility in their wise management and use. To further the knowledge of Michigan resource use, this chapter describes the state's climate, soil, and vegetation resources. Additionally, it identifies problems related to their use and management and concludes with a discussion on the history of forest exploitation and the contemporary importance of the wood-products industry.

The Weather and Climate Resources of Michigan

Whether the Ice Age ended or the world is in just another interglacial stage is a topic of serious investigation by meteorologists, climatologists, and other earth scientists. Newspapers and popular magazines find it profitable to publish interesting articles on the subject which invariably stimulate classroom questions. It is clearly evident that climate patterns have changed drastically throughout the last two billion years and it is safe to assume that very long-term climate patterns are still in transition. When another significant change in climate will occur in

Michigan is subject to speculation. Considering the immediate future, however, Michigan's climate will undoubtedly remain in the *humid continental* realm which has dominated the region with its four distinct seasons since the retreat of the last ice front.

Climate Regions

Latitude, topographic relief, relative location to large expanses of land and water, worldwide semipermanent wind, and pressure systems are the primary controllers of Michigan's local atmospheric conditions. World climate regions are determined by averaging and plotting data from about a quarter century of officially recorded daily weather occurrences. A common method used to regionalize the occurrence of climates was developed by a German botanist Köppen and later revised by Trewartha at the University of Wisconsin. In their system, Michigan is divided into Humid Continental warm summer Daf and Humid Continental cool summer Dbf regions. The transition zone between these two uniform climate regions occurs generally along the Bay-Muskegon Line with actual division shifting according to annual weather conditions. The Humid Continental title description and letters Df signify that Michigan is a snow-forest region that is affected by a continental land mass and is constantly moist with enough precipitation occurring to support trees. The lower-case "a" indicates the area where the warmest summer month averages above 22°C (71.6°F) while the lower-case "b" indicates the area where the warmest month averages below that temperature. The Daf climate is most similar to the American Midwest with its long warm summers while the Dbf climate is similar to Moscow with its short cool summers and long cold winters. Of course, each climate has advantages and disadvantages and are a perpetual source of comment by those with individual preferences.

Latitude, Wind, and Topographic Relief

The earth latitudes determine the amount of solar insulation or the effective heat which is received at the earth's surface from the sun. With a degree of latitude change poleward or about 112 km (70 mi), temperature averages shift about .5°C (1°F). In the case of Michigan's extreme latitude stations, a slightly greater yearly average temperature range exists, with Adrian averaging 9°C (49°F) while Houghton-Hancock averages 4°C (38°F). Michigan's midlatitude location places it in an area with prevailing westerly winds. In the summer when the Bermuda High Pressure center is located over southeast United States, winds from the southwest prevail. In winter months, winds from the west and northwest are most common, but vary frequently for short periods as cyclonic storm fronts moving at about 320-3,200 km (200-2,000 mi) per day pass across the state. In the eastern Upper Peninsula, easterly winds occur in late fall and early winter as a result of early winter anticyclones moving eastward across Canada as the major storm track shifts south.

Local Topography and Temperature. Hot air is commonly known to rise, yet as it increases in elevation it is cooled at the rate of 1.9°C (3.5°F) per 300 m (1,000 ft). Therefore, the elevation of a community is an important factor affecting its temperature. Michigan's *highest elevation,* 604 m (1,980 ft) is at Mount Curwood (Baraga County), and *lowest elevation* is on the shoreline of Lake Erie at 174 m (572 ft).

In the eastern Upper Peninsula lies a gently undulating lowland at about 180 m (600 ft) above sea level which then rises to about 300 m (1,000 ft). The Upper Peninsula's western uplands average about 420-480 m (1,400-1,600 ft) of elevation along the Keweenaw escarpment.

The Lower Peninsula topography varies in elevation between the former lake beds at 175 m (582 ft) in Monroe to the moraine uplands generally ranging between 240-300 m (800-1,000 ft). The Lower Peninsula maximum elevations are found in Osceola and Wexford counties at over 510 m (1,700 ft).

The weather stations at Cadillac, 388 m (1,295 ft) of elevation, and East Tawas, 177 m (590 ft) of elevation, and at the same latitude, illustrate the influence of local relief on temperatures which annually average 5.8°C (42.5°F) and 7.2°C (45.1°F) respectively. Manistee also on line with Cadillac and East Tawas but sited at an elevation of 175 m (582 ft) illustrates with its 8.1°C (46.6°F) annual average temperature the slight warming influence of Lake Michigan. In the Upper Peninsula annual average temperature also reflects the influence of local relief variations. Seney has an average temperature of 5.4°C (41.8°F) at 213 m (710 ft) elevation, but is usually warmer than Kenton sited at 350 m (1,167 ft) elevation which has an average temperature of 4.6°C (40.4°F).

Lake Influence on Temperature

Temperatures, dates of growing seasons, and cloudiness are affected by the Great Lakes which make Michigan unique in comparison to other states in the Humid Continental region. Orchardists in the Fruit Belt which extends one to two counties inland along Lake Michigan have capitalized on a climate subregion whose temperatures are altered by the prevailing west winds and the fact that the lake water warms and cools more slowly than its adjacent land. Because springtime warming temperatures are retarded, so also is the blossoming of the fruit trees until most danger of frost passes. Later in the year warmer temperatures lingering in the fall allow fruits to have enough time to ripen.

The July and January temperatures of Madison, Wisconsin, Muskegon, and Lansing illustrate the moderating influence and seasonal reversal of temperatures due to Lake Michigan lying between the two states (table 6.1).

TABLE 6.1
Season Reversal of Temperature Due to Lake Michigan

City	Average January Temperature °C	Average January Temperature °F	Average July Temperature °C	Average July Temperature °F
Madison, Wisconsin	−8	17.5	21.6	71
Muskegon, Michigan	−3.8	26.0	21.0	69.9
Lansing, Michigan	−4.2	24.3	21.7	71.1

SOURCE: Norton Strommen, *Climate of Michigan.*

On warm summer days when the prevailing wind is light, the lake shores often develop *lake breezes* which may extend inland for a few kilometers. These localized winds blow when warm air over land begins to rise allowing the cooler air over the lakes to move inland. Frequently, on some of the larger inland lakes at night, a similar air flow occurs, but on a smaller scale. Throughout the state, shoreline communities receive their highest amount of heat when the winds are from the land. During the winter months the opposite is true as the air over land is the coldest.

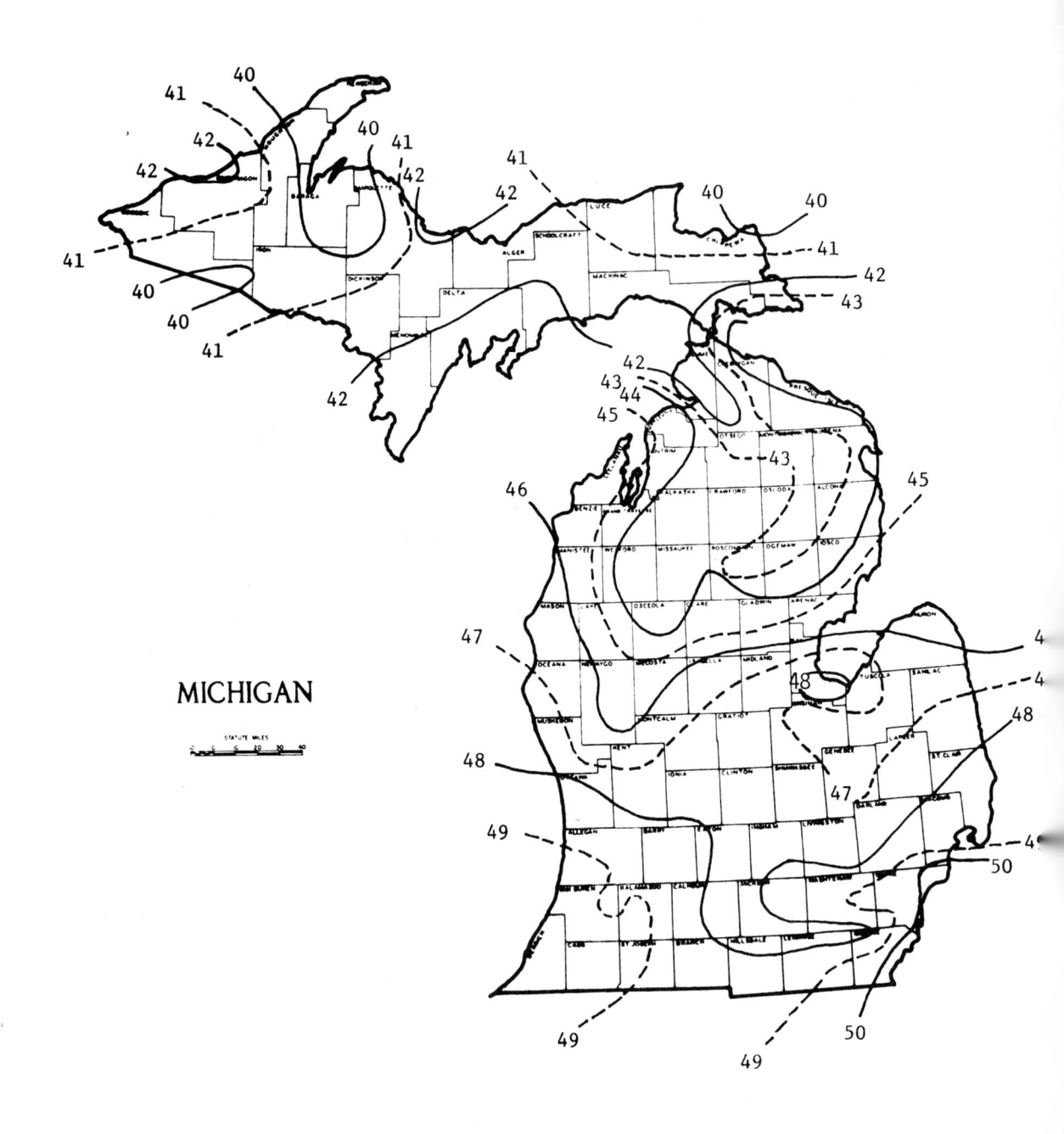

Figure 6.1. Mean annual temperature 1940-1969 in degrees Fahrenheit. (Map: Michigan Weather Service.)

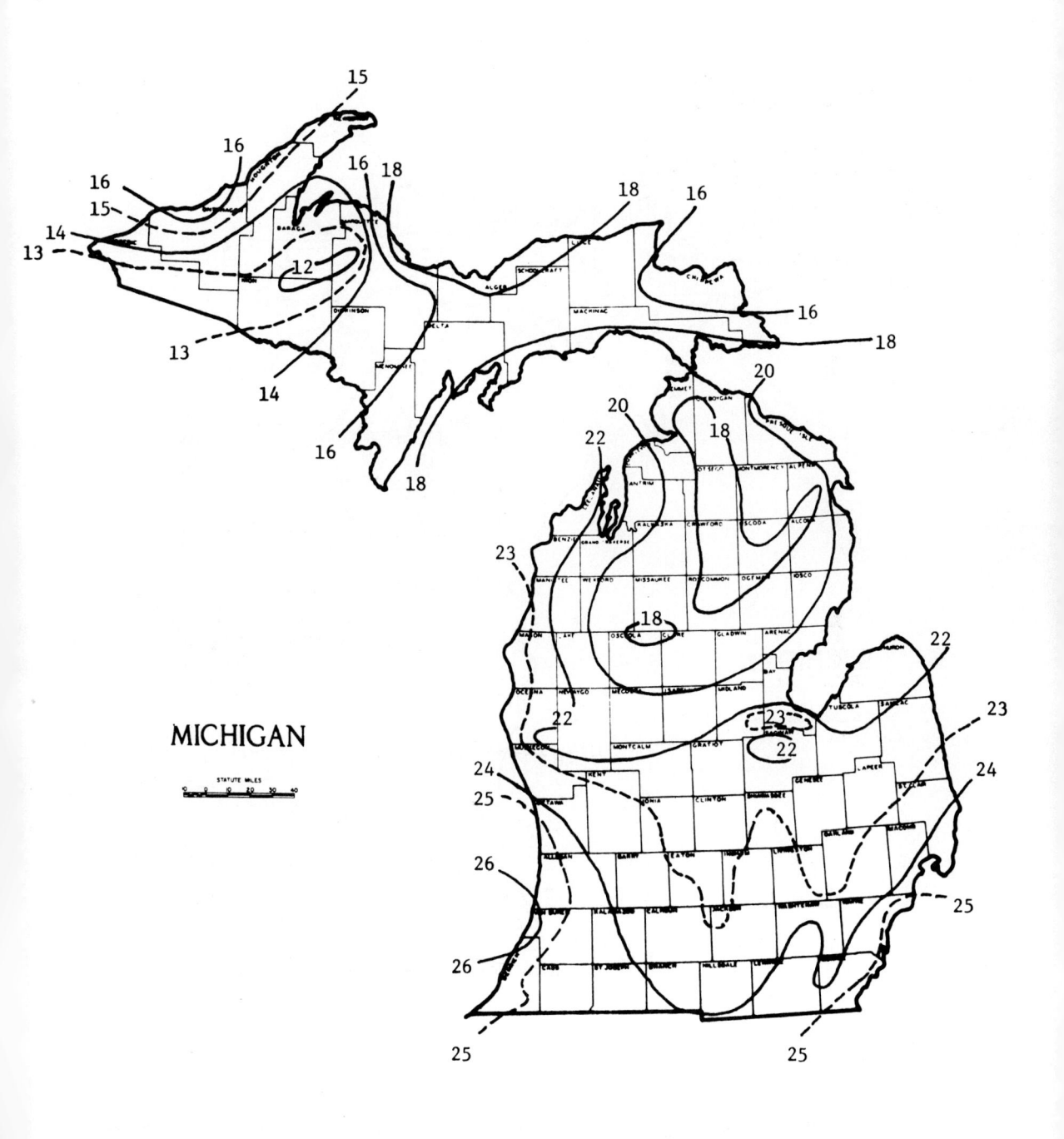

Figure 6.2. Mean annual January temperature in degrees Fahrenheit. (Map: Michigan Weather Service.)

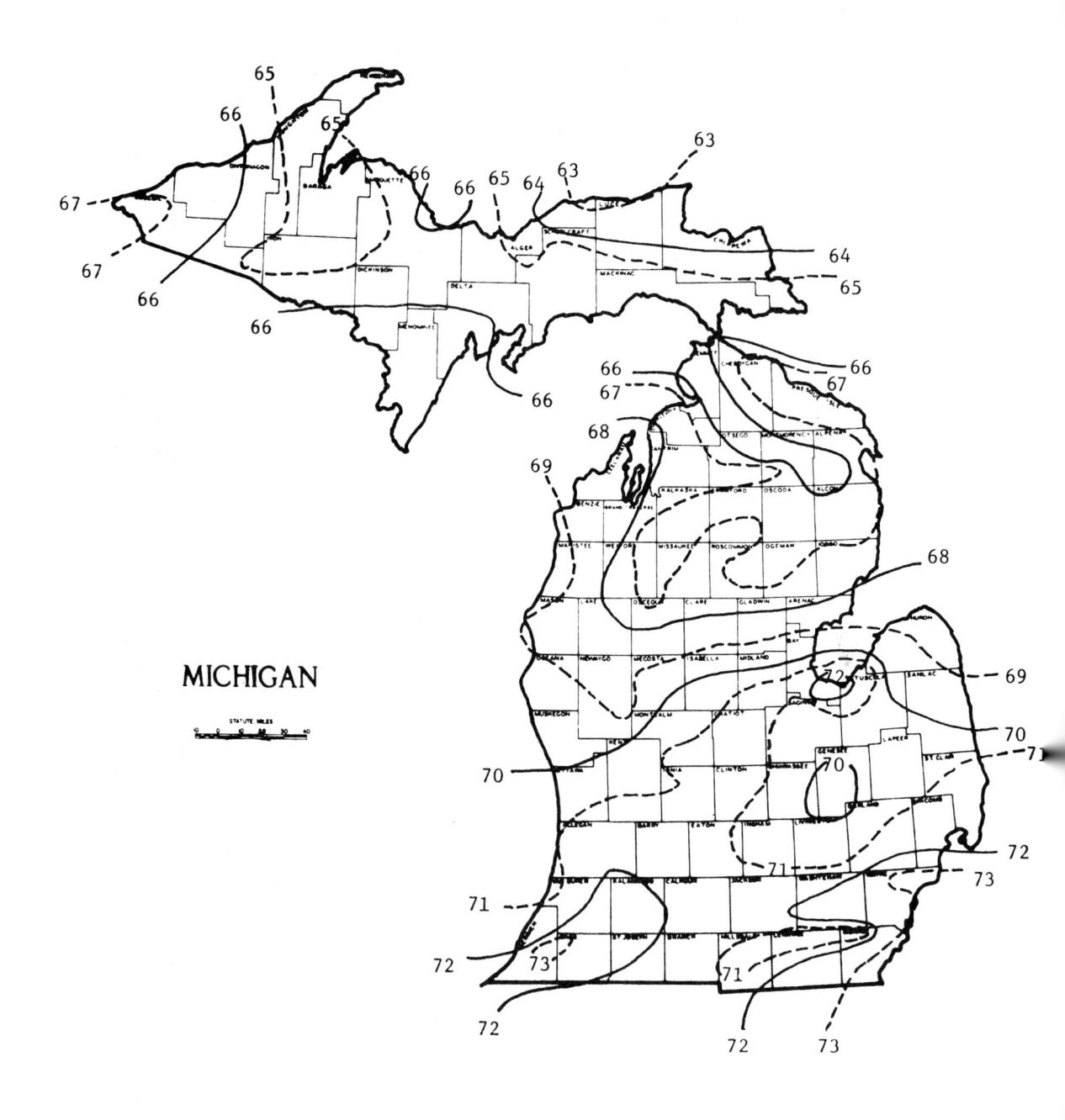

Figure 6.3. Mean annual July temperature in degrees Fahrenheit. (Map: Michigan Weather Service.)

Continental Influences on Temperatures

The influence of the continent and inland peninsular location has the greatest impact on the places in Michigan which record consistently high and low temperatures, as well as the wide range of temperatures recorded between seasons. *Mio,* on July 13, 1936, blistered with the *state's record high of 44.4° C (112° F)* while on the same day Saginaw and Newaygo were only .5° C (1° F) cooler. Bay City's temperature in July 1911 rose to 43.3° C (110° F) because of the impact of the land being a more dominant influence in summer in spite of its shoreline location. Detroit and Ann Arbor records stand at 40.6° C (105° F) although several other communities have records slightly higher. The great range in Humid Continental temperatures is demonstrated by *Vanderbilt,* near Gaylord, which recorded the state's *record low −46.1° C (−51° F)* on February 9, 1934, while its local high of 42.4° C (108° F) was established in July of 1936. Mio, in 1918 cooled to −43.9° C (−47° F) while in comparison, Detroit's lowest temperature is only −31.1° C (−24° F). Several cities have recorded temperatures above 37.8° C (100° F) and lows of below −34° to −40° C (−30° to −40° F). Seldom, however, have temperatures dropped below −29° C (−20° F) in the immediate vicinity of the Great Lakes which again act as a protection for the Fruit Belt orchards. In total, the *average annual* temperatures range between 10° C (50° F) in the southern tier of counties to 4.4° C (40° F) north of Sault Ste. Marie and the Keweenaw area.

Great Lakes Freezing Pattern

The Great Lakes rarely develop a complete covering of ice except at the narrow straits, channels between islands, and shallow water areas. It is generally assumed that an ice bridge between Isle Royale and the Minnesota shore allowed the state's moose herd to become established on that island. Usually for a few weeks each year the Mackinac Strait is frozen solid enough for the operation of snowmobiles on it. Unfortunately, tragic drownings occur when the ice unexpectedly begins to shift and open. Annually, law enforcement and Coast Guard personnel and other individuals risk their lives to rescue persons who are carried into open water on ice sheets when warming trends, winds, and currents break the ice free from shores of the lakes and bays.

Degree Days and Heating Requirements

One of the most reliable figures available for determining building heating and insulation needs is degree days (DD) figured for each weather station in Michigan. The DD index is based on 18.5° C (65° F), the point at which heating or cooling requirements are slight or none. In figuring the degree day index, each day's mean Fahrenheit temperature is subtracted from sixty-five. This daily figure is then totaled for the entire year. If the mean daily temperature is over sixty-five degrees Fahrenheit, no degree day units occur.

The advantage of the degree day index is that it provides a quick calculation for insulation and heating requirements in comparison to average temperature, i.e., Benton Harbor with 6,355 DD requires about one-third less heat energy units as Champion in Marquette County, which has 9,592 DD. Further, Champion requires about 15 percent more heating units than the city of Marquette with 8,320 DD (table 6.2).

TABLE 6.2
Selected Michigan Average Annual Degree Days,
Snow Accumulation, and Temperatures by Station

Station	Degree Days*	Snow Accumulation in Inches	Average Temperature °C	Average Temperature °F
Southern Lower Peninsula				
Adrian	6,548	30	9.4	48.9
Alma	6,901	39	8.7	47.7
Ann Arbor	6,396	29	9.7	49.5
Bay City	6,804	39	8.9	48.1
Benton Harbor	6,355	58	9.7	49.5
Detroit	6,232	31	10.0	50.1
Flint	6,885	42	8.7	47.6
Grand Rapids	6,998	80	8.7	47.6
Kalamazoo	6,373	70	9.8	47.6
Lansing	6,909	48	8.7	47.7
Mt. Pleasant	7,090	33	8.3	47.0
Muskegon	6,696	93	8.9	48.2
Port Huron	6,620	35	9.1	48.5
Northern Lower Peninsula				
Alpena	7,933	66	6.7	43.8
Big Rapids	7,491	62	7.6	45.6
Cadillac	8,427	71	5.8	42.5
Pelston	8,763	98	5.2	41.4
Traverse City	7,720	85	7.1	44.8
Upper Peninsula				
Champion	9,592	139	4.0	39.1
Escanaba	8,505	51	5.7	42.3
Houghton	8,342	89	3.6	42.9
Ironwood	8,906	42	5.2	41.3
Marquette	8,393	105	5.9	42.6
Sault Ste. Marie	9,048	105	4.7	40.6

*Based on degrees Fahrenheit.
SOURCE: *Climate of Michigan,* 2nd ed., Michigan Weather Service, 1971.

Sunshine and Cloudiness

Although cloudiness is neither popular with native residents nor fall and winter visitors to the state, the Great Lakes do contribute to an abundance of cloudy days. In the late summer when cooler air masses form and, in turn, are carried eastward over Lakes Michigan and Superior, the warmer lake water causes an unstable thin layer of moist air to develop in the lower atmosphere. This air when carried upward produces condensation, cloudiness, and often snow flurries during the fall and early winter. In December, Lansing receives 27 percent of possible sunshine in comparison to Madison, Wisconsin, which receives 42 percent. Cloudiness decreases as the lake water cools, but usually remains a significant weather factor until February. The communities most exposed to the west winds off the lakes in the western Lower

Peninsula, the Keweenaw Peninsula, plus northern Alger and Luce counties are among the most cloudy regions in the nation during the seasonal transition. In dramatic contrast, during the summer months the cooler water of the lakes tends to prevent convectional air currents and the western parts of the state receive nearly 70 percent of possible sunshine which is a higher rate than Ohio or Indiana for that time of year. Both the fruit and tourist industries immensely profit from this high percent of summer sunshine.

The Frost Free Growing Season

Activities in Michigan as in other midlatitude places, are geared to the four seasons—spring, summer, fall, and winter. Most important to the state's agricultural economy is a fifth season better known as the *frost free period* or "growing season." Unlike the typical four seasons which are determined worldwide by the specific dates of the equinox and solstice, the frost free period in Michigan varies considerably and is determined by the average dates of the last killing frost of spring and the first killing frost of fall. The average number of days in between these two days becomes the length of the "growing season" (fig. 6.4). The regional patterns based on the number of days in the frost free period are a more reliable indicator of what plants can be raised in the state as each plant varies in the number of days required to complete its life cycle. The diversity of frost free days, between a low of 60-70 in the interior north of the Lower Peninsula and the western Upper Peninsula, and 187 days at Benton Harbor, makes it possible to grow a wide variety of crops under natural sunlight conditions. Nevertheless, several foods common in the Michigan residents' diet cannot under natural conditions be raised, including citrus fruits, bananas, and coffee. Yet, with usually less than half the days of the year free of frost, Michigan citizens have been able to create a strong agricultural economy. The actual dates for the "growing season" will vary; for Benton Harbor the dates are from April 25 to October 29, while the Champion area has only the days between June 14 and August 31 to grow unprotected crops. Some places in the Upper Peninsula have occasionally had frost in every month. At the opposite extreme, Detroit in 1946 had 218 consecutive frostless days.

Precipitation

Michigan receives annually an average of 79 cm (31 in) of precipitation in a typical variety of forms common to the Humid Continental climate region including: cyclonic front rain storms, 20-40 convectional thundershowers, orographic rainfall on the end moraine belt margins, as well as snow, sleet, hail, and ice storms plus occasional blizzards. Of the total precipitation, 55-60 percent falls during the normal growing season which reduces the need for the widespread use of expensive irrigation systems on the farmlands (fig. 6.5). Nevertheless, since the early 1970s, farmers in Gratiot, Montcalm, and Isabella counties have paid commercial cloud-seeding operators to introduce silver iodide into promising clouds to increase rainfall. In the operation, ground generators vaporize the silver iodide 48-64 km (30-40 mi) upwind from the precipitation target area. In addition to extending the life of rain clouds by 10-15 minutes, it is claimed that the size of hailstones is reduced. Nonetheless, there is some concern among some earth scientists that cloud seeding often does no more than cause rain to fall in one place at the expense of another, a potential source of tension.[1]

1. L. R. Brown, P. L. McGrath, B. Stokes, "Twenty-two Dimensions of the Population Problem," Worldwatch Paper No. 5 (March 1976), p. 37.

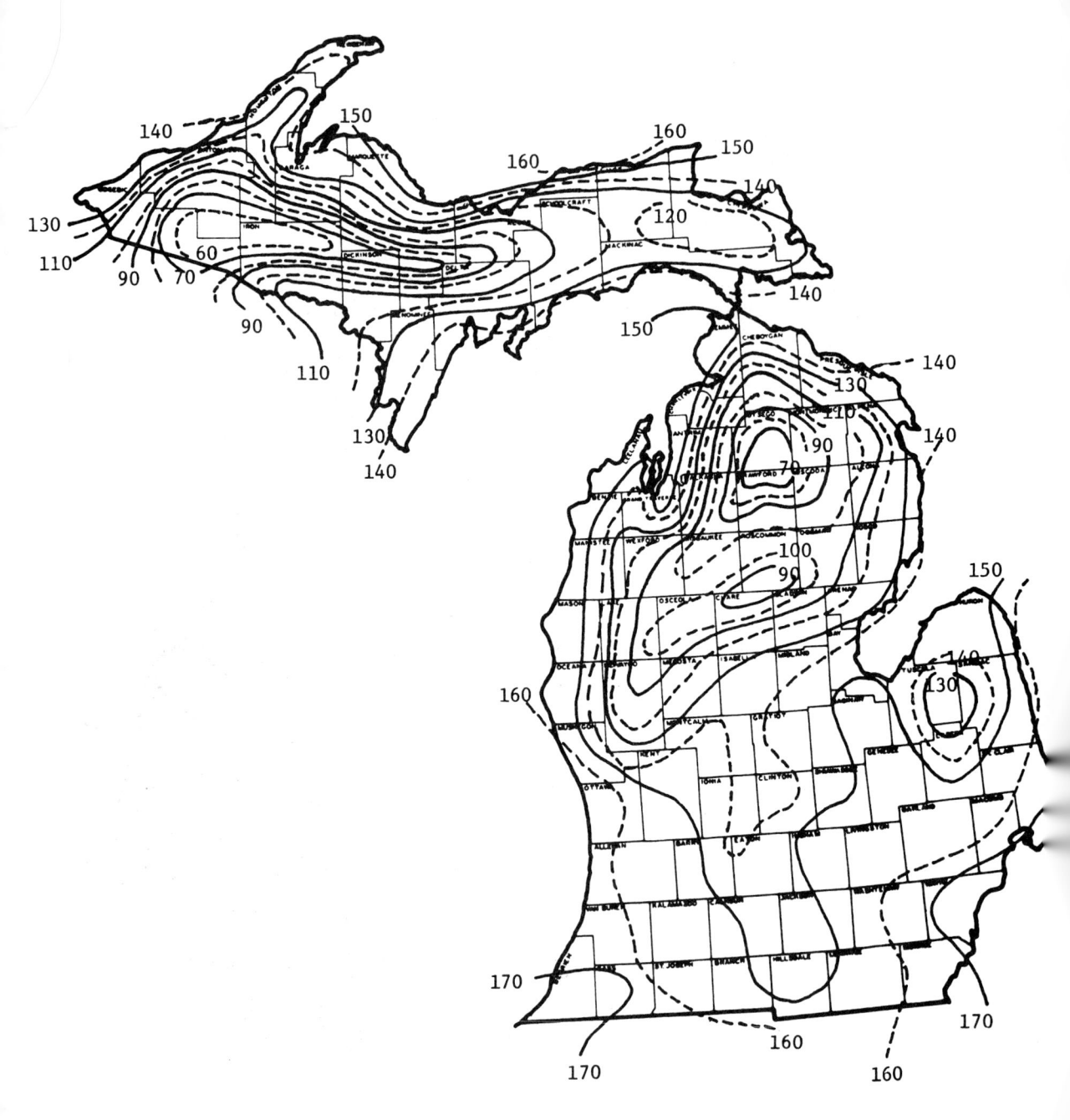

Figure 6.4. Average number of days in growing season based on 1921-1950 data. (Map: Michigan Weather Service.)

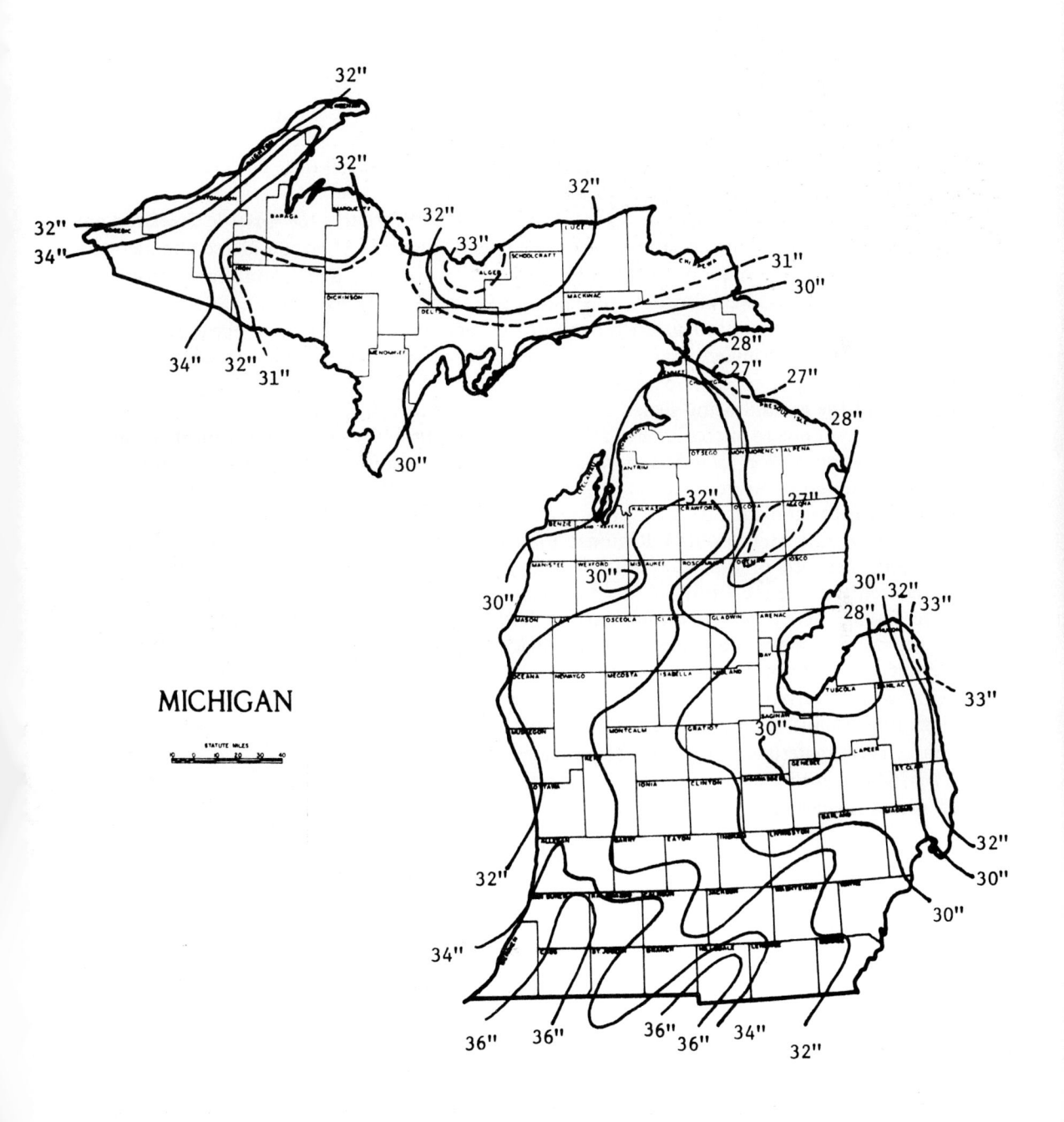

Figure 6.5. Mean annual precipitation in inches 1940-1969. (Map: Michigan Weather Service.)

Exceptional Rainfalls Recorded. Berrien County which has the state's longest growing season also receives the greatest amount of precipitation, 94 cm (37 in) while Cheboygan and Presque Isle counties receive only 69 cm (27 in). Up to the 1930s the maximum deluge of rain in a five-minute storm was at Detroit on August 17, 1926, when 2.2 cm (.86 in) was recorded. Between 1961 and 1967 that record was broken five times with a new established record set at 3 cm (1.20 in) on July 19, 1967. On the same date 12.7 cm (5 in) of rain fell in 90 minutes from a thunderstorm centered over Royal Oak. In the brief storm, over $10 million in losses were suffered due to flooding and storm drainage system failures. The greatest monthly total of rain, 41.1 cm (16.2 in) fell during June, 1883, in Battle Creek.

Illustrating the problem of drought is the fact that in February, 1877, Battle Creek did not receive any recordable precipitation. Further, while Michigan must be considered a moderately well-watered place, it is not uncommon for places in the southern and central Lower Peninsula to have periods of 3-5 weeks without precipitation in the late summer and fall.

Storm Sewer Design and Precipitation. Sewers designed to carry peak waters of a mathematically determined chance occurrence of precipitation and runoff, based on official records, are subject to error because of increased rates of runoff caused by the absorption capacity of the ground being sealed off due to concrete and asphalt. Further, sewer design is subject to error due to microclimate variations which occur in the state's industrial areas caused by the creation of *heat islands* and *dust domes* which can cause isolated increases in convectional precipitation not recorded at official weather stations sometimes miles away at airports or water treatment plants.

The Detroit Metropolitan Regional Planning Commission established in 1960 a supplemental network of rain gauges in Wayne, Oakland, and Macomb counties after it was recognized that the local rainfall pattern might actually be a microclimate variation and that sewer failures were related to the uneven distribution of rainfall. Today that data can be utilized by engineers to more accurately figure needs in designing and replacing sewer systems in the Detroit and suburban areas. Without sufficient networks of rain gauges to determine microweather variations, engineers in urban areas should add a factor which allows for variations from runoff records in the design of storm sewers. This is necessary due to impervious construction materials continually being added to the land and other cultural development. Thus, when figuring storm sewer design plus cost and benefit rates related to 10, 20, and 50 year storm requirements, cultural impacts, as well as natural occurrences should be considered.

Snowfall

Michigan receives annually some of the heaviest snowfalls east of the Rocky Mountains. The maximum average snow accumulation is 457 cm (180 in) in the Keweenaw Uplands (fig. 6.6). The Moraine Highlands of the northwest Lower Peninsula portions of Crawford, Otsego, and Kalkaska counties receive an annual average of over 330 cm (130 in). These officially recorded measurements are a result of *orographic precipitation*. Orographic snowfall, like rain, occurs when: (1) moisture is picked up by the prevailing westerly winds as they pass over Lakes Michigan and Superior, (2) when the air mass is abruptly uplifted by landforms and the moisture is condensed, and (3) the excess falls as snow if the critically low temperature is reached. Orographic precipitation is generally associated with areas of great relief, however, the

Figure 6.6. Mean annual snowfall in inches 1940-1969. (Map: Michigan Weather Service.)

belt of moraines along the former glacial lake beds are high enough to alter snowfall distribution patterns. In the southeastern section of the state, the lowest snowfall averages are found to be about 76 cm (30 in) annually. The snowfall accumulation averages increase to the north and westward into the interior hill lands.

The northern Upper Peninsula is on the margin of the Sub-Arctic Dcf climate region which dominates Alaska and extends south into the middle of Lake Superior and the tip of Isle Royale. As a result of occasional shifts of the Dcf southward, Upper Peninsula communities take pride in recording snow accumulations and in good natured betting as to which town will win the annual "snow sweepstakes." Herman in 1975-76 claimed over 762 cm (300 in) of snow just short of Calumet's record of 802 cm (316 in) claimed in 1950. In a survey taken during the winter of 1972-73 by undergraduates in anthropology and sociology at Michigan Technological University, 301 words or word groups were discovered to be in use to describe local snow and snow conditions. In general, "Tech Toots," MTU students, humorously classify snow as "Copper Country Sunshine."[2]

Impressive Snow Records for Discussion. Occasionally snowstorms with accompanied blowing and drifting paralyze the metropolitan areas. The Detroit region was especially affected on December 1-2, 1974, when 47.5 cm (19 in) of snow fell. The record single snowstorm in the state occurred at Calumet between January 15-20, 1950 when 115.2 cm (46.1 in) accumulated. At Ishpeming and at the Dunbar Forest Station 69 cm (27 in) were recorded in a 24- hour period on October 23, 1929, and March 29, 1947, respectively. While it is either fun or boring to list snowfall records, depending on one's point of view, the economic, transportation, and health consequences of the snow on the state cannot be ignored. Snow removal is big business including employment, equipment, brines, and salts for clearing streets and highways. The cost in deaths from snow removal activities, while not high in comparison to auto deaths, are no less tragic and warrant continued health care warning efforts. Additionally, further research and development of less stressful snow removal methods to replace existing equipment and shovels are necessary.

Severe Local Storms: Tornadoes, Lightning, Ice

Tornadoes. In comparison to the well-known tornado belt states to the southwest, Michigan, with a long-term average of four tornadoes per year, has a low rank. However, since the mid-1950s, Michigan has averaged ten tornadoes per year and in 1973, had 34. Some of the increase can, no doubt, be attributed to better detection, reporting, and more widespread distribution of residents. The cost of tornado damage has also risen significantly in recent years. About 90 percent of the state's tornadoes occur in the densely urbanized southern part of the state between the months of March through July. More significant is Michigan's high death rate as a result of tornadoes. Between 1953-1969, Michigan had 218 deaths from 198 tornadoes, which places the state second in the nation, only surpassed by Texas which had 234 deaths with 1,758 tornadoes (table 6.3). Major tornado losses occurred in 1953 when 116 persons lost their lives in a single tornado which struck Flint and on Palm Sunday, April 11, 1965, when a series of tornadoes laid waste to $51 million worth of property in several southern counties.[3]

2. Eleanor L. Delong, "Tech Toots and Snow Descriptors," *Michigan Academician,* vol. VII no. 4 (Spring 1975), pp. 489-99.
3. Norton Strommen, *Climate in Michigan* (East Lansing: Michigan Cooperative Extension Service, undated), p. 3.

TABLE 6.3
Tornadoes and Loss of Life 1953-1969

State	Number Tornadoes	Number Deaths	Number of Deaths per 10,000 Sq Mi Land
Michigan	198	218	37
Ohio	180	100	24
Illinois	371	108	19
Indiana	377	146	40
Missouri	496	98	14
Kansas	876	131	16
Oklahoma	1,042	121	17
Texas	1,758	234	9

SOURCE: *Tornado*, U. S. Department of Commerce, NOAA, 1975.

Ice Storms. Severe storms involving various forms of ice occur throughout the state with varying degrees of disruption and damage. Hailstorms occur with about 5 percent of the state's 20-40 thunderstorms causing at times local damage to field crops and window glass. Sleet and ice coatings which accumulate on trees and power lines and other exposed surfaces are a constant environmental hazard throughout the state especially if the ice storm is accompanied by wind. The state's most damaging ice storm occurred in March of 1976, when over 600,000 Detroit Edison and Consumers Power customers were without electricity due to breakage of power lines, hundreds of power poles, and trees which blocked access roads. In some places the power outages lasted for more than a week. Oakland County, the Thumb Area, and the Ionia-Greenville areas were most affected. Fruit trees in the Fruit Belt were also broken. Thousands of gallons of milk were lost due to both the lack of electric power and blocked roads preventing milk from being trucked to processing plants. Over 1,000 linemen and tree trimmers from Michigan, Indiana, Illinois, Kentucky, and Ohio were used by Consumers Power Company to restore emergency service. To place this storm in perspective, a severe storm in the Detroit area generally stimulates 5,000 phone calls; during the March, 1976, ice storm, Detroit Edison received 225,000 storm-related calls. A comparable increase in numbers of calls were received by law enforcement agencies.

Lightning Thunderstorms. The hot summer days commonly produce cumulonimbus clouds accompanied by lightning, spewed from electrically charged, towering, and rapidly rising thunderheads. While thundershower rains are beneficial to crops, they also are a danger to humans. National climatological records indicate that lightning accounts for more deaths annually than tornadoes. In Michigan the situation is reversed as the state has more tornado deaths in comparison to the average of 2-3 lightning deaths per year. In the decade 1957-1967, lightning-related injuries to people in Michigan more than quadrupled. Based on records dating since 1897, June and August are the months when most injuries occur, while July has produced the most fatalities. Nearly 60 percent of lightning deaths happen between noon (1200 hr) and 6 p.m. (1800 hr) while 25 percent occurred between 6 p.m. (1800 hr) and midnight (2400 hr). Wayne, Macomb, and Mecosta counties are the top three counties in both lightning injuries and deaths. The time of lightning accidents correlates with the periods of most outdoor activity.

Thus, with increases in leisure time and Daylight Savings Time, the need for education regarding actions to be taken during lightning storms to insure safety will undoubtedly have to be increased to keep Michigan below the national averages.

Great Lakes Storms. When fall comes to the Great Lakes region, nature paints the landscape in gorgeous hues of brilliant leaved trees, which brings delight and pleasure to residents and color tourists alike. For sailors on the Great Lakes the yellow waving leaves warn of disaster, for all too often the result of challenging the Great Lakes in November is a frigid watery grave. Since the earliest days of Great Lakes shipping, severe November storms, a product of the worldwide system of cooling air masses and shifting of the pressure cells, have endangered ships and lives more than clutching ice. In the pioneer era on November 18, 1842, fifty ships were wrecked on the stormy waters of the Great Lakes. In the early twentieth century, eleven ore boats with all hands aboard were lost on November 10, 1913. In 1940, the Armistice Day storm toll was less than twenty-seven years earlier, even though the gale winds were more intense. In the modern era, the SS Carl Bradley sank in Lake Michigan on November 18, 1958, with a loss of thirty-five lives. Eight years later, the SS Daniel J. Morrell was claimed by Lake Huron. On November 10, 1975, one of the newest, largest, and modern ore carriers of the Great Lakes fleet, the SS Edmund Fitzgerald sank near Whitefish Bay due to the raging waves of Lake Superior, with the loss of twenty-eight on board.

The fierceness of Great Lakes storms, including waves sometimes up to 9 m (30 ft), plus other unique conditions of plying the Great Lakes have led to the policy, since the opening of the St. Lawrence Seaway, of requiring licensed Great Lakes captains to temporarily join the crew of ocean vessels which enter the lake waters.

Wind and Solar Energy

For centuries fishermen and farmers have harnessed wind and sun to reduce the toil of their occupations. Until rural electrification in the twentieth century, narrow pyramids of angle iron supported spinning windmills lifting water on tens of thousands of farms across the state. During the transition to electricity, based on nonrenewable resources, especially coal, natural gas, and imported oil, the small technologically less-efficient sun and wind powered systems were eliminated from the landscape. The oil embargo of 1973 stunned and challenged the citizens of Michigan like other Americans into reevaluating potential sources of energy and sites for establishing innovative power plants. Michigan with its high amounts of cloudiness cannot equal sunnier states in potential solar energy use. However, a solar energy research institute in Michigan can be justified based on the university and industrial know-how agglomerated in the southeastern counties, plus the state's ability to mass produce solar energy systems.

The greatest national potentials for wind-powered turbines are found in other states to the south and west. Throughout the United States by 1995, perhaps as much as 20 percent of the nation's energy will be produced by capturing the power of somewhat constant moderate to high winds. In Michigan most weather stations and airports report average wind speeds of about 16 KPH (10 MPH), except for those along Lake Michigan which average about 19 KPH (12 MPH), a speed economically feasible to justify the installation of the large NASA-type wind generator. During the mid-1970s, research done by Michigan State University engineers led to the establishment of pilot wind-electric generation projects at Hart in Oceana County and at the Ludington Pump-Storage Electric Facility.

Michigan Meteorites

One of the most intriguing physical phenomena which occasionally occurs in Michigan is the passing or falling of a meteorite. Witnesses to the passing of a meteor are treated to a brilliant fireball of yellow or orange which can even be traced in the daylight sky. People in an area where a meteorite falls experience only a flash of light and a tremendous booming sound. The three most common meteorites found are: (1) iron or *siderites,* composed chiefly of iron-nickel alloys, (2) stones or *aerolites,* composed mostly of ferromagnesian silicate minerals, and (3) stony-irons, *siderolites,* composed of metal and stone materials. Of the three types, aerolites are by far the most common. Since 1883 eight meteorite falls have been documented in Michigan: Grand Rapids, 1883; Allegan and Iron River, 1889; Reed City, 1895; Rose City, 1921; Seneca, 1923; and Kalkaska, 1947. Star Siding and Star Creek, east of Shingleton, Alger County, probably were named for a "fallen star," however, the large flattened piece of metal displayed for several years in the community was identified by Von Del Chamberlain, astronomer of the Abrams Planetarium at Michigan State University, as a piece of slag. Doubtless, there are other real meteorites in Michigan which have been found. They are potentially of great scientific value and should be brought to the attention of professional astronomers.[4]

Michigan's Soil

Deep abiding love for a homeland has often been expressed by a person literally kneeling and kissing the soil upon returning home from a harrowing experience. With millions of gardeners in the United States, the attachment to the soil has remained compelling even with the development of an urbanized citizenry. While the dependency of agriculture on soil is obvious, the successful operation of much of our technologically advanced society is also inseparably tied to the basic knowledge of soils. Commonplace highways, sidewalks, water-septic systems, building foundations, and power poles are all dependent for smooth operation on the soil in which they are installed. Even though the dependence of humans on soil has not diminished, its misuse, destruction, and the ignorance concerning it may be at its peak in the state.

After four decades of efforts by the Soil Conservation Service (SCS) and cooperating landowners to diffuse the beneficial practices of soil management including cover cropping, contour plowing, minimum tillage, no till, and windbreak plantations, continued educational efforts are still necessary to reduce soil losses. At construction sites the need to minimize vegetation removal and maximize its reestablishment to thwart soil erosion is just as important as in agriculture. Keeping soil losses at development sites to a minimum also helps to prevent the clogging of public sewers and waterways. Preparation of Environmental Impact Statements (EIS) for highway and other construction projects is a promising step toward reducing the tons of soil loss. However, the use of EIS's is too recent to evaluate their contribution to soil protection.

Soil and Its Classification

Soil is the collection of natural elements either organic, inorganic, gas, or chemical in the earth's crust which supports the growing of vegetation. The cross section or profile of a soil is

---

4. Von Del Chamberlain, *Meteorites of Michigan,* Geological Survey Bulletin No. 5 (1968), pp. 1-42.

used for classification based on various characteristics, i.e., texture, structure, thickness, horizon color, and chemical composition. For convenience, soil scientists label the major horizons with capital letters as they occur beneath soil surface from A to D. "A" horizon includes the surface layers to which organic matter has been added by plants plus fine mineral particles and soluble materials moving down through the layer by water action. The "B" or subsoil horizon includes the layers in which some of the fine particles and some of the less soluble materials have been deposited by percolating water. The "C" horizon is slightly weathered to unaltered material beneath the subsoil. "D" horizon is bedrock material. Most Michigan soils are classified as *transported soils* as a result of being carried to their place of deposition.

Characteristics of Poor Drainage. "A" and "B" horizons appearing gray or splotched with gray flecks have been mottled by moisture and indicate poor drainage plus a lack of aeration. Such soils are generally unsuited for installation of private septic systems or require specially designed systems to make them work safely. Poor drainage has always been a factor to be contended with by Michigan farmers, but increasingly mottled soil has had to be dealt with by homeowners beyond urban sewer systems, as well as recreational homeowners and health department personnel who issue the permits for private sanitary systems. Most prospective landowners in Michigan would benefit both their later peace of mind and pocketbooks if they would seek assistance from qualified soil scientists prior to land purchase and development. Local health departments, agricultural agencies, and engineers can provide assistance to laymen in evaluating soils.

Basic Soil Knowledge for Nonprofessionals. The diversity of specialized qualities needed in soils for various uses has led to the development of several classification systems. The lack of uniformity in soil classification systems has thwarted the sharing of soils research knowledge by scientists throughout the world and between fields of specialization. Additionally, soils education for the urbanizing layman has also been slowed.

Two systems of soil classification are generally used by Michigan engineers. Highway engineers use a system approved by the American Association of State Highway Officials (AASHO) while most other engineers use the *unified system* adopted by the U.S. Army Corps of Engineers. Both systems differ from the classification system used by the United States Department of Agriculture that is based on the percentage of sand, silt, and clay-sized particles in soil texture. The AASHO soil classification system is divided into seven principal groups with twenty quality divisions based on the performance of soil material in the field according to gradation, liquid limit, and plasticity index. A-1 consists of gravelly soils that have high bearing strength while A-7 soils are clayey, have low strength when wet, and are poorest for subgrade. In the unified system, soils are identified according to performance as a construction material, their plasticity, and texture: (1) coarse-grained, (2) fine-grained, and (3) highly organic groups.

Soil Types and Causes of Differences. Soils in general acquire their distinct qualities from six natural factors: climate, vegetation, parent material, slope, drainage, and time. In the most common world regionalization of soils, Michigan soils are classified in the: (1) podzol, (2) gray-brown podzolic, and (3) mixed organic-bog soils groups which are concentrated in north Eurasia, New England, and the Great Lakes Regions (fig. 6.7).[5]

---

5. *Goode's World Atlas,* 14th ed. (Chicago: Rand McNally & Co., 1974), pp. 20-21.

Figure 6.7. General soil regions of Michigan and limits of white pine, beech vegetation. (Map: Whiteside, Schneider and Cook, *Soils of Michigan,* Michigan State University after J.O. Veach.)

The word *podzol* is Russian in origin and means "ash soil." It is a soil which tends towards acidity and is developed under forested conditions. As a group, the *gray-brown soils* are among the most productive soils in the world for agriculture. They are slightly acidic and lacking somewhat in nutrients, particularly phosphorous, but respond rapidly to soil improvement practices. Plowing under green legumes has proven especially helpful to agricultural yields. In comparison to the considerably less productive, more acidic true podzol to the north, the gray-brown podzols are somewhat more conducive to erosion on cultivated slopes. The northern podzols developed under coniferous vegetation with long winters and are generally poorly suited for agriculture due to their nutrient deficiencies. However, acid fruits, such as most species of berries, garden vegetables, potatoes, and other root crops, do well especially with the addition of fertilizer, liming, and more intensive labor.

In unraveling Michigan's complexity of soils, forty-one types of agricultural soils have been identified. Today their spatial patterns are being reevaluated with the use of air photo interpretation in addition to field borings. The modern post-World War II county soil maps being slowly and painstakingly produced, provide an excellent source of information for landowners, laymen, and community commissions on the management and use of the state's valuable soil resources (fig. 6.8).

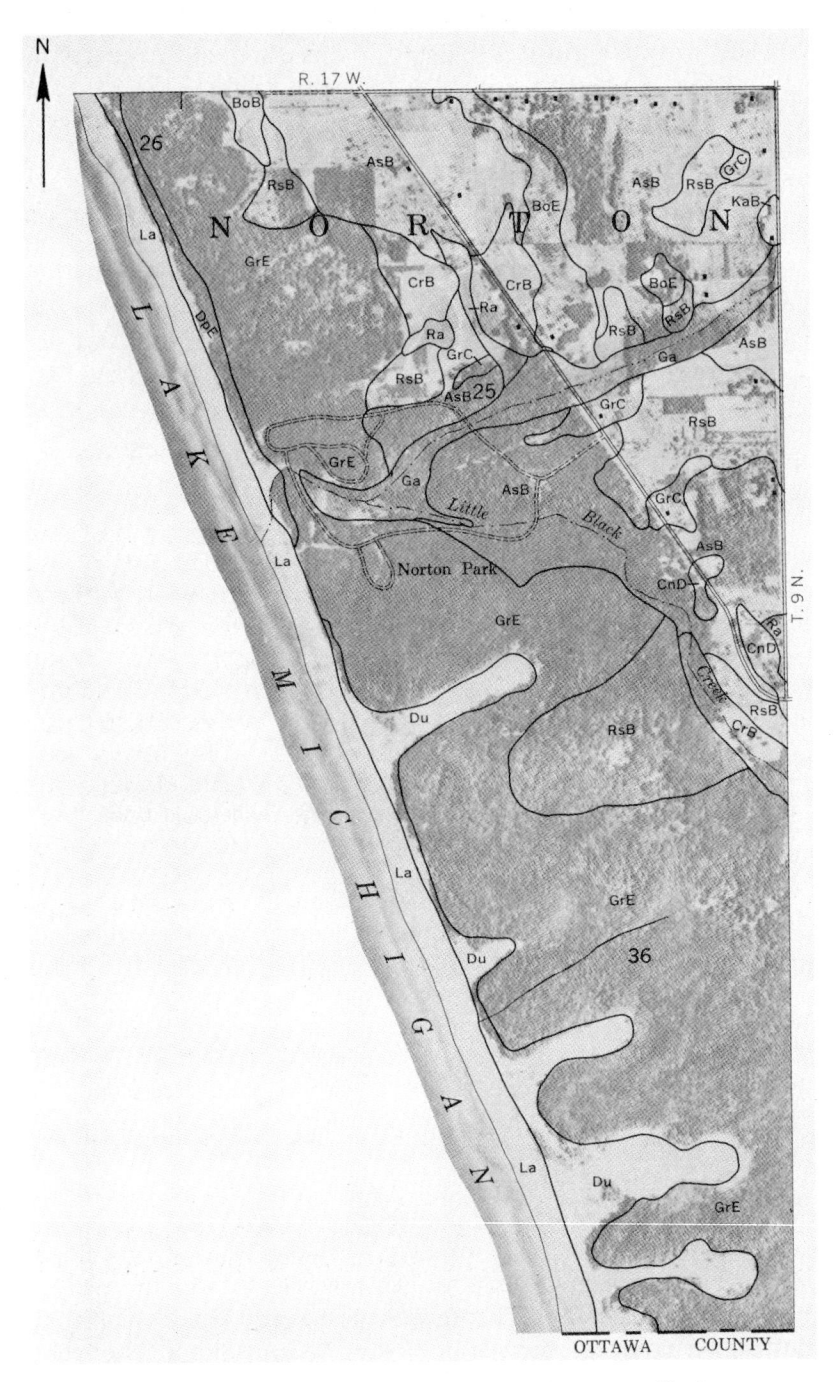

Figure 6.8. Modern soil survey map, Norton Township, Muskegon County. (U.S. Department of Agriculture.)

Michigan's Forests, Logging, and Wood Products Industry

The centuries of occupance by Indians, French, British, and early American frontiersmen, left basically untouched a magnificent virgin climax forest of decidious and coniferous trees whose size and variety were awesome. Interrupting the forest stronghold were more than a score of large grassland prairies and oak openings which appeared as far north as Newaygo County, but were concentrated in the southwestern counties of Berrien, Cass, St. Joseph, Branch, Kalamazoo, Calhoun, Barry, and Eaton. The edges of these openings whose grassland appeared to pioneers as a wavy sea, and dotted with islands of burr oaks and other hardwoods, frequently became the most densely populated area on the rural frontier. The edges of the openings and prairies were an advantage to the early settlers in gaining land already cleared of trees, plus having a forest readily at hand to satisfy their demand for wood. By avoiding thick forested stands of trees which required hours of toil to clear, crops could be immediately established. Hay marshes and former Indian farmland also had an early attraction because of their natural supply of fodder and a cleared space for immediate planting.

Nineteenth Century Perception of the Environment

The American pioneer perception and governmental policy relating to the forests of Michigan were that the forest should be cleared and the land used extensively for farming. Trees, of course, then became of secondary importance to cleared land especially after the necessary farm buildings were constructed. With such a perception operating, the sawing, girdling, chopping, grubbing, and burning of the southern hardwood deciduous forest commenced on a large scale and with the consciences of the pioneer clear. Unlike northern Michigan which developed an organized system of timber harvest and outside marketing, commercial lumbering failed to materialize in southern Michigan because of the basic interest in quickly establishing a self-sufficient pioneer farm settlement pattern. However, in a pioneer, farm-oriented society, wood still played an important role in meeting needs.

Each species of trees had its specialized uses for housing, barns, fences, furniture, utensils, tools, wheels, wagons, dams, bridges, roadways, and industry. To insure a continued supply of wood for fire maintenance and new items, small woodlots isolated near the rear of the farms or on poorly drained low quality land, were left uncleared. Frequently, these woodlots had their regenerative capabilities stifled by livestock pasturage which eliminated shoots of trees, leaving weakened homogeneous stands of mature trees. In spite of questionable pioneer forest management practices, it is in these woodlots plus in parks and state forests where the remnant natural forest survives in southern Michigan. In traveling through the southern Michigan countryside one can still gain a glimmer of the original forest-soil-topography associations such as: oak-hickory-walnut association on well-drained land, maple-beech-birch, and elm-ash-cottonwood associations on the more moist soils.

After a century and a half of placing woodlot and forest management in a secondary role in the southern Michigan farm-industry economy, coupled with the recent increase of non-farmer woodland ownership, professional foresters in the early 1960s concluded that:

> Poor cutting practices are probably a more critical feature of forest management in southern Michigan than urbanization . . . Unless many forest landowners can be motivated to adopt better forestry practices, timber output in the study area is unlikely to increase.[6]

6. Con H. Schallau, *Small Forest Ownership in the Urban Fringe Area of Michigan,* Lake States Forest Experiment Station Paper No. 103 (August 1963), pp. 15-16.

The obvious result of the years of waste and ignorant forest management practices is increased costs for today's wood products' users both in dollars and energy for transportation.

Exploitation of the Northern Pine and Hardwood Forest

The mid-nineteenth century witnessed the birth of Michigan's nationally prominent logging era. Michigan's logging fame came as a result of the depletion of the New England forests coupled with demands by industrialists, woodworking manufacturers, and city dwellers for lumber. Starting in the Saginaw Valley in the 1830s and progressing river by river, the white pine and later mixed hardwoods were rapidly stripped from the land. The peak of cutting was reached in the 1890s. By 1910 the cooling rainment of trees was gone, fires had charred the mammoth stumps, and fauna had been driven from their forest and river homes. Additionally, depression faced the boom lumber communities which established themselves to the "inexhaustible timber" or hoped-for success of farming.

The historic removal of trees from Michigan's forest land did not require the efforts of the romantic and legendary giant Paul Bunyan—what was necessary and did occur, was the arming with axes and saws of thousands of short, slightly-built men often desperate for money. This army of chore boys, cutters, teamsters, blacksmiths, cooks, top loaders, skidders, and river hogs, led by a cadre of lumber barons, cruisers with an eye for a calculator, foremen, clerks, scalers, and barn bosses, were more than equal to their forest adversary, the tree. In the century 1840-1940, 165 billion board feet of white pine were removed. Temporary logging camps were successively built, moved, or abandoned leaving relics of: smokey dim-lit bunkhouses, dining halls, offices, and barns. A few of these former campsites have survived and become small towns. At the Hartwick Pines State Forest, a typical logging camp has been reconstructed to help preserve the exuberance of the time. The camps were occupied by males only, whose rousting voices were mixed with the snort of oxen, whinny of horses, incessant clangs, whacks and buzzes, and creaks of chains, axes, saws, big wheels, and the logging railroad. The work in the woods lasted for six winter months which dovetailed nicely for young farmers trying to make capital improvements on their small farms. For others, it was a welcome retreat from the normal society which included women.

Health Care for the Woodsmen. The work was not only accident-prone, it was also a threat to health as men labored wet with sweat and snow from dawn to dark. By the 1870s, less romantic but still heroic, women of the Sisters of Mercy began their extension of organized health care to the lumberjacks. St. Mary's Hospitals and Training Schools were eventually established in several logging centers such as at East Saginaw, 1872, Bay City, 1878, and Big Rapids, 1879. These were then opened to those woodsmen and others paying $5 for an annual hospitalization certificate which provided board, medicine, doctor's fee, and care by the Sisters. In receiving patients, it was claimed, no distinction would be made regarding creed or country.

The National Demand for Timber

Clear cutting of the Michigan forests also served to meet the great national demands for wood. By 1875, it was estimated by General Brisbin of the U.S. Army Intelligence that 25 million acres of trees were used in fencing the nation's farms at a cost of $1.8 billion which represents a higher price for fencing than the original purchase price of the pioneer land.

Railroad ties for 71,000 miles of railroad, which had to be replaced every seven years in the nineteenth century, required 40,000 acres of mature trees annually. In 1871 the city of Chicago required 10,000 acres of virgin trees for residential firewood.

To feed the demand for wood, the lumbermen in the 1870s cleared yearly approximately 13,200 ha (33,000 ac) of forest and doubled that rate in the peak years of the 1890s. In the process, Michigan rose to the top in billions of board feet of timber cut. The production of 21 million board feet of white pine in 1969 may appear to be a large figure, however, it is dwarfed by the yield of over 4 billion board feet eighty years earlier. Slashings from logged trees and fires went together like fleas and dogs. Fires, surprisingly perhaps, were frequently thought of as an advantage which would further "clear the land" and be a benefit to the farmers whom it was assumed would follow the ax with their plow.

Logging Decline of the Twentieth Century. By the end of the first decade of the twentieth century the logging boom was over. Also gone were jobs for 100,000 men who would have to find other jobs and places to work. Silence replaced the ring of the ax, whine of the millsaws, bellows of men on their photographed brag loads, the crash of logs at the rollaways, the excited voices of men in brawdy houses and taverns. Finally the silence gave way to the tramp of feet boarding a train whose chugging would carry it into the sunset of forests still further west. Small communities which had sprung up along rivers and railroad lines to serve the activities of the men in the woods, soon found that agriculture could not support the local economy. Ghost towns began to dot the landscape and county government's tax delinquency lists lengthened as farmers abandoned their land rather than incur more losses in a disarrayed economy. In short, hardships replaced hard labor within the northern pinery.

Post-White Pine Era Transition. After the clearing of the large virgin white pine, lumbermen shifted to hardwoods which were mixed with the pines or stood in groves due to local natural conditions. Elm, basswood, beech, and maple became prized furniture and veneer woods. The Bird's Eye Maple Veneer Works at Escanaba grew to national importance. Cedar, tamarack, and hemlock, at first passed over, later assumed importance. For a short time the cedar swamps in the eastern Upper Peninsula became the base point for figuring freight cost shipment of cedar posts. Pines looking like toothpicks in comparison to the former giants which grew to 1.8 m (6 ft) in diameter were hauled to mills if they could produce a 5 × 10 cm (2 × 4 in) board. The harvesting of the few remaining accessible virgin trees and dredging of logs stuck in river bottoms and banks, supplied furniture plants for a few more years in: Escanaba, Cadillac, Traverse City, Kenton, Onaway, Ludington, Manistee, Alpena, and Grand Rapids. Later some of the plants diversified their sources of supply as they were no longer able to rely on Michigan timber.

The Beginnings of Renewal of the Forests

As early as 1887 Bela Hubbard and people in government foresaw the eventual high cost of the rampaging logging practices and raised the warning in regard to what was happening to the land and people plus voiced a plea to plan for the future:

> . . . the next cycle of ten years will find little white pine timber left in the state . . . the destruction by fires seems likely soon to equal all other causes, . . . Wonderful progress indeed, but attended by what waste of this great natural store-house of wealth, and with how little provision of the future![7]

7. Hubbard, *op. cit.*, pp. 375-76.

As the forest clearing continued its boom into the 1890s, the state land policy remained, based on its original two assumptions: (1) that private ownership of the cutover lands was preferable to public ownership, and (2) that practically all the land was potentially suitable for agriculture. As a result of this policy, real estate agents and "land sharks" were provided with an unparalleled opportunity to promote the sale of submarginal property for farming with its short growing season, sandy, droughty podzol soil, and a costly transportation system linking it to the distant markets.

It may seem incredible in light of contemporary knowledge, but to lure unsuspecting people to Roscommon, it was claimed that:

> Roscommon County will grow more and better wheat, oats, rye, speltz, timothy hay, clover seed, beans, field peas, potatoes, cabbage, sugar beets, turnips and rutabagas to the acre than any other county in the state, or in Illinois, Indiana or Ohio.[8]

Property bought by the uninformed, lured by such puffery, soon became listed on the lengthening roll of tax delinquent land.

What to do to ward off and reduce the hardships caused by the loss of the forest and the disruption to the state's largest industry became a focal point of discussion and decision making. This led to the creation of an independent Forestry Commission in 1887, demands for state parks in 1888 by the Michigan State Sportsmen's Association, a Tax Homestead Law in 1893, and a permanent Forestry Commission in 1899. In 1903 the Legislature withdrew from sale "all delinquent state tax, homestead, swamp, and primary school lands" in a few specified townships and placed them under the control of the Forestry Commission. These actions brought a more cognizant and realistic policy based on the partial understanding of the true environmental difficulties of the state's northern lands. Further, the twentieth century land policy allowed for both public and private land ownership in the state which has reduced the problem of tax delinquency.

Contemporary Forestry in Michigan

In the half century following the 1920s forest demise, the healing process of tree growth has noticeably advanced, trees once again bring cooling shade, roots hold soil in place, and in the regenerated forest nearly a million deer roam. The Depression Era Civilian Conservation Corps' planting of millions of seedlings is also beginning to yield its bounty. Sawdust, once burned or dumped into the lakes, as at "Sawdust Beach" near Manistique, is no longer dumped but processed into useful particle board.

In spite of numerous advances in the wise management of the state's forest land, Michigan's contemporary forest industry can be described as important, promising, but still minor in the nation's overall forest production. In area of total *forest land, Michigan ranks twelfth* with 7.7 million ha (19.3 million ac), placing it ahead of both Wisconsin, Minnesota and all other Lake states. In *commercial timber land,* that land capable of producing commercial trees, Michigan ranks fifth with 7.2 million ha (18.8 million ac) or 3.7 percent of the nation's total (table 6.4).

By stating that Michigan moved from ninth to fifth rank in commercial forest land in the United States between 1960-1970, it would be easy to infer and claim that the reforestry of

---

8. Samuel T. Dana, "Resource Problems of Michigan, "Conservation Reprint Series No. 1, Eastern Michigan University (1960), pp. 3-4.

TABLE 6.4
Great Lakes States Commercial Timber Land 1970

State	National Rank	Million Hectares	Million Acres
Michigan	5	7.52	18.8
Minnesota	10	6.72	16.8
Wisconsin	19	5.80	14.5
New York	20	5.76	14.4
Ohio	27	2.56	6.4
Indiana	34	1.52	3.8
Illinois	37	1.44	3.6

SOURCE: U. S. Statistical Abstract 1975, Table 1108, p. 653.

Michigan has been accomplished. However, most disquieting is the fact that between 1962 and 1970 the actual amount of commercial forest land in the state declined by 128,400 ha (321,000 ac) and continues to decline. The loss of commercial forest land, many foresters project, will continue for several decades. In comparison to the loss of commercial forest land, throughout the midtwentieth century the amount of immature timber growth has surpassed timber harvest. Forest inventories and evaluations still point to a significant opportunity to increase the forest capacity as less than 50 percent of the identified commercial forest land is fully stocked (fig. 6.9).

Contemporary Ownership of Commercial Forest Land. Educators, mass media, foresters, and businessmen share the efforts in determining and in diffusing knowledge concerning the most beneficial forest management practices based on sound economic, ecologic, and ethical principles. Ultimately, decisions by individual landowners hold the key to what will happen to Michigan's remaining forest land. An increasingly fragmented ownership pattern dominates the commercial forest lands today, unlike any ownership pattern in the past. Since World War II, forest parcels have become smaller as a result of increased private recreational landholding, population increase, and highway construction bisecting woodlots.

Farmers, recreationalists, and other nonindustrial private owners hold the majority of the state's commercial forest land (table 6.5). Michigan's twenty-nine state forests, three national forests, and forest industries combined, have less area in commercial forests than the small private holdings.

TABLE 6.5
Ownership of Michigan Commercial Forestland

Class of Ownership	Percent of Ownership
Private (nonindustrial)	54
State of Michigan	20
United States	13
Commercial Forest Industries	12
County-Schools-Municipal	1

SOURCE: *Forests for the Future,* DNR, March 1974, p. 14.

MAJOR FOREST TYPES - MICHIGAN

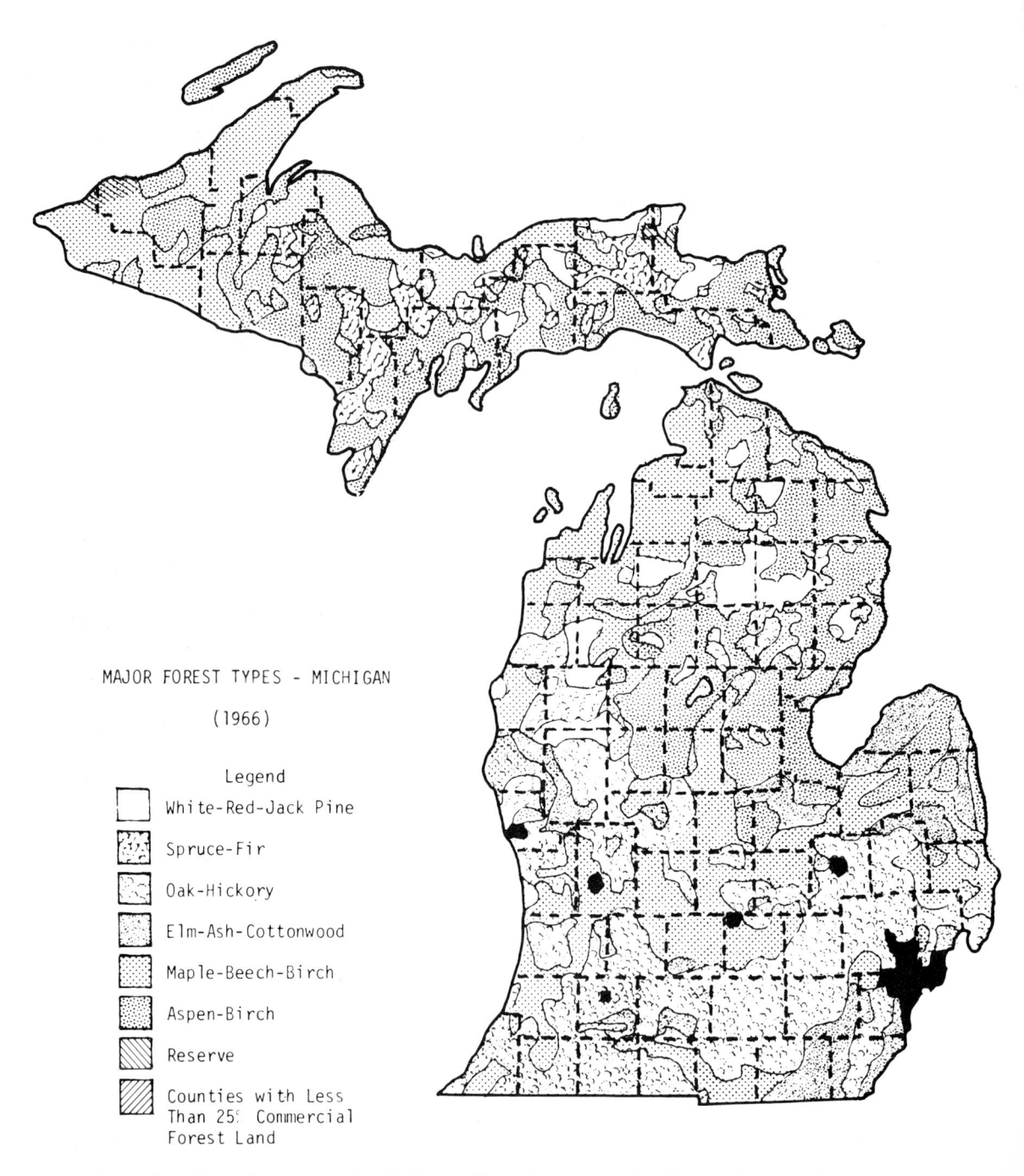

(1966)

Legend
- White-Red-Jack Pine
- Spruce-Fir
- Oak-Hickory
- Elm-Ash-Cottonwood
- Maple-Beech-Birch
- Aspen-Birch
- Reserve
- Counties with Less Than 25% Commercial Forest Land

Figure 6.9. Major forest types in Michigan. (Map: *Forests for the Future,* Michigan Department of Natural Resources.)

Multiple-Use Forest Management. During the past several decades the multiple-use concept of management has dominated the forest land recovery era. In these years state forest land perhaps has been best known to the public for its recreational opportunities for camping, hiking, hunting, fishing, trail bike riding, nature study, snowmobile riding, and other outdoor activities. As forest re-stocking has progressed with replantings and natural seeding, the demand for more recreational space in the state forests has also increased and will undoubtedly continue to do so. From these indicators a more intense conflict between those desiring to designate portions of the state forest for primary forest production and those who desire to use the same land for other public use, thus decreasing forest production capability, can be anticipated. Further debatable is the question of the sale of state land to private interests.

Wood Products and Population. Basing increased demand for wood products on expected population increases is a traditional evaluation factor. Today because of the changing characteristics of American families, additional sociological factors should be considered for the projection of timber needs. The trends toward more single heads of households either through divorce or remaining unmarried, tends to force the duplication of basic housing needs which translates into more wood products. Similarly, second homes also consume large quantities of wood. The role of petrochemicals is also a complex one to evaluate as trends cross. On one hand, petrochemical plastics are replacing woods, while on the other hand, the limited supply of oil stimulates the use of wood as a substitute for oil. The need to find efficient and economically sound methods to expand the recycling of wood products is necessary and will probably increase as tree resources become more valuable.

Industrial Wood Production. As Michigan entered the decade of the seventies, 50,000 workers who possessed a variety of skills from cutters to high quality furniture makers were occupied in the wood products industry. Rough logs, valued at $56 million were delivered by nearly 500 standing timber cutting firms to 390 primary wood product plants, 300 saw mills, and 12 veneer log mills. The pulp, lumber, and veneers produced by these operators added a value of $187 million to the rough logs. In contrast, the value added by secondary production of wood products into paper, boards, wood furniture, and other finished wood products is $386 million. The economic importance of Michigan's forest industry can be further illustrated by the fact that only 4.4 percent of all manufacturing employment is in the wood products industry, but it generates 5.3 percent of the value added by manufacturing.

Species of Trees Timbered. In the 1970s it is estimated that about 175 million cubic feet of industrial roundwood is cut yearly. Over three-fourths of these logs are from deciduous hardwood species, especially aspen which is used as a pulpwood (table 6.6). Other hardwoods such as maple, beech, oak, and birch are utilized in furniture, veneers, and industrial pallets. Of the total annual production of timber in Michigan, 54 percent goes into pulp, 36 percent is saw logs, 2 percent is used in veneers and 8 percent is used in other processes. By 1995 it is projected that pulpwood production will increase to 70 percent of the total harvest of trees. At the same time employment in timber harvesting is expected to drop from 9,300 man years to 4,800 man years between 1965 and 1995 as more efficient cutting methods are implemented. On the other hand, forest management opportunity should increase. During the 1970s, Mecosta, Osceola, Isabella, and Otsego counties have participated in the expansion of forest industries based on second growth timber. Traditional wood processing centers such as Kalamazoo (paper), Grand Rapids (furniture), Manistee (board), and Escanaba (veneers), have continued operations throughout the twentieth century by adapting to the changing characteristics of Michigan's forest.

To help insure a steady supply of timber to meet the over 198 kg (440 lb) and 18 sq m (200 bd ft) of lumber per capita used annually which is expected to increase by seventy or more percent by 2000 A.D., Michigan forest products industries have encouraged individual participation in the privately sponsored American Tree Farm System (ATFS). In 1949 Michigan became the 24th state to join the ATFS in which a tree farm is defined as: an area of *privately owned, tax-paying* forest land dedicated to the growing of *repeated* forest crops for commercial purposes. By the mid-1960s, Michigan had 1,000 participants, was the tenth ranked state in the nation and fourteenth ranked in numbers of acres certified as a tree farm with 520,000 ha (1.3 million ac). Most private tree farms are located in the northern Lower Peninsula, however, the largest acreages are located in the Upper Peninsula with one tree farm containing 114,800 ha (287,920 ac).

TABLE 6.6
Major Pulpwood Producing Counties by Peninsula 1969

Upper	1000 Standard Cords	Lower	1000 Standard Cords
Menominee	83	Lake	69
Iron	76	Alcona	49
Dickinson	64	Oscoda	43
Delta	63	Clare	37
Marquette	61	Manistee	36
Baraga	54	Montmorency	35

SOURCE: *Timber Production Now and 1985,* Project 80 & 5, MSU Cooperative Extension Service, Table A-5.

Specialty Forest Products

Maple syrup, with its delightful taste, and Christmas trees, with their promise of peace on earth, contribute to mankind's enjoyment of life. In the quest to satisfy the first of these desires, over 2,000 commercial and noncommercial producers carry on the early springtime tradition of maple syruping borrowed from the native Indians. What the value of the mature "sugar bush" trees is has not been estimated, however, 323,000 liters (85,000 gallons) of syrup are annually produced with ever-increasing retail prices. Twenty-five counties share in the production which represents 5.5 percent of the nation's total. Vermontville, in Eaton County, and Nashville, in Barry County, both have New England heritages and have been able to further share the spirit of "sugaring" with their annual festivals.

Christmas trees grown in Michigan have historically been an important segment of the national market. In 1955, Michigan's share of the market amounted to 6 percent. By the 1970s, the state's share of the market had nearly tripled. Approximately 5.25 million Christmas trees were produced in 1971, half were used in Michigan and over 1.5 million were certified for shipment west of the Mississippi River, the remainder being marketed east of the Mississippi River.

Annual production is expected to decline somewhat during the 1970s but expand to 9 million trees in 1985 as seed stocks, planting, and market expectation are brought into balance with artificial tree competition. Christmas tree plantations are found in most counties north of the Bay-Muskegon Line, Luce County in the Upper Peninsula, and in several southwestern counties. Scotch pine, spruce, and balsam fir represent the most cultivated species.

In this chapter dealing with Michigan vegetation, the emphasis has been placed on the cutting and renewal of the once forested lands of Michigan, and the economic importance of wise management of the forest resources. In placing emphasis on the state's trees, the complex of Michigan's less economically important wildflowers and other plant life has not been presented. This does not imply that they are less important in the environment. Unmeasurable, but certainly of value, are their colors, soil-holding capabilities, and aesthetic beauty which help to make Michigan an attractive place to live and tour. Questions on how to better utilize wildflowers need to be raised, such as, can they replace roadside grasses which have to be mowed, and can they be introduced to stabilize highway cuts? As mushroom collecting has helped to stimulate the economy of hamlets in the Manistee National Forest, such as Mesick, perhaps foraging for other less popularized forms of food will increase bringing both enjoyment and natural foods to the tables of state residents from the diversity within Michigan vegetation complexes.

Photo Essay B

THE NATURAL ENVIRONMENT OF MICHIGAN

B-1   The apple blossom, Michigan's official state flower.

B-2
- a. Top left: Twin whitetail fawns
- b. Top right: Whitetail buck in velvet
- c. Lower left: Black bear cub
- d. Lower right: Elk, Pigeon River State Forest

B-3   Forest Lakes area of Grand Traverse County, T26N-R10W. (Photo: Traverse City Area Chamber of Commerce)

B-4   Lumbermen's Memorial northwest of East Tawas.

B-5   Northern mixed forest of broadleaf and needleleaf trees near Cliff, Keweenaw County along US-41.

B-6   Lake of the Clouds, Ontonagon County. A late Precambrian lava flow of amygdalioidal basalt formed the top layer of exposed rock.

B-7   Miner's Castle, Pictured Rocks National Lakeshore, formed out of late Cambrian sandstone by glacial lake wave action.

B-8   Tahquamenon Falls flows over resistant sandstone of Cambrian age.

B-9   Sinkhole in middle Devonian age limestone near Posen, Presque Isle County.

B-10   Grand Marais sand dune south shore of Lake Superior.

B-11   Sleeping Bear Dune near Glen Arbor.

B-12   Silver Lake sand dune.

Unless otherwise indicated, photos courtesy Michigan Travel Commission.

B-1

B-2 a.

b.

B-3

B-4

B-5

B-6

B-7

B-8

B-9

8-10

8-11

12

> "... in a democracy the ideal is never quite reachable; there is always more to be done. The difference between what is and what might be lies in the initiative of citizens who are willing to strive together to create something better."
>
> Takeo Miki, Prime Minister Japan, 1976

Chapter Seven

Population and Settlement

Collectively the people of Michigan are no different than all societies since the beginning of human occupance of the earth who have had to calculate and make judgments on the balance between their population and resources in order to insure survival. In the present-day, religion, scientific knowledge, and technological advancements have not removed the need for a clear understanding of Michigan's population and settlement patterns in relationship to the world. Due to the state's rate of population increase and rate of resource depletion of the last century, there is an intense need for mass knowledge of the state's population structure in order for its citizens to make rational individual and democratic decisions.

The goal of this chapter is to describe, analyze, and place in time and space relationship the complexity of Michigan's population structure. In accomplishing this goal the following factors will be briefly presented: population distribution and composition (ethnic, racial, sex), historic and contemporary population growth, and pioneer settlement patterns.

Growth and Composition of Michigan's Contemporary Population

Starting with Michigan Territory's first census in 1810, the state's human resource base grew from 4,767 to one million in the late 1860s and reached over 9.2 million in 1975 (table 7.1). In the sixteen decades since the opening of the land office, settlement by the state's residents diffused from the tiny communities huddling near the shadows of the Upper and Lower Straits' forts to 1,350 communities named on the official state highway map. Three-fourths of the state's inhabitants are agglomerated in eleven Standard Metropolitan Statistical Areas (SMSA) which include twenty-one cities over 50,000 population (fig. 7.1 and table 7.2).[1] According to the Michigan Department of Commerce Special Populations Office, 11 percent of the state's

---

1. An SMSA is an area of one or more counties which has a central city or a spatially close combination of cities totaling 50,000 or more which function together socially and economically.

people are physically disabled to the extent that traditional building designs cause mobility difficulties. By the mid-1970s there were 2,322,000 rural residents living in communities of less than 2,500, on farms, or in other rural nonfarm settings.

TABLE 7.1
Michigan Population Growth and Daily
Increase by Decade 1810-1975

Date	Michigan Population	Average Daily Increase by Decade
1810	4,767	
1820	8,896	1
1830	31,639	6
1840	212,267	49
1850	397,654	50
1860	749,113	96
1870	1,184,059	119
1880	1,636,937	124
1890	2,093,890	125
1900	2,420,982	89
1910	2,810,173	106
1920	3,668,412	235
1930	4,842,325	321
1940	5,256,106	113
1950	6,371,766	305
1960	7,823,194	397
1970	8,875,083	288
1975	9,270,000 est.	216 est.

SOURCE: *Michigan Statistical Abstract*, 10th ed., 1974, p. 7.

TABLE 7.2
Michigan Nonregional Center Cities with 50,000 People 1970

Rank	Region Number	City	Population
4	1	Warren	179,260
6	1	Livonia	110,109
7	1	Dearborn	104,199
8	1	Ann Arbor	99,797
10	1	St. Clair Shores	88,093
11	1	Westland	86,749
13	1	Royal Oak	85,499
14	1	Pontiac	85,279
15	1	Dearborn Heights	80,069
16	1	Taylor	70,020
17	1	Southfield	63,285
18	1	Sterling Heights	61,365
19	1	Roseville	60,529
20	8	Wyoming	56,560
21	1	Lincoln Park	52,984

SOURCE: U.S. Census 1970, Table 24, pp. 24-102 to 24-104.

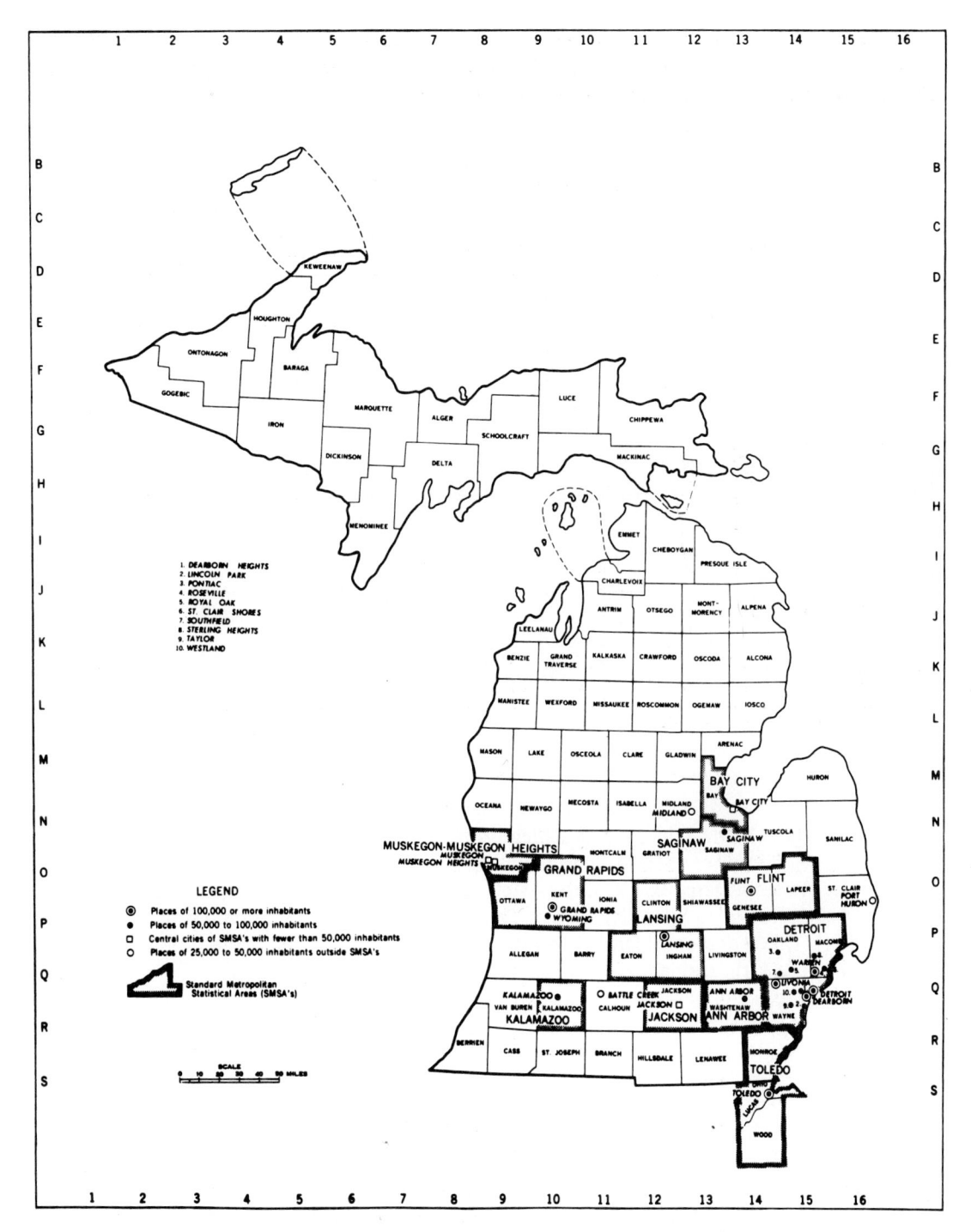

Figure 7.1. Michigan Standard Metropolitan Statistical Areas 1970. (Map: U.S. Census Bureau.)

Michigan's Birth Rate, Death Rate, Natural Increase

The initial worldwide skyrocketing increase in human population from 1 to 4 billion coincides with Michigan's rapid increases in population. Michigan pioneer young people readily participated in the economically and socially acceptable practice of producing large families to help make small labor intensive family farms profitable and offset the losses due to infant mortality. Following Genesis 1:28 immigrants were also welcomed to fill the land and take dominion over its fish and fowl as they fled more densely populated and oppressed regions of the world. Michigan's physicians and scientists joined others in working earnestly to overcome the ravages of a host of diseases and death, and to prolong life. By 1975 the world's density of population had climbed to 170 per sq km (65 per sq mi), while Michigan's density reached 250 per sq km (96 per sq mi), including the Great Lakes water area (table 7.3).

TABLE 7.3
Selected Densities of Population in Comparison to Michigan* 1974

Density Lower than Michigan	Sq Km	Sq Mi	Density Higher than Michigan	Sq Km	Sq Mi
Ontario	49	19	Cambodia	281	108
Chile	83	32	Ireland	291	112
Finland	94	36	Burma	294	113
Sweden	122	47	Asia	346	133
USA	148	57	Europe	437	168
Mexico	190	73	China	577	222
Malaysia	229	88	France	650	250
Egypt	242	93	E-W Germany	1,492	574
Morocco	250	96	Netherlands	2,233	859

*Michigan Density 250 sq km (96 sq mi).
SOURCE: *Goodes World Atlas,* 14th ed., 1974, p. 229.

Birth Rate. During the 1970s Michigan's birth rate (BR) declined at nearly the same rate as the nation's, however, its imbalance in comparison to the death rate still results in a substantial number of new citizens. By 1975, the state's lowest annual BR of 14-15 per 1,000 of the total population resulted in 137,414 live births. This was the lowest actual number of infants born since 1945 (111,557) and considerably less than 1957 when a birth rate of 28 produced a "baby boom" of 208,488, the single highest birth year in the state's history.

Death Rate. For several years Michigan's death rate (DR) has slowly declined and fluctuated at about 8-9 deaths per thousand of the total population resulting in about 78,000 deaths yearly and a significant funeral business enterprise. Although Michigan has what is classified as an effective medical care system, several nations have lower death rates than Michigan including: Costa Rica 6; Israel, Japan, Cuba, and Puerto Rico 7; plus Poland and Spain 8.5. One factor in further lowering the state DR may be the institution of a more comprehensive statewide health care delivery system.

Death and the Funeral Service Industry. Since the dawn of history, ceremonial burial or cremation has been a part of the ritual of the living to pay final respects to the departed.

Today the funeral service industry has evolved as society's institution to provide for the bereaved at the time of death. The mortuary-cemetery and associate flower businesses are prominent not only within the state's economy, but also as enduring landscape features. Michigan's 2,500 funeral service employees operate 750 mortuaries which serve the families of the over 78,000 which die annually. These funeral services generate receipts of $68 million and payrolls of over $14 million yearly. As an end result of the post-World War II "population explosion" the funeral industry undoubtedly will expand with a "death explosion" in about 2020 A.D. In the post-World War II era as homes became smaller and churches less desired for funerals, private funeral homes were expanded in size and ornateness to accommodate church-like chapels, but still reflect the atmosphere of "home" through their architectural design.

The sale of burial and crematory rights are regulated by the Cemetery Commission of the Department of Commerce. Since the enactment of PA 290 in 1972, the Cemetery Commission has the authority to regulate sale of markers, monuments, and vaults. Vaults made of concrete are frequently required in cemeteries to lower maintenance costs and prevent injury from collapsed grave sites which were common in the wooden outer case era. Within Michigan there are 129 cemeteries licensed by the state and 3,240 cemeteries not required to be licensed such as: municipally owned, church owned, private family owned, abandoned, and nonprofit under 4 ha (10 ac) cemeteries. About 320 cemeteries care for 40 percent of the state's burials. As urban sprawl has engulfed open spaces, cemeteries are increasingly used for many purposes other than their original use including: wildlife observation, hiking, bicycling, and stone rubbing.

Cremation increased from 1,708 to 3,002 in the five years between 1969 and 1974. Undoubtedly, given the increased cost of land and cemetery maintenance, divorce and remarriage rates, plus mobility of modern society, the trend toward cremation will continue. Further, the number of crematories can also be expected to increase (table 7.4).

TABLE 7.4
Crematories Under Regulation of Michigan
Cemetery Commission 1976

Crematory	Place
East Lawn Memory Garden	Okemos
Flint Memorial Park	Mt. Morris
Michigan Memorial Park	Flat Rock
North Shore Memory Garden	Harger Shores
Southern Michigan Crematory	Ann Arbor
Sunrise Memorial Garden	Muskegon
White Chapel Memorial Cemetery	Troy
Evergreen Cemetery	Detroit
Forest Lawn	Detroit
Woodlawn Cemetery	Detroit
Woodmere Cemetery	Detroit
Graceland Memorial Park	Grand Rapids
Rosedale Memorial Park	Grand Rapids
*Pontiac Municipal Cemetery	Pontiac

*Not under state regulation.
SOURCE: State Cemetery Commission, August, 1976.

The "ZPG Myth." Confusion over whether Michigan has attained ZPG can be reduced if the following points are understood: (1) Michigan's population is a distinct entity within the nation and world, but not separate from it, (2) ZPG measured by fertility ratio alone tends to ignore the fact that actual zero growth is at a point where births equal deaths at the same time as immigration equals emigration, (3) population stability in Michigan requires a long-term balance between births-deaths-migration. Because of the present imbalances in births-deaths-migration, the attainment of actual ZPG is several years away. The daily BR-DR imbalance in the state is about 150, resulting in an increase of about 55,600 annually. This increase accompanied with foreign and domestic immigration has resulted in Michigan growing at a higher rate than its adjacent states and the nation in recent years.

Interstate Migration into Michigan. In contrast to the pioneer era of migration to Michigan, modern-day interstate migration is dominated by the three adjacent southern states (table 7.5). Additionally, people from the "Sun Belt States" of California, Florida, and Texas, plus the mid-South have sought employment and the benefits of Michigan's social opportunities in significant numbers. Between 1965 and 1970, an estimate of over 75 persons per day came to reside in Michigan from other parts of the nation. By the mid-1970s due to the post-Vietnam War economic adjustments, the flow decreased significantly and may have reached a point where there was more out than in migration.

TABLE 7.5
Number of Residents in Michigan in 1970
Residing in Another State in 1965

Rank	State	Number	Rank	State	Number
1	Ohio	58,350	7	Pennsylvania	18,036
2	Illinois	50,381	8	Wisconsin	17,801
3	California	40,127	9	Texas	17,486
4	Indiana	36,433	10	Kentucky	16,004
5	New York	23,761	11	Tennessee	15,446
6	Florida	18,880	12	Alabama	15,439

SOURCE: *Michigan Statistical Abstract,* 10th ed., 1974, pp. 75-76.

There is no doubt that the 1970s have witnessed a slowing in the *rate of increase;* nevertheless, the *actual increase* in numbers is still significantly greater than the pioneer or turn of the century periods and will continue to remain higher into the next century. During the next ten to twenty years another million is expected to be added to the state's population, which is a considerably shorter period of time than the six decades it took to reach the state's first million (table 7.6).

In studying daily increases of population shown in table 7.1, the recent decline in the daily increase rate can be seen. In spite of the slowing in daily population increase, Michigan still must meet the needs of people at three times the daily rate of the boom pioneer era with less per capita raw materials and land resources available. Further, it can be hypothesized that the rapid daily increase in population is related to the difficulty contemporary society has in transmitting its morals-ethics and folkways to its children.

TABLE 7.6
Michigan Past and Future Population with Approximate Rates and
Dates to Add One Million 1810-1990

Million Population	Dates to Add 1 Million	Approximate Number Years to Add 1 Million
1	1810-1870	60
2	1870-1890	20
3	1890-1915	25
4	1915-1923	8
5	1923-1934	11
6	1934-1946	12
7	1946-1955	9
8	1955-1962	7
9	1962-1973	11
10.1 est.	1973-1985	12
10.5 est.	1990	—

SOURCE: *Michigan Statistical Abstract,* 10th ed., 1974, pp. 7, 81.

Sex Ratio of Michigan Population

As Michigan has passed through its four stages of population growth—boom frontier, large foreign immigration, interurban-auto age suburbanization, and postwar rapid population increase—its *sex ratio* (the number of males per 100 females) has fluctuated and indicates a reversal in the balance between the sexes (table 7.7).

TABLE 7.7
Michigan Sex Ratio 1900-1990 and Estimated Population by Sex 1975-1990

Sex Ratio 1900-1970		Estimate Male-Female Population 1975-1990 (in millions)			
		Date	Male	Female	Sex Ratio
1900	106	1975	4.52	4.75	95
1920	110	1980	4.71	4.99	94
1940	105	1985	4.91	5.22	94
1960	98	1990	5.07	5.42	93.5
1970	96				

SOURCE: U.S. Census, Michigan 1970; Michigan Statistical Abstract, 10th ed., 1974, p. 81.

The post-war shift in the male-female composition of the state's population illustrates the decline in immigration which is dominated by males 18-35, as well as the lengthening gap in life expectancy between males and females. The population graphs by age and sex for Michigan and Keweenaw, Mecosta, and Lake counties illustrate the diversity in the local composition of Michigan counties, variation from the state average, the lack of economic opportunity for males (especially blacks) in Lake County, the dominance of males in mining in the western Upper Peninsula and college-aged persons in Mecosta County (figs. 7.2, 7.3, 7.4, 7.5). The wide range of age and sex composition of the state's communities necessitates both business and government to adapt their services to meet the needs created by unique population demands, i.e., law enforcement, parks and recreation, shopping facilities, education, and life-styles of female senior citizens.

GENERAL POPULATION CHARACTERISTICS

Population by Age: 1970 and 1960
NUMBER IN THOUSANDS

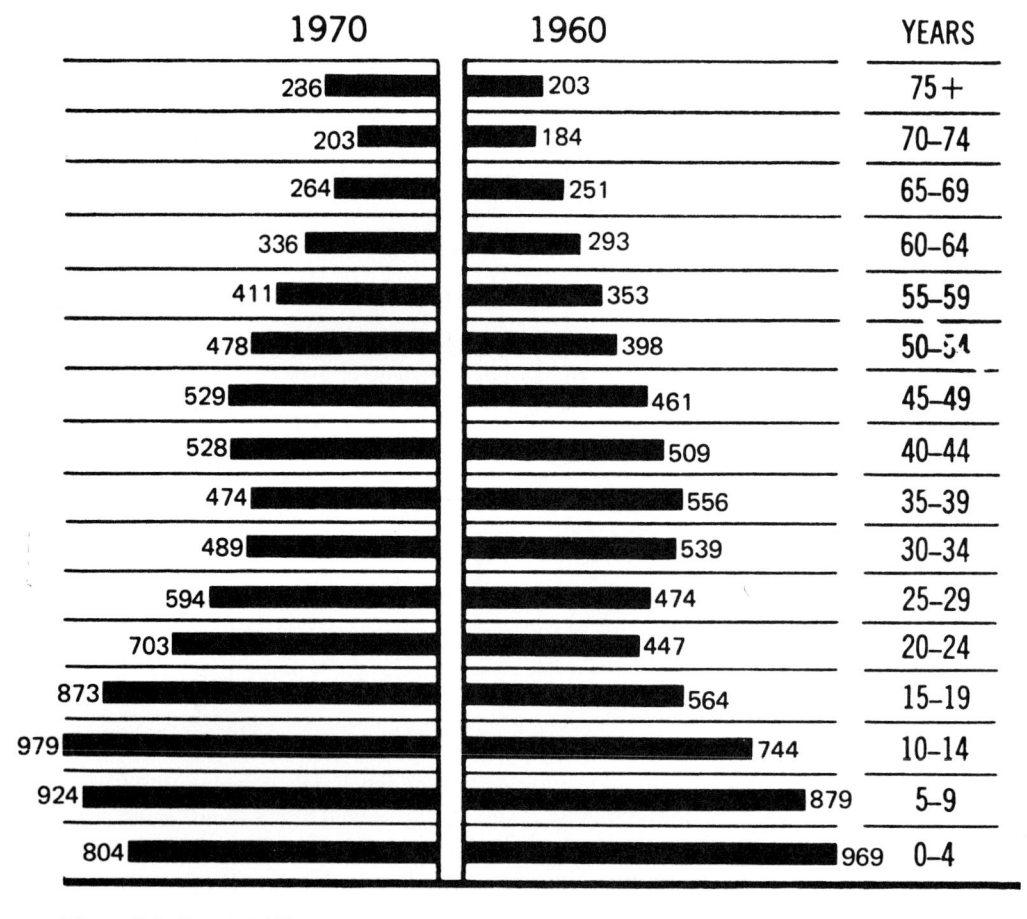

1970	1960	YEARS
236	203	75+
203	184	70–74
264	251	65–69
336	293	60–64
411	353	55–59
478	398	50–54
529	461	45–49
528	509	40–44
474	556	35–39
489	539	30–34
594	474	25–29
703	447	20–24
873	564	15–19
979	744	10–14
924	879	5–9
804	969	0–4

Figure 7.2. Graph of Michigan population by age 1960 and 1970. (U.S. Bureau of Census.)

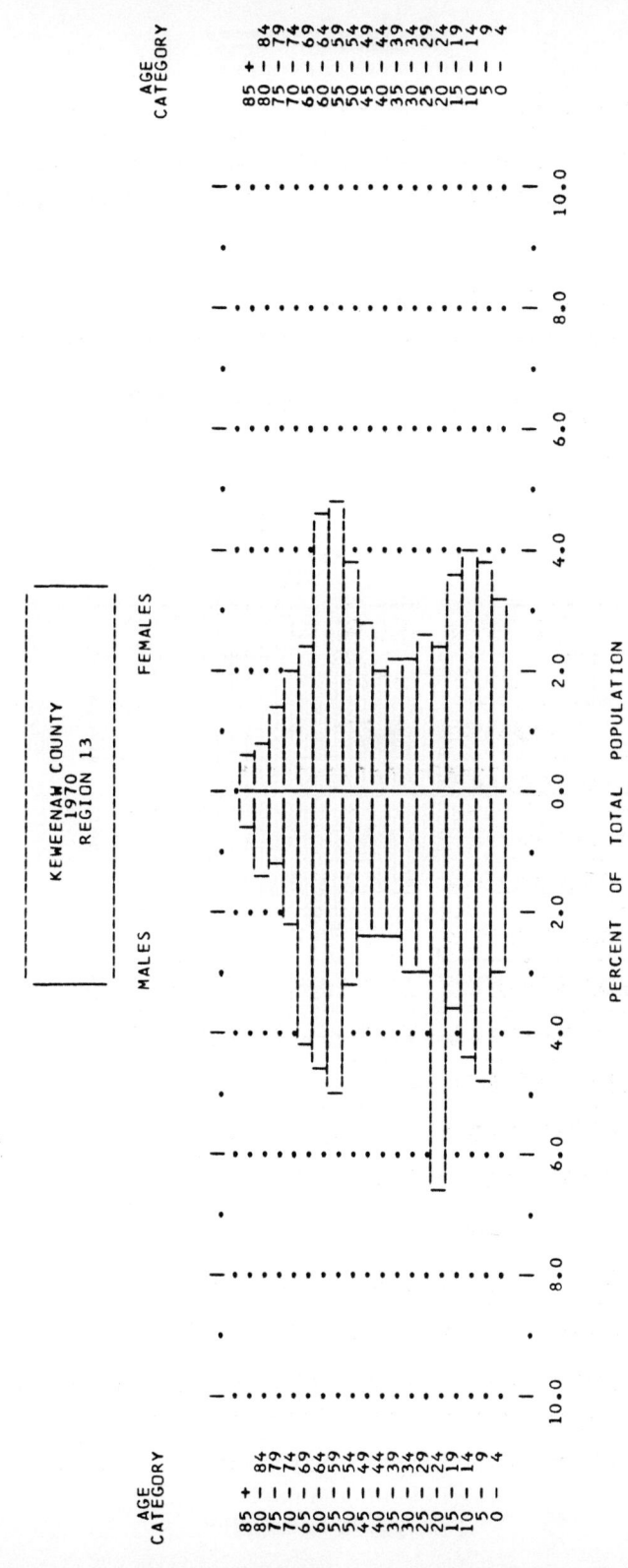

Figure 7.3. Population by age and sex Keweenaw County 1970. (Graph: J. Cook, P. Christine, *et. al.*, Ferris State College.)

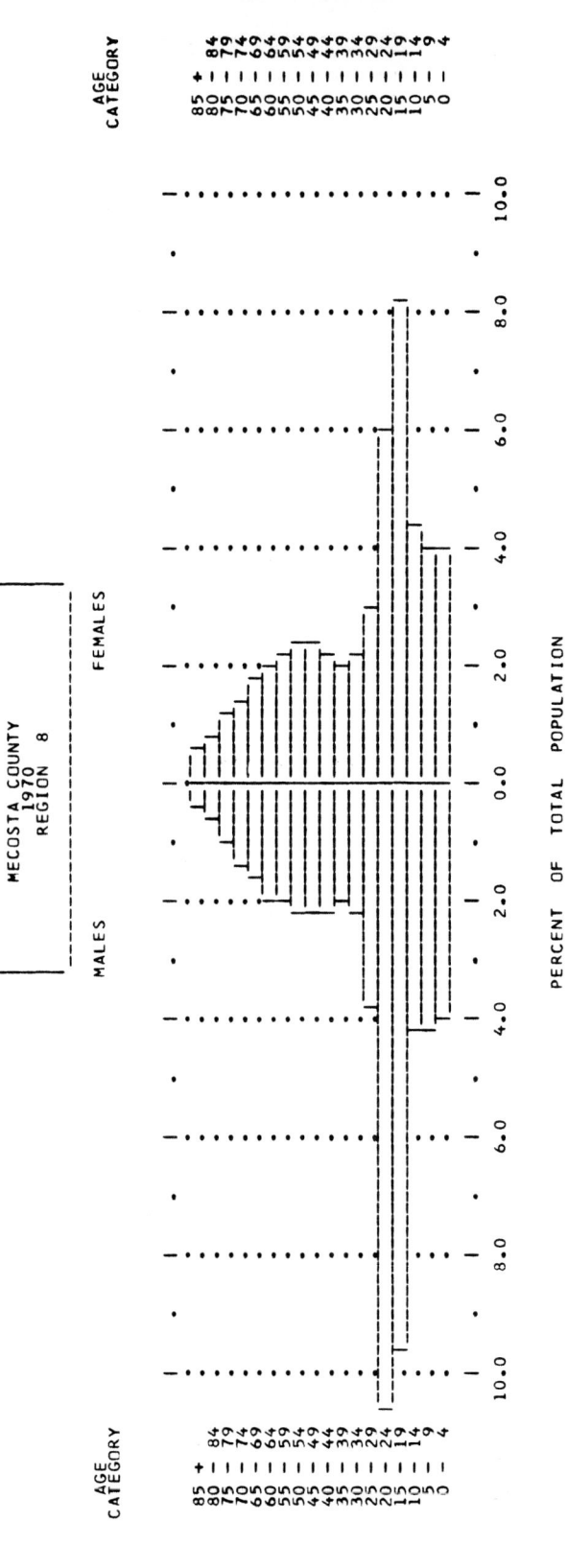

Figure 7.4. Population by age and sex Mecosta County 1970. (Graph: J. Cook, P. Christine, *et. al.*, Ferris State College.)

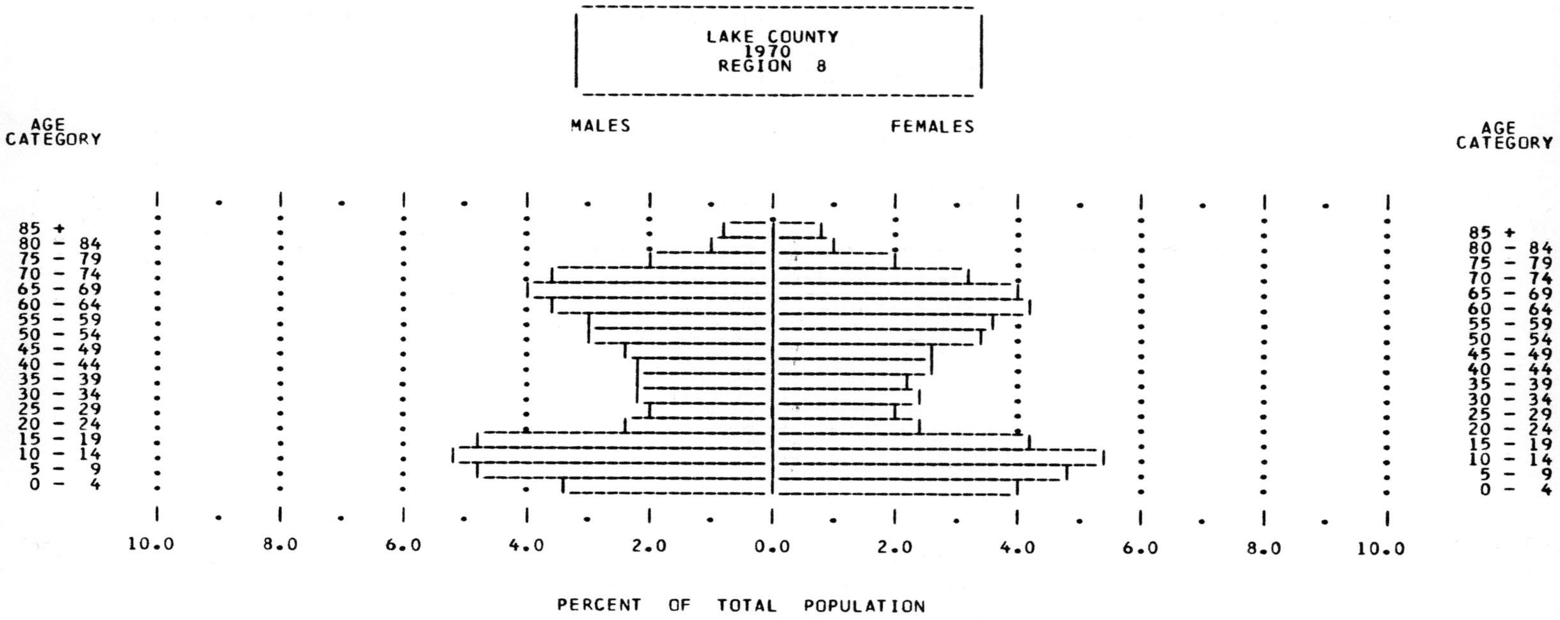

Figure 7.5. Population by age and sex Lake County 1970. (Graph: J. Cook, P. Christine, *et. al.*, Ferris State College.)

Historic Migration Influences on Michigan's Population

The Erie Canal and Myth

The Erie Canal's completion in 1825, its popular use by pioneer families migrating to the West, and the fact that between 1830 and 1840 Michigan had the highest percent increase in population in the United States, are frequently linked, to suggest that the canal caused immediate and rapid pioneer settlement in the state.

A careful analysis of both land sales records and population totals reveals, however, that forces other than the Erie Canal led to the pioneer boom of the 1830s. Land sales at Detroit and later Monroe increased significantly during the Erie Canal construction period 1818-1825. Significantly, in the five years after the canal's completion, land sales were considerably less than the precompletion levels (table 7.8).

TABLE 7.8
Certified Land Sales in Acres at Detroit 1820-1836

Year	Acres	Year	Acres	Year	Acres	Year	Acres
1820	2,860	1824	61,919	1828	17,433	1832	177,635
1821	7,494	1825	92,332	1829	23,409	1833	771,503
1822	20,068	1826	47,125	1830	70,441	1834	136,598
1823	30,173	1827	34,964	1831	217,943	1835	405,331
						1836	1,475,725

SOURCE: John T. Blois, *Gazetteer of the State of Michigan* (Detroit: Sydney F. Rood & Co., 1838), p. 74.

Further, in the immediate years after the completion of the Erie Canal, more people chose to settle in Ohio, Indiana, and Illinois than in Michigan and those states' land sales surpassed Michigan sales until 1832 (tables 7.9, 7.10).[2]

There is no single explanation for the decline in migration and land sales in Michigan between 1825 and 1830, although economic depression in the source area of the state's migrants (New York and New England) may have had a bearing on movement and land sales. Nonetheless, the states to the south continued to attract pioneers in greater numbers than Michigan. In addition to economic factors, several other forces were at work: (1) the lack of a good road into the peninsula from Ohio through the Black Swamp between Detroit and Toledo, (2) the intervening opportunity of good farmland with easier access in the Ohio Wabash River valleys, (3) the Tiffin Report which emphasized the negative aspects of Michigan's wetlands and sand plains, (4) President Madison's transfer of three-fourths of Michigan's War of 1812 bounty lands to Illinois and Missouri because: ". . . [they] are so covered with swamps or lakes, or otherwise unfit for cultivation. . ."[3] Perhaps, the most reasonable explanation for land sales slackening in Michigan after the completion of the Erie Canal is that speculators prematurely pushed sales up prior to 1825 and then had to wait for the surge of pioneers to fill Ohio's Erie shore and the Wabash Valley before spilling into Michigan.

2. Monroe Land Office sales trends were similar to Detroit's. *American State Papers,* Public Lands VI, p. 630.
3. U.S. Congress, House, *Military Bounty Lands,* HD No. 81, 14th Congress 1st Session, Feburary 6, 1816.

TABLE 7.9
1810-1840 Population of Michigan, Illinois, Indiana, and Ohio

Year	Michigan	Illinois	Indiana	Ohio
1810	4,764	12,282	24,520	230,760
1820	8,765	55,162	147,178	581,295
1830	31,639	157,445	343,031	937,903
1840	212,267	476,183	685,866	1,519,467

SOURCE: *Conpendium of the Ninth Census: 1870,* pp. 38, 40, 58, 80.

TABLE 7.10
Land Sales Receipts 1823-1837 USA, Ohio, Illinois, Indiana, Michigan ($1,000)

Year	Ohio	Illinois	Indiana	Michigan	Total USA
1823	158	76	203	38	807
1824	243	58	724	94	1,500
1825	194	82	223	136	1,292
1826	169	110	250	75	1,130
1827	215	81	263	55	1,405
1828	208	121	315	33	1,219
1829	277	282	490	90	2,163
1830	199	402	604	185	2,409
1831	442	420	713	403	3,366
1832	544	261	685	323	2,803
1833	695	381	692	563	4,173
1834	599	440	843	623	6,064
1835	828	2,688	2,078	2,272	16,165
1836	1,665	4,003	4,063	5,242	24,934
1837	590	1,271	1,571	969	6,941

SOURCE: Carstensen, *The Public Lands,* p. 233.

Territorial Inland Settlement 1817-1829

Lacking an overwhelming demand for land in the first years after the Land Office's opening, settlement away from the Detroit core was relatively orderly, deliberate, and intuitively logical. As early as the summer of 1816 Governor Cass wrote to Commissioner Meigs concerning the location of the lands that should first be brought on the market.

> . . . The first object is to settle the margin of the lakes and rivers and the lands in the immediate vicinity of the present settlements. This is uniformly the course, which the current of emigration takes and must take. . . [The settler] He is the pioneer to begin the road, which is to be traveled. But we must not expect him to begin at the wrong end, [and] to do all and leave nothing for others. By settling the country on the margin of the lakes and principal water courses we shall soon have a strong and increasing population.[4]

4. Letter, Lewis Cass to Josiah Meigs, June 16, 1816, Michigan Historical Commission, Archives, Cass Letter Book, sheets 121-22.

When the pioneer household goods finally went westward to bring comfort in the first inland communities, they left from the established river settlements (Frenchtown, Detroit, and the small trading post at Mt. Clemens). The new communities which were situated on the major rivers (Clinton, Huron, and Raisin) clung to within 48 km (30 mi) of Detroit or the waterfront.

First Interior Communities

The first inland settlements starting at Rochester and Pontiac between 1816-1818 corresponded to increased pioneer settlement at Mt. Clemens and Monroe. Several years intervened before the next inland endeavors were undertaken. Between 1823 and 1825 communities were established in Washtenaw County. Starting as Woodruff's Grove, Ypsilanti became the first settlement and was followed successively by Ann Arbor and Dexter further upstream on the Huron. Concurrent with Washtenaw's first nuclei was the initial occupation of Lenawee County up the Raisin River west of Monroe County. Tecumseh's development was started in 1824 and a Quaker Colony two years later began to prosper at Adrian. After the establishment of these frontier hamlets, further community development was curtailed as a result of the contraction of migration through Detroit following the completion of the Erie Canal.

Although some new settlers did continue to arrive during the next few years, they tended to fill the vacant areas between the old and new occupied areas. In addition to settlement in the southeast, community establishment also began taking place in the southwest, being fed at first by the unabating migration from Indiana's Ft. Wayne nucleus and later by the Chicago Road out of Detroit. By the fall of 1829, Jackson was founded. St. Joseph and Cass counties also were organized, making them independent counties in the area west of Washtenaw and Lenewee counties.

Closing the Frontier. By the end of the 1830s the frontier had been pushed north of the present-day M-46 from Port Sanilac to Muskegon. As the frontier gave way to farms and forest lumbering, scores of hamlets, villages, and towns sprang up on the rivers and Indian trails to serve the free enterprise market needs of the rural settlers. By the 1850s nuclei on the Keweenaw Peninsula and Traverse Bay were settled while in the next two decades the pioneers occupied the shores inland from Lakes Michigan and Huron. Steadily the virgin forest of the Lower Peninsula was reduced to a shrinking circle as if in defense. By the turn of the century, the Michigan frontier closed and the list of Michigan place names had grown to over five thousand spaced every 8-16 km (5-10 mi), some to grow from hamlet, village, town, and city into the top rank in the hierarchy of places as a metropolitan city, while others now fill Dodge's three-volume collection of *Michigan Ghost Towns*.

The pioneers, carrying their culture as baggage from New England, New York, Pennsylvania, Ohio, and Canada, introduced Eastern place names: New Boston, New Baltimore, Ithaca, and Genesee. County seat developers commonly platted their centers by adopting the distinctive Middle Atlantic courthouse square which originated in Philadelphia in 1682. Initially, the land of most market and governmental centers was concentrically organized with a CBD, churches, and parks. The advent of railroads and automobiles along with population growth had their influence on the internal structures of towns and cities. City land-use patterns were modified into sectors of activity along the roads and rail lines. Larger cities frequently developed a multiple nuclei pattern of land spatial organization with several business, residential, and industrial areas.

The communities which could not adapt or survive the loss of competitive transportation access, forest decline, podzolized soils, or short growing seasons, have left their names as a legacy of the past in county atlases of the 1876-1900 era. Frequently communities in adapting to change, or for other reasons, adopted new names. Thus, Bucklin, Leonard, Bronson, and Jacksonburg became respectively, Redford, Big Rapids, Kalamazoo, and Jackson.

Race and Ethnic Groups of Michigan

Since the frontier days, the Great Lakes region has attracted large groups of foreign-born to its farms, mines, industries, and other economic opportunities. Detroit has the greatest diversity of ethnic, racial, and religious settlements; however, population heterogeneity is found in most parts of the state (table 7.11). As a result of American society no longer feeling culturally threatened by large numbers of foreign immigrants, Detroit and other communities today find it popular and economically rewarding to promote and sponsor ethnic festivals. Thus, modern sociologists use this fact and the language requirements of the Voting Rights Act to debate the issue of the validity of the "melting pot theory" as it applies to Michigan.

TABLE 7.11
Racial Composition of Michigan 1860-1970

Year	White	Black	Indian	Mongolian Japanese	Chinese	Filipino	Other
1860	736,142	6,799	6,172	0	0	0	0
1880	1,614,560	15,100	7,249	1	27	0	0
1900	2,398,563	15,816	6,354	9	240	0	0
1920	3,601,627	60,082	5,614	184	792	NA	NA
1940	5,039,643	208,345	6,282	139	924	NA	NA
1960	7,085,865	717,581	9,701	3,211	3,234	1,134	2,468
1970	7,833,474	991,066	16,854	5,221	6,407	3,657	18,404

SOURCE: *Michigan Statistical Abstract,* 10th ed., 1974, p. 50.

Most ethnic communities in Michigan emerged as a result of the process of communication between the first migrants' relatives and friends, which created a *mean information field* of knowledge about Michigan. As the migration process continued, the pull of the desire to live in proximity to those with similar traditions, language, and religion tended to concentrate the ethnic groups. The "melting pot" or American acculturation process is evident in many communities by the decline of ethnic neighborhoods, the common use of the English language, intermarriage, and economic mobility.

Location of Ethnic Groups

A half century ago one out of every two persons in Michigan was foreign-born or a son or daughter of an immigrant. In the Upper Peninsula the concentration was even higher; ten counties had 75 to 90 percent foreign-born residents or their first generation descendants. Canadians primarily settled in the eastern lowland half of the Upper Peninsula and for several decades the counties bordering Lake Huron. In the eastern Upper Peninsula, Polish in Detour and Raber townships, Hollanders in Pickford and Rudyard townships, and Swedes in Moran, Hiawatha, and Doyle townships, became dominant ethnic groups. In the south central part of the Upper Peninsula, Germans, Swedes, and Belgians remain the dominant ethnic groups of Menominee, Delta, and Dickinson counties. Small French settlements are found in Lake and Homer townships.

From Alger County west, citizens of Finnish heritage dominate the settlement of the Upper Peninsula and have dotted the landscape with Lutheran Churches and saunas. Further indicative of the strength and core area of the Finns is the location of the nation's only Finnish College, Suomi, in Hancock. Even though most Michigan "Finns" are second generation Americans, a discerning listener can detect a pleasant distinctive accent when traversing the Finnish area of the state.

In the larger and more accessible Lower Peninsula a greater diversity of foreign culture groups are found (table 7.12). In some areas the acculturation process has erased most of the distinctive landscape features such as the rural Irish in Washtenaw, Kent, and Allegan counties. On the other hand, the "Irish Hills" in Lenawee County reveal their nonurban heritage. The influence of the larger and more recent ethnic groups, i.e., Germans, Polish, Dutch, and Arabs

TABLE 7.12
Nationality Composition of Michigan 1880 and 1970

Rank 1970	Nation	1970*	1880**
1	Canada	353,154	148,866 (1)
2	Poland	214,085	5,421 (3)
3	Germany	184,192	89,085
4	United Kingdom	148,612	54,763
5	Italy	117,064	505
6	Netherlands	72,763	17,177 (1)
7	USSR	65,606	1,560
8	Austria	40,730	1,025
9	Hungary	39,202	193
10	Sweden	33,639	9,412
11	Czechoslovakia	32,176	—
12	Mexico	31,067	—
13	Yugoslavia	30,375	—
14	Ireland	28,667	43,413
15	Greece	19,519	—
16	Lithuania	16,908	—
17	Norway	12,899	3,520
18	France	12,149	3,203
19	Denmark	11,951	3,513
20	Cuba	3,231	—
	Total foreign-born	424,309	388,508
	Total mixed foreign-born-national parentage	1,259,961	—

*Includes both foreign-born and mixed foreign-national parentage.
**Foreign-born only.
(1) indicates rank in USA.
SOURCE: *Michigan Statistical Abstract,* 10th ed., 1974, Table 1-24, p. 77; *Michigan Manual* (?) 1887, pp. 395-96.

still have easily recognizable features which are characteristic of their culture and identify their migrating to Michigan. In addition to place and street names marking the core of nationality group agglomerations in urban areas, are structures of fundamental institutions; churches, schools, fraternal organizations, and workers' halls. On the rural landscape, barn types and cultivation of traditional plants provide a lasting reminder of Michigan as a "mecca for foreigners" (table 7.13).

TABLE 7.13
Ethnic-Race-Religious Groups Location and Cultural Landscape Features

Group	Settlement Areas	Dominant Migration Period	Cultural Landscape Features
Polish	Detroit, Hamtramck, Jackson, Wyandotte, Posen, Minden	Post-Civil War	Polish National Alliance and Polish Roman Catholic Union Halls; place names: Krakow, Pulaski
German	Southwest of Ann Arbor, Frankenmuth, Westphalia, Weidman, Monroe, Osceola, and southern Menominee counties; Bismark and Metz Townships in Presque Isle County	1840-1850	Beer, eating and drinking "Old German," "Heidelberg" establishments, fore bay barns, rhubarb; place names: Hamburg, Zilwaukee, Hanover, Riga
Dutch	Ottawa and Allegan counties, s.w. Missaukee County, Antrim County, mixed in Kent and Kalamazoo counties, Atwood	Mid-1840s to 1914	Christian Reformed Church, tulips, businesses inactive on Sundays, barn with low pitch gable roof
Blacks	Urban: inner city of metropolitan communities, Inkster, River Rouge, Benton Harbor, Muskegon Heights. Rural: Sumpter Township, Wayne County; Calvin Township, Cass County; Idlewild, Lake County; Morton, Wheatland Townships, Mecosta County	Pre-Civil War, WWI and WWII	Martin Luther King Schools, store front churches, soul food, ribs
Arab	Dearborn: largest Arab-Moslem center in North America	Post-WWII	Arabic signs, eating places, mosques
Jewish	Southfield, Oak Park, Jackson	1860-1890	Synagogues, Yeshivath Beth Yehudah College, kosher shops
Lithuanian	Grand Rapids	Post-WWII	
Finnish	Kaleva, central and west Upper Peninsula	1860-1890	Saunas, Suomi College, Finnish Lutheran Churches
Amish	Nottawa, Colon Townships, St. Joseph County; Langston, Montcalm County	1910-1920 1970s	Plain clothes, horse-powered vehicles and equipment, no power lines to homes or farm buildings

The Complexity Explosion and Urban Communities

The readily observable modern-day maze of Michigan freeway intersections is evidence of a complexity explosion which can in part be attributed to the combined effects of the postwar surge in marriages, births, divorce, home ownership, and urbanization. Another aspect of the complexity explosion on Michigan has been the effect of the rip tide of migrations from rural areas to the cities and later a reverse flow to the suburbs. These migration tides have further strained the ability of local governments to satisfy the needs of citizens as urban communities became functionally *underbound*. In recent years increasing numbers of people are relocating from suburbs into communities of 12,000 to 50,000. As these twentieth century migrations have occurred, computer mapping processes and statistics have identified Michigan as a leading place for criminal activity (figs. 7.6, 7.7).

Additionally, during the migration process the state's black citizens have tended to be segregated and concentrated in the central cities. The pent-up frustrations of blacks and lack of their mobility have periodically been expressed in riots, burning, looting, and "turf" conflicts.

In spite of the gloomy picture which a list of urban problems presents, cities with their agglomerations of skilled people still possess elements of the highest attainment in civilization including: medical facilities where life-sustaining atomic "pacemakers" are implanted, unequaled museums and libraries, financial institutions, professional sports, newspapers and communication centers, plus a diversity of activity which gives any urban place character and excitement.

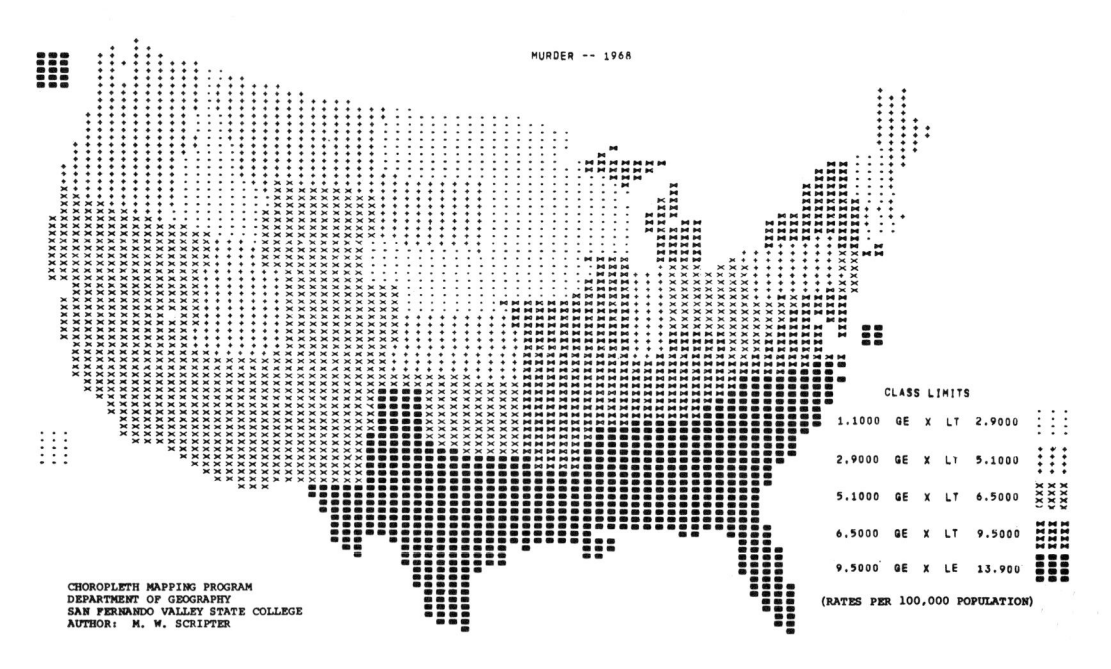

Figure 7.6. Murder distribution in United States 1968. (Source: *Journal of Geography*, April 1971, used with permission.)

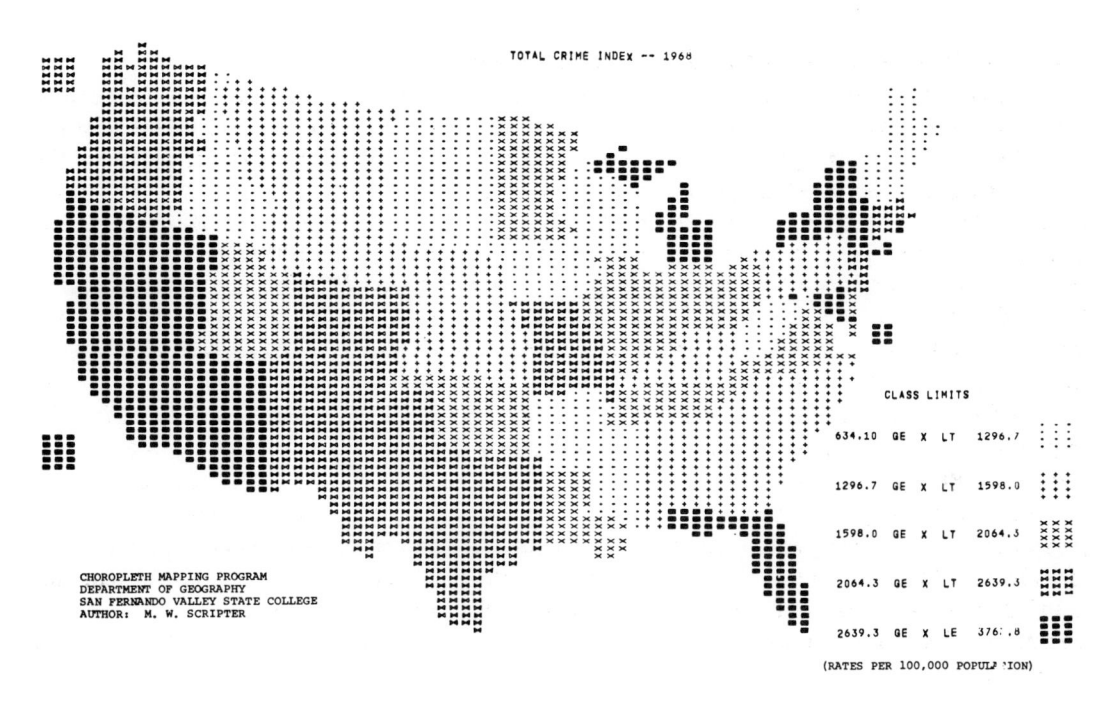

Figure 7.7. Total index of crime distribution for the United States. (Source: *Journal of Geography,* April 1971, used with permission.)

> *"Every kingdom divided against itself is brought to desolation; and every city or house divided against itself shall not stand."*
>
> Matthew 12:25

Chapter Eight

Population and Settlement Patterns of Michigan's Fourteen Planning and Development Regions

This chapter is devoted to establishing an understanding of Michigan based on its fourteen Planning and Development Regions which were created between 1968 and 1973. A comparative profile of the regions is drawn by describing those features which give each region a unique identity. Included within each regional summary are the identification of: (1) the region's population and settlement features, (2) major employment and production activities, (3) intraregional linkages, and (4) higher education and recreational activities. Table 8.1 provides an introductory statistical summary of the comparative land-water area and population composition by race for each region.

Detroit, Region One: Michigan's Core Area

The Detroit region encompasses seven counties of southeastern Michigan which forms the core area of the state with 53 percent of its population. The region's outer ring of major cities, Monroe, Ann Arbor, Pontiac, and Port Huron, lie 40-80 km (25-50 mi) from Detroit. These cities are still separated from the region's core by vestiges of agricultural activities and open space similar to the situation of a half century ago when a green belt intervened between the city and its older satellite suburbs, Wyandotte, Dearborn, Farmington, Royal Oak, St. Clair Shores, and the enclave cities of Hamtramck and Highland Park. The region's sectors along I-75, I-94, I-96, and its airport area have acquired in recent years the region's characteristic urban, industrial, and high population density patterns.

TABLE 8.1
Population and Land-Water Areas of Michigan's Planning and Development Regions 1970

Region Number	Regional Center	Non-Great Lakes Area					Population		
		Water		Land			Total	Negro	Regional Center Population	Regional Center Percent Nonwhite
		Square Kilometers	Square Miles	Square Kilometers	Square Miles				
1	Detroit	187	72	11,840	4,554	4,731,655	780,138	1,511,482	45
2	Jackson	55	21	5,356	2,060	262,054	9,117	45,484	14
3	Kalamazoo/ Battle Creek	164	63	7,381	2,839	466,977	22,793	85,555/ 38,931	11/ 21
4	Benton Harbor/ St. Joseph	75	29	4,355	1,675	263,360	26,842	16,481/ 11,092	59/ 1
5	Flint	21	8	4,784	1,840	559,733	60,707	193,317	29
6	Lansing	21	8	4,412	1,697	378,423	14,699	131,546	10
7	Saginaw/ Bay City	276	106	22,360	8,600	690,284	29,271	91,849/ 49,449	25/ 2
8	Grand Rapids	156	60	15,714	6,044	662,222	27,649	197,649	12
9	Alpena	421	162	12,576	4,837	94,107	146	13,805	1
10	Traverse City	536	206	12,301	4,731	158,333	396	18,046	1
11	Sault Ste. Marie	398	153	9,121	3,508	48,861	796	15,136	3.7
12	Marquette/ Escanaba	278	107	17,997	6,922	165,744	1,283	21,967/ 15,368	3/ 1
13	Ironwood	382	147	15,881	6,108	89,742	101	8,711	—
14	Muskegon	73	28	4,170	1,604	303,908	17,128	44,631	15

SOURCE: *Michigan Statistical Abstract*, 10th ed., 1974; *General Population Characteristics Michigan 1970*, Bureau of the Census.

Population and Settlement Features

Detroit, the sixth largest city in the nation, and its functional region are similar to most major metropolitan regions in the nation. The central city has declined in population from 1.85 million in 1950 to 1.5 million in 1970. Even the region's SMSA lost an estimated 200,000 residents between 1970 and 1974. On the other hand, the total Region One population rose from 4.18 million in 1960 to 4.73 million in 1970, indicating a strong migration trend away from the older settled centers of population into the less densely populated counties. In the intraregional migration process, the city of Detroit's black population has risen from 16.2 percent in 1950 to approximately 50 percent in the mid-1970s.

Centripetal-Centrifugal Forces. In the past, several centripetal forces have drawn people to the Detroit area. Especially important attractions have been: (1) access by highway or the Detroit River allowing cheap movement of bulk manufactured goods and raw materials, (2) employment opportunities including a higher wage scale, (3) outstanding educational opportunities in its public schools, universities, law, medical, and technical institutions, (4) enriching cultural attractions including historical and art museums, libraries, and theaters, (5) excitement of its professional major league sports, and (6) recreation-health facilities of its neighborhood and regional parks (Belle Isle and River Rouge) and hospitals (Ford and Detroit Osteopathic). In the post-World War II era, several centrifugal forces have contributed to the wave of changing land-use rings which have swept across the region pulling people away from the central city. One of the most important has been Detroit's tradition of spreading out horizontally in opposition to the patterns of New York City, Chicago, and San Francisco which have traditions of extensively developing vertical space by the construction of skyscrapers. Prior to the mid-1950s "skyscraper boom," Detroit had one "cathedral of commerce" over 150 m (500 ft) tall and eleven over 90 m (300 ft) tall. By 1974 the number of skyscrapers in each of the above categories stood at a modest one and twenty respectively. In comparison, the skylines of other major United States cities underwent significant vertical transformations in attempting to "save the cities" (table 8.2).

TABLE 8.2
Vertical Space Enclosure in Major USA Cities 1954 and 1974

City	Number Buildings Over 150 m (500 ft) 1954	1974	City	Number Buildings Over 150 m (500 ft) 1954	1974
New York	36	90	Los Angeles	0	6
Chicago	9	24	Dallas/Fort Worth	2	5
Boston	0	6	Houston	0	7
Pittsburgh	3	5	Atlanta	0	2
San Francisco	0	9	Cincinnati	1	1
Detroit	1	1	Cleveland	1	2

SOURCE: *Journal of Geography,* vol. 75, no. 3 (March 1976), pp. 156-57.

Automobiles, Shopping Centers, and the Low Profile Tradition. The region's strong attachment to horizontal space development can perhaps be linked to the mystique of the automobile to solve problems. To take advantage of the mobility of the automobile and reduce the problem of CBD congestion, it is not surprising that Detroit pioneered in the 1950s the development of the extensive regional shopping center concept for retail trade. The internationally recognized Northland Shopping Center situated in Southfield was the first of a series of large centers which now form a crescent around the city. The seeming conflict in names (Northland and Southfield) is illustrative of the politically fragmented nature of the urban areas; the shopping center is both north of Detroit and the Baseline, while Southfield is in the southern tier of townships in Oakland County.

In coping with the problems generated by unprecedented population growth and migration, only time will tell whether the Detroit Region will be best served by the low density sprawl pattern with its multiple nuclei commercial centers, or by returning to the historical precedent of a strong CBD surrounded by varying concentric rings of warehouses, manufacturing, and residential land uses.

The Detroit Renaissance Center is a bold attempt by the Downtown Detroit Development Corporation to set into motion the critical mass which will stimulate renewed development on the waterfront. The Renaissance complex consists of a civic center plaza, four octagon-shaped thirty-nine-story office buildings around a seventy-story cylindrical-shaped hotel. When completed, the Detroit Renaissance Center will be one of the most dramatic riverfront service-retail trade centers in the nation.

Crime as a Region-Shaping Force

In the past the river, automotive genius, accessibility, and individual motivation have been dominant forces shaping the region. By the 1970s crime must be added to the list of potent forces (fig. 8.1). Violent crime and war are axiomatic in that those who possess the means to flee danger do so with little or no regard to surrounding resources in order to gain the immediate goal of survival. Undoubtedly, the fleeing to the suburbs and small towns has had its immediate reward of peace; however, the cost in lost agricultural and open space, resources expended in transportation or duplicate structures, and time away from families in journeys to work, have also been devastating losses. In spite of the migration out of the central cities for any reason, crime has followed. A slowing in the rate of crime-related unwise and unnecessary land transformation may be attained with a mass realization that, for the foreseeable future, a heterogeneous ethnic and racial population composition will be the state's norm and will have to be accommodated in a nation devoted to equality.

Employment and Production Activities

The Detroit Region is one of the world's foremost manufacturing areas. Automobile production is of course the dominant activity comprising 23 percent of the domestic automobile production and 19 percent of the United States truck production. In recent years a significant shift in employment has taken place with 60 percent of Detroit's labor force engaged in non-manufacturing activities such as wholesale-retail trade, finance, service, and construction. Manufacturing activities account for over 30 percent of the labor force. In addition to motor vehicles and equipment, the manufacture of primary metals, machinery, chemicals, printing and publishing, food processing, and metal fabrication are major production activities.

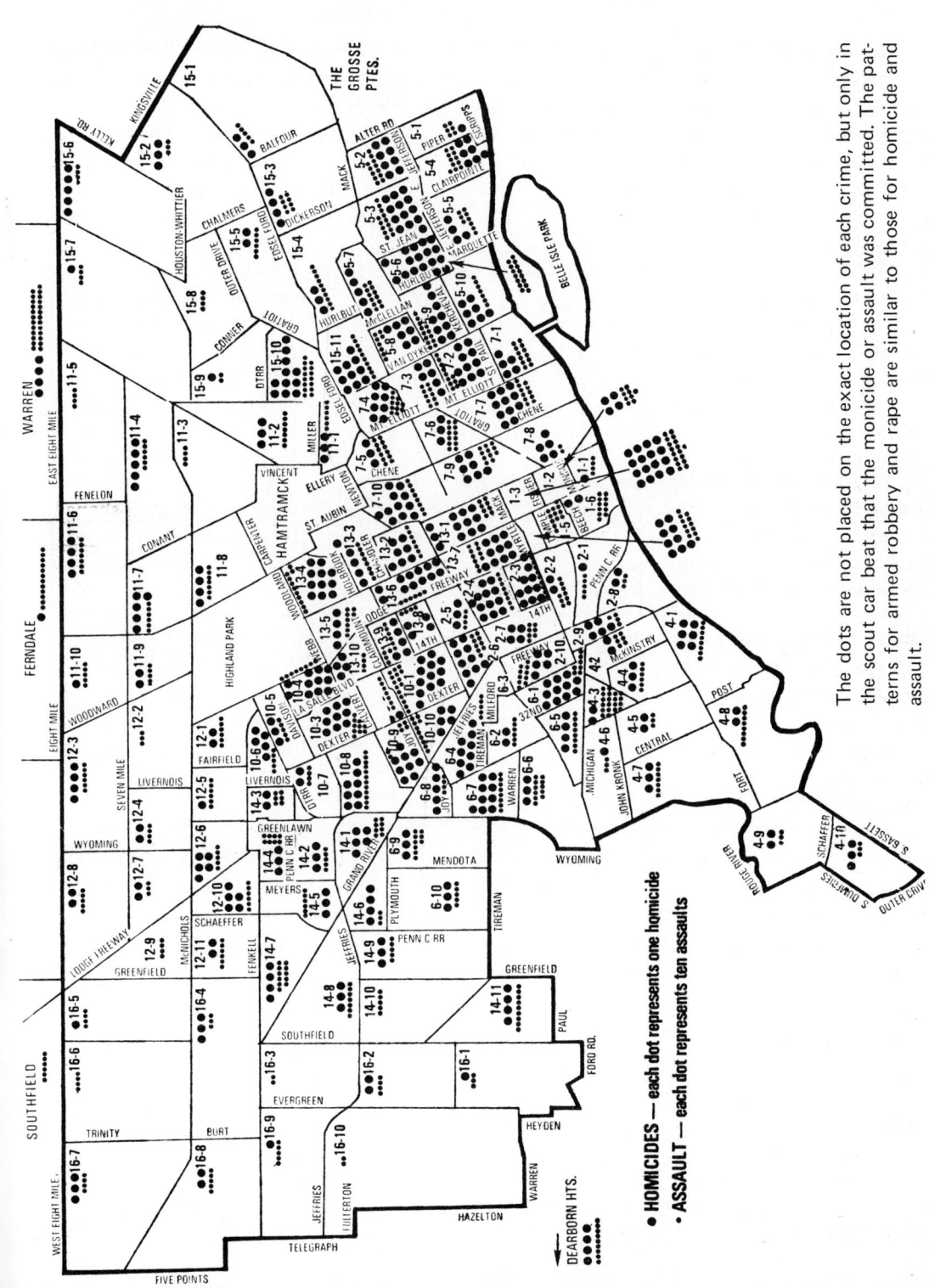

Figure 8.1. Murder and assault pattern in Detroit. (Map: *The Detroit Free Press*, December 13, 1973.)

The dots are not placed on the exact location of each crime, but only in the scout car beat that the homicide or assault was committed. The patterns for armed robbery and rape are similar to those for homicide and assault.

• HOMICIDES — each dot represents one homicide
· ASSAULT — each dot represents ten assaults

The high degree of employment-political interdependency within the Detroit Region is evident by comparing the maps of industrial corridors and political units, and the table of Place of Work by County (figs. 8.2, 8.3 and table 8.3). A further illustration of the region's community interdependency is the fact that the Detroit Region accounts for 65 percent of the state's cross-county line journeys to work.

TABLE 8.3
Region One: Place of Work by County

Area	Total Population	All Workers	Work in County of Residence	Work Outside County of Residence	Place of Work Not Reported
Wayne	2,669,604	963,470	754,475	139,500	69,495
Oakland	907,871	335,961	205,736	112,375	17,850
Macomb	626,938	226,117	120,451	95,831	9,835
Washtenaw	234,103	96,118	76,045	11,632	8,441
Monroe	118,479	41,262	20,034	19,292	1,936
St. Clair	120,175	39,694	28,611	8,233	2,850
Livingston	58,967	20,786	10,276	8,542	1,968
Region One	4,734,508	1,723,408	1,215,628	395,405	112,375
State	8,875,083	3,173,241	2,351,876	601,705	219,660

SOURCE: *1970 Census of Population General Social and Economic Characteristics–Michigan U.S. Department of Commerce,* Table 119, pp. 537-43; *1970 Transportation Related Data SEMCOG Region,* 1972, Table 7, p. 9.

Selfridge Air National Guard Base is the major military facility in the Detroit Region occupying 240 ha (600 ac) of marshland northeast of Mount Clemens. The level of the land at the base averages approximately one meter below the surface of Lake St. Clair. To prevent flooding and insure operation of the base, a seawall and 101 km (63 mi) of underground drainage system are used to pump up to 72,200 liters (19,000 gal) of water per minute from the site (fig. 8.4).

Education and Recreation

The Detroit Region has been a leader in Michigan and world higher education since 1809, when the Territorial Legislature passed the first school law, and 1817, when the University of Michigan was founded in Detroit, to the present-day when over thirty colleges and universities are concentrated in the region. The library at the University of Michigan, Ann Arbor, is an unequalled resource in the interior of North America. Eastern Michigan University, founded in 1849 as the first teacher training institution west of New York, continues to earn international acclaim with an expanded role. Wayne State University complements the core area's educational-cultural complex which also includes the Detroit Historical Museum, Institute of Arts, and Detroit Public Library with its outstanding Burton Collection of maps and Michigan History. Foreboding a decline in educational excellence in the state is the fact that by the mid-1970s, Michigan ranked thirty-fourth nationally in both percentages of collected tax revenue

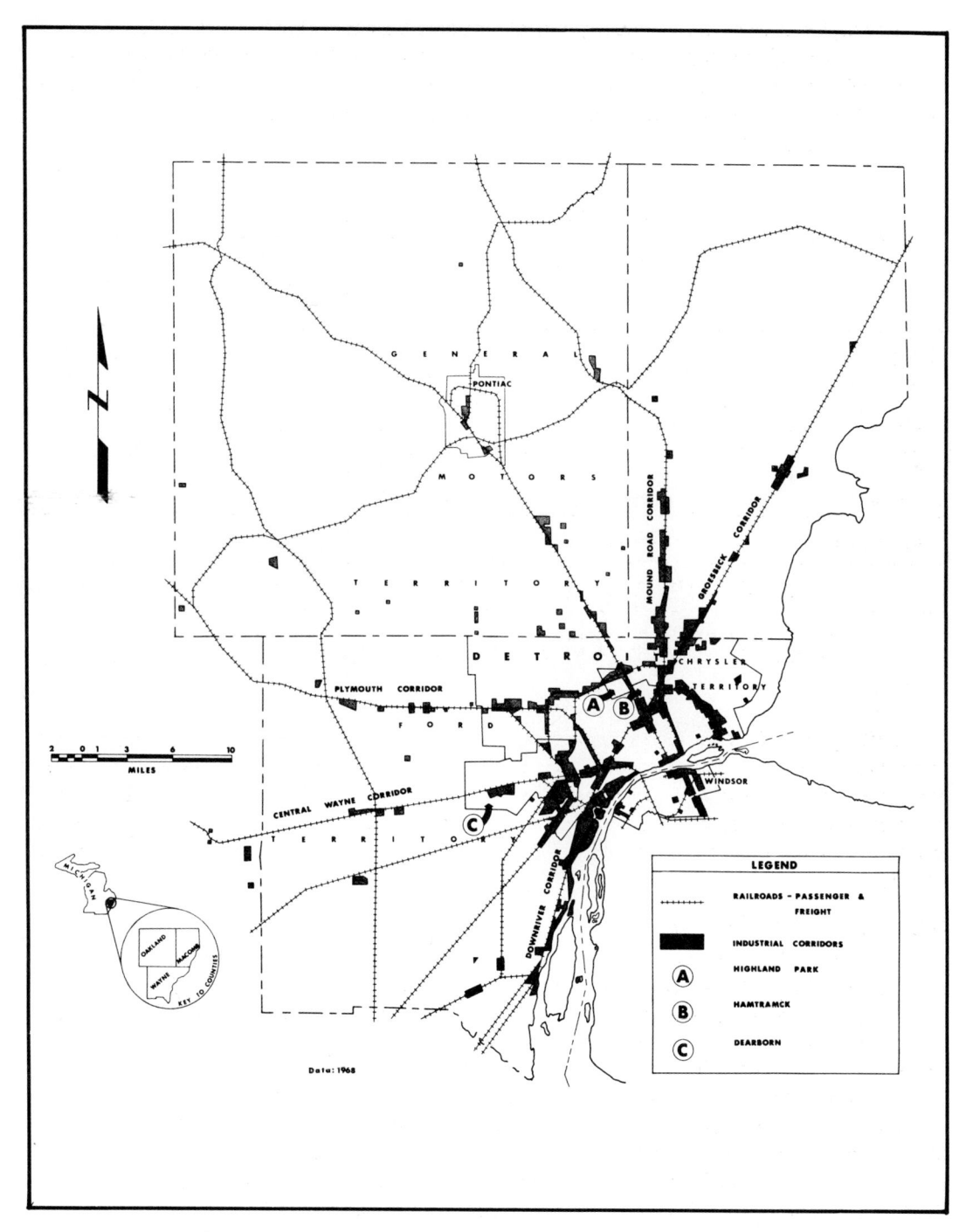

Figure 8.2. Industrial corridors of Metropolitan Detroit. (Map: R. Sinclair, *The Face of Detroit.*)

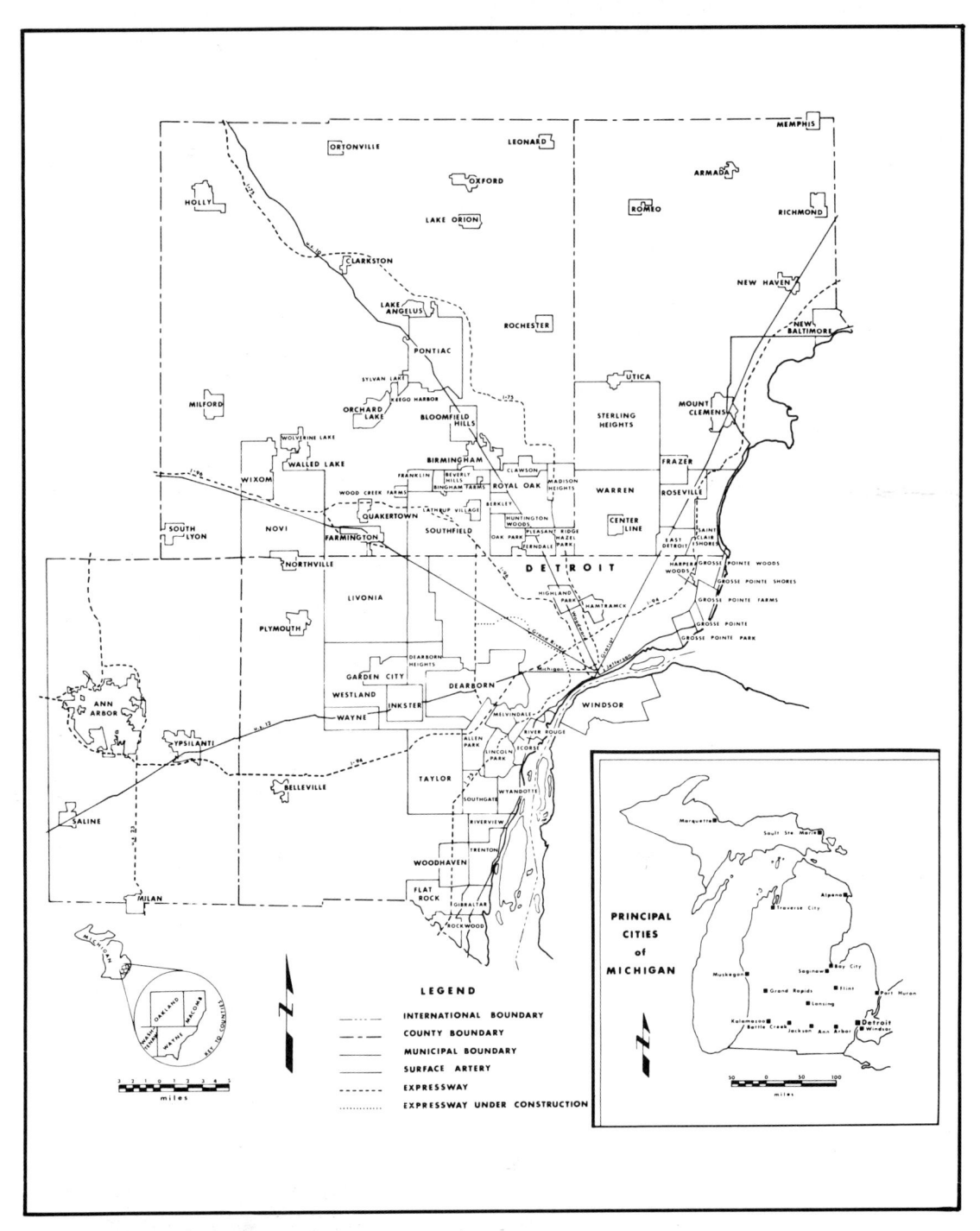

Figure 8.3. Political units of Metropolitan Detroit. (Map: R. Sinclair, *The Face of Detroit.*)

Figure 8.4. Selfridge Air National Guard Base on Anchor Bay of Lake St. Clair. (Photo: Michigan Air National Guard.)

allocated to higher education and its appropriations per student. In the mid-1960s, Michigan's four-year colleges and universities received 20 percent of the state's general fund-general purpose expenditures. Since then, although dollars allocated have increased, the percentage has declined to less than 15 percent. As recently as 1966-67 Michigan ranked seventh in the nation in the amount of state appropriations per capita for higher education. Ten years later its rank fell to twenty-sixth. In contrast to the percentage decline in education allocations is the blossoming of other human service facilities on the landscape including mental and public health clinics and social welfare service offices.

To serve the recreational needs of the core population area of the state, the DNR operates sixteen state parks and recreation areas within the region (table 8.4). Of the total state parks in the region, one-third of them are located in lake-studded Oakland County. Belle Isle and River Rouge Park in Detroit are complemented by the river-oriented Huron-ClintonMetropolitan Park System. In the shadows of the world headquarters of Ford Motor Company in Dearborn is Greenfield Village and Henry Ford Museum which attract over a million people annually to view the Midwest's most unique collection of Americana.

TABLE 8.4
Region One: State Parks and Selected Historic Attractions

State Park	Acres	Number Camp Sites	Historic Site	Place
Algonac	981	390	Fort Street Presbyterian Church	Detroit
Bald Mountain	3,100	80	Mariner's Church	Detroit
Brighton	4,706	258	Belle Isle	Detroit
Dodge-4	136	None	Moross House	Detroit
Highland	5,402	60	Detroit Cornice and Slate	Detroit
Holly	6,942	190	Fort Wayne	Detroit
Island Lake	3,420	104	Grosse Isle	Grosse Isle
Lakeport	565	256	River Rouge Plant	Dearborn
Maybury	929	None	Nankin Mills Nature Center	Westland
Ortonville	3,996	54	Old Observatory U of M	Ann Arbor
Pinckney	9,613	310	Statue George Custer	Monroe
Pontiac Lake	3,645	50	Cranbrook Culture Center	Bloomfield Hills
Proud Lake	3,434	207	Clinton-Kalamazoo Canal	Rochester
Rochester-Utica	862	None	General Motors Technical Center	Warren
Seven Lakes	1,378	None	St. Clair River Tunnel	Port Huron
Sterling	997	192	Grist Mill	Parshallville

SOURCE: *Michigan's Historic Attractions,* Michigan History Division, 1973; *Michigan State Parks,* DNR—Michigan Tourist Council, 1975.

Jackson, Region Two: The Auto Parts, General Livestock and Corn Production Area

Region Two is composed of Jackson, Lenawee, and Hillsdale counties which occupy a northeast-southwest belt of moraines, outwash channels and till plains in south central Lower Michigan. The rich soils and flatlands of the lake plain in western Lenawee County and its proximity to the Detroit-Toledo markets contribute significantly to the region being one of the state's two most valued farming areas. Other influences on the region's land-use include I-94, recent oil discoveries, the Jackson manufacturing complex, and the attractions of the Irish Hills recreation area. The city of Jackson with a population of about 50,000 since 1920 is the regional center for fifty-nine townships, eight cities, and twenty villages (fig. 8.5). The county seats of Adrian and Hillsdale, plus Tecumseh are the region's secondary centers, however, the comparison shopping and educational activities in Toledo and Ann Arbor also are factors in shaping the region's economic patterns.

Population and Settlement

Region Two's population of over a quarter million, increased by less than 20,000 or 7.2 percent between 1960-1970, the slowest rate of any of the state's nine metro-city regions (table 8.1). In the same decade, the sex ratio changed significantly from 101.5 to 97.9. Combined, these figures are indicative of: (1) the lessening impact of the males confined to the State Prison outside Jackson, and (2) the slower diffusion of industry in agriculturally significant parts of the region. In contrast, during the 1970s the urbanization of the landscape and loss of agricultural land has been more visible following the expansion of Budd Company in Clinton, General Motors Upholstery Plant and Stauffer Chemical in Adrian. Further urban transformation has been stimulated by those desiring to live in small towns but maintaining employment in the Detroit, Lansing, and Kalamazoo Regions.

Historically, Jackson was similar to most pre-Civil War communities of southern Michigan with its active participation in the Underground Railroad. Politically, the support for abolition of slavery and greater equality coalesced into the formation (with Ripon, Wisconsin) of the Republican Party "under the Oaks" in 1854. By 1870 the forces of accessibility and progressive attitudes had combined to make the city the third largest in the state with a population of 11,447 including 359 blacks. By the 1970s over 65 percent of the region's blacks (table 8.1) resided in homes within the city limits of Jackson. The several maps of Jackson, 1870-1960, illustrate one model of changing housing patterns which has occurred in the nation during the last century with the concentration of black citizens in the central city. It can be observed that the restriction of black housing to certain areas appears to have occurred in the World War I era when European immigration declined and southern blacks were actively recruited by northern industrialists for employment (figs. 8.6, 8.7, 8.8, 8.9).

Employment and Production Activities

Jackson, beginning with the St. Joseph Indian Trail, followed by its hub location in the Michigan Central rail network and freeway connections, has always had a high degree of accessibility. These accessibility factors have been important in the location of the Consumers Power main offices and the concentration of auto parts and other electronic and aircraft manufacturing (Kelsey-Hayes, Goodyear, Clark Equipment, Aeroquip, Walker Muffler, Hayes-Albion, Yardman, and Sparton) in the area. While Jackson is no longer the "corset capital of the world," the modern-day offshoot, hygienic medical braces and supports, is still an important employer. Michigan's largest consulting and design engineering firm, Commonwealth Associates, is located in a modern glass structure in downtown Jackson. In the mid-1930s, Tecumseh Products located in Tecumseh because of timely financial support for their manufacture of refrigerator compressors and subsequently captured the world market.

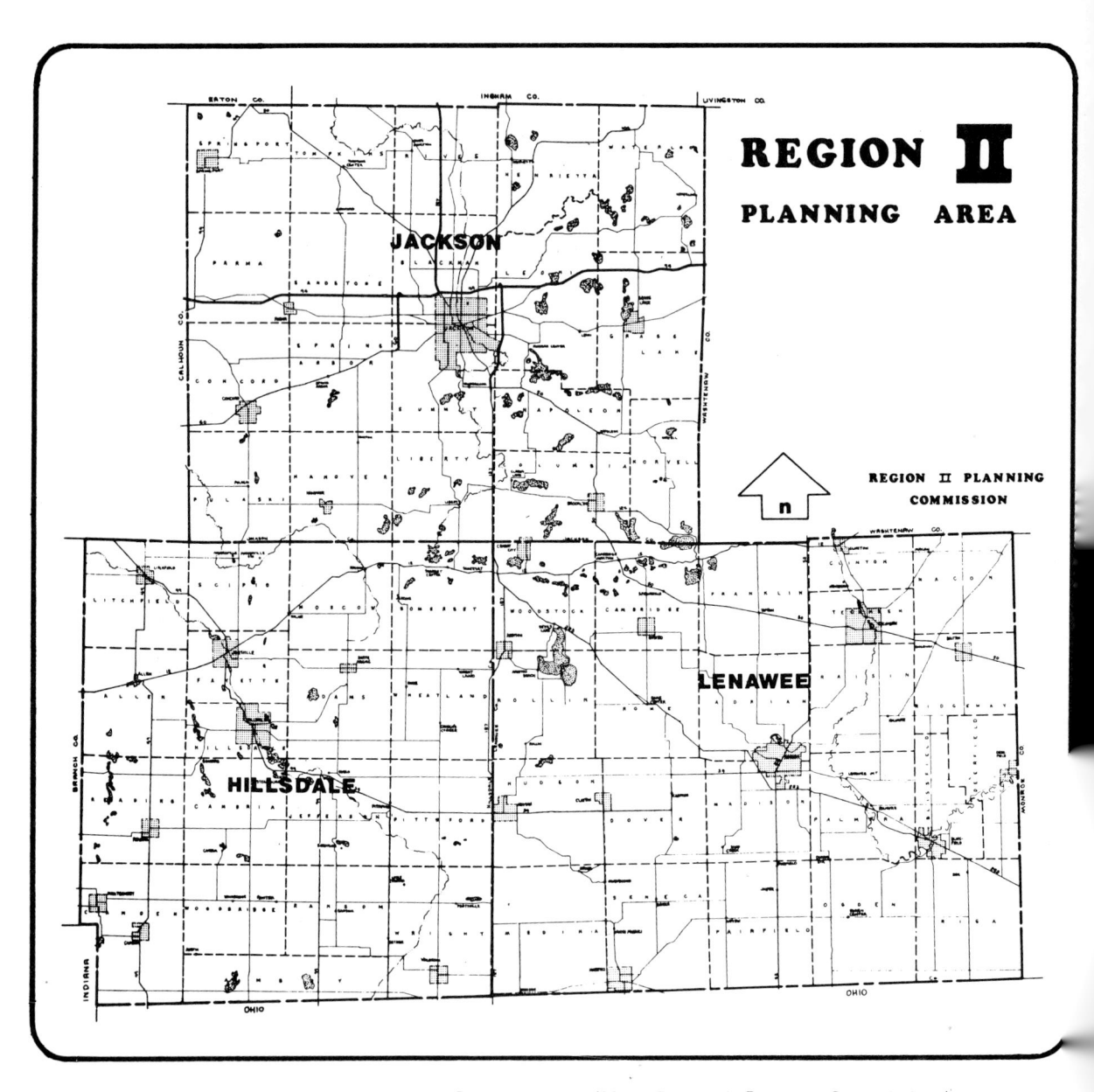

Figure 8.5. Region Two—Jackson Planning Area. (Map: Region II Planning Commission.)

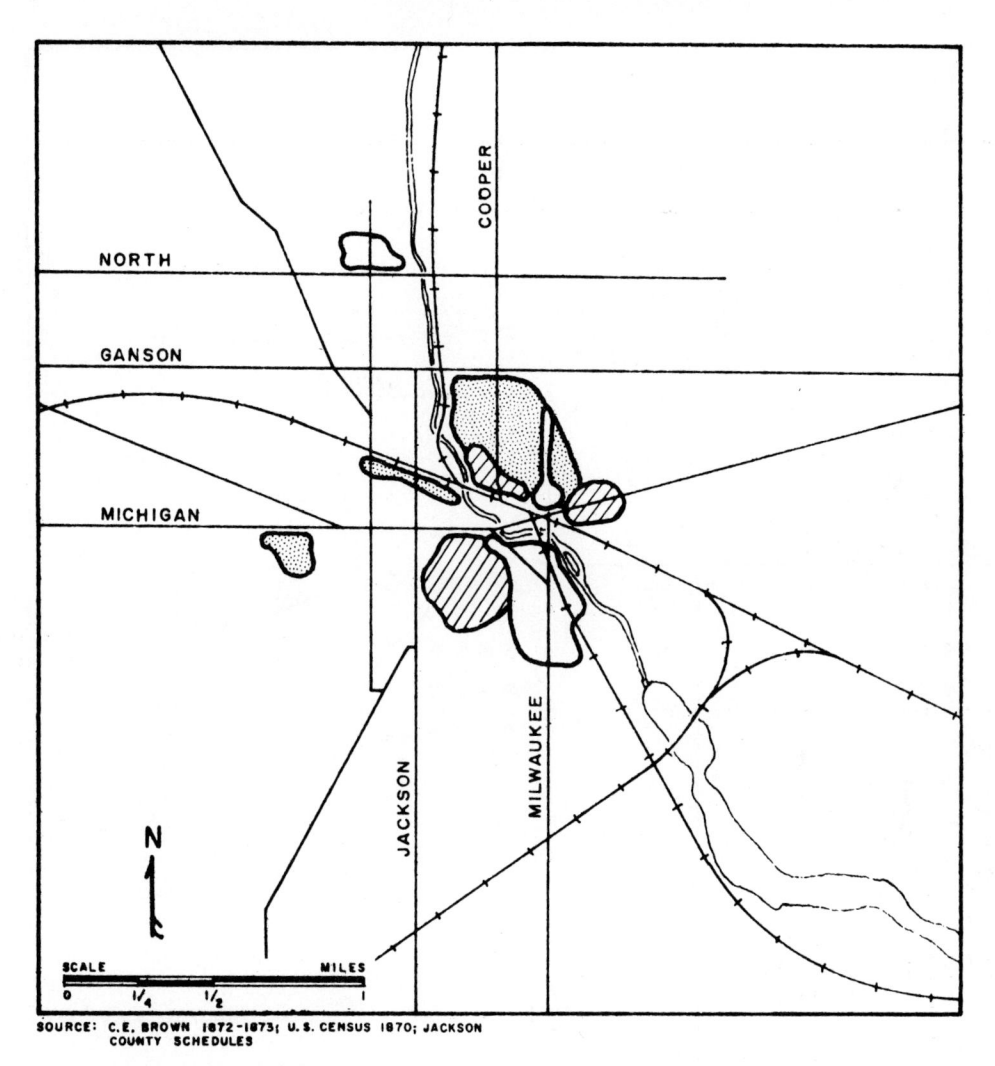

Figure 8.6. Negro and foreign-born housing pattern, Jackson 1870.

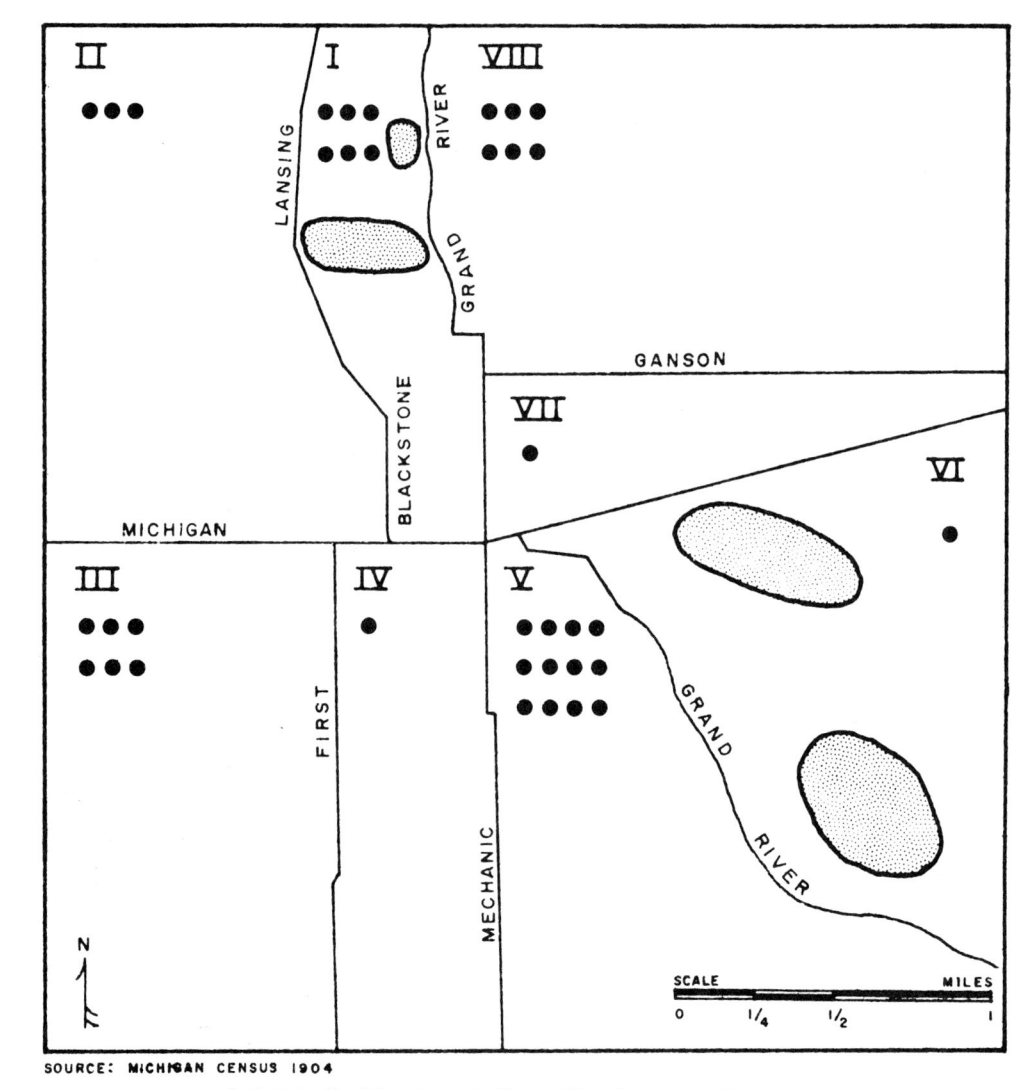

NEGROES-POLISH

1870-1910

● = 10 NEGRO RESIDENTS BY WARDS - 1904

◯ POLISH SETTLED AREA: 1870-1910

II WARD NUMBER

Figure 8.7. Negro and Polish housing pattern, Jackson 1910.

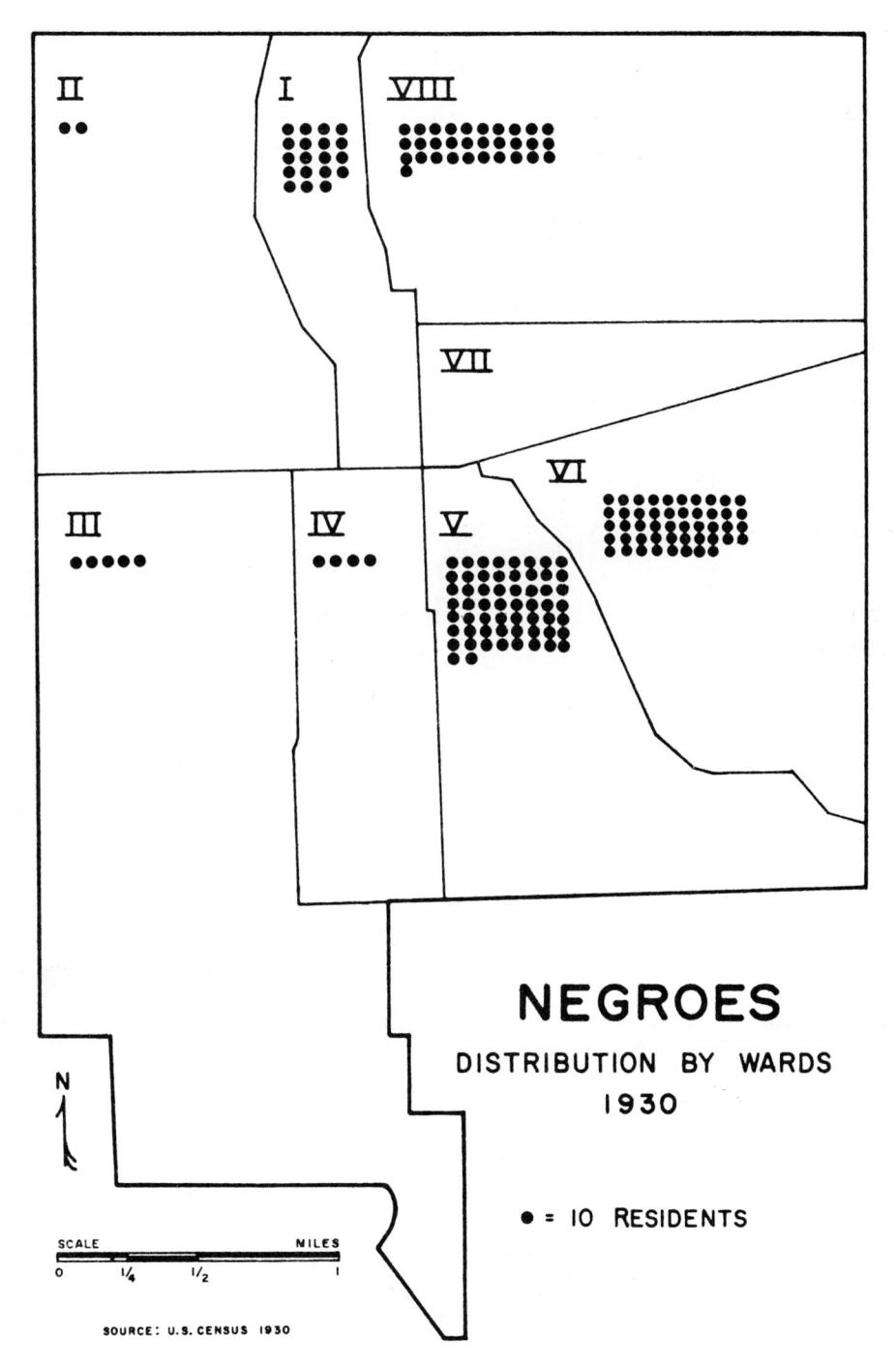

Figure 8.8. Negro distribution by wards, Jackson 1930.

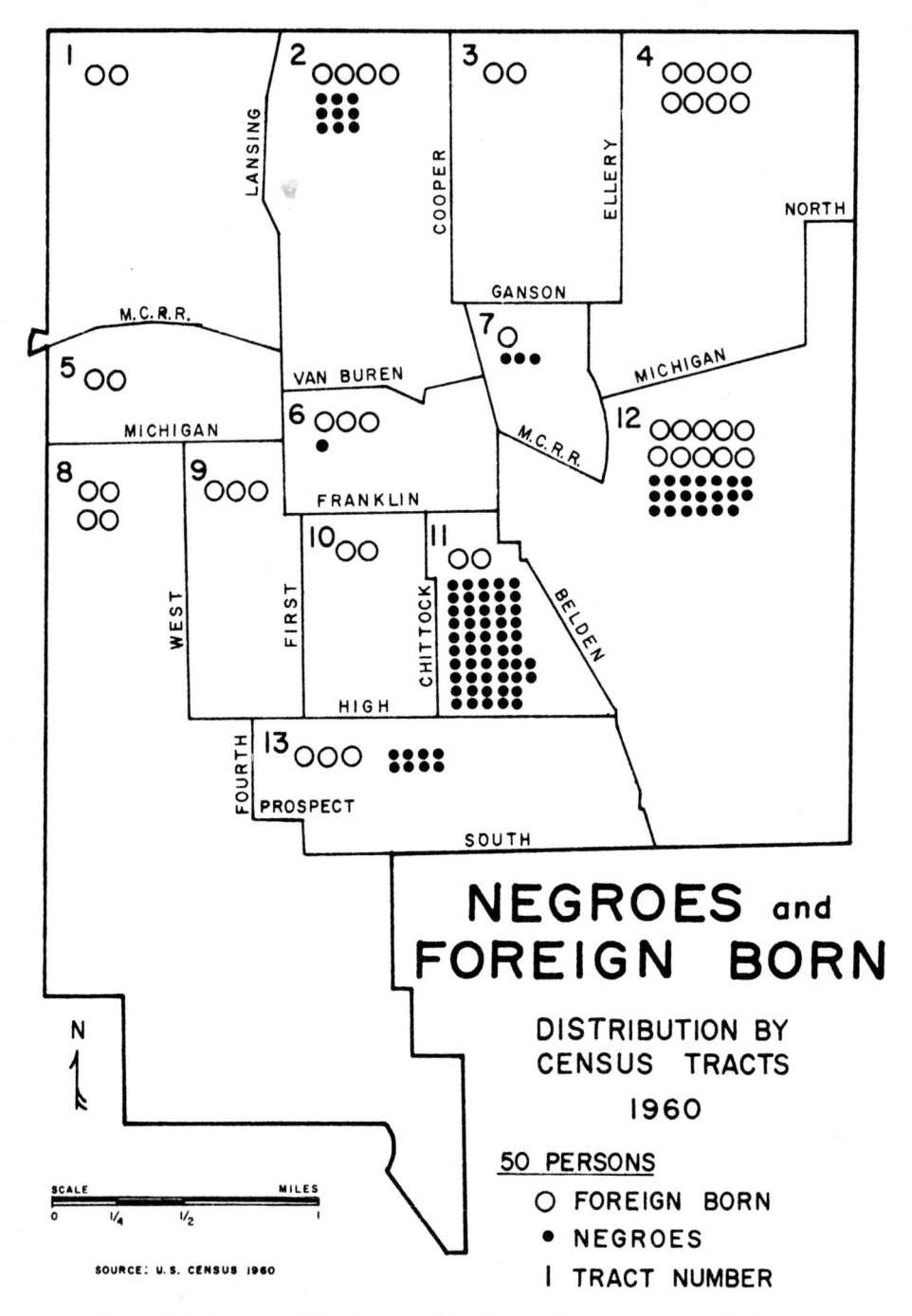

Figure 8.9. Negro and foreign-born distribution by census tract, Jackson 1960.

Education and Recreation

In contrast to other southern Michigan regions, higher education in this area is primarily supported by church and private funding. Its four-year institutions include Adrian, Siena Heights, Hillsdale, and Spring Arbor, while Jackson Community College, a two-year institution, is the only public college.

The periodic weekend or seasonal recreational attractions of the region including three State Parks are also significant economic and land-use factors (table 8.5). The soothing lighted artificial cascades in Jackson overcome the lack of waterfalls in southern Michigan. Other major facilities include Ella Sharp Park, Wamplers Lake and Waterloo State Parks, and the Jackson Harness Raceway. The Irish Hills attraction has been strengthened by the commercialization of skiing, rennovation of historic Walker Tavern, and the Michigan International Speedway at Cambridge Junction.

TABLE 8.5
Regions Two, Three, Four: State Parks and Selected Historic Attractions

State Park	Acres	Camp Sites	Historic Site	Place
Region Two			Region Two	
Cambridge	183	None	Hidden Lake Gardens	Tipton
Hayes	654	210	1839 Post Office	Jackson
Waterloo	17,053	424	Old Central Hall	Hillsdale
Region Three			Region Three	
Fort Custer	2,866	None	West South Street District	Kalamazoo
Yankee Springs	4,972	368	Bristol Inn	SE Hastings
Region Four			Region Four	
Van Buren	326	205	Berrien County Courthouse	Berrien Springs
Warren Dunes	1,499	249	Father Allouez Memorial	Niles

SOURCE: *Michigan Historic Attractions,* Michigan History Division, 1973; *Michigan State Parks,* DNR–Michigan Tourist Council, 1975.

Kalamazoo-Battle Creek, Region Three: A Pharmaceutical and Cereal Products Manufacturing Area

Region Three consists of the Kalamazoo SMSA and the counties of Barry, Calhoun, St. Joseph, and Branch (table 8.1). The region's rivers, St. Joseph, Kalamazoo, and Thornapple, a tributary of the Grand, flow into Lake Michigan resulting in a tendency to separate the region from the state's southeast-eastern core area. By the 1830s the region's prairies had attracted settlers, and settlements were established at Sturgis, Kalamazoo, Marshall, and in northwestern Branch County. Since the 1850s when the Detroit-Chicago Railroad line was completed, the transportation route including I-94 between those two principal national cities has been the most powerful cultural force shaping the region. Other important external forces include the expansion of the Lansing area and the conurbanization of South Bend-Elkhart-Mishawka in northern Indiana.

Population and Settlement

The region, although always having some manufacturing, has tended, in comparison to southeastern Michgain, to have a lower percentage of urbanization, industrialization, and black population. Black settlement in the region is still negligible in Barry and Branch counties. However, between 1940 and 1970, the diffusion of World War II industrial production into the area was a strong factor in the increased percentage of urban black population in the counties of Calhoun (3.2 to 8.4), Kalamazoo (1.2 to 4.8), and St. Joseph (.4 to 2.2).

Battle Creek is the region's largest urban subcenter. Historically its large number of vegetarians led to the development of Kellogg and Post cereal processing factories in that city. Marshall, Albion, Coldwater, Sturgis, Three Rivers, and Hastings are the region's smaller important satellite communities lying within 70 km (42 mi) of Kalamazoo (fig. 8.10).

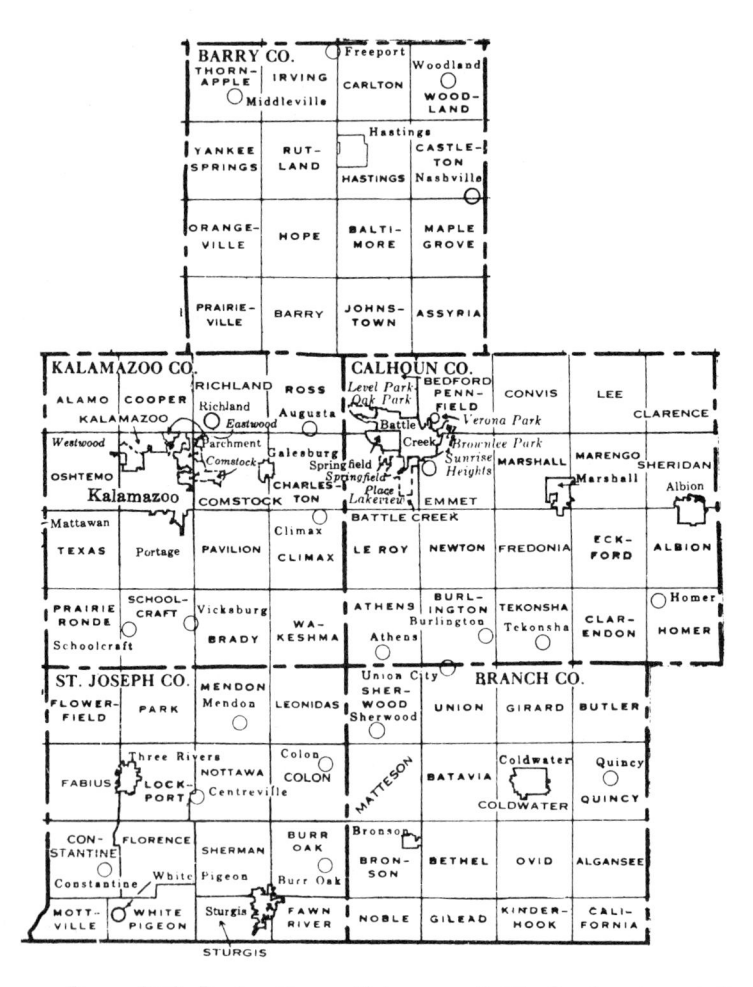

Figure 8.10. Region Three—Kalamazoo-Battle Creek, minor civil divisions. (Map: U.S. Bureau of Census.)

Employment and Production Activities

The most important value added by manufacturing activity found in the regional center is the production of pharmaceuticals and chemicals. Other regional activities are furniture, dairy processing plants, musical instruments, and pulp-paper mills. Automobile-related activites include machine tools, truck transmissions, and taxicab production.

Education and Recreation

Western Michigan Univeristy, founded in 1903 as a teacher training institution, has, with a greatly diversified curricula, grown into the state's fourth largest university enrolling over 22,000 and employing more than 800 professional faculty. The region's four smaller private and public colleges, Kalamazoo, Nazareth, Glen Oaks, and Kalamazoo Valley Community College, serve both specialized and liberal arts interests. A strong recreational influence from Chicago is found in Barry County (table 8.5). Scenic hills, numerous lakes, and the Yankee Springs State Park attract thousands into the region annually from the states and communities lying adjacent to the south and west. Since World War I, Fort Custer has contributed to the twentieth century military needs of the state and nation. Today, the sounds of grunts and exploding shells are mixed with the more tranquil sounds of hikers, bird watchers, and other recreational pursuers.

Benton Harbor-St. Joseph, Region Four: A Fruit Raising and Processing Area

Region Four consists of Berrien, Cass, and Van Buren counties and is unique in several comparisons with the other regions of Lower Michigan (table 8.1). Its location in close proximity to Chicago and South Bend coupled with the frequent interaction with people from those two communities provides a strong influence on the region's social, economic, and transportation organization. Using the state's longest growing season advantageously, the orchardists and fruit processors have taken the opportunity to develop the region into the state's most valuable fruit-producing area.

Population and Settlement

Benton Harbor, a predominantly black community of 16,000, and St. Joseph, a city of 11,000, combine to form the regional center for the area's quarter million residents. These two cities in addition to Niles (13,000) and Dowagiac (6,500), in opposition to recent small city trends in Michigan, have declined in population since 1960. However, the county seat communities of Cassopolis (2,108) and Paw Paw (3,160), with dissimilar racial composition, have continued to grow. Thus, typical generalizations about community size and racial composition do not fit the Region Four population situation. Historically, Berrien and Cass counties have been noted for their populations of black citizens. However, Berrien County with 11.2 percent black residents, has a nonwhite population percentage which is the same as the state's average black population percentage.

A binding force which helps to maintain the regional identity is the Benton Harbor News-Palladium, one of four regional newspapers in Michigan with a circulation greater than the number of citizens in the community in which it is printed. Until the early 1930s the interurban railway (IRW) was a dominant cohesive force with its connections between Benton Harbor,

Watervliet, Dowagiac and South Bend-Chicago through Niles. The Benton Harbor-Chicago Interurban connection lasted until 1934 when it became the last IRW to discontinue operation in Michigan.

Employment and Production Activities

Since prohibition, Van Buren County and Paw Paw have developed into the state's leading wine-producing region. The emergence of wine making as an outstanding activity illustrates in part the strong locational advantages held by the most diversified part of the Fruit Belt. It also indicates a major shift away from an earlier prohibitionist position, as Van Buren County was the first to "go dry" under the 1887 local option law passed by the State Legislature. The two shoreline counties of the region reveal the greatest land-use devoted to fruit raising which is dominated by peaches, but includes significant yields of grapes, apples, pears, and plums. All three of the region's counties participate in seasonal processing activities. Paper production in Niles and several small wood products plants remain active as a legacy to the lumber era which reached Van Buren County in the 1870s.

Education and Recreation

Warren Dunes State Park is increasingly important to the region's recreational economy. A critical threat to the region's dunes is sand mining and private development which continually reduce the amount of dunelands along the Lake Michigan shore for recreation. The region's innovative Blossom Festival was one of this century's earliest tourist festivals which capitalized on the promotion of a regional product (table 8.5).

Region Four is a center for Seventh Day Adventist activities connected with the location of Andrews University in Berrien Springs. In 1870, those people advocating a vegetarian diet and holding similar religious beliefs established a college in Battle Creek complementing the cereal plants which grew out of vegetarian diet interests. In 1901 the school was relocated in Berrien Springs and named Emmanuel Missionary College. Several years later, in 1960, it merged with Potomic University to form the present-day institution. The House of David is another vegetarian sect which organized in the area in 1903. The religious group operates a summer resort, cold storage plant, a printing establishment, and farms.

Flint, Region Five: An Automobile Manufacturing Area

Region Five is composed of Genesee, Lapeer, and Shiawassee counties. Flint, the state's third largest city, is the regional center. Owosso, Fenton, Flushing, Lapeer, and Grand Blanc are the region's subcenters which have been built on the moraine belts south of the extensively farmed Saginaw Lowland. Genesee County contains 80 percent of the region's half million residents, while 90 percent of the region's black citizens are agglomerated within the city limits of Flint (table 8.1).

Lying between the centers of General Motors activity in Flint and Detroit are the high-class suburbs of Region One, Bloomfield Hills and Birmingham, whose country clubs and eating establishments act as informal business centers to discuss styling, design, mileage, engineering, and financial matters of interest to automobile executives.

Employment and Production Activities

In the late nineteenth century Flint attained a reputation as a quality wagon and carriage manufacturing center (fig. 8.11). By 1900 its annual production reached 100,000. Building on its vehicle heritage, Flint adapted its factory facilities and later became the state's most specialized auto production center. Today one can look over the skyline of Flint and observe an expanse of a dozen auto plants operated by the Buick, Chevrolet, and AC Spark Plug Divisions of General Motors Corporation (GM). Flint's auto production activities are closely linked to Detroit and are guided from the international headquarters of GM at the Grand Boulevard *New Center Area* in Detroit. Flint, as the state's second largest automotive production center, also has the nation's lowest SMSA industrial diversification index which underlines its high degree of dependency on the economic health of the automobile industry.

ESTABLISHED IN 1869.

CARRIAGES

Top Phætons, Open Phætons.   Top Buggies, Open Buggies.

Platform Wagons,

THREE-SPRING WAGONS.

I have now on hand and am building the best and largest stock of FINE WORK ever made in Michigan. Every job made in my establishment in 1877 will be of the very Best Quality, and Finished in the best style. Parties intending to buy will do well to call and examine my work and get prices.

W. A. PATTERSON,

125 Saginaw Street, Flint, Mich.

Figure 8.11. 1877 Flint carriage, buggy and wagon advertisement. (Source: C. Young, *Citizen Century*.)

During this century's first two decades when the world's largest GM manufacturing complex was being organized, Jackson was the leading auto center outside Detroit. Between 1904 and 1907, Jackson was even the "Home of Buick." O. W. Mott, brother of C. S. Mott, was induced by W. C. Durant to come to Michigan from New York to manage the Jackson Imperial Wheel Factory where Buicks were then assembled. W. M. Eaton, GM's first president was also from Jackson. Why then did Buick and GM become so important to Flint? Pound, in his history of General Motors, suggests that Jackson may well have continued as the headquarters of Buick if financial capital could have been raised there as easily as it was in Flint. The argument that the Flint Wagon and Carriage Business alone was the critical location factor is questionable as Jackson also had a national reputation for wagon production. Thus, the critical location factor for the Flint auto center appears to be the financial support which Durant received in Flint. Although Jackson remained as the state's second-ranked auto assembly center until World War I, by 1926 Jackson totally ceased auto assembly operations, and Flint emerged unchallenged in the automobile production field outside the Detroit area. In the process of coalescing auto production in Flint, the automotive brain power of C. S. Mott, C. W. Nash, and W. P. Chrysler was drawn to Flint. Because of their productive efforts, combined with those in Detroit, the face of the earth continues to be transformed and the world's people adapt themselves to the mobility that automobiles provide.

In addition to automobile production, the regional center produces building insulation, foundry products, paper cartons, steel tanks, varnishes and paints, tools and dies, and furniture. In Genesee County, McLaren, St. Joseph, and Flint Osteopathic Hospitals are second to GM in providing nonpublic funded employment. Agricultural production, meat-packing, and dairy-processing activities also give diversity and some economic stability to the region.

Education and Recreation

Easily overlooked in Flint is the quiet revolution of education which can be seen in the burning lights both day and night in the schools throughout the community. In the contemporary era, nighttime school or campus lighting may at first be interpreted as just vandal and crime deterrents. In Flint, lighting is indicative of a community school concept at work, supported by the Mott Foundation which keeps the school facilities open after normal school hours to all age groups for both educational and recreational activities. Another pioneer educational program operates at General Motors Institute which is noted for its technical programs devoted to the improvement of automobiles. Additional higher education activities are found at the C. S. Mott Community College and Flint College of the University of Michigan which adjoin each other in the city's cultural center. The cultural center includes a planetarium, library, art facility, and theater. Only one state park has been established in Region Five (table 8.6).

Lansing, Region Six: The Capital Area

The decision to relocate the state capital from Detroit to Ingham County in 1847 has transformed Region Six into a culturally unique place in Michigan. The region encompasses three counties, Ingham, Eaton, and Clinton, which reached a population of over 400,000 in 1974. Of the total, less than 4 percent are nonwhite citizens; characteristically though, 84 percent of the black residents live in Lansing, the regional center (table 8.1).

TABLE 8.6
Regions Five, Six, and Seven: State Parks and Selected Historic Attractions

State Park	Acres	Camp Sites	Historic Site	Place
Region Five			Region Five	
Metamora-Hadley	683	211	Linden Mill	Linden
Region Six			Region Six	
Sleepy Hollow	2,685	None	State Capitol	Lansing
Region Seven			Region Seven	
Lakeport	565	256	Shiawassee National	T11N-R4E
Port Crescent	209	181	Wildlife Refuge	Sec. 20
Sleeper	963	335	Saginaw Post Office	Saginaw
Bay City	196	285	Frankenmuth Community	Frankenmuth
Gladwin	381	45	Grindstone City	Grindstone City
N Higgins Lake	429	201	Pioneer Huron City	Huron City
S Higgins Lake	305	500	Midland Center for Arts	Midland
Rifle River	4,329	165	Beechwood/Cobblestone Farm	Farwell
Tawas Point	175	202	Gypsum Quarries	Alabaster
			Lumberman's Monument	T24N-R7E Sec. 32

SOURCE: *Michigan Historic Attractions,* Michigan History Division, 1973; *Michigan State Parks,* DNR–Michigan Tourist Council, 1975.

Population and Settlement

Building on a base of local economic diversification, it is expected that by the year 2000, the Lansing Region will have to accommodate 145,000 new residents which represents about one out of every dozen people expected to be added to the state population in the next quarter century.

Undoubtedly, both the growth of the region and state growth will necessitate continued expansion of the central capitol complex which is concentrated into ten square blocks. Visually, the domed capitol sandstone building completed in 1878 appears as an architectural contrast to the 1960s low, functional, modernistic, box-shaped government office buildings which are separated by pleasant, tree-lined, pedestrian malls (fig. 8.12).

Decision to Locate Capital in Lansing. The original State Legislature was understandably beset with many initial statehood problems. Thus, it postponed for a decade the selection of the location for the capital. After ten years of arguments and politicking, the final decision was made in favor of the wilderness site near the confluence of the Grand and Red Cedar rivers. Persuasive arguments for an interior location included: (1) the well-remembered capture of Detroit in the War of 1812, (2) a more central location to better serve the entire state, (3) a smaller more tranquil place than the state's largest city for deliberations. Several communities could have fulfilled the capital site requirements and actively competed with each other for the designation. Marshall and Jackson even had designated land for the capitol building site. Nonetheless, community pride prevented many representatives from voting for a town other than their own. Thus, the Lansing Township and Ingham County interests which did not have as thriving a town as others to the south, were able to sway support to the neutral wilderness site. The slow growth of the capital area in its early stages illustrates the typical premature settlement model. When the community was incorporated twelve years after it became the capital, it still had only 1,500 residents. The economic base of the region was finally secured by the location of the State Agricultural College in 1855 6.4 km (4 mi) to the east, the completing of the railroad in the Civil War era, and the post-Civil War industrial boom.

Figure 8.12. The Lansing Capital Complex and central business district. (Photo: Michigan Travel Commission.)

Employment and Production Activities
In addition to the influences of governmental administration, higher education especially linked to agriculture, motor vehicle production (Oldsmobile, Reo, White), and commerce have been significant factors in minimizing the cyclical traumas which affect the strictly automotive dominated communities of Michigan. In the contemporary era, 150 industries contribute to the

economic stability of the Lansing Region. Abrams Aerial Survey Company in Lansing has been a pioneer corporation in air photo services throughout the world.

Lansing, like most cities, has been faced with the vexing problem of a deteriorating downtown area and the loss of city employment opportunities. In addition to urban renewal and the creation of downtown pedestrian-parking malls out of former streets, Lansing community leaders made the decision to maintain and expand its Lansing Community College adjacent to the CBD along the Grand River which was cleared of blighted buildings during the decade 1965-1975. By keeping the community college in the city, it forms a nucleus to attract young people to the center of the city. In the renewal process, Lansing adopted the innovation of combining parking ramps with other commercial activities. By locating businesses on the ground and basement levels and stacking parked cars above, valuable urban land space was preserved and the site is better able to generate money and taxes.

Education and Recreation

In East Lansing are found the internationally important extensive agricultural research fields of Michigan State University. The university offers Baccalaureate Degrees in 130 programs and Graduate Degrees in seventy areas of study. The city, along with the highrise dormitories of the university, houses the state's largest student body (45,000) which helps to form it into Region Six's second largest city.

Physiographically, the region occupies rolling recessional moraines and eskers which is notably devoid of inland lakes. However, the Grand River with its tributaries, Red Cedar, Looking Glass, and Maple, provide the area with canoeing and water fowl recreation opportunities. The Sleepy Hollow State Park Water Impoundment, formed during the mid-1970s, is designed to diversify and add to the water surface contact sports opportunities for the area's residents. Complementing the Sleepy Hollow project are the Danville State Game Area and Rose Lake Wildlife Research Area.

Saginaw-Bay City, Region Seven: The Eastern Transition Area from the Agricultural-Industrial South to Forested North

Region Seven consists of thirteen counties. They extend from agriculturally bountiful Sanilac County through the industrial metropolis of its region centers Saginaw-Bay City, to the northern forest and recreation lands of Roscommon and Iosco counties. Dominating the state's largest region physiographically is the extensive, flat, lacustrine Saginaw Lowland. This flat plain of the region is carved by the numerous tributaries of the Saginaw River. Today the wounds caused by the logging era are covered by a second growth forest which provides an illusion of what the region was like before 100,000,000 logs were floated to more than 100 sawmills lining the 6.4 km (10 mi) of river between Saginaw and Bay City. The river and the logs propelled the two cities to prominence as an important ship-building center which has been followed in the modern era by automobile-related production.

Population and Settlement

Lying in an arc around Saginaw-Bay City are several smaller places which serve the region as farm market and industrial centers. The most prominent of these are: Marlette, Ithaca,

Alma-St. Louis (mobile homes); Frankenmuth (beer brewing, Christmas decorations, restaurants); and Mount Pleasant (education-petroleum). Functioning as county administrative centers are Tawas, West Branch, Roscommon, Gladwin, Standish, Caro, Sandusky, and Bad Axe. Midland, the home of Dow Chemical, with a population of 35,000 is the region's third largest community (table 8.1).

Intra-Regional Population Migration. The population migration pattern in Region Seven is similar to Region Four in which the regional centers have declined in population, while the area's other large communities and fringe areas have gained population regardless of racial composition.

Saginaw with a black population of 22,000 declined 6.5 percent between 1960-1969. In comparison, Bay City with only 686 black citizens witnessed a decline of 7.8 percent. On the other hand, industrial Midland gained 27 percent and Mount Pleasant increased 38 percent with both cities having 150-300 black citizens in residence. Such a population migration and growth pattern is illustrative of nonracial factors stimulating change and strongly suggests other *push-pull factors* which include: (1) aging character and rising maintenance costs of housing, (2) congestion brought on by traffic, (3) high incidence of crime, and (4) higher taxes and declining city services. During the 1960s Iosco County witnessed a 50 percent population increase, third to Livingston and Macomb counties, each with a 54 percent increase. These counties illustrate the concept of the classic *pull factors* of migration: i.e., perception of (1) lower taxes, (2) lower land prices, (3) newer trouble-free housing, (4) increased status of a new home, (5) nostalgia for rural America with its fresh air and space for children to play, and (6) a more conducive atmosphere for out-of-door activities and patio living. Propelling the migration and longer journeys to work are the general availability of the motorized triple-geared chariot of mass affluence, plus credit financing and the high density of good roads.[1] Undoubtedly, linked to the high degree of interregional mobility are several physical-social factors, including crime. The occurrence of crime in Clare, Ogemaw, Gladwin, and Roscommon counties is above the state's Index Crime average. Roscommon County is not only well above the average in water area recreation facilities, but also bank deposits.

Employment and Production Activities. Bay City is the most northerly industrial and international port city in Michigan. In World War II and later years, warships were built for both the United States and other nations. Now freighters are constructed in its shipyards. Bay City's industrial production includes petrochemicals, cranes, shovels, automotive parts, transformers, welding machines, and sugar. In metropolitan Saginaw, manufacturing has been closely tied to automotive activities since 1910. Twelve General Motors plants and four plants of Eaton Corporation are sited in or near the regional center. Usually more than 20,000 people earn livings from work in GM's central foundry, the Chevrolet and GM Steering Gear Divisions. Many products are processed in Saginaw from foreign countries under a law which allows foreign raw materials to enter the area and then be redirected abroad without import or export duties. Wickes Corporation which originated in the logging era now distributes through a state network of outlets, lumber, home supplies, and manufactured buildings.

Farm Activities. East of the urban-industrial I-75 corridor is found Michigan's highest dollar value farming area, specializing in cash crops and dairying. Seen throughout the farming

---

1. C F. Heller, E. C. Quandt, H. A. Raup, *Population Patterns of Southwestern Michigan* (Kalamazoo: Western Michigan University, 1974), pp. 55-56.

area are fields and large storage facilities for dry navy beans, sugar beets, hay, corn, and several truck vegetable crops. Sanilac and Huron counties lead in dairy production while dairy-processing plants are concentrated in Saginaw and Bay City. Huge storage facilities for wheat and other grain exports pierce the skyline.

Wurtsmith Air Force Base at Oscoda in Iosco County is another basic contributor to the region's economy. Evidence of the growing economic strength of Region Seven is the expansion of branch financial institutions, parcel delivery services, and regional utility management into western Mecosta County from Bay City, Mt. Pleasant, and Alma respectively.

Education and Recreation. Central Michigan University and Saginaw Valley College are the Saginaw-Bay City Region's two public four-year institutions. The Clarke Historical Collection at Mount Pleasant with its holdings of county maps and histories is of special interest to geographers. Complementing these institutions are three postwar community colleges, Kirtland, Mid-Michigan, and Delta, plus two four-year private colleges, Alma and Northwood Institute. Along Saginaw Bay and into the interior, waterfowl sports and forest camping are important activities in the nine State Parks and several State Wildlife Areas found within the region (table 8.6). The Tittabawassee River State Forest covered by aspen, oak, lowland hardwoods, and brush, contrasts sharply with the bent windbreak poplar trees which sectionalize the flat lowlands. As one travels northward into the forested area, evidence of the beavers' survival and resurgence can be observed. The floodings which they cause, although troublesome at times, are beneficial to wetland wildlife and habitat management. Cedar swamps and open fields are important for their winter protection for deer, tourist viewing, and picture taking.

In contrast to the recreational activities of the region's forested north is the Saginaw Civic Center. The center includes facilities for ice hockey and other sports events, performing arts, circuses, and conventions. Over half a million people annually attend events in the Saginaw Civic Center. Since the construction of the civic center, completed in 1972, Saginaw's position as a major Michigan convention center has been strengthened.

Grand Rapids, Region Eight: The Heartland of the Western Lower Peninsula

The nine counties which compose Region Eight are the core area of the western Lower Peninsula. The regional center, Grand Rapids, has been the state's second largest city for more than a century. Currently its SMSA which includes Ottawa County in Region Fourteen, ranks sixty-fifth in population in the nation (table 8.1).

Population and Settlement

In the quarter century following World War II, Grand Rapids, the contiguous suburbs of Wyoming (57,000), Kentwood (21,000), East Grand Rapids (13,000), Walker (12,000), and Grandville (11,000), received the region's most significant increases in population and became a part of the urbanized core. Holland (27,000) lying 48 km (30 mi) southwest of Grand Rapids is split by the Allegan-Ottawa County Line and functions with Region Fourteen—Muskegon. Big Rapids (12,000), a county seat and site of Ferris State College on the Muskegon River 90 km (55 mi) north of Grand Rapids, acts as a regional subcenter. Except for Ludington (9,000) which adds port and recreation activities to its functions, the other six county seat towns are considerably smaller in population: Allegan, Reed City, White Cloud, and Stanton range in size between Baldwin's 600 and Ionia's 6,300 (fig. 8.13).

Idlewild, a Rural Retreat for Northern Blacks. In the early twentieth century and continuing to the Black Movement of the 1960s, south central Lake County was a "rural retreat" for blacks seeking a rural life-style and for nationally famous Negro entertainers who sought a quiet recreation area. Idlewild became the center of the community which includes Webber, Cherry Valley, Pleasant Plains, and Yates townships. Although nearly a quarter of Lake County's population is composed of black residents, their total number of approximately 1,275 is nearly the same as in 1950.

Idlewild's single-family dwellings reflect the American acculturation process. However, the structures reflect the low economic condition of the area even though twentieth century period architectural styles and building materials have been used in their construction. In contrast, the Grand Rapids inner city black areas reflect the effort of the community to redress the conditions of the economically deprived with housing projects, new schools, park space, and swimming pool improvements.

Employment and Production Activities

Historically the region's identity has come from logging, lumbering, and the creative crafting of wood into world famous, high quality furniture. The contemporary era's economy is much more diversified and responds to a variety of social and economic conditions. Nevertheless, with over seventy-five firms engaged in furniture design and production, Grand Rapids is still the center of the national industry. The historical antecedents of the coalescing of the furniture industry in Grand Rapids can be traced to the 1840s. The original location of woodworking was in a two-block long by one-half-block wide area hugging a speculatively created canal, whose locks were never installed, to bypass the Grand Rapids. At that site were assembled the first dozen cabinet, chair, and woodworking shops which competed to satisfy the local market and soon saturated it with their products. In a quest for economic survival, other markets were penetrated by raising the quality of the Grand Rapids furniture so that it could better compete in the local region and later with furniture made in Boston and Cincinnati. By raising the furniture's quality a reputation for high style and durable wood products was established. Further, pride, creativity, and skilled labor of the early craftsmen were perhaps the most important factors in establishing the furniture industry which still shapes the region and gives Grand Rapids prominence.

In analysis today, it can be observed that the locational advantages of Grand Rapids for furniture making and distribution were equalled or surpassed by several Michigan communities which were located in the hardwood forest region of the Lower Peninsula. At first Grand Rapid's disadvantage of lying north of the Detroit-Chicago transportation route was overcome by the use of the Grand River for navigation. Although in the mid-1970s the shallow draft navigation channel is open only to Eastmanville, in the pioneer era, thousands of pieces of furniture were sent to midwestern markets via steamboats which plied upstream to Grand Rapids from Grand Haven. With the completion of a railroad line to Detroit in 1858, Boston, New York, and Cincinnati began to feel the greater impact of the wood artisans' labor. In 1861, in Peoria, Illinois, and later in St. Louis, warerooms were established to affect "warehouse direct" shipping. As rail passenger service increased, the woodworkers filled cars with beautiful seats, sideboards, and other furnishings. Adapting to twentieth century markets, furniture

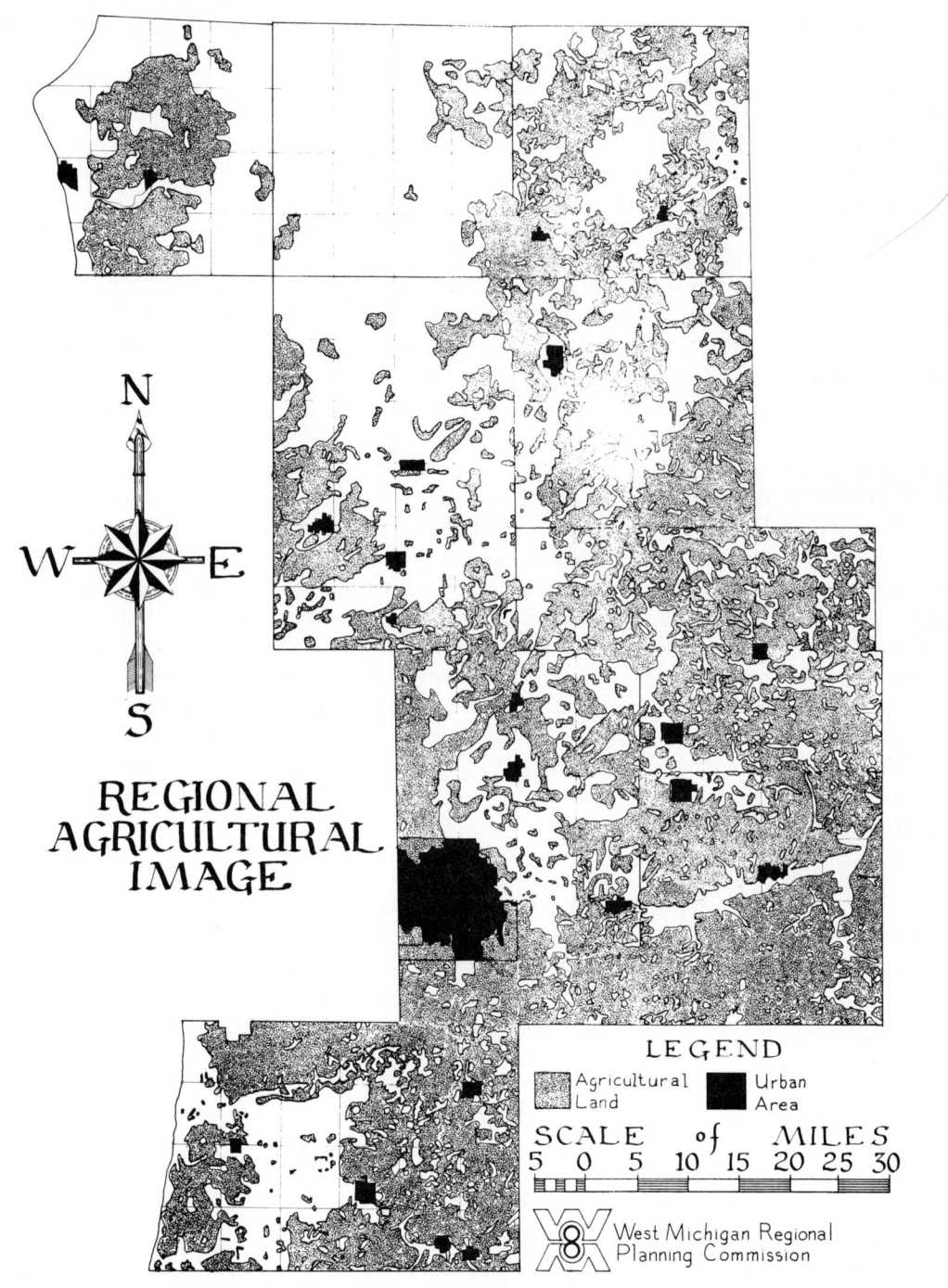

Figure 8.13. Region Eight—Grand Rapids agricultural land and urban center patterns. (West Michigan Regional Planning Commission.)

203

manufacturers expanded the production of school chairs, institutional furniture, stadium seats, and introduced high quality steel office furniture.

Complementing wood in the Grand Rapids economy are the fabricated metal industries which employ 13,000 and metal stamping industries. Nonelectrical machinery, die casting, metal plating, and other hardware production provide a strong tie to the construction industry. Chemicals, pharmaceuticals, gypsum mining and processing, dairy processing and distribution, plus publishing, are also significant in the regional economy. The region's link to Detroit can be traced by the flow of locally made auto parts, as well as the operation of one of the Detroit founded J. L. Hudson retail outlets in the ring of modern shopping centers which surround Grand Rapids. Auto parts production also occurs in Big Rapids, but parts manufacturing is more significant in the local economy of Evart, located on US-10, the extension of Detroit's Woodward Avenue.

Big Rapids' economy is dominated by Ferris State College with a student body of over 9,000. Ferris is noted for its blend of unique 2-5 year technical and professional programs in automotive, allied health, air conditioning, and avionic technical courses, as well as education, pharmacy, optometry, and business programs. Japan's investments penetrated the region in the early 1970s with the acquisition of a General Electric plant in Edmore and Magna-Lock Corporation in Big Rapids.

Specialized production activities are found in several county seats and in the region's smaller centers which include: Edmore (potatoes), Fremont (baby foods), Reed City (cottage cheese), and Ionia (plastics and State Reformatory). Shoe production is important in both Rockford and Big Rapids whose plants of Wolverine World Wide manufacture Hush Puppy shoes and other leather clothing accessories. Ludington continues to maintain its Wisconsin ties with its ferry service and further diversifies its economy with the manufacture of: magnesium pellets used in fire bricks, Dow chemicals, small kitchen products, and wire grates for stove and refrigerator shelving. It is also an important center for Lake Michigan-oriented activities including: seawall construction, the innovative pump-storage hydroelectric power plant, and the experimental use of wind power.

Education and Recreation

The location of Calvin, Aquinas, Grace Bible, and Grand Rapids Baptist colleges, plus Calvin Theological and St. Joseph Seminaries in Kent County indicates the profound influence of Christian Reformed and other religious denominations in higher education activities of the region. Montcalm and West Shore Community colleges in Stanton and Scottville, respectively, provide the region with two-year and more locally-oriented community programs.

No other region in Michigan has as many covered bridges as the Kent-Ionia County area of Region Eight. The preservation of these historic bridges adds a diversity to pleasure driving and color touring, which have developed into important regional activities (table 8.7). In the transition to the northern forest and recreation area, hunting, fishing, camping, canoeing, snowmobiling, and other outdoor activities are important. Increasingly the conflicts between motorized and nonmotorized vehicle users are thorny management problems facing the local and regional governmental bodies. In the resurgence of the Manistee National Forest, deer, partridge, turkey, and other small game have become common sights. Additionally, during the 1970s signs of bear and bald eagles are increasingly reported which give encouragement to further environmental management efforts.

TABLE 8.7
Regions Eight and Fourteen: State Parks and Selected Historic Attractions

State Park	Acres	Camp Sites	Historic Site	Place
Region Eight			Region Eight	
Ionia	3,826	None	Heritage Hill	Grand Rapids
Ludington	4,156	414	Hall-Fowler Library	Ionia
Newaygo	257	99	Windmill Gardens	Fremont
White Cloud	89	80	Norton Mound Group	Grand Rapids
Region Fourteen			Region Fourteen	
Grand Haven	48	172	Hackley House	Muskegon
Hoffmaster	1,030	333	9th St. Christian Reformed Church	Holland
Holland	142	342	De Zwaan Windmill	Holland
Muskegon	1,125	346	Escanaba Park	Grand Haven
Mears	50	179	Muskegon Waste Water Facility	T10N-R14W
Silver Lake	2,078	250		Sec. 19
			Muskegon Harbor	Muskegon

SOURCE: *Michigan Historic Attractions,* Michigan History Division, 1973; *Michigan State Parks,* DNR–Michigan Tourist Council, 1975.

Alpena-Gaylord, Region Nine: The Northeast Forest, Recreation, and Limestone Area

Region Nine is situated in the northeastern part of the Lower Peninsula and consists of eight counties. Lake Huron, the AuSable River and the north-south highways which bisect the peninsula have been and continue to be the major forces shaping the region.

Population and Settlement

Alpena and Gaylord are the regional centers for the area's approximately 100,000 people whose less than 1 percent nonwhite citizens are primarily located in Crawford County (table 8.1). The region has the lowest density and most rural population of any found in Lower Michigan. Thirty-three percent of its land is publicly owned and nearly 75 percent is forested. Forestry, combined with the region's limestone mining activities, make it most similar to an Upper Peninsula area. Alpena, the region's largest city, is situated 176 km (110 mi) from Bay City, Traverse City, and Cadillac, the closest communities with populations over 10,000. Situated approximately 96 km (60 mi) from Alpena are the county seat communities of Cheboygan, Gaylord, and Grayling. The population in these communities illustrates the impact of I-75 on development. Cheboygan, the region's second largest city (5,553) sited several miles east of I-75 declined in population after the highway's construction. On the other hand, Gaylord and Grayling, adjacent to I-75, increased 17 and 6 percent, respectively. Undoubtedly, these two communities' more southernly location, nearby military activity, and Gaylord's deliberate attempt to create a unique identity were also factors in their growth.

The counties of Alcona, Crawford, Montmorency, and Oscoda are without urban populations, and Oscoda does not have an incorporated town or village. One factor limiting even rural community incorporation in the region is taxes, as an unincorporated village is not required by state law to furnish police and fire protection or many other services.

Because of out-migration the population of Region Nine has fewer of the most productive age group, twenty-five to forty-four year-olds, proportionately than the rest of the state. The existing imbalance in age structure poses serious implications for future development of the region. People under fourteen and over sixty-five years of age make a demand on the community for social and welfare services such as education, recreation, and medical assistance. Yet, they are least able to meet the cost of services.

Overcoming the Problem of Out-Migration. In the early 1960s Gaylord's CBD had an "on the skids" appearance and was representative of many county seats of northern Michigan which possessed a high proportion of blighted and empty buildings. As a solution, Gaylord's civic leaders adopted a plan of community renewal which included for the CBD an Alpine architectural theme using natural stone and timbers. Further, there were efforts to secure new businesses based on the local resources of second growth timber and its 345 cm (136 in) average annual snowfall. Today the successful cooperative efforts between city-county government, national chain store operators, local financial leaders, and the community with its renewed pride, are uniquely imprinted on the landscape. Contrary to usual operation, three national chain stores modified their prototype designs to fit the community standard. The county and city government combined their efforts to create an innovative joint governmental building which reflected the community image (fig. 8.14). Nearly fifty business establishments which have been built or remodeled since the plan's inception have an Alpine facade but maintain a modern functional interior. The strengthened image as a community with pride is reflected in its week-long Alpine Festival held each July.

In addition to the greater access brought by I-75, the area's economy has been strengthened by a US Plywood plant and many ski-related recreational establishments. The adaptive use of the old CBD and off-street parking has strengthened the city in its competition with outlying mini-shopping centers, yet it has not preserved the traditional concentric zone pattern of land use which characterized small cities a century ago. In the outlying parts of Otsego County and the region, ten-acre half-mile long and narrow land divisions are frequently interspersed with large hunt club holdings (T30N-R2W). The fragmentation of the land into slightly over ten-acre parcels is done to avoid regulation under the 1967 Subdivision Control Act.

Employment and Production Activities. Alpena has combined the advantages of its protected site on Thunder Bay at the mouth of the Thunder Bay River with its access to the limestone quarries which lie between it and Rogers City, to concentrate the region's greatest diversity of economic activities. Paper making since 1875 and concrete block machinery since 1897 are Alpena's two oldest industries, however, cement production employs the most. Complementing industries include: hydraulic air cylinders, sheet metal, and a metals foundry. Auto parts, hardboard, and plywood production are located in both Alpena and Gaylord. Paper is produced in Cheboygan. The economic interdependency between the counties and adjacent regions is found in the significant amount of commuting across county lines (fig. 8.15). In the region as a whole, an average of one out of four employed persons travels into another county to his place of work. In a comparison of extremes, 37 percent of Alcona's labor force crosses into another county for work while only 10 percent of Alpena's employed labor commutes to another county.

Figure 8.14. Otsego County-City Building, Gaylord. (Photo: Michigan Travel Commission.)

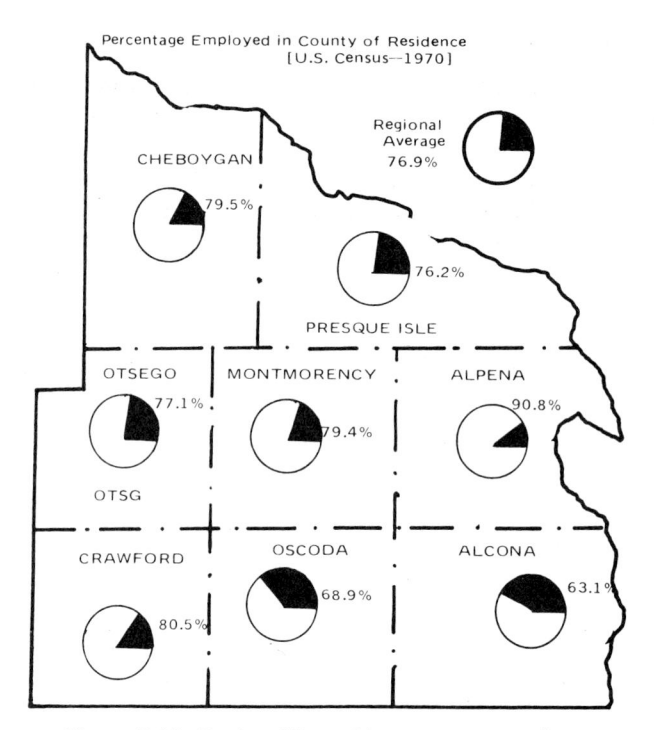

Figure 8.15. Region Nine—Alpena, percent of employed who cross a county line in their journey to work. (Map: Northeast Planning and Development Commission.)

Camp Grayling. Camp Grayling was initially known as Camp Ferris when it was established in 1913 in honor of the late Governor and US Senator Woodbridge N. Ferris. The military reservation now comprises 52,000 ha (130,000 ac) in Crawford and Otsego counties plus Kalkaska County in Region Ten. At the camp military training including infantry, artillery, and armor usually takes place between May and November 14. The facilities are primarily used by National Guard troops from three states (Michigan, Ohio, and Indiana), however, US Army Reserves and Marines from the Midwest and mid-South also utilize the reservation. Additionally, the air-to-ground target ranges are used year-round by air units from all parts of the nation. The reservation is generally considered a division (16,000 persons) sized training facility for live fire and maneuver tactical training. Today, most personnel reach the camp by truck; yet in the pre-World War II era, artillery units with their horses would march from Detroit, usually taking sixteen days. Military facilities at Camp Grayling have contributed much to stabilizing the local economy. In addition to the constant threat of fire and ignorant handling of dud ammunition, real estate development adjacent to the military reservation has become an increasingly difficult environmental management problem. At odds are the military's need for adequate training space, protection of its seven decades of capital improvements bought with taxpayer contribution, and those who have more recently built on nearby property and clamor for quiet.

Education and Recreation

Alpena Community College's contribution to the region is more than that of just an institution for higher education. It also has an effect on slowing the rate of out-migration.

Region Nine has the largest number of state parks and recreation areas in the state. As a result of their use, the region can be considered one of Michigan's major leisure time centers (table 8.8). It has twelve ski areas and twenty-one snowmobile trails and other areas for trail bikes, tobogganing, ice boating, and other outdoor activities. Of an estimated 4,000-5,000 campsites in the region, 50 percent are scattered along the Lake Huron shoreline.

TABLE 8.8
Regions Nine and Ten: State Parks and Selected Historic Attractions

State Park	Acres	Camp Sites	Historic Site	Place
Region Nine			Region Nine	
Harrisville	94	229	Camp Grayling	Grayling
Hartwick Pines	9,138	46	Au Sable River	Grayling
Aloha	76	300	Oscoda Courthouse	Mio
Burt Lake	406	365	Pine Stump Preserve	Deward
Cheboygan	932	78	Huron Cement	Alpena
Clear Lake	290	200	Old Presque Isle Lighthouse	Presque Isle Harbor
Hoeft	300	146	Limestone Quarry	Rogers City
Onaway	158	101	Mackinac Bridge	Mackinac City
Otsego Lake	62	203	Alpena Courthouse	Alpena
Region Ten			Region Ten	
Benzie	2,295	200	Fort Michilimackinac	Mackinac City
Interlochen	187	551	L'Ambre Croche Area	Cross Village
Mitchell	32	270	Beaver Island	Lake Michigan
Orchard Beach	201	175	National Music Camp	Interlochen
Petoskey	305	90	Sleeping Bear Dune	Glen Arbor
Traverse City	39	330	Point Betsie Lighthouse	Betsie Point
Wilderness	6,925	210	Old Waterworks	Manistee
Young	563	300		

SOURCE: *Michigan Historic Attractions,* Michigan History Division, 1973; *Michigan State Parks,* DNR—Michigan Tourist Council, 1975.

Of the several state parks, Hartwick Pines is most important with its few remaining acres of original white pine. Annually 120,000-170,000 visitors are attracted to the restored lumber-camp buildings and equipment displays.

Traverse City, Region Ten: The Cherry Capital Area

Region Ten in northwestern Lower Michigan gains its regional identity from its leadership in cherry production and its recreationally attractive natural environment. Nature, in providing the region with a unique combination of climate, sand dunes, and drumlin fields, carved its shoreline into a host of picturesque bays, points, and small peninsulas including: Betsie,

Pyramid, and Big Rock Points; Leelanau, Old Mission, and Waugoshance Peninsulas; plus Good Harbor, Grand Traverse, Little Traverse, and Cecil Bays. The region's land of moraines and outwash channels are studded with jewellike lakes including the long narrow walloon, Charlevoix, Torch, Elk, Leelanau, and Platte plus the more circular Mitchell and Cadillac, as well as numerous other inland lakes (fig. 8.16).

Figure 8.16. Traverse City on the west arm of Grand Traverse Bay with the Boardman Lake and River in the foreground. (Photo: Traverse City Area Chamber of Commerce.)

Population and Settlement

The Old Mission established by Protestant missionaries in 1839 to serve the local Indians predated the settlement of Traverse City which was founded in 1849. Omena, south of the resort community of Northport on the Leelanau Peninsula, became the "New Mission" in 1852 after many local Indians had immigrated to Wisconsin and Canada. In the century following its settlement, Traverse City grew into the largest community between Midland and Marquette. Thus, in the contemporary era, Traverse City's regional influence extends well into the Upper Peninsula. Possessing over 2,000 Class A overnight accommodations, Traverse City is frequently used by traveling salespersons as a temporary business center. The five counties which make up the core of the region (Antrim, Benzie, Grand Traverse, Kalkaska, and Leelanau) attract a peak daily visitor population of over 72,000 in August (fig. 8.17). In spite of the recently developed commercialization of downhill and cross country skiing and snowmobiling, the seasonal fluctuation in tourism is great.

1974 Average Number of Visitors Per Day
5 County Area

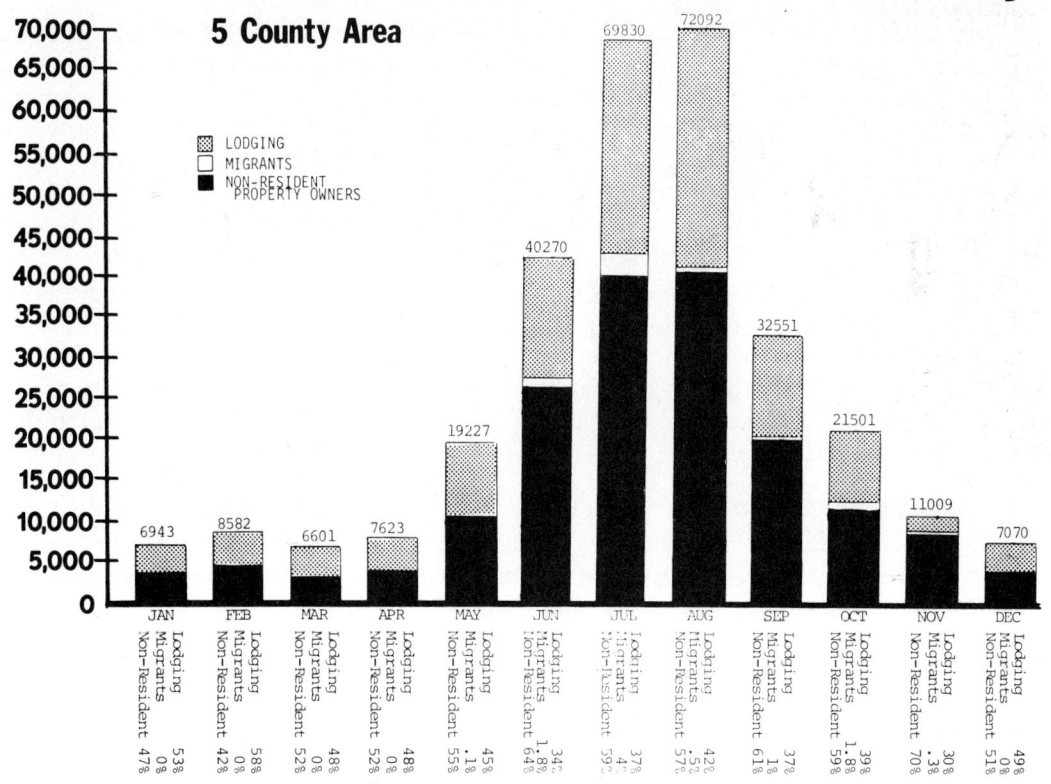

Source: SEASONAL POPULATION OF THE GRAND TRAVERSE AREA: Antrim, Benzie, Grand Traverse, Kalkaska and Leelanau Counties. PUBLISHED BY: The Grand Traverse Area Data Center, 13247 W. Bay Shore Drive, Traverse City, Michigan. Phone (616) 947-2501

Figure 8.17. Average number of visitors per day by month to Antrim, Benzile, Grand Traverse, Kalkaska, and Leelanau counties. (Graph: Traverse City Area Chamber of Commerce.)

Employment and Production Activities

Cadillac, with a population of approximately 10,000 situated 64 km (40 mi) southeast of Traverse City, is the region's second largest city and functions as a major retail, communication, and recreation center for the southern part of the region. Industrial metal production, boat building, and wood products complement its emphasis on recreation activities centered around Mitchell State Park and the Manistee-Huron National Forest. Other important population and retail centers tied primarily to recreation include: Petoskey (6,400), Boyne City (3,000), and Mancelona. In addition, Kalkaska and Manistee are important oil and paperboard producing centers.

Enhancing the high quality of living in the Traverse City Region is its concentration of medical personnel and health care facilities. Combined, Munson Medical Center, the Traverse City State Hospital, Grand Traverse Medical Care Facility, and the Traverse City Osteopathic Hospital are the city's leading employers. Grand Traverse County also has the state's lowest physician-resident ratio. Other leading activities in the region's center include: the manufacture of clocks, furniture and wall accessories, frozen pies and desserts, along with small automotive stampings and trim.

The Cherry Capital. Cherries, both tart and sweet, are the leading product of both Leelanau and Grand Traverse counties and give the region its identity within the Fruit Belt and nation. Michigan leads the nation in tart cherry production followed by New York, Wisconsin, and Pennsylvania. There are about 735 orchards in the Grand Traverse Bay area with an average of 3,265 trees each. The Old Mission Peninsula has the highest density of cherry trees with an average of 58,760 per sq km (22,600 per sq mi). Most red tart cherries are locally canned or frozen for later use in food products while maraschino cherries are mostly sweet cherries which are bleached, colored, then canned.

As the demand increases for housing sites within the cherry growing area, many orchards are being sacrificed. When projections are made about the future, the loss of orchards tends to warn of a possible threat to the stability of the fruit industry. While long-term concern is warranted, a short-run comparison of cherries produced in 1960-1964 and 1970-1974 periods indicates that cherry yields increased from 168 to 264 million kg (374 to 587 million lb) in the Grand Traverse area.

Education and Recreation

Higher education needs in Region Ten are met by two community colleges: North Central Michigan at Petoskey and Northwestern Michigan at Traverse City. In addition, the University of Michigan, Michigan State University, and Central Michigan University provide extension classes at several locations. The National Music Camp and Interlochen Arts Academy at Interlochen provide a unique center for the training of outstanding musicians from all parts of the nation.

Eight state parks are found in the region in addition to the Manistee-Huron National Forest and the Sleeping Bear Dune National Lake Shore, which includes the former D. H. Day State Park at Glen Arbor. Interlochen State Park with 551 camping sites on 75 ha (187 ac) has the largest number of camp sites in the state system (table 8.8).

As Traverse City has removed blighted buildings from its shoreline to protect and improve the shoreline by providing more open space, the question of waterfront balance between the spatial needs of its small port, which supplies the area with coal, and park use continually has to be assessed.

The Upper Peninsula, Regions Eleven, Twelve, Thirteen: The North Country of Forest, Mining, and Recreation

The three regions of the Upper Peninsula comprise fifteen counties which vary in size and number between three and six per region (table 8.1). The sex ratio for the total population of over 305,000 exceeds 100 for each region which reflects the Upper Peninsula's preponderance of male-oriented functions: mining, technical education, historic migration, military, and the State Prison (fig. 7.3). In the past, migration into the peninsula has tended to increase the male segment of the population. Projections of population by county to the year 1990 indicate a decline of over 36,725 can be expected.

Population and Settlement

Viewing the population and settlement pattern of the entire Upper Peninsula, the even spacing and variation in size of its communities are similar to a theoretical model advanced by the German geographer, Christaller, to explain the spatial organization and hierarchy of cities developed as a result of marketing, transportation, and administration. Marquette, the Upper Peninsula's principal city, is centrally located on the south shore of Lake Superior. Situated approximately 232 km (145 mi) from Marquette are Sault Ste. Marie and Ironwood, the regional centers for the east and west ends of the peninsula. At intervals of about 96 km (60 mi) from Marquette are Escanaba and Menominee while Houghton-Hancock is situated nearly halfway between Marquette and Ironwood but at a greater distance due to the configuration of the Keweenaw Peninsula. St. Ignace also varies from the uniform distance model due to the narrowing of the eastern end of the peninsula. The few other urban centers found have had their sites and populations historically influenced by either mining, forestry, or county seat administration. The larger of this group include Ishpeming, Negaunee, Iron River, Iron Mountain, Kingsford, Gladstone, Munising, and Manistique.

Employment and Production Activities

Oftentimes when the Upper Peninsula is mentioned, only the Soo Locks, mining of copper or iron, hunting-fishing, and the falls of the national and state parks come to mind. However, the area embraces a much wider diversity of economic opportunities especially in its urban communities. Service activities, especially higher education and transportation have become significant twentieth century employers. The labor involved in overcoming the geographic space of the area is reflected in the 1,400 jobs in Marquette and Escanaba linked to trucking and ore shipments. Other important production activities include Cliffs-Dow Chemical (Marquette), cranes (Iron Mountain, Escanaba), hydraulic valves (Iron Mountain), armaments and electric motors (Gladstone), pulpwood movers and welding equipment (Escanaba), helicopters (Menominee), wooden toys and ten pins (Iron River), and maple flooring (Ironwood). Smaller in scale but illustrative of the nation's trend toward according pets human status and their increased use as child substitutes is found in the pet casket, flower planter, and pet bed production in Gladstone and pet food processing in Menominee.

Out-Migration and the Quest for More Employment Opportunities. In comparison to the northern Lower Peninsula, there has been less success in slowing the wave of young men and women out of the Upper Peninsula into the distressed urban regions of southern Michigan to find employment. In the decade of the 1950s eight Lower Michigan counties, all in the North, lost population while in the decade of the 1960s, only one (Presque Isle) declined. In the same time period, twelve Upper Peninsula counties lost population with Gogebic, Iron, Luce, and Mackinac declining more than 10 percent. Only Baraga, Delta, and Marquette counties have witnessed population growth between the 1950s and 1970s. The consequences of out-migration, if continued, can be expected to be reflected in louder demands from the Upper Peninsula for industrialization, government assistance, and political pressure to equalize enforcement of environmental protection measures between established and newer industries. In the regional development of economic opportunities, the Upper Peninsula faces several obstacles including: (1) comparatively small market area population, (2) time and monetary costs of land transportation to existing markets, (3) costs to overcome cold and snow, (4) the size and skills pool of its labor force, and (5) population versus areal representation in the State Legislature. On the other hand, the Upper Peninsula possesses several advantages which hold potential for economic stability; i.e., (1) friendly welcome to new employers, (2) natural environment, (3) network of public institutions providing initial basic money for the region, (4) outstanding low unit cost bulk shipping facilities, and (5) improved highway and continued railroad transportation linkages.

Education and Recreation

A potent weapon in helping to stabilize the economic base of a frontier area is for the core area to extend public supported facilities into the region. The Upper Peninsula with three public four-year institutions—Michigan Technological (Houghton-Hancock), Northern (Marquette), and Lake Superior (Sault Ste. Marie); plus two community colleges: Bay De Noc (Escanaba) and Gogebic (Ironwood), illustrate the attempt to not only slow the region's "brain drain" but also to greatly expand local employment and attract educated people into the area. The State Hospital at Newberry, State Prison at Marquette, and new administrative regional centers complement the economic impact of the colleges. Suomi College at Hancock continues to represent the region's Finnish heritage. The peninsula's outdoor recreation industry is built on a foundation of seventeen state parks, two national forests, a national lake shore, and the state's only national park, which are evenly spaced throughout the area (table 8.9). Complementing the region's tradition of ski jumping is the soaring "ski flying" ramp at Copper Peak in Gogebic County which now challenges the nerves and skills of the world's outstanding ski jumpers. The state's highest density of log cabin and log farm buildings is in the Upper Peninsula which reflects the area's more recent pioneer settlement. These log structures serve not only as a reminder of past conditions, but also provide scenic subjects for photos. The cabins also hold a potential as examples for the accurate restoration and preservation of authentic log buildings which have to a great extent been lost in Lower Michigan, or have been less than accurately replicated, such as the "log cabin" in Lansing's Arboretum Park which was quickly fashioned out of telephone poles and perched off the ground.

TABLE 8.9
Upper Peninsula Regions: State Parks and Selected Historic Attractions

State Park	Acres	Camp Sites	Historic Site	Place
Region Eleven			**Region Eleven**	
Brimley	151	270	Soo Locks	Sault Ste. Marie
Detour	403	22	Schoolcraft House	Sault Ste. Marie
Muskallonge Lake	172	150	St. Ignace Mission	St. Ignace
Straits	120	322	Baraga House	Sault Ste. Marie
Tahquamenon Falls	19,244	319	Mackinac Island	Straits of Mackinac
Region Twelve			**Region Twelve**	
Fayette	357	80	John Burt House	Marquette
Indian Lake	567	302	Ore Docks	Marquette
Palms Book	308	None	Jackson Mine	Negaunee
Van Riper	1,044	227	Ski Hall of Fame	Ishpeming
Wells	974	155	Pictured Rocks	Munising
Region Thirteen			**Region Thirteen**	
Baraga	56	137	Lac Vieux Desert Trail	
Bewabic	200	52	Chippewa Burial Ground	T42N-R34W Sec. 11
Fort Wilkins	190	163		
Lake Gogebic	361	167	Copper Peak	T49N-R46W Sec. 32
McLain	401	90		
Porcupine Mountains	58,327	183	Suomi College	Hancock
Twin Lakes	175	62	Calumet Fire Station	Calumet
			Cliff Mine	near Phoenix
			Houghton County Historical Museum	Lake Linden

SOURCE: *Michigan Historic Attractions,* Michigan History Division, 1973; *Michigan State Parks,* DNR–Michigan Tourist Council, 1975.

Muskegon, Region Fourteen: The West Shore Area of Lower Michigan

Region Fourteen comprises three counties which front on the west shore of the Lower Peninsula: Ottawa, Muskegon, and Oceana. Although it is the smallest state region, it has a population as large as the entire Upper Peninsula (table 8.1). In comparing its settlement pattern, newspaper circulation, and economic activities, the region is most similar to Region Four. The city of Muskegon, the regional center, has a black population which comprises 15 percent of its total while its suburb community Muskegon Heights with 17,300 citizens, has 52 percent black residents. In contrast, Muskegon's other adjoining suburbs, Norton Shores (22,271) and Roosevelt Park (4,176), and Grand Haven (11,644), a satellite city 21 km (13 mi) south, have less than 1 percent nonwhite residents.

The State Planning and Development Regional boundary between Grand Rapids and Muskegon is poorly placed from a social and economic function point of view. Several small towns including Jenison, Lamont, Marne, plus Allendale which function economically with Grand Rapids are placed in Region Fourteen. This is one area in the state which would be well served by a shift from county to township boundaries for regional organization. Such a shift in boundaries would allow regional organizations to better serve the social-economic needs of their areas. The map from *Muskegon Country* produced by the Muskegon Area Development Council and Muskegon Chamber of Commerce perhaps better illustrates the actual Muskegon Region in relation to the Grand Rapids Region (fig. 8.18).

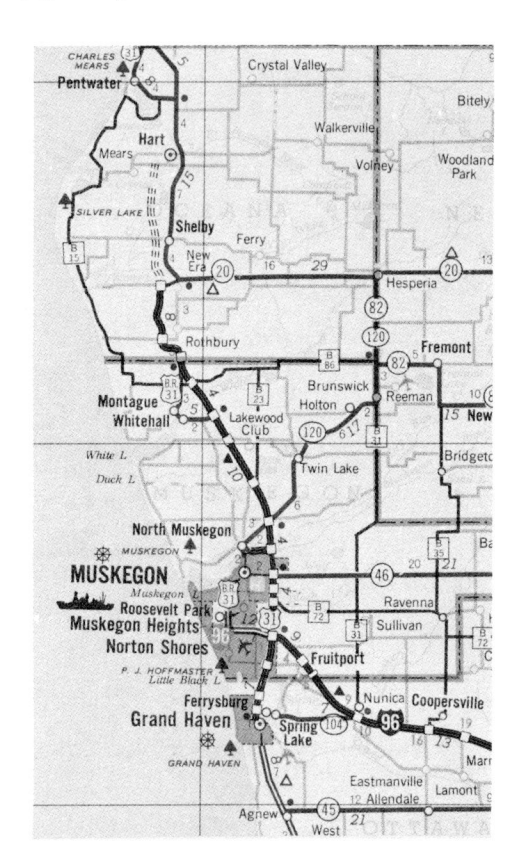

Figure 8.18. Muskegon Service Area based on the Muskegon Area Development Council publication *Muskegon Country.* (Map: Michigan Department of State Highways and Transportation.)

Population and Settlement

Physiographically, Region Fourteen occupies a former lake bed and outwash plains with a border of sand dunes. Draining this region are the Grand, Muskegon, White, and Pentwater rivers which in logging days greatly extended the region's influence into the hinterland.

However, with the creation of modern railroad and highway networks, the service and market area of the Muskegon Region have been truncated. In the process, Newaygo, Big Rapids, and White Cloud were drawn into the Grand Rapids Region. Strengthening Muskegon's postlumber era dominance as a regional center has been its gradual modernization of its port facilities. Its channelization, pier, and port warehouses combine with its industry to make it the major international and domestic port on Lake Michigan. The major limiting factor which the city has to face in comparison to Milwaukee (717,000) located directly across Lake Michigan, is the size of its hinterland. Milwaukee has half a continent at its "backdoor" while Muskegon must share the small Lower Peninsula with both Detroit and Saginaw. Further, the port of Grand Haven also competes with Muskegon for Lake Michigan shipping activity.

North of the urbanizing Ottawa and Muskegon counties, is rural Oceana County in which even its Fruit Belt market centers, county seat, and recreational communities (Shelby, Hart, and Pentwater) have remained nonurban in character. However, with the extension of the US-31 freeway and continued growth as in the 1970s, the two villages nearest Muskegon will soon become urbanized. Economically, Oceana County is the region's most active area in relation to the seasonal canning and freezing of fruit.

Employment and Production Activities

Muskegon is unique on the west shore of the Lower Peninsula with its concentration of manufacturing and professional sports facilities. It is the operation of these facilities which gives the regional center a cityscape similar to other urban regions of southern Michigan. Muskegon is linked to Detroit with the production of auto parts, pattern equipment, piston rings, and gas pumps; however, nonmotor vehicle manufacturing provides a larger share of the employment opportunities. Significant regional products include paper, metal furniture, air suspension systems, wire products, boats, electric cranes, organic chemicals, and concrete products. Primary manufacturing includes furnaces and foundries for iron, steel, brass, and aluminum castings. In Muskegon is the Western Division Office Center for General Telephone Company which also has its State Administrative Office in Norton Shores.

Education and Recreation

Grand Valley State Colleges established in 1960 is the region's most recent complex for higher education added to the landscape and it complements the new campus of Muskegon Community College and two private institutions, Hope and Western Theological Seminary. The region possesses six state parks which are sited to take advantage of the sand, sun, and fun possibilities of the Lake Michigan shoreline (table 8.7). These parks on Lake Michigan play a significant role in the state's efforts to preserve the sand dunes. Other tourists are annually drawn to the region for the fishing and boating sports which are also important to the local economy. The L. C. Walker Arena is used for various forms of entertainment in downtown Muskegon including International League Ice Hockey.

Photo Essay C

MICHIGAN SETTLEMENT FEATURES 1830-1976

C-1 Relic pioneer log cabin and lilac bush, Beaver Island.

C-2 Old Mission Church, Grand Traverse County, typical of nineteenth century construction methods and design.

C-3 Berrien County Courthouse in Berrien Springs, constructed in 1830s.

C-4 The Clinton Inn, relocated to Greenfield Village, is a typical example of a mid-1800s stagecoach inn.

C-5 A typical farmhouse and barn constructed in the late nineteenth century and early twentieth century north of Walloon Lake on US-131.

C-6 Typical central business district buildings constructed between 1880 and 1930 in a small county seat town, St. Johns.

C-7 Traffic on US-25 in Detroit in the late 1930s. (Photo: Michigan Department of State Highways and Transportation)

C-8 General Motors and Fisher Buildings at Grand Boulevard and Second in the 1920s New Center Area of Detroit.

C-9 Typical post-World War II automobile plant built in Ypsilanti along I-94.

C-10 Vandenberg Center, the city-county governmental core of Grand Rapids, 1975.

C-11 The Detroit skyline and downtown waterfront with the Renaissance Center on the right.

(Unless otherwise indicated, photos courtesy Michigan Travel Commission)

C-1

C-2

C-3

C-4

C-5

C-6

C-7

C-8

C-9

C-10

C-11

> "In the long run whatever proves to be biologically incorrect will never be economically sound."
>
> H. Leibundgut, Switzerland

Chapter Nine

Michigan's Economic Geography

This chapter on the economic geography of Michigan deals with the spatial structure of the economic activities of the state. Its focus is primarily upon the production of goods and services which are vitally essential to the state's economy and well-being of those who provide them. Although there are over one thousand activities identified in the United States Standard Industrial Classification System, most of which are represented in Michigan, geographers tend to be most interested in those which are closely related to the land in the production of goods and services. It is perhaps impossible to gain universal agreement as to which activities are most important to individuals and the state in terms of human effort, however, there should be little doubt that those which are devoted to food, shelter, mobility of individuals and ideas, transmission of knowledge, plus maintenance of health are near the head of any list.

Michigan's Labor Force and Diversity of Production Activities

The distribution of Michigan's labor force of over four million is similar to the general population. However, there is some skewing toward urban centers accounted for by the historic migration of workers over sixteen years of age to job opportunities in metropolitan centers. In spite of improved economic opportunities in areas outside southeastern Michigan, the Detroit SMSA still possesses half of the state's civilian labor force. Further, the Detroit SMSA's percent of the work force continues to increase although the city of Detroit's portion of state employment has declined from 17 to 13 percent in the 1970s (table 9.1).

TABLE 9.1
Civilian Labor Force and Unemployment 1970-1975 (in millions)

Place	1970 Labor Force	1970 Percent Unemployed	1975 Labor Force	1975 Percent Unemployed
USA	82.7	4.9	94.0	8.6
Michigan	3.6	6.7	3.9	12.5
Detroit SMSA	1.69	7.0	1.9	13.5
City of Detroit	.63	8.2	.52	17.4

SOURCE: *Michigan Statistical Abstract 1974,* Table V-1, p. 193, and Draft 1976.

Diversification of the Economy Dominated by Motor Vehicles, Agriculture, and Recreation

Motor vehicles, agriculture, and recreation industries are the three well-known foundation stones of Michigan's economy. In the last quarter century, there has been progress toward diversifying the industrial base. Continued diversification appears to be the key to moderating the contemporary reputation which the state has acquired, "If the national economy catches cold, Michigan gets pneumonia." Michigan's unemployment rate has tended in recent years to be significantly greater than the national average (table 9.1). Within the state, unemployment rates also vary considerably with communities dominated by motor vehicle and related industries, plus the Upper Peninsula usually has the highest rates (table 9.2).

TABLE 9.2
Unemployment Percent for Selected Michigan Areas

Place	1973	1974	1975
Ann Arbor	4.1	7.1	12.2
Battle Creek	4.8	7.4	12.0
Flint	5.7	13.2	15.0
Grand Rapids	4.9	7.3	11.0
Kalamazoo	4.2	6.0	10.1
Lansing	4.1	7.7	11.7
Upper Peninsula	7.7	8.7	12.0

SOURCE: *Economic Report of the Governor,* 1976, p. 13.

A slow but steady progress toward diversification can be illustrated by the distribution of manufacturing establishments by industry groupings and employment. Nevertheless, the economic diversity developed up to the late 1960s was not enough to prevent the severe economic dislocations or employment dominance by the motor vehicle production industry in the mid-1970s (table 9.3).

TABLE 9.3
Distribution of Employment in Michigan Manufacturing Industries 1975

Category	Average 1975 Employment
Durable Goods:	
Lumber-wood	11,200
Furniture	19,400
Primary metals	91,100
Fabricated metals	113,300
Nonelectric machinery	143,500
Electrical machinery	37,600
Motor vehicles and equipment	358,100
Other durable goods	43,700
Nondurable Goods:	
Food and kindred	50,900
Apparel and textile mill products	25,400
Paper and allied products	23,700
Printing publishing	33,100
Chemicals and allied	44,700
Other nondurable goods	32,200
Total	1,030,900

SOURCE: *Economic Report of Governor,* 1976, p. 15

Within Michigan's diversifying economy, electrical equipment, machinery, chemicals, apparel, food processing, publishing, plastics, and instruments are those sectors which have the greatest employment. One of the contributions geographers can make in future years is in the identification of not only the locational attributes and land-use requirements of those industries, but also which can be most easily expanded within the growing interdependent world economy.

Government Service and Agricultural Employment

Employment in government service activities represents about 16 percent of the state labor force. The funneling of federal funds to local governments enables those units to increase their employment. Employment in state colleges as a part of the state economy has tended to level in the 1970s after that sector of state employment expanded rapidly in the 1960s.

In 1880 when most people lived and worked in rural settings, the state's total labor force was only 569,204 of which 42 percent were employed in agriculture. In contrast, by the mid-1970s full-time agricultural employment declined to 52,500 or 1.4 percent of the labor force.

In analysis, these statistics only hint at the profound upheaval which has occurred as the state's economy mutated from one of primary industries (agriculture-mining) to secondary industries (manufacturing), and finally to one increasingly dependent upon tertiary service industries (public utilities, health, education, government, transportation, and recreation). In the next several pages the basic industries of each of the three broad classifications (primary, secondary, and tertiary) will be discussed, including agriculture, automobile, and recreation industries.

Agriculture: Primary within the Michigan Economy

In a society spurred by manufacturing and recreation which has an image of abundance, whose farmers are generally known for high productivity but are isolated from their consumers who have come to expect an unending computerized flow of high quality foods at low cost, it is not surprising that many citizens lose consciousness of the actual status and land needs of agriculture. Agriculture within our technological society is still a primary industry, not only in classification, but also in providing sustenance for human survival and economic viability to the state.

Agricultural Production Trends and Leading Products

Depending on systems and considerations in measurement, agribusiness in Michigan is the state's second or third largest industry in source of income. Michigan farmers received over $1.7 billion for their products in 1975 which was 4 percent less than the record high volume of production in 1974. By adding the costs of processing, transportation, and marketing, agribusiness is worth about five billion dollars. In a similar range of economic value, tourism ranks with agriculture as a major land-oriented industry and basic activity within the state's economy. In production, Michigan leads the nation in four products (tart cherries, dry edible navy beans, pickling cucumbers, and blueberries) and ranks fifth or higher with thirteen other products (table 9.4).

Decline in Farm Numbers

The decline in number of farms and increase in farm size is a generally known fact of twentieth century American rural life. Less well-known is the actual loss of land devoted to agriculture after farm consolidation and post-Vietnam era production increases (table 9.5).

The decline in number and acres in farms is attributable to several factors including: (1) extensive farming based on motorized machinery, (2) transfer of land used for animal feed production to human food production, (3) release of rural people for urban jobs, and (4) increased yields linked to scientific agriculture.

Does Less Equal More? The twentieth century has brought a paradox in Michigan agriculture in which seemingly fewer acres in farms have coincided with higher yields. Further, this increase in scientific agriculture has come at an apparent blinding rate. For instance, in 1924, 823,000 cows produced 1,870 mil kg (4,156 mil lb) of milk while in 1972 only 427,000 cows produced slightly more, 2,212 mil kg (4,916 mil lb) of milk. However, in relation to total state population, yield per person actually decreased from approximately 450 kg (1,000 lb) to 243 kg (540 lb) annually. Shortages in dairy products have been averted by the substitution of nondairy products such as margarine and soft drinks, decreases in milk consumption, and reduction in export of dairy products. In spite of actual per capita decreases in dairy production, proven scientific management practices diffused throughout Michigan's dairy herds undoubtedly could in the short run still reverse the yield-population downward trend. Finally, after a half century of changing farm production and marketing practices, balancing the exports to the Toledo milkshed with imports from Wisconsin, Michigan in the 1970s meets only 92 percent of its milk demand. Thus, it must supplement 8 percent of its basic food need by additional import. Milk is not an isolated case, but represents the lowest import food within the state's basic diet. A pertinent question which now needs to be raised for the state's citizens to

TABLE 9.4
Michigan Rank in Agricultural Products 1975

Commodity	Rank in Nation	Percent USA Production
Crops:		
Cherries, tart	1	76.4
Cucumbers, processing	1	19.2
Dry beans	1	26.2
Blueberries	1	39.0
Apples	3	9.5
Asparagus	3	9.2
Celery	3	5.6
Carrots	4	5.9
Cherries, sweet	4	17.6
Grapes	4	1.3
Maple syrup	4	8.2
Prunes and plums	4	2.8
Red clover seed	4	8.5
Spearmint	4	7.0
Cauliflower	5	1.7
Pears	5	2.0
Strawberries	5	3.0
Cantaloupe	6	1.7
Green pepper	6	2.9
Peaches	6	2.3
Snap beans, processing	6	4.5
Tomatoes, processing	6	.7
Corn, sweet	7	5.3
Onions	7	5.6
Rye	7	3.9
Tomatoes, fresh market	7	1.9
Sugar beets	8	6.0
Cabbage, fresh market	9	3.0
Corn, for grain	9	2.6
Corn, for silage	9	3.9
Oats	9	3.2
Popcorn	9	1.3
Snap beans, fresh market	10	2.2
Cucumbers, fresh market	10	3.1
Lettuce	10	.4
Livestock:		
Cheese, creamed cottage	4	6.2
Milk	6	3.8
Milk cows, on farms	6	3.7
Ice cream	7	4.4
Creamery butter	9	2.4

SOURCE: *Michigan Agricultural Statistics,* June 1976, p. 3.

answer is: How much food or dairy imports can be economically tolerated before decisive action is taken to insure continued high per capita yields and a viable Michigan economy?

TABLE 9.5
Farms, Farm Size, and Farmland 1920-1975

Date	Number Farms	Land in Farms Ha (mil)	Land in Farms Acres (mil)	Average Size Farm Ha (mil)	Average Size Farm Acres (mil)
1910	206,960*	7.6	18.9	37	92
1920	196,447	7.6	19.0*	39	97
1930	169,372	6.8	17.1	40	101
1940	187,589	7.2	18.0	38	96
1950	155,589	6.9	17.2	44	111
1960	111,817	5.9	14.7	53	132
1970	77,946	4.8	11.9	61	153
1975	80,000	5.0	12.4	62	155

*Peak number.
SOURCE: *Michigan Statistical Abstract 1974*, Table IX-1, p. 328; *Michigan Agricultural Statistics*, June 1974, p. 13. (These two sources conflict in actual figures, but show the same trend.)

Michigan Agriculture in Comparison to Other States

In comparison to other states Michigan ranks 21st in value of agricultural products sold, and 31st in amount of land in farms. California, Iowa, and Texas rank the highest in receipts from agricultural sales. Regionally within the United States, each of the Great Lakes states surpasses Michigan in both amount of farmland and value of products sold which provides a stabilizing influence within their economies (table 9.6).

TABLE 9.6
Great Lakes State Farm Comparisons 1969

State	Number of Farms	All Land in Farms (million acres)	Average Size in Acres	Rank in Value	Value of Farm Products Sold (million dollars)
New York	52,000	10.1	196	16	$ 979
Ohio	111,000	17.1	154	11	1,246
Indiana	101,000	17.5	173	10	1,400
Illinois	124,000	29.9	242	4	2,612
Michigan	78,000	11.9	153	21	829
Wisconsin	99,000	18.1	183	9	1,455
Minnesota	111,000	28.8	260	7	1,748
USA	2,730,000	1,063.3	390		45,609

SOURCE: *United States Statistical Abstract 1975*, Table 1,036, p. 614.

Cash receipts from Michigan farm products are about equally divided between livestock and crop production with dairy and corn receipts the most prominent in the two categories. Table 9.7 and the several agricultural product maps illustrate the distribution of agricultural activity within the state (figs. 9.1 through 9.11).

TABLE 9.7
Usual County Rank for Selected Agricultural Products

Product	1	2	3	4
Corn	Lenawee	Branch	Huron	Ionia
Winter wheat	Huron	Lenawee	Saginaw	Tuscola
Oats	Sanilac	Huron	Tuscola	Lenawee
Soy beans	Lenawee	Monroe	Saginaw	Shiawassee
Dry beans	Huron	Tuscola	Saginaw	Gratiot
Sugar beets	Saginaw	Tuscola	Bay	Huron
Sheep	Washtenaw	Jackson	Lenawee	Eaton
Milk cows	Sanilac	Huron	Clinton	Kent
Hogs	Cass	Lenawee	St. Joseph	Branch
Chickens	Huron	Allegan	Ottawa	Tuscola

SOURCE: *Michigan Agricultural Statistics,* June 1976, pp. 66-67; *Michigan Statistical Abstract 1974*, p. 335.

TABLE 9.8
Crop and Livestock Comparisons 1880-1975

Product	1880 Production	1880 USA Rank	1975 Total Production
Corn	32,461,452 bu	12	157,240,000 bu
Wheat	35,532,543 bu	4	38,760,000 bu
Oats	18,190,793 bu	9	20,720,000 bu
Barley	1,204,316 bu	9	1,056,000 bu
Rye	294,918 bu	15	700,000 bu
Potatoes (Irish)	10,924,111 bu	4	8,076,000 bu
Hops	266,010 lb	4	—
Horses	378,778 head	10	171,000 head
Milch cows	384,578 head	11	421,000 head
Other cattle	466,660 head	13	1,219,000 head
Sheep	2,189,389 head	4	140,000 head
Swine	964,071 head	18	715,000 head
Number of farms	154,000	11	80,000

SOURCE: *Michigan Agricultural Statistics 1976;* "Michigan Manual" 1887 (?), p. 397.

Michigan's present agricultural production in comparison to its 1880 production illustrates a shift from general farm production to a greater specialization of production. Corn, rye, and cattle (beef) have been greatly increased in production while hops, sheep, and swine have declined (table 9.8).

Summary of Leading Michigan Agricultural Products

Corn. Corn, or maize, since its domestication and introduction to Michigan by the native Indians centuries ago has been important in sustaining life in Michigan. Today corn is

One dot = 1,000 planted acres

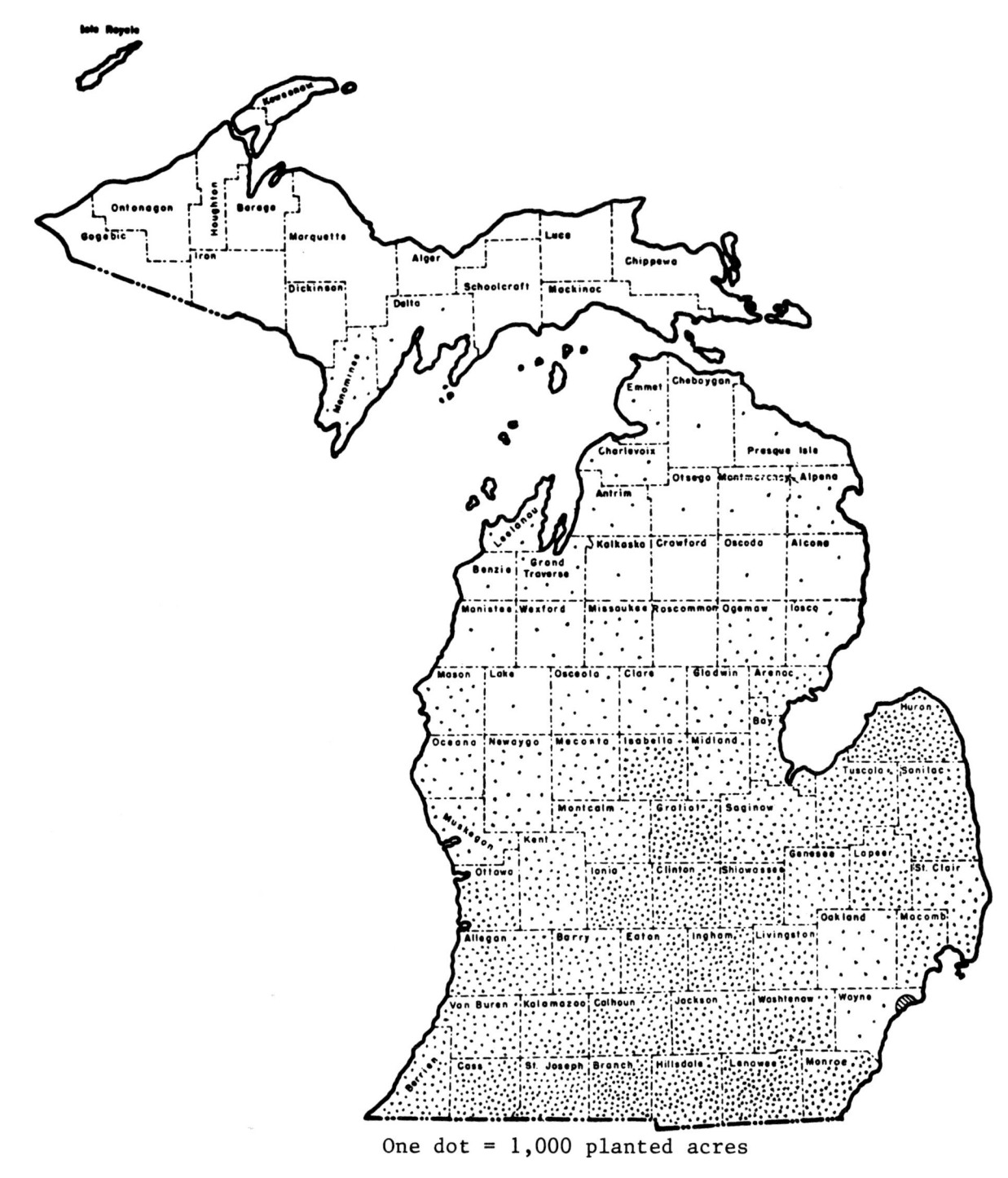

Figure 9.1. Corn. (Map: Michigan Department of Agriculture.)

One dot = 500 planted acres

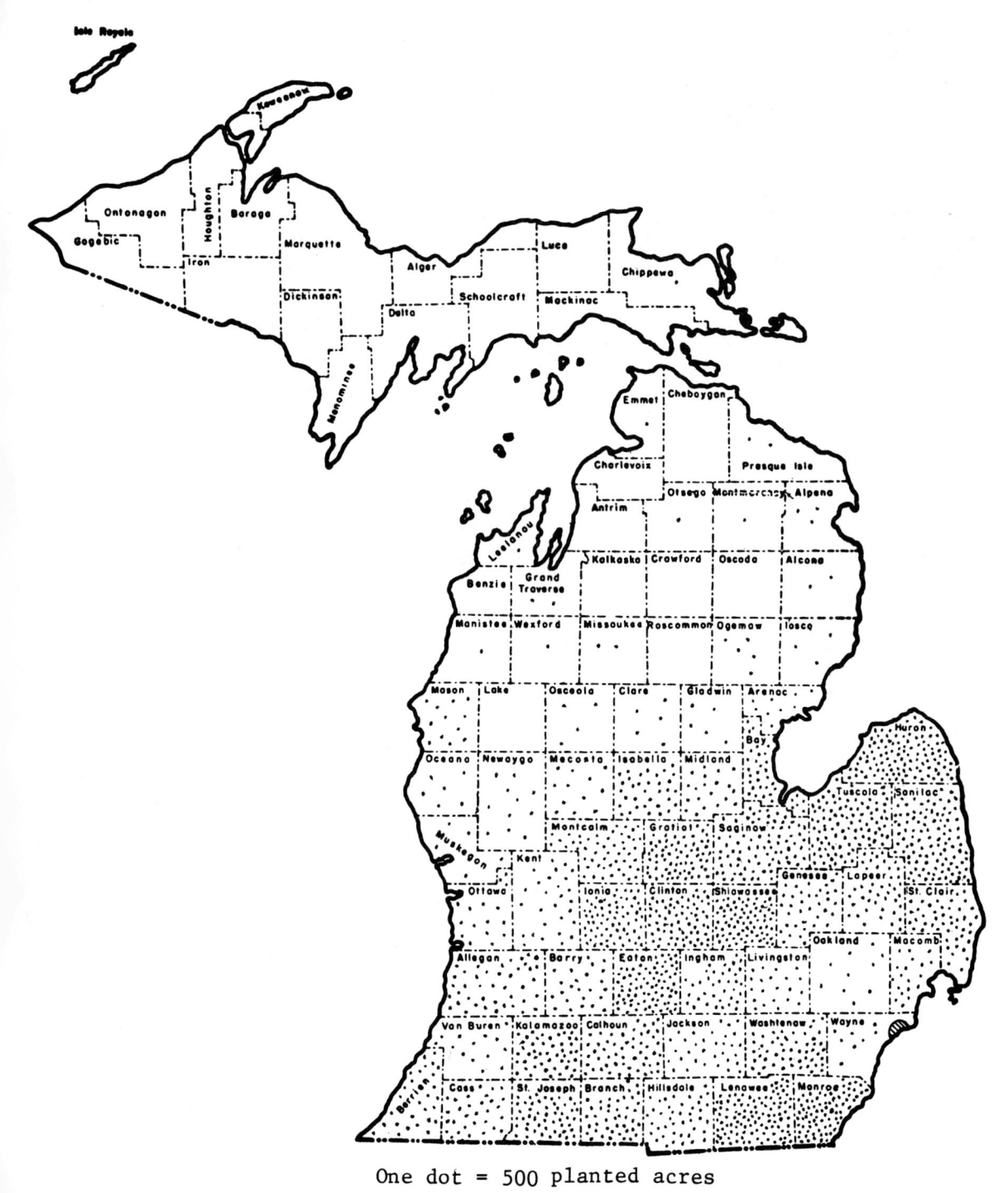

Figure 9.2. Wheat. (Map: Michigan Department of Agriculture.)

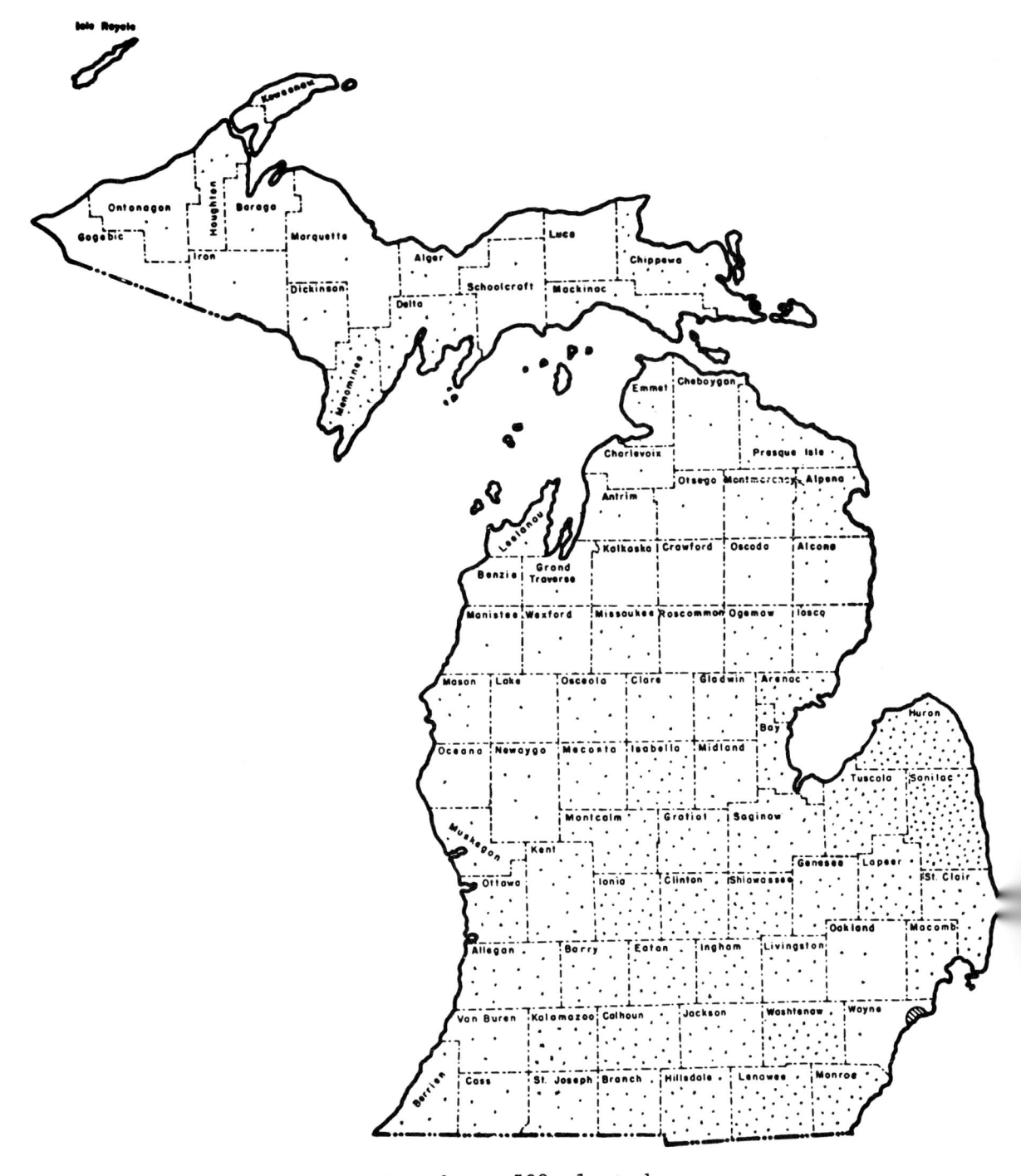

One dot = 500 planted acres

Figure 9.3. Oats. (Map: Michigan Department of Agriculture.)

Figure 9.4. Dry beans. (Map: Michigan Department of Agriculture.)

One dot = 1,000 planted acres

One dot = 1,000 planted acres

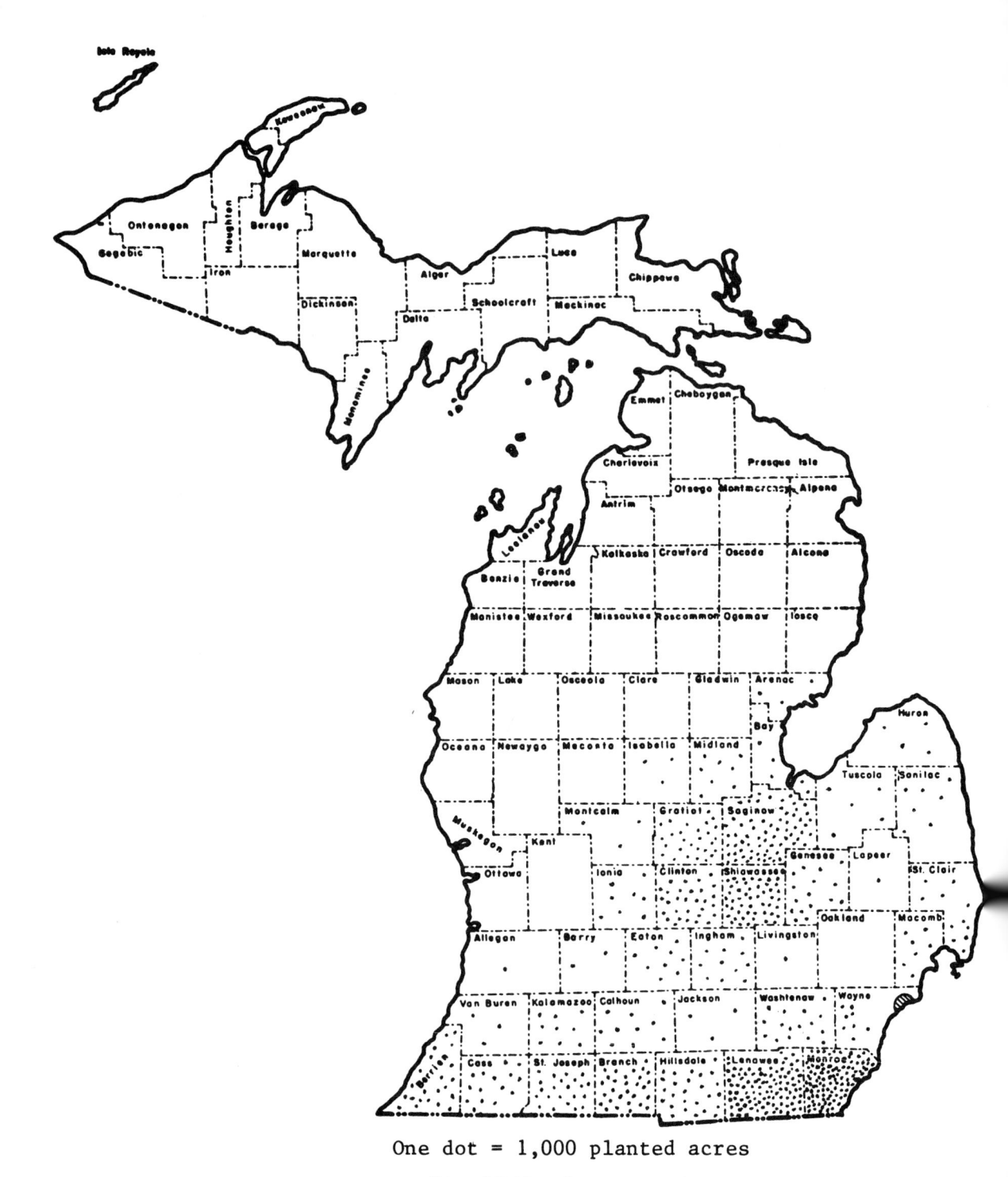

Figure 9.5. Soybeans. (Map: Michigan Department of Agriculture.)

One dot = 100 planted acres

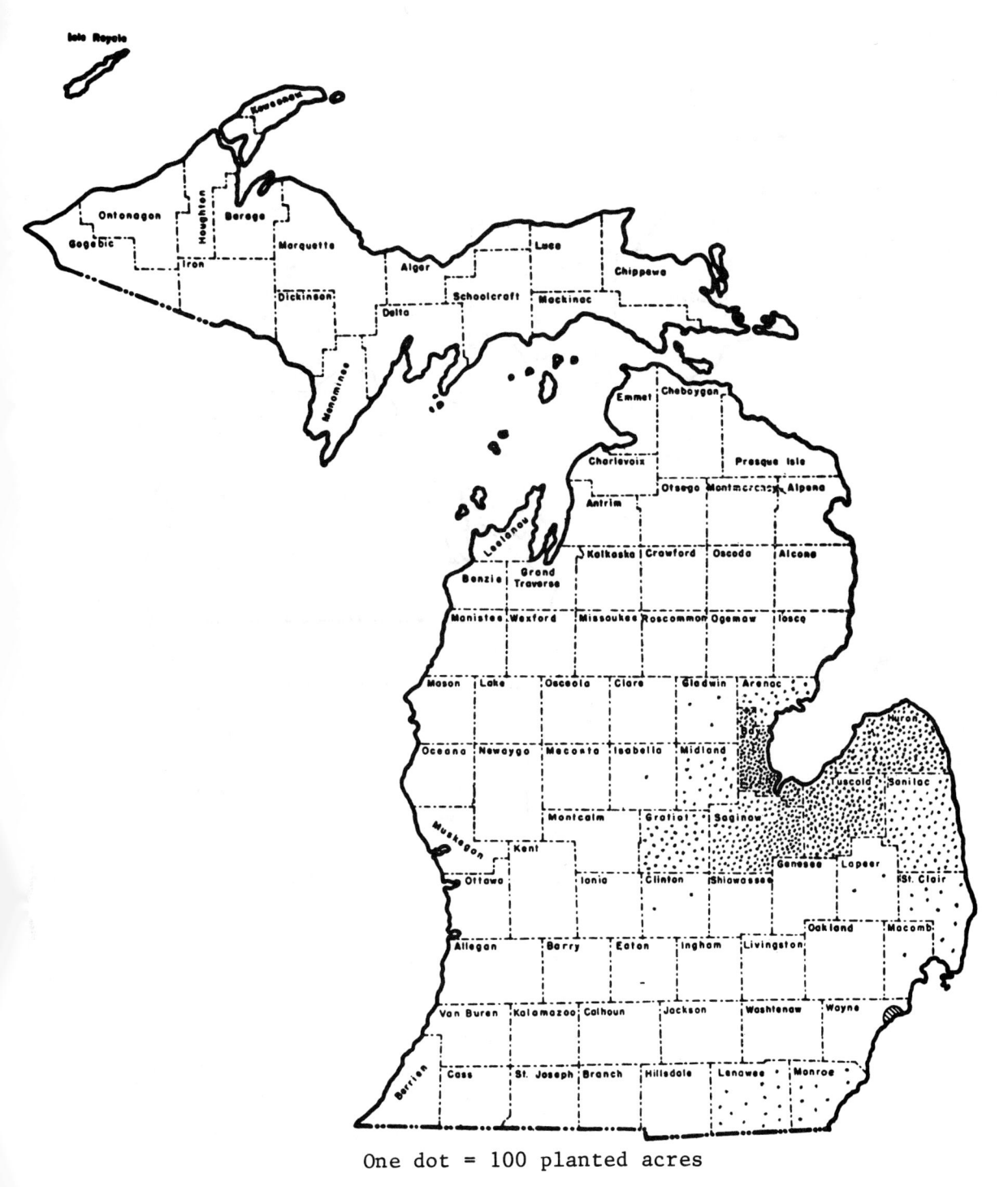

Figure 9.6. Sugar beets. (Map: Michigan Department of Agriculture.)

Each dot = 500 head

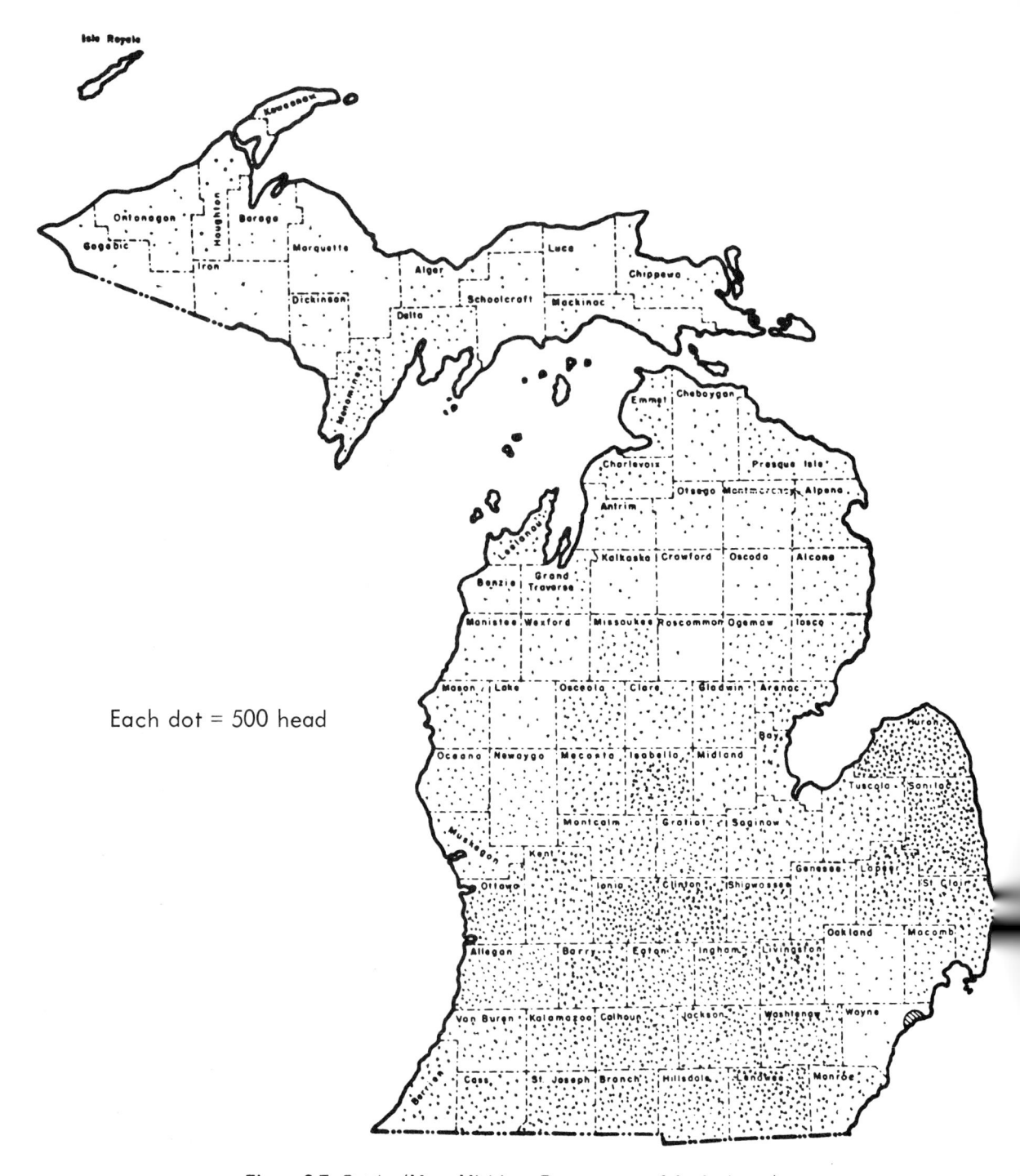

Figure 9.7. Cattle. (Map: Michigan Department of Agriculture.)

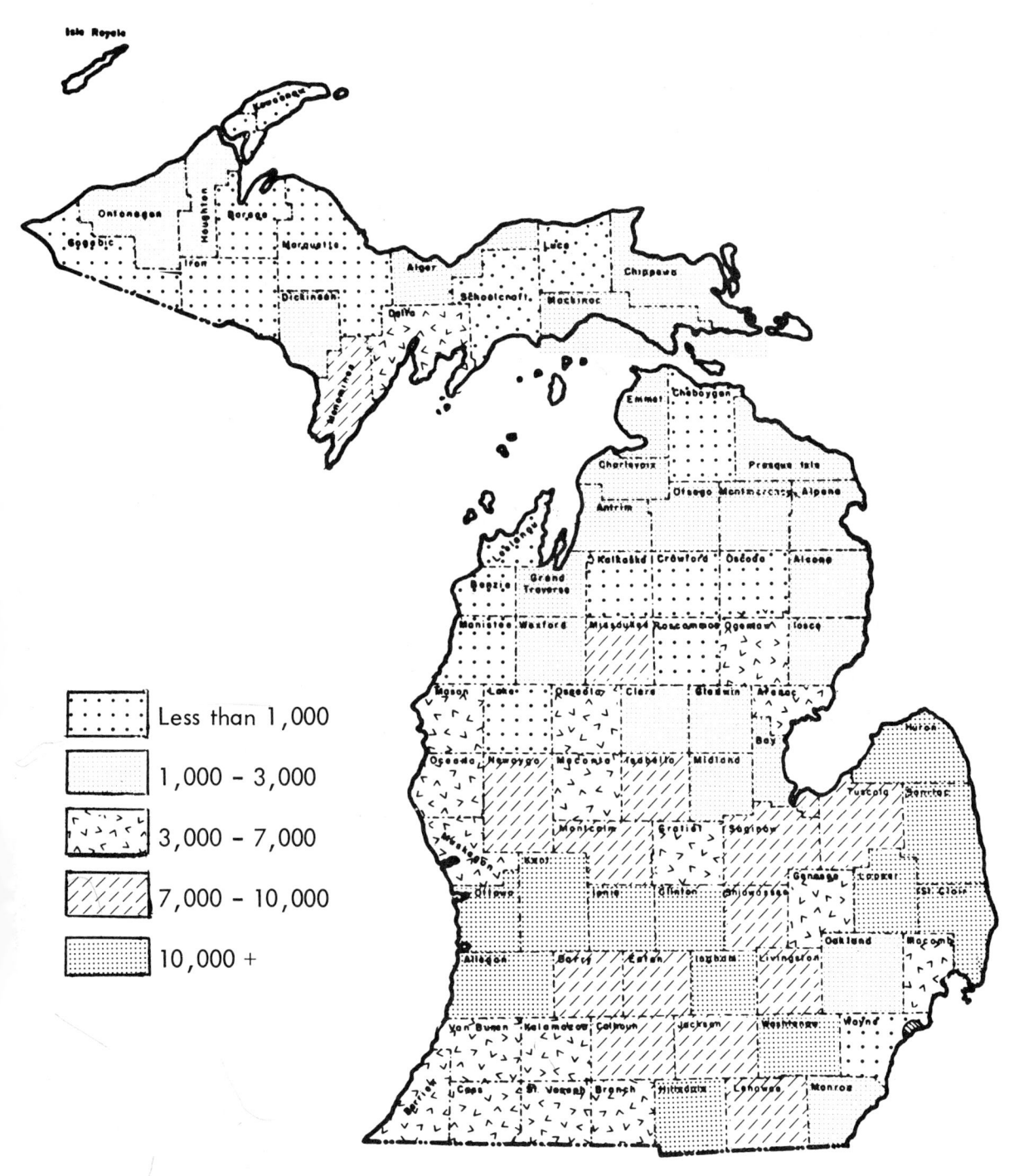

Figure 9.8. Milk cows. (Map: Michigan Department of Agriculture.)

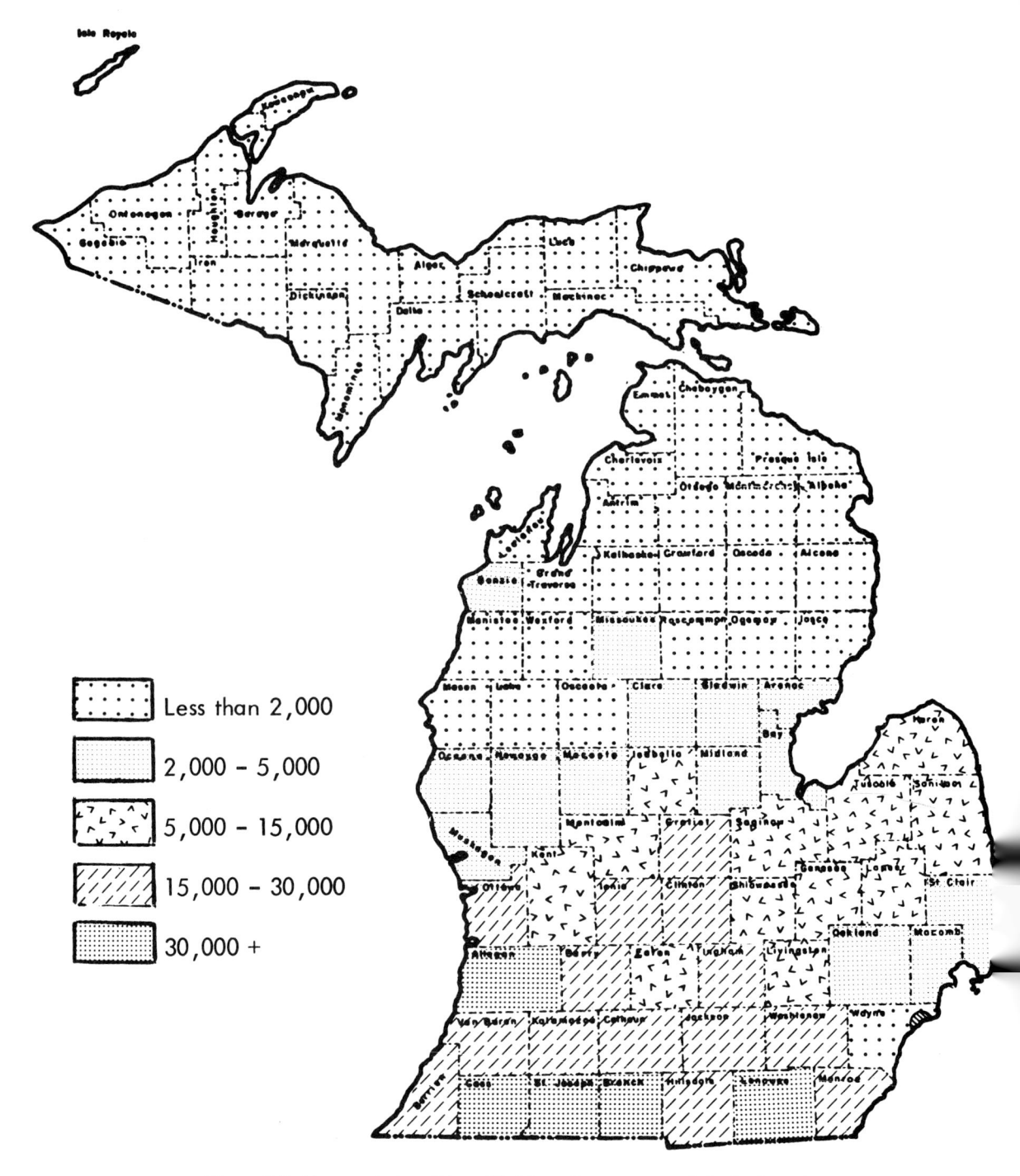

Figure 9.9. Hogs and pigs. (Map: Michigan Department of Agriculture.)

Each dot = 5,000 birds

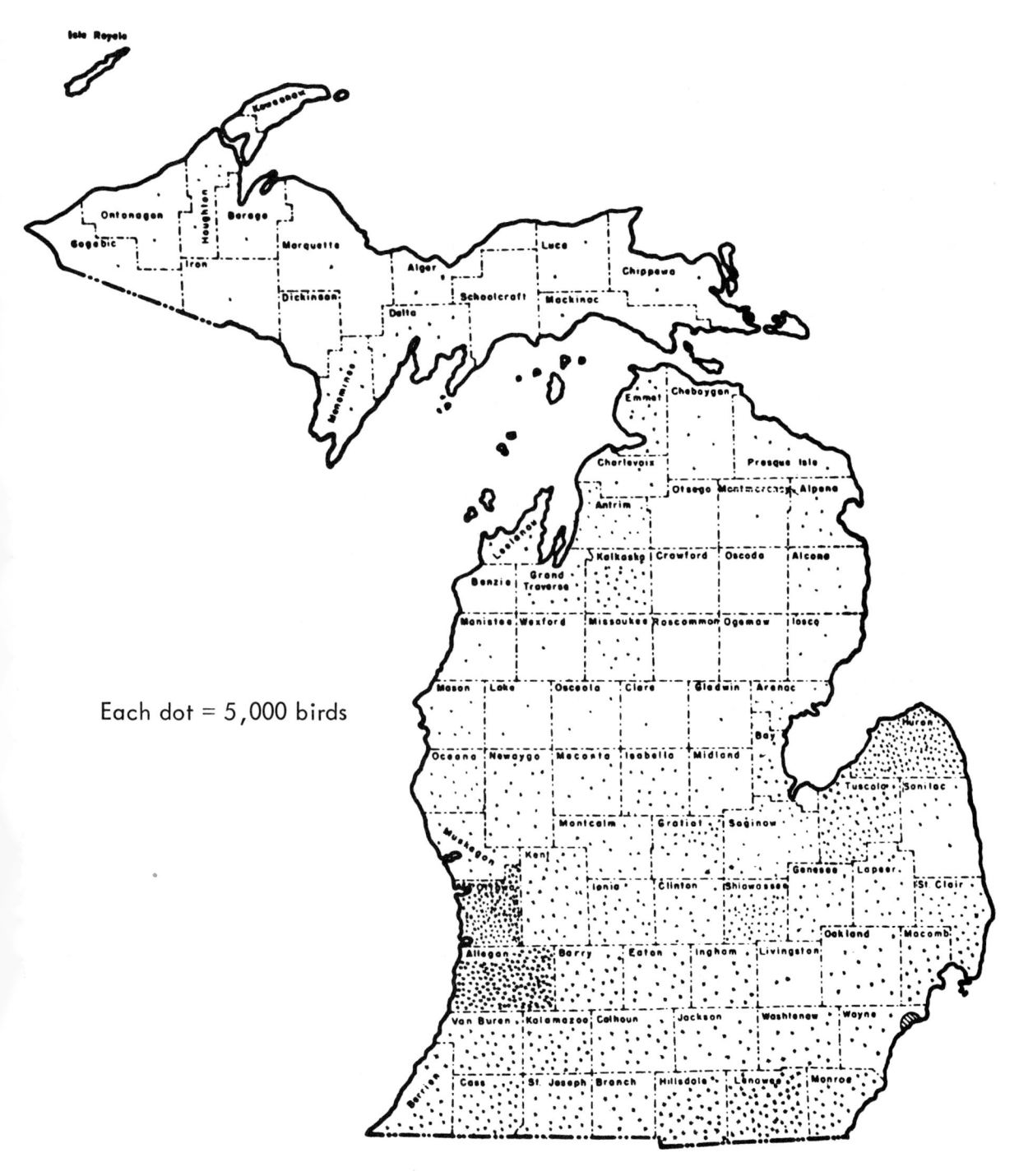

Figure 9.10. Egg producing chickens. (Map: Michigan Department of Agriculture.)

Each dot = 250 head

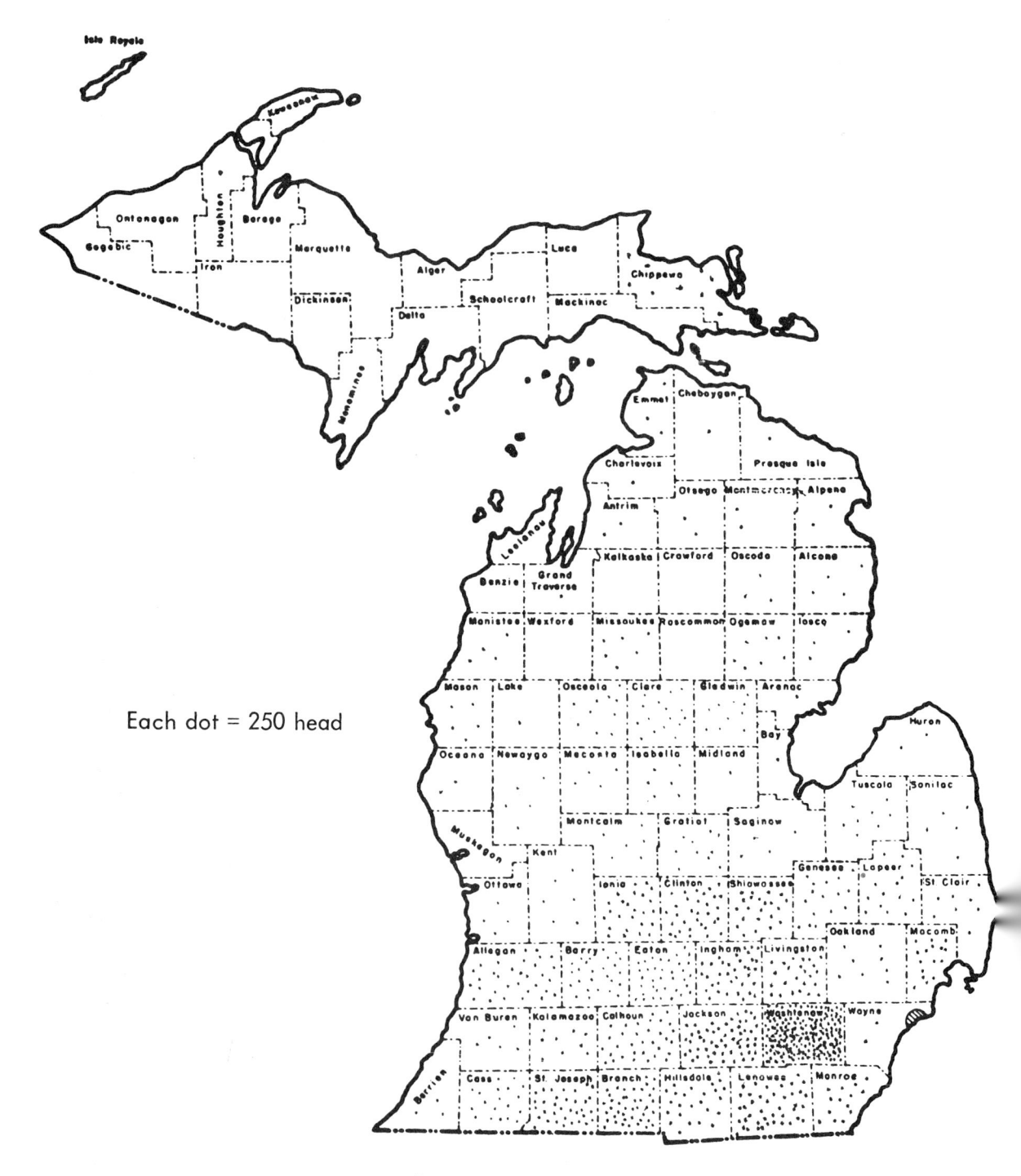

Figure 9.11. Sheep. (Map: Michigan Department of Agriculture.)

the state's leading crop in both area planted and cash value. The majority, 80 percent, is grown for use as a livestock feed grain while the remainder is harvested as silage. Plant population averages a density of 40,000-45,000 per ha (16,000-18,000 per ac) in central Lower Michigan and exceeds 50,000 per ha (20,000 per ac) on some farms. Row width which previously controlled density, is no longer determined by the girth of a work horse. Silage corn is less geared to the frost-free season, as it is harvested in late summer before the kernel is fully matured. Of the corn harvested, 70 percent is usually stored for later use or marketing while 20 percent is marketed directly after harvest or drying. Local farm market elevators receive two-thirds of the corn harvest, while Toledo is the market for about one-fifth of it. The remainder is marketed at Saginaw, Chicago, and by trucker buyers. By the mid-1970s the amount of corn artificially dried surpassed the amount dried naturally in the field or in storage resulting in an increased dependency on propane gas.

Sweet Corn. Sweet corn has the second largest acreage of Michigan freshmarket vegetable crops. The counties within and near the Detroit metropolitan area are the leading producers. Nationally, Michigan ranks seventh in sweet corn production.

Dry Navy Beans. Michigan is the largest producer of *dry beans* in the United States. Among Michigan's field crops, however, dry beans rank second in crop value and fourth in acreage. The pea or edible "navy" bean is the leading variety of beans sown. Planting usually begins in June with harvesting taking place in late summer or early fall.

Hay. Hay in Michigan is valuable within the state's agricultural economy, ranking third in value as a field crop and second in area. Hay contributes to stabilizing soil on sloping land and protecting it from erosion. Two hay cuttings are most common, they usually occur on hot sunny days in June and August with a third cutting sometimes made in early fall. Alfalfa is the dominant plant comprising 80 percent of hay fodder. Its increase in production coincides with the decline in timothy which was a favored horse hay. Although hay is produced in huge quantities in the Thumb and south central parts of the state, Michigan ranks only nineteenth in national production.

Soybeans. Since the mid-1920s and during the national crop quota post-World War II period, soybean production has steadily increased in the southern Lower Peninsula. In addition to its uses for manufactured products, oils, livestock meal, and meat supplement, it also is a product which holds great potential for expanded exports, especially into Europe.

Winter Wheat. Wheat is the fifth ranking field crop in Michigan in both area planted and value. Winter varieties of wheat, which are planted in the fall and combined the following summer, comprise the majority of the Michigan wheat crop. Seventy-five percent of the winter wheat consists of soft white varieties of which Michigan farmers are the nation's primary producers. The milled soft white wheat is extensively used by commercial bakers in cookies, crackers, and as a blend with other flours. In the past Michigan has been the leading producer; however, with adverse weather conditions in 1973, the state fell to fourteenth rank nationally. Further illustrative of wheat decline in Michigan is a comparison with 1880 when 35.5 million bushels were raised while in 1973 only 19 million bushels were raised, but in 1975, 38 million bushels were produced.

Sugar Beets. Sugar beet production in Michigan can be traced to the Franco-Prussian War of 1871, however, major commercial production occurred in Michigan beginning in the 1890s. Sugar beets, whose refined product is indistinguishable from its tropical cane competitor, are usually one of the first crops planted in spring. Normally over one-quarter of the crop is sown by the last week of April with harvesting extending from mid-September to mid-November. Like fruits and cucumbers, sugar beets in the past have been dependent upon migrant labor. In recent years the need for migrant laborers has been reduced by the planting of monogerminating beet seed.

Oats. Unlike corn which has quadrupled in production during the last century, *oats* with an average 19 million bushels produced yearly in the 1970s is only slightly higher than the 18.1 million bushels recorded in 1880. Oats is used as a cereal, livestock, and poultry grain. Planting occurs in early spring and the grain is harvested in midsummer. Among the field crops, oats ranks sixth in acreage and eighth in crop value.

Potatoes. Sandy loam soils, of which much of the state is covered, are ideally suited for the raising of potatoes. Michigan produces both a summer and fall crop. The summer production comes generally from the Saginaw Bay area while the fall varieties are harvested throughout the state; leading production areas include Montcalm, Presque Isle, and Lenawee counties. The bulk of the harvest is marketed in the SMSA counties and Toledo for direct table use or processed into chips and frozen products. Further capitalizing on the importance of potatoes in local economies are the Potato Festivals held each July in Edmore and Munger.

Michigan Livestock

The total of all cattle on Michigan farms has generally been decreasing since the mid-1940s although there has been a slight upswing since 1970. Seven Michigan counties average more than one milk cow per 12 hectare (1 per 32 ac) which include: Sanilac, Huron, Lapeer, Clinton, Ionia, Ottawa, and Ingham. The amount of milk sold as whole milk has been increasing steadily from 90 percent in 1960 to 97 percent in the 1970s. Michigan's main manufactured products from milk include American cheese, creamed cottage cheese, ice cream, and butter. During the last two decades the production of American cheese and butter has declined while cottage cheese and ice cream has risen. The dairy manufacturing industry has undergone a tremendous change during the last thirty years which is witnessed by the decline in number of processing plants (table 9.9).

Milk, in spite of momentous changes in production and processing methods, is the state's leading agricultural product in dollar value producing over $375 million annually. Most of the state's procution is marketed by truck into the SMSAs. The milk production of the thirteen counties of the northwestern Lower Peninsula is extensively marketed in Regions Nine and Ten.

The Coming Beef Cattle Revolution. Feed cattle for beef production are second to dairy cattle in value of the state's livestock. The trends in beef production and consumption indicate a decrease in consumption and number of production operations but an increase in feedlot size. According to the analysis in *Project 80 and 5* of the Cooperative Extension Service, the number of feedlots will decline from 1,700 to about 1,000 in 1985. In the same time the number of cattle fed per lot will increase from 175 to 530 head. With increased mechanization it is expected that approximately 200 people will feed 50 percent of the state's cattle in 1985.

Hog-Swine Production. Southern Michigan lies on the edge of the Great Midwest Corn-Hog Belt. However, as a state, Michigan ranks seventeenth with 1.2 percent of the nation's live pork production. Nearly a million pigs are marketed each year while by 1985 produc-

TABLE 9.9
Number of Dairy Processing Plants 1940-1970

Year	Butter	Cheese (Excl. Cottage Cheese)	Cond. Evap. Milk	Ice Cream
1940	271	61	39	783
1945	205	55	46	612
1950	138	47	42	811
1955	98	39	30	623
1960	55	37	20	430
1965	41	35	16	231
1970	16	16	11	121

SOURCE: *Dairy Trends in Michigan,* 1973, p. 14.

tion is expected to rise to 1.3 million. During the decade of the late seventies and early eighties while production is increasing, the number of hog raisers is expected to decline from 11,000 to 4,000 with only 700 farms producing two-thirds of the state total.

Sheep. Michigan sheep industry, which ranked fourth nationally in 1880 and now ranks twentieth, is at an important crossroads. Either sheep raising will continue to decline becoming a part-time enterprise with only a few larger efficient producers or new technology and production methods will be adopted with several large operations specializing in lamb production. If the industry continues "as is" the number of ewes will decline by over half by 1985. On the other hand, Michigan resources and consumer demand potentially could support a tripling to 300,000 or more breeding ewes. Nationally, the Sheep Industry Development Program is geared to disseminate new technology and emphasize intensive full-time operations. One critical dependent related to the expansion of the sheep industry is the control of loose and feral dogs.

Horses. The popularity of raising horses for recreational use is reflected in the rapid increase in their number from a low of 34,000 in 1960 to over 171,000 in the early 1970s. By 1985 it is expected that the state's horse population may reach 400,000. This tripling in numbers is based on more leisure time, trend towards suburban-exurban living, greater emphasis on family recreation, and respect and love for horses. The support of 400,000 horses requires 540,000 tons of feed grain, 60,000 tons of high protein feed, 1.2 million tons of hay and 400,000 acres of open pasture. If the horse population continues to increase as projected, their numbers will be greater than in 1880 (when the state had 378,778 head which were primarily work species), but less than the peak of 700,000 at the beginning of World War I.

Specialty Products—Fruits, Poultry, and Vegetables

Thousands of Michigan farmers and processors are engaged in the production of scores of agricultural commodities which are classified in categories other than the state's major food products. Many of these specialized commodities hold significantly higher ranks within the state and nation than the major farm products. Tables 9.10, 9.11, and 9.12 attempt to summarize the diversity, rank, and area of production of several of Michigan's lesser known agricultural products.

TABLE 9.10
Selected Facts on Vegetable Production and Location 1975

Vegetable	Location of Production	Comments
Asparagus	Van Buren, Oceana, Berrien, Cass Counties	First in acreage of Michigan's fresh market crops with 15,000 planted annually. National Asparagus Festival in Hart-Shelby in June.
Snap beans	Antrim, Mason, Mecosta, Sanilac, Van Buren Counties	Ranks 6th in USA with 30,000 tons produced in 1975. Acreage planted has declined in recent years.
Cabbage	Kent, Saginaw, Lake, and East Lowland Counties	Ranks 9th in USA with 74 million pounds raised in 1975.
Carrots	Newaygo east through Clinton to St. Clair Counties	Second in volume of fresh vegetable production with 56,650 tons produced in 1975. Ranks 4th in USA production.
Celery	Allegan, Kent, Lapeer, Muskegon, Ottawa Counties	Sixty-five producers grow 90.5 million pounds on 2,400 acres which ranks Michigan 3rd in USA.
Cucumbers	Thumb and Saginaw Lowland Areas	Ranks 1st in USA (pickle variety) with 129,000 tons produced in 1975 on 30,400 acres.
Lettuce	Ingham, Jackson, Lapeer, and Macomb Counties	Ranks 10th in USA with 19.5 million pounds. Continual research to adapt mechanical harvesters to replace hand labor.
Mint (spearmint, little peppermint)	Clinton, Calhoun, Eaton, Ingham, and Shiawassee Counties	Ranks 4th in USA. Until 1940 when fungus nearly destroyed crop, Michigan was world leader in peppermint oil production. Now spearmint dominates with 3,600 acres planted.
Onions	Newaygo, Ottawa, and Allegan Counties	Ranks 5th in USA, 1st in Michigan volume of fresh vegetable crop market outside Michigan and into Europe.
Tomatoes	Monroe, Lenawee, Macomb, Berrien Counties	Ranks 6th (processing), 7th (fresh market) in USA with 63 million tons (processing), 38 million pounds (fresh).

SOURCE: *1976 Michigan Food Facts,* Michigan Department of Agriculture.

A World View and the Future Needs of Michigan Agriculture

In evaluating agricultural production and Michigan's ranks in comparison to the rest of the nation, it can be observed that Michigan residents share with most citizens of the United States access to abundant supplies of a wide variety of foods. In comparison to the world, the food it produces is nutritious and at levels of quality, quantity, and price which normally satisfy public

TABLE 9.11
Selected Facts on Fruit Production and Location 1975

Fruit	Location of Production	Comments
Apples	Berrien, Kent, and Van Buren Counties	Ranks 1st in USA in production of Northern spies, Jonathons in total product rank 3rd. 1975 production 720 million pounds.
Blueberries	Allegan, Berrien, Muskegon, Ottawa, Van Buren Counties	Ranks 1st in USA in replacing New Jersey. Thirty-two million pounds produced in 1974.
Cantaloupe	Bay, Berrien, Monroe, Van Buren, and Macomb Counties	Ranks 6th in USA with 16.5 million pounds produced in 1975. Introduced into New World by Columbus in 1494 after diffusing from Iran into Europe.
Cherries	Leelanau, Grand Traverse, Oceana, Berrien Counties	Ranks 1st in USA in tart production with over 75 percent annual yield. Ranks 4th in sweet production with 27,000 ton yield in 1975.
Grapes	Berrien, Van Buren Counties	Ranks 4th in USA with 55,000 tons, major products include wine, jams, and juices.
Peaches	Fruit Belt south of Oceana County	Ranks 6th in USA.
Pears	South half of Lake Michigan Fruit Belt	Ranks 5th in USA, Bartlett chief variety and used for canning. Fifteen thousand tons produced in 1975.
Prunes-Plums	Grand Traverse, Leelanau, Oceana, Berrien Counties	Ranks 4th in USA with 18,000 tons produced in 1975.
Rhubarb	Berrien County—outdoors, Macomb County—hothouse	Ranks 1st in production from low, windowless hothouses and 2nd in outdoor varieties. Decline from about 300 families producing in 1955 to 50 in 1975, primarily German and Belgian.
Strawberries	Alpena, Houghton Counties and Lake Michigan Fruit Belt	Ranks 5th in USA with 16.5 million pounds yield in 1975 from 3,100 acres. Fresh market sale accounts for 75 percent of production.

SOURCE: *1976 Michigan Food Facts,* Michigan Department of Agriculture.

demand. In light of post-World War II seminal work on agriculture done by scientists associated with the UN, FAO, Club of Rome, Green Revolution, and scholarly texts by George Borgestrom *The Hungry Planet* and *The Food and Population Dilemma,* the begging question is what is the trend of Michigan's food production in terms of the forseeable future? Three trends appear to be clearly emerging: (1) Michigan farmers and land will be expected to produce more food, (2) Michigan's agribusinesses will be expected to engage in increasing foreign

TABLE 9.12
Selected Food Products, Location, and US Rank 1975

Product	Location of Production	Comments
Butter	Clinton, Huron, Mecosta, and St. Joseph Counties	Ranks 9th in USA with 23 million pounds produced in 1974.
Cheese	Arenac, Clare, and Osceola Counties	Ranks 4th in USA with 53 million pounds of cottage cheese but 17th overall in cheddar and American process production.
Chicken	Allegan, Kent, Huron, Ottawa, and Oscoda Counties	Ranks 19th in USA with 4.2 million birds.
Eggs	Widespread	Ranks 18th in USA, 5.6 million hens average 232 eggs yearly, movement toward marketing precooked, preshelled eggs to restaurateurs and other large users.
Honeybees	Widespread	Ranks 13th in USA, 5.1 million pounds. Bees are critical to pollination of fruits and plants, 80,000 farms dependent on the efforts of 112,000 bee colonies.
Ice Cream	Wayne, Genesee, Ottawa, Kent Counties	Ranks 7th in USA with 38.7 million gallons produced.
Maple syrup	Vermontville, Shepherd	Ranks 4th in USA with 98,000 gallons weighing legal minimum of 11 pounds a gallon.
Mushrooms (commercial)	Macomb, Berrien, Allegan Counties	Ranks 3rd in USA with 15 million pounds annual production.
Turkey	Ottawa, Allegan, Gratiot, Barry, and Lenawee Counties	Ranks 21st in USA with 700,000 birds, produced under indoor factorylike conditions, 16.1 million pounds.
Wine	Paw Paw, Hartford, Harbert, Buchanan, Fennville, Detroit	Ranks 4th in USA with 15,800 acres producing 5,000 tons of wine grapes.

SOURCE: *1976 Michigan Food Facts,* Michigan Department of Agriculture.

sales, and (3) Michigan farm prices, land planted, and production goals will be more closely related to national and international food market demands.

Michigan Agricultural Land Requirements: A Projection to 2000 A.D.

The Michigan Department of Agriculture (MDA) completed in 1973 an investigation of farmland requirements for Michigan. In summary, it was determined that in order to ensure that Michigan's growing population will continue to have adequate supplies of desirable foodstuffs in the future, food demands and production capabilities must be forecast and a manageable land-use plan created. Further, the MDA put the public on notice that a certain minimum area of land resources which are agriculturally significant must be maintained and reserved exclusively for food production. The concluding pages of this section on Michigan agriculture are excerpted from the Michigan Department of Agriculture's Land Requirement Projection to 2000 A.D.

To identify the amount of land that will be needed, the MDA made calculations based on very conservative estimates, projections and . . . assumptions. The necessity of stopping encroachments upon agricultural lands is strongly underscored by the conservative bias of this estimate.

Assumptions

1. Although agricultural technology will advance to a point well beyond current technology, society will continue to impose limitations which will limit per acre yields during the remainder of this century to what are essentially today's levels.
2. There will not be significant changes in consumer food preferences or consumption rates during the rest of this century.
3. Through the year 2000, Michigan agriculture will continue to produce the same proportion of foodstuffs per capita, for both the state and the national markets, as it does at this time.
4. Michigan will have the same percentage of the national population in 2000 A.D. that it had in 1970; the U.S. Bureau of Census' lowest projected fertility rate (1.8 births per woman) is reasonable, and there will be a continuation of 1960 to 1970 gross migration trends.
5. There will be no severe economic depression, major war, or other similar catastrophe.

Projections of agricultural land needs made by other analysts and planners appear to rely heavily upon an assumption not a part of this projection: that agricultural technology will continue to increase yields so that increasing amounts of foodstuffs can be produced on fixed acreage or that a constant amount of foodstuffs can be obtained from a diminishing number of acres. The Michigan Department of Agriculture believes that such an assumption is unreasonable, not because the technology will not be discovered, but rather because society has shown an increasing disposition to assert constraints upon such technology . . . The Michigan Department of Agriculture does not believe that environmental concerns of paramount importance today will be considered unimportant in the future.

Other projections have estimated a need for as little as 2.5 million acres of crop land in Michigan in the year 2000. These projections have probably been based on assumptions of rapidly increasing per acre yields, extrapolation of the historic trend of agricultural crop land in Michigan since World War II, and an assumption that Michigan citizens' food needs will be increasingly provided from sources outside the state. As shown in figure 9.12, a curve fit mathematically to the points which describe the history of agricultural land use in Michigan since World War II suggests that in the year 2000 we will have 2.5 million acres of agricultural crop land. Were we to arrive at that acreage, our ratio then of four humans to one acre of agriculturally productive land would be substantially higher than the ratio of humans to crop acres in Taiwan today. Massively increased amounts of foodstuffs would have to be imported into Michigan if our diet in the year 2000 were to avoid taking on the characteristics of today's diet in Taiwan.

. . . .

Of the food which Michiganders presently consume, what proportions of the major staples are grown in the state? More than eight times the edible beans and 1.7 times the beets for sugar we consume are grown here; the surpluses are exported from the state. Even now, however, Michigan relies very heavily upon imports from outside the state. We produce only 37.4 percent of the amount of the wheat needed in Michigan, 28 percent of the soybeans and hogs, 65.3 percent of the corn, 70.4 percent of the potatoes, 21 percent of the cattle, 91.7 percent of the milk and 46.7 percent of the eggs. It is therefore of paramount importance to Michigan that our sister states continue to supply us with increasing amounts of foodstuffs up to and past the year 2000. This they cannot do unless they, too, move vigorously today to reserve agricultural lands in their jurisdictions; we in Michigan have no assurance that this is being done.

Acres In Millions

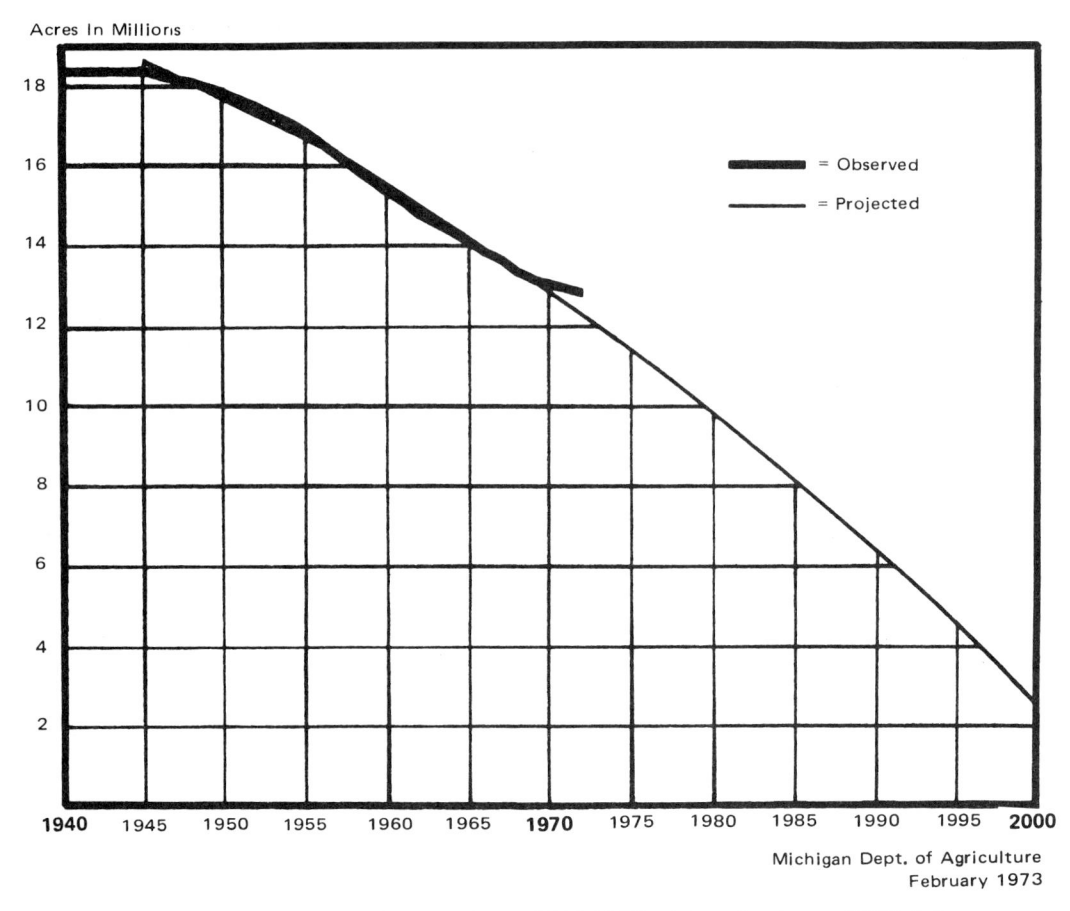

Michigan Dept. of Agriculture
February 1973

Figure 9.12. Trend of land in farms 1945-1972 with projection to 2000 A.D.

. . . .

The U.S. Department of Commerce, Bureau of the Census, in cooperation with the U.S. Department of Agriculture, conducts censuses of agriculture at five year intervals. [The census in Michigan], conducted in 1969, identified 5,501,729 acres of harvested crop land and 1,090,891 acres of crop land used only for pasture or grazing; these two figures add to 6,592,620 acres of crop land in Michigan in foodstuff production.

Excluded from the 6,592,620 figure are 1,987,771 acres of crop land identified with soil improvement crops, crop failure, cultivated summer fallow, and idle crop lands. Neither have [been] included either 1,843,581 acres of farm wood lands (whether pastured or not) or 1,476,717 acres now being used for house lots, barn lots, ponds, roads, wasteland or pastureland other than crop land and woodland pasture. This has been done, again, in the interest of conservatism even though it is apparent to an agriculturalist that the 75,000 farms in the state require about five acres each for the house and barn lots incident to the farming operation—more than a third of a million acres—and virtually every farm utilizes some lands in field roads or ponds, while substantial numbers have swamps or gullies which render some lands unuseable.

Using the premises thus developed, projected is the Michigan agricultural land need in the year 2000 from the equation:

$$\frac{\text{Michigan population in the year 2000}}{\text{Michigan population in the year 1970}} \times \begin{array}{c}\text{Michigan harvested,}\\ \text{pastured and grazed}\\ \text{crop lands in the}\\ \text{year 1969}\end{array} = \begin{array}{c}\text{Michigan harvested,}\\ \text{pastured and grazed}\\ \text{crop lands in the}\\ \text{year 2000}\end{array}$$

$$\frac{10{,}704{,}000}{8{,}875{,}000} \times 6{,}592{,}256 = 7{,}951{,}256$$

The case, then is clearly and conservatively made for reserving 7,951,256 acres for agricultural production in the year 2000. But, will there be nearly eight million acres of agricultural crop land available in Michigan at that time on which to grow foodstuffs for our grandchildren? The stark and unpleasant truth of the matter is that there will almost certainly not be.

The 1969 Census of Agriculture identifies 11,900,689 acres of land in agriculture in Michigan. [The MDA has taken] the decidedly conservative position that 1,987,771 acres of "All other crop land," 1,476,717 acres of "All other land" and 1,843,581 acres of "Woodland including woodland pasture" have no food production utility.[1] These increments of land sum to 5,308,069 acres and that number subtracted from the 11,900,689 acres of agricultural lands of all kinds indicates that there were only 6,592,620 acres of suitable agricultural land available in Michigan in 1969 for the growing of foodstuffs—a deficit 1,358,636 acres as against the projected need of 7,951,256 acres in the year 2000.

Does this mean that the Michigan Department of Agriculture believes there will be famine in Michigan in 2000? This is a possibility, and [is viewed with] utmost concern. Returning to and reviewing the initial assumptions, [it is found] that a number of things might happen to forestall severe, protracted and widespread food shortages:

1. If famine should seem likely, society may relax constraints on application of food production technology, even though the constraints were originally imposed in hopes of precluding environmental damage.
2. We may be willing to accept changes in our food preferences away from meat protein sources and toward alternative vegetable protein sources, or less protein altogether.
3. Michigan may become a more thoroughly food deficient state and import from our sister states and foreign countries a greater proportion of our foodstuffs per capita than at present. This presupposes, of course, that those states and countries will have surpluses and that Michigan will have the wealth to import them.
4. Michigan may lose part of its population, the projected fertility rate may drop below 1.8 births per woman, and migration into Michigan may cease.
5. Though it is an undesirable direction from which to accept help, war or another catastrophe may diminish the population which must be fed in Michigan in 2000 A.D.
6. Lastly, any acute food shortage of significant duration will be accompanied by sharply rising food prices. It will then become economic to farm some lands classified in the 1969 Census of Agriculture as "All other crop lands." It may also be that persons who know how and possess the capability will undertake labor-intensive growing of foodstuffs for their own personal use.

It is of absolutely critical concern that conversions of agricultural crop lands stop immediately. . . . We will then expect to identify specific areas where land must be preserved for agricultural use.

The essential and emphasized conclusion to be drawn from this initial study is that land use plans for Michigan must not further reduce land available for intensive agricultural production in the state. The specific identity of the required minimum of 7,951,256 acres—some of which must necessarily come from

---

1. Timber production needs are not included in this MDA study, which is limited to food production needs.

those categories of land acknowledged to be inferior—must be performed quickly, and a statewide land use plan must be adopted which will ensure the continued availability of these lands for agricultural production.[2]

The Economic Geography of the Automobile Industry

Those who use the word "Detroit" interchangeably with the phrase "Automobile Industry" know that Michigan's economy and employment are heavily dependent on the manufacture of motor vehicles. Not to belabor the point, but to illustrate the industry's concentration and spatial patterns in Michigan, the following summary is presented.

One-third of all automobiles produced in the United States are assembled in Michigan factories. Further, 40 percent of the industry's employees live in the state. The motor vehicle industry directly accounts for 11 percent of the state's total employment, but indirectly, through related industries, accounts for over two-thirds of manufacturing employment and one-quarter of total employment. Table 9.13 indicates the distribution of employment by the "Big Three" automakers by state while table 9.14 illustrates the diffusion of production by community in Michigan during a peak year of production.

TABLE 9.13
Average Number Employees in Automobile Production by State 1972

State	General Motors	Ford	Chrysler	Percent of Total
Michigan	245,294	114,680	91,400	49.3
Ohio	92,488	34,619	14,300	15.4
Indiana	53,718	4,166	14,200	7.8
New York	41,150	5,095	3,650	5.4
Illinois	16,750	8,443	6,300	3.4

SOURCE: *Michigan Statistical Abstract 1974*, p. 402.

TABLE 9.14
Passenger Cars Assembled by City 1973 (in thousands)

City	Production	City	Production
Dearborn	240	Pontiac	327
Detroit	706	Warren	5
Flint	374	Wayne	160
Hamtramck	511	Willow Run	318
Kalamazoo	6	Wixom	175
Lansing	474	Total Michigan	3,298

SOURCE: *Michigan Statistical Abstract 1974*, p. 402.

2. *Michigan Agricultural Land Requirements: A Projection to 2000 A.D.,* (Lansing: Michigan Department of Agriculture, February 1973), Mimeograph, pp. 1-11.

Cyclic Production Activities

When car production booms as in 1955, 1965, and 1973, the state's economy appears healthy and booms with it. The record automobile production of 1973 led to nearly 400,000 jobs directly and over 600,000 indirectly, however the subsequent decline from 9.6 million to less than 7 million cars assembled in 1975 caused a direct employment decrease of 20 percent (table 9.15). The cyclic expansion-contraction of the motor vehicle industry is registered of course with the periodic scurry of activity around unemployment offices. More closely linked to the landscape are the spurts and slowing in community capital improvement projects, as well as in the maintenance of private and public facilities. In recent years blight spawned by temporary unemployment has been reduced by the institution of extended and supplemental unemployment benefits.

The Automobile Realm Centered on Southeast Michigan

Automobile assembly and decision-making activities are centered in metropolitan Detroit, however the realm of influence of vehicle production expressed on the landscape is spread throughout the southern Great Lakes Region. The realm of the automobile industry can be best described as the area of spatial interaction, convergence, and areal association with the automobile company headquarters of Michigan. Integral parts of the motor vehicle industry which function with metropolitan Detroit include: (1) the rubber plants of Kitchener, Ontario, and Akron, (2) electronics and hydraulic research laboratories in Columbus and Dayton, (3) steel mills and foundries in Buffalo, Chicago, Gary, and Cleveland, and (4) the machine tool shops of Cincinnati and Windsor. The necessary interaction within the auto realm is manifested in the flow of materials and people by highway, railroad, and air. Telephone calls between the interdependent cities are also great.

Boundary of the Automobile Realm. The automobile manufacturing realm stretches from Oshawa, Ontario, south to Cincinnati, and northwest to Milwaukee. The area contains about 90 percent of the motor vehicle employment of both the United States and Canada. The

TABLE 9.15
United States Automobile Production for Selected Years 1900-1975 (in millions)

Year	Passenger Cars	Total	Year	Passenger Cars	Total
1900	.004	.004	1955	7.9	9.20
1910	.181	.187	1958	4.2	5.12
1915	.89	.96	1960	6.7	7.90
1920	1.90	2.22	1965	9.3	11.13
1929	4.58	5.35	1970	6.5	8.28
1932	1.13	1.37	1971	8.5	10.66
1940	3.71	4.47	1972	8.8	11.31
1945	.069	.72	1973	9.6	12.68
1950	6.66	8.00	1974	7.3	10.07
1952	4.3	5.56	1975	6.7	8.98

SOURCE: *Face of Detroit a Spatial Synthesis,* Wayne State University, 1970, p. 37; *Economic Report of the Governor,* 1976, p. 123.

key to the boundary of this industrial areal association of communities is the placement of the activities within one-shift truck driving distance of Detroit prior to the 88 kph (55 mph) speed limit instituted in 1974 (fig. 9.13).

Land Use Patterns in the Automobile Center

Three primary factors can be identified which have shaped the locational pattern of the automobile industry centered on Detroit in addition to the birth of men near Detroit who were motivated to relieve human dependency on the horse. The three critical factors include: (1) the availability of risk capital, (2) railroad facilities, and (3) open space for industrial development. Unlike the steel, chemical, and refining industries which have concentrated in the adjacent Downriver heavy industry suburbs, automobile manufacturing has not been strongly attached to the Detroit waterway. An analysis of mode of transportation further illustrates the discontinued use of water shipment of motor vehicles (table 9.16). The location of Ford's Rouge complex on the River Rouge tributary may be attributed to the steel mills of Ford which are one of the complex's major facilities.

Stages of Land-Use Development Near Auto Plants. Between the turn of the century and the present, automotive plant location and land-use change have followed three steps. These stages included: (1) occupation of large existing or new plant location on a major railroad with open space well beyond builtup area, but close enough to tap its labor supply, (2) location of complementary metal and machine industries in vicinity, (3) sprawl of residential development in surrounding open space. The continued succession of these stages has further resulted in the emergence of industrial corridors which follow the primary railroads leading into the city (fig. 8.2).

Corporation Territory. Within the heart of the automobile realm, a spatial pattern of corporate identity has emerged based on the residential and social patterns of corporation employees. There is a natural tendency for employees not only to reside on routes of access to their place of employment but also to identify with the companies which employ them. Further, management personnel tend to take an interest in the communities where their plants are located. However, this interest may not be political due to residential restrictions nor does this

TABLE 9.16
Method of Shipment of Motor Vehicles by Percent 1950-1974

Year	Highway	Railroad	Waterway	Total Vehicles Transported (in thousands)
1950	72	21	7	8,003
1955	82	12	5	9,169
1960	87	10	3	7,869
1965	59	40	1	11,057
1970	45	55	0	8,239
1974	45	55	0	10,058

SOURCE: *Economic Report of the Governor,* 1976, p. 38.

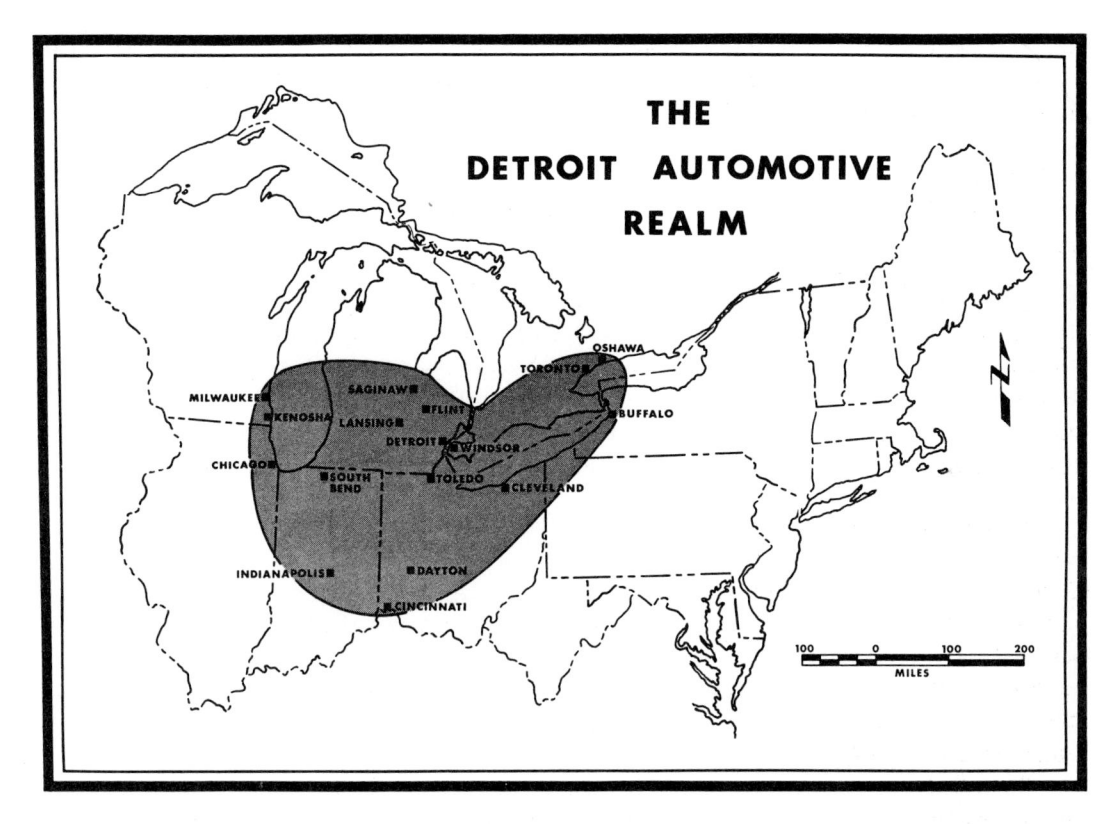

Figure 9.13. The automobile realm. (Map: R. Sinclair, *The Face of Detroit.*)

corporate territory equate with the negative attributes of "company towns" of the bygone mining era. Thus "corporate territory" in the modern sense is envisioned as a much less dominant presence and control of the landscape (fig. 8.2). "Ford Territory" in a general sense, lies to the west of the city of Detroit, centering on Dearborn and extending west and southwest into Washtenaw County. In this area are found the Rouge plants, their modern glass skyscraper main administrative buildings on spacious lawns along the Southfield Freeway, their research facilities, Greenfield Village, Henry Ford Museum, Henry Ford Community College, and many Ford plants built since World War II. "General Motors Territory" lies to the northwest of its New Center-Detroit Headquarters established in the 1920s extending into Oakland County and beyond, along Woodward Avenue. Most of General Motors' major divisions and research facilities are sited along its northwest axis. The GM Technical Center houses 6,000 scientists at Mound and Twelve Mile Road in a unified plan of cubic-shaped glazed brick structures on a site including ponded water and Calder sculptures. "Chrysler Territory" is considerably smaller and is centered in Detroit's East Side and Highland Park. Hamtramck and southern Macomb

County are also embraced within its general territory. During and since the Vietnam era there has been a greater tendency for all corporations to locate plants in each of the historic industrial corridors, nevertheless, the emotional, social, and economic identity to the "corporate territories" persists as a legacy of the past locational decisions of the industry.[3]

Michigan's Leisure Time Industry

The antecedents of Michigan's leisure time industry can be traced to the frontier days when occasional travelers were provided with accommodations, however humble, and other "away from home" needs for a fee. From the tourists Michigan received not only basic economic benefits, but their favorable reports encouraged further economic development which would have lasting impact on the state's landscape. Darby's observations of 1819 in *A Tour from the City of New York to Detroit* illustrates both the difficulty in measuring the economic geographic influence of travelers, as well as their value economically:

> . . . the soil is good in general, some of it excellent, and all part well situated for agriculture and commerce. . .[4]

In the modern era, the size, variety, and dispersal of firms engaged in leisure time activities from the sale of fish bait worms to the management of professional sports teams make the determination of the economics of leisure in the state gross product difficult and undoubtedly imprecise. Nevertheless, most measures rank the "recreation" industry with agriculture behind heavy industry within the state's economy. From a geographic point of view, leisure time activities have their own unique time and space characteristics. Most distinctive between *recreation* which is "the refreshment of the body and mind" and the *recreation or leisure time industry* is that the latter is based on revenues generated from the land, facilities, travel, and sales or services provided people in their pursuit of recreation or business away from home. Leisure time activity "away from home and job" may be exhausting and classified as a part of the broad recreation industry, but may *not* be recreational in reality (table 9.17). Therefore, leisure time industry may be a preferable classification for Michigan's second or third largest economic activity.

The Michigan Department of Commerce estimates that there are over 72,000 travel related businesses in the state and these businesses employ more than a half million people. It is further estimated that over 31 million tourist-type business trips of over 160 km (100 mi) are made annually in the state including nonrecreational and leisure time travel. Forty-eight percent of Michigan's long-distance travelers come from outside the state. Those people, it is found, generally stay longer and spend more in leisure pursuits than resident travelers. Thus, nonresidents generally contribute more than half of Michigan's travel-related revenues. Unlike other states with large metropolitan centers, Michigan has generally been unable to attract a significant influx of convention and business travel. As a result only 17 percent of Michigan's annual business travel is to conventions.

---

3. Robert R. Sinclair, *Face of Detroit* (Detroit: Wayne State University, National Council for Geographic Education, U.S. Office of Education, 1970), pp. 28, 35-40.
4. William Darby, *A Tour from the City of New York to Detroit* (Chicago: Americana Classics Quadrangle Books, 1962), pp. 199-200 (reprint of First Edition, New York, 1819).

TABLE 9.17
Leisure Time Terms and Space Relationships

Term	Time/Space Relationship
Recreation	Anyplace and time but refreshing to mind or body.
Tourism	Constant travel with only one day/night at a place, meals different place each 24 hours.
Tourist	Travels more than 100 miles from home or 50 miles with an overnight lodging.
Vacation	Little travel from home or place of temporary lodging, most meals at one place.
Resort	Temporary residence of one week or more at group of commercial cottages or living units.
Seasonal resident	Owns or rents a single-family dwelling for a season, most meals at site.
Weekenders	Much travel, but return to single place to sleep.
Camper	Carry own shelter to place of stay, may travel much (tourist) or stay in one place (vacationist).
Day camper	Travel to campground for day use of facilities, usually swimming, fishing, hiking.
Wreck creationist	Exhausted traveler, damager of nature or recreation facilities.

Modified from: R.N. Pearson, *Papers Michigan Academy of Science Arts and Letters,* Vol. 47, 1962.

Origin of Michigan Travelers

Citizens from the states of Ohio, Illinois, and Indiana contribute to Michigan's travel industry in both the greatest number and revenue. Based on state park use, Ohio leads nonresident visits with 30 percent of the total while Illinois and Indiana make up 25 and 19 percent, respectively. Generally more than one-third of all vacation or similar trips taken by Michiganians are spent in the state. In comparison, only between 10-12 percent of Indiana, Ohio, and Illinois vacationers seek recreation places in their own states. Florida, in the Sun Belt, is Michigan's chief competitor for vacationers who travel there from adjacent states. Ontario, Wisconsin, and Minnesota also have great potential for competition because of their lakes and forests. Land ownership is also a significant attraction for both Michigan and nonresident vacation travelers. Eleven percent of outstate and 16 percent of resident vacationists own their own property in Michigan recreation areas.

Attractions for Michigan Tourists. A basic question for which an answer must be determined if the state is to maintain and further capitalize on its tourist-leisure time industry economically is: What do people seek in the state? A corollary would be; Can the major attractions be improved and are they in need of protection? About one-third of the people who take their longest trip in Michigan seek outdoor recreation, nearly one-third of the people make their longest journey to visit friends and relatives, and about 16 percent are attracted for sightseeing and special events. Swimming and fishing are mentioned nearly 30 percent of the time by vacationers making them the most popularly sought outdoor recreation attractions. Regionally, the state parks and other historic attractions in the western Lower Peninsula draw the greatest proportion of visitors, nearly one-third, while the East, Upper Peninsula, and Southeast Tourist Council Regions attract 20-25 percent annually.

Professional Sports. Professional sports typically are businesses which require population of metropolitan size for support, but also draw statewide attendance occasionally for leisure time visits. Most professional major league sports are concentrated in Detroit (baseball, basketball, hockey, tennis, and power boating) while football has been lured to Pontiac with its air-supported roofed stadium. Horse racing, like football, is also concentrated in the Detroit suburbs, Hazel Park, Northville, Livonia, as well as Jackson. Minor league hockey is well developed in Port Huron, Kalamazoo, Saginaw, and Muskegon while Grand Rapids supports basketball. These professional teams plus metro-city libraries, museums, and night life also serve as attractions for Michigan tourists.

State Parks and Camping

Since 1921 the DNR and the former Michigan Conservation Department have played a vital role in the leisure-time industry. The DNR has led in park development, fishing-boat launch site acquisition, hunting-fishing research, snowmobile and other trail improvements, resource education at Higgins Lake, as well as acquiring land specifically for recreational use and wildlife protection. The activities of the DNR in relation to resource management and legislation are not only critical for the protection of the environment but also for the state's recreation industry. The Michigan park system includes eighty areas which are used by twenty million people annually. Of the visitors to state parks, one-third are campers and the remaining two-thirds day-camp users. Annually half a million camp permits are issued for the use of the state's approximately 15,000 campsites (table 9.18).

State parks, local parks, and private campgrounds, which number approximately 340, have increased to accommodate the demands of the state's growing population and leisure time industry. Nevertheless, shortages in camp facilities commonly disappoint thousands as "Sorry Full" signs are placed at park entrances (fig. 9.14). In the early 1970s nearly 60,000 requests for camp permits were turned down and 25,000 day users were denied entrance to state parks annually.

Density of Campsites. John Steinbeck in *America and the Americans* observed that people in our society appear "afraid to be together and afraid to be alone." The weekend agglomeration of people in "camp cities" onto sites of about 180 sq m (2,000 sq ft) would support his observation and bring to question the assumption that the majority of campers are seeking open space or a wildernesslike experience. The creature comfort facilities located in both private and state campgrounds lead the landscape interpreter to the conclusion that campers are seeking something other than temporarily low housing densities or avoidance of fellow human beings. Investigation reveals that many campers, although forming temporarily actutely dense shelter areas do seek: (1) quiet retreat away from hyperstimulated urban living, especially the telephone, (2) temporary nonbinding social relationships, and (3) access to the rudiments of the modern home. A sense of safety is also important. Thus, while people may be more densely agglomerated in campgrounds than in most residential areas, if peace and quiet are maintained and modern facilities available, campers will tolerate and can find enjoyment in what otherwise

TABLE 9.18
Most Used State Parks by Category 1973

Park	Total Attendance	Campers	Day Use
Holland	1,071,159 (1)	151,302	919,857 (1)
Warren Dunes	1,068,726 (2)	169,933	898,793 (2)
Yankee Springs	765,744 (3)	155,503	610,241
Ludington	625,606	247,190 (1)	378,416
South Higgins	409,938	215,803 (2)	194,135
Waterloo	564,303	193,038 (3)	371,265
Grand Haven	730,076	69,213	660,863 (3)

SOURCE: *Twenty-Seventh Biennial Report 1973-1974,* Department of Natural Resources, pp. 215-16.

would be considered unacceptably high-housing densities. Another important space aspect of campgrounds is that high-density campsite areas be adjacent to common grounds or open space for play, walking, or just viewing. In the organization of campground space, private campgrounds tend to have narrower widths for campsites in comparison to state parks, which undoubtedly is a function of reducing the cost of extending water, electrical, and sewer lines to individual campsites.

Campground Amenities. The economic geographic necessities to expand and support the camping aspect of the Michigan travel industry includes several features with varying priorities. High priority items include in addition to space: (1) access to water whether natural lake or pool for swimming, (2) electrical power to campsites, and (3) modern baths with hot showers. The obvious importance of water is seen in the location of most campgrounds near it and the immediate construction of swimming pools by private developers where natural lakes and beaches appear inadequate. The high priority for electricity at campsites is not only evident from the modern recreational vehicles (RV) with electric lights, refrigerators, TV antennas, and air conditioners, but also from the park records which show that as early as the 1930s underground electric hookups were installed at Otsego Lake State Park. Human attraction to water is further evident by the demand for showers especially with hot water, as all but seventeen state parks which allow camping have shower facilities.

Recreational Shelters. The last quarter century has witnessed an expansion in the size and value of seasonal and vacation homes. This is due to their more frequent use, as well as their being a hedge against the time when they may be converted into a year-round dwelling. Consequently, northern Michigan zoning laws now frequently require minimum floor spaces and lot sizes which were common for full-sized homes built in pre-World War II times.

The simple tent, which has not changed much in exterior space, has witnessed a revolution in suspension systems which allows greater interior space. Nevertheless, affluence and desire for greater comfort has brought about the adoption of pop-up campers, travel trailers, and motor lodges. In space these modern camp shelters are miniaturizations of contemporary homes and contain what many in the less-developed world would consider luxurious amenities. In comparison to the expedient log cabin of the pioneer period, modern recreational vehicles are smaller which reflects their mobile and temporary use. Log cabins typically were about 3.6 × 5.4 m (12 × 18 ft) while today's typical travel trailer or motor lodge ranges be-

Figure 9.14. Sign of the times.

tween 5.4-7.2 m (18-24 ft) long and 2.1 m (7 ft) wide. Retirees increasingly are found vagabonding in 9-10.5 m (30-35 ft) motor lodges which include many of the features of a modern home. One of the problems which increasingly confronts campground managers and users is the rapidly rising use of electricity and its abuses in use such as air conditioning vehicles when individuals are away, decorative lighting, and charging of battery-operated tools from home for "free." Such overloads not only waste resources but cause unnecessary expansions in electrical distribution systems. Other "out of place" problems which continually plague park managers which are basically people problems are: (1) dog control including running loose, barking, and defecating on paths and beaches, (2) broken glass and metal pull tabs which are littered on beaches, (3) trees damaged by youths who, unrestrained, fantasize as pioneers welding hatchets and chop and scar random trees, (4) path-bank erosion, and (5) undisciplined vandalism. Although data is limited on the subject, it can be hypothesized that there is a relationship between the increased use of area lighting, lockable hardside vehicles, and security patroling to campground thefts and disturbances (fig. 9.15).

Hunting-Fishing

For over a century hunting and fishing sportsmen have had a significant impact on the allocation, use, and revenues generated from Michigan's land and water resources. These activities in comparison to the travel industry as a whole, tend to attract considerably fewer nonresidents. For instance, of the one million fishing licenses and trout stamps issued annually, about 12 percent are granted to nonresidents. Additionally, nonresidents comprise less than 2 percent of the state's half million licensed small game and deer hunters. To meet the demands of these activities, the state manages sixty-five Game and Wildlife Areas comprising an area of 200,809 ha (502,024 ac) of which 111,503 ha (278,757 ac) are presently owned by the state's citizens. To facilitate fishing, the DNR maintains nearly 600 public access sites to water areas of which 250 are in the northern Lower Peninsula. Van Burean County with twenty-five access sites has the largest number of any county.

The coho and other large fish planting and management activities of the DNR associated with the Great Lakes and selected inland lakes has stimulated the development of 360 charter fishing boat businesses. Undoubtedly, with further expansion of the sport fisheries program, that segment of the fishing industry can be expected to increase and may draw more nonresident fishermen.

Until the development of paved roads and winter sports which extended and increased leisure time activities in the North, that area's economy and human activity were paced by the opening of the trout season and close of the deer season Although mushrooming, snowmobiling, skiing, trail riding, and winter weekending have had a stabilizing impact, deer season usually is the peak activity period in the North. Deer hunting activity results in the movement of 700,000 people, school closings in some districts of the northern Lower Peninsula and Upper Peninsula, as well as some businesses converting to 24-hour operations. Electric generation networks redistribute their power while the logistics of storing and distributing the short-term peak demands for gasoline, food, paper products, and alcoholic beverages, taxes the storage and distribution facilities in Regions Seven through Fourteen.

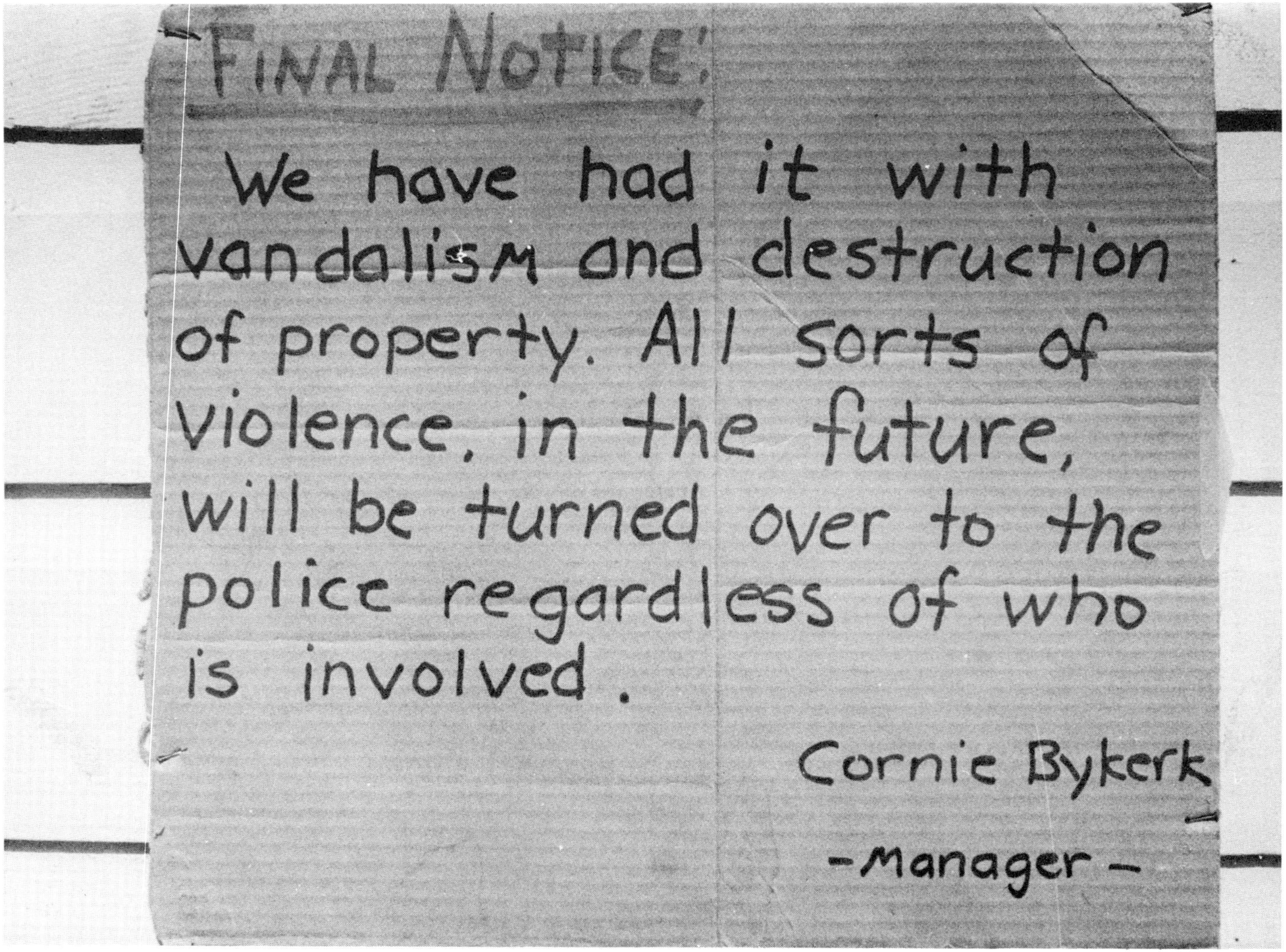

Figure 9.15. Sign at private campground 1976.

Snowmobiling-Skiing

Skiing and snowmobiling in the last quarter century have become major contributors to the economy of the northern counties. Unlike camping, hunting, and fishing, the state has been less directly involved in the expansion of these activities. Nevertheless, fifty-five ski resorts dot the map and landscape with their characteristic lodges, lifts, and forest-cleared slopes. Approximately two-thirds of the state's private ski areas are located in the Upper and northern Lower Peninsula with most sited in areas which receive more than 175 cm (70 in) of snowfall annually. In addition to downhill skiing, cross country skiing facilities are marketed at twenty-five resorts.

Snowmobiles. The national and Michigan ownership pattern of snowmobiles reflects the state's large population, Snow Belt location, and general economic affluence. It is estimated that Michigan has 1.3 million snowmobilers who operate a half million vehicles of which 379,000 are licensed for operation off the owner's private property. Snowmobilers have the use of 4,016 km (2,510 mi) of state-groomed public trails in addition to many additional designated scramble and operation areas on state land. In total, there are approximately 160 state-private land snowmobile trails and areas identified by the Michigan Travel Commission. Of these, only nineteen are located south of the Bay-Muskegon Line while forty-four are located in the Upper Peninsula. Generally, the Keweenaw Peninsula with its extreme north location has the longest season for this outdoor activity. Traverse City and Sault Ste. Marie have capitalized on the competitive spectator aspect of the powerful sounding machine with their long distance track races. Both Wisconsin and Minnesota with 10,400 and 8,800 km (6,500 and 5,500 mi) of state-groomed trails, respectively, have been more active in developing public trails. Although Michigan is a major snowmobile use state, production of the vehicles is very limited in Michigan. Troy is the only Michigan community which is the headquarters of a snowmobile production business of which there are twenty-nine nationally. In comparison, Wisconsin is the headquarters for four companies and Minnesota for six companies. Jackson and Grand Rapids have businesses which supply parts for snowmobiles.

The introduction and rapid diffusion of snowmobiles is typical of the *culture lag* theory with material technology advancing ahead of nonmaterial cultural institutions, such as government and education which ultimately manage the innovation from a health and safety point of view. Conflicts have emerged over the operation of snowmobiles on the right-of-ways of highway and county roads, operation by prepuberty aged youths, constant noise emissions above 82 decibels, undisciplined operation which is detrimental to plant and animal life, and trespassing. Law enforcement agencies are challenged with how to deal with the mobility gained which increasingly is used by thieves to gain access to vacant seasonal homes. In addition to their obvious economic value, snowmobiles have brought benefits which include emergency assistance mobility in heavy snow periods, as well as greater mobility for shopping, neighbor interaction, and social trail riding and snowmobile lodge partying.

Expanding the Leisure Time Industry

Research done for the Michigan Travel Commission reveals that the primary source of vacation planning information is "friends and relatives," 52 percent, while having "been there before," 12 percent, is another major influence of drawing people to Michigan. It follows then that the traditional business maxim "a satisfied customer" is one key to the growth of

Michigan's leisure time industry. Thus, to maintain or expand the economic value of the industry requires the protection of those things which have initially drawn people to the state—access to outdoor recreational environments and facilities, especially quiet areas. Less developed, but potentially useful in cementing the recreation foundation stone in Michigan's economy is expanding the emphasis on the public interaction with historical sites and fine arts. Frequently overlooked is the fact that Interlochen State Park, near the National Music Camp, has the fourth highest camping use within the state park system even though its total use figure is relatively low. If the Michigan tourist industry is to continue to prosper, its virtues must be protected and continually be made known in competition with the other states.

Economic Development and International Trade

In Michigan, as in any political entity, the quest for economic stability is an endless task for each generation. Reforestation, fisheries research and development, and iron beneficiation are but a few examples of profitable labor in the past to help make Michigan a desirable place to live. More recently international trade, foreign investments in Michigan, certified industrial parks, and school consolidations have been important contributions to the state's economy.

Michigan's International Trade

The reputation as the world's motor vehicle center, the operation of the St. Lawrence Seaway, plus the establishment of trade offices in Tokyo and Brussels, helped Michigan attain in 1975 first rank among the states in value of products exported. Exports totaled $3.5 billion of which $3.2 billion were manufactured goods, i.e., transportation and construction equipment, processed foods, metal products, chemicals, and pharmaceuticals. Agricultural products represent about 5 percent of the state's gross manufacturing output. However, farm exports including related transportation and marketing costs comprise nearly 20 percent of total agricultural sales. Michigan's 1975 leadership in exporting was somewhat unusual due to the influences of inflation/recession, depreciation of the dollar, floating exchange rates, and OPEC (Organization of Petroleum Exporting Countries) countries' purchases. More typical is a nearly balanced export-import of goods and services which reflects the state's increased import demands for machinery, transportation equipment, iron-steel, other metals, and food. In number of export-related jobs, Ohio which ranks below Michigan in dollar volume of export goods, has more—66,600 in 1975 compared to Michigan's 56,000.

Foreign Investment in Michigan. Since the 1920s foreign investment and partial or full control of Michigan-located business firms has been relatively modest. During the 1970s the number of foreign-owned or joint-venture firms located in the state increased to over forty. Foreign investment in Michigan firms is dominated by capital from Canada, Japan, and the United Kingdom. The foreign-owned firms are dispersed in thirty-three communities with Detroit and its metropolitan area the most active center of foreign operations (table 9.19). Initial employment in foreign firms is still modest totaling approximately 11,000 jobs.

New Corporate and Industrial Investment in Michigan. Michigan, in the post-Korean War era, has witnessed a doubling in the annual rate of chartering new profit-making corporations and has tripled its number of out-of-state incorporations of firms located in the state (table 9.20). In the two decades after 1955, the cyclic weakening of the state's economy is

TABLE 9.19
Foreign Investments in Michigan by Nation and Community 1975

Nation	Product	Michigan Location
Belgium	Machine tools	Detroit
Canada	Steel tubing	Sault Ste. Marie
	Paperboard	Birmingham
	Chemical	Troy
	Truck attachments	Alpena
	Strapping	Port Huron
	Construction machines (tractors)	Detroit
	Phone equipment	Port Huron
	Gasoline pumps	Muskegon Heights
	Cookies	Springfield
France	Oil refining	Alma
	Steel wire	Bridgman
	Casings	Muskegon
Germany	Chemicals	Wyandotte
	Machine tools	Detroit
	Metal presses	Southfield
	Machine tools	Troy
	Metal stamps	Detroit
	Steel springs	Edwardsburg
Japan	Warehouse	Ferndale
	Bearings	Ann Arbor
	Music instruments	Kentwood
	Pianos	South Haven
	Magnetics	Edmore
	Polyfoam	Coldwater
	Pottery	Mt. Clemens
	Machine tool accessories	Big Rapids
Liechtenstein	Photo equipment	Ann Arbor
Netherlands Antilles	Electronics	Benton Harbor
Sweden	Steel strip	Benton Harbor
Switzerland	Sheet aluminum	Jackson
	Cement	Dundee
	Foundry machinery	Holly
	Epoxy resins	Lansing
United Kingdom	Food machinery	Saginaw
	Pneumatic tools	Detroit
	Chemicals	Plymouth
	Electric gears	Jackson
	Seed sorting machinery	Lowell
	Animal food	Adrian
	Cookies	Grand Rapids

SOURCE: Michigan Department of Commerce, International Division.

TABLE 9.20
New Incorporations and Industrial Commercial Failures 1955-1975

Year	New Incorporations Profit Making	Foreign Out-of-State Ventures	Industrial Commercial Failures
1955	4,619	379	211
1956	4,337	389	413
1957	3,842	461	512
1958	3,900	404	547
1959	4,812	527	496
1960	4,800	499	524
1961	4,788	497	564
1962	5,135	601	523
1963	5,102	528	371
1964	5,825	593	285
1965	6,152	627	222
1966	6,315	640	215
1967	6,341	715	191
1968	7,700	825	290
1969	9,586	1,064	251
1970	8,378	1,054	336
1971	8,270	1,082	321
1972	9,202	1,175	558
1973	9,709	1,093	563
1974	9,342	1,009	652
1975	9,996	926	NA

SOURCE: *Economic Report of the Governor*, 1976, p. 114.

apparent by the number of industrial and commercial failures which normally average 200-250 yearly, but generally spurt to over 500 in times of automobile production declines, such as 1956-1962, and 1972-1974 (tables 9.15 and 9.20). In the periods of decreased auto production, outstate incorporation tends to increase, which undoubtedly indicates periodic efforts by the state government and business communities to gain economic improvement through greater efforts to expand the flow of non-Michigan capital into the state.

The Michigan Business Climate. In recent years there has developed considerable concern by Chambers of Commerce, state government leaders, and economists in what is referred to as "Michigan's business climate." Most attention is generally focused on the overall economy and its relation to workmen's compensation, tax rates, and welfare rates. These relationships are also critical in land-use planning. It is counterproductive to plan for or allocate land for activities which will not be used, however well-suited physically, due to other social-economic factors. Workmen's compensation in relationship to the state's three automobile corporations is an illustration of the dilemma between attempts for social progress and economic expansion. At times individual abuse of the state's social welfare system has been detrimental to Michigan's economy. Comparatively, during the mid-1970s Chrysler Corporation made 89 percent of its workmen's compensation payments in Michigan while only 63 percent of its employees were located in the state. Similarly Ford Motor Company paid 80 percent of its workmen's compensation in the state while only 56 percent of its workers resided in Michigan. For General Motors the figures are 71 percent and 41 percent, respectively. State level social benefit costs as a business location factor can be further illustrated with the Campbell, Wyant and Cannon Foundry of South Haven. In 1974 its workmen's compensation costs in its Michigan plant were $938 per employee for Michigan workers. In comparison, its compensation costs in its Indiana plant were $259 per employee. In a study conducted by the Wisconsin State Department of Revenue on business tax systems of fifteen states, Michigan was ranked with the highest third being grouped with New York, Illinois, California, and Iowa. On balance Michigan generally is considered a state that provides much to its citizens and businesses for taxes in good highways, education, and government services.

Energy costs have a further bearing on economic expansion in the state as its manufacturing economy is energy intensive. While the average Michigan housing unit requires 5,400 cu m (180,000 cu ft) of gas per year, manufacturing industries use an average of 11,250 cu m (375,000 cu ft) per production worker. Similarly, while the average household uses 6,500 kilowatt hours of electricity per year, a production worker uses an average of 46,500 kilowatt hours per year. As a result, in a limited financial and energy situation, Michigan's economic decision makers are confronted with serious investment and energy costs in planning the expansion of durable goods manufacturing.

Food and Michigan Tractor Production

With little fanfare Michigan's motor vehicle industry has diversified and profited from Canadian tractor manufacturing investments which has led to Michigan becoming North America's largest producer of farm and light industrial tractors. The tractor industry located in the Detroit region has expanded based on: (1) the international demand for food, (2) the historic technical "know how" of automotive-tractor corporations, (3) the developing nations securing "new wealth" based on resource exports, and (4) the global operation of Michigan tractor manufacturing which can meet any world market. It is estimated that about 25 percent of the quarter million North American produced tractors are made by Ford's tractor operations in Troy and Romeo plus Canada's Massey-Ferguson's plants located on the Southfield Freeway in Detroit and at its Wayne plant.

Mobile Home Industry

In the years of the Vietnam War, mobile homes became a significant part of the single-family dwelling housing market. Until 1963, Michigan, with centers of production at Marlette and Alma, produced nearly 15 percent of the nation's mobile homes. In spite of the quadrupled expansion of the industry in one decade, Michigan's share of mobile home production declined drastically to less than 2 percent in 1975 (table 9.21).

The dramatic decline of the mobile home industry and the cyclic failure of businesses are less than exciting things to describe or for persons to read about. Nevertheless, if Michigan is to mature with an economy of stable health and vigor, students of geography, as well as other disciplines, can play an exciting role in determining the locational dynamics of decline and then participate in decisions and steps necessary to moderate the causes of economic reversals which

TABLE 9.21
Michigan-USA Mobile Home Production 1963-1975

Year	Sold in Michigan	Produced in Michigan	Produced in USA	Michigan Percent of USA Total
1963	5,616	21,876	150,840	14.5
1966	11,737	16,204	217,300	7.5
1969	19,676	19,506	412,690	4.7
1972	17,983	14,779	601,250	2.5
1974	12,095	5,718	330,855	1.7
1975	6,089	NA	NA	NA

SOURCE: *Economic Report of the Governor*, 1976, p. 56.

bring with it its blight and human misery. Professor James Wheeler, a geographer at the University of Georgia, has found that the expansion of the factory-built home industry in nine southeastern states is most critically associated with: (1) access to market, (2) access to labor supply, (3) access to materials, and (4) labor costs.

Planning for Modern Industrial Expansion

Industry, like agriculture, transportation, or recreation activities, is best suited to sites with specific characteristics. Since the 1960s many communities in Michigan, as in other parts of the nation, have recognized the advantages of planning for industrial growth by designating certain areas as *Industrial Parks*. By protecting land suitable for industry from random development, communities gain the potential of economic benefits resulting from guided expansion. Further, industrial parks allow older industries to modernize by relocating on a more competitive site within the community, thus protecting the local tax base. By 1976 Michigan had certified one hundred industrial parks in six counties of the Upper Peninsula and thirty-two counties of the Lower Peninsula.

Industrial developers have long recognized the need for uniformity in use of the term "industrial park." The expression designates certain kinds of districts or subdivisions set aside for sites to be occupied by groups of industrial facilities. However, areas designated by the name range from the highly sophisticated, organized industrial district, to an isolated cornfield completely lacking in basic services and amenities.

To give prospective occupants a better idea of what they can expect to find in an industrial park and assure them of high quality site characteristics and services, the Michigan Department of Commerce has adopted a set of standards for qualified developments to be known as "Certified Industrial Parks."

Using criteria established by the Michigan Professional Industrial Development Association, the department has pioneered a program for rating and certifying industrial parks. Landowners are still free to call their acreage anything they choose but only those meeting the established standards are entitled to the state certification.

To be eligible, an industrial park must meet the following basic requirements:
1. Minimum size of 16 ha (40 ac).
2. Land zoned for industrial use.
3. Area has both external and internal paved streets.
4. Area has water and sanitary sewer installed.

The criteria used for rating proposed state certified industrial parks used by the Michigan Department of Commerce places highest value on sanitary sewers, community and auxiliary services (table 9.22).[5]

TABLE 9.22
Criteria and Point Scale Used for Certifying Industrial Parks

Criteria	Maximum Points
Sanitary sewers	13
Community and auxiliary services	13
Municipal water service	10
Storm sewers	9
Paved streets	9
Protective covenants and restrictions	9
Soil characteristics	7
Highway accessibility	6
Airport facilities	6
Rail accessibility	5
Grading and clearing	4
Special park features	4
Harbor facilities	3
Natural gas service	2

SOURCE: Michigan Department of Commerce.

Education and Economics

The economic importance of quality education has been a basic concern of Michigan residents since the enactment of the Northwest Ordinance. In the years after the post-World War II "baby boom," school administrators and citizens were first overwhelmed by the pupil numbers, then challenged by the two-pronged responsibility to: (1) transmit the basics of American culture and values to the youth and (2) provide the pupils with skills and reasoning abilities in preparation for jobs or college. To meet the needs of the burgeoning population and complexity explosion, massive school consolidation and specialized school transportation programs were initiated. These programs obviously brought an end to the once commonplace one-room schoolhouses which now appear on the landscape as churches, granaries, homes, museums, or as decaying buildings. Replacing the small wooden gable-roofed structures are sprawling one-story flat-roofed brick and glass facilities located on central sites or outlying areas depending on community sentiment and available space. The land space demand whether for a consolidated or urban school district, also underwent a dramatic change. Whereas less than 2 ha (5 ac) were adequate for a 500 pupil Junior High building in 1918, the spatial needs to serve 500 pupils expanded to 12-16 ha (30-40 ac) in the 1960s. With consolidation, transportation became frequently the second largest item of operating expenses for rural school districts and now provides a dilemma for school boards and officials as energy costs rise. Undoubtedly,

---

5. Office of Economic Expansion, *1976 Michigan Plant Location Directory* (Lansing: Michigan Department of Commerce), p. ix.

the savings in transportation costs by the use of applied geometry and computer assisted network theory for the routing of school buses will have to be more widely adopted than at present.

School Consolidation. Between 1952 and 1970 the number of Michigan school districts declined from 4,532 to 625. By 1976 the number of districts was further lowered to 590 (table 9.23). Unfortunately, many school district boundaries which have been created as a result of rapid school consolidation do not entirely fit functional community interaction patterns. Nevertheless, consolidated school districts do provide an indication of the contemporary local political-social geographic pattern and area of space which functions between village-city levels of government and the county level.

TABLE 9.23
Public School District Consolidation with Number of Teachers and Pupils 1952-1970

School Year	Number Districts	Number Teachers	Number Pupils (in millions)
1952-53	4,532	42,528	1.17
1957-58	2,499	55,794	1.51
1962-63	1,580	68,099	1.79
1967-68	712	85,346	2.07
1970-71	624	90,672	2.17
1974-75	590	--	2.13
1980-81	--	--	1.93*

*Estimated
SOURCE: *Michigan Statistical Abstract,* 1972, p. 138; *Economic Report of the Governor,* 1976, p. 61.

Nonpublic school education has also changed significantly in the recent decades, however, nonpublic school building abandonment has been much less pronounced on the landscape. Between 1960 and the mid-1970s nonpublic school enrollment declined from 16 to 9 percent of the total Michigan kindergarten-twelfth grade (K-12) enrollment. In those same years, secondary private schools declined in operation from 230 to 170 high schools. On the other hand, parochial elementary schools have declined less than 10 percent from their expansion peak of 763 in 1966 to about 700 in operation in the 1970s.

Two-year community or junior colleges have witnessed two rapid growth periods in the twentieth century. The decades of the teens and twenties were the years of diffusion of the junior colleges affiliated with urban high school districts (Grand Rapids 1914, Highland Park 1918, Flint 1923, Port Huron 1923, Muskegon 1926, Jackson 1928, and Dearborn 1938). In the 1950s and 1960s the two-year institutions expanded their role consistent with the modern-day community college movement which included an open door policy plus a goal to serve a wider segment of local populations. Twenty-nine community colleges now serve the state from both modernistic urban campuses to smaller rural campuses. Student growth rates of 12 to 15 percent have been common in most of the two-year colleges, however, in the late 1970s the rate of growth is expected to slow to about 10 percent annually as the legislature and community college districts adjust their financing formulas.

Photo Essay D

LEISURE TIME AND AGRICULTURE

D-1   Canoeing, Belle Isle Park, Detroit. (Michigan Travel Commission)

D-2   Commercial sport fishing on the Great Lakes. (Michigan Travel Commission)

D-3   Promotional sign for salmon fishing.

D-4   State park camping, Harrisville. (Michigan Travel Commission)

D-5   National Arts Academy, Interlochen, Grand Traverse County (Michigan Travel Commission)

D-6   Snowmobiling. (Michigan Travel Commission)

D-7   Ski flying, Copper Peak, Gogebic County. (Michigan Travel Commission)

D-8   Tractor and grain binder typical of 1930s.

D-9   Grain threshing operation typical of pre-World War II era.

D-10   Family farm with cattle, recreational horses, and fruit trees. Barns with gable and gambrel roof types. (Michigan Travel Commission)

D-11   Agribusiness beef operation, Tecumseh Township, Lenawee County. (*Michigan Farmer*)

D-12   Demonstration of 14-bottom plow for use on lacustrine plains. (*Michigan Farmer*)

D-13   Migrant laborers picking cucumbers. (Michigan Travel Commission)

D-14   Mechanized grape harvest, Paw Paw area. (Michigan Travel Commission)

D-15   Bean harvest, Saginaw Lowland. (*Michigan Farmer*)

D-16   Sugar beet storage before processing, Saginaw region. (*Michigan Farmer*)

D-17   Three-row corn picker-sheller. (*Michigan Farmer*)

D-18   Land-use for agriculture and other modern-day needs is a serious problem, Port Austin, Huron County. (Michigan Travel Commission)

D-1

D-2

D-3

D-4

INTERLOCHEN

Ottawa Indians once lived in the pine forest between lakes Wahbekaness and Wahbekanetta. In the late 1800's white men came and cut the pines, leaving only a small forest between the lakes. This virgin pine was purchased in 1917 by the state and became part of one of the first state parks. When the lumber era ended, the Wylie Cooperage mill occupied the Indian village site, making barrels until the hardwood ran out. Willis Pennington's summer hotel, opened in 1909, was popular with fishermen until automobiles and better roads drew them elsewhere. Then in 1918, Camp Interlochen, one of Michigan's first girls' recreation camps, was opened, followed in 1922 by Camp Penn Loch for boys. In 1928, by arrangement with Willis Pennington, Joseph E. Maddy and Thaddeus P. Giddings established the National High School Orchestra Camp. It grew rapidly in scope, size, and reputation, becoming the National Music Camp in 1931, and affiliating with the University of Michigan in 1942. Interlochen Arts Academy was chartered in 1960 to provide year-round training in the creative arts.

MICHIGAN HISTORICAL COMMISSION REGISTERED SITE NO. 225

D-5

D-6

D-7

D-8

D-9

D-10

D-11

D-12

D-13

D-14

D-15

D-16

D-17

D-18

"Transportation is a measure of the relations between areas and is therefore an essential part of Geography."

Edward Ullman

Chapter Ten

Michigan's Transportation and Communication Systems

In this chapter transportation and communication as a means of linking places together is presented in relation to Michigan's economy. In its broadest sense, transportation-communication includes the means to transmit people, materials, energy, and ideas from one place to another. Based on historical tradition of transportation network development, it can be observed that communication systems are axiomatic to an area's people for military security. However, in the contemporary era well-functioning transportation-communication networks are critical to the well-being of society and enable it to agglomerate people, raw material for manufacturing and service activities, plus the distribution of finished products and services. Typically land-use patterns and decisions to locate industrial, commercial, and residential activities are directly related to accessibility to one or more modes of transportation. The mode of transportation-communication that is most critical in the location of an activity is usually dependent upon the weight and judgment values placed on time, modal costs, as well as rate structures and continuity of accessibility throughout the seasons.

Land values are profoundly affected by accessibility and have most recently been visible by the scramble to acquire property near freeway interchanges. In the past, central business district property commanded the highest prices with the intersection having the greatest number of pedestrian crossings becoming known as the 100 percent corner. City address systems frequently have been modified through the years in many cities to accommodate persuasive businesses to carry the Number One or One Hundred address. Banks and department stores are the most typical land users for 100 percent locations. Residential locations in relationship to places of work, market, or education, historically have been within one hour's journey. Such a time factor is still influential in determining settlement patterns regardless of mode of modern transportation. On the other hand, Michigan's seasonal second home boom was triggered when freeways were extended out from metro-communities which made the "North" accessible on weekends within two-four hours driving time as opposed to five-six hours or more in the prefreeway era or by public transportation. An underlying factor, but rarely focused on in the contemporary era, is that modern settlement patterns and location decisions are based on the common expectation that people and goods will have freedom from highway robbery both literally and figuratively. Due to the past practice of abusing transportation-communication rights and ease of establishing monopolies, it is not surprising that the state and national governments have been granted power to regulate the various communication networks through the Michigan Public Service Commission, Department of Highways and Transportation, and police agencies.

Highways in Michigan

Historic Territorial Roads

The Great Lakes, rivers, and Indian trails were, of course, the initial transportation routes of Michigan. After the American Government gained control of the peninsular region, Detroit had to be defended and improved territorial roads connecting it to the rest of the Northwest Territory became a necessity. Nonetheless, frontier road construction lagged nearly as much as Michigan territorial settlement. By the land boom of the 1830s, only three roads had been started and only one completed. In 1827, nearly a decade after Secretary of War Calhoun had stressed the need for roads for national defense, a stagecoach-worthy road was completed through the Black Swamp to link Detroit and Ohio. The state's first major military road to the northwest of Detroit was started in 1816 leading to Pontiac and Saginaw following the Saginaw Trail. This route later became Woodward Avenue and parts of M-1, US-10, and I-75. The first road west was the Chicago Military Road linking Detroit with Fort Dearborn, then at the site of Chicago. The Chicago Military Road followed parts of the Old Salk and St. Joseph Indian Trails. The road was authorized for construction by Congress in 1825, and its route was partly marked in the same year. The Chicago Road is the contemporary route of US-12 (formerly US-112) and originally directed settlement into the most southerly tier of counties after it passed west of Ypsilanti. Three other major roads were constructed in the 1830s territorial period: (1) the Territorial or St. Joseph Trail which followed the former US-12 between Ann Arbor and Benton Harbor west of Ypsilanti which is now paralleled by I-94, (2) the Grand River Road (Detroit-Muskegon) which reached Grand Rapids in 1837, later known as US-16 and is now paralleled by I-96, and (3) the Detroit-Fort Gratiot or Port Huron Road, formerly US-25 which is now paralleled by I-94. LaPlaisance Bay Trail (Monroe-Cambridge Junction), now part of M-50, and Pontiac Trail (Pontiac-Ann Arbor) were also pioneer routes which are studded with farmhouses, pioneer plantings, and vestiges of the territorial era. When the military roads were completed, stagecoach and wagon travel became common modes of land travel and increased movement rates to 24-32 km (15-20 mi) per day.

Early Statehood Road Building

Federal road building in Michigan ceased with statehood in 1837. However, state road improvements continued basically under township administration and the over 200 Plank Road Companies chartered by the state. The companies charged tolls for road use which were to be used for their continued improvements and maintenance. Oftentimes soil and drainage problems outran the available money or other uses were found for the revenues generated which sometimes created hostile feeling.

For several decades railroads and the 1850 Constitution curtailed broad interest in highway building and improvements. In the 1890s a "good roads" reawakening began when the safety bike was introduced with uniform-sized wheels. Independent bike clubs and those in the League of American Wheelmen organized in 1879, were reinforced by motorists in the early twentieth century in demanding better roads. In 1905, as a result of the growing political pressure to alleviate the hazards of sand, mud, and ruts, Michigan's 1850 Constitution was amended to relieve the prohibition of the state from being:

> . . . a party to, or interested in any work of internal improvement, nor engage in carrying on any such work. . . .

The 1905 Constitutional Amendment further permitted the state to participate in building public wagon roads and was approved by vote in all counties.

Twentieth Century Road Building

Prior to the passage of the Road Amendment (1903-1905), Horatio S. Earle, who was the president of the American Wheelmen in 1901, acted as the state's unconstitutional, unpaid Highway Commissioner and became Michigan's first legal commissioner in 1905. The twentieth century impact on highway construction can be measured from the length and type of roads developed in the state up to 1905 (table 10.1).

TABLE 10.1
Michigan Road Lengths and Type 1905

Road Type	Kilometers	Miles
Unimproved		
Clay	48,000	30,000
Sand	41,600	26,000
Swamp	4,800	3,000
Improved		
Gravel	12,320	7,700
Stone/macadam	392	245
Total System	107,112	66,945

SOURCE: "History of Michigan Highways," Michigan Department of State Highways and Transportation, May 1974.

In 1909, Michigan's stature as a road-building state increased with the pouring of the world's first mile of concrete highway on Woodward Avenue between Six and Seven Mile Roads through a wet, poorly drained area adjacent to present-day Palmer Park.

Citizen Participation in Road Building. In 1907, Michigan repealed a law which permitted citizens to substitute work for their road tax, however, the idea of citizen responsibility and active participation in good road construction continued. In 1913, the State Trunk Line Act was passed to create 4,800 km (3,000 mi) of highways to link the state's larger cities, major transportation points, and major cities near the state boundary. The enthusiasm generated by the anticipated value of the Trunk Line System led to the first Road Bee Day in Michigan in 1913. So successful was the road improvement venture that Governor W. N. Ferris issued a proclamation officially setting aside June 4-5, 1914, as statewide Road Bee Days.

In 1919, license plate fees began to be charged based on vehicle weight. The system was related to the ability of improved road surfaces and soil to support vehicles under thaw conditions. Initially half the fees were returned to the county registering the vehicles. After 1945, college communities felt an inequality in the revenue distribution system. The inequality resulted from students tending to register vehicles in their hometown, thereby reducing the funds available in college counties to maintain roads where the cars were operated nine months of the year.

Snow Removal. Up to World War I, snow removal from roads was uncommon. As a result, many auto owners blocked and stored their autos in private and commercial garages. When the United States entered the war, there was an increased demand for snow removal and all-weather roads to transport war material. By 1918, snow removal was initiated on five routes and, by 1921, some of the mining region's roads in the Upper Peninsula were plowed. Today the entire State Highway System is included in the snow removal program. At the county level, high priority is given to opening school bus routes which also influences the selection of contemporary country homesites.

Highway Construction 1920-1970

In the mid-twentieth century several factors of geographic interest combined to stimulate the transformation of the landscape by road building and increased highway travel in the state. Between 1920-1925, the state's $50 million bond program for highway construction was combined with $31 million federal-county funds to activate the largest road-building boom up to that time in the state's history (fig. 10.1).

During the Depression, improved roads and long distance travel were further stimulated. First, there was a gradual consolidation of township roads into county systems. Second, and most important, was the opening of the first Travel Information Center in 1935 on US-12 near the Indiana border and the creation of the nationally famous roadside park system which now totals 103 roadside parks. The number of rest areas on freeways alone has risen to 66 with 27 additional ones planned. The thirties also witnessed the modification of the earlier state highway condition map into a more easily used format. Additionally there was wide circulation of oil or insurance company highway maps for use by motorists. The cover of the 1930 Auto Owners Insurance Map encouraged tourism with the heading: "Tour in Michigan's Scenic Wonderland—the Playground of a Nation." As tourism increased, auto ferry service across the Straits of Mackinac also began to accelerate. In spite of the fact that annual automobile production declined between 1929 and 1950, Highway Department studies showed that highway travel increased 18 percent even in the Depression years, 1930-1936. For over a third of the century, 1938-1972, the State Constitution required that gasoline and weight taxes be only for highway purposes, effectively curtailing any major diversity of use within route right-of-ways during that period.

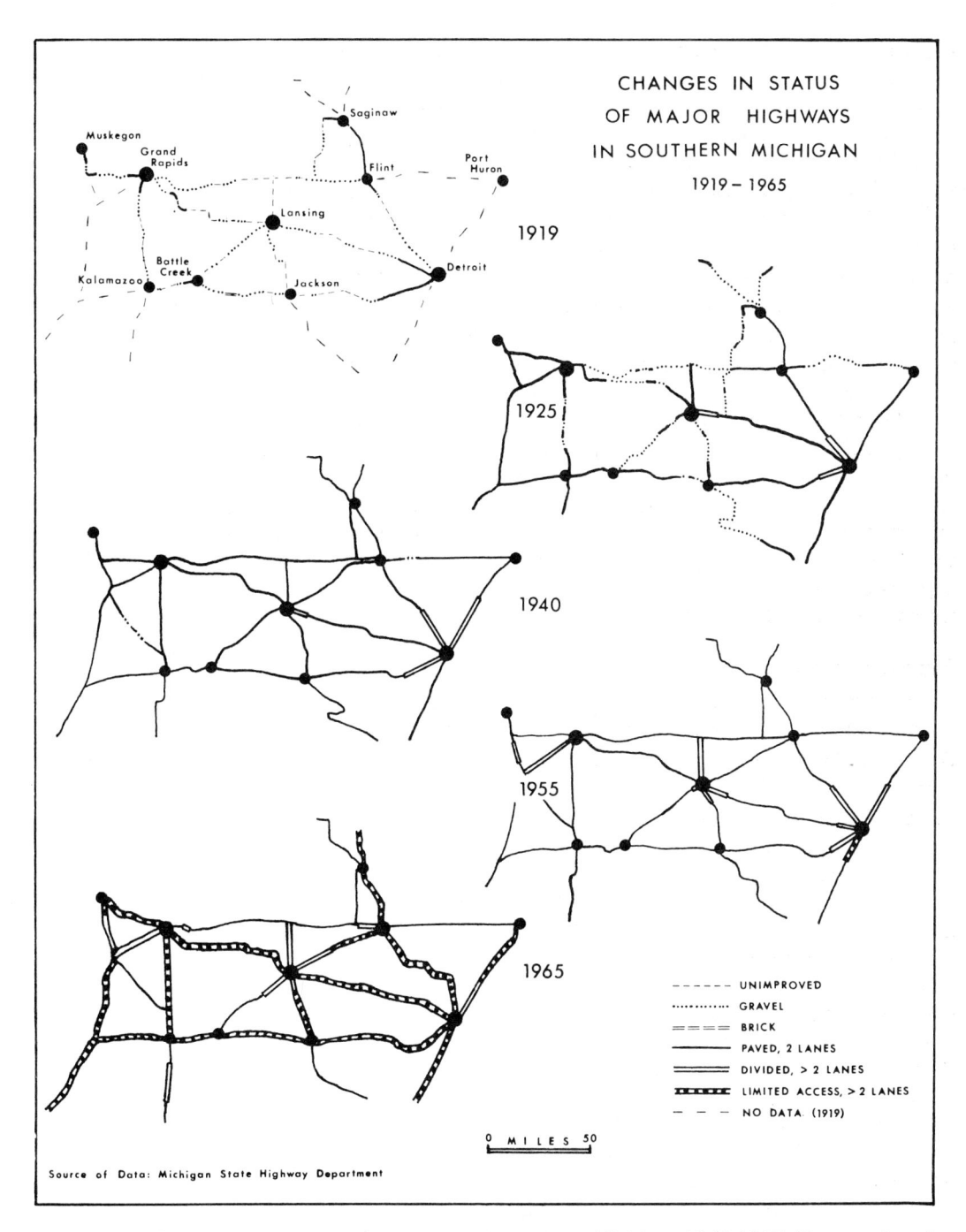

Figure 10.1. Change in status of major highways in southern Michigan 1919-1965. (Source: *Annals Association of American Geographers,* Vol. 59, No. 2, 1969, used with permission.)

The World War II and Freeway Era. During World War II when Michigan's people and industries produced one-eighth of America's entire war output, over 75 percent of the material was transported at some point on the state highways. As the war was fought, the modern chapter of freeway construction began with the hurried laying of the Detroit Industrial or Willow Run Expressway. The divided highway was necessary to carry workers to the huge Bomber Plant near Ypsilanti. In the 1970s the original expressway was reconstructed as a part of I-94. In 1947 the first step in modern urban freeways was begun with the $200 million Lodge and Ford Freeways in Detroit jointly financed by the local, state, and national governments. During President Eisenhower's administration the National Defense Highway Act (NDHA) was signed into law which initiated the development of 1883 km (1,177 mi) of state freeway construction of which 1,704 km (1,065 mi) were completed by 1975. The NDHA freeways are routed to connect the nation's SMSA cities and strategic defense localities with divided roadways of at least two lanes in each direction with all crossings closed or separated. In addition to the NDHA routes which are financed 90 percent by the federal government, Michigan has constructed 800 km (500 mi) of other freeways which received 50 percent federal financing (table 10.2).

TABLE 10.2
Total Length of Michigan Highway Network by Category

Year	Category of Highway	Kilometers	Miles
1975	State highways	14,920	9,325
1974	County roads	140,488	87,805
1974	City streets	29,654	18,534
1975	Freeways (state system)	2,564	1,603
	Total	185,062	115,664

Economic Interdependency on Roads

Approximately three-fourths of the raw materials used in Michigan factories and their finished products move by truck on the state highways. Nearly all of the state agricultural production is transported on state roads. Additionally, the leisure time industry relies on all-weather highway accessibility. In spite of continued dependency on highway travel, each generation has to decide how much of the state's gross product and land resources should and can be spent on highways.

Costs and Savings in Time-Space Convergence

The steady twentieth century improvement in highway surfaces has converted the time needed to overcome space. The increase in speed of highway travel since 1900 has been over five-fold from less than 16 kph (10 mph) on unimproved dirt roads to 88 kph (55 mph) on a paved two-lane road or freeway. In comparison, the road improvements of the 1900-1925 period brought greater rates in time-distance savings than the 1940-1965 freeway era (fig. 10.2).

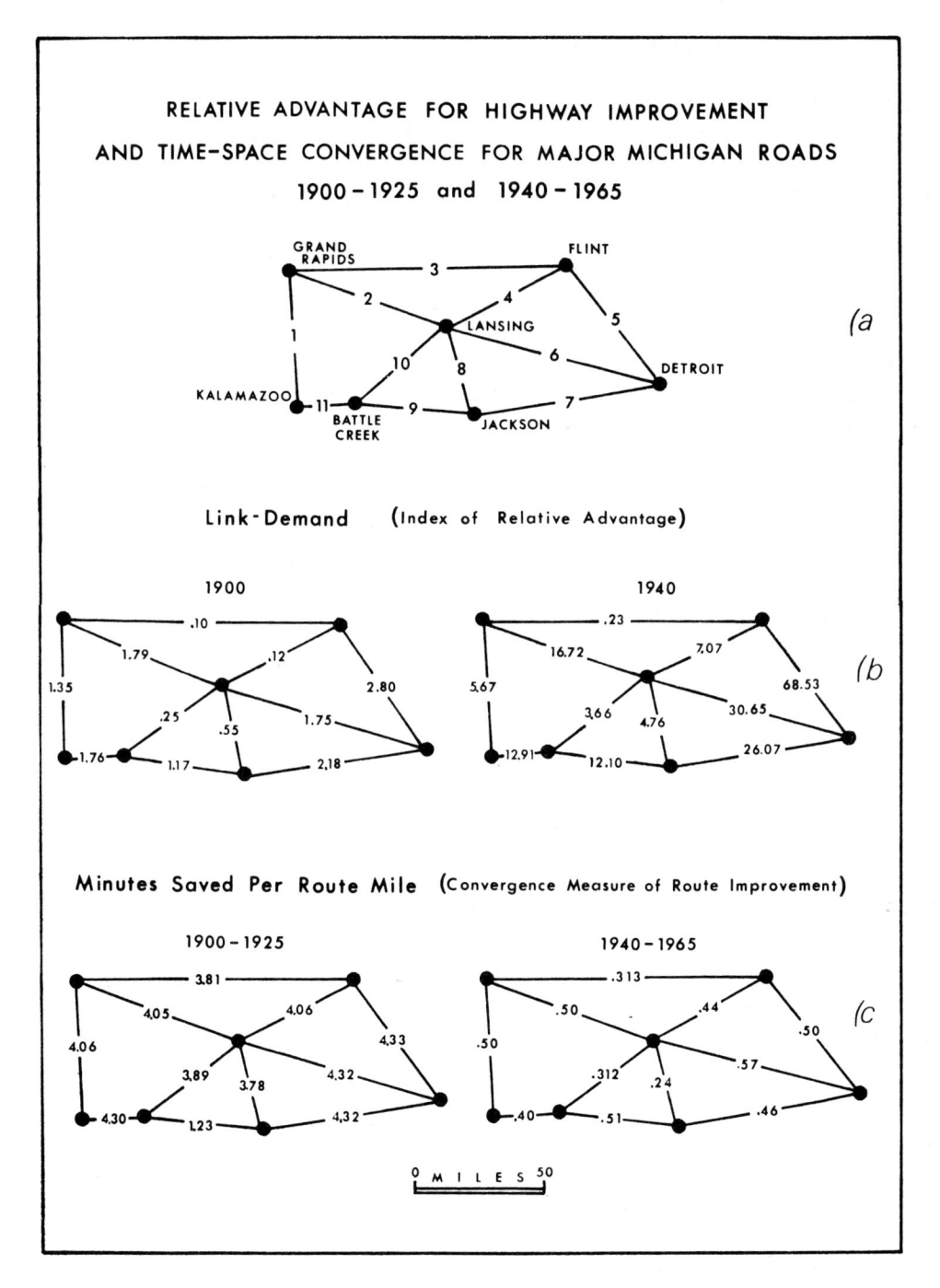

Figure 10.2. Relative advantage of highway improvements. (Source: *Annals Association of American Geographers,* Vol. 59, No. 2, 1969, used with permission.)

In recent years there has been little improvement in the speed of mobility within CBDs. The overall twentieth century convergence of time-space has not been without its monetary and environmental costs. In dollars, between 1960 and 1975, the State Highway Department spent between $152 million and $279 million annually for right-of-way acquisition, engineering costs, construction, and maintenance of the 14,920 km (9,325 mi) in the State Highway System. In comparison, in 1976 an average mile of county road could be hard-surfaced for $30,000-$60,000 while the average freeway mile costs generally average one million dollars. In area, a county road with a right-of-way of 20 m (66 ft) requires 31, 363 sq m (348,480 sq ft) per mile while a freeway mile of a modest width of 90 m (300 ft) requires the use of 142,560 sq m (1,584,000 sq ft) of land. The trend towards more and wider right-of-ways has caused critical concerns to not only environmentalists, but also local governments which lose tax rights on the right-of-ways, as well as witness the community loss of forest and agricultural land (fig. 10.3).

The I-696 Completion Dilemma. The completion of I-696 between I-75 and Northwestern Highway north of Detroit has been a classic battle in freeway location. Since 1950 each suburb between Baseline Road and 16 Mile Road has registered opposition to the right-of-way crossing their territory. The political sparring between Detroit and Pleasant Ridge illustrates the economic clout gained through the use of the 1969 National Environmental Quality Act which prohibits use of park lands and other public recreational facilities for highway use unless: ". . . no prudent and feasible alternative" exists. When Pleasant Ridge voters rejected an offer of $500,000 for a small portion of park land near 10 Mile and Woodward, the Michigan Highway Department (MHD) offered the city of Detroit $1.5 million for .404 ha (1.01 ac) of its Zoological Park including the relocation of its railroad and rail station. As delays continue over the years, the projected cost to complete the 12.8 km (8 mi) of freeway has risen to $112 million.[1]

Highway Numbering and Location Systems

By the midtwenties, the multitude of highway numbers in each state caused bewildered motorists to demand a simplified system of route identification. Thus, in 1925 the federal government in cooperation with the states, created the US highway numbering system which changed many state trunk line numbers to US highway numbers. For example, in the Jackson area, M-17 became US-12 and M-14 became US-127, and other large Michigan cities gained equally by the reduction in the road numbering confusion.

Today Michigan is a part of the nationally integrated US and Interstate highway numbering system which consistently numbers east-west highways with even one- or two-digit numbers and north-south routes with odd numbers. United States highways are numbered north to south and east to west which places US-2 in the Upper Peninsula, US-12 in the southern Lower Peninsula, US-23-25 in the eastern part of the southern Lower Peninsula, US-31 in the western Lower Peninsula and US-41 in the western Upper Peninsula. The interstate numbering system uses the same consistency, but numbers the freeways south to north and west to east which places I-96 north of I-94 and I-69 west of I-75. Unfortunately, some inconsistency has been introduced into the system; i.e., I-94 runs north of I-96 between Detroit and Port Huron, US-24 runs due north from the state line to Pontiac, and US-29 is located in Washington, D.C. and along the Eastern Seaboard rather than in the Midwest.

1. *Detroit Free Press,* February 29, 1976, p. B 1.

284

Figure 10.3. Michigan's basic highway network. (Map: Michigan Department of Natural Resources.)

Three-digit numerals also have a route meaning in the US system, such as US-131 indicates a relatively short length state highway parallel to a long distance US route, in this case, US-31, which extends through several states. In the Interstate system even numbered prefix digits indicate a loop of freeway into a city which reconnects with the main Interstate freeway, such as I-496 in Lansing. Odd prefix digits indicate freeway spurs which lead into cities or link with other highway networks, such as I-196 between Benton Harbor and Grand Rapids. To further identify microgeographic space on the Interstate route, interchanges are identified according to the closest mile post which are numbered from the west and south borders of the state. The Michigan or M-designated highways are numbered unsystematically, thus no geographical location can easily be determined by route number alone.

Local County Road Identification Systems. Since the early 1970s, Michigan, in cooperation with the counties, has instituted a designated multicounty road letter-number system. In the Designated County Road system, the state is divided into eight letter areas. Areas A, B, and C lie to the west of US-127, US-27, and I-75 in the Lower Peninsula and Areas D, E, and F lie to the east of the major highways that bisect the Lower Peninsula. The Upper Peninsula is divided into Areas G and H. The state intercounty roads are further identified similar to the Interstate numbering system with east-west routes carrying the area letter and even numbers, while north-south roads carry the area letter and odd numbers. Numbering is started in the south and west.

At the local county level, seventeen counties, mostly in the western Lower Peninsula, have capitalized on the advantages of systematic numbering of county section line roads. Generally the local county systems are not uniformly linked to the historic Baseline and Principle Meridian. As an example, without uniformity in numbering county roads the State Police at Reed City must contend with responding to places which may have the same road name. In four adjacent counties, Wexford, Lake, Newaygo, and Mecosta, each uses a numbering system with similar road numbers but none are connected to each other such as Twelve Mile Road.

Highway Bridges and Tunnels

Because Michigan is comprised of peninsulas and separated by narrow straits, bridges and tunnels have become important highway and railway linkages. In addition to the three Michigan-Canadian bridges: the Ambassador Bridge (Detroit), the Blue Water Bridge (Port Huron), and International Bridge (Sault Ste. Marie), the Mackinac Bridge crossing the Straits of Mackinac since 1957 is also notable. By 1974, the bridge had carried its 25 millionth motor vehicle. When the bridge was first proposed in 1884 many judged that the "Big Mac" could not be built contending that the strait was too wide and unsuitable bedrock conditions existed. To overcome the Mackinac breccia, the two tall suspension towers were placed in bedrock at sites 60 m (200 ft) below the water. Thirty-three marine foundations support the 6.4 km (4 mi) long uninterrupted steel superstructure. When completed the Mackinac Bridge was the world's longest total suspension bridge, 2,503 m (8,344 ft) from cable anchorage to cable anchorage. The "Big Mac" Bridge and Detroit-Windsor Tunnel are the few places requiring tolls in the entire Michigan highway network which reflects the desire to make the state as accessible as possible for tourists. When the Blue Water Bridge bonds were paid, its toll was reduced to a nominal twenty-five cents. The International Bridge at the Soo carries nearly 900,000 vehicles annually with its bonds expected to be paid in 1992.

First International Tunnel. The world's first international submarine railway tunnel was opened between Port Huron and Sarnia in 1891. Up to that time, the St. Clair River was the only gap in a rail line that linked Toronto with Chicago. For years the Grand Trunk Railroad used barges to move up to 1,000 rail cars a day across the river. The cost to use the barge system was high as ice jams caused delays and loading-unloading the barges was also time-consuming.

Engineers at the time said a bridge would have to be high enough to accommodate the passage of vessels in one of the world's busiest waterways. In comparative costs, tunneling was cheaper; therefore, the tunnel idea was implemented. Quicksand under the river necessitated special tunneling techniques; using a tunnel shield, cast iron lining, and compressed air. These tunneling methods were first used in North America at Port Huron but now are in common use.

After two years of labor, the nearly 12,000 feet of tunneling (2,290 feet under water) was completed. Tunnel operations were electrified in 1908 and dieselized in 1958. In 1938 the Blue Water Bridge was opened complementing the tunnel connection between Michigan and Ontario.

Rediversifying the Michigan Transportation System

Public knowledge gained by the Ecology Movement of the sixties led in 1972, the year before the OPEC oil embargo, to state legisation to encourage diversification in modes of transportation and greater emphasis on public transportation improvements. Created at that time was a General Transportation Fund (GTF) to finance public transportation including local bus systems. By Executive Order, the Highway Commission was reorganized into the Department of State Highways and Transportation with an advisory Public Transportation Council (PTC). The size and importance of the State Transportation Department is easily observable in Lansing as it occupies one of the four major buildings in the Capitol Complex in addition to occupying an Upper Peninsula Office at Escanaba and District Offices in Southfield, Jackson, Kalamazoo, Grand Rapids, Saginaw, Alpena, Cadillac, Newberry, and Crystal Falls. The short-term impact of the PTC can be illustrated by the fact that in 1973 only nine of Michigan's largest cities provided local bus service. By 1975, Metro-bus Service operated in twelve communities and Dial-A-Ride (DART) systems operated in twenty-eight communities.

Nonmotorized Transportation

Since the turn of the century there has been a shared need between bicyclists and motorists for hard surface routes. Michigan "good roads" advocates supported the national movement which brought about the reorganization of the American Wheelmen into the American Roadmakers Association, which later became the American Road Builders Association. In the early 1970s bicycle production surpassed automobile production for the first time in several decades. Michigan citizens, of course, participated in the bike sale resurgence and, as a result, demanded safer paths to operate on, not in direct competition for space with motor vehicles. *Public Act 327-1972 requires that* communities receiving motor vehicle tax funds shall expend reasonable amounts to establish and maintain nonmotorized paths. In 1975 the Department of Highways-Transportation spent $1 million to establish bicycle lanes in twenty stretches of state highway right-of-ways to serve a portion of the state's three million bicyclists. In determining location of nonmotorized paths, the following priority of factors is used based on an Attorney General's position paper: (1) safety, (2) function—to link residents to places of work, education, and markets, (3) recreational use, (4) sporting use. In most cases the modern-day state non-motorized paths are 2.4 m (8 ft) wide shoulder pavings with a solid white line separating motorists and nonmotorists. The largest, most complex bike project when completed will be the 64 km (40 mi) path running along both sides of the right-of-way fence of I-275 from Newport to Novi.

The State-Highway Transportation Commission also has approved a 61 km (38 mi) combination equestrian-hiking-bicycle path to be operated by the DNR along an abandoned railroad right-of-way between South Haven and Kalamazoo. Local and state efforts to preserve abandoned railroad right-of-ways for contemporary nonmotorized use is frequently a difficult and thorny legal problem due to the wording of original land-use agreements between rail companies and earlier property owners. Although some property owners have expressed opposition to the recreational use of former railroad routes, the railroad right-of-ways hold great potential for both leisure time use and future transportation modes in urban and rural areas which would possibly preclude future generations from having to repurchase right-of-ways.

Railroads in Michigan

Shortly after Michigan received statehood, it assumed the role of trunk line railroad builder under the massive program of internal improvements. According to former Governor Felch, the original idea of the Legislative Committee on Railroads was to have only a single road from Detroit to St. Joseph. However, the legislators from the counties to the north and south passed an amendment to build three roads across the state. These three railroad routes were designated to extend across the state: (1) the Central, to connect Detroit and the St. Joseph River mouth; (2) the Southern, to link Monroe with New Buffalo; and (3) the Northern, not constructed, which was to join the mouth of the Black River (Port Huron) with navigable water of the Grand River in Kent County or its mouth in Ottawa County. The Central route became the state's most important rail line successively as a part of the Michigan Central, New York Central, and Penn Central systems. Jackson, throughout the years had been the "Hub City" within these systems and provides a model for railroad expansion in Michigan.

Historical Development of Michigan Railroads 1837-1960s

In the planning stages for Michigan railroads the Legislature defeated a motion to have the tracks laid simultaneously from the east and west sides of the peninsula. Construction was directed to begin at Detroit. Thus, the financial resources allocated for the railroad's construction first benefited the most easterly communities, especially Detroit from its initiation, as well as Jackson. The Central Railroad reached Jackson on the twenty-ninth of December, 1841. For three years, 1841-1844, Jackson profited as the Central Railroad's western terminal. Later Marshall (1844), Battle Creek (1845), and Kalamazoo (1846) were the Central's terminal communities before the state sold the Central and Southern Railroads. Their sale to individual Boston financial interests brought about Jackson's railroad advantage. The critical point for Jackson was that the Southern Railroad Charter, when it was granted, required the completion of the formerly authorized route of the Jacksonburgh-Palmyra Railroad.

In 1858, the Michigan Southern Railroad finally completed construction of the Jackson Branch. Until the late 1860s the City of Jackson was the only interior point where the two major competing railroads approached each other which resulted in Jackson gaining considerable advantage in transportation rates.

Michigan's Lag in Railroad Building. Although there had been a rush of railroad activity after the Erie and Kalamazoo Railroad pioneering success in the 1830s, Michigan lagged far behind other old-Northwest states in miles of tracks laid between 1840-1860. In these early years in Michigan only 760 km (475 mi) of tracks were laid while in Illinois and Ohio, 4,411 km and 3,720 km (2,757 and 2,325 mi) were set in place, respectively. Even Iowa out-distanced Michigan with 1,086 km (679 mi) of railway. Undoubtedly, the state's isolation between the Great Lakes and its sparse northern population accounted for the low amount of trackage.

By the summer of 1870, Jackson had developed into the dominant center of the Michigan rail network, the number one passenger station on the Michigan Central Railroad, and ranked second in freight shipped; only Detroit handled more (table 10.3, fig. 10.4).

TABLE 10.3
Michigan Central Railroad Report 1870

Rank	City	Passengers	Tons Freight Shipped
1	Jackson	72,482	67,969
2	Detroit	71,927	70,169
3	Kalamazoo	65,946	28,427
4	Chicago	48,879	63,749
5	Ann Arbor	45,538	8,694

SOURCE: *Jackson Weekly Citizen,* July 19, 1870, p. 5.

The earliest decline of railroad functions in Michigan can be traced to 1904 when the last ten railroad locomotives were produced in the Jackson locomotive works. As locomotive production was phased out, the Michigan Central Railroad utilized engines made at Schenectady, New York, and Lima, Ohio, as well as Baldwins from Philadelphia.

Depression Years and Diesel Era. While the railroads continued to function during the Depression, they were not as active as in preceding years. Freight tonnage carried decreased from 1.3 to 1.2 million tons and daily freight trains operating through southern Michigan dropped from fifty-six to fifty. Passenger trains serving the southern counties decreased by eight, to sixty. Steam railroads continued to lead in the hauling of freight and long distance passenger service through World War II.

In the mid-1940s the diesel era began with the Michigan Central Railroad integrated into the larger New York Central system, which later became a part of the Penn Central System. As a result of these consolidations, Detroit became the state's major rail center and Cleveland, Ohio and Elkhart, Indiana assumed enlarged maintenance and classification roles.

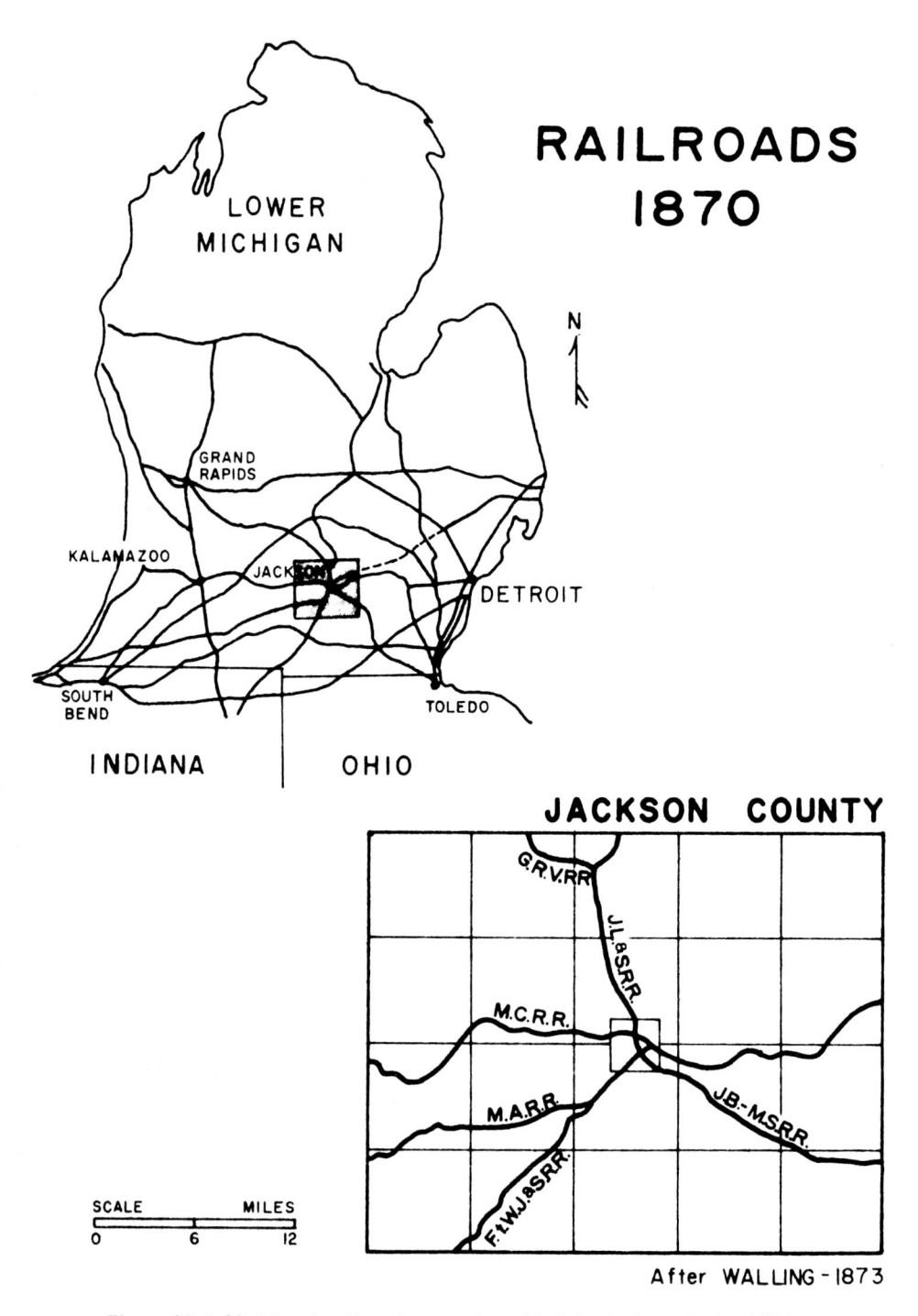

Figure 10.4. Michigan's railroad network and hub in Jackson in the 1870s.

The Railroad Resurgence

The decade of the 1970s witnessed the reorganization of the twenty railroads which operate in Michigan and the elimination of many branch lines. Private, state, federal, and in one instance, a local community, have joined to revive rail service in Michigan for both freight and limited passenger service. Intercity rail service by 1973 had declined to the one Amtrak line, Detroit-Chicago. By 1975 the use of PTC general transportation funds supported Amtrak service on three additional lines: (1) Port Huron-Chicago, (2) Detroit-Buffalo-New York, and (3) Jackson-Ann Arbor-Detroit.

Freight Service. Freight service in Michigan since the implementation of the Railroad Revitalization and Regulatory Reform Act (RRRRA) of 1976 is provided by four major rail systems (table 10.4).

TABLE 10.4
Major Michigan Rail Systems and Connected Communities 1976

System	Rail Center	Linked Communities
Grand Trunk Western	Durand	Port Huron, Bay City, Grand Haven, Detroit, South Bend
Chesapeake-Ohio	Saginaw	Port Huron, Toledo, Ludington, Edmore, Elmdale
	Holland	Benton Harbor, Hart, Petoskey
	Grand Rapids	Detroit, Manistee, Traverse City
Soo Line	Escanaba-Marquette	Eben, Faithorn, Sault Ste. Marie, Calumet, Montreal-St. Ignace, Raco
ConRail	Jackson	Detroit, Lansing, Grand Rapids, Kalamazoo, Three Rivers
	Kalamazoo	Grand Rapids, Vicksburg, Elkhart, Indiana, Menden, Michigan City, Indiana
	Vassar	Millington, Colling, Munger
	Toledo	Clinton, Lenawee Junction, Detroit to Utica

SOURCE: Official Railway Map of Michigan 1976; Railroad Reorganization in Michigan, *Michigan Farm Economics*, June 1976.

To preclude the abandonment of 1,459 km (912 mi) of freight lines, the state, under the Transportation Preservation Act, is subsidizing three newly-formed railway companies operating on Penn Central tracks; (1) the Michigan Northern, 832 km (520 mi) linking Grand Rapids, Walton Junction, Traverse City, and Mackinac City; (2) Hillsdale County Railway, 64 km (40 mi) linking Jonesville, Quincy, Litchfield, Hillsdale, and Montgomery; and (3) the Detroit-Mackinac, 170 km (106 mi) linking Linwood in Bay County with Otsego Lake. The Ann Arbor Railroad and Car Ferry between Frankfort and Kewaunee, Wisconsin, is also subsidized. How long Michigan's reshaped rail network continues to operate and exist depends on not only its refinancing, but also imaginative use, modernization, transfer of ownership or leases of right-of-ways, service, revamping of freight structures, and natural resource supplies (fig. 10.5).

**CURRENT DISPOSITION
OF PENN CENTRAL AND ANN ARBOR RAIL LINES IN MICHIGAN**
(Only Lower Peninsula affected)

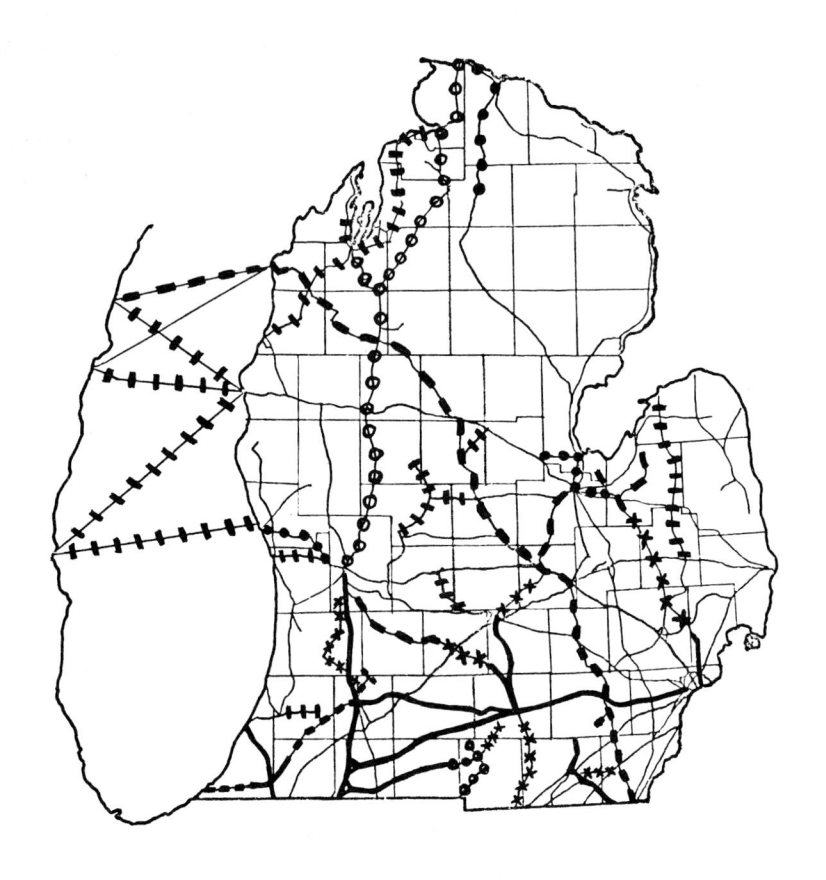

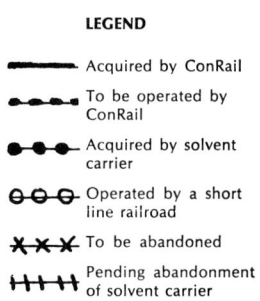

LEGEND

― Acquired by ConRail
▪▪▪▪ To be operated by ConRail
●●● Acquired by solvent carrier
ΘΘΘ Operated by a short line railroad
✗✗✗ To be abandoned
┼┼┼ Pending abandonment of solvent carrier

Figure 10.5. Michigan and ConRail reorganization of the Penn Central and Ann Arbor rail network. (Map: *Michigan Farm Economics,* June 1976.)

Method of Shipping Motor Vehicles and Coal. Railroad shipment has become the dominant mode of transportation for moving automobiles and coal in the Detroit area (table 9.16). Water transportation has been affected the greatest by change in modes, but truck transportation has also been affected. The *unit-train* has become the principal competitor of Great Lakes shipping. By using the cost-reducing, specialized, one-product rail haulage system to move Appalachian coal the 96 km (60 mi) from Toledo to Detroit utility plants, the lake vessel tonnages have declined significantly.

Figure 10.6 illustrates the flow pattern of coal into Michigan from the eastern coal fields to Detroit, Traverse City, and Marquette, and from the Illinois Field into the port of Muskegon. One of the manifestations of the energy-environmental crises is the anticipated reversal in direction of supply coming about with the massive movement of low sulfur western coal across the Great Lakes from Northwestern ports.

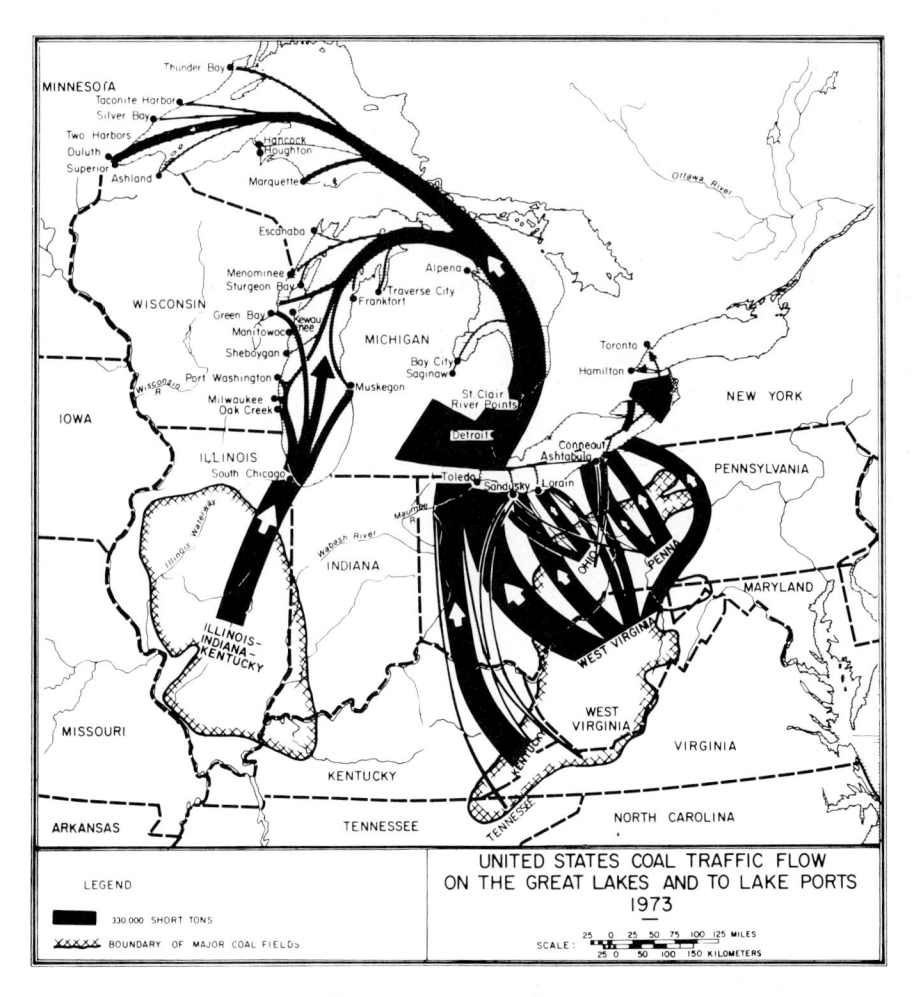

Figure 10.6. Flow of coal to Greak Lakes ports. (Map: University of Wisconsin Sea Grant College Program, Technical Report No. 230.)

Truck-Railroad Competition for Use and Space. In Michigan land-use management, the relative cost of transportation is important. In the competition for land space to transport goods and people, railroad's movements are less costly especially in relationship to energy needed to move a product by truck (table 10.5).

TABLE 10.5
Relative Energy Efficiency of Freight Transportation by Mode

Mode	BTU's per Ton Mile	Ton Miles per Gallon
Airplane	63,000	3.7
Truck	2,400	58
Railroad	750	200
Pipeline	NA	300
Lake Vessel	NA	600
Barge (Tow)	500	250

SOURCE: *The Great Lakes Transportation System,* University of Wisconsin Sea Grant Program Technical Report 230, 1976, pp. 121-3.

In the quest to save time and gain efficiency through scale of operation, truck sizes have increased. The legal length for a truck in Michigan is 16.5 m (55 ft), however, in 1975 the Legislature authorized experimental permits for tandem trucks of up to 29.9 m (100 ft) in length. At opposition concerning the length of trucks is the position of (1) the Bureau of Public Roads statement:

> The question of whether highways could be built at less cost if there were no heavy trucks becomes largely academic, since the design of the major routes must be held to defense standards,

and (2) the position of the national American Automobile Association whose studies indicate that the use of oversized trucks can increase pavement and maintenance costs by as much as 20 percent.[2]

Great Lakes Transportation

For more than two centuries the Great Lakes strategic straits have provided Michigan with trade advantages. As the City of Detroit evolved from a trading settlement and fortress to a modern metrocity, several factors interacted to diminish the public visibility of the waterway. Thus, in contemporary times when transportation in Michigan is mentioned there is a tendency to overlook Detroit's high rank as an international lake port (table 10.6).

Michigan has numerous ports with varying degrees of capability and specialization. Of the ports, Detroit is by far the dominant one (fig. 10.7). Detroit's advantage has been its location. Generally the Port of Detroit has been able to control a consistent 15-20 percent of the value-volume of United States direct overseas commerce through the Seaway.

---

2. "A Salute to the Trucking Industry," *Grand Rapids Press,* September 26, 1975, p. 7 F; "The 'Super Truck'—Too Big?" *Motor News* (November 15, 1975), p. 16.

TABLE 10.6
Major Great Lakes Port Clusters Ranked by Weight of General Cargo 1975

Port Cluster	Exports (Short Tons) Weight	Rank	Imports (Short Tons) Weight	Rank
Chicago	1,392,242	1	835,680	2
Detroit	794,049	2	854,063	1
Duluth	239,407	3	27,098	6
Cleveland/Loraine	201,106	4	201,631	3
Milwaukee/Kenosha	182,082	5	183,948	5
Toledo	125,443	6	185,208	4

SOURCE: *Great Lakes Transportation System,* University of Wisconsin Sea Grant Program, pp. 145-46.

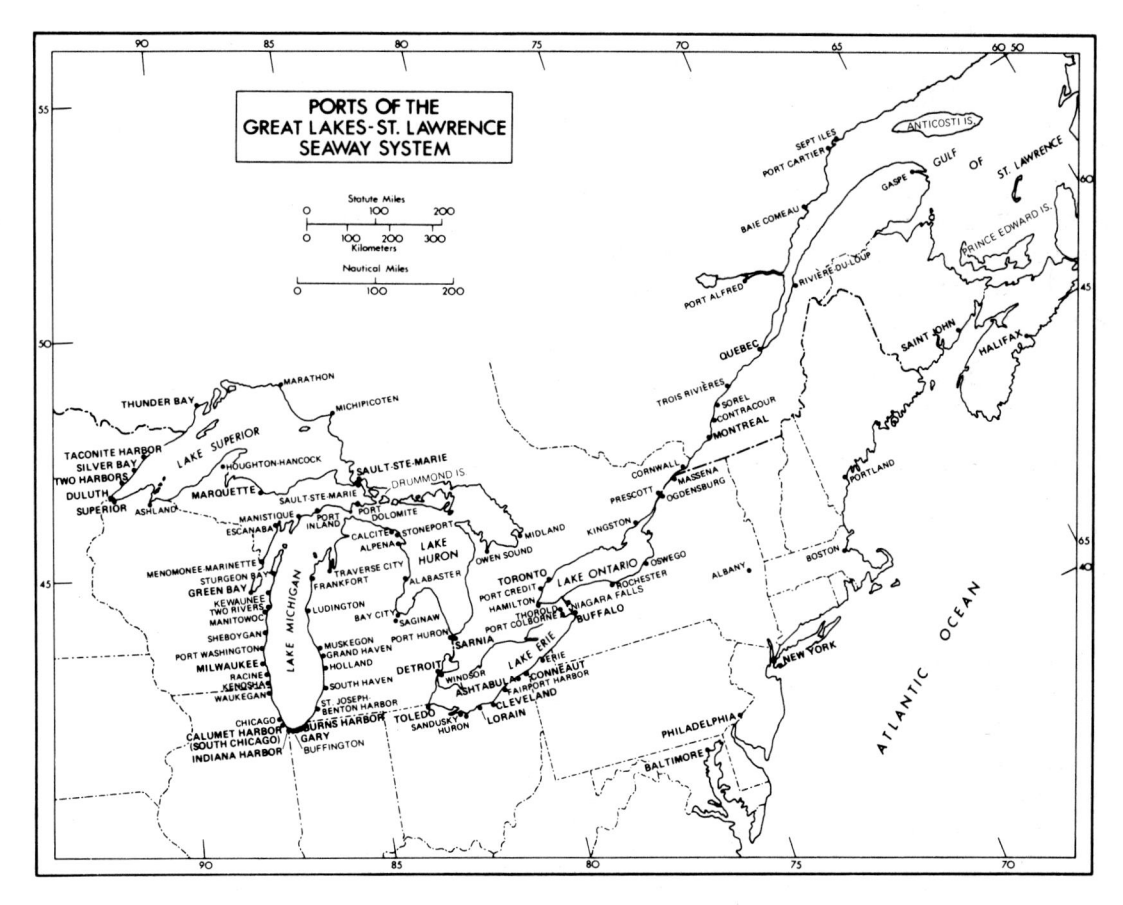

Figure 10.7. Ports of the Great Lakes. (Map: University of Wisconsin Sea Grant College Program, Technical Report No. 230.)

TABLE 10.7
Characteristics of Major Great Lakes Vessel Types

Vessel Types	Length (ft)	Beam (ft)	Draft (ft)[1]	Cargo Tonnage	Employment
Pre-Seaway "Canaller" (Lake Service)	258	43.5	14.00	3,000	Great Lakes-St. Lawrence[2] Pre-Seaway Canal System
Pre-Seaway "Canaller" (Lake-Overseas Service)	258	43.5	14.00	1,600[3]	Great Lakes–Overseas Direct via Pre-Seaway Canal System
Cuyahoga River Laker	630	68.0	25.75	18,000	Great Lakes, St. Lawrence[4]
"Maximum Laker" (pre-1970; post-1959)	730	75.0	25.75	28,000	Great Lakes, St. Lawrence west of Sept. Isles, Quebec
"Maximum Laker" (post-1970)	1,000	105.0	25.75	57,500	Great Lakes, west of Welland Ship Canal
Typical Great Lakes-Overseas General Cargo Liner	500	75.0	24.00	9,000	Great Lakes–Overseas Direct
Typical Lake-Ocean Bulk Carrier	600	75.0	25.75	25,000	Irregular Great Lakes-Ocean Service

1. Maximum draft normally allowed for transit of lock system.
2. Obsolete since opening of enlarged Seaway System in 1959.
3. On Seaway draft; additional 1,000 tons on 18-foot draft east of Montreal.
4. Dimensions limited by Cuyahoga River at Cleveland, Ohio.
SOURCE: *Great Lakes Transportation System,* University of Wisconsin Sea Grant Program, p. 14.

Telephone Company Territory. Until the mid-1930s two or more telephone companies could compete in the same territory. When operations were duplicated in a city it meant that a customer who wanted to call any local phone subscriber had to have and pay for phones from each company. The confusion and costly duplication of service began to be minimized when the state's more than 200 telephone companies filed with the Michigan Public Service Commission (MPSC) maps of their service territory. Eventually, these were refined into maps of exclusive service territory. Today any service area changes have to be approved by the MPSC. Since the 1930s many service boundary changes have been made as the number of independent companies decreased to fifty-three territories in 1976. The territory of Michigan Bell Telephone, the state's largest telephone company with headquarters in Detroit and Southfield, has remained basically unchanged. However, Michigan Bell's growth has been in number of its stations. Since the pre-World War II Kingsbury Agreement, the General Telephone Company has been most active in merging the territories of small and home-operated independent companies. For several years the state's third largest telephone company was Continental Telephone which operates thirty exchanges mostly in the Thumb Area and northern Lower Peninsula. However, in the 1970s, Mid-Michigan Telephone Company at Stockbridge surpassed Continental in number of subscribers (table 10.8).

TABLE 10.8
Location of Telephone Company and Number of Main Stations,
Michigan Telephone Network 1976

Location	Number of Main Stations	Location	Number of Main Stations
Alba	348	Kingsley	1,298
Allendale	2,288	Lennon	1,285
Au Gres	1,743	Chesaning (Mesick)	1,208
Delton (Banfield)	917	Stockbridge (Mid-Michigan)	27,292
Baraga	1,429	Watton (Midway)	688
Delton (Barry)	3,341	Chesaning (Midwest)	3,256
Blanchard	767	Morenci	1,386
Bloomingdale	1,037	Munising	3,153
Camden	3,935	Chesaning (Northern)	505
Branch (Carr)	629	Blissfield (Ogden)	380
Chesaning (Central)	6,677	Ontonagon	3,815
Chatham	1,367	Parma	1,507
Brimley (Chippewa)	517	Traverse City (Peninsula)	601
Clayton	509	Pigeon	1,124
Climax	829	Chesaning (Public Service)	2,494
Concord	1,242	Adrian (Sand Lake)	941
Pinconning (Continental)	26,705	Perry (Shiawassee)	2,964
Deerfield	1,890	Brooklyn (Southport)	8,072
Detroit (Michigan Bell)	3,003,138	Springport	1,233
Zeeland (Drenthe)	440	Pigeon (Twining)	351
Carney (Drummond)	765	Augusta (United)	1,143
Elsie (Farmers)	441	Carney (Upper Peninsula)	1,137
Muskegon (General)	385,828	Waldron	417
Hadley	749	Westphalia	818
Hickory Corners	986	Winn	478
Chesaning (Island)	248	Millington (Wolverine)	5,193
Kaleva	1,148		

( ) Name of Telephone Company if different from company headquarters location.
SOURCE: Michigan Public Service Commission as of 12/31/75.

Indicative of the mobile nature of Michigan society is the operation of seventeen Radiotelephone Companies, listed by the Michigan Public Service Commission, which serve business and professional persons. These radio answering services are located in all but the three smallest regional centers in the state, plus the cities of St. Joseph, Petoskey, Holland, Southfield, Big Rapids, and Battle Creek.

Telephone Consolidation and Territorial Expansion Problems. Several hundred square miles of territory in Michigan are not served by any telephone company especially in the state's sparsely populated northeastern Lower Peninsula, as well as parts of half the counties in the Upper Peninsula. The combined movements of school consolidation and telephone company mergers has confronted the MPSC, school administrators, and telephone companies with having to deal with the problems of toll charges between home and school due to boundary mismatches. Other boundary-toll charge problems sometimes emerge in the extension of rural

World Reputation Problem

In spite of Detroit's favorable location and the use of its water shipping facilities since the opening of the St. Lawrence Seaway in 1959, it has been referred to as the "most controversial and least appreciated port on the Lakes." The root of the world port reputation problem may be traced to the minimal public contribution to port and water transportation in comparison to highway, railway and airports. For years ships stood offshore waiting terminal berths, a condition which has diminished with some consolidation efforts. Nevertheless, in 1976, several Detroit and other terminal operators still make separate arrangements to bring ships into the Lakes. Internationally, this function is usually performed by a Public Port Authority. Promotional work is directly associated with Detroit and Michigan's ability to improve its reputation as a world port. In expenditures for promotion, the Port of Detroit spends less than 20 percent of the comparable averages for Toronto, Toledo, Duluth, Chicago, Milwaukee, and Cleveland. The Port of Detroit has considerably more capability than is commonly known; it can handle 12 m (40 ft) containers for "door-to-door" shipping. This capability, although still somewhat on a small scale, is an important advantage for origin packaging, reduced handling, substitution of cardboard for wood crating, theft control, and worker injury reduction.

Trend Toward Load Centers. Inescapably, Detroit and Michigan will be affected by the worldwide growing trend toward centralization of commerce at a relatively few *load centers*. The technology of ship load capabilities has raced ahead of implementation of advance port technology (table 10.7).

Michigan port terminals will be required to respond to the need for deeper channels, provide for intermodal transfer facilities, which generally require large land areas, and to adapt aging physical facilities for modern competitive load centers. Traditionally the nation and Great Lakes states have depended upon local and private initiative for port development. This policy has produced competition and the existence of a considerable resource in general and specialized ports. Yet, it also has produced redundances in facilities. The question which Michigan residents must respond to is: Can or will local ports adequately serve the state in its efforts to diversify its economy, as well as adapt to shifting traffic technological, economic, and environmental requirements?

Conclusions reached in *The Land and the River,* a 1976 report of the Detroit-Wayne County River Front Development Task Force, were that sufficient water traffic and Detroit's hinterland warranted significant further development of the Port of Detroit. Given a modern load center, a Detroit regional facility could, by 1985, increase tonnage handled by seven million, add $500-540 million to the state and local economy, and create nearly 5,000 jobs.

Closing Michigan's Utility Frontier

The Telephone in Michigan

The telephone was introduced into Michigan at Detroit sixteen months after Alexander Graham Bell and his young assistant closed the time-space interval with the historic words, "Mr. Watson, come here, . . ." On July 26, 1877, C. C. Reed, Telegraph Superintendent of the Michigan Central Railroad received two telephones mailed to him by Bell. Later that year phones were introduced into Jackson and Grand Rapids. Within one year, more distant places such as Big Rapids, established private telephone systems to connect businesses, banks, and railroads.

service. For instance, two families may build homes on opposite sides of a previously vacant extent of county road. If the telephone company service boundary is described as (1) in the middle of the road, or (2) along the section line, then the two families could be charged a toll or be served by two different companies to telephone across the road. However, if the exchange or company boundary is described as a "rural common boundary," then either adjacent company may cross the boundary the distance of "a pole and drop" or 150 m (500 ft) if underground wire is used, to serve a new customer. However, usually the first company to install service on the common rural boundary will serve both sides of the road.

Telephone rates for an exchange area are usually determined by the (1) identification of a base rate area (BRA) which is served by one-party connections, and (2) tariffs charged according to zones or distances away from the BRA. In the majority of tariff areas, a maximum of four-party lines will be used after 1978. Michigan Bell uses the zone rate concept while General Telephone uses a half-mile distance cost measurement for rural service (fig. 10.8).

In the 1970s Michigan averaged sixty-one telephones per one hundred people. Southfield, having a central exchange function, is one of seven metropolitan cities in the nation with more telephones than people, the others being: Washington, D.C., Cambridge, Brookline, Champaign, Palo Alto, and San Francisco. Rural farm telephone service has steadily increased. By the mid-1970s all but 5 percent or 4,000 farm families were subscribers of telephone service.

Electric Power Distribution

Until the mid-to-late nineteenth century the darkness of Michigan's nighttime landscape was only penetrated by the twinkling flame of various oils, waxes, and wood torches. After 1850, in a few larger city homes and businesses, and on streets, gas lights came into use. The widespread use of energy to "turn night into day" began with Edison's small incandescent lamp. Edison's boyhood roots were in Port Huron where he sold newspapers on the Grand Trunk Railroad. Later Ford preserved much of one of his laboratories at the Edison Institute in Dearborn. Nonetheless, most of Edison's "one percent inspiration and ninety-nine percent perspiration" of his adulthood was performed at Menlo Park in New Jersey. In addition to Edison, two other Michigan persons, the Foote brothers of Jackson's Consumers Power Company, had a major impact on the diffusion of electricity. Michigan's pattern of nighttime glow, recorded by satellite photos, reflects not only the relative size of the state's cities, but also the efforts to reduce auto accidents and crime.[3]

Historical Beginnings of Electricity in Michigan.
The founders of Consumers Power, William A. and James B. Foote, pioneered the transmission of high voltage power. Originally from Adrian, they became interested in electricity after a generator had been placed in the flour mill in which they worked. In 1885, they installed Jackson's first street lighting system after selecting that city for their work site and electric promotions due to its accessibility and connections as the Rail Hub. Although Edison Electric Light Company preceded the Footes in Jackson, the brothers envisioned a mass market network based on street lighting and home use, not a limited store lighting system which was set up in the formative days. Further, the Footes' major concern was to create an interconnected electric transmission system to supply several cities. To foster such a network, hydroelectric power and high voltage flow was

---

3. A fine example of the nighttime light pattern of the Eastern United States can be found in *National Geographic,* vol. 150, no. 1 (July 1976), p. 25.

LOCAL TELEPHONE TARIFF

BASE RATE AREA - Enclosed by the following boundary:

Starting at the center of the west line of Section 3, Big Rapids Township; east two miles; south to the center of the Muskegon River; westerly along the center of the Muskegon River to the east-west center line of Section 23; west to a point ¼ mile east of the west line of Section 23; south to 14 Mile Road; westerly along 14 Mile Road and the south line of Section 22 to a point ¼ mile west of 205th Avenue; north to the east-west center line of Section 22; west to the west line of Section 22; north to the starting point.

EXCHANGE SERVICE AREA - Enclosed by the boundary designated below.

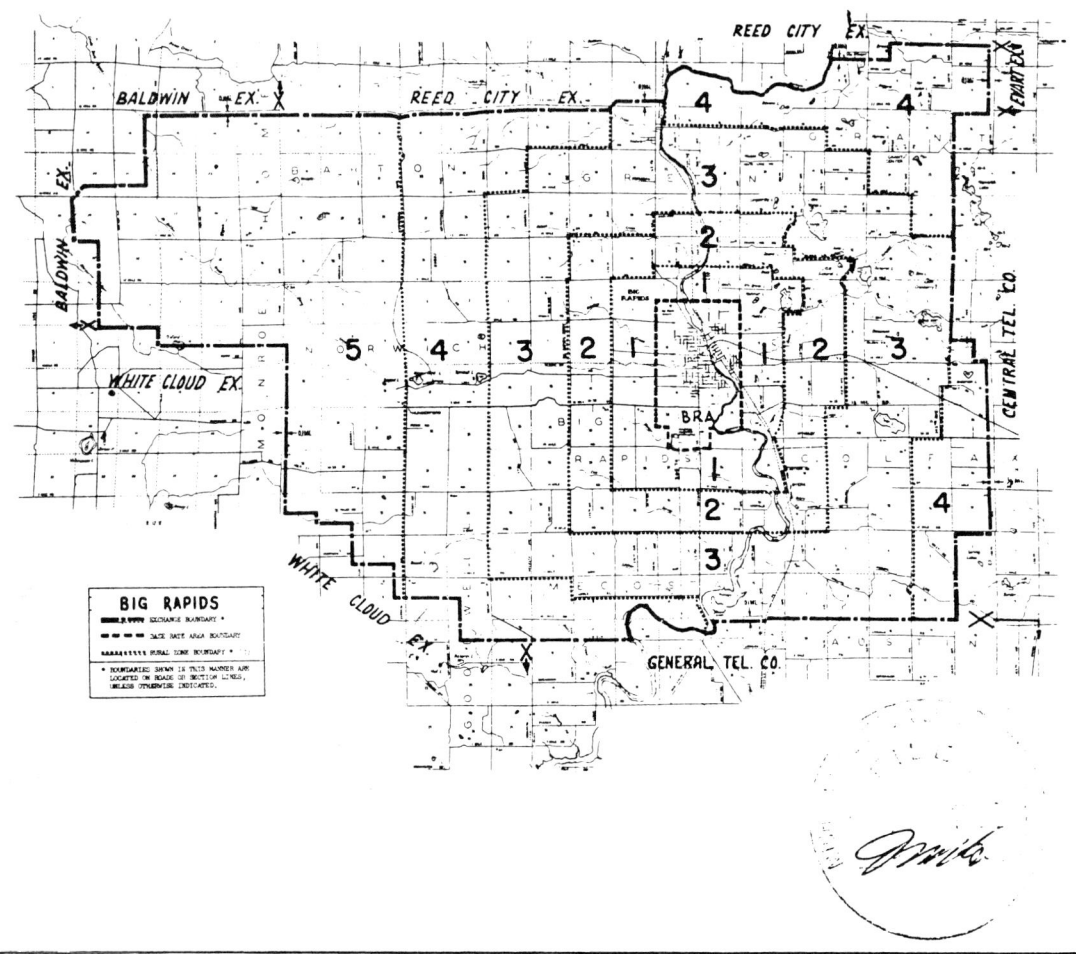

Issued under authority of Mich.Pub.Serv.Comm.Order dated Oct. 16, 1969, Case No. U-353

Issued: November 5, 1969   Effective: November 10, 1969

By W. C. Patterson, Senior Vice President
Detroit, Michigan

Figure 10.8. Base Rate Area and Local Telephone Tariff Zones for Big Rapids. (Map: Michigan Public Service Commission.)

deemed necessary; the former based on cost considerations, and the latter, to overcome the problem of transmission line losses. Prior to the organization of Consumers Power as a holding company in 1910, the foundation for operations were laid with the construction of the Rogers Dam in 1905-1906, the Croton Dam in 1911, and later the huge Hardy earth dam was added upstream in 1931 creating a 1,588 ha (3,970 ac) impoundment on the Muskegon River.

Contemporary Electric Distribution and Problems. The traditions of high voltage generation and long-distance transmission technology pioneered in the state during the last century, provide the state with the basis for continued electrical innovation. In 1920 only 8 percent of Michigan farms had electricity, however, soon after the end of World War II, 97 percent of the homes were connected to a power network. The postwar years also brought the shift to atomic power (Monroe, South Haven, Charlevoix, Midland) and the joint Detroit Edison- Consumers Pump Storage Plant at Ludington. In recent years Michigan's electrical demand grew at 7 percent annually with doubling of use each ten years. Forecasts for future electric generation expansion by Detroit Edison and Consumers Power for the next decade are estimated at about 4.5 percent. Thus, the need to encourage continued energy conservation and restrained demand should be apparent.

Contemporary electric distribution is accomplished by seventy-one utility companies which include forty-two municipal, fourteen private, and fifteen REA Cooperatives. Detroit Edison, Consumers Power, and the Lansing Board of Power and Light are the state's three largest distributors. Unlike telephone utilities, the number of electric utilities have remained relatively stable in recent decades.

Regulation of Territorial Expansion of Electric Companies. During the past thirty years, the extension of electric distribution facilities by cooperatives and the privately-owned electric companies has resulted in extensive duplication of facilities in many areas within the State of Michigan. The proximity of facilities has resulted in numerous disputes between cooperatives and the privately-owned electric companies as to their respective rights to serve existing customers and prospective customers. With a desire to minimize the number of such disputes to come before the MPSC, the Commission initiated rules governing the extension of single-phase electric service in areas served by two or more utilities. The rules are designed to: (1) substantially reduce the number of disputes between the cooperatives and the privately-owned utilities, (2) reduce the expenses of both the cooperatives and the privately-owned utilities in the litigation, (3) result in a saving of taxpayers' money in the processing and hearing of disputes by the MPSC, and (4) curtail the uneconomical duplication of electric distribution facilities in the state.

Under the MPSC rules, "distances" are determined by direct measurement from the closest point of a utility's existing distribution facility to the customer's meter location and not by the *circuit feet involved in extensions*. Further, existing customers are not allowed to transfer from one utility area to another, however, prospective customers for single-phase service located within 90 m (300 ft) of the distribution facilities of two or more utilities may have the service of their choice. Prospective customers for single-phase service located at a distance greater than 90 m (300 ft) and within 792 m (2,640 ft) from the distribution facilities of two or more utilities have to be served by the closest utility. Prosepctive customers for single-phase service located more than 792 m (2,640 ft) from the distribution facilities of any utility may have the services on the following basis: where such extension will be located within one mile of another utility's distribution facilities, extension of service cannot be made by a utility without first giving the MPSC and any affected utility ten days' notice of its intention by filing a map showing the location of the proposed new distribution facilities, the location of the prospective customers' meters and the location of the facilities of any other utility in the area. If no objections to the proposed extension are received within the ten-day notice period, the utility may construct extension lines into previously unserved territory.

Natural Gas Franchise Areas and Pipeline Distribution

Michigan's natural gas distribution areas and the number of companies holding franchises to serve parts of the state are considerably smaller in comparison to telephone and electric service. Only eleven companies hold natural gas franchises of which nine operate pipelines for its transportation. Over 300 township-sized areas between Amboy Township on the Ohio border and Bliss Township at the Straits of Mackinac are outside natural gas service areas. Most of these unserved natural gas areas lie northwest of a line drawn between Muskegon and Tawas. Over two-thirds of the Upper Peninsula, especially its eastern and northwestern sections, also lie beyond franchised natural gas company territory.

Pipelines used to transport and distribute natural gas in Michigan vary in size between 10 cm (4 in.) well head lines to 105 cm (42 in.) pipes along short distances into the storage fields. The greatest convergence of pipelines is in the vicinity of the Austin Gas Storage Fields of the Michigan Consolidated Gas Company. The primary transporter of gas into the state, however, is the Michigan-Wisconsin Pipeline Company which moves 45 percent of the gas coming into Michigan from the Gulf of Mexico, Louisiana, Texas, Oklahoma, and Canada. The major line extends between Berrien and Mecosta counties which in some places is three 55-105 cm (22-42 in.) pipes wide. The major Michigan Consolidated pipeline, which is geared to consumption distribution, connects the Austin Fields with the Detroit Region One area. The Great Lakes Transmission Company operates a 90 cm (36 in.) line from Ironwood to Port Huron to carry natural gas from the Canadian Prairie Field to Sarnia, Ontario. Consumers Power Company operates a 65 cm and 90 cm (26 in. and 36 in.) trunk line between St. Joseph and Livingston counties which ties into the Michigan Gas Storage Company's main line from the Clare County Gas Fields. Table 10.9 outlines the gas utility and Michigan franchised companies, including their major pipeline locations, and storage areas.

Fuel Oil and Coal Transportation. In the Upper Peninsula by the 1970s, fuel oil became the primary space heating fuel replacing coal and wood. In the Lower Peninsula, 26-50 percent of the homes are also heated by fuel oil except inside an arc of counties from Bay through Kent to Wayne which are primarily served by natural gas rather than truck delivered fuel oil or LP gas.

Michigan Aviation

At Greenfield Village thousands annually pay homage to the Wright Brothers by visiting their Cycle Shop which was formerly located in Dayton, Ohio. The photographs displayed in the adjacent building, formerly a funeral home, well document their aviation history at Kitty Hawk. Less well-known are the controversial aviation pioneering exploits of Augustus Herring on the shores of Lake Michigan at St. Joseph in the 1890s. In St. Joseph was built a powered, controlled, heavier-than-air machine which is claimed to have been flown October 22, 1898.[4]

4. Leslie W. Flott, "Augustus Herring . . . Aviation Pioneer," *Chronicle,* vol. 10, no. 3 (1974), pp. 2-8.

TABLE 10.9
Michigan Franchised Gas Utilities and Pipeline Companies 1976

Pipeline and Gas Utility	Major Pipeline*	Major Storage Area*
Michigan Consolidated	Clare-Presque Isle, Clare-Cheboygan, Mecosta to Oakland	Mecosta, Montcalm, Isabella, Gratiot, St. Clair
Consumers Power	St. Joseph-Livingston, Clinton-Allegan	St. Clair, Osceola Allegan, Macomb
Michigan Gas Utilities	St. Joseph-Hillsdale, St. Joseph-Calhoun, Berrien, Allegan	—
Southeastern Michigan Gas	St. Clair-Tuscola, Jackson-Hillsdale	—
Michigan Power	Berrien, Cass, St. Joseph, Ottawa-Allegan	—
Northern Natural Gas	Marquette-Keweenaw, Gogebic-Marquette	—
Battle Creek Gas	Calhoun-Barry	—
Citizens Gas Fuel	Lenawee	—
Peninsular Power Company	Keweenaw	—

Franchise Gas Utility	Franchise Area*	Major Storage Area*
Lake Superior Power District	Gogebic, Ontonagon	—
Wisconsin Public Service Corporation	Menominee	—

Pipeline Company	Major Pipeline*	Major Storage Area*
Michigan-Wisconsin	Berrien-Mecosta, Lenawee-Washtenaw	Newaygo, Mecosta, Osceola, Clare, Montcalm, Isabella
Pan Handle Eastern	Calhoun-Washtenaw-Lenawee-Monroe-Wayne	Livingston
Michigan Gas Storage	Clare-Saginaw, Clare-Washtenaw	Clare, Missaukee
Dow Chemical	Crawford-Midland	Crawford, Missaukee
Great Lakes Transmission	Gogebic-St. Clair	—

*By counties.
SOURCE: Michigan Gas Pipeline Map; Michigan Consolidated Gas Company, Engineer Services, December 31, 1975, @ 1 m X 1 m.

In contrast to the past, Michigan's pioneering today in aviation is "safe landings" rather than takeoffs. In 1975 with the commissioning of solid-state precision microwave landing systems, Antrim County Airport in Michigan and an airport at St. Paul, Minnesota, became the world's first airports to install the innovative landing devices. These instruments mark the beginning of a worldwide transition to a more accurate, reliable, and less costly landing system. The airport located at Bellaire (Antrim County) was initially selected because of the advantages the microwave landing system have in areas of rough terrain and heavy snow accumulation. In contrast, air navigation in the Upper Peninsula in 1975 was upgraded by more traditional methods with the painting of air marking signs on fifty rooftops for visual orientation and navigation.

Michigan Aviation Facilities

In the contemporary era, the state's aviation system includes 375 airports of which about 200 are licensed, 21 handle commercial air service, and 14 have air control towers. Facilities range from simple grass landing takeoff strips similar to the pre-World War I era to 33 airports having runways longer than 1,200 m (4,000 ft) and 84 with lighted and paved runways. Between 1960 and 1975 the number of pilots doubled, now totaling approximately 26,150 which operate 6,300 registered aircraft.

Detroit Metropolitan Airport accounts for more than three-fourths of the total volume of the state's ten million air passengers arriving and taking off. Passenger volume to a large extent reflects population and accessibility. Airline scheduling is also a factor which has been instrumental in increasing movements at airports other than Detroit (table 10.10). Marquette which serves about 50,000 passengers annually is the Upper Peninsula's leading airport while Grand Rapid's Kent County Airport is the state's second largest, handling a half million passengers yearly.

TABLE 10.10
Aircraft Operation at FAA Traffic Control Tower Airports 1973

Tower Location	Total Operations	Tower Location	Total Operations
Ann Arbor	116,330*	Jackson	74,750
Battle Creek	66,458	Kalamazoo	143,940
Detroit City	204,255	Lansing	155,099
Detroit Wayne	268,701	Muskegon	81,350
Detroit Willow Run	190,214	Pontiac	212,638
Flint	149,897	Saginaw Tri City	74,627
Grand Rapids	145,037	Michigan Total	1,767,819

*1971 est.
SOURCE: *Michigan Statistical Abstract* (1974), Table XIII, p. 442.

Movement of mail by air transport is also dominated by the Detroit airports. Of a total of 180 million tons of mail lifted in 1970, 162 million tons were handled at Detroit.

Airport and Air Service Expansion. In 1973, Michigan aviation entered a period of uncertainty due to the cost and availability of fuel. Further airport expansion is affected by the costs of modernization, level land, and environmental noise considerations. Commuter airlines which expanded rapidly in the 1960s to serve the smaller northern cities and specialized needs, decreased to three in the 1970s. On the other hand, the 88 kph (55 mph) automobile speed limit, instituted for fuel saving, has been a contributing factor in the greater use of corporate aircraft to offset slowed land travel. Unlike other commercial airlines, commuter air service is operated under a Civil Aeronautics Board (CAB) exemption. Under the CAB special permits, 5,625 kg (12,500 lb) is the maximum gross weight per operation which includes passengers, fuel, and cargo. To help increase the economic viability of air transportation and secure suitable sites for air facilities, the federal and state governments have evaluated and are considering the possibility of establishing regional airports in northern Michigan.

Communication by Newspaper, Radio, Television, and Mail

Newspaper Circulation

The dissemination and diffusion of news and advertising, as well as social events and sports information is, of course, fundamental to the well-being of Michigan citizens. Education has also been a basic responsibility of publishers since the day in 1809 when Michigan's first printing press at Detroit impressed its initial product, a child's spelling book. On August 31, 1809, Michigan's first newspaper, the *Michigan Essay or Impartial Observer* was printed; however, it was not until 1817 that *The Detroit Gazette* became regularly distributed.

Two decades later in the fall and winter of 1836-37, printing equipment, including a Washington hand press from the *Niagara Falls Journal,* was sent to Grand Rapids. Enroute the ship was wrecked at Alpena, but the press was saved and delivered by sailboat to Grand Haven. The last leg of the journey was made by sledding the press up the frozen ice of the Grand River pulled by six teams of dogs.

In the contemporary era of publication, the Michigan Press Association lists 57 daily papers and over 375 weekly and semiweekly newspapers. The *Detroit Legal News* with a specialized circulation of 2,500 is the smallest daily in circulation while *The Detroit News* (683,450) and *The Detroit Free Press* (602,100) have both the greatest production and statewide circulation. Fourteen Sunday papers totaling 2.2 million newspapers are published in Michigan. Of these, *The Detroit News* dominates circulation by nearly 150,000 with its sales of 850,000 Sunday newspapers. Since the pioneer days educational textbook and trade magazine publishing has become a specialized field. In these specialized publishing fields, Detroit has less dominance statewide while Ann Arbor, Lansing, Grand Rapids, and Hillsdale have emerged as the most significant centers. Each of these smaller cities possesses the locational advantage of higher education activities in their communities while Lansing with its capital role also is the location of the headquarters of many statewide organizations.

Radio

KDKA in Pittsburgh is generally considered to be the nation's first radio station. However, WWJ operated by the Detroit News was also a forerunner nationally, as it started regularly scheduled braodcasting known as 8ML in August 1920. By the end of the decade of the twenties, ten other Michigan stations were operating in a total of eight communities including Houghton in the Upper Peninsula (table 10.12). Detroit and the Michigan State Police pioneered in the use of radio equipped patrol cars also in the 1920s.

In the decade of the seventies, the number of commercial radio stations had increased to 209, which is double the number operating as recently as 1958. Public Service Radio was pioneered by several state colleges, but WKAR at Michigan State University is the only one to have stayed in operation since 1922. Specialized farm programs, weather conditions, commodity prices, and other agriculturally-related information characterized the initial programs to introduce noncommercial radio. WUOM, WCMU, WGVC, and other college or education/cultural spirited organizations continue the tradition of noncommercial educational broadcasting.

TABLE 10.11
AM Radio Stations in Operation Since 1920s

Station	City	Year	Contemporary Power and Time of Operation (Watts)
WWJ (8ML)	Detroit	1920	5,000 24 hrs
WJR (WCL)	Detroit	1922	50,000 24 hrs
WKZO	Kalamazoo	1923	5,000 0530-0105 hrs
WEXL	Royal Oak	1923	1,000 day, 250 night 24 hrs
WOOD (WASH)	Grand Rapids	1924	5,000 0500-0100 hrs
WBCM	Bay City	1925	1,000 day, 500 night 24 hrs
WDEE	Detroit	1925	50,000 day, 5,000 night 24 hrs
WXYZ (WGHP)	Detroit	1925	5,000 24 hrs
WIBM	Jackson	1925	1,000 day, 250 night 24 hrs
WKBZ	Muskegon	1926	1,000 0530-2400 hrs
WHDF	Houghton	1929	1,000 0600-2230 hrs

SOURCE: *Michigan Statistical Abstract* (1974), Table XII-5, pp. 466-74; *Michigan History Magazine*, Vol. XXi (winter, 1937).

In 1941, WWJ-FM began initial operations of FM broadcasting. By 1960, only nineteen FM stations were in operation. A dozen years later, eighty-four FM stations were broadcasting; seven with over 100,000 watts of power, two (WOOD, WOMC) with over 200,000 watts, and one (WJFM-FM) in Grand Rapids which operated with over 500,000 watts. As a result of the freedom of airwaves, both Canadian and Wisconsin radio stations can create *information fields* more easily in the state than can newspapers. Thus, in the Detroit Region and other border areas, out-of-state stations provide a major communication link with the state's international neighbor and Great Lakes neighbor states.

Television

Television has had not only controversial impact on the social and education traditions of American society, it also has had its distinctive landscape influences. Most apparent of course, has been the ubiquitous home antenna. More critical to geographers, however, are the sites of the necessary communication towers which relay the signals. In an era of rapidly changing land-use patterns, consideration needs to be given to the protection of the unique highland sites which have advantages for communication, as well as water towers. Balanced against site protection, especially along the Michigan Divide, are the engineering costs to use less-suitable sites. The popular use of television has also had its impact on the once attractive motion picture theaters which dotted most Michigan towns and cities after the innovative first showing of a movie at the Detroit Grand Opera House in 1896.

Commercial television, like earlier communication innovations, was introduced by WWJ-

TV in 1947. Within a year, WJBK-TV and WXYZ-TV began telecasting affiliated with the major national radio-television networks. Between 1958 and 1972 the most active era of television expansion took place in the state with the number of commercial TV stations doubling to twenty-two. Public television and Cablevision also began to gain more general support in the 1970s. From a geographic viewpoint, there still appears to be a lag, especially by advertisers, in pinpointing the location of business activity. The lack of community name given in advertising and news telecasting is especially apparent to northern Michigan residents with cable connections to a variety of Michigan metrocommunities. Disorientation to place is introduced because most communities have a Michigan Avenue and other commonly duplicated street names.

Post Office and Mail Distribution

Since the appointment of Benjamin Franklin as Postmaster by the Continental Congress in 1775, the United States Post Office has been the most obvious and continuous link between local communities and the federal government. Except for churches and courthouses, Class I post offices generally have had the most distinctive and monumental architectural style in communities throughout Michigan.

To handle the collection, sorting, and distribution of the deluge of hundreds of thousands of letters and packages each day, post offices have become increasingly functional and factorylike in appearance as well as frequently located in rented space. Consolidation of Class 3 and 4 post offices into larger service areas has slowly reduced the numbers of the once ubiquitous and affectionately revered social gathering and gossip places. By the mid-1970s approximately 960 post officties were located in 890 communities in the state. To process the mail with computer-assisted machinery, nineteen postal Sectional Center Facilities (SFC) have been established in eleven cities (table 10.12). Additionally, to cope with the millions of packages sent annually, two Bulk Mail Centers (BMC) have been located in Grand Rapids and Allen Park, a suburb of Detroit. The Detroit BMC occupies a 19 ha (48 ac) tract and a 30,150 sq m (335,000 sq ft) facility. At Detroit an average of 130,000 parcels and 30,000 sacks of mail are

TABLE 10.12
Michigan Sectional Center Facilities and Number of Post Offices 1976

SFC Number*	City	Percent Mail Handled	Number of Post Offices
480	Royal Oak	12	73
481-2	Detroit	18	86
483	—		
484-5	Flint	10	71
486-7	Saginaw	4	100
488-9	Lansing	12	86
490-1	Kalamazoo	10	96
492	Jackson	4	64
493-5	Grand Rapids	18	103
496	Traverse City	2	69
497	Gaylord	4	80
498-9	Iron Mountain	6	133

*First three numbers of Zip Code.
SOURCE: *National Zip Code Directory 75-76*, U.S. Postal Service, pp. 1696-1697.

processed each day by the center's 600 employees. The Grand Rapids BMC has approximately the same volume.

Urban-Rural Mailing Addresses. Typically, land which has been subdivided has two location identification systems: (1) legal survey description linked to the Federal Survey System, and (2) a local postal mailing address. In urban areas, commonly, the mailing address consists of a number and street name. Thus, location of a home is fairly easy once the proper street is identified. In rural areas mailing addresses typically are by postal route number and roadside box number. To locate a rural place, especially when the post office is closed or at night, finding the address such as, Route 3, Box 217, can be an insurmountable task. The location of rural homes or a home in a rural subdivision from the mailing address alone is made more difficult in that postal authorities may be unwilling to divulge a house location due to invasion of privacy concerns. Further, rural addressing systems by route and box number are rarely published or available to the public (fig. 10.9). With increasing development of rural housing and the demand for public services, especially law enforcement, fire, medical, and school-home contact, undoubtedly students of geography and public administration should consider the creation of a more easily used rural mail address system. Perhaps one of the public utilities' systems based on the Federal Survey System holds the greatest promise for universal adoption.

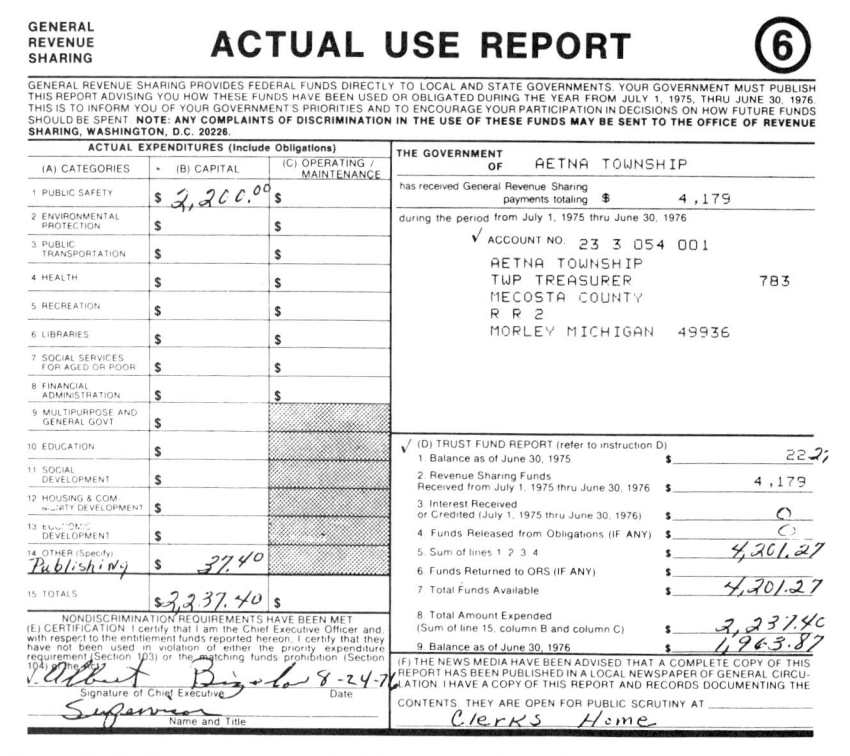

Figure 10.9. Rural route postal addresses provide only orientation to a general area. Specific location of a home or governmental office can only be determined with additional information. (Source: *The Pioneer,* Big Rapids, August 27, 1976, p. 5 A.)

Photo Essay E

TWENTIETH CENTURY WATER AND HIGHWAY TRANSPORTATION

E-1   Ore-loading dock, Marquette.

E-2   Soo Locks, Sault Ste. Marie.

E-3   Great Lakes freighters, Detroit River.

E-4   Detroit harbor terminal.

E-5   Unique Houghton-Hancock lift bridge.

E-6   Bluewater Bridge connecting Port Huron and Sarnia, Ontario.

E-7   International Bridge, Sault Ste. Marie.

E-8   Mackinac Bridge.

E-9   1907 AAA Pathfinder tour.

E-10   1914 sand road, Meridian Township, Ingham County.

E-11   Snowplow in operation in early 1920s.

E-12   Michigan's pioneer Willow Run expressway east of Bomber Plant July 31, 1942.

E-13   The Grand River at I-96, I-296, and US-131 in Grand Rapids.

E-14   Dial-A-Ride bus in Houghton-Hancock.

E-15   Typical bicycle path and shoulder paving 1975.

Photo credits: E-1 to E-8 Michigan Travel Commission, E-9 to E-15 Michigan Department of State Highways and Transportation.

E-1

E-2

E-3

E-4

E-5

E-6

E-7

E-8

E-9

E-10

E-11

E-12

E-13

E-14

E-15

> "They agree and disagree in order to develop understanding."
> **Unknown**

Chapter Eleven

The Quest for a Quality Environment

Deeply embedded in American culture is the ethic to make a living and organize society in such a way as to enable the following generation to have a less rugged life than the previous one had. In most instances the application of the ethic has been an apparent unbounded success with seemingly unending technological advancements especially in agriculture, health, and industry. In the process of attaining a comparatively high standard of living, higher per capita gross product incomes, and more leisure time, the quality of the environment has deteriorated. Although "quality" is a difficult concept to measure, quality of the environment of an area can be judged by the purity of air and water, the condition of the land after resource removal, the success of police and health officials in managing deviant behavior, as well as by the threats communities face from floods and chemical wastes entering the life support system. This chapter will focus on each of these quality factors by describing the programs past generations introduced to protect the environment, as well as present-day conditions of land/human relations and activities to insure a healthy society.

As Michigan citizens strive to make wise environmental decisions in relation to present and future economic needs, Frank Borman's observations from outer space should provide a philosophical basis for the management of the state's and the earth's resources:

> When you are privileged to view the earth from afar, when you can hold out your thumb and cover the earth's whole image with your thumbnail, you realize that we are really, all of us around the world, crew members on the space station earth. . . If nothing else, it should impress all humans with the absolute fact that our environment is bounded, that our resources are limited, and that our life support system is a closed cycle.

To secure for third-century Americans and other generations following, a quality environment plus the pursuit of life, liberty, and happiness, requires of Michiganians balancing and rebalancing private individual rights and public responsibilities within the democratic framework. The democratic process and wise environmental decision-making require not only a lifelong educated and well-informed citizenry, but also moral and ethical judgment.

National Forest Management

The establishment of Michigan's five areas that comprise the state's three national forests reflects the most active periods of the nation's conservation-environment movement. In 1909, nearly two decades after the passage of the initial Forest Reserve Act, Michigan's first two National Forest areas were established. The first two units were the Marquette, later renamed the Eastern Unit of the Hiawatha National Forest, and the Huron, now a part of the Huron-Manistee National Forest. During the Depression, three additional areas were made parts of the national forest system: the Ottawa National Forest, the Western Unit of the Hiawatha National Forest, and the Manistee National Forest. All totaled, 1,076,062 ha (2,690,155 ac) are owned and under the control of the Department of Agriculture United States Forest Service within the boundaries of the state's national forests (table 11.1).

TABLE 11.1
Michigan National Forests

National Forest	Date Established	Total Area of Forest Hectares	Total Area of Forest Acres	Percent in National Forest Ownership	Supervisors Office Location
Hiawatha	1962	504,164	1,260,411	68	Escanaba
East Unit	1909		NA	NA	
West Unit	1931		NA	NA	
Huron-Manistee*	1964	802,540	2,006,350	45	Cadillac
Huron	1909		691,444	61	
Manistee	1938		1,314,906	38	
Ottawa	1931	609,016	1,522,540	60	Ironwood
Total		1,915,720	4,789,301	56	

*1945-1964 known as Lower Michigan National Forest.
SOURCE: *Guide for Managing the National Forests in the Lake States* (Draft), February 1975, p. 5.

During the 1960s-1970s the responsibilities for diversified management of the national forests were expanded by several Congressional Acts including: (1) Multiple Use-Sustained Yield, 1960; (2) Wilderness Preservation, 1964; (3) Land and Water Conservation for Outdoor Recreation, 1964; and (4) Forest and Rangeland Renewal, 1974. Today the supervisors of Michigan's national forests are confronted with how to allocate a finite land base for a variety of uses. Further, some of the demands made on the national forests are incompatible, yet remain the responsibility of the forest managers to best satisfy the demands of the people, as well as meet future demands on the forest.

Multiple Use and Management Trade-offs

Economically, where two or more goods or services can be produced from the same land, maximizing the production of one usually leads to the serious reduction in the output of others. Therefore, in the management of national forest land-uses, an optimized mix of activities is strived for and, at the same time, attempts are made to minimize the conflicts between uses. In addition to a high priority for timber management, considerations for fish and wildlife, fire control, land acquisition, mineral potential, outdoor recreation, river management, water quality, and wetlands preservation are included as priority items in national forest management plans.

People and Property Protection. Protection of national forest users and property has always been a significant task for forest supervisors. In recent years, the greatly increased public use of the Michigan national forests has drastically raised the law enforcement needs on the national forest lands. The cooperative efforts of state and local enforcement agencies have been strengthened with the passage of Public Law 92-82, the Cooperative Law Enforcement Act. This act enables the U.S. Forest Service to reimburse local agencies for costs incurred in enforcing state and local laws and ordinances on national forest land. Further, the Federal Magistrate System provides magistrates to try petty offenses that take place on national forest land. Historically, some northern counties have had to struggle with the problem of diminished property taxes as a result of large areas of land in the public national and state forests.

Off-Road Vehicles in the National Forests. During the economic expansion years of the 1960s mechanized-motor driven "off-road vehicles (ORV's) and portable sound systems including radios, televisions, tapes, and CB radios, came into general recreation use. The large number of ORV's and the loud use of sound equipment has created a significant impact on the forest environment, traditional users of the public land, as well as local economies. In February 1972 Presidential Executive Order 11644 was issued which directed the establishment of policies which would assure that the use of ORV's on federal public land would be controlled and directed so as to, (1) protect the resources, (2) promote the safety of all users, and (3) minimize conflicts among various users of federal land. To create a policy which will satisfy the passive bird watcher, as well as the operator of a roaring "dirt digger" cycle is obviously no simple task, but calls for compromise.

In the control and management of ORV's, several options are available, however, neither no policy nor a policy of prohibition are acceptable. On the other hand, permitting ORV's to be operated on designated roads and trails, but curtailing unrestricted cross-country travel could be satisfying to most. By limiting operation to designated routes and areas, the usually preferred ORV experience can be met, as well as provision for effective resource protection, user safety, and minimization of user conflicts.

In establishing non-ORV and restricted electronic broadcast quiet areas, the principle of locating areas as close to major population centers as possible is generally desirable. Situating quiet areas close to population centers minimizes travel time and energy resource needs for the majority of people in order that they may interact with places of natural tranquility.

The Innovative Muskegon Waste Water System

Similar to the pattern of national forest development, the treatment of sewage has followed the peaks of the conservation-ecology movements. Municipal sewage systems were introduced at the turn of the century while during the Depression years *primary* (removal of settleable solids) and *secondary* (removal of 65-90 percent of biological-chemical substances) processes were perfected and widely diffused in southern Michigan cities. In spite of these pioneering efforts, the "solution to pollution by dilution" ethic remained popular as widespread direct discard of wastes into the air and waterways continued, especially during World War II. In the 1960s, most municipalities including those north of the Bay-Muskegon Line were faced with a mounting challenge of how to accommodate the ever-increasing sewage produced by residents and industry, as well as protect ground and surface waters. Even primary and secondary treatment which removed over two-thirds of sewage contaminants proved in the long-run inadequate.

Popular Concern for Clean Water

By the mid-twentieth century parents across Michigan were saddened when confronted with the realization that lakes and streams in which they had swum and fished had become poisoned by wastes to the point that they were unsafe for use by their children. The heightening of awareness and support given to the environmental movement spawned the addition of phosphate removal and tertiary treatment to existing or new sewage plants. These processes, if working properly, generally removed over 98 percent of water contaminants before returning the water to rivers. Sludge, which is produced at most Michigan sewage treatment plants, unlike in Milwaukee, is still considered a waste and either incinerated or deposited in a landfill.

Recycling of Waste Water

The Muskegon Waste Water System is an innovation which began operation in 1973, designed to better utilize and protect the waters of west central Michigan. In this system, municipal waste water from fourteen communities serving 140,000 people and 200 industries is recycled by a land-processing system. The total system is an adaptation of two traditional operations: (1) municipal sewage treatment, and (2) agricultural spray irrigation. It is theorized that the innovation in processing waste water will not only reduce river-lake pollution problems, but also be a contribution to agricultural expansion.

How the System Works. The Muskegon Waste Water System has nine steps in its basic operation which are summarized below.

1. *Collection* of the metropolitan area sewage is accomplished by a 21 km (13 mi) intercepter system and pumped 18 km (11 mi) to the 4,000 ha (10,000 ac) recycling site.
2. *Initial treatment* including three days of aeration and mixing is equivalent to secondary treatment (fig. 11.1).
3. *Settling and stabilization* takes place in settling basins in the summer or in one of two 340 ha (850 ac) storage lagoons in the winter and heavy rain periods.
4. *Disinfection by chlorination* is done when the liquid is drawn out of the lagoons or basin and, at that point, the water is felt to be safe for body contact.
5. *Spray irrigation* is accomplished by fifty-five center pivot 250 and 420 m (750 and 1,400 ft) ground directed low pressure rigs covering 2,400 ha (6,000 ac) of the site's sandy low fertility soil (fig. 11.2).
6. *Crop production,* especially corn for livestock, is profitable on the generally poor soil by the enrichment of the waste water nutrients and phosphates (fig. 11.3).

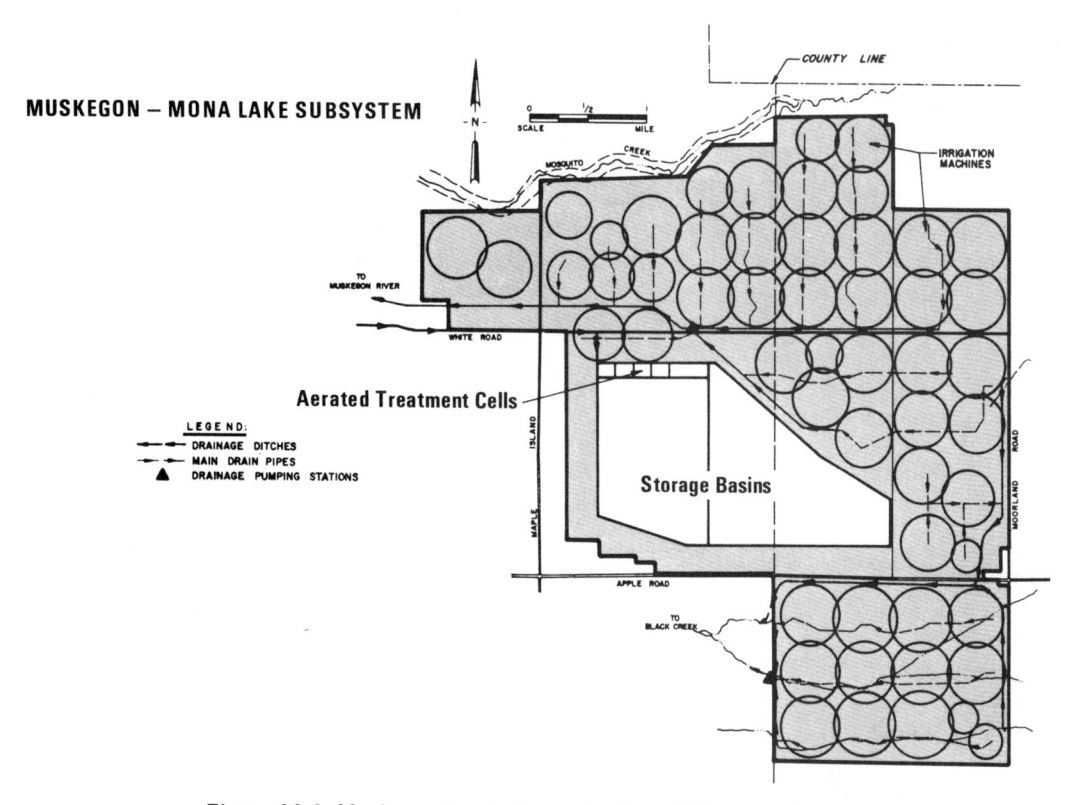

Figure 11.1. Muskegon Waste Water facility. (Diagram: Teledyne Triple R.)

Figure 11.2. Center pivot sprayer in operation at the Muskegon Waste Water facility.

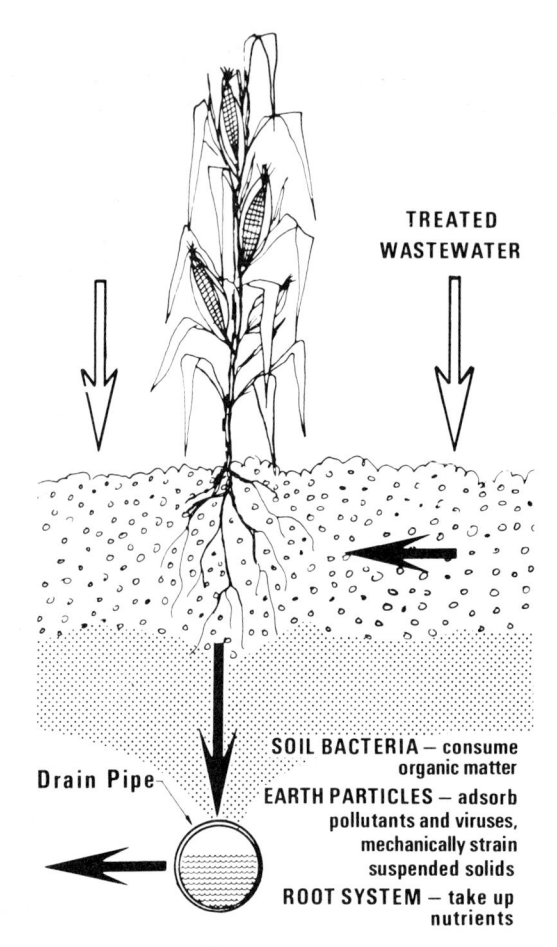

Figure 11.3. Method of waste water use at the Muskegon Waste Water facility. (Diagram: Teledyne Triple R.)

7. *Purification* is furthered by soil filtration in which suspended matter, discolorations, and heavy metals are removed or trapped.
8. *Monitoring* of ground water is done by several test wells on a scheduled basis.
9. *Return to surface waterways* takes place by an underground drainage system which also prevents waterlogging of the site.

The Muskegon facility is designed to serve the needs of the county until 1992 and a population of 170,000 with an average sewage flow of 163,400,000 liters (43 million gal) per day. In spite of the innovative work and hope generated by the facility, occasional odor and the accumulation of heavy metals (mercury, chrome, platinum, and nickel) in the soil are problems yet to be solved. The successful diffusion of the system to other areas is directly related to the availability of sandy soil, relatively level terrain, and treeless open sites.

In addition to Musekgon's innovative waste water system which is one of the largest in the nation, about forty other spray or spread of waste water on farm crops have been initiated. Harbor Springs has also experimented with spray irrigation for Christmas tree raising. Middleville, Wayland, Leoni Township (Jackson), Ravenna, and the Ottawa County Infirmary at Eastmanville have waste water farm systems. Michigan State University has established a four-lake, weed harvest for cattle feed, and a spray irrigation system for continued research. Between 1948 and 1971 a dozen Michigan industries adopted a system of deep well "waste baskets" in which industrial wastes are pumped 150-1,800 m (500-6,000 ft) underground into sandstone or limestone rock structures below fresh water supplies. Little is known about the impact of the wastes in these deep wells.

Misplaced Chemicals in the Environment

The billion dollar chemical industry in Michigan which ranks tenth nationally in value added by manufacturing obviously provides significant economic diversity and employment opportunities for thousands of residents. Unfortunately, as a result of chemical production activities and handling, as well as indiscriminate use of lead shot in hunting and salt for ice removal, many health threatening substances have been misplaced in the environment both unintentionally and intentionally. Until recently the cumulative effects on the *food chain* of such chemicals as DDT (dichlord-diphenyc-trichloroenthane), PCB (polychlorinated biphenyl), PBB (poly-brominated biphenyl), mercury, phosphates, and other substances have been meager. Each of the chemicals has made a useful contribution to society such as their use in insect control, high-powered electrical equipment, fire retardant, and a host of other industrial, agricultural, and domestic products. By the 1970s, dangers to the food chain and human health became apparent enough for the state to ban the sale of DDT and foods having an excess of 5 ppm of PCBs.

To control, remove, and find safer substitutes for health-threatening chemicals has, of course, challenged chemical scientists and engineers. In meeting the chemical waste problem and environmental protection requirements, Michigan's chemical industry has been able to maintain a position of national leadership. Dow Chemical Company and Dow Corning scientists developed a diphenyl oxide insulator fluid for use in capacitors and a silicone-based insulator for use as a transformer fluid. The substitute fluid breaks down in the enviornment forty times more rapidly than similar fluids containing PCBs. In Michigan, as in the nation, environmental protection costs in relation to jobs has stirred controversy. Sylvia Porter, the noted business news columnist, has observed that pollution control while displacing some workers, tends to generate jobs, as well as stimulate profitable recovery of traditional wastes. A statement by Dow Chemical Company chairman, Carl A. Gerstacker, cites one example of the desirable economic impacts of pollution reduction at Dow Corning's Hemlock plant:

> Solving pollution problems is good business as well as good citizenship. It can be profitable . . . an investment of $2.7 million at one Dow Silicon metal factory to recover chemicals previously lost to the atmosphere . . . amounted to the savings of $900,000 per year.[1]

---

1. Sylvia Porter, *Grand Rapids Press* (November 14, 1975), p. 13 B; Dow Chemical Corporation, Public Relations Department, August 19, 1976.

Control efforts have not always proved so measurably profitable in dollars and cents. Nevertheless, the reduction in chemical contaminants in fish in Michigan water has been notable since 1969 except for PCBs (table 11.2).

TABLE 11.2
DDT, PCBs, and Mercury in Fish (in parts per million) 1969-1974*

Fish Species	Lake Michigan				Fish Species	Lake St. Clair	
	PCBs		DDT			Mercury	
	1969	1974	1969	1974		1969	1974
Lk. Trout	13	23	20	8	Walleye	29	10
Coho	11	13	12	5	Rock Bass	13	4
Chubs	5	6	9	1	Perch	11	2

*5 ppm maximum allowance for consumption and 2 ppm in Canada.
SOURCE: *Michigan Natural Resources,* March-April 1976, p. 6.

As recently as 1948, the Detroit River received a daily average of 38,000 liters (10,000 gal) of oil from one steel plant, 38,000 liters (10,000 gal) from an auto plant, and 57,000 liters (15,000 gal) from smaller industries and city sewers. By the mid-1970s oil dumping into the Detroit River had ceased. Sixty industries which line the shore have installed millions of dollars worth of in-plant pretreatment and recovery facilities. Chlorides and phosphorous have also significantly declined with the innovation in combating one pollutant with another, such as pickle liquors left over from steel processing used to reduce phosphorous in sewage effluent. Pioneering work done by the Detroit Water Department in using liquid oxygen to eliminate organic material from waste water has been adopted at one hundred other sewage plants nationwide. Because of cooperative efforts and compromise the once oily foul Detroit waterway is recovering and rewarding its users today with ". . . fishing in great abundance" as Cadillac wrote in 1702.

Michigan State Police and a Quality Environment

A quality environment includes one in which people can live without the fear or presence of major crime (murder, rape, aggravated assault, burglary, larceny, and vehicle theft). Students of geography, with those in other disciplines, have both a responsibility and an active role to play in the reduction of what has become an increasingly costly problem in terms of personal violence, property, and economic losses. In 1971, a research study for the Governor indicated that the total cost of crime in Michigan was $1.77 billion. Distributionally, most of the state's *index* or major crime is located in the large urban areas and along the interstate highway corridors of southern Lower Michigan. In comparison, though, the highest percent growth of total crime between 1970-1975 occurred in the central and northern Lower Peninsula plus the central and western Upper Peninsula. (fig. 11.4).

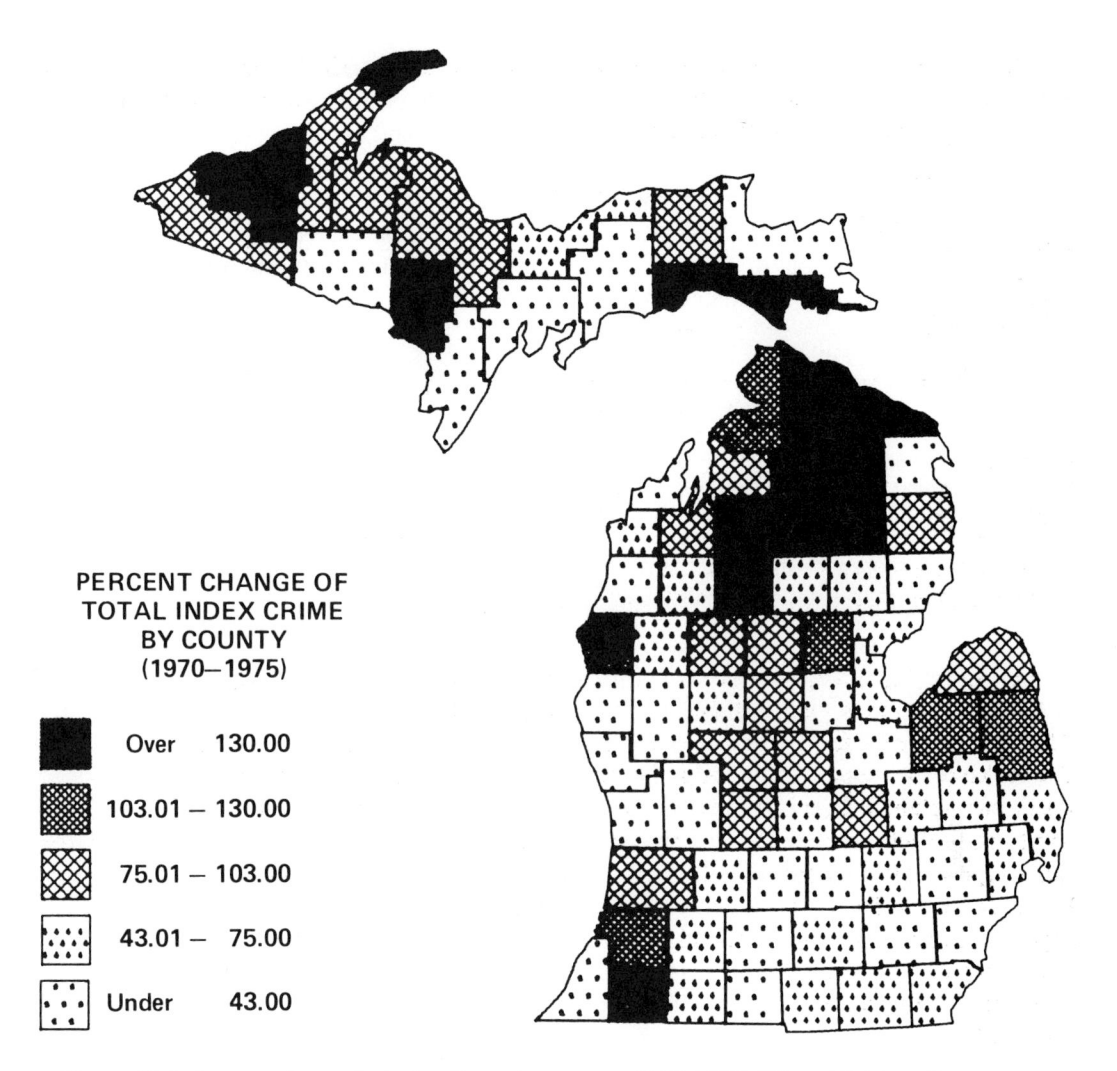

Figure 11.4. Percent change in Index Crime by county 1970-1975. (Map: Michigan Department of State Police.)

Another analytical tool for allocating law enforcement resources is the per capita rate of crime. In 1975, there were 6,825 index crimes per 100,000 population. For all reported crimes the rate was double or 13,055 per 100,000 population. By an analysis of index crimes per 100,000 population, it can be concluded that violent crime is a result of a multitude of factors other than simple density of population or a basic phenomenon of the urban landscape. For instance, per capita index crime may be low or high in rural or urban areas as demonstrated by the following county index crime rates for 1975: Keweenaw, 3,352; Alcona, 8,657; Kent, 5,610; Wayne, 9,247; and Roscommon, 10,363.

Since 1968 Michigan has participated in the distribution of funds under the Crime Control Act and Law Enforcement Assistance Administration (LEAA). Because the state has over 500 police agencies, the allocation of federal money, equipment, and personnel resources supported by LEAA has been primarily directed to the state's fourteen Planning and Development Regions. By utilizing the regional approach, the traditional law enforcement situation of crime being generally mobile, but enforcement jurisdictionally isolated, is being reduced. At the statewide level of operation, Michigan has sixty-three State Police Posts and four major correctional institutions (Jackson, Ionia, Marquette, and Muskegon), plus a Federal Prison at Milan (table 11.3).

TABLE 11.3
Number of State Police Posts by Region and Police Reporting Agencies

Planning and Development Region Number	Number of State Police Posts	Type of Reporting Agency	Number of Police Agencies
1	9	Cities/Villages	361
2	3	County Sheriffs	83
3	3	Townships	56
4	5	Special	9
5	4	State Police	1
6	1	Total	510
7	10		
8	6		
9	3		
10	4		
11	3		
12	6		
13	4		
14	2		

SOURCE: 1976 Uniform Crime Report, Department of State Police, p. 7; 1976-1977 Michigan Official Transportation Map.

Mental Health Service Areas

The rapid growth of population, trends toward depersonalization, changes in traditional social institutions especially in family and employment expectations, as well as other variables of modern stressful life, have resulted in both the need and creation of Mental Health Services at numerous sites. This section describes the organizational structure of the state's Mental Health Service areas.

Organizationally, there are three major components of the Michigan Mental Health System: community based programs, state facilities, and central office activities of the Department of Mental Health located in Lansing.

Community Based Mental Health Programs

In 1963 began the rapid diffusion of modern mental health services and facilities in the state. Public Act 54-1963 allows any county or combination of adjoining counties to establish a Community Mental Health Board which then may qualify for state funds. In the dozen years following the passage of PA 54, fifty-one Boards serving seventy-six counties have been formed. The remaining counties are expected to be organized into four additional service areas (fig. 11.5).

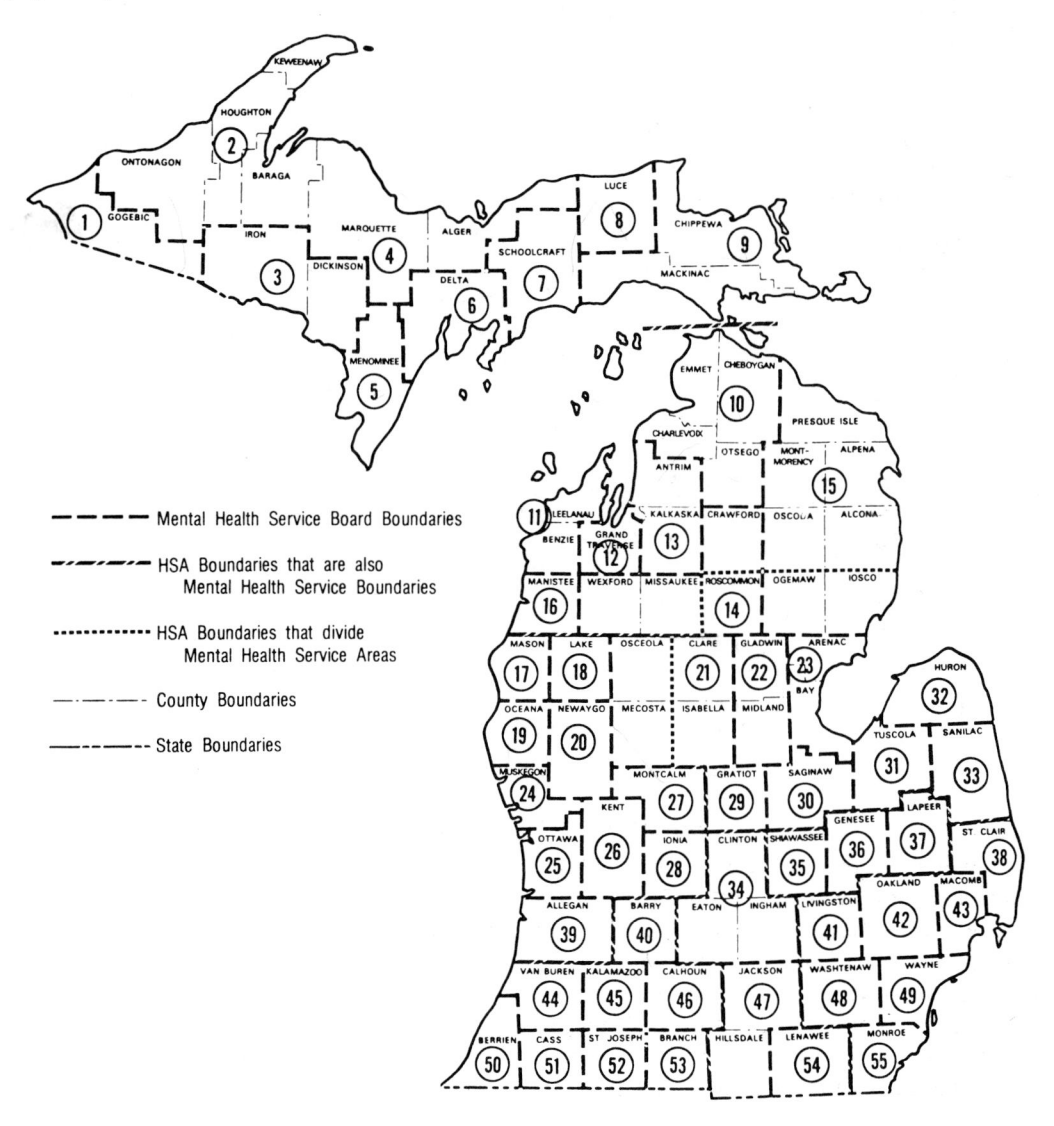

Figure 11.5. Community Mental Health Board Service Areas. (Map: Michigan Department of Mental Health.)

325

Under Michigan Law, six services are required to be provided by Community Health Boards: (1) 24-hour intervention, (2) prevention, (3) out-patient, (4) aftercare, (5) day programs, and (6) public information. Substance Abuse Services are funded separately. Frequently, directly linked to the state-supported Mental Health Board activities, are Community Mental Health Centers established under federal law. These centers are to insure a comprehensive range of mental health services to persons in "a specified geographical area" including day care, specialized children's services, elderly screening, and halfway house service. Community Mental Health Centers are established with catchment areas based on population usually between 75,000-200,000, however, variances of up to 25 percent are allowed. Therefore, state-funded Community Mental Health Board service areas and federally-funded Community Mental Health Centers catchment areas may not coincide (fig. 11.6).

State Facilities for Mental Health

The first state hospital to operate in Michigan was opened in 1859 at Kalamazoo for the "humane, curative, scientific, and economical treatment of insane persons." State centers for the mentally retarded began to be established in 1895. Lapeer was the location of the state's first home for the "feeble-minded and epileptic." Until the Mental Health Movement of the 1960s, the State Hospitals were the only public treatment facilities available to the mentally ill. In contrast to the present day, both the State Hospitals and State Asylums were designed to protect patients from the stress of life basically by isolation of the facilities from contact with community residents except for local employment opportunities. In recent years the pattern has changed with mental health services more locally based and visible.

In the contemporary era the Department of Mental Health operates twenty-five in-patient residential facilities, ten state hospitals for the mentally disturbed, and twelve centers for the mentally retarded (fig. 11.7). Additionally, a research clinic (Detroit), a medical center (Pontiac), and a center for Forensic Psychiatry (Ann Arbor) are also operated by the state (fig. 11.8). The state hospitals and centers service areas are based on regions with their boundaries coinciding with county lines while the three specialized facilities serve the entire state.

Flood Plain Management

Since the arrival of humans in Michigan, residents have occupied and placed valued structures on the thousands of kilometers of flood plain adjacent to waterways. Today, the continued growth of settlement results in additional encroachment on the flood plain. Yearly, as a result of flooding, newspapers and television report with banner headlines, "River Runs Berserk" with a subsequent story enumerating damage to property, as well as listing those injured or killed. In April 1975, a flood in central Lower Michigan cost an estimated $61 million in property damage, as well as loss of life. In August of the same year, $73 million of damage occurred to agricultural property alone. In the contemporary era floods may not be truly water, but rather flood chemicals, as the liquid frequently includes gasoline or oil along with sewage and other chemical substances carried by the torrent. Through the years, flood protection works, site improvements, and limited zoning have been initiated in some cities to protect citizens and communities from floods. Nevertheless, development on flood plains has still taken place in most parts of the state faster than structural or other control measures can alleviate the problem.

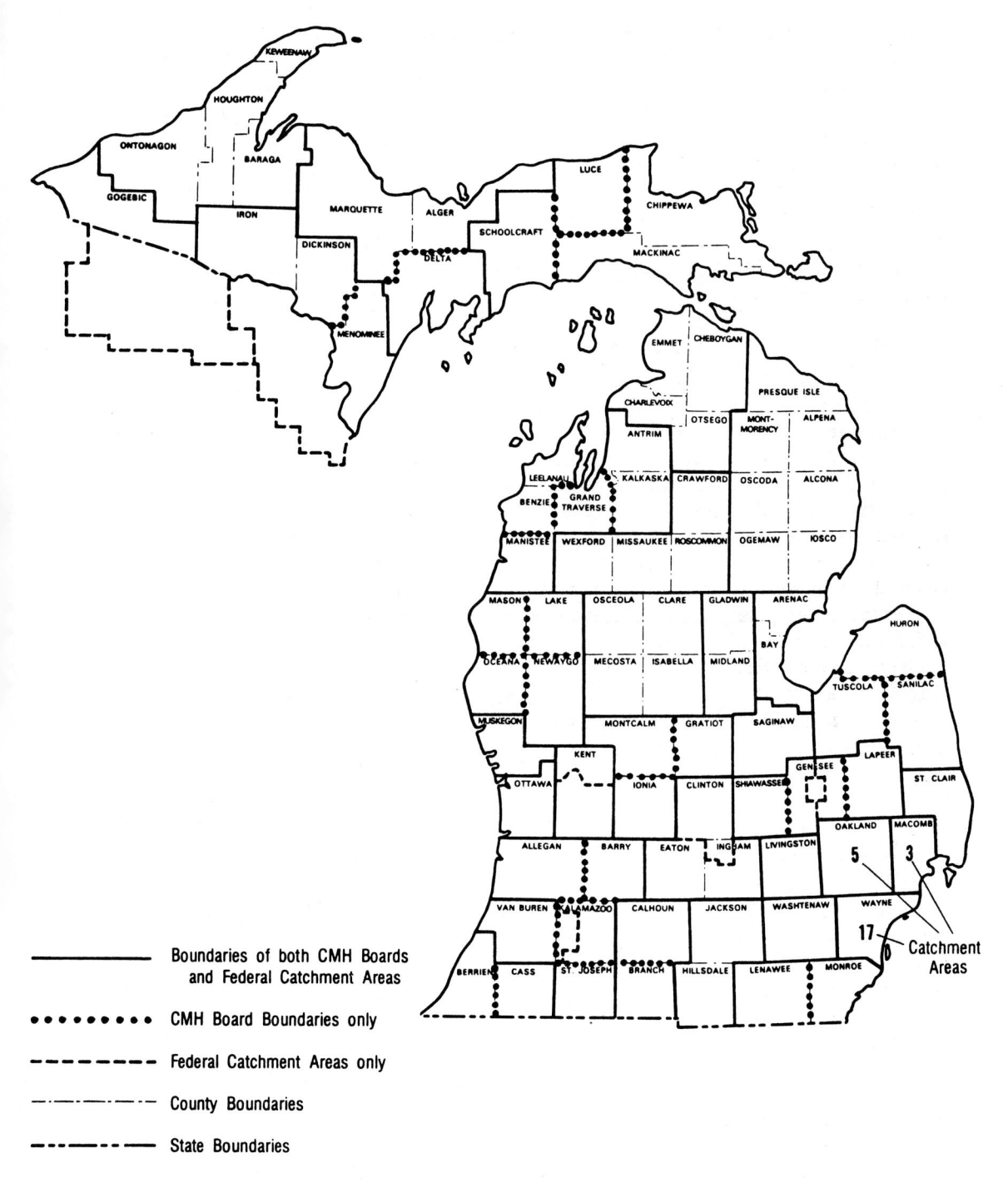

Figure 11.6. Federal Mental Health Catchment Areas. (Map: Michigan Department of Mental Health.)

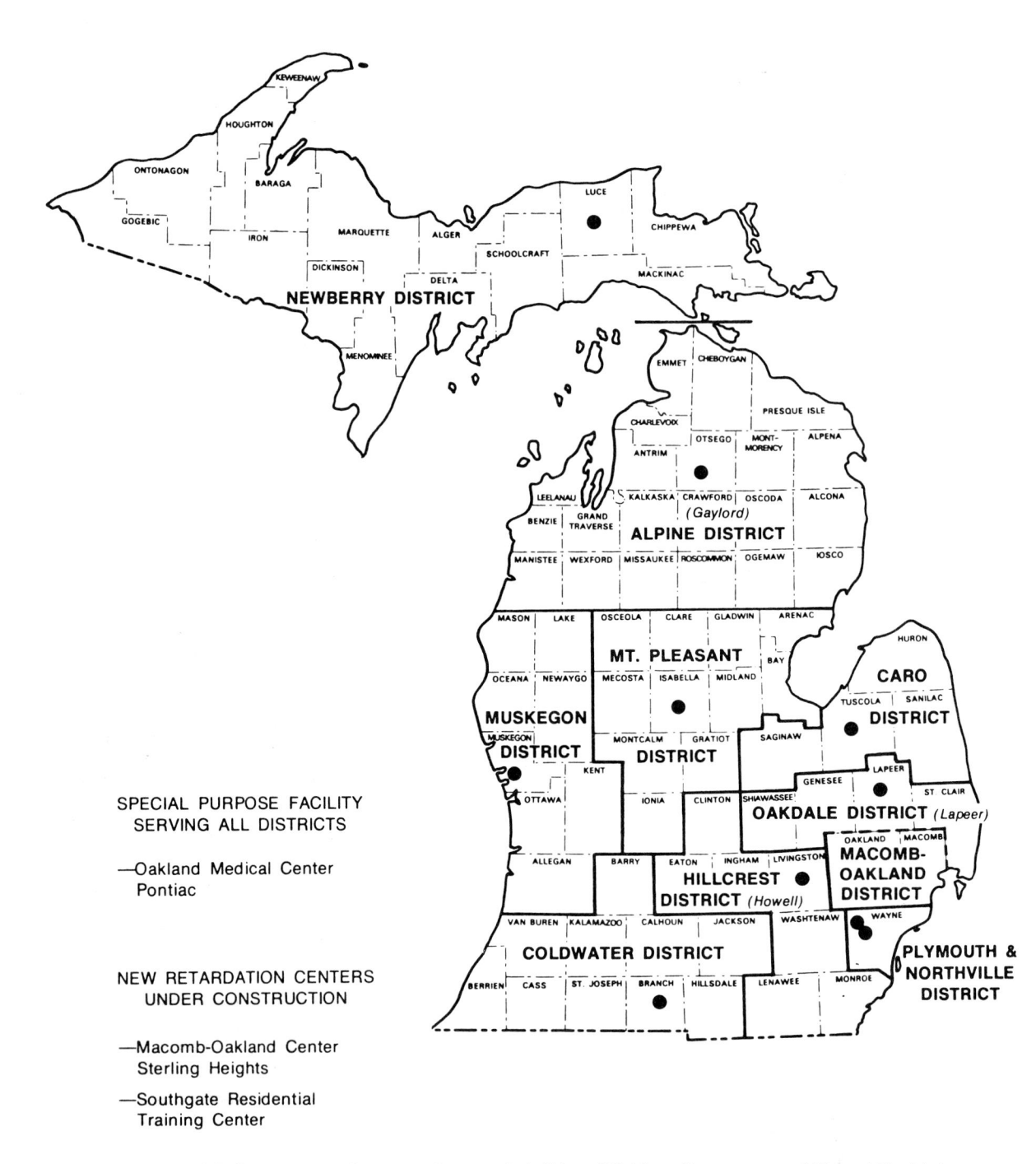

SPECIAL PURPOSE FACILITY
SERVING ALL DISTRICTS

—Oakland Medical Center
  Pontiac

NEW RETARDATION CENTERS
UNDER CONSTRUCTION

—Macomb-Oakland Center
  Sterling Heights
—Southgate Residential
  Training Center

Figure 11.7. State centers for mentally retarded. (Map: Michigan Department of Mental Health.)

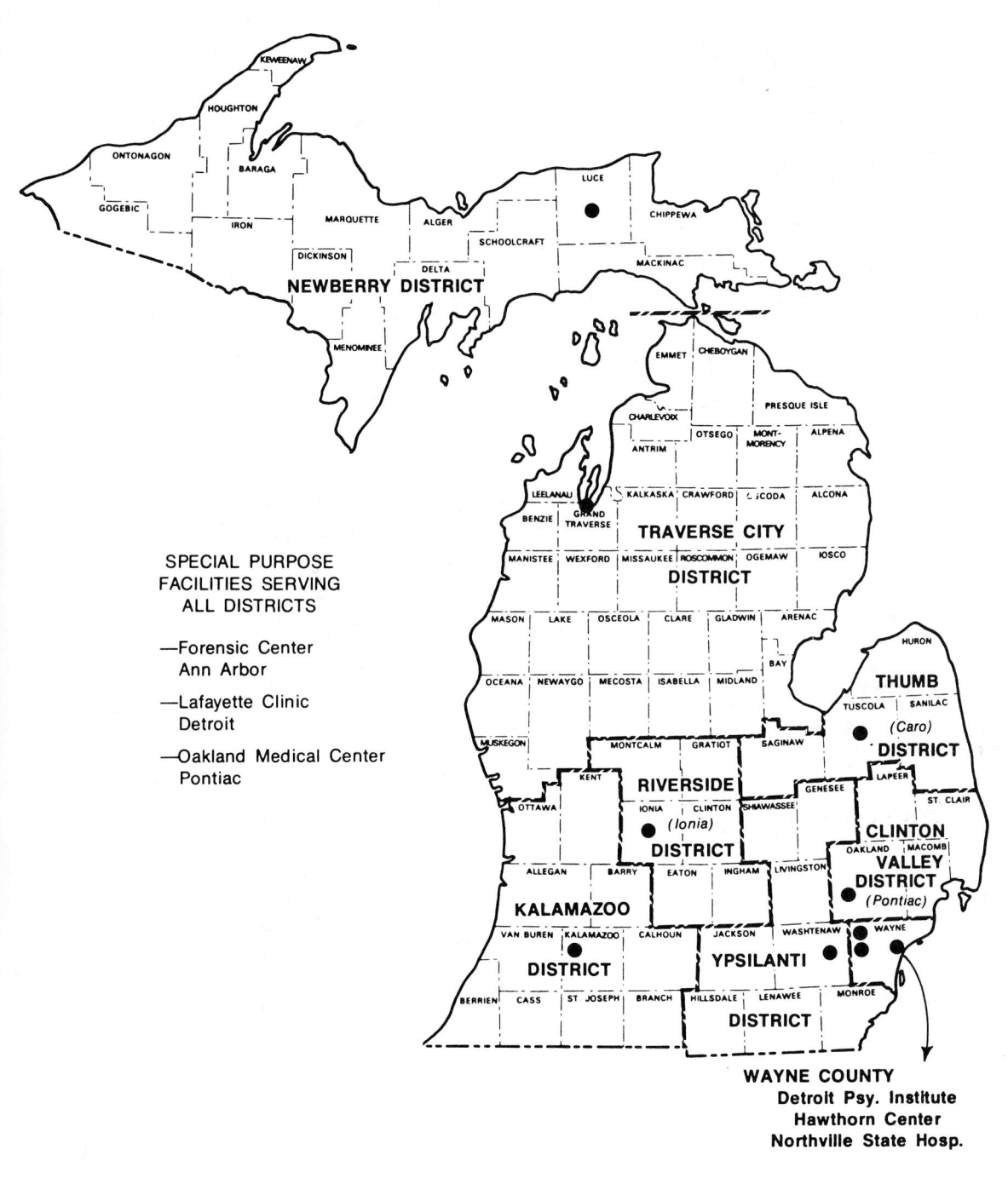

Figure 11.8. State hospitals for mentally ill. (Map: Michigan Department of Mental Health.)

Photo Essay F

HOUSES AND WATER

F-1 Lake Michigan penetrates sea walls September 1974, Grand Haven Township, Ottawa County. (Photo by B. Mills, Land Resources Division, Department of Natural Resources)

F-2 Bluff erosion undermines a lakeside home, Laketon Township, Muskegon County, July 1976. (Photo by B. Mills, Land Resources Division, Department of Natural Resources)

F-3 Wintertime shore erosion behind ice margin, Grand Haven Township, Ottawa County, February 1975. (Photo by B. Mills, Land Resources Division, Department of Natural Resources)

F-4 Flooding in commercial district of Lansing, April 21, 1975. (Photo by J. Royer, Information and Education Division, Department of Natural Resources)

F-5 Flooding in vicinity of sewage treatment plant, Lansing, April 21, 1975. (Photo by J. Royer, Information and Education Division, Department of Natural Resources)

F-6 Residential area flooding, Lansing, April 21, 1975. (Photo by R. Harrington, Information and Education Division, Department of Natural Resources)

F-1

F-2

F-3

F-4

F-5

F-6

Reducing Flood Losses

Based on scientific knowledge, Corps of Engineer studies, DNR, and community experience, there is little reason to doubt that flood problems can be significantly reduced through awareness, careful evaluation of flood hazards, and decisions which implement both structural flood proofing, as well as land-use planning and zoning controls. In spite of the knowledge of how to reduce flood losses, there are many who are willing to gamble their property and lives against periodic losses due to torrents of water sweeping the scenic or valuable lowland adjacent to rivers. Compounding the problem is the fact that citizens, cities, and townships have been reluctant to implement comprehensive flood plain management systems sometimes due to the expectation that federal "disaster" assistance at the time of loss will offset any damage. Insurance companies may describe losses as an "Act of God," but, in fact, it is most often the acts of people, individually and collectively, which cause much flood damage. Vegetation removal, engineering standards which are unsuited for dynamic population settlement patterns, out-moded slogan of "100 Year Flood," disregard for locating businesses, roads, and homes in flood plains without flood-proof designs, continuously compound the problem of periodic flooding. To gain the advantage of using flood plains, including their generally fertile soil and scenic views, requires sensitive cooperation and restraint in lowland use. Land-use planning can assist individuals and community leaders in decision making. In 1969 Common Pleas Judge Richard S. Lowe of Pennsylvania observed the result of unrestrained land development:

> History has proven time and again that absolute and unbridled freedom of individual choice has resulted in improvident and ludicrous land-use patterns which have obstructed the free flow of surface waters and thereby necessitated inordinately expensive public works or equally expensive disaster relief measures.[2]

Flood Plain Uses in the Modern Era

It is possible for Michigan residents to use the flood plains and gain both economic and health benefits. In urban areas flood plains can effectively be used for golf courses, parking lots, intensive park use, hiking, and forest reserves. In certain instances, business structures or homes can safely occupy the flood plain if structures are designed to withstand floods by elevation on pillars or by installing flood proof walls and opening devices. In rural areas agricultural uses, especially permanent grasses, are compatible with flood waters. However, other crops and plowed open land are subject to losses through erosion which adds sediments to stream bottoms.

Mapping the Flood Plain. Accurate mapping of flood plains is essential to the success of the Subdivision Control Act of 1967 and its 1972 Revision. The Act requires that a building's lower floor (not basement) and opening to below grade levels be at least 30 cm (1 ft) above the flood plain. The success of the National Flood Insurance Program as well as land-use planning and individual land development decisions also rest on the availability of accurate flood plain maps. Detailed maps for most of Michigan's waterways are not yet widely available. However, the Army Corps of Engineers and DNR do have useful data for some rivers (fig. 11.9).

Without the implementation of scientific and common sense flood plain management knowledge, professors and students of philosophy and logic may be expected to reflect increas-

---

2. *Flood Plain: Handle with Care,* Department of the Army Corps of Engineers (March 1974), p. 9.

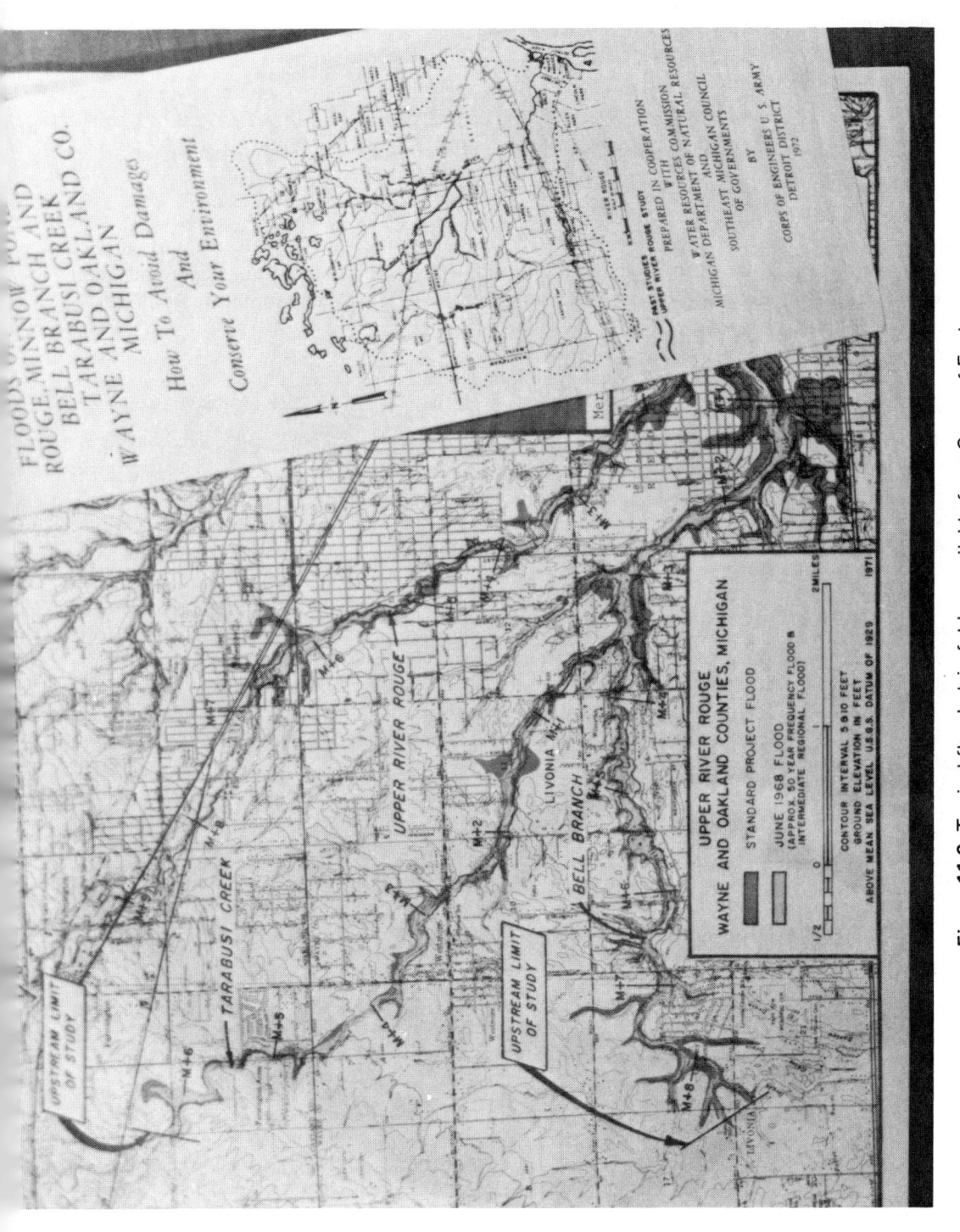

Figure 11.9. Typical flood plain folders available from Corps of Engineers.

ingly on the obligation of not only citizens or law enforcement officers to risk their lives to rescue careless flood victims, but also of taxpayers to underwrite property damages due to imprudent use of the flood plain.

Land Use Management, Open Space and Historic Site Preservation

Michigan's political history and heritage of guided land development has been traced in Chapter 3. This concluding section outlines the recent twentieth century activities which provide a basis for continued restrained development of the state's land. The establishment of national and state forests, Department of Conservation in 1921, and urban zoning represents three sporadic but major steps in protecting and improving Michigans's environment. By the 1970s Governor Milliken concluded that:

> No area is more critical to man's relationship with the environment than land use. Yet, in no area is regulation more fragmented, standards less certain, and decisions more shielded from the people.[4]

To challenge the critical problems of land management, the state established a Special Commission on Land Use in 1970 and an Office of Land Use within the DNR. However, through the representative government process, no statewide land use program has been implemented.

PA 116-1974 Farmland and Open Space Preservation Act

The passage in 1974 of PA 116 was another significant step which recognized the relationships between a growing population, resource depletion, and the haunting rapid loss of agricultural land and historic sites. Although this Act cannot be considered as a substitute for a comprehensive land use program, it does serve as an interim measure for the temporary preservation of farmland and land around historic sites. In the operation of the Act, one milestone feature is an adaptation of the traditional property and income taxes to include actual land use. Under PA 116, a landowner may enter into an agreement with the State of Michigan which ensures that a designated parcel of land remains in a particular use for an agreed upon length of time, usually a minimum of ten years. As an incentive to curtail fragmentation and development, a basic part of the agreement provides for income and property tax benefits. The Act applies to farms over 16 ha (40 ac) and those 2-16 ha (5-40 ac) which yield an income of $200 per acre or an income of $2,000 (fig. 11.10). Undeveloped nonagricultural open land suitable to conserve natural or scenic resources plus designated historic, river front, and shoreland areas identified under the Natural Rivers Act and Shoreline Protection and Management Act are also eligible for inclusion in the tax benefits of PA 116.

The quest for the preservation of critical lands for future generations under PA 116 also marked a milestone in the cooperative efforts of people and organizations which had been accustomed to being on opposite sides during the Environmental Movement of the Sixties, but came to understand that:

> We have not inherited the land from our Father [rather] we have borrowed it from our children.

> Not the end, but hopefully a commencement.

---

4. *Michigan's Future Was Today* (Department of Natural Resources, Office of Land Use, September 1974).

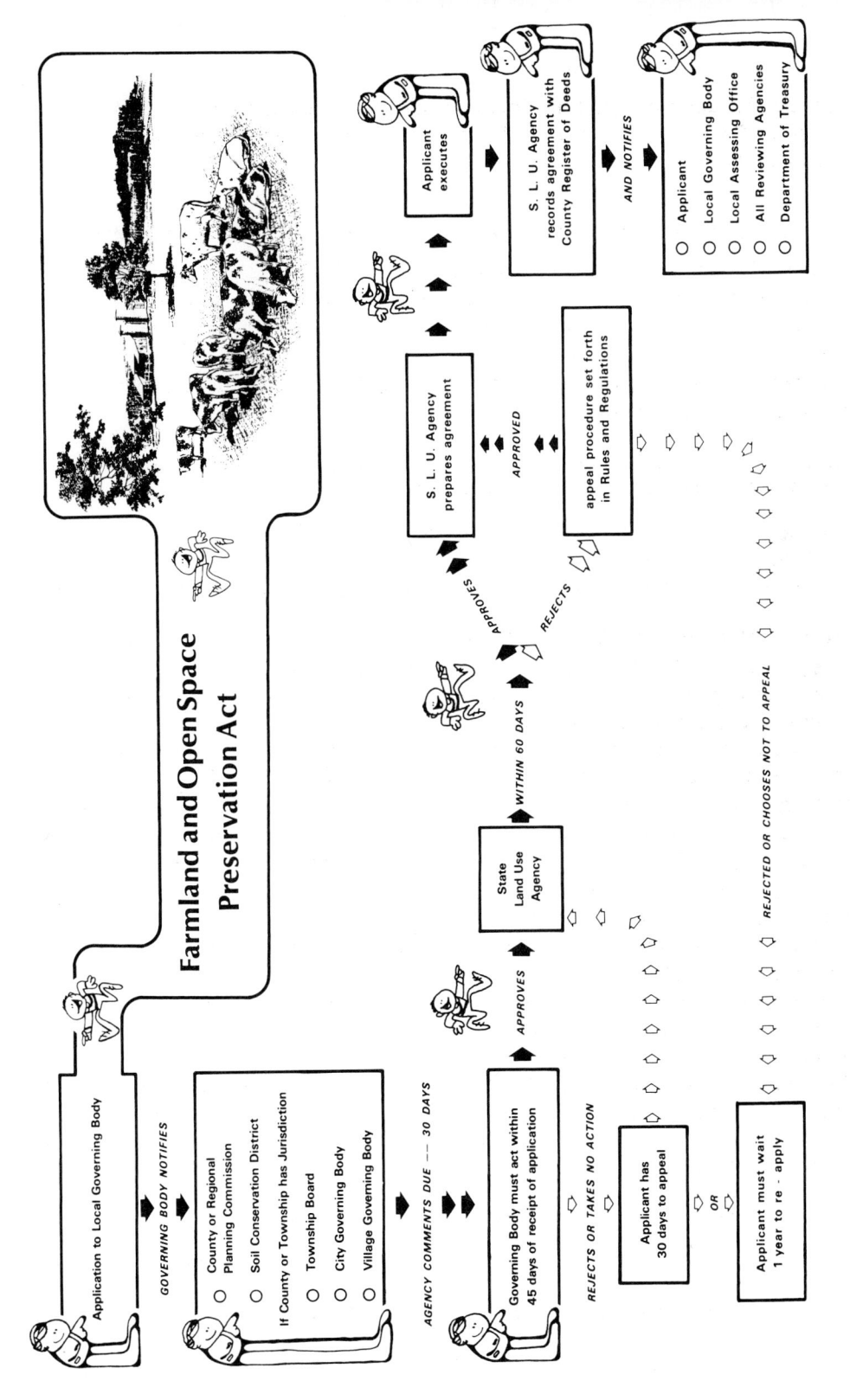

Figure 11.10. Application process for open space and farmland preservation under PA 116. (Diagram: R. Webster, Michigan Department of Natural Resources.)

List of Sources

General References

Bald, F. Clever. *Michigan in Four Centuries.* New York: Harper and Brothers, Publishers, 1954.

Broek, Jan O. M. *Geography: Its Scope and Spirit. Social Science Seminar Series.* Columbus: Charles E. Merrill Books, Inc., 1965.

Brown, A. S.; Houdek, J. J.; and Yzenbaard, J. H. *Michigan Perspectives: People, Events, Issues.* Dubuque, Iowa: Kendall/Hunt Publishing Company, 1974.

Davis, Charles M. *Readings in the Geography of Michigan.* Ann Arbor: Ann Arbor Publishers, 1964.

Dunbar, Willis F. *Michigan: A History of the Wolverine State.* Grand Rapids: William B. Eerdmans Publishing Company, 1965.

Espenshade, Edward, Jr. *Goode's World Atlas,* 14th ed. Chicago: Rand McNally, 1974.

Fuller, George N. *Economic and Social Beginnings of Michigan.* Lansing: Wynkoop Hallenbeck Crawford Co. State Printers, 1916.

Graduate School of Business Administration, *Michigan Statistical Abstract,* 9th ed. East Lansing: Michigan State University, 1972.

Graduate School of Business Administration, *Michigan Statistical Abstract,* 10th ed. East Lansing: Michigan State University, 1974.

Hatcher, H. and Walter, E. A. *A Pictorial History of the Great Lakes.* New York: Bonanza Books, 1963.

Hathaway, Richard J. *Dissertations and Theses in Michigan History.* Lansing: Michigan History Division, *ca.* 1972.

Hudgins, Bert. *Michigan: Geographic Backgrounds in the Development of the Commonwealth,* 4th ed. Detroit: Copyright by Bert Hudgins, 1961.

Jacobson, Daniel. "Man the Chooser and Mankind's Most Important Choices." *The Journal of Geography,* LXIX (September, 1970), 326-34.

Karpinski, Louis C. *Bibliography of Printed Maps of Michigan 1804-1880.* Lansing: Michigan Historical Commission, 1931.

Michigan Department of Natural Resources. *Mapping and Photography Directory.* Office of Land Use, January, 1976.

Michigan Department of Natural Resources. *Twenty-Seventh Biennial Report 1973-1974.* Lansing: State of Michigan.

Michigan, State of. *Michigan Manual* (?) Title page missing. Lansing: 1887 (?) 695 pp.

Michigan State University. *A Look into the Future,* Research Report 180 through 194. Project '80 and 5. East Lansing: Agricultural Experiment Station and Cooperative Extension Service, 1973.

Morrison, Paul C. "Geographer's Mirror of Michigan: A Bibliography of Professional Writings." *Michigan Academician,* L (1965), 493-518.

Nesbit, Robert C. *Wisconsin: A History.* Madison: University of Wisconsin Press, 1973.

Parkins, Almon E. *The Historical Geography of Detroit.* Lansing: Michigan Historical Commission, 1918.

Romig, Walter. *Michigan Place Names.* Grosse Pointe: By the author, 979 Lakepoint Rd. *ca.* 1971.
Rosenboom, E. H., and Weisenburger, F. P. *A History of Ohio.* Columbus: The Ohio Historical Society, 1973.
Senninger, Earl J., Jr. *Atlas of Michigan,* 3rd ed. Flint: Flint Geographical Press, 1970.
United States Bureau of Census. *Statistical Abstract of the United States, 1975,* 96th ed. Washington, D.C., 1975.
United States Department of Commerce. "Metric Conversion Card," Sp. pub. 365. Washington, D.C.: National Bureau of Standards, November, 1972.
United States Department of Interior. *The National Atlas of the United States.* Washington, D.C.: Geological Survey, 1970.
Wood, L. H. *Geography of Michigan: Physical, Industrial and Sectional.* Kalamazoo: Horton-Beimer Press, 1914.
The World Book Encyclopedia. Chicago: Field Enterprises Educational Corporation, 1973.

Chapter One

Brunn, Stanley. "A New United States," A Map. 1973.
Ferry, Mary B. (Curator of the Michigan Museum). "Michigan's Seal and Flag." Undated, 8 pp.
Funk and Wagnalls New "Standard" Dictionary of the English Language. New York: Funk and Wagnalls, 1956.
The Grand Rapids Press. Islands, February 21, 1971, p. 1 B; Upper Peninsula Left Out, July 14, 1974, p. 1 F.
Michigan Department of Attorney General, "Process for Obtaining Statehood," Opinion no. 4911. Lansing: Department of Attorney General, January 22, 1976.
"Michigan's Official Gem." *Michigan Natural Resources,* May-June, 1972, p. 16.
"Polar-Equator New State Trail." *Michigan Natural Resources,* September-October, 1974, p. 27.
The Oxford English Dictionary. Oxford: Clarendon Press, 1933.
The Random House Dictionary of the English Language, Unabridged ed. New York: Random House, Inc., 1966.
United States Department of Interior. *Islands of America.* Washington, D.C.: Bureau of Outdoor Recreation, 1970.
Websters New World Dictionary of the American Language, 2nd ed. New York: World Publishing Company, 1970.
"When You Find a Petoskey Stone." *Michigan Natural Resources.* September-October, 1972, p. 30.

Chapter Two

Angelo, Frank. *Yesterday's Michigan. Seemann's Historic Series,* no. 5. Miami, Florida: E. A. Seemann Publishing, Inc., 1975.
Broek, J. O. M. and Webb, J. W. *A Geography of Mankind.* New York: McGraw-Hill Book Company, 1968.
Brown, Ralph H. *Historical Geography of the United States.* New York: Harcourt, Brace and World, Inc., 1948.
Burton, Clarence M. "The Boundary Lines of the United States under the Treaty of 1782." *Michigan Pioneer and Historical Collections,* XXXVIII (1912) 130-39.
―――. "Moravians at Detroit." *Michigan Pioneer and Historical Collections,* XXX (1901) 51-63.
Butler, Albert F. "Thoreau's Week in Michigan." *Michigan Natural Resources,* May-June, 1976, pp. 16-20.
Claspy, Everett. *The Potawatomi Indians of Southwestern Michigan.* Dowagiac, Michigan, 1966.

Cooley, Thomas M. *Michigan: A History of Government.* Boston: Houghton Mifflin Co., 1913.
Fancher, Isaac A. *Past and Present of Isabella County.* Indianapolis: B. F. Brown and Company, 1911.
Fitting, James E. *The Archaeology of Michigan: A Guide to the Great Lakes Region.* Bloomfield Hills, Michigan: Cranbrook Institute of Science, 1975.
———. "Archaeology in Michigan: Present Knowledge and Prospects," *Great Lakes Informant,* Ser. 1, no. 1. Lansing: Michigan History Division, 1973.
Ford, Clyde R. "The Indian Way of Life." *This Is Michigan: A Sketch of These Times and Times Gone By.* Lansing: Michigan Historical Commission, 1953.
"French Map From 1749 . . ." *Michigan Natural Resources,* September-October, 1974, p. 30.
Grand Rapids Press. Spanish-English, April 22, 1976, p. 5 A.
Greenman, Emerson F. "The Indians of Michigan." Info. Ser. no. 1. Lansing: Michigan Historical Commission, Feb. 20, 1957. (mimeographed)
Hinsdale, Wilbert B. *Archaeological Atlas of Michigan.* Ann Arbor: University of Michigan Press, 1931.
———. *Distribution of the Aboriginal Population of Michigan,* Occ. Paper 2. with map. Ann Arbor: The Museum of Anthropology of the University of Michigan. Reprinted 1968.
Hubbard, Bela. *Memorials of a Half-Century.* New York: G. P. Putnam's Sons, 1887.
Kyser, Dewayne. "The American Indian in Isabella County." *The Peninsular,* I (1974), 14-19.
"Mackinac Island State Park 1895-1976." *Michigan Natural Resources,* May-June, 1976, pp. 42-43.
McLuhan, T. C. *Touch the Earth: A Self-portrait of Indian Existence.* New York: Promontory Press, 1971.
Michigan Department of State. "Michigan Indians." *Great Lakes Informant,* Ser. 1, no. 4 Lansing: Michigan History Division, 1975.
Michigan Historical Commission. *The Origin and Meaning of the Name Michigan.* Info. Ser. no. 3. Lansing: March 14, 1957. (mimeographed).
Mullally, Lee J. "A Historical Analysis of the American Indians of Lansing, Michigan." *The Peninsular,* I (1974), 20-26.
Petersen, Eugene T. *France at Mackinac: A Pictorial Record of French Life and Culture 1715-1760.* Mackinac Island: Mackinac Island State Park Commission, 1968.
"Proclamation of 1763." *Michigan Pioneer and Historical Collections* XXXVI (1908) 19.
Redford Historical Commission. "Map of Redford Township 1876." Reprint from *Atlas of Wayne County.* 1876.
Snell, Charles J. "This Was Fort Lernoult, 1782." *Michigan Natural Resources,* January-February, 1976, pp. 39-41.
Spain—U.S. Chamber of Commerce. "The Spain-U.S. Chamber of Commerce Celebrates the United States Bicentennial and Spain's Role in United States History, A Map." *ca.* 1976.
United States Constitution Sesquicentennial Commission. "The United States at the Time of the Ratification of the Constitution." Washington, D.C.: 1937-1939. Reprint of "New and Correct Map of North America," 1783.
Walton, Ivan. "Indian Place Names in Michigan" *Midwest Folklore,* vol. no. 1. (1955), 23-34.

Chapter Three

Armour, David A. "The Revolution Begins" *Michigan Natural Resources,* March-April, 1972, pp. 2-5.
Bald, F. Clever. "The Contest for the Great Lakes." *This Is Michigan: A Sketch of These Times and Times Gone By.* Lansing: Michigan Historical Commission, 1953.
Brown, Alan S. "Surveys and Surveyors in Frontier Michigan." *Great Lakes Informant,* Ser. 1 no. 3. Lansing: Michigan History Division, 1975.
Brunn, Stanley D. *Geography and Politics in America.* New York: Harper and Row, Publishers, 1974.

Carstensen, Vernon, ed. *The Public Lands.* Madison: The University of Wisconsin Press, 1968.

The Detroit Free Press. "Solve Problems via Regionalism" October 23, 1973, p. 7 A.

Farmer, Silas. *History of Detroit and Wayne County and Early Michigan.* Detroit: Silas Farmer and Co., 1890.

Felch, Alpheus. "The Indians of Michigan and the Cession of Their Lands to the United States by Treaties." *Michigan Pioneer and Historical Collections,* XXVI (1894-1895), 247-97.

George, Mary Karl. "Drums Along the Maumee." *Michigan Natural Resources,* March-April, 1972, pp. 17-32.

International Joint Commission. *The Annual Report of the International Joint Commission United States-Canada.* Washington-Ottawa, May, 1974.

Jefferson, Mark S. W. "Note on the Expansion of Michigan." *Report: Michigan Academy of Science,* (1902), 88-91.

Jenks, W. L. "History and Meaning of County Names of Michigan." *Michigan Pioneer and Historical Collections,* XXXVIII (1912) 439-77.

Martin, Lawrence. *The Physical Geography of Wisconsin,* 3rd ed. Madison: The University of Wisconsin Press, 1965.

McDonald, James R. *A Geography of Regions.* Dubuque, Iowa: Wm. C. Brown Company Publishers, 1972.

Michigan Department of Education. *County Evolution in Michigan 1790-1897,* Occ. Paper no. 2. Lansing: State Library Services, 1972.

Michigan Department of State. "History of Michigan Counties." Undated 4 pp.

Michigan Geological and Biological Survey. *Biennial Report of the Director and Report on Retracement and Permanent Monumenting of the Michigan-Ohio Boundary,* Pub. 22, Geol. Ser. 18. Lansing: State Printers, 1916.

"Michigan Started Here." *Michigan Natural Resources,* May-June, 1974, pp. 22-25.

Office of Criminal Justice Programs. "Interim Regional Guidelines for Fiscal Year 1974." July 27, 1973.

Office of the Governor. "An Investigation of Locally Established Regional Bodies in Michigan." Informational Memorandum Ala. December, 1970.

Office of the Governor. *Planning and Development Regions for Michigan.* Tech. Rep. no. 14. February, 1968.

Parke, Harvey. "Reminiscences." *Michigan Pioneer and Historical Collections,* III (1881), 572-76.

Price, Edward T. "The Central Courthouse Square in the American County Seat." *The Geographical Review,* LVIII no. 1 (January, 1968) 29-60.

Smith, Herbert H. *The Citizens Guide to Zoning.* West Trenton, N.J.: Chandler-Davis Publishing Company, 1965.

Treat, Payson J. "Origin of the National Land System Under the Constitution." *The Public Lands: Studies in the History of Public Domain.* Madison: The University of Wisconsin Press, 1968.

United States Congress. *An Ordinance for the Government of the Territory of the United States, Northwest of the River Ohio.* Facsimile Reprint: National Archives Washington, D.C.

United States Supreme Court. *Report of Special Master State of Michigan vs. State of Ohio.* No. 30 original. October Term 1970.

United States Supreme Court. "State of Michigan vs. State of Wisconsin." *Supreme Court Reporter,* XLVII no. 9 Original. Decided November 22, 1926. 272 U.S. 398.

United States Supreme Court. *Michigan vs. Wisconsin in Equity.* No. 19 Original. (Argued January 5, 1926—Decided March 1, 1926), 270 U.S. 295.

United States Supreme Court. *Report of Special Master State of Michigan vs. State of Ohio,* no. 30 Original October term 1970. Quoting: Hening's *Statutes of Virginia,* XI (1782-1784), XII (1785-1788).

Waldron, Clara. *One Hundred Years—A Country Town.* Tecumseh: Thomas A. Riordian, 1968.

Chapter Four

Anderson, Alan Jr. "Earthquake Prediction." *Saturday Review of the Sciences,* February, 1973, pp. 25-33.

Boyum, Burton H. *The Marquette Mineral District of Michigan.* Ishpeming, Michigan: The Cleveland-Cliffs Iron Co. 1975.

Consumers Power Company and The Detroit Edison Company. *Ludington Pumped Storage Hydroelectric Plant.* Undated.

Dorr, J. A. and Eschman, D. F. *Geology of Michigan.* Ann Arbor: University of Michigan Press, 1971.

Empire Iron Mining Company, Palmer Michigan. Ishpeming, Michigan: The Cleveland Cliffs Iron Co., *ca.* 1976.

Finster, Chester. "Geology." Unpublished draft mimeographed, 62 pp. with maps. *ca.* 1965.

Gilluly, J.; Waters, A. C.; and Woodford, A. O. *Principles of Geology.* San Francisco: W. H. Freeman and Co., 1955.

The Grand Rapids Press. Earthquake, February 3, 1976, p. 1 A. Earth Shrinking, October 16, 1975, p. 1 E. Oil in Michigan, June 9, 1974, p. 1 B. Pigeon River Oil, May 12, 1976, p. 14 A. Saltbeds "N" Waste, May 12, 1976, p. 12 A.

Iron Mining Today. Cleveland: American Iron Ore Association, *ca.* 1976.

Ives, Robert. "Down the Well." *Michigan Natural Resources,* July-August, 1971, pp. 2-7.

Kelley, Robert W. *Guide to Michigan Fossils.* Lansing: Michigan Department of Conservation. Undated.

Leopold, Aldo. *A Sand County Almanac.* New York: A Sierra Club/Ballantine Book, 1966.

Leverett, F. B. and Taylor, F. *The Pleistocene of Indiana and Michigan and the History of the Great Lakes,* Monograph 53. United States Geological Survey, 1915.

Lewis, Jerry D. *Michigan Mineral Producers 1975,* Annual Directory 9. Lansing: Geological Survey Division, 1975.

Marquette Iron Mining Company: Republic, Michigan. Ishpeming, Michigan: The Cleveland-Cliffs Iron Co., *ca.* 1976.

Martin, Helen M. *Outline of the Geologic History of Michigan.* Lansing: Geological Survey Division, May, 1952.

"Mineral Values Rose in 1973." *Michigan Natural Resources,* September-October, 1974, p. 26.

Michigan Department of Conservation. *Fourth Biennial Report 1927-1928.* Lansing: State of Michigan.

Michigan Department of Natural Resources. *Running Out of Everything.* Lansing: Mineral Lands Subcommittee of the State Essential and Unique Lands Advisory Committee, November 19, 1973.

Milepost Interstate 75: *The Michigan Bicentennial Highway.* Lansing: Winkelman's, Automobile Club of Michigan in Cooperation with State Agencies. 1976.

Preifer, Ray. "The Pigeon River Country." *Michigan Natural Resources,* July-August, 1974, pp. 22-25.

Segal, T. and Segal, G. "14 Years of 24 Karat Mining." *Michigan Natural Resources.* November-December, 1975, pp. 7-9.

Thatcher, Charles. "Pigeon River Perspectives." *Michigan Natural Resources,* May-June, 1976, pp. 2-9.

The Tilden Mining Company. Ishpeming, Michigan: The Cleveland-Cliffs Iron Co., *ca.* 1976.

Wieber, J. M. "A Billion Tons of Iron Ore." *Michigan Natural Resources,* November-December, 1975, pp. 16-17.

Chapter Five

Brater, E. F.; Armstrong, J. M.; and McGill, W. *Michigan's Demonstration Erosion Control Program,* Update Evaluation Report. Lansing: Michigan Department of Natural Resources, August 1975.

Brater, Ernest F. and Cortright, Michelle, ed. *Beach Erosion in Michigan: An Historical Review.* Lansing: Michigan Department of Natural Resources. Undated.

Buckler, W. R. and Winters, H. A. "Rates of Bluff Recession at Selected Sites Along the Southeastern Shore of Lake Michigan." *Michigan Academician,* VIII no. 2 (Fall 1975), 179-86.

Cutler, Irving. *Chicago: Metropolis of the Mid-Continent,* 2nd ed. Dubuque, Iowa: Kendall/Hunt Publishing Company, 1976.

Fuller, George N. ed. *Geological Reports of Douglass Houghton: First State Geologist of Michigan 1837-1845.* Lansing: The Michigan Historical Commission, 1928.

"Guide to Cleaning Out Water Weeds." *Michigan Natural Resources,* May-June, 1973, p. 31.

Kelley, Robert W. *Michigan's Sand Dunes: A Geologic Sketch.* Lansing: Geological Survey Division, 1962.

Kelley, R. W., and Farrand, W. R. *The Glacial Lakes around Michigan,* Bull. no. 4. Lansing: Geological Survey, 1967.

Lake Hydraulics Laboratory. *Low Cost Shore Protection for the Great Lakes.* University of Michigan: 1952. Reprint 1975, Michigan Water Resources Commission.

Michigan Department of Conservation. "Map of the Surface Formations of the Northern Peninsula of Michigan." Pub. 49. Geological Survey Division, 1957.

Michigan Department of Conservation. "Map of the Surface Formations of the Southern Peninsula of Michigan." Pub. 49. Geological Survey Division, 1955.

Michigan Department of Natural Resources. *Report of Special Environments.* Lansing: Office of Land Use, April, 1974.

Michigan Department of Natural Resources. *Michigan's Natural Rivers Program.* Lansing: May, 1975.

Michigan Department of Natural Resources. *Erosion.* Lansing: April, 1976.

United States. *American State Papers,* Public Lands. III, VI.

United States Army. *Help Yourself: A Discussion of the Critical Erosion Problems of the Great Lakes and Alternative Methods of Shore Protection.* Chicago: Corps of Engineers, North Central Division, Undated.

Chapter Six

Brown, L. R.; McGrath, P. L.; and Stokes, B. "Twenty-Two Dimensions of the Population Problem." *Worldwatch Paper 5.* Washington, D.C.: Worldwatch Institute. March, 1976.

Chamberlain, Von Del. *Meteorites of Michigan,* Bull. 5. Lansing: Geological Survey, 1968.

Dana, Samuel T. "Resource Problems of Michigan," An Address Before the Michigan Natural Resources Conference. January, 1955. Michigan State University Publication L no. 1 July, 1955. Reprinted Ypsilanti: Division Field Services, Eastern Michigan University. March 1960.

DeLong, Eleanor L. "Tech Toots and Snow Descriptors." *Michigan Academician,* VII no. 4 (Spring 1975), 489-500.

The Detroit Free Press. Ice Storm, March 7, 1976, p. 1 A. Ice Storm, March 12, 1976, p. 3 B.

The Grand Rapids Press. Cloud Seeding, April 21, 1976, p. 9 B. Flooding, March 6, 1976, p. 1 A. Flooding, March 9, 1976, p. 1 B. Ice Storm, March 3, 1976, p. 1 A. Ice Storm, March 4, 1976, p. 1 A. Ice Storm, March 5, 1976, p. 1 A. Ice Storm, April, 20, 1976, p. 1 A. November Storms February 8, 1976, p. 1 B. Snow in U.P., May 7, 1976, p. 11 C. Solar Energy, May 3, 1976, p. 7 B. Wind Power, March 1, 1976, p. 7 B. Wind Power, April 25, 1976, p. 1 B. Wind Power, May 21, 1976, p. 6 A.

Gray, John, ed. "Pine Days" *Some of the Best from Michigan Natural Resources, ca.* Mid- 1970s, pp. 33-48.

"Here Comes the Sun." *Michigan Natural Resources,* July-August, 1974, pp. 2-7.

Lotbiniere, Michel C. *Fort Michilimackinac in 1749.* Translated by Marie Gerin-Lajoie. *Mackinac History,* II, Leaflet 5. 1976.

Michigan Department of Agriculture. *Climate of Michigan by Stations,* 2nd revised ed. E. Lansing: Michigan Weather Service, December, 1971.

Michigan Department of Agriculture. *Michigan Snow Depths.* E. Lansing: Michigan Weather Service, May, 1974.

Michigan Department of Agriculture. *Supplement to the Climate of Michigan by Stations:* Mean Temperature Maps for the Period 1940-1969. East Lansing: Michigan Weather Service, June 1974 reprint October 1975.

Michigan Department of Agriculture, *Supplement to the Climate of Michigan by Stations:* Mean Precipitation Maps for the Period 1940-1969. East Lansing: Michigan Weather Service. June 1974 reprint October, 1975.

Michigan Department of Agriculture. *Supplement to the Climate of Michigan by Stations:* Mean Snowfall Maps for the Period 1940-1969. East Lansing: Michigan Weather Service. June 1974 reprint October 1975.

Michigan Department of Natural Resources. *Forests for the Future,* Forestry Subcommittee Report to Essential and Unique Lands Committee. Lansing: Office of Land Use, March 1974.

Michigan Extremes Temperature and Precipitation by Station for Period of Record Through June 1974. East Lansing: Michigan Department of Agriculture, Weather Service, October, 1974.

Michigan State University. *Recommended Standards for Drainage of Michigan Soils.* East Lansing: Cooperative Extension Service, January 1963.

Nurnberger, Fred V. and Oshel, M. W. *Michigan Temperatures Annual Extremes of Record 1888-1974.* East Lansing: Michigan Department of Agriculture, Weather Service, May 1975.

The Pioneer, Big Rapids. Flooding, September 3, 1975, p. 2. Ice Storm, March 12, 1976, p. 2. Soil Drainage, March 13, 1976, p. 20. Wood Chipping, August 30-31, 1975, pp. 10-11.

St. Mary's Parish. *Centennial Brochure 1873-1973.* Big Rapids: Copyright by Ronald J. Schinderle and J. R. Schauble, 1973.

Schallau, Con H. *Forest Owners and Timber Management in Michigan,* Research Paper LS-9. Lake States Forest Experiment Station: U.S. Department of Agriculture, March, 1964.

———. *Small Forest Ownership in the Urban Fringe Area of Michigan,* Station Paper No. 103. Lake States Forest Experiment Station: U. S. Department of Agriculture, August, 1962.

Strommen Norton. *Climate of Michigan.* East Lansing: Michigan Cooperative Extension Service, undated.

———. *Urban Influences of Rainfall in the Detroit, Michigan Area.* East Lansing: Michigan Department of Agriculture, Weather Service, undated.

The Sunday News. Detroit. November Storms, February 23, 1976, pp. 10-11 A. Solar Energy, February 8, 1976, p. 8 A.

"Twister Tally Shows State Low." *Michigan Natural Resources,* September-October, 1974, p. 30.

United States Department of Agriculture. *Soil Survey Muskegon County Michigan.* Washington, D.C.: U.S. Government Printing Office, October, 1968.

United States Department of Commerce. *Detroit: Local Climatological Data.* Asheville: National Oceanic and Atmospheric Administration, December, 1974.

United States Department of Commerce. *Lightning Fatalities and Injuries in Michigan 1897-1966,* CI ser. no. 2. East Lansing: Environmental Science Services Administration, October, 1967.

United States Department of Commerce. *Tornado.* Washington, D.C.: National Oceanic and Atmospheric Administration, undated. (Should not be mistaken for 1969 booklet of same title by Environmental Science Services Administration.)

VanRiper, Joseph E. *Man's Physical World.* New York: McGraw-Hill Book Co., Inc., 1962.

Whiteside, E. P., Schneider, I. F. and Cook, R. L. *Soils of Michigan,* Sp. Bull. 402. East Lansing: Soil Science Department, Michigan State University. 1956.

Works Progress Administration. *Log Marks of Michigan.* East Lansing: Michigan Agricultural Experiment Station, 1941. Reprint: Social Science Division, Muskegon Community College, 1971.

Chapter Seven

Anderson, Thomas D. "Use of the Rule of 70 in Teaching About Population." *The Journal of Geography,* LXXV no. 4. (April, 1976), 227-30.

Blois, John T. *Gazetteer of the State of Michigan.* Detroit: Sydney L. Rood and Co. 1838.

Borgstrom, George. *The Food and People Dilemma.* North Scituate, Massachusetts: Duxbury Press, 1973.
Cook, J. M., Christine, P. and Students. Computer Graphs: Population by Counties of Michigan 1960-1970. Big Rapids: Ferris State College School of Business, 1976 (unpublished).
Harries, Keith D. "The Geography of American Crime." *The Journal of Geography,* LXX, no. 4. (April 1971), 204-213.
Jacobson, Daniel. "Lansing's Jewish Community: The Beginnings." *Michigan Jewish History,* XVI, no. 1 (January 1976), 5-17.
Kuhn, Madison. "Tiffin, Morse and the Reluctant Pioneer." *Michigan History,* L (June 1966), 111-38.
Letter, Lewis Cass to Josiah Meigs, June 16, 1816. Michigan Historical Commission, Archives, Cass Letter Book, Sheets 121-22.
Michigan Department of Management and Budget. *Population Projections of the Counties . . . 1970 through 1990.* Lansing: Planning and Analysis Division, October, 1974.
Peters, Bernard C. "Settler Attitudes Toward the Land as Revealed in the Pioneer Poetry of Kalamazoo County." *Michigan Academician,* VI, no. 2. (Fall 1973), 209-17.
Poles in Michigan, I, Detroit: The Poles in Michigan Associated, 1953.
Rugg, Dean S. *Spatial Foundations of Urbanism.* Dubuque, Iowa: Wm. C. Brown Company Publishers, 1972.
Sale, R. D. and Karn F. D. *American Expansion: A Book of Maps.* Homewood, Illinois: The Dorsey Press, Inc., 1962.
"St. Joseph County." *Michigan Pioneer and Historical Collections,* III (1881), 610.
Schnell, G. A. and Monmonier, M. S. "U.S. Population Change 1960-70." *Journal of Geography,* LXXV no. 5. (May 1976), 280-91.
Thaden, J. F. "Ethnic Settlements in Rural Michigan." *Michigan Agricultural Experiment Station Quarterly Bulletin,* XXIX no. 2. (November 1946), 102-11.
———. *Map: The Farm People of Michigan According to Ethnic Stock: 1945.* East Lansing: Agricultural Experiment Station, Michigan State College.
United States Bureau of Census. *General Population Characteristics: Michigan,* PC (1)-B24. Washington, D.C.: 1970.
United States Congress. House. *Military Bounty Lands.* H. D. no. 81, 14th Congress, 1st Sess. February 6, 1816.

Chapter Eight

Boas, Charles W. "Locational Patterns of the Michigan Passenger Automobile Industry." *Readings in the Geography of Michigan.* Edited by C. M. Davis. Ann Arbor: Ann Arbor Publishers. 1964 pp. 259-63. Reprint from *Michigan Academician,* LXIV.
Brown, C. Exera. *Jackson City Directory for: 1872-1873.* Jackson: VanDyne's Printing House, 1872.
The Detroit Free Press. Murder Map, December 13, 1973, p. 9 A.
"Downtown Is Looking Up." *Time: The Weekly Newsmagazine.* July 5, 1976, pp. 54-62.
Dunbar, Willis S. "Bay City," "Flint," "Saginaw." *The World Book Encyclopedia,* II, VII, XVII, (1973).
Escanaba Area Chamber of Commerce. *Escanaba, Michigan.* Encino, California: Windsor Publications, Inc., 1971.
Ford, Larry R. "The Urban Skyline as a City Classification System." *The Journal of Geography,* LXXV, no. 3 (March 1976), 154-64.
"The Gaylord Story: Modern Renaissance of a Small Town." *The Gaylord Area Business Directory. ca.* 1970. pp. 3-13.
Grand Traverse Bay Region, Form 865. Traverse City: Printed By Traverse City High School. *ca.* 1970.

Greater Jackson Chamber of Commerce. *Greater Jackson , Michigan.* Jackson: *ca.* 1976.

Greater Saginaw Chamber of Commerce. *Saginaw Michigan.* Windsor Publications Inc., 1972.

Hart, John F. "A Rural Retreat for Northern Negroes." *The Geographical Review,* L no. 2. (April 1960), 148-67.

Heller, C. F.; Quandt, E. C.; and Raup, H. A. *Population Patterns of Southwestern Michigan.* Kalamazoo: The New Issues Press, Institute of Public Affairs Western Michigan University, 1974.

Kent County Planning Department. *A Data Profile: Grand Rapids Metropolitan Area.* Grand Rapids: 1967.

Lydens, Z. Z. ed. *The Story of Grand Rapids.* Grand Rapids: Kregel Publications, 1966.

Michigan Academy of Science, Arts, and Letters. "Tax Revenue Allocated to Higher Education in Michigan Low." *The Academy Letter,* no. 69-70. May-June, 1976, pp. 7-8.

Michigan Department of Census. *Census of Michigan: 1904. Population,* I.

Michigan Department of Commerce. *County and Regional Facts for . . . Hillsdale, Jackson, Lenawee Counties.* Lansing: Office of Economic Expansion, Cooperative Extension Service, undated.

Michigan Department of State. *Michigan's Historic Attractions.* Lansing: Michigan History Division, 1973.

Michigan National Guard. *Camp Grayling: Official Visitors Guide.* undated.

Muskegon Area Development Council. *Muskegon Country, Michigan.* Windsor Publications Inc., 1973.

Northeast Michigan Regional Planning and Development Commission. *The Northeast Michigan Region.* Rogers City: June, 1973.

Operation Action-U.P. Council. *The Good Life Is Even Better in Michigan's Upper Peninsula,* rev. ed. Marquette: Operation Action-U.P. 1968.

Pound, Arthur. *The Turning Wheel: The Story of General Motors Through Twenty-Five Years 1908-1933.* Garden City, New York: Doubleday Doran and Co., Inc., 1934.

Region II Planning Commission. *Population: Jackson, Lenawee, and Hillsdale Counties.* Detroit: U.S. Department of Housing and Urban Development, 1975.

Saginaw Civic Center. *Let Us Entertain You.* Saginaw: *ca.* 1972.

Sinclair, Robert. *The Face of Detroit—A Spatial Synthesis.* Detroit: Wayne State University, National Council for Geographic Education, U.S. Office of Education, 1970.

Southeast Michigan Council of Governments. *1970 Transportation Related Data SEMCOG Region.* December, 1972.

Thompson, Donald C. "Grand Rapids: A Furniture Legend." *Chronicle,* Historical Society of Michigan, II no. 3 (1975), 3-10.

Triennial Atlas and Plat Book Otsego County, Michigan. Rockford, Ill.: Rockford Map Publishers, Inc., 1969.

Twin Cities Area Chamber of Commerce. *Twin Cities Area: Benton Harbor/St. Joseph.* Paxton Advertising, Inc. 1972.

United Community Services. *200 Years in the Life of Our Community.* Detroit: 1976.

United States Bureau of Census. *Ninth Census of the United States:* 1870. Michigan Population, Jackson County Schedules.

United States Bureau of Census. *Fifteenth Census of the United States: 1930.* Population, II.

United States Bureau of Census. *Eighteenth Census of the United States: 1960.* Population, I.

Wakefield, Larry, ed. *Traverse City Area Michigan.* Traverse City: Village Press, July, 1972.

West Michigan Regional Planning Commission. *Recreation and Open Space Inventory and Analysis.* Grand Rapids: April 1976.

Western Upper Peninsula Regional Planning Commission. *Open Space and Recreation Inventory and Interim Plan.* Houghton: Western Upper Peninsula Regional Planning Commission, October, 1972.

Western Upper Peninsula Planning and Development Region. *Natural Resource Analysis.* Houghton: Western Upper Peninsula Planning and Development Region. June, 1974.

Young, Clarence H. *Citizens Century 1871-1971.* Flint: Citizens Commercial and Savings Bank, 1971.

Chapter Nine

Chermayeff, Serge and Tzonis, Alexander. *Shape of Community: Realization of Human Potential.* Harmondsworth Middlesex, England: Penguin Books Ltd., 1971.

Ching, Derek. "Some Aspects of Snowmobiling—A Foreign Geographer's Viewpoint." Paper read before Geography Section, Michigan Academy Science Arts and Letters, 1973.

Colling, Peter. "Mini Motor Rovers." *Great Lakes Sportsman,* March-April, 1976, pp. 30-34.

Darby, William. *A Tour from the City of New York to Detroit.* Chicago: Americans Classics Quadrangle Books, 1962. Reprint of First Edition, New York: 1819.

The Detroit Free Press. Tractors, May 2, 1976, p. 1 B.

The Grand Rapids Press. Exports, April 21, 1976, p. 7 C; Taxes, April 29, 1976, p. 2 E; Tax Systems, May 2, 1976, p. 10 B.

McBeath, Sandy. "Coho Madness." *Michigan Natural Resources,* September-October, 1973, pp. 12-16.

Michigan Crop Reporting Service. *Corn Harvesting and Marketing Statistics 1975.* Lansing: Michigan and United States Department of Agriculture, 1976.

Michigan Crop Reporting Service. *Dairy Trends in Michigan 1973.* Lansing: Michigan and United States Departments of Agriculture, 1973.

Michigan Crop Reporting Service. *Michigan Agricultural Statistics 1974.* Lansing: United States Department of Agriculture, 1974.

Michigan Crop Reporting Service. *Michigan Agricultural Statistics 1976.* Lansing: United States Department of Agriculture, 1976.

Michigan Crop Reporting Service. *Michigan County Estimates Livestock-Dairy-Poultry 1965-1973.* Lansing: Michigan Department of Agriculture. October 1973.

Michigan Crop Reporting Service. *Michigan Planting and Harvesting Data 1966-1974.* Lansing: Michigan and United States Departments of Agriculture, June 1975.

Michigan Department of Agriculture. *Annual Report of Food Inspection Regulatory Activities . . . Year Ending June 30, 1975.* Lansing: Bureau of Consumer Protection, 1975.

Michigan Department of Agriculture. *Michigan Agricultural Land Requirements: A Projection to 2000 A.D.* Lansing: February, 1973. Mimeographed, 11 pp.

Michigan Department of Agriculture. *1976 Michigan Food Facts.* Lansing: 1976.

Michigan Department of Commerce. *Annual Report 1972-1973.* Lansing: August 1974.

Michigan Department of Commerce. *1976 Michigan Plant Location Directory.* Lansing: Office of Economic Expansion, 1976.

Michigan Economic Action Council. *Recommendations for Short Term Action.* E. Lansing: Michigan Action Council, August, 1975.

Michigan Economic Action Council. *Toward Growth with Stability—Recommendations for Long Term Action.* E. Lansing: Michigan Economic Action Council. June 1976.

Michigan Travel Commission. *Michigan Winter Sports Guide: Ski Michigan/Snowmobile Michigan.* Lansing: Michigan Department of Commerce 1975-1976. (Maps)

Michigan Travel Commission. *Summary of the Travel Product Market Analysis Study.* Lansing: Department of Commerce. March, 1976. Mimeographed, 6 pp.

Milliken, William G. *Economic Report of the Governor 1976.* Lansing: March, 1976.

Mowat, John S. "Unemployment Crisis," A Special Report. Lansing: State Representative Mowat, *ca.* 1976.

Office of Economic Expansion. *1976 Certified Industrial Parks.* Lansing: Michigan Department of Commerce. 1976.

Pearson, Ross N. "The Terminology of the Recreation Industry." *Readings in the Geography of Michigan.* Edited by C. M. Davis. Ann Arbor: Ann Arbor Publishers. 1964. Reprinted from *Michigan Academician* vol. 47. 1962.

The Pioneer, Big Rapids. Snowmobiles, July 20, 1976, p. 5.

The Sunday News. Detroit, Community Colleges, May 16, 1976, p. 9 A.

Vinge, C. L. and Vinge, A. G. *Economic Geography.* Totowa, New Jersey: Littlefield, Adams and Co., Inc., 1966.

Wheeler, James O. "Location of Mobile Home Manufacturing: A Multidimensional Scaling Analysis." *The Professional Geographer,* XXVIII, no. 3 (August 1976), 261-66.

Chapter Ten

Berndt, Clarence F., Jr. "Michigan Railroads 1837-1846: A Study in Internal Improvements." Unpublished Master's Thesis, Department of History, Michigan State University. 1967.

Consumers Power Company. *Hardy Dam.* Jackson: undated.

Dann, Richard R. "The 'Super Trucks' Too Big?" *Motor News.* Dearborn: November 15, 1975. p. 16, 36.

The Detroit Free Press. Bulk Mail, March 12, 1976, p. 10 D; I-696, February 29, 1976, p. 1 B.

Felch, Alpheus. "Minutes of Annual Meeting, 1893." *Michigan Pioneer and Historical Collections,* XXII (1894), 11-17.

Flott, Leslie W. "Augustus Herring . . . Aviation Pioneer." *Chronicle,* Historical Society of Michigan, 10, no. 3 (1974), 2-8.

General Telephone News, July 16, 1976.

The Grand Rapids Press. Trucking, September 26, 1975, pp. 1-16 F; Extension of Freeway, May 9, 1976, p. 1 A.

Hurst, Michael F. E. *Transportation Geography Comments and Readings.* New York: McGraw-Hill Book Company, 1974.

Janelle, Donald G. "Spatial Reorganization: A Model and Concept." *Annals of the Association of American Geographers,* 59, no. 2 (June 1969) 348-65.

Kelley, Robert L. "History of Radio in Michigan." *Michigan History,* XXI (1937), 5-19.

Laboratory for Computer Graphics and Spatial Analysis. "CALFORM Map from Solar Energy Study." *Context.* Cambridge: Harvard University, May, 1976. p. 9.

Luther, Hardy E. "High Voltage Transmission." *Michigan History,* LI (1967), 95-113.

Michigan Consolidated Gas Company. *Michigan Gas Pipeline Map,* with Franchise Areas. 1 m. × 1 m. December 31, 1975.

Michigan Department of Attorney General. *A Position Paper . . . : Building a Healthy and Safe Environment with the Bicycle.* Lansing: March 27, 1973.

Michigan Department of Commerce. *Michigan 1970-1975 State Airport Plan.* Lansing: Michigan Aeronautics Commission, 1971.

The Land and the River. Lansing: Office of Economic Expansion, June, 1976.

Michigan Department of State Highways and Transportation. *History of Michigan Highways and the Michigan Department of State Highways and Transportation.* Lansing: May, 1974. Mimeographed 11 pp.

Michigan Public Service Commission. "Rules Governing Extension of Single-Phase Electric Service," Case No. U2291. March 24, 1966.

Michigan State Highway Commission. *Annual Report 1974.* Lansing: Department of State Highways and Transportation.

Michigan State Highway Commission. *Annual Report 1975.* Lansing: Department of State Highways and Transportation.

Morrison, Roger L. "The History and Development of Michigan Highways." University of Michigan Official Publications, XXXIX, no. 4. April 6, 1938. Reprint from *Michigan Alumnus Quarterly Review.* Autumn 1937, pp. 59-73.

Patrick, Michael and Ferres, Bernie. "Railroad Reorganization in Michigan," *Michigan Farm Economics,* no. 401. E. Lansing: June 1976. (includes map).

Schenker, E.; Mayer, H. M.; and Brockel, H. C. *The Great Lakes Transportation System.* Tech. Report 230. Madison: University of Wisconsin Sea Grant College Program, January, 1976.

The Sunday News. Detroit, ConRail, April 25, 1976, p. 3 J.

White, Peter T. "This Land of Ours—How Are We Using It." *National Geographic,* 150, no. 1 (July 1976), 20-67.

Chapter Eleven

Brown, Allan S. "Caroline Bartlett Crane and Urban Reform." *Michigan History,* LVI, No. 4 (1972), 287-301.

Bryan, M. Leonard. "Flooding of Monroe County, Michigan: A Comparison of Three Remote Sensor Data Sets." *Michigan Academician,* VIII, no. 4 (Spring 1976), 425-40.

Charles F. Kettering Foundation. *New Ways.* Spring 1976.

"Chemical Clean-up Paying Off." *Michigan Natural Resources,* July-August, 1974, p. 20.

Cowels, Gay. "Return of the River." *Michigan Natural Resources,* January-February, 1975, pp. 2-6.

The Grand Rapids Press. Pollution Control Profit, November 14, 1975, p. 13 B.

Hall, Dennis. "The Land Is Borrowed from Our Children." *Michigan Natural Resources,* July-August, 1975, pp. 2-9.

Hepp, Ralph E. and Ott, Stephen L. "Farmland and Open Space Preservation Act." Extension Bulletin, E. 792, no. 40. May, 1975.

Hugg, Lawrence. "A Medical Geography of Tuberculosis in Michigan: An Alternative Framework for Health Care Organization." *The Michigan Academician,* VII, no. 3. (1975), 293-302.

"Lead Pellet on Way Out." *Michigan Natural Resources,* May-June, 1973, p. 33.

McDowell, Norris. "Trails for Everyone." *Michigan Natural Resources,* July-August, 1974, pp. 10-13.

Michigan Department of Mental Health. *Michigan State Plan for Comprehensive Mental Health Services 1976.* Lansing: State of Michigan, 1976.

Michigan Department of Natural Resources. *Michigan's Future Was Today.* Lansing: Office of Land Use, September, 1974.

Michigan Department of State Police. *Uniform Crime Report 1975,* 17 ed. East Lansing: State of Michigan.

Morscheck, Richard. "Minding Our PCB's." *Michigan Natural Resources,* March-April, 1976, pp. 4-7.

Muskegon County Department of Public Works. *Muskegon County Where Wastes Are Resources.* Muskegon: Muskegon County Board of Commissioners. ca. 1974.

Office of the Governor. *Program Policy Guidelines 1975-1976.* Lansing: April, 1974.

Platt, Rutherford H. *Land Use Control: Interface of Law and Geography,* Res. Paper No. 75-1. Washington, D.C.: Association of American Geographers. 1976.

Reinking, R. L. and Zilinski, R. E. "Effect of Deicing Salt of Sodium Content of Lake Macatawa, Michigan." *Michigan Academician,* VII, no. 3 (1975), 373-82.

Sheaffer, John R. *Introduction to Flood Proofing an Outline of Principles and Methods.* Chicago: Center for Urban Studies, The University of Chicago. April, 1967.

―――. "Reviving the Great Lakes." *Saturday Review.* November 7, 1970. pp. 62-65.

Tanner, Howard. "Putting Waste in Its Place." *Michigan Natural Resources,* November-December, 1972, pp. 2-7.

Teledyne Triple R., *Waste Water Systems.* Muskegon: ca. 1974.

United States Army. *Flood Plain Handle with Care,* EP 1105-2-4. Washington, D.C.: Corps of Engineers, March, 1974.

United States Army. *Guidelines for Reducing Flood Damages.* Vicksburg, Mississippi: Corps of Engineers, May, 1967.

United States Forest Service Eastern Region. *Guide for Managing the National Forests in the Lake States,* draft. United States Department of Agriculture, February, 1975.

United States Forest Service, Huron-Manistee National Forest. *Interim Plan for the Management of Off Road Vehicles on the Huron-Mainstee National Forest,* draft. Cadillac: United States Department of Agriculture. April, 1975.

Wasbotten, Tom. "Solving the 1% Problem." *Michigan Natural Resources,* September-October, 1975, pp. 2-7.

Wilson, Wallace. "Danger Flood Plain." *Michigan Natural Resources,* May-June, 1976. pp. 28-31.

Index

Abrams, 135, 199
Acculturation, 34, 169, 202
Adrian, 35, 66, 107, 120, 126, 168, 185, 191, 263, 298
Aeroquip, 185
Agassiz, 94
Agriculture, 38, 200, 201, 203, 212, 225-50, 273, 276, 284
Alabama, 160
Alabaster, 86, 197
Alamo, 34
Alba, 298
Albion, 90
Alcona, 100, 146, 205
Alfalfa. *See* Hay
Alger, 127, 135, 170
Algonquian, 13, 18
Allegan, 135, 170, 171, 202, 244, 245, 246, 303
Allendale, 298
Alma, 90, 126, 200, 263
Alpena, 5, 65, 86, 89, 126, 141, 176, 205, 209, 245, 263
Alpena Community College, 209
Amasa, 80
Amboy, 302
American Indians, 15-24, 47-50, 169
Amish, 171
Andrews University, 194
Ann Arbor, 125, 126, 156, 159, 171, 175, 184, 185, 224, 263, 291, 304, 326
Antrim, 98, 100, 171, 211, 244, 304
Apples, 32, 149, 227, 245
Aquinas College, 204
Arab, 171
Archaic period, 16
Area, 7, 8, 61, 176, 228, 249
Arenac, 246
Asia, 158
Asparagus, 227, 244
Atlanta, 177
Atwood, 171
Audrey, 33

Au Gres, 298
Augusta, 298
Austria, 170
Automobiles, 178, 181, 194-96, 204, 217, 250-54, 293
Aviation, 294, 302-5

Bad Axe, 200
Baldwin, 66, 202
Banfield, 298
Bank deposits, 200
Baraga, 146, 298
Barley, 229
Barry, 100, 139, 191, 192, 193, 246, 298
Baseline, 49, 57
Battle Creek, 130, 176, 194, 224, 298, 303, 304
Bay, 245, 291
Bay City, 88, 90, 125, 126, 140, 176, 201, 205, 291, 306
Bay De Noc Community College, 214
Bay-Muskegon Line, 147, 261, 318
Beans, 227, 229, 233, 241, 244
Bedrock, 76, 78, 79
Beef. *See* Livestock
Belgians, 170, 263
Bellaire, 5
Benton Harbor, 126, 127, 171, 176, 193, 194, 263, 291
Benton Harbor News—Palladium, 193
Benzie, 61, 100, 211
Berrien, 130, 139, 193, 244, 245, 246, 302
Berrien Springs, 191, 194, 220
Bessemer, 80
Big Rapids, 96, 126, 140, 201, 204, 217, 263, 296, 298, 300
Bike Trails. *See* Nonmotorized Transportation
Birmingham, 194, 263
Birth Rate, 158, 160
Bismark, 171
Bitley, 96
Blacks, 169, 171, 176, 185, 187-90, 193, 194, 202, 205

353

Black River, 103, 107
Black Swamp, 166, 278
Blanchard, 298
Bliss, 302
Blissfield, 298
Bloomfield Hills, 184, 194
Bloomingdale, 298
Blossom Festival, 194
Blueberries, 227, 245
Bois Blanc, 49
Borgestrom, 245
Borman, 315
Boston, 177, 202
Boundary, 41, 42, 44, 46, 47-56, 299-302
Boundary claims, 35, 43
Boundary proposals, 8, 11, 14, 43
Boyne City, 98, 212
Boyne Falls, 98
Branch, 91. 139, 191, 298
Bridges, 85, 204, 286, 287, 311, 312
Bridgman, 263
Brimley, 298
Brines, 85, 86
British, 27, 28, 35-40, 41-44, 170, 262, 263
Brooklyn, 298
Brule, 25
Buchanan, 246
Budd Company, 185
Buena Vista, 34
Buffalo, 23
Buick, 195
Burma, 158
Burt, 54, 57, 59
Business climate, 264, 265
Butter, 246

Cabbage, 227, 244
Cadillac, 27, 29
Cadillac (city), 121, 126, 141, 205, 316
Calder, 222, 253
Calhoun, 139, 191, 244
Calhoun, Secty. of War, 278
California, 34, 91, 160, 265
Calumet, 82, 132, 215, 291
Calvin College, 204
Cambodia, 158
Cambrian, 84, 151, 152
Cambridge Junction, 191
Camden, 298
Campau, 33
Campbell, Wyant and Cannon, 265
Camp Ferris. *See* Camp Grayling
Camp Grayling, 208

Campgrounds, 180, 184, 191, 197, 205, 215, 256-59, 260, 270
Canada, 50, 89, 169, 170, 262, 263, 302
Canals, 107, 110
Cantaloupe, 245
Carney, 298
Caro, 200
Carr, 298
Carrots, 227, 244
Carry Mission, 50
Cartier, 25
Cass, 139, 167, 168, 171, 193, 244
Cass City, 110
Cassopolis, 65, 193
Celery, 227, 244
Cement, 86
Cemetery, 159
Central, 82, 298
Central Business District (CBD), 168, 199, 206, 221, 222, 277, 284
Central Michigan University, 201, 212
Centrifugal, 177
Centripetal, 177
Champion, 125, 126
Champlain, 25
Charlevoix, 86, 89, 98, 100, 301
Charlotte, 90
Chatham, 298
Chavey, 33
Cheboygan, 91, 100, 130, 205
Cheese, 227, 243, 246
Chemicals, 85, 321, 322
Chene, 33
Cherronesus, 13, 14
Cherry, 212, 227, 245
Chert, 98
Chesaning, 298
Chicago, 11, 107, 110, 177, 193, 202, 289
Chickens, 229, 239, 246
Chile, 158
China, 158, 169
Chippewa County, 89, 100
Chippewa tribe, 19, 21, 49
Christaller, 213
Christmas trees, 146, 321
Chrysler, 181, 196, 250, 253
Churches, 29, 39, 170, 194, 204, 210, 219
Cicot, 33
Cincinnati, 177, 202, 251
Citizens Gas Fuel, 303
Clare, 146, 200, 246, 303
Clark Equipment, 185
Clay, 98

354

Clayton, 298
Cleveland, 77, 80, 177, 295
Cliff, 82
Climate, 119-34
Climax, 298
Clinton, 185, 196, 220, 244, 246, 291
Clover, 227
Coal, 88, 293, 302
Cobalt, 83
Coldwater, 263
Colon, 171
Commerce, 96
Commonwealth Associates, 185
Community College. *See* individual name
Commuting, 206, 208
Complexity explosion, 172
Concord, 298
Concord Bridge, 38
Connecticut, 36, 41
Consumers Power Company, 185, 299, 301, 303
Copper, 82-83
Copper Harbor, 82
Copper Peak, 214
Coral, 85, 86, 88, 89
Core Area, 6, 201
Corn, 227, 229, 230, 241, 320
Corunna, 34
Costa Rica, 158
County evolution, 62-66
County names, 2, 62
County seats, 65-66
Coureurs de bois, 27, 30, 36
Courthouse square, 168
Cranbrook, 88
Crawford, 47, 96, 205, 303
Cremation, 159
Crime, 172, 173, 178, 179, 200, 260, 261, 299, 317, 322, 323, 324
Cross, 88, 209
Crystal Falls, 65, 80
Cuba, 158, 170
Cucumbers, 227, 244
Cultural baggage, 16, 32, 168
Culture lag, 261
Czechoslovakia, 170

Daily population increase, 156, 160
Dallas, 177
Dams, 105
Dana, 119, 142
Darby, 253, 254
DDT, 321, 322
Dearborn, 156, 171, 176, 184, 250

Dearborn Heights, 156
Death rate, 158, 160
Deerfield, 298
Degree days, 125, 126
Delta, 89, 146, 170
Delta Community College, 201
Delton, 298
Denmark, 170
Density, 158, 256
Dequindre, 33
Des Moines, 47
Des Rocher, 33
Detour, 28, 169
Detroit, 15, 26, 27, 29, 30, 32, 33, 37-40, 62, 65, 91, 115, 125, 126, 127, 130, 133, 159, 166-69, 171, 175-84, 194-97, 202, 204, 208, 217, 221-24, 250-54, 263, 265, 270, 278, 282, 284, 286, 288, 289, 291, 293-98, 304-7, 309-11, 326, 335
Detroit Edison, 133
Detroit Free Press, 305
Detroit Legal News, 305
Detroit News, 305
Devonian, 84, 85, 86
Deward, 209
Dexter, 168
Dickinson, 146, 170
Dowagiac, 19, 193
Dow Chemical Company, 85, 200, 204, 213, 303, 321
Doyle, 170
Drayton Plains, 96
Drenthe, 298
Drift, 94, 95
Drumlins, 96, 98
Drummond, 298
Drummond Island, 35, 84
Du Bois, 33
Du Boisville, 33
Dubuque, 47
Duluth, Minnesota, 295
Dunbar, 132
Dundee, 86, 263
Durand, 291
Durant, 196
Dutch. *See* Netherlands
Dutoise, 33

Earle, 279
Earthquakes, 91
East Grand Rapids, 201
Eastern Michigan University, 180
East Lansing, 199

Eastmanville, 321
East Saginaw, 140
East Tawas, 121
Eaton, 139, 196, 244
Eaton Corporation, 200
Eben, 291
Ecology, xxi, xxii
Economic, xxi, xxii, 223-67
Edison Institute, 299
Edmore, 204, 263, 291
Education, 23, 24, 180, 184, 191, 193, 194, 196, 199, 201, 204, 209, 212, 214, 217, 267, 268, 298
Edwardsburg, 263
Eggs, 239, 246
Egypt, 158
Eisenhower, 282
Electric power, 299, 301, 302
Elevation, 120
Elk, 3
Elmdale, 291
Elsie, 298
Emmanuel Missionary College, 194
Emmet, 23
Empire, 80
Employment—production, 178, 180, 185, 193, 194, 195, 198, 199, 200, 202, 206, 212, 213, 217
Energy, 89-91, 134, 265, 294, 299-303
Environment, 148-53, 315-38
Erie Canal, 166, 167
Erosion, 115-18, 331, 332
Escanaba, 65, 126, 145, 176, 213, 214, 291, 316
Esker, 95, 96
Ethnic groups, 169-71
Europe, 158
Eutrophication, 99
Evart, 96, 204
Extended rivers, 103

Fallen Timbers, 43
Farmington, 175
Farwell, 197
Fayette, 84
Felch, 80
Fennville, 246
Fenton, 194
Ferndale, 263
Ferris State College, 201
Ferris, W. N., 208, 280
Filipino, 169
Finland, 158, 170, 171
Fishing, 26, 33, 259, 270
Fish ladder, 105
Flat Rock, 49, 90, 159

Fletcher Park, 86
Flint, 88, 126, 132, 176, 194-96, 224, 250, 304, 307
Flint College, U of M, 196
Flint Junior College, 268
Flood plain, 326, 332-36
Florida, 160
Flushing, 194
Foote, 299
Ford, 181, 184, 250, 252, 253
Foreign investments, 262-64
Forest industry, 139-47, 150, 199, 200, 202, 204
Fort Brady, 44
Fort Dearborn, 278
Fort Greenville, 49
Fort Harmar, 48
Fort Lernoult, 38, 44
Fort Mackinac, 26, 28, 37, 38, 73
Fort McIntosh, 48
Fort Michilimackinac, 27, 28, 29, 34, 37, 39, 73
Fort Pontchartrain, 30, 39
Fort St. Joseph, 25, 34
Fort Shelby, 39
Fort Stanwix, 48
Fort Wayne, 44
Fossils, 88, 89
France, 25-36, 158, 170, 263
Frankenmuth, 110, 171, 197, 200
Frankfort, 291
Franklin, 41
Freeways. *See* Roads
Fremont, 204
French family names, 33
Frenchtown, 26, 29, 31, 168
Frey, 40
Frost-free season, 127, 128, 193
Fruit, 32, 212, 243, 245
Fruit Belt, 121, 125, 193, 217, 245
Fuel oil, 302
Funeral industry, 158, 159
Furniture, 202-4
Fur trade, 26-29, 35-39
Future, 8, 11, 12, 244-50, 296

Garden Peninsula, 84
Gas, 89-91, 302, 303
Gaylord, 5, 205-7, 307
General Motors, 181, 194-96, 221, 250, 253
General Motors Institute, 196
General Telephone Company, 217, 298, 299
Genesee, 23, 168, 194, 246
Geodesy, xxii
Geo-disciplines, xxi, xxii

Geographic Method, xvii
Geology, xxii, 75-91
Geometry, xxii, 268
Geomorphology, xxii, 93-98
German, 158, 170, 171, 213, 263
Gerstacker, 321
Ghost towns, 168
Glaciation, 93-98, 106-15
Gladstone, 213
Gladwin, 200
Glen Arbor, 209
Glen Oaks Community College, 193
Gogebic, 100, 103, 214, 272
Gold, 83
Grace Bible College, 204
Grand Blanc, 194
Grand Haven, 103, 116, 215, 217, 291
Grand Rapids, 65, 85, 86, 88, 126, 135, 141, 145, 159, 171, 176, 222, 224, 263, 286, 287, 291, 304, 306, 307, 314
Grand Rapids Baptist College, 204
Grand Rapids Junior College, 268
Grand River, 103, 105, 107, 199, 202
Grand Traverse, 245
Grand Valley State Colleges, 217
Grandville, 101
Grapes, 227, 245
Gratiot, 100, 127, 246, 303
Gravel, 98
Grayling, 4, 65, 205, 208, 209
Great Lakes, 7, 8, 13, 84, 106-18, 294-96
Great Lakes Transmission Company, 303
Great Seal, 4
Greece, 8, 170
Greenfield Village, 184, 220, 302
Greenman, 20
Greenville, 9, 49
Grenoble, 25
Grindsone City, 197
Grosse Isle, 85, 184
Growing season. *See* Frost-free season
Gulf of Mexico, 302
Gypsum, 86

Hadley, 298
Hamtramck, 171, 175, 250, 253
Hancock, 82, 170, 213, 215, 311
Harger Shores, 159
Hart, 134, 217, 291
Hartford, 246
Hastings, 66, 191
Hay, 241, 243
Hayes-Albion, 185

Haymarsh State Game Area, 99
Health care, 140, 158, 196, 212, 324-29
Heartland, 7
Hemlock, 321
Herman, 132
Herring, 302
Hesse, Department of, 42
Hiawatha, 169, 316
Hickory Corners, 298
Higgins, 100, 115
Highland Park, 175
Highland Park Junior College, 268
Highways. *See* Road and Transportation
Highway numbering systems, 284-86
Hillsdale, 90, 184, 191, 291
Hinge line, 111
Hinsdale, 19
Historic sites, 72-74, 184, 191, 197, 205, 207, 209, 215, 271
History, xxii, xxiii, 13-40, 41-71, 139-42, 278-82, 288-91, 296-301, 302-7, 326
Hogs. *See* Swine
Holland. *See* Netherlands
Holland, City of, 201, 291, 298
Holly, 263
Honey, 246
Hops, 229
Horses, 229, 243
Houghton, 42, 82, 100, 120, 126, 213-15, 245, 306, 311
House of David, 194
Housetypes, 73, 74, 219, 220, 266
Houston, 177
Howell, 96
Hubbard, 141
Hudson, 49
Hungary, 8, 170
Hunting, 259
Huron, 19, 197, 246
Hydrologic, 99-112, 127, 130, 326, 330-36

Ice Age. *See* Glaciation
Ice cream, 227, 243, 246
Ice storms, 133
Iconography, 3
Idlewild, 171, 202
Illinois, 7, 13, 46, 84, 143, 160, 167, 202, 228, 229, 250, 265
Imlay, 107
Indiana, 7, 13, 84, 127, 143, 160, 167, 168, 228, 229, 250, 265
Indian trails. *See* Roads
Industrial Parks, 266, 267

Industrial products, 225, 263
Ingham, 23, 196, 198, 244, 313
Inkster, 171
Inland lakes, 99-102
Interlochen, 209, 212, 262, 271
International Joint Commission, 44
International trade, 262-65
Interurban railway, 193
Ionia, 204, 324
Iosco, 86, 200
Iowa, 47, 265, 289
Ireland, 158, 170, 187
Irish Hills, 96, 185, 191
Iron, 77-81, 84, 146
Iron Mountain, 65, 80, 213, 307
Iron River, 80, 135, 213
Ironwood, 6, 8, 54, 65, 80, 126, 176, 214, 302, 316
Isabella, 23, 90, 127, 145, 303
Isabella Reservation, 21, 22
Ishpeming, 77, 83, 213, 215, 237
Islands, 1, 19, 35, 42, 84
Isle Royale, 1, 7, 42, 82, 125
Israel, 158
Italy, 170
Ithaca, 65, 77, 168, 199

Jackson, 61, 65, 81, 86-88, 103, 168, 169, 171, 176, 184-91, 196, 244, 263, 284, 288-91, 304, 306, 307
Japan, 158, 169, 204, 262, 263
Jefferson, 13, 14, 38, 55
Jewish, 171
Jonesville, 291
Journey to work, 180, 208
Junior Colleges. *See also* Community College names, 268

Kalamazoo, 49, 103, 107, 126, 139, 145, 169, 171, 176, 191-93, 224, 250, 288, 289, 291, 304, 306, 307, 326
Kalamazoo Valley Community College, 193
Kaleva, 171, 298
Kalkaska, 90, 96, 135, 211, 212
Kame, 95, 96, 98
Kansas, 89
Karst topography, 86, 152
Kelsey-Hayes, 185
Kent, 170, 171, 204, 244, 245, 246
Kenton, 141
Kentucky, 160
Kentwood, 201, 263
Kettle, 96

Keweenaw, 42, 100, 125, 127, 161, 213
Keweenaw fault, 82, 100
Kingsford, 213
Kingsley, 298
Kinross, 98
Kirtland Community College, 201
Kirtland's warbler, 3
Knox, 47

Labor force, 223, 224
Lachine, 86
Lac Illinois, 13
Lake breeze, 121
Lake County, 146, 161, 165, 171, 202, 244
Lake levels, 115
Lake Superior Power District, 303
Lake Superior State College, 214
Land claims, 33
Land office, 62
Land use, 168, 244-50, 252-54, 334, 336, 337
Langston, 171
L'Anse Reservation, 22, 23
Lansing, 23, 24, 121, 126, 176, 196-99, 214, 224, 250, 263, 286, 291, 304, 306, 332
Lansing Community College, 199
Lapeer, 194, 244, 326
L'Arbre Croche, 19
Lead, 83, 321
Leisure time, 184, 191, 194, 196, 199, 201, 204, 211, 212, 214, 217, 254-62, 269-72
Leelanau, 98, 211, 245
Lenawee, 61, 184, 229, 244, 246
Lenawee Junction, 291
Lennon, 298
Leoni, 321
Leopold, 75
Lettuce, 227, 244
Libraries, 180, 196, 201
Liechtenstein, 263
Lightning, 133
Lima, Ohio, 289
Limestone, 84-86, 206
Lincoln Park, 156
Linden, 197
Linwood, 291
Litchfield, 291
Lithuania, 170, 171
Livestock, 229, 236-40, 242, 243
Livonia, 156, 335
Livingston, 180, 200, 303
Location, 5-8
Locks, 103, 110, 310
Logging. *See* Forest industry

Logos, 9, 10
Long lot farms. *See* Ribbon farms
Long Rapids, 86
Los Angeles, 177
Lost Peninsula, 52, 53
Lotbiniere, 115
Louisiana, 30, 302
Lowe, 334
Lowell, 263
Luce, 100, 127, 147
Ludington, 36, 85, 134, 141, 201, 204, 291
Lumber. *See* Forest industry
Lutheran, 170

Mackinac, 26-29, 35, 37, 38, 49, 85, 100
Mackinaw City, 115, 209
Macomb, 23, 100, 130, 133, 180, 244-46, 303
Macon, 107
Madison, President, 166
Madison, Wisconsin, 121
Malaysia, 158
Mancelona, 212
Manistee, 85, 90, 141, 145, 146, 209, 291
Manistique, 213
Manufacturing industries. *See* Employment-production
Maple syrup, 146, 227, 246
Marl, 98
Marlette, 199
Marquette, 8, 61, 65, 80, 100, 125, 126, 146, 176, 213, 215, 291, 304, 310
Marshall, 65, 86, 191
Marysville, 85
Mason, 90, 244
Massachusetts, 36, 41
Mather, 80
Matthew, 175
Mayville, 85
McNiff, 40
Mean information field, 169
Mecosta, 89, 99, 100, 133, 145, 161, 171, 244, 246, 302, 303
Melting pot, 169
Melvindale, 90
Menominee, 5, 19, 103, 146, 170, 171, 213
Mental health service areas, 324-29
Mental map image, 1
Mesick, 298
Mesozoic, 88
Meteorites, 135
Metz, 171
Mexico, 158, 170
Michigan Basin, 75, 77

Michigan Bell Telephone Company, 297-99
Michigan Consolidated Gas Company, 90, 302, 303
Michigan Divide, 306
Michigan Gas Utilities, 303
Michigan Meridian, 49
Michigan-Ohio boundary, 50-53
Michigan Power Company, 303
Michigan statehood, 3, 4, 8, 47, 50
Michigan State University, 88, 134, 135, 199, 212, 305
Michigan Technological University, 132, 214
Michigan Territory, 46, 47
Michigan-Wisconsin Pipeline Company, 302, 303
Michilimackinac, 26, 27, 29, 34, 37
Middleville, 321
Midland, 85, 90, 197, 200, 301, 303
Mid-Michigan Community College, 201
Mid-Polar-Equator Trail, 5
Migration, 160, 169, 170
Miki, 155
Milk, 226, 227, 229, 243
Millington, 291, 298
Milwaukee, 8, 47, 217, 295
Minden, 171
Mining, 39, 77, 79-83, 85, 113
Minneapolis, 8
Minnesota, 7, 42, 80, 125, 143, 228, 261
Mint, 227, 244
Mio, 125, 209
Missaukee, 96, 171, 303
Missionary efforts, 27
Mississippi, 46, 103, 110, 146
Mississippian, 78, 79, 86
Mitchell map (1755), 51
Mobile home industry, 265, 266
Modern geography, xxiii
Monroe, 16, 65, 84, 89, 121, 166, 168, 171, 175, 180, 184, 229, 245, 303
Montcalm, 90, 127, 171, 303
Montcalm Community College, 204
Montgomery, 291
Montmorency, 91, 146, 205
Montreal River, 54
Moose, 3, 125
Moraine, 95-97, 107, 108
Moran, 33, 169
Morenci, 298
Morley, 308
Morocco, 158
Morton, 171
Mott, 196
Mott Community College, 196

Mt. Clemens, 168, 180, 263
Mt. Morris, 159
Mt. Pleasant, 21, 90, 200
Multiple-use, 145, 317
Munger, 242, 291
Munising, 213, 215, 298
Murder, 172, 179, 322
Museums, 180, 184
Mushrooms, 147, 246
Muskegon, 23, 65, 69, 85, 90, 103, 115, 121, 126, 159, 168, 176, 215-17, 244, 263, 270, 304, 306, 317-21, 331
Muskegon Community College, 217, 268
Muskegon Heights, 171, 263

Napoleon, 86
Nash, 196
Nashville, 146
National Forests, 145, 204, 212, 214, 316, 317
National Parks, 1, 7, 10, 28, 214
Natural increase, 158, 160
Natural Rivers Act, 106, 336
Nazareth College, 193
Negaunee, 84, 213, 215
Netherlands, 158, 169, 170, 171, 263
Newaygo, 77, 125, 139, 217, 244, 303
New Baltimore, 168
Newberry, 214
Newspapers, 193, 305
New York, 8, 36, 41, 107, 143, 160, 166, 168, 178, 202, 228, 250, 265, 289
Niagara Falls, 27, 110, 112
Niagara reef, 90
Nickel, 83
Nicolet, 13
Niles, 34, 191, 194
Nonmotorized transportation, 287-88, 314
North Central Michigan College, 212
Northern Michigan University, 214
Northern Natural Gas, 303
Northport, 210
Northwestern Michigan College, 212
Northwest Ordinance, 1, 44-46, 52
Northwest Territory, 44, 45, 278
Northwood Institute, 201
Norway, 170
Nottawa, 171
November storms, 134

Oakland, 61, 96, 100, 130, 180, 184, 253
Oak openings, 139
Oak Park, 171
Oats, 227, 229, 232, 242, 243

Oceana, 69, 134, 215, 217, 244, 245
Off-road vehicles (ORVs), 317
Ogden, 298
Ogemaw, 77, 200
Ohio, 7, 49, 50-55, 84, 127, 143, 160, 166-68, 228, 250, 262, 289, 291
Oil, 89-91
Ojibwa, 19
Okemos, 18, 159
Oklahoma, 302
Old Mission, 115, 210, 212, 219
Olivet, 96
Omena, 210
Onaway, 141
Onions, 227, 244
Ontario, 5, 158, 251
Ontonagon, 19, 100, 298
Open space, 159, 336, 337
Ordovician, 84, 89
Osceola, 18, 90, 121, 145, 171, 246, 303
Oscoda, 146, 201, 205
Otsego, 90, 91, 145
Ottawa County, 61, 69, 171, 201, 215, 244-46, 331
Ottawa tribe, 18, 19, 49
Outlets, 107, 109-11
Owosso, 194
Oxford, 96

Paleo-Indians, 15, 16
Paleozoic, 79, 84-90, 93
Palo, 34
Pan Handle Eastern, 303
Parke, 59
Parma, 298
Parshallville, 184
Paw Paw, 193, 194, 246
PCBs, 321
Peaches, 194, 227, 245
Peat, 98
Pelston, 126
Peninsular Power Company, 303
Pennsylvania, 160, 168, 334
Pennsylvanian, 78, 79, 88
Pentwater, 216
Peoria, Illinois, 202
Perception of environment, 25, 139
Permian, 76, 88
Perry, 298
Peterson, 80
Petoskey, 86, 212, 291, 298
Petoskey stone, 4, 86
Petroleum, 89-91

Philadelphia, 289
Phoenicians, 25
Phoenix, 215
Pictured Rocks, 84, 151
Pigeon, 298
Pigeon River State Forest, 3, 90, 91
Pinconning, 298
Pine Run, 110
Pipeline, 294, 302, 303
Pittsburgh, 178
Platinum, 83
Pleasant Ridge, 284
Pleistocene, 93-99, 106-12
Plums, 227, 245
Plymouth, 263
Poland, 158, 170, 188
Political geographic evolution, 35, 41-71, 182
Pontiac, 36, 156, 159, 168, 175, 250, 278, 304, 326
Popcorn, 227
Population, 18, 23, 26, 39, 145, 155-73, 175-77, 185, 192, 193, 197, 199, 200-202, 205, 206, 210, 213, 214, 216, 258, 268
Portages, 26, 27, 42
Port Huron, 6, 8, 86, 107, 112, 126, 184, 263, 291, 299, 311
Port Huron Junior College, 268
Port of Detroit, 294-96
Porter, 321
Posen, 171
Post offices, 307-8
Potatoes, 229, 242
Potawatomi, 18-20, 22, 48
Potomic University, 194
Prairies, 139
Precambrian, 76-84, 91, 151
Precipitation, 127-32
Presque Isle, 89, 100, 103, 130, 171, 209
Problems, 5
Public Acts, 116, 159, 206, 288, 316, 334, 336, 337
Puerto Rico, 158

Quebec, 27, 35, 37, 41
Quince, 32

Raco, 291
Radio, 305, 306
Railroad, 191, 202, 288-94
Ranks, 7, 227-29, 244-47, 257
Rapid City, 98
Ravenna, 321
Rebound, 111

Recreation. *See* Leisure time
Redford, 33, 115, 169, 335
Reed City, 65, 96, 135, 202, 204
Regional centers, 70, 176
Regional concept, 66-68
Regions, 66-71, 175-217
Relative location, 5
Religion, 20, 27, 29, 30, 39, 46, 115, 169, 204, 210, 212, 219
Renaissance Center, 178, 222
Republic, 80
Rhubarb, 245
Ribbon farms, 30-33
River Rouge, 171, 252
Rivers, 100, 102-6, 210, 326, 332-36
Roads, 166, 175, 277-88, 312-14
Rochester, 168, 184
Rockford, 204
Rockwood, 91
Rogers City, 86, 206, 209
Rogers Dam, 301
Romeo, 265
Roscommon, 100, 142, 199-200
Roseville, 156
Royal Oak, 130, 156, 175, 306, 307
Rush-Bagot, 44
Rye, 227, 229

Saginaw, 35, 49, 88, 90, 103, 115, 125, 176, 194, 197, 199-201, 217, 229, 244, 263, 278, 291, 304, 306
Saginaw Valley College, 201
Salt, 84, 85
Sand dunes, 112-14, 153
Sand Lake, 298
Sandstone, 86, 87
Sandusky, 107, 200
San Francisco, 177
Sanilac, 100, 199, 244
Santiago, 34
Sargent, 44
Sault Ste. Marie, 26-28, 44, 49, 98, 125, 126, 176, 213, 215, 263, 291, 310, 312
Schenectady, New York, 289
School consolidation. *See* Education
Schoolcraft, 62, 85, 89, 100
Scipio, 90
Scottville, 204
Selfridge, 180, 183
Seneca, 135
Settlements. *See* Population and Regions
Seventh Day Adventist, 194
Sex ratio, 161, 213

361

Shale, 86
Shape, 8
Sheep, 229, 240, 243
Shelby, 217
Shepherd, 246
Sherwood, 80
Shiawassee, 100, 194, 197, 244
Shingleton, 135
Shoes, 204
Shoreline, 7, 8
Shoreline erosion, 115-18, 331, 332
Siena Heights College, 191
Silurian, 76, 78, 79, 84, 85
Silver, 83
Skiing, 261, 272
Skyscrapers, 177
Sleeping Bear Dune, 113, 212
Smith, 40
Snowfall, 130-32
Snowmobiling, 261, 272
Snow removal, 280, 313, 321
Soils, 135-38
Soumi College, 170, 171, 214
South Bend, 193, 291
Southeastern Michigan Gas Company, 303
Southfield, 115, 156, 178, 263, 297
South Haven, 115, 263, 301
Soybeans, 229, 234, 241
Spanish, 25, 34, 35, 158
Spring Arbor College, 191
Springfield, 263
Springport, 298
SMSA—Standard Metropolitan Statistical Area, 155-57, 195, 201, 224
Standish, 200
Stanton, 202, 204
Star Creek, 135
Star Siding, 135
State capital, 196-99, 176, 214, 224, 250
State game areas, 259
State Motto, 4, 41
State Parks, 28, 184, 191, 193, 194, 196, 197, 199, 201, 205, 209, 212, 214, 215, 217, 256, 257, 271
State Police, 322-24
State Prisons, 86, 87, 185, 204, 213, 214, 324
State Seal, 4
State symbols, 3, 4
State of Superior, 8, 11
Stauffer Chemical, 185
Sterling, 40
Sterling Heights, 156
St. Clair, 90, 112, 180, 244, 303

St. Clair Shores, 156, 175
St. Joseph, 65, 103, 139, 168, 171, 176, 193, 229, 245, 288, 298, 302
St. Ignace, 27, 49, 85, 213, 215, 291
St. Lawrence Seaway, 294-96
St. Louis, Michigan, 85, 200
St. Louis, Missouri, 8, 34, 202
St. Mary's River, 103, 112, 310
St. Paul, Minnesota, 304
Stockbridge, 298
Straits of Mackinac, i, 19, 27, 110, 125, 286, 312
Strawberries, 245
Stuart, 50
Sturgis, 107, 191
Sub-arctic climate, 132
Sugar beets, 227, 229, 235, 241, 242
Sugar Island (St. George's), 19, 35, 42
Sumpter, 171
Sunshine, 126, 127
Surveys, 31, 39, 40, 42, 49, 52, 55-61, 308
Suttons Bay, 98
Sweden, 158, 170, 263
Sweet corn, 17, 227, 241
Swine, 229, 238, 242, 243
Switzerland, 263

Tahquamenon Falls, 84, 103, 152
Taiwan, 247
Tawas, 200, 302
Tax delinquent land, 142
Taylor, 156
Tectonic plates, 91
Tecumseh, Chief, 15
Tecumseh, City of, 66, 168, 185
Tecumseh Products, 185
Tekonsha, 107
Telephone, 296-99
Television, 306, 307
Temperature, 120-26
Tennessee, 160
Texas, 89, 91, 160, 302
Tiffin, 166
Tilden, 80
Till, 94-98
Till plains, 94-96
Tipton, 191
Toledo, 43, 50-53, 90, 115, 166, 185, 291, 293, 295, 296
Tomatoes, 227, 244
Topography, 120, 121
Tornadoes, 132, 133

Toronto, 287
Townships, 59-61
Tractor production, 265
Transportation, 26, 27, 295, 297, 302-5, 309-14
Traverse City, 115, 126, 141, 176, 205, 209-13, 291, 298, 307
Treaties, Indian, 47-50
Treaty of Ghent, 42
Treaty of Paris, 35, 41
Tree farm system, 146
Trenton, 90, 91
Troy, 159, 261, 263, 265
Trucking, 294
Tunnels, 286, 287
Turkeys, 246
Twining, 298

Ubly, 107, 109
Ullman, 277
Underground railroad, 185
Unemployment, 224
Union of Soviet Socialist Republics, 170
United Kingdom, 170, 262, 263
Unit train, 293
University of Michigan, 6, 88, 180, 212
Upper Peninsula, 8, 10, 11, 19, 26, 50-52, 54-57, 77-83, 98, 100, 103, 110, 112, 120, 126, 127, 132, 146, 169-71, 213-15, 224, 261, 298
Uranium, 83
Urban patterns, 172, 179, 181, 182, 186-90, 192, 206, 213, 216
Utica, 291

Valders, 110
Valley trains, 96
Van Buren, 193, 194, 244, 245
Vanderbilt, 125
Vassar, 110, 291
Vegetables, 227, 244
Vermontville, 146, 246
Vicksburg, 291
Vikings, 25
Virginia, 36, 41, 44, 45
Von Del Chamberlain, 135
Voting Rights Act, 35
Voyageurs, 27

Wakefield, 80
Waldron, 298
Walker, 201

Walker-Muffler, 185
Walton Junction, 291
Warren, 156, 184, 250
Watton, 298
Washington, President, 38, 43, 47, 64
Washtenaw, 61, 168, 170, 180, 229, 303
Waste water systems, 317-20
Waterfalls, 103
Watershed, 100, 102, 103
Watervliet, 194
Wayland, 321
Wayne, 43, 44, 62, 91, 130, 133, 171, 180, 246
Wayne, City of, 250, 265
Wayne State University, 180
Weidman, 171
Wells, deep, 77, 85
West Branch, 90, 200
Western Michigan University, 193
Westland, 156, 184
Westphalia, 171, 298
West Shore Community College, 204
Wexford, 121
Wheat, 32, 229, 231, 241
Wheatland, 171
Wheeler, 266
White Cloud, 202, 217
Wickes Corporation, 200
Wildlife, 149, 159
Williamsburg, 86
Windmills, 32, 134
Wine, 246
Winn, 298
Wisconsin, 7, 8, 46, 52, 54-56, 84, 93, 103, 143, 160, 228, 261, 302
Wolverine World Wide, 204
Woodland Period, 16-18
Wood products. *See* Forest industry
Woodruff's Grove, 168
Workmen's Compensation, 264
Wurtsmith, 201
Wyandot tribe, 20, 21, 45
Wyandotte, 20, 85, 171, 175, 263
Wyoming, 156, 201

Yardman, 185
Ypsilanti, 96, 107, 168, 222, 278
Yugoslavia, 170

Zeeland, 298
Zero population growth, 160
Zinc, 83

SUMMARY OF SIGNIFICANT HISTORICAL GEOGRAPHIC EVENTS AND DATES

ca. 3.5 billion BP-600 million BP	Oldest precambrian rock (iron-copper) formed
ca. 11,500 BP	Final retreat of glaciers from Great Lakes basins
ca. 11,000 BP	Arrival of Paleo-Indians
ca. 2000 BP	Modern Great Lakes shapes formed
ca. 1000 AD	Corn introduced to Monroe County area
ca. 1618	Arrival of French explorers
1668	Mission at Sault Ste. Marie established
1681	Earliest known use of Michigan on a map
1701	Detroit founded by French
1760-1796	British occupy the peninsulas
1805	Michigan Territory created
1807	Treaty of Detroit—major southeast Lower Peninsula Indian land cession
1815	Beginning of Federal land surveys
1815	County government established—Wayne County
1825	Creation of civil townships authorized by Congress
1835	"Toledo Strip" dispute with Ohio
1835	First operating railroad: Erie and Kalamazoo RR
1837	Michigan statehood
1895	First state park—Mackinac
1909	World's first poured concrete road—Woodward Avenue, Detroit
World War II	First state freeway—Willow Run
1945	Regional organizations authorized by state legislature